Lee Adams' Supercharged C++ Graphics

Lee Adams

Windcrest®/McGraw-Hill

NOTICES

Turbo C++™, **Borland C++**™	Borland International, Inc.
Pizazz™	Application Techniques Inc.
MetaWINDOW™, **MetaWINDOW/Plus**™	Metagraphics Software Corp.
Lee Adams™	Lee Adams
HALO®, **HALO Professional**™, **Dr. Proto**™	Media Cybernetics, Inc.
IBM PC®, **PS/2**®	International Business Machines Corp.
Hercules®	Hercules Computer Technology, Inc.
MS-DOS®, **Microsoft**®, **QuickC**®	Microsoft Corp.
Zortech C++™, **Flash Graphics**™	Zortech Inc.
Intel®, **i486**™, **i860**™	Intel Corp.
Dan Bricklin's™	Daniel Bricklin
PageGarden™, **Software Garden**®	Software Garden, Inc.
Genus Microprogramming™, **pcxGrab**™, **PCX Programmer's Toolkit**™	Genus Microprogramming, Inc.

FIRST EDITION
FIRST PRINTING

© 1992 by **Lee Adams**.
Published by Windcrest Books, an imprint of TAB Books.
TAB Books is a division of McGraw-Hill, Inc.
The name "Windcrest" is a registered trademark of TAB Books.

Library of Congress Cataloging-in-Publication Data

Adams, Lee.
    [Supercharged C++ graphics]
    Lee Adams' supercharged C++ graphics / by Lee Adams.
      p. cm.
    Includes index.
    ISBN 0-8306-6489-0 (h)   ISBN 0-8306-3489-4 (p)
    1. Computer graphics. 2. C++ (Computer program language)
I. Title. II. Title: Supercharged C++ graphics.
T385.A332 1991
006.6'6—dc20   91-20266
                        CIP

TAB Books offers software for sale. For information and a catalog, please contact TAB Software Department, Blue Ridge Summit, PA 17294-0850.

Acquisitions Editor: Stephen Moore
Book Editor: David Harter
Production: Katherine G. Brown
Book Design: Jaclyn J. Boone
Cover Design: Sandra Blair Design, Harrisburg, PA
Cover Photograph: Lee Adams   WP1

Contents

_____PART ONE_____

HIGH-PERFORMANCE
PROGRAMMING SKILLS

2 *Programming an animation sequence*   *40*

3 *Programming a pointing device*   *67*

PART TWO

BUILDING 2-D GRAPHICS APPLICATIONS

_____*PART THREE*_____

BUILDING 3-D GRAPHICS APPLICATIONS

PART FOUR

ANIMATION

APPENDICES

Acknowledgments

The following development tools and utilities were provided for the author's use during preparation of the program listings in the book.

Zortech C++ 2.12 Developer's Edition, from Zortech Incorporated, 4-C Gill St., Woburn MA, 01801 USA.

Borland C++ 2.0, from Borland International, Inc., 1800 Green Hills Rd., Scotts Valley CA, 95066-0001 USA.

PCX Programmer's Toolkit 4.0, from Genus Microprogramming, Inc., 11315 Meadow Lake, Houston TX, 77077 USA.

Pizazz Plus 2.0, from Application Techniques, Incorporated, 10 Lomar Park Dr., Pepperell MA, 01463 USA.

HALO Professional 2.0, from Media Cybernetics, Inc., 8484 Georgia Ave., Silver Spring MD, 20910 USA.

MetaWINDOW/Plus 3.7b, from Metagraphics Software Corporation, 4575 Scotts Valley Dr., Scotts Valley CA, 95066 USA.

How to get the most from this book

This book provides you with the C++ programming skills you need to take timely advantage of the growing worldwide market for graphics applications on personal computers. The graphics features you have seen in commercial software can be a part of your own graphics programming toolkit.

If you are interested in C++ graphics programming, you are poised at the threshold of opportunity. Industry analysts say this is the decade of graphics on personal computers. Computer graphics programming has become an integral part of today's software products.

Computer graphics programming is made up of such diverse disciplines as 3-D modeling and rendering, simulations and animations, image analysis and retouching, computer vision and image processing, morphing and tweening, desktop publishing, recreation and games, learning and tutorials, and much more.

Computer graphics enhance our ability to solve complex problems, to understand a wide range of data, and to express creative ideas. Computer graphics are changing the visual arts and design, engineering and architecture, industrial design and manufacturing, mathematics and medicine, physics and biology, and entertainment and advertising.

The book will help you broaden your C++ programming skills so you can position yourself to take maximum advantage of this strong graphics trend on personal computers. If you want to develop serious graphics applications for business, science, medicine, engineering, or design—if you want to write graphics software for the entertainment and recreation markets—this book will help you get your program up and running.

The book is packed with solutions. It contains nearly a megabyte of source listings—nearly 14,000 lines of demonstration programs (see FIG. 1) and class libraries (see FIG. 2). The code is supported by numerous drawings and screen images accompanying the easy-to-follow text. *Lee Adams' Supercharged C++*

PROGRAMMER'S QUICK REFERENCE		
TOPIC	DEMONSTRATION	CLASS LIBRARY Appendix E
interactive draw/paint graphics	SKETCH.CPP in Chapter 6	LIB2D.HPP LIB2D.CPP
interactive 3D graphics	OBJECTS.CPP in Chapter 9	LIB3D.HPP LIB3D.CPP
desktop publishing graphics	DESKTOP.CPP in Chapter 7	PUBLISH.HPP PUBLISH.CPP
display animation	STRIDES.CPP in Chapter 10	BLITTER.HPP BLITTER.CPP
kinetic animation	HIT.CPP in Chapter 12	KINETIC.HPP KINETIC.CPP
GUI graphics	GUI.CPP in Chapter 5	BITBLT.HPP BITBLT.CPP
pointing device control	CLICK.CPP in Chapter 3	MOUSE.HPP MOUSE.CPP
self-controlling bitblts	BLOCK.CPP in Chapter 4	BITBLT.HPP BITBLT.CPP
autodetect of graphics adapter	STARTUP.CPP in Chapter 1	LIB2D.HPP LIB2D.CPP
tweening for cel animation	CEL.CPP in Chapter 11	LIB2D.HPP LIB2D.CPP
programming an animation sequence	BOUNCE.CPP in Chapter 2	BLITTER.HPP BLITTER.CPP
compiling the demos with Turbo C++	discussion in Appendix A	LIB2D.HPP LIB2D.CPP
compiling the demos with Borland C++	discussion in Appendix B	LIB2DBC.HPP LIB2DBC.CPP
compiling the demos with Zortech C++	discussion in Appendix C	LIB2D.HPP LIB2D.CPP

1 Topical reference to the demonstration programs.

Graphics follows the same here-is-how-it-is-done approach made popular by previous books in Windcrest/McGraw-Hill's C graphics series.

The book does not adopt a dogmatic, purist approach to object-oriented programming (OOP). Rather, it masterfully mixes C++ techniques with already proven C graphics routines, using OOP where efficiency and productivity are best realized. You get the best of both worlds, taking full advantage of the power of C++ while prudently safeguarding the investment you have in C.

Who should use the book

If you use a personal computer and you are interested in computer graphics programming, then you will want to read this book.

CLASS LIBRARIES	
(source code in Appendix E)	
LIB2D.HPP	declaration file for class Physical Display and class Viewport.
LIB2D.CPP	implemention file containing methods for class Physical Display and class Viewport, providing a set of graphics language bindings to control the physical display, viewports, bitblts, lines, circle, fills, and other low-level drawing functions.
LIB3D.HPP	declaration file for class Model3D.
LIB3D.CPP	implementation file containing methods for class Model3D, providing 3D modelling and shading functions with automatic backplane hidden surface removal.
MOUSE.HPP	declaration file for class PointingDevice.
MOUSE.CPP	implementation file containing methods for class PointingDevice, providing low-level interactive control over a mouse.
BITBLT.HPP	declaration file for class Bitblt.
BITBLT.CPP	implementation file containing methods for class Bitblt, providing bitblt objects (graphic arrays) capable of storing, displaying, removing, saving, and loading themselves.
BLITTER.HPP	declaration file for class Blitter.
BLITTER.CPP	implementation file containing methods for class Blitter, providing high-speed overwrite bitblt animation.
PUBLISH.HPP	declaration file for class Layout.
PUBLISH.CPP	implementation file containing methods for class Layout, providing text-pouring functions for desktop publishing.
KINETIC.HPP	declaration file for class Kinetic3D.
KINETIC.CPP	implementation file containing methods for class Kinetic3D, providing 3D routines for kinetic-based 3D animation using the laws of physics.

2   Functional reference to the class libraries.

Supercharged C++ Graphics is an advanced text that picks up where many other books leave off. It is easy to read and the material is presented in a way that is easy to absorb. It provides the information you need to begin developing world-class graphics software. The book has been designed to be suitable for beginner, intermediate, and advanced programmers.

Beginner programmers

If you are new to C++ programming, you can use the sample programs in the book just like training wheels on a bicycle. The demos get you up and running fast. Before you know it you don't need them anymore—you are writing your own high-performance code.

Intermediate and advanced programmers

If you are a corporate programmer building software products for departmental use or for your company's clients—or if you are a professional developer creating applications for the retail market—this book will help you create a software product that is more efficient, effective, and competitive.

If you are an intermediate or advanced amateur programmer interested in writing shareware, freeware, or even commercial software, this book will introduce you to some advanced graphics techniques that can be fine-tuned to compete head-on against packaged software products.

Managers and project leaders

The book is designed to be useful to engineers, scientists, systems analysts, programmers, and managers who are involved in managing a graphics software development project.

About the book

The book is a learning tool. It does not attempt to be complete. There is just not enough space in one book to cover everything about C++ graphics programming. Instead, the book attempts to be useful. It achieves that by using example-rich discussions. It provides sample working code for substantive C++ graphics applications. You will not find any toy programs here—every demonstration program, every class library, and every algorithm can be put to use in developing your own serious software project. The book is a software engineering toolkit, ready for you to use as a springboard to your own programming goals in today's vibrant graphics software marketplace.

Special features of the book

The book's entire production team was keenly aware of the book's main purpose, which is to teach C++ graphics programming. As the book passed along the production process—from my original manuscript to the revisions of the technical editor—from the art director's layout to the press operator's lithography—the book benefitted from that mutual goal.

The book lays flat. This is important if you use the book while you are at your computer. The book is self-contained. Although computer graphics programming is a diverse field, all the routines you need to run the demonstration programs are in the book. The advanced graphics features provided by the demonstration programs are made possible by the use of class libraries in appendix E. See FIG. 3. These class libraries are like software toolkits, providing the low level 2-D and 3-D graphics routines that act as linchpins for the advanced graphics images of the demonstration programs.

This approach to C++ graphics programming makes it possible to build advanced, complex, and sophisticated programs using source listings that are easy to understand. It keeps the size of each program listing at a reasonable length, in spite of the high quality on-screen graphics produced by the demos. It also helps to promote cross-compiler compatibility. See FIG. 4.

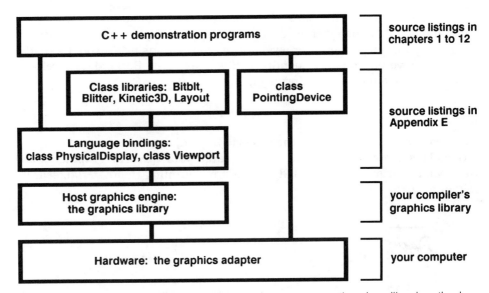

3 Interdependencies between the demonstration programs, the class libraries, the language bindings, the host graphics engine (graphics library), and the hardware.

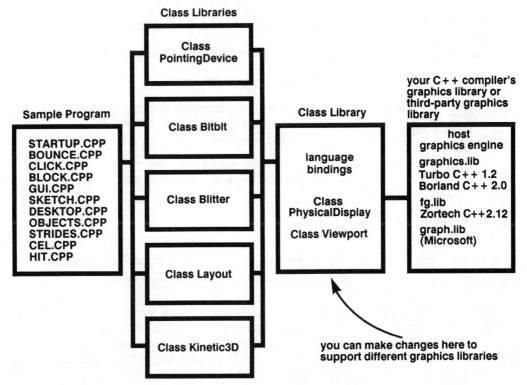

4 The design of the demonstration programs and class libraries strives to be independent of the host graphics engine or graphics library being used by the C++ programmer.

The appendices at the back of the book provide the no-nonsense, practical, hands-on guidance you need to get the sample applications up and running on your own computer system. If you are using Turbo C++, the information you need is in appendix A. If you are using Borland C++, refer to appendix B. If you are using Zortech C++, see appendix C.

Icons

The book uses icons placed on the edges to flag important sections of text. See FIG. 5. This ensures that essential items catch your eye. The graphics make the book easier to read—especially if you are skimming the material, searching for a particular topic.

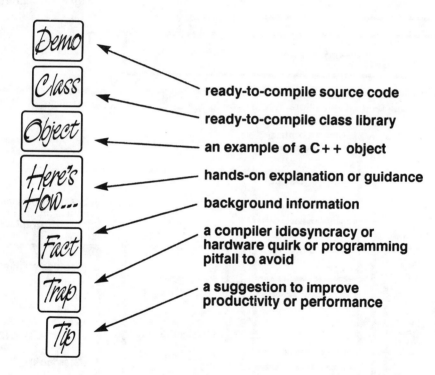

ready-to-compile source code

ready-to-compile class library

an example of a C++ object

hands-on explanation or guidance

background information

a compiler idiosyncracy or hardware quirk or programming pitfall to avoid

a suggestion to improve productivity or performance

5 Icons are placed on the left margin of the book to help flag your attention to important sections.

The book distinguishes between the different types of source code presented in its pages. Icons on the sides help you understand the purpose of the code. A listing accompanied by the Demo icon is a complete, full-length demonstration program ready to compile, link, and run with Turbo C++, Borland C++, and Zortech C++. A listing marked with the Class icon is a C++ class declaration or class implementation listing, ready to compile, link, and run with Turbo C++, Borland C++, and Zortech C++.

Hardware and software compatibility

The principles and all the program listings in the book support cross-compiler development. They have been designed to work with Turbo C++ 1.2, Borland C++ 2.0, and Zortech C++ 2.12. The source listings also offer nominal compatibility with Microsoft's anticipated C++ compiler, still under production as this book goes to press. The powerful preprocessor directives #if, #elif, and #endif have been used in the source code to ensure compatibility with the Turbo C++, Borland C++, and Zortech C++ implementations of the C++ programming language and the AT&T C++ 2.0 specification.

A special autodetect module is present in the methods for class PhysicalDisplay in the class implementation listing, LIB2D.CPP, presented in appendix E. This routine allows each demonstration program to adapt itself at startup to support the best graphics possible on your computer system. Most demonstration programs in *Lee Adams' Supercharged C++ Graphics* explicitly support all popular graphics adapters, including VGA, EGA, MCGA, CGA, and Hercules.

The code supports the concept of platform-independent graphics. Source code that is dependent on a specific graphics library—either the BGI library of Turbo C++ and Borland C++, or the Flash Graphics library of Zortech C++, or Microsoft's graph.lib—has mostly been limited to the class libraries in appendix E. This means that the demonstration programs are relatively easy to adapt to other C++ compilers as they become available. Perhaps even more important, the multi-module programming approach used throughout the book makes it possible to convert the demonstration programs and class libraries to third-party graphics libraries like HALO Professional, MetaWINDOW, MetaWINDOW/Plus, and others. See appendix F for further discussion.

Error-free program listings

The program listings are photographic copies of listings produced on my laser printer. This is your assurance of error-free program listings. The source code in the book is exactly the same code distributed on the companion disks. It is taken directly from my hard disk where it has been meticulously tested with Turbo C++ 1.2, Borland C++ 2.0, and Zortech C++ 2.12 in many different graphics modes on three different computer systems.

Program format

Each program listing and class library adheres to a consistent format. See FIG. 6. The source code in the book is formatted to make the code easy to understand. Each program listing and code fragment carries line numbers down the left margin. This provides a reliable method for referring to the code in the text. The line numbers were added when the listings were printed using Dan Bricklin's laser printer driver, PageGarden version 1A.

C++ compilers do not recognize line numbers in source code, however. Do not type the line numbers if you are typing in the program listings from the book.

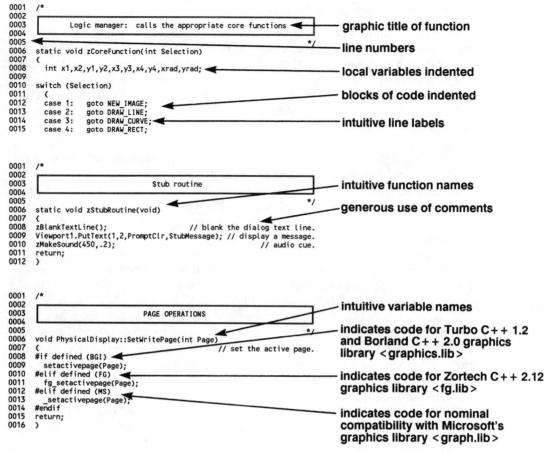

```
0001  /*
0002
0003        Logic manager:  calls the appropriate core functions
0004
0005                                                              */
0006  static void zCoreFunction(int Selection)
0007  {
0008    int x1,x2,y1,y2,x3,y3,x4,y4,xrad,yrad;
0009
0010  switch (Selection)
0011    {
0012    case 1:    goto NEW_IMAGE;
0013    case 2:    goto DRAW_LINE;
0014    case 3:    goto DRAW_CURVE;
0015    case 4:    goto DRAW_RECT;
```

— graphic title of function
— line numbers
— local variables indented
— blocks of code indented
— intuitive line labels

```
0001  /*
0002
0003                         Stub routine
0004
0005                                                              */
0006  static void zStubRoutine(void)
0007  {
0008  zBlankTextLine();                        // blank the dialog text line.
0009  Viewport1.PutText(1,2,PromptClr,StubMessage); // display a message.
0010  zMakeSound(450,.2);                          // audio cue.
0011  return;
0012  }
```

— intuitive function names
— generous use of comments

```
0001  /*
0002
0003                      PAGE OPERATIONS
0004
0005                                                              */
0006  void PhysicalDisplay::SetWritePage(int Page)
0007  {
0008  #if defined (BGI)                      // set the active page.
0009    setactivepage(Page);
0010  #elif defined (FG)
0011    fg_setactivepage(Page);
0012  #elif defined (MS)
0013    _setactivepage(Page);
0014  #endif
0015  return;
0016  }
```

— intuitive variable names
— indicates code for Turbo C++ 1.2 and Borland C++ 2.0 graphics library < graphics.lib >
— indicates code for Zortech C++ 2.12 graphics library < fg.lib >
— indicates code for nominal compatibility with Microsoft's graphics library < graph.lib >

6 The source code listings are presented in a format intended to make learning easy.

Each demonstration program listing and class library listing is generously sprinkled with remarks. This policy swells the length of each listing, but the comments make it easier for you to understand what the code is doing.

Blocks of code are indented in the listings. Run-ons from previous lines of code are also indented. The Turbo C++, Borland C++, and Zortech C++ editors were set to a tab setting of two spaces during preparation of the code. A small tab value like this keeps complex code from running past the right edge of the screen. Set your own Turbo C++, Borland C++, or Zortech C++ editor to tab two spaces if you are using the companion disks to *Lee Adams' Supercharged C++ Graphics*.

Program title blocks

Each full-length demonstration program begins with a formal title block. See FIG. 7. This header provides important information, including the name of the source file, the purpose of the code, and the list of source files and class

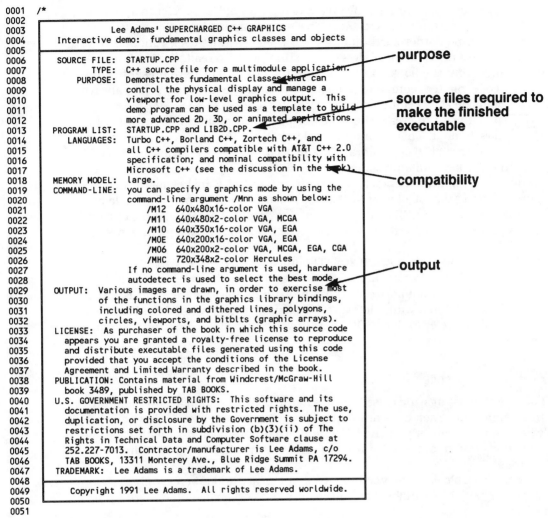

```
0001  /*
0002
0003               Lee Adams' SUPERCHARGED C++ GRAPHICS
0004        Interactive demo:  fundamental graphics classes and objects
0005
0006      SOURCE FILE:  STARTUP.CPP
0007             TYPE:  C++ source file for a multimodule application.
0008          PURPOSE:  Demonstrates fundamental classes that can
0009                    control the physical display and manage a
0010                    viewport for low-level graphics output.  This
0011                    demo program can be used as a template to build
0012                    more advanced 2D, 3D, or animated applications.
0013     PROGRAM LIST:  STARTUP.CPP and LIB2D.CPP.
0014        LANGUAGES:  Turbo C++, Borland C++, Zortech C++, and
0015                    all C++ compilers compatible with AT&T C++ 2.0
0016                    specification; and nominal compatibility with
0017                    Microsoft C++ (see the discussion in the book).
0018     MEMORY MODEL:  large.
0019     COMMAND-LINE:  you can specify a graphics mode by using the
0020                    command-line argument /Mnn as shown below:
0021                         /M12  640x480x16-color VGA
0022                         /M11  640x480x2-color VGA, MCGA
0023                         /M10  640x350x16-color VGA, EGA
0024                         /MOE  640x200x16-color VGA, EGA
0025                         /M06  640x200x2-color VGA, MCGA, EGA, CGA
0026                         /MHC  720x348x2-color Hercules
0027                    If no command-line argument is used, hardware
0028                    autodetect is used to select the best mode.
0029     OUTPUT:  Various images are drawn, in order to exercise most
0030              of the functions in the graphics library bindings,
0031              including colored and dithered lines, polygons,
0032              circles, viewports, and bitblts (graphic arrays).
0033     LICENSE:  As purchaser of the book in which this source code
0034        appears you are granted a royalty-free license to reproduce
0035        and distribute executable files generated using this code
0036        provided that you accept the conditions of the License
0037        Agreement and Limited Warranty described in the book.
0038     PUBLICATION: Contains material from Windcrest/McGraw-Hill
0039        book 3489, published by TAB BOOKS.
0040     U.S. GOVERNMENT RESTRICTED RIGHTS:  This software and its
0041        documentation is provided with restricted rights.  The use,
0042        duplication, or disclosure by the Government is subject to
0043        restrictions set forth in subdivision (b)(3)(ii) of The
0044        Rights in Technical Data and Computer Software clause at
0045        252.227-7013.  Contractor/manufacturer is Lee Adams, c/o
0046        TAB BOOKS, 13311 Monterey Ave., Blue Ridge Summit PA 17294.
0047     TRADEMARK:  Lee Adams is a trademark of Lee Adams.
0048
0049        Copyright 1991 Lee Adams.  All rights reserved worldwide.
0050
0051
```

purpose

source files required to make the finished executable

compatibility

output

7 Each source code listing contains an informative header.

libraries which must be linked together to produce the finished executable program.

The title block also provides information about the performance and features of the finished program. If command-line arguments are supported, they are explained here. If you are using a VGA, for example, you can coerce most demonstration programs in *Supercharged C++ Graphics* to run in a different mode. Simply type a designated keyword when you run the program from the operating system prompt. Turbo C++, Borland C++, and Zortech C++ also support a simulated command-line prompt during an interactive C++ programming session. If you are using Turbo C++, see appendix A for more information on this technique. If you are using Borland C++, refer to appendix B. If you are programming with Zortech C++, see appendix C.

The graphic border surrounding each program title, each function title, and each class method title makes each listing easier to read. If you are typing the listings from the book you can ignore the boxes. They are present in the source code on the companion disks, but because the boxes are always enclosed inside /*...*/ comments the compiler ignores them.

Here's How... If you want to create the boxes in your own program listings, here is how to do it. This technique works with the Turbo C++, Borland C++, and Zortech C++ editors. Ensure that Num Lock is disabled. Hold down the Alt key while pressing a sequence of ASCII codes on the numeric keypad. Use the numeric keypad at the right end of your keyboard, not the numbers along the top of your keyboard. The upper left corner of the title box is created by typing ASCII 201. To display this graphic character at the current cursor position, hold down Alt while you type 2 0 1 on the keypad, then release the Alt key.

The horizontal line is ASCII 205. The upper right corner is 187. The lower left and lower right corners are ASCII 200 and 188. The vertical line is 186. The vertical line with a horizontal stub protruding towards the right is ASCII 204. The vertical line with a leftward horizontal stub is ASCII 185. For other line-characters, refer to the ASCII chart in your Turbo C++, Borland C++, and Zortech C++ manual.

Programming style

The program listings and class libraries in the book maintain a consistent programming style. Each constant name is typed in all uppercase characters. A leading z character is prepended to help avoid name conflicts with existing constants which are built into the compiler's libraries and third-party libraries.

Each variable name is typed in mixed uppercase and lowercase characters. Whenever possible, variables are given intuitive, self-explanatory, descriptive names.

Each program function and class method is typed in mixed uppercase and lowercase characters. Functions are given descriptive names that help explain their actions. Each program function name starts with the z prefix in order to help avoid name conflicts with library functions.

Screen prints

Each demonstration program in the book is accompanied by at least one screen print. This visual feedback can be used as a benchmark by which to judge the graphics output on your own computer system.

Each screen print was produced directly from my own VGA-equipped personal computer. This is your assurance that the C++ routines in the book generate high quality graphics output.

The screen images were stored in PCX format by pcxGrab, a utility from

Genus Microprogramming, developers of the PCX Programmer's Toolkit. Pizazz, the screen printing utility from Application Techniques, was used to size and dither the image before generating hard copy output on the author's LaserJet IIP printer.

The demonstration programs in *Lee Adams' Supercharged C++ Graphics* run in full color on VGA and EGA adapters. They run in black-and-white on MCGA, CGA, and Hercules adapters. Each screen print in the book is printed in black and white. For programs that use 3-D modeling and shading, some minor conflicting patterns have been printed because of the need to translate a multicolor image to a black and white print.

Illustrations

In addition to demonstration programs, class libraries, code fragments, pseudocode, and text discussion, the book contains many drawings, illustrations, and graphics prints. A simple, well-designed drawing can often explain a concept that might otherwise take many paragraphs to describe. The use of graphics in the book reflects my unshakeable conviction in the strength and power of graphics in communicating—especially computer graphics.

How the book is organized

Lee Adams' Supercharged C++ Graphics is organized to give you practical, hands-on experience with computer graphics. Using an easy-to-follow format, important fundamentals are introduced in Part One. They become linchpins for more advanced programming techniques presented in parts two, three, and four.

The book does not force you to adopt a dogmatic approach to learning the material. If you are a beginner or intermediate C++ programmer, you might benefit from following the book from start to finish. The sample programs and the text discussion build upon material presented earlier. If you are an intermediate or advanced C++ programmer you might prefer to skip from section to section in random order, picking topics that interest you. Most chapters are presented as individual packets of information. They can be studied independent of each other.

Part One: High-performance programming skills

Part One introduces some fundamental C++ programming skills that form the foundation for many of the demonstration programs and class libraries in the book.

Chapter 1 provides an overview of graphics application development using C++. It discusses C++ extensions to C, const variables, overloaded functions, classes, inheritance, and other C++ paradigms that will make your graphics programming more productive. A sample program, STARTUP.CPP, is used to exercise many of the low-level graphics methods in class PhysicalDisplay and class Viewport.

Chapter 2 teaches you how to program an animation sequence. Frame and bitblt methods are discussed. A sample program, BOUNCE.CPP, is used to demonstrate the powerful bitblt techniques in the class library BLITTER.CPP.

Chapter 3 discusses programming a pointing device. A sample program, CLICK.CPP, shows you how to take full advantage of the class methods in MOUSE.HPP and MOUSE.CPP.

Chapter 4 focuses on programming for keyboard and disk. A fully interactive sample program, BLOCK.CPP, lets you manipulate a self-controlling bitblt image on the display. The powerful methods in class Bitblt provide graphics capable of displaying, moving, erasing, saving, and loading themselves.

Part Two: Building 2-D graphics applications

Part Two provides instruction in interactive GUI graphics, interactive draw/paint graphics, and desktop publishing graphics.

Chapter 5 describes GUI graphics, also known as graphical user interfaces. The methods of class Bitblt are used to build a sample program, GUI.CPP, that provides a menuing system to act as a front end for your own C++ graphics programs.

Chapter 6 shows you some routines used in interactive paint/draw software. A sample program, SKETCH.CPP, provides an interactive drawing and painting toolkit with which you can experiment.

Chapter 7 deals with interactive desktop publishing graphics. A timely discussion of page layout components gives you a solid understanding of the intricacies involved. A sample program, DESKTOP.CPP, exercises the powerful page layout methods found in the class library PUBLISH.CPP, pouring text from a standard ASCII file onto a page design.

Part Three: Building 3-D graphics applications

Part Three introduces the challenging field of interactive 3-D graphics on personal computers.

Chapter 8 introduces you to the theory behind 3-D computer-generated images. Concepts like rotation, translation, extrusion, facets, edges, and camera are explored. The underpinnings of the class library LIB3D.HPP are explained.

Chapter 9 provides hands-on experience in using C++ to build an interactive 3-D modeler and shader. A sample program, OBJECTS.CPP, provides working code for your experimentation.

Part Four: Creating animation software

Part Four focuses on the animation capabilities of personal computers, including display animation, cel animation, and kinetic animation.

Chapter 10 teaches you versatile techniques for using display animation in your own programming projects. A sample program, STRIDES.CPP, provides a professionally animated example of a running cartoon character. A thorough discussion of tricks used by professional animators gives you the background you need to successfully tackle any animation project.

Chapter 11 describes some interesting aspects of computer-assisted cel animation. Tweening, morphing, and onionskin techniques are discussed. An interactive sample program, CEL.CPP, automatically generates in-between images (tweens) from two images that you provide (keyframes).

Chapter 12 is a hands-on tutorial with kinetic animation, where the laws of physics can be used to control 3-D animation sequences. Using the C++ class library KINETIC.CPP, a sample program animates a 3-D sphere as it ricochets off the walls of a 3-D container.

Appendices

The appendices provide practical help in getting the demonstration programs up and running on your computer system.

Appendix A shows you how to compile the sample programs with Turbo C++. Appendix B provides guidance for Borland C++. Appendix C is a step-by-step guide for running the sample programs with Zortech C++. Appendix D describes the nominal compatibility provided by the listings for Microsoft's anticipated C++ compiler.

The complete source code for the C++ class libraries used by the demonstration programs is presented in appendix E. Included are .hpp class declaration listings and .cpp class implementation listings. You get seven high-powered C++ class libraries for graphics output, viewports, self-displaying bitblts, 3-D modeling, desktop publishing, high-speed animation, and more. Appendix E contains nearly 6500 lines of code to support the 7000 lines of code found in demonstration programs in the main body of the book. Appendix G provides tips for trapping runtime errors in your C++ programs.

A glossary provides a collection of names, definitions, acronyms, and descriptions that are common to computer programming in general, and to C++ and graphics programming in particular.

What you need to use the book

In spite of the sophisticated on-screen images produced by the demonstration programs, you need only a personal computer and a typical C++ compiler to begin exploring the potential of computer graphics.

Hardware required

If you have an IBM-compatible personal computer equipped with an Intel 8086, 8088, 80286, 80386, or 80486 microprocessor, then you have the platform you need to run the demonstration programs in the book.

You will need graphics hardware too. VGA, EGA, MCGA, CGA, and Hercules adapters are supported by the program listings in the book. A VGA adapter provides the best color and resolution—and it can emulate the modes of other adapters. Most of the demo programs will start up in the 640×480×16-color analog mode if a VGA is present.

Next best is an EGA adapter. Most of the demonstration programs will use the 640×350×16-color mode if an enhanced monitor is available. If you are using a standard color display with your EGA, the demo programs will start up in the 640×200×16-color mode.

If an MCGA adapter is present, the programs will use the 640×480× 2-color mode. If you are using a CGA adapter, the demo programs will run in the 640×200×2-color mode. If your system has a Hercules adapter installed, the demonstration programs will start up in the 720×348×2-color mode, subject to the limitations of the graphics library and mouse driver being used.

To use the C++ compilers that are supported by the demonstration programs in the book you will need a hard disk in your computer. 640K of RAM is also advisable.

Software required

You can compile, link, and run the demonstration programs with Turbo C++, Borland C++, and Zortech C++. During the preparation of the program listings I used Turbo C++ version 1.2, Borland C++ version 2.0, and Zortech C++ version 2.12.

The companion disks

The companion disks for *Lee Adams' Supercharged C++ Graphics* contain all the source code from the book. And the listings in the book contain all the source code in the companion disks—nothing is missing. The companion disks save you the time and trouble of keying in the program listings, so you can concentrate instead on learning about C++ graphics programming.

The companion disks are available in both 5.25-inch and 3.5-inch format. See the publisher's ad at the back of the book for further information.

If you intend to adapt material from this book

The source code and information presented in this book can be used to write commercial-quality software. Other readers have taken material from previous books, expanded upon it and fine-tuned it, and have used it to help them create profitable software products.

If you intend to adapt material from this book to write commercial software, corporate software, shareware, or freeware, then it is important that you read and understand the License Agreement and Limited Warranty. See FIG. 8.

About the license agreement and limited warranty

Other books about C++ programming contain source code, but often impose limitations on your right to lawfully distribute the code as part of your software product. This book takes a different approach. The "License Agreement" per-

8 The source code in the book can be used to help build your own applications, subject to the royalty-free license.

mits you to use the program code in the development of your own software, no matter whether you plan to distribute your product in the commercial, corporate, shareware, or freeware marketplace. After all, the source code is probably one of the reasons why you acquired the book in the first place.

The main purpose of the source code in the book is to teach. The program code has been designed to be easy to read, easy to understand, and easy to test. It is optimized for browsing. It is not optimized for speed. Even so, it is an excellent starting point from which to build your own C++ applications. By plugging the sample code into your own C++ source files, you can get your application prototype working sooner. You can always return later to optimize the code for maximum speed and minimum size.

Some limitations apply

It is important for you to understand that a few simple limitations apply to your use of the program code. The "License Agreement" in FIG. 8 explains your rights and your responsibilities.

A copy of the "License Agreement" and "Limited Warranty" is also included on the companion disks in a text file named READ_ME.DOC.

Additional material

If you enjoy the material in this book, or if you want further information about specialized topics, additional information can be found in my other books in the Applied C Graphics series from Windcrest/McGraw-Hill. A catalog of current titles about programming is available by writing to the publisher. See the information at the back of the book.

Demonstration programs

The book contains 12 full-length, ready-to-run C++ demonstration programs and seven C++ class libraries. The plug'n'play demo programs are provided in the main body of the book. The class libraries are provided in appendix E.

The demonstration programs are designed to be linked with the appropriate class libraries. Detailed instructions for compiling, linking, and running each demonstration program is provided in the appropriate chapter. Further compiler-specific information is provided in the appendices.

Cross-compiler development

The source code in *Lee Adams' Supercharged C++ Graphics* has been designed to support cross-compiler development. This means you can use your favorite C++ compiler to compile, link, and run the demonstration programs in the book. Turbo C++, Borland C++, and Zortech C++ are explicitly supported. Nominal compatibility is provided for Microsoft's anticipated C++ compiler. If you are using Turbo C++, refer to appendix A for guidance in compiling the demonstration programs and class libraries. If you are using Borland C++, refer to appendix B. If you are using Zortech C++, read appendix C.

Platform independence

The source code in *Lee Adams' Supercharged C++ Graphics* has been designed to provide a significant degree of platform independence. This means you can run most of the demonstration programs on a VGA, EGA, MCGA, CGA, or Hercules graphics adapter. If you are using a VGA, the sample programs run in the 640×480×16-color mode. If you are using an EGA and enhanced display, the programs run in the 640×350×16-color mode. If you are using an EGA and standard display, the demos run in the 640×200×16-color mode. If you are using an MCGA, the sample programs run in the 640×480×2-color mode. If you are using a CGA, the demonstration programs run in the 640×200×2-color mode. If you are using a Hercules adapter, the sample applications run in the 720×348×2-color mode. If you are using a VGA, you can use a command line argument to force the demonstration programs to run in the EGA, MCGA, or CGA modes. If you are using an EGA, you can use a command line argument to force the demonstration programs to run in the low-resolution EGA mode or the CGA mode.

C++ demonstration programs

STARTUP.CPP provides a test suite for the low-level graphics routines in class PhysicalDisplay and class Viewport, found in LIB2D.CPP. A runtime autodetect routine is demonstrated, providing language bindings to the graphics libraries of Turbo C++, Borland C++, Zortech C++, and Microsoft.

BOUNCE.CPP demonstrates high-speed bitblt animation using overwrite graphic arrays. The program utilizes the specialized animation methods of class Blitter in BLITTER.CPP.

CLICK.CPP demonstrates a fundamental interactive mouse application, relying upon the low-level mouse methods of class PointingDevice provided in MOUSE.CPP.

BLOCK.CPP provides interactive control over a bitblt image using nondestructive graphic arrays. The program demonstrates the methods of class Bitblt, which provides bitblt objects capable of displaying, moving, and erasing themselves—in addition to being able to save themselves to disk and load themselves from disk.

GUI.CPP demonstrates a graphical user interface menu system that can be used as a front end for graphics programs. The demo relies upon the methods of class Bitblt, class PhysicalDisplay, and class Viewport.

SKETCH.CPP is an interactive draw/paint toolkit. It exploits the methods of class PhysicalDisplay and class Viewport found in LIB2D.CPP.

DESKTOP.CPP demonstrates text-pouring methods useful for creating desktop publishing software with C++. It relies on the methods of class Layout in PUBLISH.CPP.

OBJECTS.CPP is a full-featured, interactive 3-D modeling and shading toolkit. The demonstration program exercises the 3-D methods of class Model3D, found in LIB3D.CPP.

STRIDES.CPP is an anatomically exaggerated animation of a running cartoon character. The sample program uses the methods of class Blitter, class PhysicalDisplay, and class Viewport.

CEL.CPP demonstrates an interactive morphing and tweening editor that can generate in-between images from two keyframes you draw. The program relies upon class PhysicalDisplay and class Viewport.

HIT.CPP illustrates 3-D kinetic animation, providing a real-time simulation of a 3-D sphere ricocheting off the walls of a container. The demonstration relies on the methods of class Kinetic3D in KINETIC.CPP.

C++ class libraries

LIB2D.HPP is the declaration file for class PhysicalDisplay and class Viewport.

LIB2D.CPP is the implementation file for class PhysicalDisplay and class Viewport, providing a set of low-level graphics language bindings for Turbo C++, Borland C++, Zortech C++, and Microsoft's anticipated C++ compiler.

LIB3D.HPP is the declaration file for class Model3D.

LIB3D.CPP is the implementation file for class Model3D, providing methods for creating fully shaded solid 3-D models with hidden surface removal.

MOUSE.HPP is the declaration file for class PointingDevice.

MOUSE.CPP is the implementation file for class PointingDevice, providing low-level control for mouse input.

BITBLT.HPP is the declaration file for class Bitblt.

BITBLT.CPP is the implementation file for class Bitblt, providing bitblt objects capable of displaying, moving, erasing, saving, and loading themselves.

BLITTER.HPP is the declaration file for class Blitter.

BLITTER.CPP is the implementation file for class Blitter, providing specialized methods for high-speed bitblt animation.

PUBLISH.HPP is the declaration file for class Layout.

PUBLISH.CPP is the implementation file for class Layout, providing text-pouring methods for desktop publishing functions.

KINETIC.HPP is the declaration file for class Kinetic3D.

KINETIC.CPP is the implementation file for class Kinetic3D, providing methods to support 3-D kinetic animation and collision detection.

LIB2DBC.HPP is the declaration file for class PhysicalDisplay and class Viewport for use with Borland C++.

LIB2DBC.CPP is the implementation file for class PhysicalDisplay and class Viewport for use with Borland C++.

MOUSEBC.CPP is the declaration file for class PointingDevice for use with Borland C++.

Why use C++

C has been the language of choice for many software developers up to now. Most serious applications are written in C, with critical portions of the program hand-coded in assembly language.

Today's C development platform is richly endowed. It offers versatility, power, and portability. In addition to the built-in runtime libraries of C, numerous toolkits are available from third-party suppliers. These add-ins give C programmers the power they need to tackle advanced applications like graphics, communications, database, screen management, menuing, TSRs, pointing devices, overlays, multitasking, and more.

With all these advantages, why would anyone want to switch to C++? The answer is simple. This is one of those situations where you can have your cake and eat it too.

The C++ superset

C++ is a superset of C. That means it possesses all the features and all the functionality of C. In fact, you can use your C++ compiler as a standard C compiler if you wish. Then, as you become comfortable with the productivity advantages offered by C++, you can gradually add some C++ code to your programs. Your migration from C to C++ can be at your own pace. C++ prudently allows you to safeguard the investment you have already made in C. There are no burned bridges along the road to C++. C++ does not ask that you abandon the past as you build for the future.

Graphics advantages of C++

C++ offers immediate and significant advantages for graphics programmers. C++ concepts like encapsulation, inheritance, and polymorphism are more than just mere jingoism. As this book shows, C++ can be immediately put to work providing you with self-controlling graphic images capable of displaying themselves, moving themselves, erasing themselves—even saving themselves to disk and reloading themselves if needed. And, best of all, you need to write the code only once! C++ takes care of all the low-level work if you decide you want more self-controlling objects in different sizes, colors, or shapes. If you want to add yet more capabilities to your object, C++ will conveniently append your new code to existing code, rocketing your productivity to new highs. And that is just one example of the power of C++.

C++ can boost your performance, enhance your productivity, and increase your profitability. C++ can turn your computer into a partner in your software projects—a partner that gladly toils in the back shop, working hard to make you look good up front.

Part One

High-performance programming skills

1
Graphics application development using C++

In the early 1990s, a new programming language roared onto the scene. New compilers suddenly appeared in the marketplace, unashamedly making brazen claims for improved productivity and reusable code. During the year 1990, interest in the new upstart began to swell in spite of its curious name, C++ (see-plus-plus). A product named Zortech C++ aggressively staked out a share of the market and began to build up a loyal cadre of followers. By the fall of 1990, Turbo C++ was already providing stiff competition for Zortech C++. By the spring of 1991, Turbo C++ had been joined in the marketplace by its superset Borland C++, and Microsoft was talking about introducing a C++ compiler by year's end. Almost overnight, C++ had become a part of the mainstream. C's revered position as the most popular programming language was seriously threatened. Or was it?

The C programming language was developed in the middle 1970s at the AT&T Bell Laboratories by Dennis Ritchie. C was originally designed as a systems programming language. It quickly became the language of choice for serious software developers. C offered many of the features found in high-level languages like BASIC, Pascal, and Fortran. At the same time, C retained much of the power and direct access to hardware provided by a low-level language like assembly language.

The C++ programming language was developed in the early 1980s at the AT&T Bell Laboratories by Bjarne Stroustrup. C++ was designed as a simulation language intended to rely upon *object-oriented programming* (OOP). Stroustrup's first implementations of C++ were as *translators*, or programs that acted as preprocessors to a standard C compiler. The C++ preprocessor translated C++ source code into C source code, which in turn was provided to the C compiler for parsing and compiling. C++ compilers capable of accepting C++ source code and producing native object code began to enter the market in the early 1990s.

C++ provides two important improvements to the C programming language. First, it offers extensions, such as new keywords and features, to C. Second, it adds the productivity-boosting power of object-oriented programming to C.

Perhaps even more important, however, is the manner in which C++ meshes with C. Because it is a superset of C, you can use your C++ compiler as a regular C compiler. This means you can gradually make the transition to C++ programming.

Fact C++ is a superset of C.

C++ extensions to C

C++ provides significant extensions to the C programming language. These extensions fall into four broad categories. They are comments, variables, functions, and memory allocation.

C++ comments

C++ supports the comment tokens provided by C. This format specifies that all characters following the /* character sequence are ignored by the compiler until the */ character sequence is encountered. The following example is a legitimate comment in C and C++ source code:

```
/* this is a comment */
```

C++ provides another comment format. All characters following the // double slash token are ignored by the compiler up to the end of the current line of the source code. The following line is a valid comment in C++ source code:

```
// this is a comment
```

Most C compilers will flag this as a syntax error.

The // comment format makes it easier to add remarks to your source code. You don't have to concern yourself with properly terminating a comment, because the remark automatically ends at the end of the current line. If you want to insert a comment that exceeds one line, simply revert to the /*...*/ format.

Trap Many C compilers do not recognize the // comment format.

C++ variables

C++ provides a number of improvements to the way C programmers have traditionally handled variables in their programs. Two of the most useful extensions are the positioning of variable declarations and the C++ const keyword.

Position of variable declarations

C programming protocol dictated that all variables local to a function be declared before any executable statements. Global variables needed to be declared outside of any function and before the executable statements that used the variables.

C++ loosens the restrictions on where and when you declare variables in your source code. First, C++ allows you to declare a variable anywhere in your program, provided that the declaration is made before the variable is used by the program. Second, C++ allows you to declare a new variable at the moment you first use the variable in your program. The following loop construction is an example.

```
for (int Count = 1; Count < 10; Count ++)
```

In this example the variable Count is declared to be of type int at the same time it is assigned the value of 1. This declaration feature of C++ helps keep you moving forward as you write code, rather than continually moving back in the source code to add variable declarations to support the code you are about to write.

C++ const variables

Constants are variables whose values do not change during the execution of the program. As FIG. 1-1 illustrates, C++ provides more control over how these constants are handled by the compiler. The const keyword is prepended to the line that declares the type and assigns a value to the constant variable.

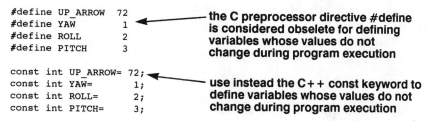

1-1 The C++ const keyword indicates constant variables that do not change during program execution.

Any variable declared with the const variable type qualifier is a read-only variable, except at the moment when it is first initialized. You can declare and initialize a const variable wherever you can declare an ordinary variable. You must, however, initialize a const variable with a constant such as 27, .70711, 28044, and so on. You cannot assign a regular variable to a const variable.

Many C++ programmers consider C's #define directive to be obsolete.

C++ functions

C++ provides a number of significant extensions to the way C programmers use functions. Two important extensions are default function arguments and function overloading.

Default function arguments

A default function argument is an argument that the compiler automatically provides when the function is called. The following example illustrates the concept.

```
static int DrawDot(int, int, int Color = 4);
```

This sample line of code is a function declaration. It declares a function named DrawDot( ) that returns a value of type int. Drawdot( ) is declared as static, meaning its visibility is limited to the source file in which it is declared. Draw-Dot( ) expects to receive three arguments when it is called, all of type int. If you call DrawDot( ) and provide only two arguments, the compiler will use a value of 4 as the third argument. If you call DrawDot( ) and provide three arguments, the compile will use the three arguments you provide—and will not use the default argument. If you provide three arguments, you are overriding the default argument.

Suppose, for example, that DrawDot( ) sets a single pixel on the display. The first argument might be the x coordinate. The second argument might be the y coordinate. The third argument might be the color. If your program calls DrawDot( ) repeatedly with the color 4 as the third argument, it makes more sense to use 4 as a default argument. If, from time to time, you need DrawDot ( ) to set a pixel to a color other than 4, simply provide the desired color as the third argument. Otherwise, just call Drawdot( ) with two arguments.

A function can be declared with more than one default argument, but the default arguments must always be the final arguments in the function's argument list. Also see FIG. 1-6 later in this chapter for an example of multiple default arguments.

Trap Default arguments must always be the last arguments in a function declaration.

Function overloading

The C++ feature of function overloading refers to the practice of calling different functions via the same function name. Consider the following example, which declares three different functions, each of which draws a line on the display.

```
static void DrawTheLine(int, int);
static void DrawTheLine(int, int, int);
static void DrawTheLine(int, int, int, int);
```

The definition for the first version of DrawTheLine( ) might contain graphics drawing statements that draw a line. The function might expect to receive an x coordinate and a y coordinate in the argument list. The line would be drawn from the current position to the xy position. The line would be drawn as a solid line using the current system color.

The definition for the second version of DrawTheLine( ) expects to receive three arguments when it is called. The first argument might be the x coordinate. The second argument might be the y coordinate. The third argument might be the desired color. The function would draw a solid line from the current position to the xy coordinates in the color desired.

The definition for the third version of DrawTheLine( ) expects to receive four arguments when it is called. The fourth argument might specify the line style to be used—solid, dotted, dashed, patterned, and so forth.

The C++ compiler will produce code that automatically selects the appropriate version of DrawTheLine( ), based upon the number and type of arguments used in the function call. Different function definitions (executable blocks of code) can use the same function name provided that their argument lists are different. Consider the following example, which continues the DrawTheLine( ) series.

```
static void DrawTheLine(float,float,float,float);
```

Although this version of DrawTheLine( ) contains four arguments, it will not be confused with the earlier example that also contains four arguments, because the previous version contains four arguments of type int. This example employs four arguments of type float, which might be used if the function were expected to draw a parametric curve instead of a simple straight line.

Function overloading can make your programming easier by providing a common function name to functions that are just variations on a theme. Also see FIG. 1-6 later in this chapter for an example of function overloading used in class methods, where it is known as *polymorphism.*

C++ new and delete keywords

C++ provides two new keywords that make it easier to allocate and deallocate memory during program execution. See FIG. 1-2. The new operator allocates memory from the free store. The delete operator returns a block of previously allocated memory to the free store. The free store is the heap or far heap, depending on the memory model you are using. It is free memory.

C++ new operator

The new operator is used to allocate an appropriate block of memory for a data type, structure, or array. The operator will automatically allocate the correctly sized block of memory. As FIG. 1-2 shows, the new operator results in source code that is easier to read. It also removes much of the low-level tedium from the programmer's shoulders.

Tip The new operator is easier to use than C's family of malloc functions. It results in source code that is easier to read and maintain.

C++ delete operator

The delete operator returns to the free store memory that was previously allocated by the new operator. Figure 1-2 shows just how handily this is accomplished.

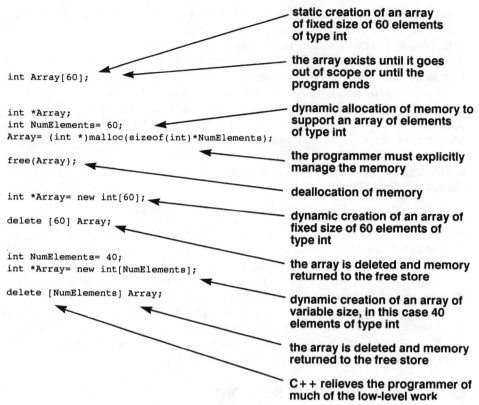

```
                                                   static creation of an array
                                                   of fixed size of 60 elements
                                                   of type int

                                                   the array exists until it goes
int Array[60];                                     out of scope or until the
                                                   program ends

int *Array;                                        dynamic allocation of memory to
int NumElements= 60;                               support an array of elements
Array= (int *)malloc(sizeof(int)*NumElements);     of type int

free(Array);                                       the programmer must explicitly
                                                   manage the memory

                                                   deallocation of memory
int *Array= new int[60];
                                                   dynamic creation of an array of
delete [60] Array;                                 fixed size of 60 elements of
                                                   type int

int NumElements= 40;                               the array is deleted and memory
int *Array= new int[NumElements];                  returned to the free store

delete [NumElements] Array;                        dynamic creation of an array of
                                                   variable size, in this case 40
                                                   elements of type int

                                                   the array is deleted and memory
                                                   returned to the free store

                                                   C++ relieves the programmer of
                                                   much of the low-level work
```

1-2 The C++ operators new and delete provide powerful memory allocation capabilities during program execution.

Allocating dynamic arrays

Probably the single most important benefit of the new and delete operators is their ability to allocate and deallocate dynamic arrays in a consistent and simple manner. A dynamic array is an array that is allocated at runtime, often using a variable dimension instead of a constant dimension. This is a significant improvement over C's capabilities, as shown in FIG. 1-2. The new and delete operators can also be used to create and destroy C++ objects. A C++ object is an instance of a class.

C++ classes

In addition to the extensions to C that have already been described, C++ brings something entirely new to your development environment—the awesome power of object-oriented programming.

Object-oriented programming revolves around the concept of objects. An object is an instance or an occurrence of a new structure type just like a variable is an occurrence of a data type. This new type of structure possesses some unique properties that bring a new vitality to programming.

A new type of structure

This new type of structure provided by C++ is called a *class*. A C++ class is similar to a C structure, but with some important differences. Whereas a C structure is a variable type that is a collection of data elements, a C++ class is made up of both data and the functions that operate on the data. Declaring a class in C++ is akin to declaring a structure in C, except that this new variable type contains both data and functions. The data are called *data members*. The functions are called *member functions*.

Fact A C++ class is a variable structure that is made up of both data and the functions that operate on the data.

After you have used C to declare a structure type, you can create numerous variables of that type. Likewise in C++, after you have declared a class you can create numerous variables of that type. Each occurrence of the class is called an *instance*, or an *instantiation*, or an *object*.

Using objects in your programming will mean you can take full advantage of encapsulation, inheritance, and polymorphism.

Encapsulation

Encapsulation refers to the bundling together of a group of data and the functions that operate on the data. Because you can treat the data and the functions as an object, you do not have to concern yourself with detail. Encapsulation hides a lot of the complexity from you. This means you can work, think, and plan in broader terms—at a higher level of abstraction. C++ encapsulation is like an automatic transmission in a automobile—you no longer have to worry about changing gears anymore, you can instead focus your attention on the road, the traffic signals, and the street signs.

Inheritance

Inheritance refers to the concept of building a new class from classes you have already created. This means you can reuse code. For example, if you want to add a few new features to a class that is already working correctly, you can use C++ inheritance to derive a new class that possesses all the properties of the existing class. Then you simply add the new code to the new class. The C++ compiler takes care of all the low-level work involved in reusing the existing code—you just concentrate on the new enhancements. Because the former class still exists, it can be used by other parts of your program without any unexpected side effects.

Tip C++ inheritance makes it easy to reuse code that you have already tested and debugged.

The new class that you derived from the existing class is called a *derived* class. The existing class is called a *base* class. A derived class possesses all the features—both data members and member functions—of the base class.

Classes can be derived from numerous other classes to numerous levels of derivations, creating a hierarchy of classes.

Polymorphism

Polymorphism refers to the act of using the same name to accomplish different purposes. The C++ features of default arguments and function overloading were described earlier in this chapter. Both are examples of polymorphism.

C++ encapsulation

In C, before you can use a variable in your program you must declare it and initialize it. In C++, before you can use an object in your program you must declare a class and define it. Declaring a class involves naming it and identifying its data members and its methods (member functions). Defining a class involves providing the definitions (executable routines) for the methods of the class.

After you have declared and defined a class you can create as many instances of it in your program as you need. Conceptually, each instance of the class is an object, containing its own set of data and the functions that operate on the data. In practice, however, the C++ compiler generates code that uses the same block of executable code for a method that may belong to many objects of the class.

Each instance is an object that contains all the features of the class. As FIG. 1-3 shows, you can create C++ objects as either static or dynamic. A *static* object is created during compilation and remains available until it goes out of scope or until the program terminates. A *dynamic* C++ object is created at runtime by the C++ new operator and remains valid until destroyed by the C++ delete operator or until the program terminates.

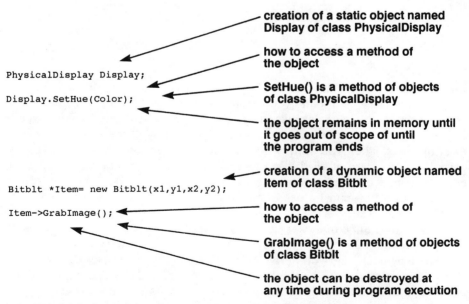

1-3 The C++ operators . and -> are used to access the data members and member functions of an object.

Constructors and destructors

Initialization of an object is performed when the object is created. A special method of the class called a *constructor* is automatically called whenever you create an object of the class. See FIG. 1-4. In many ways the constructor is just like any other C or C++ function, except that it never returns a value, not even void. Constructors can assign values to data members (class variables) that were declared when the class itself was declared.

Conversely, whenever an object is destroyed a special method of the class called a *destructor* is automatically called. Destructors are usually used to release memory allocated by methods of the class.

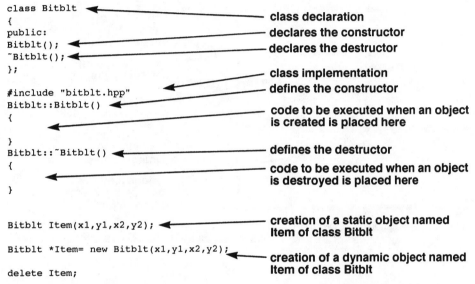

1-4 C++ constructors and destructors are called automatically whenever an object is created or destroyed.

Class declaration files

The C++ source code that declares a class is usually placed in its own source file with the .hpp extension. See FIG. 1-5. This class declaration file is #included in any other C++ source file that requires the services offered by the methods of the class.

Class implementation files

The C++ source code that defines the methods of a class is usually placed in its own source file with a .cpp extension. See FIG. 1-5. This source file is called a *class implementation* file, because it contains the source code that implements the methods of the class. As FIG. 1-5 shows, the .hpp class declaration file is #included in the .cpp class implementation file.

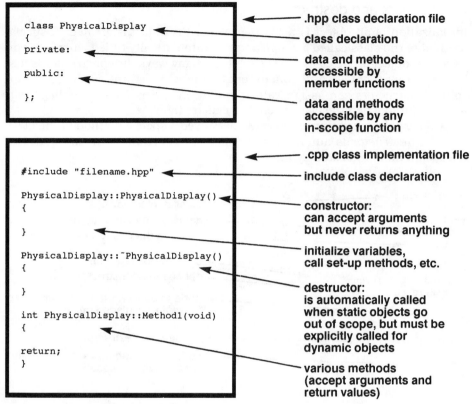

1-5 Encapsulation hides program complexity from the C++ programmer, making it possible to use higher levels of abstraction and to think in broader terms when designing applications.

Segregation of the class declaration and the class definition into separate files makes it easier to manage your C++ projects. In addition, if you decide to market some of the classes you create, you can keep your definitions confidential by distributing the class implementation file in .obj format. By distributing the class declaration file in .hpp source code format you allow your users to take full advantage of all the features offered by your class, including inheritance and polymorphism. Your users can customize your class, yet your proprietary source code remains your secret.

C++ polymorphism

Figure 1-6 depicts one way to take advantage of C++ polymorphism in your programming. By using default arguments and function overloading you can use a common method name to access a variety of different functions.

Some of the source code shown in FIG. 1-6 is taken directly from class Viewport, provided as LIB2D.HPP and LIB2D.CPP in appendix E. As the dem-

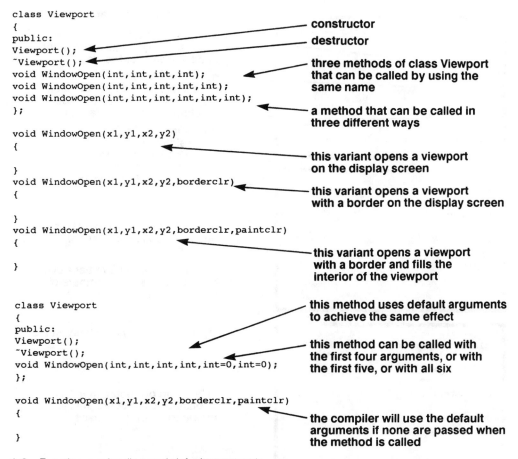

```
class Viewport
{
public:
Viewport();                                    ← constructor
~Viewport();                                   ← destructor
void WindowOpen(int,int,int,int);              ← three methods of class Viewport
void WindowOpen(int,int,int,int,int);            that can be called by using the
void WindowOpen(int,int,int,int,int,int);        same name
};                                             ← a method that can be called in
                                                 three different ways
void WindowOpen(x1,y1,x2,y2)
{
                                               ← this variant opens a viewport
}                                                on the display screen
void WindowOpen(x1,y1,x2,y2,borderclr)         ←
{                                                this variant opens a viewport
                                                 with a border on the display screen
}
void WindowOpen(x1,y1,x2,y2,borderclr,paintclr)
{
                                               ← this variant opens a viewport
                                                 with a border and fills the
}                                                interior of the viewport

class Viewport
{                                              this method uses default arguments
public:                                        to achieve the same effect
Viewport();
~Viewport();                                   ← this method can be called with
void WindowOpen(int,int,int,int,int=0,int=0);    the first four arguments, or with
};                                               the first five, or with all six

void WindowOpen(x1,y1,x2,y2,borderclr,paintclr)
{
                                               ← the compiler will use the default
                                                 arguments if none are passed when
}                                                the method is called
```

1-6 Function overloading and default arguments.

onstration program later in this chapter illustrates, you can set up a viewport on the display screen by calling the WindowOpen( ) method of class Viewport. Depending upon the number of arguments you pass to the method the viewport will be transparent, or transparent and outlined with a border, or filled and outlined with a border.

C++ inheritance

By using the inheritance capabilities of the C++ programming language you can reuse your code by incorporating it into new classes that you write. See FIG. 1-7.

Public, private, protected members

The data members of a class can be declared as either private, protected, or public. A public data member is visible to all functions and methods that are

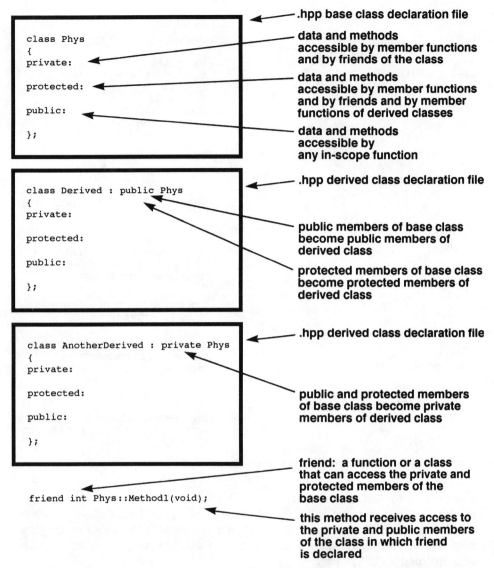

1-7 Inheritance provides the opportunity for C++ programmers to reuse existing code when building new modules.

in scope. A private data member is visible only by methods of the class and by friends of the class. A protected data member is visible only by methods of the class, by friends of the class, and by methods of derived classes.

Friends of a class

A method of a class can be declared to be a friend of another class. A friend can access all the data members and methods of the other class. It can act as if it were a method of the class, although it is not.

Derived class

A derived class is a class that incorporates all the features of the base class from which it is derived. The private, protected, and public qualifiers used in the class declaration for the base class determine which data members and methods are inherited by the derived class. As FIG. 1-7 shows, C++ inheritance can become quite a complex undertaking. Although inheritance makes it possible to reuse code, it significantly reduces the readability of your C++ source code.

Building programs with C++

Building graphics programs with C++ involves many of the same skills used to create graphics software with C. In particular, the principle of multimodule programming can significantly reduce your workload and increase your productivity.

Multimodule programming

The practice of placing class declarations and class implementations into separate source files was described earlier. This is the paradigm followed by the demonstration programs and class libraries in the book. See FIG. 1-5.

The demonstration programs are found in the main body of the book. The class libraries—the .hpp class declaration files and the .cpp class implementation files—are presented in appendix E. Each demonstration program in the main body of the book #includes the appropriate .hpp file for each class whose members it needs to use. Your C++ compiler will link the demonstration program with the class implementation file to produce the finished .exe file. The linker knows which files to link together because of the contents of the project list you provide to your Turbo C++, Borland C++, or Zortech C++ compiler. The compiler knows how to call the methods of the class you are using by the .hpp class declaration file you have incorporated via the #include directive.

Here's How... If you are using Turbo C++ you might benefit from reading appendix A, which describes how to compile and run the demonstration programs. If you are using Borland C++, see appendix B. If you are using Zortech C++, you might want to review appendix C.

Essential parts of C++ graphics programs

The demonstration program later in this chapter demonstrates the essential parts of a typical C++ graphics program. These essential parts, which relate to the runtime functioning of the program, include language bindings, startup and shutdown, detection of the user's graphics hardware, graphics output, and text output.

Language bindings

The language bindings are the source code routines that call the library functions provided by the graphics toolkit you are using. The language bindings are found in LIB2D.CPP in appendix E. In particular, class PhysicalDisplay and class Viewport call the runtime library routines of either Turbo C++'s graphics.lib, Borland C++'s graphics.lib, Zortech C++'s fg.lib, or Microsoft's graph.lib, depending upon which compiler you are using. As described later in this chapter, class PhysicalDisplay provides low-level routines for managing the display; class Viewport provides low-level routines for managing viewports on the display and for generating graphics in the viewports. In its default configuration, class Viewport provides one viewport whose size is the size of the display screen.

Startup and shutdown

An essential ingredient of any graphics program is a well-managed startup process. This includes the sign-on banner, copyright notice, automatic detection of the user's graphics adapter, setting the graphics mode, and launching of the program itself. Of equal importance is a graceful and clean shutdown, usually restoring the screen mode to its previously existing state.

Detection of graphics hardware

The demonstration programs in the book are capable of detecting a VGA, EGA, MCGA, CGA, and Hercules graphics adapter, no matter whether you are using Turbo C++, Borland C++, or Zortech C++ to compile the code. The actual code that performs this task is provided in class PhysicalDisplay, found in the LIB2D.CPP class library in appendix E.

Graphics output

Graphics output refers to the lines, rectangles, fills, bitblts, and other imagery generated at runtime. In most cases the demonstration programs in the book rely upon the class libraries in appendix E for graphics output. These class libraries in turn rely upon the language bindings in LIB2D.CPP to call the appropriate functions from your graphics library.

Text output

When your program is running in a graphics mode, text output can be provided by either using the default system font or custom fonts. Custom fonts can be stroked or bitmap.

The C++ standard output stream, cout, provides a handy method for display text using the built-in system font of your computer. The cout variable is more versatile and powerful than C's printf( ) function. The demonstration programs in the book use cout to display a diagnostic message if the autodetect routine fails to find an acceptable display adapter at program startup.

A sample program: STARTUP.CPP

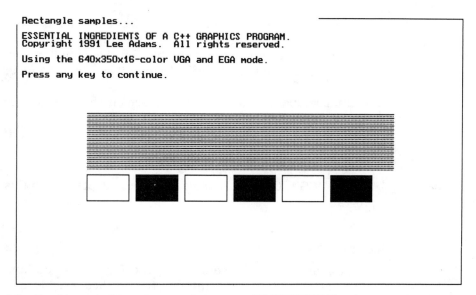Figure 1-8 depicts a typical display produced by the sample program STARTUP.CPP, whose complete source code is provided in FIG. 1-11 at the end of the chapter. The program provides a test suite that exercises the language bindings found in the class libraries in appendix E. After detecting the graphics adapter in your computer system, the program switches to a graphics mode and generates a series of line styles, rectangles, fills, bitblts, and viewport samples in order to verify the integrity of the programming platform. After you have successfully compiled, linked, and run STARTUP.CPP, you should experience no difficulty using the other demonstration programs in the book.

```
Rectangle samples...
ESSENTIAL INGREDIENTS OF A C++ GRAPHICS PROGRAM.
Copyright 1991 Lee Adams.  All rights reserved.
Using the 640x350x16-color VGA and EGA mode.
Press any key to continue.
```

1-8 Graphics output from the sample program STARTUP.CPP. The demonstration program tests solid and dithered lines in each of 16 colors, and rectangles in both hollow and solid styles.

How to compile and link the sample program

The program listing presented in FIG. 1-11 contains the complete source code for the main module of the C++ demonstration program called Essential Ingredients of a C++ Graphics Program. If you are using the companion disks to the book, the source code is in the file named STARTUP.CPP. Two C++ source files are needed to build the finished .exe file. These are STARTUP.CPP from FIG. 1-11 and one of the class libraries in appendix E.

[Class] The class library that provides the language bindings and low-level graphics routines for this demonstration program is found in FIG. E-2 in appendix E. This listing contains the implementations for class PhysicalDisplay and class Viewport. If you are using the companion disks to the book, this file is named LIB2D.CPP. The class declarations are presented in FIG. E-1 in appendix E. If you are using the companion disks to the book, this file is named LIB2D.HPP.

You can compile, link, and run this demonstration program using either Turbo C++, Borland C++, or Zortech C++. If you are using Turbo C++, you might wish to read appendix A for guidance in compiling, linking, and running the demonstration program. If you are using Borland C++, you can find the appropriate information in appendix B. If you are using Zortech C++, refer to appendix C.

You must create a Turbo C++ or Borland C++ project list to advise your compiler which source files to bind together to build the finished .exe file. If you are using Zortech C++, you must name the files on the compiler command line field. Refer to the appendices described earlier if you are unfamiliar with this technique.

After a successful compile and link the startup screen should resemble the screen print shown in FIG. 1-8.

How to run the demonstration program

You need a VGA, EGA, MCGA, CGA, or Hercules graphics adapter to run this demonstration program.

Using the editor to run the program

[Here's How...] To run the program under the control of your Turbo C++, Borland C++, or Zortech C++ editor, make sure that the finished .exe file is in the default directory. If you used Turbo C++ or Borland C++ to compile the program, the appropriate graphics driver must be in the default directory. If you are using a VGA or EGA, the EGAVGA.BGI file must be present. If you are using an MCGA or CGA, the CGA.BGI file must be located in the default directory. If you are using a Hercules graphics adapter, the HERC.BGI file must be available. These graphics drivers are installed on your hard disk by the Turbo C++ and Borland C++ installation utilities. If you used Zortech C++ to compile the demonstration program, the appropriate graphics drivers have already been linked into the finished executable code by the Zortech linker.

You need a VGA, EGA, MCGA, CGA, or Hercules graphics adapter to run the demonstration program STARTUP.CPP. The built-in autodetect routine will detect the graphics hardware in your computer system and will set up the best graphics mode supported by your computer hardware. To override the autodetect routine use the Turbo C++, Borland C++, or Zortech C++ editor to simulate a command line argument. The header in FIG. 1-11 provides a set of mnemonics you can use. See the appendices for guidance in using this technique with your particular compiler. If you are using a VGA, you can override the autodetect routine and force the demonstration program to run in an EGA, MCGA, or CGA mode. If you are using an EGA, you can force the program to run in a lower-resolution EGA mode or a CGA mode.

Running the program
from the operating system prompt

To start the program from the operating system prompt, simply enter STARTUP. The .exe file and any required graphics drivers must be present in the default directory. If the software finds a VGA present in your system, the program will start up in the 640×480×16-color mode. If an EGA and enhanced monitor are found, the 640×350×16-color mode is used. If an EGA and standard display are present, the program sets up the 640×200×16-color mode. If an MCGA is detected, the 640×480×2-color mode is employed. If a CGA is found, the 640×200×2-color mode is used. If the program detects a Hercules graphics adapter, it will use the 720×348×2-color mode.

You can force the program to start up in a different mode by adding a command line argument when you start the program from the operating system prompt. Enter STARTUP /M11 to force the 640×480×2-color mode. Enter STARTUP / M10 to force the 640×350×16-color mode. Entering STARTUP /M0E forces the program to run in the 640×200×16-color mode. Entering STARTUP /M06 tests the demonstration program in the 640×200×2-color mode.

Using the demonstration program

The program prompts you to press a key to see the next set of graphics imagery. See FIG. 1-9. First, a set of solid lines and dithered lines in a variety of hues are drawn. Next, a selection of rectangles are drawn using both outline and filled style. Then four-sided polygons are demonstrated, using both filled and outline format. Next, a six-sided, filled, outlined polygon is drawn. The floodfill function is then tested in the upper right corner of the display. The dialog line at the top of the display then indicates that the stub routine has been successfully called. Then two bitblts are captured and written to the screen. Next, as FIG. 1-10 illustrates, a transparent viewport is created. A few sample graphics are drawn in this viewport; they are clipped at the boundaries of the viewport. Then a viewport is created with a solid background and a border. Sample graphics output is written to the viewport. Finally, XOR mode drawing is demonstrated by generating a line in standard overwrite mode and in exclusive-or mode.

Programmer's Guide to STARTUP.CPP

The complete listing for the demonstration program STARTUP.CPP is presented in FIG. 1-11 at the end of this chapter. The source code con-

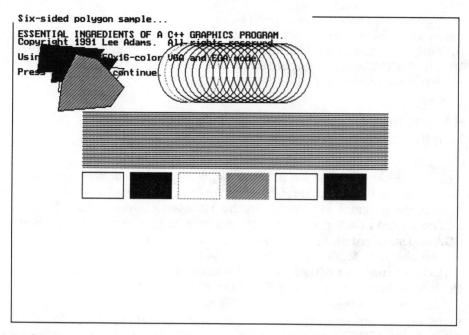

1-9 Graphics output from the sample program STARTUP.CPP. The demonstration program tests four-sided and five-sided polygons in both hollow and solid styles.

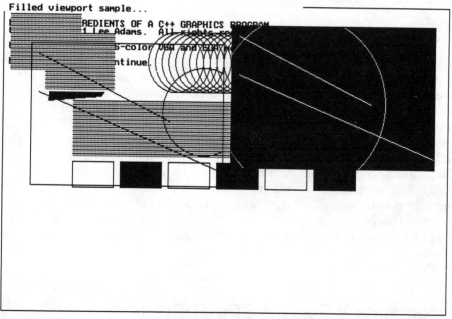

1-10 Graphics output from the sample program STARTUP.CPP. The demo tests a transparent viewport (shown at left) and a solid viewport (shown at right). All graphics drawn inside a viewport are clipped at the edge of the viewport.

sists of an informative header, conditional compilation directives, declaration of constants and macros, file include directives, function prototypes, variable declarations, and the executable functions. Because many of the functions present in STARTUP.CPP form the foundation for demonstration programs later in the book, it might be useful to explore in detail this program listing.

The header

The informative header is located at lines 0001 through 0050.

Conditional compilation

Information and source code for conditional compilation is located at lines 0051 through 0068. If you are using Turbo C++ or Borland C++, the program is ready to compile, subject to the instructions provided in appendix B. If you are using Zortech C++, change line 0067 to read #define FG and change line 0068 to read #define ZORTECH.

Constants

The C++ qualifier, const, is used to declare and assign values to ten variables at lines 0070 through 0077. The const keyword is used instead of C's #define directive, which is considered obsolete by many programmers.

Macros

A useful macro is defined at line 0083. The C++ compiler will expand the Wait-_for_any_key instruction when it again encounters this string at line 0213. Using a macro in this way can help make your C++ source code easier to read. In addition, you can change all occurrences of the macro in your source code by simply changing the definition of the macro in line 0083.

Include files

The code at lines 0085 through 0112 uses the #include directive to load in the appropriate header files and C++ class declaration files. Line 0112 loads LIB-2D.HPP, which declares the data members and methods of class PhysicalDisplay and class Viewport. These two classes are discussed later in this chapter.

Function prototypes

The function declarations—also called function prototypes—are provided in lines 0114 through 0126. These functions are visible throughout this source file and can be called by any other function in the source file. Because each function is declared with the static qualifier, they are not visible to functions located in other source files—and will not generate any naming conflict warnings if identically named functions are used in other source files.

Variable declarations

Lines 0128 through 0162 declare global variables that are visible anywhere in this source file. These variables are said to have "file scope." It is good programming practice to initialize these variables at this time by assigning a value to them.

Object declarations

Object Note line 0161, which creates an object from class PhysicalDisplay. The object is named "Display." The program will later call the methods of this object to help it manage the display. The methods are declared in the class declaration listing LIB2D.HPP and are defined in the class implementation listing LIB2D.CPP in appendix E. The object created at line 0161 is a static object. It has file scope and will remain available until the program terminates.

Line 0162 creates an object from the Viewport class. The object is named Viewport1. Note in particular how the address of the object named Display is passed to this new object. Viewport1 will need to use the methods of Display to generate graphics imagery. The object created at line 0162 is a static object with file scope. It will remain available until the program terminates.

main( )

The main( ) function is located at lines 0167 through 0350. After first checking to see if any command line arguments were used to launch the program, the code switches to an appropriate graphics mode, and then generates a variety of graphics samples, pausing to wait for your keystroke.

Filtering the command line arguments

The code at lines 0177 through 0179 filters the command line arguments. Note how argc and argv[ ] are retrieved from the argument list received when main( ) was invoked at program startup. Line 0179 calls a function located near the end of this source listing to parse the arguments.

Switching to a graphics mode

The code at line 0181 calls a function named zStartup( ) which calls a method of the object named Display. Note how the code at line 0182 then initializes the 2D routines by using the dot operator to call the Init2D( ) method of the object named Display.

The sign-on display

The switch( ) block at lines 0191 through 0210 uses a global variable named Mode to display an appropriate text string advising you which graphics mode has been invoked at startup.

The graphics test suite

The source code at lines 0215 through 0347 exercises the methods of class PhysicalDisplay and class Viewport by calling the member functions of objects Display and Viewport1, respectively. The method names are relatively intuitive. By referring to the LIB2D.CPP source code in appendix E you can readily see how the methods are used.

Terminating the program

The function at lines 0352 through 0360 calls a method of class PhysicalDisplay to terminate the graphics state and return the display to the screen mode that existed prior to startup. Note how line 0359 returns an OK code to the operating system.

The Startup( ) function

The function at lines 0362 through 0445 calls the SetupMode( ) method of class PhysicalDisplay to detect the graphics hardware. The switch( ) block at lines 0373 through 0383 forces the logic flow to jump to an appropriate block of code that initializes variables peculiar to each graphics mode. Note how the variable named CommandLineArg is used to determine if the user wants to override the autodetect routine. If so, the code jumps to line 0429, where the ForceMode( ) method of class PhysicalDisplay is used to reset the graphics mode.

The StubRoutine( ) function

The stub routine at lines 0447 through 0455 is a do-nothing routine that displays a simple message on the dialog line at the top of the display. A stub like this is handy when you are building a large and complex program. You can call the stub instead of stopping and taking the time to build a specific routine. By using the stub routine paradigm, you can concentrate your attention on getting a crude prototype up and running, rather than allowing yourself to be diverted by the necessity to write each and every function that your program requires.

Tip Use a stub routine to help get your first prototype up and running sooner.

The ClearTextLine( ) function

The code at lines 0458 through 0468 blanks the text line at the top of the display. Note how three methods of the object named Display are called to set the current color, line style, and fill style. Then a method of the object named Viewport1 is called to blank the line.

The Keyboard( ) function

The function at lines 0470 through 0498 detects and retrieves a keystroke from the keyboard buffer. This routine can detect subtle control keystrokes like F2, Ctrl+F2, Alt+F2, and others.

The Purge( ) function

The function at lines 0500 through 0508 simply keeps calling the keyboard function until the keyboard buffer is empty. This routine is helpful when you want to ensure that no unwanted keystrokes remain in the buffer after a lengthy graphics operation. Your user might have been leaning on the Esc key, for example, while your program was drawing—and your next function might not expect to receive an Esc key.

The MakeSound( ) function

The zMakeSound( ) function at lines 0511 through 0546 uses a compiler-independent method to generate a sound from the system speaker. Note how the appropriate codes are sent to the hardware ports to exert direct control over the speaker.

The Pause( ) function

The function at lines 0549 through 0567 can be used to pause for a specified length of time. The code uses the value returned by the system clock and multiplies it by the number of ticks per second. If you are using Turbo C++ or Borland C++, this value is represented by the global variable CLK_TCK. If you are using Zortech C++ it is represented by the global variable named CLOCKS_PER_SEC.

The Arguments( ) function

The function at lines 0569 through 0611, which was called by main( ) when the program started up, compares the command line argument with a set of permitted strings. The function assigns an appropriate value to the global variable named Mode. Other functions will later use Mode to help them manage graphics output.

Programmer's Guide to LIB2D.HPP

Code The complete source code for the declarations for class PhysicalDisplay and class Viewport is found in LIB2D.HPP in appendix E. The source from LIB2D.HPP must be #included at the beginning of any program that wishes to use the methods of class PhysicalDisplay or class Viewport.

The header

The informative header for the class declaration listing is located at lines 0001 through 0040.

Cross-compiler development

The preprocessor directives at lines 0046 through 0052 are used to inform the compiler which compiler-dependent blocks of code to compile. Remember, because this file is included in another file, the variables being tested will have already been defined.

Declaring class PhysicalDisplay

The code that declares class PhysicalDisplay is located at lines 0054 through 0115. The class itself is declared at line 0054. The opening brace at line 0055 opens a block of declarations that will run until the closing brace at line 0115. The private qualifier at line 0057 identifies the beginning of a set of declarations for variables and member functions that are visible only to the class itself. Outside functions will not be able to access these data members and methods. The public qualifier at line 0095 identifies member functions that can be called by any in-scope function. Note line 0096, which declares the constructor. Line 0097 declares the destructor, marked by the tilde (~) character.

It is important to note that this block of code merely declares the existence of class PhysicalDisplay. It does not provide the executable code to implement the methods of class PhysicalDisplay. Functionality will be added later in the listing LIB2D.CPP, which contains the class implementation.

Declaring class Viewport

The code at lines 0117 through 0165 declares the data members and methods of class Viewport. Note the directives at lines 0137 through 0158, which cause the compiler to compile only those blocks of code supporting either Turbo C++, Borland C++, Zortech C++, or Microsoft. Also of interest is the code at lines 0160 through 0162, which uses function overloading to declare three variants of a method named WindowOpen( ). See the discussion earlier in this chapter for more about function overloading. The method declared at line 0164 uses a default argument, also discussed earlier in this chapter.

Programmer's Guide to LIB2D.CPP

Code The source code in LIB2D.CPP, presented in appendix E, provides the graphics library language bindings that produce the low-level graphics used by most of the demonstration programs in the book. The source code calls the appropriate runtime library functions in Turbo C++'s graphics.lib, Borland C++'s graphics.lib, Zortech C++'s fg.lib, or Microsoft's graph.lib.

LIB2D.CPP is the class implementation listing for class PhysicalDisplay and class Viewport. Class PhysicalDisplay is generally responsible for managing the state of the overall display. Class Viewport is responsible for maintaining a viewport and producing low-level graphics like lines, rectangles, fills, bitblts, and so forth. Between them, these two classes form the underpinnings for almost all graphics generated by the demonstration programs in *Lee Adams' Supercharged C++ Graphics*. As the sample program in this chapter shows, it is possible to create numerous objects of class Viewport, enabling your software to easily maintain and manipulate numerous simultaneous viewports on the display screen.

The header

The informative header for LIB2D.CPP is located at lines 0001 through 0040. In addition to other information, the header describes a list of graphics adapters and graphics modes explicitly supported by the language bindings.

Conditional compilation

The code at lines 0041 through 0059 supports conditional compilation. If you are using Turbo C++ or Borland C++ the source listing is ready to compile, subject to the instructions provided in appendix B for Borland C++. If you are using Zortech C++, change line 0058 to #define FG and change line 0059 to #define ZORTECH.

Constants

The constants declared and initialized at lines 0061 through 0073 are used as decision-makers for the if( ) statements and the switch( ) blocks later in the listing.

Include files

The #include preprocessor directive is used at lines 0079 through 0092 to load in the class declaration file at line 0079 and the compiler-dependent header files.

The PhysicalDisplay class

Class The methods of class PhysicalDisplay are responsible for managing the display as a whole, setting the mode, blanking the screen, setting the current color, setting the fill style, setting the active or display page, and so on.

The constructor   The constructor for class PhysicalDisplay is located at lines 0094 through 0112. A number of variables are initialized by this block of code. The constructor is called automatically whenever an instance—an object—of class PhysicalDisplay is created.

The destructor   The destructor for class PhysicalDisplay is located at lines

0114 through 0121. The destructor is called automatically whenever an object of class PhysicalDisplay is destroyed.

Method SetupMode( )   The implementation for the SetupMode method of class PhysicalDisplay is located at lines 0123 through 0196. This block of code constitutes the autodetect routine that each demonstration program uses at startup. If you are using Turbo C++ or Borland C++, note how the detectgraph( ) library function is used to identify the graphics adapter. If you are using Zortech C++, note how the fg_get_type( ) library function is used to identify the adapter.

Method ForceMode( )   The method at lines 0199 through 0256 can be used if the user wants to override the autodetect mechanism by using a command line argument.

Method Init2D( )   The Init2D( ) method of class PhysicalDisplay, located at lines 0259 through 0295, sets the current graphics state. It uses a variable named "token" to help it initialize variables that will be required for graphics operations.

Method ShutDownGraphics( )   The method at lines 0298 through 0323 tidies up the graphics environment before switching back to the default text mode. Note in particular the block of code at lines 0300 through 0311, which frees memory that might have been used by a hidden graphics page in RAM. If a VGA is being used in the 640×480×16-color mode, not enough display memory is present on the board to support more than one page. If your program requires a hidden page for a backup function, then you must create a simulated page in RAM for that purpose, as the code in LIB2D.CPP does. (See the discussion for methods BackUp( ) and Restore( ) later in this chapter.)

Setting attributes for pens and brushes   The code at lines 0325 through 0404 sets attributes for the pens and brushes used for graphics output. Method SetHue( ) at line 0329 sets the current drawing color. Method SetWriteMode( ) at line 0342 sets the overwrite or exclusive-or drawing mode. Method SetLine ( ) at line 0358 sets the line style—solid or pattern. Method SetFill( ) at line 0371 sets the fill pattern, either solid or dithered. Method SetRGB( ) at line 0388 sets the hardware color, exerting direct control over the red, green, and blue guns of the cathode ray tube.

Graphics page operations   The code at lines 0406 through 0446 controls page operations. Method SetWritePage( ) at line 0410 controls the page to which graphics will be output. This can be either the displayed page or a hidden page. Method SetDisplayPage( ) at line 0423 controls which page is being displayed. This is not necessarily the same page to which graphics are being sent. Method BlankPage( ) at line 0436 blanks the active page.

Hidden page operations   The code at lines 1028 through 1379 provides hidden page operations. Method InitUndo( ) at line 1032 initializes a hidden graphics page either on the display adapter itself or in RAM. If the hidden page must be simulated in RAM, InitUndo( ) calls method InitHiddenPage( ) at line 1081. In that event, method FreeMemory( ) at line 1095 will be called when the graphics are shut down, in order to free the memory allocated in RAM.

Method BackUp( ) at line 1108 copies the contents of page 0—usually the displayed page—to the hidden page. The port addresses and port data used in this method are taken from various reference manuals. Method Restore( ) at line 1245 copies the contents of the hidden page back to page 0. By using these two functions a working undo function can be provided. BackUp( ) can be used to store the display image before new graphics are generated. Then, if your user wants to undo the operations, Restore( ) can be called to copy the contents of the hidden page back to the screen.

The Viewport class

Class The methods of class Viewport provide low-level graphics output, including lines, viewports, rectangles, polygons, facets, circles, bitblts, and default font output. Class Viewport relies on some of the methods of class PhysicalDisplay to get the job done.

The constructor   The constructor for class Viewport is located at lines 0449 through 0457. Note how a pointer named GenericDisplay is used to capture the address of the PhysicalDisplay object passed to the constructor. The methods of class Viewport will occasionally need to call the methods of class PhysicalDisplay to help generate graphics output.

The destructor   The destructor for class Viewport is located at lines 0459 through 0466.

Graphics viewport operations   The code at lines 0468 through 0571 provides viewports for graphics output. A viewport is a subset of the display screen. It is a rectangle on the screen. Graphics drawn in a viewport are clipped at the edge of the viewport. By creating numerous instances of class Viewport, you can use each object to set up a different viewport, making it easy to manage numerous simultaneous graphics viewports on the display at runtime.

Note in particular the three versions of method WindowOpen( ). Function overloading is used to provide a common calling protocol for three different types of windows. The first variant of WindowOpen( ) will set up a transparent viewport with no border. The second variant will create a transparent viewport with an outlined border. The third variant will build a solid viewport with a filled client area and an outlined border.

Method WindowClose( ) at line 0541 shuts down a viewport. After using this method, graphics output will no longer be clipped at the boundary of the viewport. Method WindowClear( ) at line 0558 blanks the interior of a viewport.

Low-level drawing functions   The code at lines 0573 through 0787 provides a set of low-level drawing functions. Method SetPosition( ) at line 0577 sets the current position of the graphics cursor. Method Drawline( ) at line 0590 draws a line from the current position to the specified coordinates using the current color and line style. Method DrawBorder( ) at line 0611 draws a hollow rectangle. Method DrawPanel( ) at line 0631 draws a filled rectangle using the current fill style. Method DrawPolygon( ) at line 0649 draws a filled polygon of three or more sides. Method DrawFacet( ) at line 0691 draws a hollow polygon of three, four, five, six, or more sides. Method DrawCircle( ) at line 0729 draws a circle. Method Fill( ) at line 0776 performs a standard floodfill function.

Graphic array operations   The code at lines 0789 through 0935 provides bitblt functionality. These methods are heavily used by class Bitblt and class Blitter later in the book.

Method MemBlock( ) at line 0793 allocates memory in RAM to hold the graphic array. Method GetBlockSize( ) at line 0827 can be used to calculate the number of bytes required to store the graphic array in memory. Method FreeBlock( ) frees the memory.

Method GetBlock( ) captures the image from the display and stores it as a graphic array in RAM. Method PutXOR( ) writes the graphic array back to the screen using exclusive-or logic. Method PutAND( ) and PutPSET( ) can also be used to write the graphic array to the screen.

Default font operations   The code at lines 0937 through 1026 manages text output while in a graphics mode. Method PutText( ) writes a string of text to the display at a specified position. Method SetTextRowCol( ) can be used to set the starting position for the text operation. Method ClearTextLine( ) clears the dialog line.

Extending the class library

The methods of class PhysicalDisplay and class Viewport provide a working platform from which to build your own graphics classes and methods. The demonstration program in this chapter shows how to create objects of class PhysicalDisplay and class Viewport. It also shows how to use the methods of class PhysicalDisplay and class Viewport to generate graphics output. You can expand the capabilities of LIB2D.HPP and LIB2D.CPP by either writing additional methods and inserting them directly into the source code—or you can use the powerful inheritance capabilities of C++ to create derived classes that expand the features of class PhysicalDisplay and class Viewport.

Even if you choose to use these two classes in their current implementation, you have access to some very powerful graphics methods, as the coming demonstration programs in the book illustrate. Advanced graphics like 3-D modeling, desktop publishing, and display animation can be easily built using the comprehensive graphics engine provided by the C++ methods in the LIB2D.CPP class library.

1-11 Sample program STARTUP.CPP. Supports VGA, EGA, MCGA, CGA, and Hercules adapters. This application exercises the language bindings in the class library LIB2D.CPP (see appendix E for source code).

```
0001   /*
0002
0003          ┌─────────────────────────────────────────────────────┐
0004          │      Lee Adams' SUPERCHARGED C++ GRAPHICS            │
0005          │   Interactive demo:  fundamental graphics classes and objects │
0006          ├─────────────────────────────────────────────────────┤
0007     SOURCE FILE:  STARTUP.CPP
0008            TYPE:  C++ source file for a multimodule application.
0009         PURPOSE:  Demonstrates fundamental classes that can
0010                   control the physical display and manage a
0011                   viewport for low-level graphics output.  This
0012                   demo program can be used as a template to build
0013                   more advanced 2D, 3D, or animated applications.
0013   PROGRAM LIST:  STARTUP.CPP and LIB2D.CPP.
0014       LANGUAGES:  Turbo C++, Borland C++, Zortech C++, and
0015                   all C++ compilers compatible with AT&T C++ 2.0
0016                   specification; and nominal compatibility with
0017                   Microsoft C++ (see the discussion in the book).
0018   MEMORY MODEL:  large.
0019   COMMAND-LINE:  you can specify a graphics mode by using the
0020                   command-line argument /Mnn as shown below:
0021                       /M12  640x480x16-color VGA
0022                       /M11  640x480x2-color VGA, MCGA
0023                       /M10  640x350x16-color VGA, EGA
0024                       /MOE  640x200x16-color VGA, EGA
0025                       /M06  640x200x2-color VGA, MCGA, EGA, CGA
0026                       /MHC  720x348x2-color Hercules
0027                   If no command-line argument is used, hardware
0028                   autodetect is used to select the best mode.
0029   OUTPUT:  Various images are drawn, in order to exercise most
0030            of the functions in the graphics library bindings,
0031            including colored and dithered lines, polygons,
0032            circles, viewports, and bitblts (graphic arrays).
0033   LICENSE:  As purchaser of the book in which this source code
0034      appears you are granted a royalty-free license to reproduce
0035      and distribute executable files generated using this code
0036      provided that you accept the conditions of the License
0037      Agreement and Limited Warranty described in the book.
0038   PUBLICATION: Contains material from Windcrest/McGraw-Hill
0039      book 3489, published by TAB BOOKS.
0040   U.S. GOVERNMENT RESTRICTED RIGHTS:  This software and its
0041      documentation is provided with restricted rights.  The use,
0042      duplication, or disclosure by the Government is subject to
0043      restrictions set forth in subdivision (b)(3)(ii) of The
0044      Rights in Technical Data and Computer Software clause at
0045      252.227-7013.  Contractor/manufacturer is Lee Adams, c/o
0046      TAB BOOKS, 13311 Monterey Ave., Blue Ridge Summit PA 17294.
0047   TRADEMARK:  Lee Adams is a trademark of Lee Adams.
0048          ├─────────────────────────────────────────────────────┤
0049          │    Copyright 1991 Lee Adams.  All rights reserved worldwide. │
0050          └─────────────────────────────────────────────────────┘
0051
0052          ┌─────────────────────────────────────────────────────┐
0052                       CONDITIONAL COMPILATION
0053   To compile only those blocks of code that support the C++
0054   compiler and graphics library that you are using, you should
0055   #define the appropriate tokens on lines 0067 and 0068.
0056               GRAPHICS LIBRARY
0057       Borland's graphics.lib          #define BGI
0058       Zortech's fg.lib or fgdebug.lib #define FG
```

```
0059            Microsoft's graph.lib            #define MS
0060            COMPILER
0061         Borland Turbo C++ compiler          #define BORLAND
0062         Zortech C++ compiler                #define ZORTECH
0063         AT&T-compatible C++ compilers       #define MICROSOFT
0064      Be sure you define only one compiler and one graphics library.
0065
0066                                                                       */
0067   #define BGI     1 // indicates the graphics library you are using.
0068   #define BORLAND 1 // indicates the C++ compiler you are using.
0069   /*
0070
0071   ┌──────────────────────────────────────────────────────────────┐
0071   │                        Constants                               │
0072   └──────────────────────────────────────────────────────────────┘
0073                                                                       */
0074   const int zFAIL=0; const int zEMPTY=0;
0075   const int zYES=1; const int zNO=0;
0076   const int zVGA_12H=1; const int zEGA_10H=2; const int zEGA_EH=3;
0077   const int zMCGA_11H=4; const int zCGA_6H=5; const int zHERC=6;
0078   /*
0079
0080   ┌──────────────────────────────────────────────────────────────┐
0080   │                          Macros                                │
0081   └──────────────────────────────────────────────────────────────┘
0082                                                                       */
0083   #define Wait_for_any_key  while(KeyCode==0) zKeyboard(); KeyCode=0;
0084   /*
0085
0086   ┌──────────────────────────────────────────────────────────────┐
0086   │                       Include files                            │
0087   └──────────────────────────────────────────────────────────────┘
0088                                                                       */
0089   #if defined (BORLAND)
0090   #include <time.h>         // supports clock().
0091   #include <string.h>       // supports strncmp().
0092   #include <bios.h>         // supports bioskey().
0093   #include <process.h>      // supports exit().
0094   #include <iostream.h>     // supports cout.
0095   #include <dos.h>          // supports outportb(), inportb().
0096   #elif defined (ZORTECH)
0097   #include <time.h>         // supports clock().
0098   #include <string.h>       // supports strncmp().
0099   #include <bios.h>         // supports bioskey().
0100   #include <stdlib.h>       // supports exit().
0101   #include <stream.hpp>     // supports cout.
0102   #include <dos.h>          // supports outp(), inp().
0103   #elif defined (MICROSOFT)
0104   #include <time.h>         // supports clock().
0105   #include <string.h>       // supports strncmp().
0106   #include <bios.h>         // supports _bios_keybrd().
0107   #include <process.h>      // supports exit().
0108   #include <iostream.h>     // supports cout.
0109   #include <conio.h>        // supports outp(), inp().
0110   #endif
0111
0112   #include "LIB2D.HPP"      // declarations for PhysicalDisplay class.
0113   /*
0114
0115   ┌──────────────────────────────────────────────────────────────┐
0115   │      Prototypes for functions visible throughout this file     │
0116   └──────────────────────────────────────────────────────────────┘
0117                                                                       */
0118   static void zStartup(void);          // initializes a graphics mode.
0119   static void zArguments(int, char far* far*);   // checks arguments.
0120   static void zKeyboard(void);              // checks for a keystroke.
0121   static void zQuit_Pgm(void);          // ends the program gracefully.
```

```
0122   static void zPurge(void);              // empties the keyboard buffer.
0123   static void zStubRoutine(void);               // do-nothing stub.
0124   static void zMakeSound(int,double);      // makes a specific sound.
0125   static clock_t zDelay(clock_t,double);    // CPU-independent pause.
0126   static void zClearTextLine(void);    // blanks the dialog text line.
0127   /*
0128
0129   ┌─────────────────────────────────────────────────────────────────┐
        │        Declaration of variables visible throughout this file      │
0130    └─────────────────────────────────────────────────────────────────┘
0131                                                                    */
0132   static char *StartUpArg[6]=          // legal command-line arguments.
0133          { "/M12", "/M10", "/MOE", "/M11", "/M06", "/MHC" };
0134   static int CommandLineArg=zNO;       // indicates if argument exists.
0135   static int CommandLineCompare=0;     // indicates if argument legal.
0136   static int C0=0,C1=1,C2=2,C3=3,C4=4,C5=5,C6=6,
0137          C7=7,C8=8,C9=9,C10=10,C11=11,C12=12,C13=13,
0138          C14=14,C15=15;                        // palette index codes.
0139   static int Mode=0;               // which graphics mode is being used.
0140   static int Result=0;          // captures result of graphics routines.
0141   static int CharWidth=0, CharHeight=0;   // dimensions of character.
0142   static char KeyCode=0;    // token for normal or extended keystroke.
0143   static char KeyNum=0;                  // ASCII number of keystroke.
0144   static char SolidFill[]=
0145                  {255,255,255,255,255,255,255,255};   // 100% fill.
0146   static int TextClr=7;                 // font color for regular text.
0147   static int PromptClr=7;                // font color for prompt text.
0148   static char Copyright[]=
0149                  "Copyright 1991 Lee Adams.  All rights reserved.";
0150   static char Title[]=
0151   "ESSENTIAL INGREDIENTS OF A C++ GRAPHICS PROGRAM.";
0152   static char PressAnyKey[]= "Press any key to continue.";
0153   static char StubMessage[]= "The generic stub routine was called.";
0154   static int X_Res=0, Y_Res=0;              // screen resolution.
0155   static int Facet1[10]= {40,30, 35,60, 110,55, 130,35, 40,30};
0156   static int Facet2[10]= {60,40, 55,70, 130,65, 150,45, 60,40};
0157   static int Facet3[10]= {70,50, 65,80, 140,75, 160,55, 70,50};
0158   static int Poly1[14]= {70,70, 65,100, 140,95, 160,75, 120,45,
0159                          90,40, 70,70};
0160
0161   PhysicalDisplay Display;              // the physical display object.
0162   Viewport Viewport1(&Display);                  // a viewport object.
0163   /*
0164
0165   ┌─────────────────────────────────────────────────────────────────┐
        │                        Function definitions                       │
0166    └─────────────────────────────────────────────────────────────────┘
0167
0168   ┌─────────────────────────────────────────────────────────────────┐
        │      The executive routine:  program execution begins here        │
0169    └─────────────────────────────────────────────────────────────────┘
0170                                                                    */
0171   main(int argc, char *argv[])
0172   {
0173     int NumArgs; char far* far* Arg;
0174     int LoopX1, LoopY1, LoopX2, LoopY2, LoopColor, LoopMaxHues;
0175     int LoopCount;
0176
0177   NumArgs= argc;                          // grab number of arguments.
0178   Arg= &argv[0];              // grab address of array of arguments.
0179   zArguments(NumArgs, Arg);       // check the command-line arguments.
0180
0181   zStartup();                          // establish the graphics mode.
0182   Display.Init2D(Mode,0,0,X_Res-1,Y_Res-1);   // set graphics state.
0183   Result= Display.InitUndo();   // create hidden page (unused here).
```

```
0184   if (Result==zFAIL) zQuit_Pgm();              // if hidden page failed.
0185
0186   Display.BlankPage();                            // clear the display.
0187   Display.SetHue(C7);                         // set the drawing color.
0188   Display.SetFill(SolidFill,C7);               // set the fill style.
0189   Viewport1.PutText(3,2,TextClr,Title);          // sign-on notice.
0190   Viewport1.PutText(4,2,TextClr,Copyright);     // copyright notice.
0191   switch (Mode)
0192     {          // notify user which display mode is being used...
0193     case zVGA_12H:   Viewport1.PutText(6,2,TextClr,
0194                      "Using the 640x480x16-color VGA mode.");
0195                      break;
0196     case zEGA_10H:   Viewport1.PutText(6,2,TextClr,
0197                      "Using the 640x350x16-color VGA and EGA mode.");
0198                      break;
0199     case zEGA_EH:    Viewport1.PutText(6,2,TextClr,
0200                      "Using the 640x200x16-color VGA and EGA mode.");
0201                      break;
0202     case zMCGA_11H:  Viewport1.PutText(6,2,TextClr,
0203                      "Using the 640x480x2-color VGA and MCGA mode.");
0204                      break;
0205     case zCGA_6H:    Viewport1.PutText(6,2,TextClr,
0206                      "Using the 640x200x2-color CGA mode.");
0207                      break;
0208     case zHERC:      Viewport1.PutText(6,2,TextClr,
0209                      "Using the 720x348x2-color Hercules mode.");
0210     }
0211   Viewport1.DrawBorder(0,0,X_Res-1,Y_Res-1);       // draw a border.
0212   Viewport1.PutText(8,2,PromptClr,PressAnyKey);    // show a prompt.
0213   Wait_for_any_key     // this macro was defined earlier at line 0073.
0214
0215                // demonstrate some line samples...
0216   LoopColor= 1; LoopMaxHues= 15;
0217   LoopX1= 100; LoopY1= 100; LoopX2= 540;
0218   for (LoopCount= 1; LoopCount<= LoopMaxHues; LoopCount++)
0219     {                      // draw 15 multicolored solid lines...
0220     Display.SetHue(LoopColor);            // set the drawing color.
0221     Viewport1.SetPosition(LoopX1,LoopY1);// set the current position.
0222     Viewport1.DrawLine(LoopX2,LoopY1);            // draw a line.
0223     LoopColor++;                  // increment the color variable.
0224     LoopY1+= 4;                   // increment the y coordinate.
0225     }
0226   LoopColor= 1; LoopY1= 102; Display.SetLine(0xaaaa);
0227   for (LoopCount= 1; LoopCount<= LoopMaxHues; LoopCount++)
0228     {                      // draw 15 multicolored dithered lines...
0229     Display.SetHue(LoopColor);            // set the drawing color.
0230     Viewport1.SetPosition(LoopX1,LoopY1);// set the current position.
0231     Viewport1.DrawLine(LoopX2,LoopY1);            // draw a line.
0232     LoopColor++;                  // increment the color variable.
0233     LoopY1+= 4;                   // increment the y coordinate.
0234     }
0235   zClearTextLine();
0236   Viewport1.PutText(1,2,TextClr,"Line style samples...");
0237   Wait_for_any_key
0238
0239                // demonstrate some rectangle samples...
0240   Display.SetLine(0xffff);
0241   Display.SetHue(C5);
0242   Viewport1.DrawBorder(100,164,160,191);
0243   Display.SetFill(SolidFill,C5);
0244   Viewport1.DrawPanel(170,164,230,191);
0245   Display.SetHue(C2);
0246   Viewport1.DrawBorder(240,164,300,191);
```

```
0247  Display.SetFill(SolidFill,C2);
0248  Viewport1.DrawPanel(310,164,370,191);
0249  Display.SetHue(C3);
0250  Viewport1.DrawBorder(380,164,440,191);
0251  Display.SetFill(SolidFill,C3);
0252  Viewport1.DrawPanel(450,164,510,191);
0253  zClearTextLine();
0254  Viewport1.PutText(1,2,TextClr,"Rectangle samples...");
0255  Wait_for_any_key
0256
0257                  // demonstrate some circle samples...
0258  LoopColor= 1; LoopX1= 249; LoopY1= 59;
0259  for (LoopCount= 1; LoopCount<= LoopMaxHues; LoopCount++)
0260    {                           // draw 15 multicolored circles...
0261    Display.SetHue(LoopColor);            // set the drawing color.
0262    Viewport1.DrawCircle(LoopX1,LoopY1,40);       // draw a circle.
0263    LoopColor++;                      // increment the color variable.
0264    LoopX1+= 10;                    // increment the x coordinate.
0265    }
0266  zClearTextLine();
0267  Viewport1.PutText(1,2,TextClr,"Circle samples...");
0268  Wait_for_any_key
0269
0270                  // demonstrate some polygon samples...
0271  Display.SetHue(C15); Display.SetLine(0xffff);
0272  Display.SetFill(SolidFill,C9);
0273  Viewport1.DrawPolygon(5, Facet1);   // draw 4-sided filled polygon.
0274  Display.SetLine(0xfff0);
0275  Display.SetFill(SolidFill,C12);
0276  Viewport1.DrawPolygon(5, Facet2);   // draw 4-sided filled polygon.
0277  Display.SetHue(C7); Display.SetLine(0xffff);
0278  Viewport1.DrawFacet(5, Facet3);// draw 4-sided transparent polygon.
0279  zClearTextLine();
0280  Viewport1.PutText(1,2,TextClr,"Four-sided polygon samples...");
0281  Wait_for_any_key
0282  Display.SetHue(C10);Display.SetLine(0xffff);
0283  Display.SetFill(SolidFill,C2);
0284  Viewport1.DrawPolygon(7, Poly1);  // draw six-sided filled polygon.
0285  zClearTextLine();
0286  Viewport1.PutText(1,2,TextClr,"Six-sided polygon sample...");
0287  Wait_for_any_key
0288
0289                    // demonstrate a floodfill...
0290  Display.SetHue(C7); Display.SetLine(0xffff);
0291  Viewport1.DrawBorder(530,30,610,80);
0292  Display.SetFill(SolidFill,C6);
0293  Viewport1.Fill(600,60,C7);                  // test the flood fill.
0294  zClearTextLine();
0295  Viewport1.PutText(1,2,TextClr,"Floodfill sample...");
0296  Wait_for_any_key
0297
0298                    // demonstrate a stub routine...
0299  zStubRoutine();
0300  Wait_for_any_key
0301
0302                    // demonstrate some bitblt samples...
0303  #if defined (FG)
0304    fg_color_t far *Image;
0305  #else
0306    char far *Image;
0307  #endif
0308  Image= Viewport1.MemBlock(100,100,200,160);    // reserve some RAM.
```

```
0309   Viewport1.GetBlock(100,100,200,160,Image);    // capture the image.
0310   Viewport1.PutPSET(10,10,Image);    // write bitblt to the display.
0311   Viewport1.PutPSET(60,30,Image);
0312   Viewport1.FreeBlock(Image);                    // release the RAM.
0313   zClearTextLine();
0314   Viewport1.PutText(1,2,TextClr,"Bitblt samples...");
0315   Wait_for_any_key
0316
0317                // demonstrate a transparent viewport...
0318   Viewport1.WindowOpen(40,40,319,189,C14);       // open a viewport.
0319   Display.SetHue(C15);
0320   Viewport1.SetPosition(10,10); Viewport1.DrawLine(200,80);
0321   Viewport1.SetPosition(10,50); Viewport1.DrawLine(300,140);
0322   Viewport1.DrawCircle(250,7C,60);
0323   Viewport1.WindowClose(X_Res, Y_Res);           // close viewport.
0324   zClearTextLine();
0325   Viewport1.PutText(1,2,TextClr,"Transparent viewport sample...");
0326   Wait_for_any_key
0327
0328                // demonstrate a solid viewport...
0329   Viewport1.WindowOpen(330,20,620,169,C15,C7);   // open a viewport.
0330   Display.SetHue(C0);
0331   Viewport1.SetPosition(10,10); Viewport1.DrawLine(200,80);
0332   Viewport1.SetPosition(10,50); Viewport1.DrawLine(300,140);
0333   Viewport1.DrawCircle(100,80,120);
0334   Viewport1.WindowClose(X_Res, Y_Res);           // close viewport.
0335   zClearTextLine();
0336   Viewport1.PutText(1,2,TextClr,"Filled viewport sample...");
0337   Wait_for_any_key
0338
0339                // demonstrate the XOR drawing mode...
0340   Display.SetHue(C7);
0341   Display.SetWriteMode(1);                 // set to XOR drawing mode.
0342   Viewport1.SetPosition(0,0); Viewport1.DrawLine(X_Res-1,Y_Res-1);
0343   Display.SetWriteMode(0);                  // set back to PSET mode.
0344   Viewport1.SetPosition(0,Y_Res-1); Viewport1.DrawLine(X_Res-1,0);
0345   zClearTextLine();
0346   Viewport1.PutText(1,2,TextClr,"XOR drawing sample...");
0347   Wait_for_any_key
0348
0349   zQuit_Pgm();            // tidy up and terminate the application.
0350   }
0351   /*
0352
0353   ┌──────────────────────────────────────────────────────────┐
       │                  Terminate the program                   │
0354   └──────────────────────────────────────────────────────────┘
0355                                                                  */
0356   static void zQuit_Pgm(void)
0357   {
0358   Display.ShutDownGraphics();  // graceful shutdown of graphics mode.
0359   exit(0);              // terminate the program and return an OK code.
0360   }
0361   /*
0362
0363   ┌──────────────────────────────────────────────────────────┐
       │          Detect the graphics hardware and set the        │
0364   │   highest mode permitted by the graphics adapter and monitor.  │
0365   │   The user can override the autodetect algorithm by providing  │
0366   │   an argument on the command-line when the program is started. │
0367   └──────────────────────────────────────────────────────────┘
0368                                                                  */
0369   static void zStartup(void)
0370   {
0371     int DefaultMode;
```

1-11 Continued.

```
0372  DefaultMode= Display.SetupMode();   // get results of autodetect...
0373  switch(DefaultMode)                 // ...and jump to appropriate code.
0374    {
0375    case zFAIL:       goto ABORT_PGM;
0376    case zVGA_12H:    goto VGA_mode;
0377    case zEGA_10H:    goto EGA_ECD_mode;
0378    case zEGA_EH:     goto EGA_SCD_mode;
0379    case zMCGA_11H:   goto MCGA_mode;
0380    case zCGA_6H:     goto CGA_mode;
0381    case zHERC:       goto Hercules_mode;
0382    default:          goto ABORT_PGM;
0383    }
0384  VGA_mode:          // VGA 640x480x16-color, 80x60 character mode.
0385  if(CommandLineArg==zYES)
0386    {                              // if user has requested a mode.
0387    if((Mode>zVGA_12H)&&(Mode<zHERC)) goto FORCE_USER_MODE;
0388    }
0389  X_Res=640; Y_Res=480; Mode=zVGA_12H; CharWidth=8; CharHeight=8;
0390  return;
0391  EGA_ECD_mode:       // EGA 640x350x16-color, 80x43 character mode.
0392  if(CommandLineArg==zYES)
0393    {
0394    if((Mode==zEGA_EH)||(Mode==zCGA_6H))   // permit only EGA or CGA.
0395    goto FORCE_USER_MODE;
0396    }
0397  X_Res=640; Y_Res=350; Mode=zEGA_10H; CharWidth=8; CharHeight=8;
0398  return;
0399  EGA_SCD_mode:       // EGA 640x200x16-color, 80x25 char mode.
0400  if(CommandLineArg==zYES)
0401    {
0402    if(Mode==zCGA_6H) goto FORCE_USER_MODE;   // only CGA permitted.
0403    }
0404  X_Res=640; Y_Res=200; Mode=zEGA_EH; CharWidth=8; CharHeight=8;
0405  return;
0406  MCGA_mode:          // MCGA 640x480x2-color, 80x60 char mode.
0407  if(CommandLineArg==zYES)
0408    {
0409    if(Mode==zCGA_6H) goto FORCE_USER_MODE;   // only CGA permitted.
0410    }
0411  X_Res=640; Y_Res=480; Mode=zMCGA_11H;
0412  C0=0; C1=1; C2=1; C3=1; C4=1; C5=1; C6=1; C7=1;
0413  C8=1; C9=1; C10=1; C11=1; C12=1; C13=1; C14=1; C15=1;
0414  CharWidth=8; CharHeight=8;
0415  return;
0416  CGA_mode:           // CGA 640x200x2-color, 80x25 char mode.
0417  X_Res=640; Y_Res=200; Mode=zCGA_6H;
0418  C0=0; C1=1; C2=1; C3=1; C4=1; C5=1; C6=1; C7=1;
0419  C8=1; C9=1; C10=1; C11=1; C12=1; C13=1; C14=1; C15=1;
0420  CharWidth=8; CharHeight=8;
0421  return;
0422  Hercules_mode:      // Hercules 720x348x2-color, 80x25 char mode.
0423  X_Res=720; Y_Res=348; Mode=zHERC;
0424  C0=0; C1=1; C2=1; C3=1; C4=1; C5=1; C6=1; C7=1;
0425  C8=1; C9=1; C10=1; C11=1; C12=1; C13=1; C14=1; C15=1;
0426  CharWidth=9; CharHeight=14;
0427  return;
0428
0429  FORCE_USER_MODE:    // jump to here if command-line argument legal.
0430  CommandLineArg= zNO; // first, reset token to avoid returning here.
0431  Display.ForceMode(Mode);        // ...then reset the graphics mode.
0432  switch(Mode)                    // ...then jump back to appropriate code.
0433    {
```

```
0434    case zEGA_10H:      goto EGA_ECD_mode;
0435    case zEGA_EH:       goto EGA_SCD_mode;
0436    case zMCGA_11H:     goto MCGA_mode;
0437    case zCGA_6H:       goto CGA_mode;
0438    default:            goto ABORT_PGM;
0439    }
0440
0441  ABORT_PGM:          // jump to here if no graphics hardware detected.
0442  cout << "\n\n\rThis C++ graphics programming demo requires a";
0443  cout << "\n\rVGA, EGA, CGA, MCGA, or HGA graphics adapter.\n\r";
0444  exit(-1);                     // terminate, returning an error code.
0445  }
0446  /*
0447
0448  ┌────────────────────────────────────────────────────────────────┐
        │                         Stub routine                           │
0449    │                                                                │
0450    └────────────────────────────────────────────────────────────────┘  */
0451  static void zStubRoutine(void)
0452  {       // this do-nothing routine is a placeholder for future code.
0453  zClearTextLine();                         // clear the text dialog line.
0454  Viewport1.PutText(1,2,TextClr,StubMessage);      // display message.
0455  return;
0456  }
0457  /*
0458
0459  ┌────────────────────────────────────────────────────────────────┐
        │                   Clear the text dialog line                   │
0460    │                                                                │
0461    └────────────────────────────────────────────────────────────────┘  */
0462  static void zClearTextLine(void)
0463  {                                      // clear the text dialog line.
0464  Display.SetHue(C0);                       // set the drawing color.
0465  Display.SetLine(0xffff);                  // set the line style.
0466  Display.SetFill(SolidFill,C0);            // set the fill style.
0467  Viewport1.ClearTextLine();            // call the viewport method.
0468  }
0469  /*
0470
0471  ┌────────────────────────────────────────────────────────────────┐
        │                Check the keyboard for a keystroke              │
0472    │                                                                │
0473    └────────────────────────────────────────────────────────────────┘  */
0474  static void zKeyboard(void)
0475  {       // can detect keypad keys like PgUp and control keys like F2.
0476    union AnyName{int RawCode;char Code[3];}Keystroke;
0477    char TempKey=0;
0478  #if defined (BORLAND)
0479    if (bioskey(1)==zEMPTY) { KeyCode=0; return; }
0480    Keystroke.RawCode= bioskey(0);
0481  #elif defined (ZORTECH)
0482    if (bioskey(1)==zEMPTY) { KeyCode=0; return; }
0483    Keystroke.RawCode= bioskey(0);
0484  #elif defined (MICROSOFT)
0485    if (_bios_keybrd(_KEYBRD_READY)==zEMPTY)
0486      { KeyCode=0; return; }
0487    Keystroke.RawCode= _bios_keybrd(_KEYBRD_READ);
0488  #endif
0489  TempKey= Keystroke.Code[0];
0490  if (TempKey!=0)
0491      {                                    // if a normal keystroke...
0492      KeyCode=1; KeyNum=TempKey; return;
0493      }
0494  if (TempKey==0)
0495      {                                    // if an extended keystroke...
0496      KeyCode=2; KeyNum=Keystroke.Code[1]; return;
```

```
0497     }
0498   }
0499   /*
0500
0501   ┌─────────────────────────────────────────────────────────┐
         │                Empty the keystroke buffer                │
0502   │                                                          │
0503   └─────────────────────────────────────────────────────────┘
                                                                   */
0504   static void zPurge(void)
0505   {
0506   do zKeyboard();
0507      while (KeyCode!=0);
0508   return;
0509   }
0510   /*
0511
0512   ┌─────────────────────────────────────────────────────────┐
         │                      Make a sound                        │
0513   │                                                          │
0514   └─────────────────────────────────────────────────────────┘
                                                                   */
0515   static void zMakeSound(int Hertz,double Duration)
0516   {
0517      static clock_t FormerTime=0;
0518      short Count=0;
0519      int HighByte=0, LowByte=0;
0520      unsigned char OldPort=0, NewPort=0;
0521   FormerTime= clock();
0522   if (Hertz < 40) return;
0523   if (Hertz > 4660) return;
0524   Count= 1193180L/Hertz;
0525   HighByte= Count / 256;
0526   LowByte= Count - (HighByte * 256);
0527   #if defined (BORLAND)
0528      outportb(0x43,0xB6); outportb(0x42,(unsigned char)LowByte);
0529      outportb(0x42,(unsigned char)HighByte); OldPort=inportb(0x61);
0530      NewPort=(OldPort | 0x03); outportb(0x61,NewPort);
0531      zDelay(FormerTime,Duration);
0532      outportb(0x61,OldPort);
0533   #elif defined (ZORTECH)
0534      outp(0x43,0xB6); outp(0x42,LowByte);
0535      outp(0x42,HighByte); OldPort=(unsigned char)inp(0x61);
0536      NewPort=(OldPort | 0x03); outp(0x61,(int)NewPort);
0537      zDelay(FormerTime,Duration);
0538      outp(0x61,(int)OldPort);
0539   #elif defined (MICROSOFT)
0540      outp(0x43,0xB6); outp(0x42,LowByte);
0541      outp(0x42,HighByte); OldPort=(unsigned char)inp(0x61);
0542      NewPort=(OldPort | 0x03); outp(0x61,(int)NewPort);
0543      zDelay(FormerTime,Duration);
0544      outp(0x61,(int)OldPort);
0545   #endif
0546   return;
0547   }
0548   /*
0549
0550   ┌─────────────────────────────────────────────────────────┐
         │                         Pause                            │
0551   │                                                          │
0552   └─────────────────────────────────────────────────────────┘
                                                                   */
0553   static clock_t zDelay(clock_t StartTime, double Wait)
0554   {                          // pause for a specified length of time.
0555      clock_t StopTime;
0556      clock_t NewClockTime;
0557   #if defined (BORLAND)
0558      StopTime= StartTime + (Wait * CLK_TCK);
```

```
0559  #elif defined (ZORTECH)
0560    StopTime= StartTime + (Wait * CLOCKS_PER_SEC);
0561  #elif defined (MICROSOFT)
0562    StopTime= StartTime + (Wait * CLK_TCK);
0563  #endif
0564  while ( clock() < StopTime ) {;}
0565  NewClockTime= clock();
0566  return NewClockTime;
0567  }
0568  /*
0569
0570  ┌─────────────────────────────────────────────────────────┐
       │        Retrieve the command-line arguments, if any      │
0571  └─────────────────────────────────────────────────────────┘
0572                                                           */
0573  static void zArguments(int NumArgs, char *Arg[])
0574  {
0575  if(NumArgs==1)
0576    {
0577    CommandLineArg= zNO; return;                      // if no arg.
0578    }
0579  CommandLineCompare= strncmp(StartUpArg[0],Arg[1],5);
0580  if(CommandLineCompare==0)
0581    {
0582    CommandLineArg=zYES; Mode=zVGA_12H; return;       // /M12.
0583    }
0584  CommandLineCompare= strncmp(StartUpArg[1],Arg[1],5);
0585  if(CommandLineCompare==0)
0586    {
0587    CommandLineArg=zYES; Mode=zEGA_10H; return;       // /M10.
0588    }
0589  CommandLineCompare= strncmp(StartUpArg[2],Arg[1],5);
0590  if(CommandLineCompare==0)
0591    {
0592    CommandLineArg=zYES; Mode=zEGA_EH; return;        // /M0E.
0593    }
0594  CommandLineCompare= strncmp(StartUpArg[3],Arg[1],5);
0595  if(CommandLineCompare==0)
0596    {
0597    CommandLineArg=zYES; Mode=zMCGA_11H; return;      // /M11.
0598    }
0599  CommandLineCompare= strncmp(StartUpArg[4],Arg[1],5);
0600  if(CommandLineCompare==0)
0601    {
0602    CommandLineArg=zYES; Mode=zCGA_6H; return;        // /M06.
0603    }
0604  CommandLineCompare= strncmp(StartUpArg[5],Arg[1],5);
0605  if(CommandLineCompare==0)
0606    {
0607    CommandLineArg=zYES; Mode=zHERC; return;          // /MHC.
0608    }
0609  CommandLineArg= zNO;                 // if an unrecognized argument.
0610  return;
0611  }
0612  /*
0613
0614  ┌─────────────────────────────────────────────────────────┐
       │  Supercharged C++ Graphics  --  end of source file STARTUP.CPP │
0615  └─────────────────────────────────────────────────────────┘
0616                                                           */
```

2
Programming
an animation sequence

The object-oriented features of C++ can make it easier for you to design, write, and debug animation sequences. Animation is a vital part of graphics programming. Only animation can exploit the fourth dimension of computer graphics, the element of time.

Computer animation can spin and rotate a 3-D object. Computer animation can take a fully-shaded 3-D model and make it come alive with movement on the display screen. Computer animation can use morphing and tweening routines to build 2-D cel animation. Computer animation can create arcade-style graphics. Indeed, computer animation is the most common simulation tool.

Categories of animation

The two categories of animation are called *procedural* animation and *kinetic* animation. Three methods exist for producing these two categories of animation on personal computers. These hardware-based methods are frame animation, bitblt animation, and real-time animation.

Procedural animation

Procedural animation is based upon instructions provided by either the programmer or the user. These instructions are sometimes called a *script*. The animated subjects are usually called *actors*, whether they represent living things or otherwise. The actors follow a path of motion proscribed by you or by your software customer.

Kinetic animation

Kinetic animation adheres to the laws of physics—or a simplified interpretation of those laws. Ricochets, collisions, bounces, acceleration, and other phenomena are managed according to mathematical algorithms provided by the programmer. Kinetic animation is also called *forward dynamics*.

Hardware constraints

No matter what types of graphics adapter you intend to support with your software—VGA, EGA, MCGA, CGA, or Hercules—you can produce high-speed animation. You can choose your algorithms from the three methods of bitblt animation, frame animation, and real-time animation. You can combine any of the three methods, mixing and matching as your project requires.

The only constraints are hardware-based limitations. Microprocessor clock speed, memory availability, and screen resolution are the significant factors to be considered.

Clock speed

Obviously, the clock speed of the microprocessor will affect animation rates. A 33 MHz chip will always outperform a 16 MHz chip. Some animation, however, produces more pleasing results at lower rates. The demonstration program in chapter 10 looks best when executing on a 16 MHz machine. You can, of course, use software-based delaying tactics to control excessive speed.

Memory availability

Memory availability is important for the storage of images. If sufficient quantities of RAM, extended memory (XMS), and expanded memory (EMS) are not available, then your animation images will need to be stored on hard disk—or, in a worst case scenario, on floppy disk.

Screen resolution

Screen resolution affects the drawing speed of the computer. You can write low-level graphics like lines and polygons—and bitblt objects like graphic arrays—to the 640×200×2-color mode much faster than the 640×480×16-color mode. There are four bitplanes to write in the 640×480×16-color mode and only one bitmap in the 640×200×2-color mode. If the viewable dimensions of the image are kept constant, then there are more than twice as many pixels to be written in the 640×480×16-color mode.

This chapter of *Lee Adams' Supercharged C++ Graphics* provides an overview of computer animation concepts. It is intended to give you the background you need to understand the C++ animation samples in the book. For more detailed instruction and programming examples refer to the first volume in the Applied C Graphics series, *High Performance Graphics in C: Animation and Simulation*, Windcrest/McGraw-Hill book 3049. Also consult *Lee Adams' Visualization Graphics in C*, Windcrest/McGraw-Hill book 3487, for advanced programming examples of procedural animation and kinetic animation.

Principles of frame animation

Frame animation is also called full-screen animation and page animation. The animating program creates a series of full-screen images and saves each image in a separate page buffer. After all the pages have been created, a specialized routine in the program flips the pages into the display buffer in proper sequence in order to create animation. Large images can be drawn, filling the entire page, and ample time is available to create those images, so frame animation is usually the best choice for animation of complicated, fully-shaded, 3-D solid models. No matter how complex the 3-D model, frame animation can rotate it at pleasing rates.

VGA and EGA graphics adapters each contain enough display memory to support extra graphics pages in the 640×350×16-color mode (2 pages), the 640×200×16-color mode (4 pages), the 320×200×16-color mode (8 pages), and others. If you are using Turbo C++ or Borland C++, the setactivepage( ) instruction can be used to select the page upon which graphics will be drawn. The setvisualpage( ) instruction is used to choose the page to be displayed on the monitor. If you are using Zortech C++, the fg_setactivepage( ) function selects the written-to page. The fg_setdisplaypage( ) determines the page to be displayed.

The CGA does not support multiple pages. C++ graphics programs that use frame animation on a CGA must store the extra pages in RAM, EMS, XMS, or on disk.

Two pages are usually available on Hercules adapters using the 720×348×2- color mode.

You can use the high-speed animation techniques of bitblt, frame, and real-time no matter which graphic adapters you support with your software: VGA, EGA, MCGA, CGA, and Hercules.

Choosing the graphics mode

The most productive graphics mode for frame animation using display memory on VGA and EGA graphics adapters is the 640×200×16-color mode. Because each page requires 64,000 bytes of display memory, four pages are available on an adapter carrying 256K of display memory. VGA boards carry at least 256K. Most EGA boards are equipped with 256K.

The 640×200 resolution of this mode and the availability of 16 colors means that detailed imagery can be displayed. The availability of four graphics pages means that brief loops of high-speed animation can be generated.

The 320×200×16-color mode of the VGA and EGA offers 8 pages, but the coarse resolution of this mode must be taken into consideration. The 640×480×16-color mode of the VGA offers superb resolution, but only one graphics page is available on most VGAs. The 640×350×16-color mode of the VGA and EGA provides equally good resolution, but only two graphics pages are available because each page requires a whopping 112,900 bytes of display memory.

In graphics modes offering one or two pages, you can store other images in

RAM, extended memory, expanded memory, or on hard disk. The animation drivers copy the images from the inventory onto the graphics adapter display memory during the animation sequence.

RAM-based frame animation

RAM-based frame animation uses memory up to 640K to store frames. To implement the animation sequence, the movedata( ) function is employed to copy the data from each image buffer to the display buffer. The page copying routines provided in class PhysicalDisplay, found in LIB2D.CPP in appendix E, are useful for moving images from page to page in display memory, and from RAM to display memory.

When frame animation is implemented on a VGA using the 640×480×16-color mode, or on a VGA or EGA using the 640×350×16-color mode, the extra pages for short animation sequences are often stored in RAM, because there is no room in display memory for extra images. Brief sequences of frame animation on MCGA, CGA, and Hercules adapters can be implemented in the same manner.

Storage of images. Images for frame animation can be stored in RAM, in display memory, in expanded or extended memory, in a RAM disk, or on a hard disk.

Using EMS and XMS for frame animation

Lengthy animation playbacks can be produced if frames are stored in expanded memory or extended memory. Special software drivers are required to move the image data into and out of these special memory areas. The technical specifications for writing these drivers is available at nominal cost from both Microsoft and Intel.

Disk-based frame animation

Storage of frames on a fixed disk provides an easily managed mechanism for producing lengthy animation sequences. The playback is managed by downloading each frame from disk to the display buffer. The sequence can be further optimized by downloading a series of images to hidden buffers in RAM and in display memory, and running the playback from these multiple image buffers, reducing the number of disk accesses required.

Principles of bitblt animation

Bitblt animation is also called block graphics, software sprite animation, graphic array animation, snapshot animation, partial-screen animation, arcade-style animation, and bit blitting. Bitblt (pronounced bit blit) is an acronym for bit block transfer.

C++ bitblt animation is capable of extremely fast runtime performance because only a small portion of the screen is being manipulated. Animation speeds faster than the refresh rate of the display monitor are possible.

If you are using Turbo C++ or Borland C++, you can use the imagesize( ) function to set aside memory in RAM to hold the contents of a rectangular block of the display buffer. The getimage( ) function is used to store the graphics data in RAM as a graphic array. The image can be placed at different locations on the display screen by the putimage( ) instruction. If you are using Zortech C++, fg_readbox( ) will capture a block from the display buffer and store it in a graphic array. You can utilize fg_writebox( ) to place a graphic array on the screen. The methods of class Viewport provide comprehensive support for bitblt animation. LIB2D.HPP in appendix E contains the declaration for class Viewport. LIB2D.CPP provides the class implementation.

Bitblt animation is supported by the display hardware in every graphics mode. High-resolution, multicolor modes tend to produce slower runtime speeds than lower resolution, monocolor modes such as the 640×200×2-color mode. Smaller blocks can be animated at faster rates than larger blocks. The constraining factor is the amount of data being manipulated on the screen.

Fact *Hardware Compatibility.* Bitblt animation is supported in the standard display modes by the graphics libraries of Turbo C++, Borland C++, and Zortech C++. Animation is quickest in low-resolution black-and-white modes. It is slower in high-resolution 16-color modes.

RAM-based bitblt animation

In many instances, lengthy or complex bitblt animation sequences can be implemented by using the free store to hold the graphic arrays. It is sometimes convenient to download images from disk at program startup and place them in RAM, in extended memory, or in expanded memory.

Disk-based bitblt animation

If a fast hard disk is present in the system, graphic arrays stored in binary format on the disk can be downloaded fast enough to generate realistic animation sequences. Bitblt objects created from class Viewport (provided in appendix E) are capable of saving themselves to disk and loading themselves from disk. Using the same C++ methods with a RAM disk will produce even quicker results.

Principles of real-time animation

Unlike bitblt animation and frame animation in which all images are drawn and saved before starting the animation sequence, real-time animation draws the images while it is animating. During real-time animation, microprocessor time is sliced between creating images and animating those images. During bitblt animation and frame animation, the microprocessor can focus its attention on animation, because all images already exist in memory.

Real-time animation is also called live animation, ping pong animation, hidden page animation, and dynamic page-flipping animation. A minimum of two graphics pages are required. While the software is drawing an image on one page, the other page is being displayed. When an image is complete, it is displayed on the screen. The software then begins preparing the next image on the other page. The computer user never sees the images being drawn, only the completed images. Animation speed is constrained by the complexity of the image being animated.

How to increase real-time animation speed

A number of methods can be used to improve execution times for real-time animation programs. Although real-time animation will never be as quick as frame animation or bitblt animation, the need for meaningful keyboard interaction often makes real-time animation the preferred choice. With frame animation and bitblt animation, you can animate only images which already exist. Using real-time animation, your software is creating images at the same time it is animating them, so the user can use the keyboard to interact with the animation.

Keep it simple

Keep the image simple. The more time it takes for the computer to create the image, the slower the animation rate. In real-time animation, it is the action that creates the effect. Detailing is important in real-time animation, but action is more important. If your project requires a higher priority for detail, you should use frame animation or bitblt animation.

Create a background buffer

If a complex background is required, create a generic version of the background and store it in a separate hidden page. Each frame of the animation sequence can be implemented by flipping the pages, copying the contents of the background page onto the hidden written-to page, drawing the new image on the hidden written-to page, and flipping the completed image up onto the display screen.

RAM-based real-time animation

Most real-time animation can be operated from RAM or from the on-board display memory of the graphics adapter. Because neither Turbo C++, Borland C++, nor Zortech C++ supports graphics output directed to a hidden bitmap in RAM, it is best to use the 640×350×16-color mode with the VGA and EGA. This mode provides a second page on the graphics adapter, which can be used as the hidden, written-to page.

If your real-time animation requires background images, you can use expanded memory or extended memory as convenient storage for this inventory.

Animation technique strengths and weaknesses

Each animation method has its strengths and weaknesses. Here is an overview of factors you can consider when designing your C++ animation software.

Frame animation:
Memory intensive/quick playback

Frame animation produces the quickest animation. Because all images have been created in advance you are limited to using only those existing images during the animation sequence. Because full-screen images are being manipulated, lots of RAM or disk space is needed to store those images. Animation playback is very fast because the processor dedicates all its attention to copying blocks of data from one memory location to another.

Bitblt animation:
Optimized for small images

Bitblt animation is not as quick as frame animation, but it conserves memory because only small portions of the screen are being manipulated. Bitblt animation can preserve the background imagery if logical operations like XOR and AND are used. This technique saves the time and memory required to redraw the background graphics. Your software is limited to using images that you have previously saved as graphic arrays.

Real-time animation:
Versatility at the expense of speed

Real-time animation is the most versatile method, but it is also the slowest. Because you are drawing each frame at the same time you are animating, you can change the contents of the next frame in the animation sequence. Real-time animation is the ultimate interactive mechanism.

Interactive animation concepts

Animation sequences that involve the interactive participation of the user during runtime are based on three principles: instancing of actors, a fixed camera, and a moving camera.

Actor instancing

By quickly redisplaying an actor in a position slightly offset from the previous position, the illusion of motion can be effected. Each occurrence of the actor is called an *instance*.

Bitblt animation and real-time animation provide the most useful tools for instancing.

A fixed camera

Fixed camera animation is usually associated with 3-D scenes. If the viewpoint does not change but the objects in the scene are being moved, then the camera is said to be fixed. The scene does not move, only the actors in the scene.

A moving camera

Moving camera animation is also called point-of-view animation. The entire scene and all the objects in the scene are changing on the display screen as the camera moves. The viewpoint can be moved to any location and the viewing angle can be set to any angle of yaw, roll, and pitch.

Advantages of C++
for animation programming

Class The object-oriented capabilities of C++ can be put to good use in animation programming. Bitblt actors, for example, can be designed as C++ objects, each capable of displaying itself, moving itself, and erasing itself. Because the class library takes on the responsibility for managing the bitblt, you can focus more of your attention on the subtleties of the animation presentation itself.

The demonstration program in this chapter shows how easy it is to manage the simultaneous animation of three separate actors, even though each actor is bouncing off the boundaries of the display area.

A sample program: BOUNCE.CPP

Demo Figure 2-1 depicts typical displays produced by the sample program BOUNCE.CPP, whose complete source code is provided in FIG. 2-3 at the end of the chapter. The program simultaneously animates three different actors on the display. Each actor careens off the walls of the bounding box in a never-ending frenzy of activity.

How to compile and link
the sample program

Here's How... The program listing presented in FIG. 2-3 contains the complete source code for the main module of the C++ demonstration program called "Using C++ for Object-oriented Animation of Multiple Items." If you are using the companion disks to the book, the source code is in the file named BOUNCE.CPP. Three C++ source files are needed to build the finished .exe file. These are BOUNCE.CPP from FIG. 2-3 and two of the class libraries in appendix E.

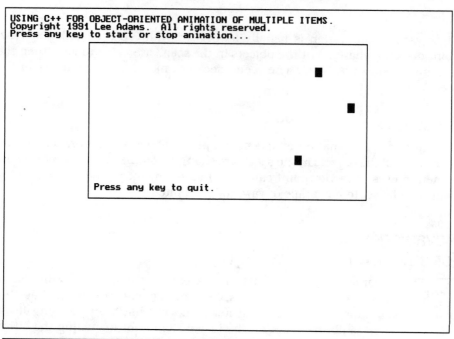

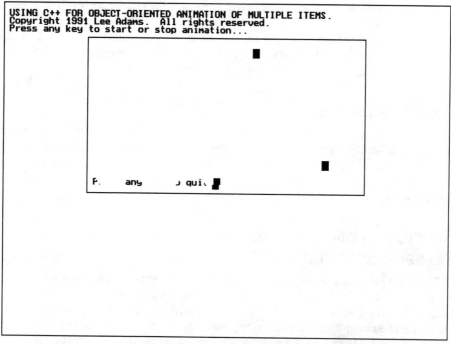

2-1 Graphics output from the animated sample program BOUNCE.CPP. Top: three moving bitblts at the start of the animation sequence. Each bitblt is a separate C++ object capable of displaying and moving itself. Bottom: because of the overwrite technique used to animate the bitblts, the caption is eventually obliterated.

The class library that provides the language bindings and low-level graphics routines for this demonstration program is found in FIG. E-2 in appendix E. This listing contains the implementations for class PhysicalDisplay and class Viewport. If you are using the companion disks to the book, this file is named LIB2D.CPP. The class declarations are presented in FIG. E-1 in appendix E. If you are using the companion disks to the book, this file is named LIB2D.HPP.

The class library that provides the bitblt animation methods for this demonstration program is found in FIG. E-10 in appendix E. This listing contains the implementations for class Blitter. If you are using the companion disks to the book, this file is named BLITTER.CPP. The class declarations are presented in FIG. E-9 in appendix E. If you are using the companion disks to the book, this file is named BLITTER.HPP.

You can compile, link, and run this demonstration program using either Turbo C++, Borland C++, or Zortech C++. If you are using Turbo C++, you might wish to read appendix A for guidance in compiling, linking, and running the demonstration program. If you are using Borland C++, you can find the appropriate information in appendix B. If you are using Zortech C++, refer to appendix C.

You must create a Turbo C++ or Borland C++ project list to advise your compiler which source files to bind together to build the finished .exe file. If you are using Zortech C++, you must name the files on the compiler command line field. Refer to the appendices described earlier if you are unfamiliar with this technique.

After a successful compile and link, the animated screen should resemble the screen prints shown in FIG. 2-1.

How to run the demonstration program

You need a VGA, EGA, MCGA, CGA, or Hercules graphics adapter to run this demonstration program.

Using the editor to run the program

To run the program under the control of your Turbo C++, Borland C++, or Zortech C++ editor, make sure that the finished .exe file is in the default directory. If you used Turbo C++ or Borland C++ to compile the program, the appropriate graphics driver must be in the default directory. If you are using a VGA or EGA, the EGAVGA.BGI file must be present. If you are using an MCGA or CGA, the CGA.BGI file must be located in the default directory. If you are using a Hercules graphics adapter, the HERC.BGI file must be available. These graphics drivers are installed on your hard disk by the Turbo C++ and Borland C++ installation utilities. If you used Zortech C++ to compile the demonstration program, the appropriate graphics drivers have already been linked into the finished executable code by the Zortech linker.

You need a VGA, EGA, MCGA, CGA, or Hercules graphics adapter to run the demonstration program BOUNCE.CPP. The built-in autodetect routine will detect the graphics hardware in your computer system and will set up the best graphics mode supported by your computer hardware. To override the autodetect routine, use the Turbo C++, Borland C++, or Zortech C++ editor to simulate a command line argument. The header in FIG. 2-3 provides a set of mnemonics you can use. See the appendices for guidance in using this technique with your particular compiler. If you are using a VGA, you can override the autodetect routine and force the demonstration program to run in an EGA, MCGA, cr CGA mode. If you are using an EGA, you can force the program to run in a lower-resolution EGA mode or a CGA mode.

Running the program from the operating system prompt

Here's How... To start the program from the operating system prompt, simply enter BOUNCE. The .exe file and any required graphics drivers must be present in the default directory. If the software finds a VGA present in your system, the program will animate using the 640×480×16-color mode. If an EGA and enhanced monitor are found, the 640×350×16-color mode is used. If an EGA and standard display are present, the program sets up the 640×200×16-color mode. If an MCGA is detected, the 640×480×2-color mode is employed. If a CGA is found, the 640×200×2-color mode is used. If the program detects a Hercules graphics adapter, it will animate the actors using the 720×348×2-color mode.

You can force the program to start up in a different mode by adding a command line argument when you start the program from the operating system prompt. Enter BOUNCE /M11 to force the 640×480×2-color mode. Enter BOUNCE /M10 to force the 640×350×16-color mode. Entering BOUNCE /M0E forces the program to run in the 640×200×16-color mode. Enter BOUNCE /M06 to test the demonstration program in the 640×200×2-color mode.

Using the demonstration program

Each actor is animated independently using overwrite logic. As FIG. 2-1 shows, the background is eventually completely overwritten, obliterating the text string near the bottom of the bounding box.

Each actor is a graphic array. See FIG. 2-2. The active image is slightly smaller than the graphic array. This results in an unused border area, which is the same color as the background over which the bitblt will be placed. By placing each new instance of the actor just slightly offset from the previous occurrence, the former image is conveniently overwritten.

If you are using a VGA or EGA, you might find it instructive to try running the demonstration program in the 640×200×2-color CGA mode to see the dramatic effect upon animation speed that a lower resolution screen mode can produce.

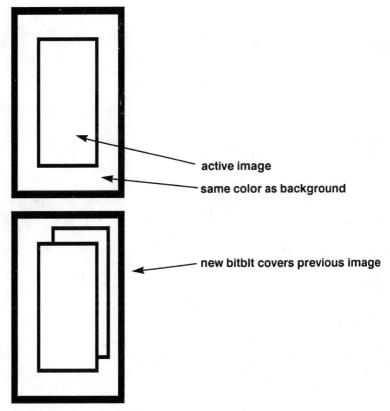

active image

same color as background

new bitblt covers previous image

2-2 The nominal border around the bitblt makes it possible to cleanly overwrite the previous bitblt during an animation sequence.

Programmer's Guide to BOUNCE.CPP

Code   The complete listing for the demonstration program BOUNCE.CPP is presented in FIG. 2-3. The source code consists of an informative header, conditional compilation directives, declaration of constants and macros, file include directives, function prototypes, variable declarations, and the executable functions.

Conditional compilation

Information and source code for conditional compilation is located at lines 0045 through 0062. If you are using Turbo C++ or Borland C++, the program is ready to compile, subject to the instructions provided in appendix B. If you are using Zortech C++, change line 0061 to read #define FG and change line 0062 to read #define ZORTECH.

Constants

The C++ qualifier, const, is used to declare and assign values to constant variables at lines 0064 through 0072.

Macros

A macro is defined at line 0078. The C++ compiler will expand the Wait _for_any_key instruction when it again encounters this string at line 0184. Using this macro makes the source code easier to read.

Include files

The code at lines 0080 through 0108 uses the #include directive to load in the appropriate header files and C++ class declaration files. Line 0107 loads LIB2D.HPP, which declares the data members and methods of class PhysicalDisplay and class Viewport. Line 0108 loads BLITTER.HPP, which declares the data members and methods of class Blitter. Class Blitter is discussed later in this chapter.

Function prototypes

Function declarations are provided in lines 0110 through 0122. These functions are visible throughout this source file and can be called by any other function in the source file. Because each function is declared with the static qualifier, it is not available to functions located in other source files.

Variable declarations

Lines 0124 through 0155 declare global variables that are visible throughout this source file. These variables have file scope.

Object declarations

Object Note line 0154, which creates an object from class PhysicalDisplay. The object is named Display. The program will later call the methods of this object to help it manage the display. The methods are declared in the class declaration listing LIB2D.HPP and are defined in the class implementation listing LIB2D.CPP in appendix E. The object created at line 0161 is a static object. It has file scope and will remain available until the program terminates.

Line 0155 creates an object from the Viewport class. The object is named Viewport1. The address of Display is passed to this new object. Viewport1 will need to use the methods of Display to generate graphics output. The object created at line 0155 is a static object with file scope. It will remain active until program termination.

main( )

The main( ) function is located at lines 0160 through 0189. After first checking to see if any command line arguments were used to launch the program, the code switches to an appropriate graphics mode, and then calls the function that manages the animation of the three actors.

Managing the animation sequence

The function at lines 0191 through 0343 manages the simultaneous animation of the three actors. Variables local to this function are declared at lines 0197 through 0223. Note in particular line 0226, where a local pointer is assigned the address of the Viewport object passed to this function. The function needs to call the methods of the object to handle all bitblt operations.

The code at lines 0228 through 0242 creates actor #1 and stores the image in a graphic array. The // comments explain in detail how the code goes about performing this task.

The code at lines 0244 through 0258 creates actor #2 and stores the resulting imagery in a graphic array. The code at lines 0260 through 0274 creates the image of actor #3 and stores the bitblt in a graphic array by using the methods of class Viewport and class Blitter.

The background for the animation sequence is drawn by the code at lines 0276 through 0282.

Notice the source code at lines 0284 through 0300. These lines calculate the collision points for each actor, based upon the width and height of the bitblt. Each actor can be a different size, as well as different color, in this animation sequence.

The animation loop is located at lines 0308 through 0342. The + = additive assignment operator is used to move each actor in a horizontal and vertical direction. The if( ) statement is used to test if a boundary collision has occurred, and to reverse the direction of movement if needed. The workhorse of the animation loop, however, is the code replicated at lines 0322, 0331, and 0340. The MoveImage( ) method of class Blitter can be relied upon to cleanly move the bitblt image from one location to another on the display screen.

By using the cut-and-paste capabilities of the Turbo C++, Borland C++, or Zortech C++ editor, you can easily add a fourth or fifth actor to this animation environment.

Terminating the program

The function at lines 0345 through 0353 calls a method of class PhysicalDisplay to terminate the graphics state. Line 0352 returns an OK code to the operating system.

The Startup( ) function

The function at lines 0355 through 0438 calls the SetupMode( ) method of class PhysicalDisplay to detect the graphics hardware. Lines 0373 through 0383 force the logic to an appropriate block of code that initializes variables for whatever graphics mode has been invoked.

The StubRoutine( ) function

The stub routine at lines 0440 through 0451 is a do-nothing routine that displays a simple message on the dialog line at the top of the display. A stub like this is handy when you are building a large, unwieldy program. By calling the stub, you can avoid taking the time to build specific routine while you are creating your first prototype.

The Keyboard( ) function

The function at lines 0454 through 0482 detects and retrieves keystrokes from the keyboard buffer. The function at lines 0484 through 0492 repeatedly calls the keyboard function until the keyboard buffer is empty. This routine ensures that no unwanted keystrokes remain in the buffer after a lengthy graphics operation.

The MakeSound( ) function

The zMakeSound( ) function at lines 0495 through 0531 generates a sound from the system speaker. Appropriate values are sent to the hardware ports, providing direct control over the speaker.

The Pause( ) function

The function at lines 0533 through 0551 pauses program execution for a specified length of time. The code uses the value returned by the system clock and multiplies it by the number of ticks per second. If you are using Turbo C++ or Borland C++, this value is represented by the global variable CLK_TCK. If you are using Zortech C++ it is represented by CLOCKS_PER_SEC. The pause function is unused in this demonstration program.

The Arguments( ) function

The function at lines 0553 through 0595 compares the command line argument with a set of permitted strings. The function assigns an appropriate value to the global variable named Mode. Mode is referenced by other functions to help manage graphics output.

Programmer's Guide to LIB2D.HPP

Code The complete source code for the declarations for class PhysicalDisplay and class Viewport is found in LIB2D.HPP in appendix E. The source from LIB2D.HPP must be #included at the beginning of any program that wishes to use the methods of class PhysicalDisplay or class Viewport. See the discussion in chapter 1 for more information about LIB2D.HPP.

Programmer's Guide to LIB2D.CPP

Code The source code in LIB2D.CPP, presented in appendix E, provides language bindings that produce low-level graphics. The routines in LIB2D.CPP call the appropriate runtime library functions in Turbo C++'s graphics.lib, Borland C++'s graphics.lib, Zortech C++'s fg.lib, or Microsoft's graph.lib.

LIB2D.CPP is the class implementation listing for class PhysicalDisplay and class Viewport. Class PhysicalDisplay manages the state of the display. Class Viewport is responsible for maintaining a viewport and producing low-level graphics. These two classes generate nearly all the low-level graphics required by the demonstration programs in the book. See the discussion in chapter 1 for further information about class PhysicalDisplay and class Viewport.

Programmer's Guide to BLITTER.HPP

Code The complete source code for the declarations for class Blitter is found in BLITTER.HPP in appendix E. The source from BLITTER.HPP must be #included at the beginning of any program that wishes to use the methods of class Blitter.

Here's Why... An interesting wrinkle in this source file is at lines 0045 and 0046. These two preprocessor directives are used to ensure that BLITTER.HPP will not be #included if it has already been #included. A previous inclusion will have defined the variable BLITTER_HPP, which would cause the test at line 0045 to fail, skipping all code until line 0081.

The source code at lines 0050 through 0071 declares data members and a method that are not visible to functions or methods outside class Blitter. The code at lines 0073 through 0078 declares methods of class Blitter that can be called by any in-scope function or method.

Programmer's Guide to BLITTER.CPP

Code The complete source code for the implementation for class Blitter is found in BLITTER.CPP in appendix E. The methods of class Blitter provide bitblt operations that are optimized for high-speed overwrite animation sequences.

Constructor

The constructor for objects of class Blitter is located at lines 0058 through 0072. The constructor expects to receive in its argument list the diagonal bounding coordinates of the bitblt being created, the horizontal and vertical resolution of the current graphics screen mode, and a pointer to the Viewport object to be used for low-level graphics output to the display.

Much of the constructor's activity is centered around initializing tokens that will indicate the state of the bitblt at runtime. The methods of class Blitter need to know if memory has been allocated, if a graphic array has already been stored in RAM, and so on.

Destructor

The destructor for class Blitter is presented at lines 0075 through 0082. The destructor is automatically called whenever an object of class Blitter is destroyed. A call to method FreeBlock( ) ensures that the memory allocated for the graphic array is released back to the free store.

Method GrabImage( )

The method at lines 0084 through 0098 captures the image from the display. Note line 0091, for example. The -> addressing notation is used to send a message to the MemBlock( ) method of an object named Generic. Generic is a pointer to the Viewport object that was passed when the bitblt was activated. A subsequent call to method GetBlock( ) stores the image in the memory allocated by method MemBlock( ).

The code at line 0096 sets a token to indicate that the bitblt is ready to be used by any client program. This token will be verified by other methods that want to write a bitblt to the display, in order to avoid generating a runtime error in the event the client program mistakenly calls for a bitblt to be displayed before it has been stored in a graphic array.

Method DisplayImage( )

The method at lines 0110 through 0126 places the bitblt onto the screen. The test at line 0116 ensures that DisplayImage( ) will not place a second bitblt on the display if the bitblt is already present. The test at line 0117 ensures that a graphic array exists. The tests at lines 0119 through 0122 ensures that the requested location for installation is legal.

The PutPSET method of class Viewport is called at line 0123 to actually write the bitblt to the display.

Method MoveImage( )

The method at lines 0128 through 0142 is the central core of this class. Method MoveImage( ) will move an already displayed bitblt a specified distance from its current location. The distance to be moved is passed to the method in its argument list. The code at line 0135 increments the current writeable location of the bitblt. The call to method PutPSET of class Viewport at line 0140 writes the bitblt to the new location.

2-3 Sample program BOUNCE.CPP. Supports VGA, EGA, MCGA, CGA, and Hercules adapters. This application demonstrates high-speed bitblt animation using overwrite logic. Each bitblt is a C++ object capable of displaying and moving itself on the screen.

```
0001   /*
0002
0003          Lee Adams' SUPERCHARGED C++ GRAPHICS
0004          Interactive demo:   fundamental bitblt objects
0005
0006   SOURCE FILE:    BOUNCE.CPP
0007          TYPE:    C++ source file for a multimodule application.
0008       PURPOSE:    Demonstrates object-oriented bitblt animation.
0009   PROGRAM LIST:   BOUNCE.CPP, LIB2D.CPP and BLITTER.CPP.
0010      LANGUAGES:   Turbo C++, Borland C++, Zortech C++, and
0011                   all C++ compilers compatible with AT&T C++ 2.0
0012                   specification; and nominal compatibility with
0013                   Microsoft C++ (see the discussion in the book).
0014   MEMORY MODEL:   large.
0015   COMMAND-LINE:   you can specify a graphics mode by using the
0016                   command-line argument /Mnn as shown below:
0017                        /M12  640x480x16-color VGA
0018                        /M11  640x480x2-color VGA, MCGA
0019                        /M10  640x350x16-color VGA, EGA
0020                        /M0E  640x200x16-color VGA, EGA
0021                        /M06  640x200x2-color VGA, MCGA, EGA, CGA
0022                        /MHC  720x348x2-color Hercules
0023                   If no command-line argument is used, hardware
0024                   autodetect is used to select the best mode.
0025   OUTPUT:   Three actors are moved around the display using
0026             high-speed overwrite animation of a graphic array.
0027   LICENSE:  As purchaser of the book in which this source code
0028     appears you are granted a royalty-free license to reproduce
0029     and distribute executable files generated using this code
0030     provided that you accept the conditions of the License
0031     Agreement and Limited Warranty described in the book.
0032   PUBLICATION: Contains material from Windcrest/McGraw-Hill
0033     book 3489, published by TAB BOOKS.
0034   U.S. GOVERNMENT RESTRICTED RIGHTS:  This software and its
0035     documentation is provided with restricted rights.  The use,
0036     duplication, or disclosure by the Government is subject to
0037     restrictions set forth in subdivision (b)(3)(ii) of The
0038     Rights in Technical Data and Computer Software clause at
0039     252.227-7013.  Contractor/manufacturer is Lee Adams, c/o
0040     TAB BOOKS, 13311 Monterey Ave., Blue Ridge Summit PA 17294.
0041   TRADEMARK:  Lee Adams is a trademark of Lee Adams.
0042
0043       Copyright 1991 Lee Adams.  All rights reserved worldwide.
0044
0045
0046                   CONDITIONAL COMPILATION
0047   To compile only those blocks of code that support the C++
0048   compiler and graphics library that you are using, you should
0049   #define the appropriate tokens on lines 0061 and 0062.
0050                   GRAPHICS LIBRARY
```

2-3 Continued.

```
0051             Borland's graphics.lib              #define BGI
0052             Zortech's fg.lib or fgdebug.lib     #define FG
0053             Microsoft's graph.lib               #define MS
0054                     COMPILER
0055             Borland Turbo C++ compiler          #define BORLAND
0056             Zortech C++ compiler                #define ZORTECH
0057             AT&T-compatible C++ compilers        #define MICROSOFT
0058       Be sure you define only one compiler and one graphics library.
0059
0060                                                                     */
0061   #define BGI      1  // indicates the graphics library you are using.
0062   #define BORLAND 1  // indicates the C++ compiler you are using.
0063   /*
0064
0065   ┌──────────────────────────────────────────────────────────────┐
       │                          Constants                             │
0066   └──────────────────────────────────────────────────────────────┘
0067                                                                     */
0068   const int zFAIL=0; const int zEMPTY=0;
0069   const int zYES=1; const int zNO=0;
0070   const int zVGA_12H=1; const int zEGA_10H=2; const int zEGA_EH=3;
0071   const int zMCGA_11H=4; const int zCGA_6H=5; const int zHERC=6;
0072   const int zENTER=13; const int zESC=27;
0073   /*
0074
0075   ┌──────────────────────────────────────────────────────────────┐
       │                           Macros                               │
0076   └──────────────────────────────────────────────────────────────┘
0077                                                                     */
0078   #define Wait_for_any_key  while(KeyCode==0) zKeyboard(); KeyCode=0;
0079   /*
0080
0081   ┌──────────────────────────────────────────────────────────────┐
       │                         Include files                          │
0082   └──────────────────────────────────────────────────────────────┘
0083                                                                     */
0084   #if defined (BORLAND)
0085   #include <time.h>          // supports clock().
0086   #include <string.h>        // supports strncmp().
0087   #include <bios.h>          // supports bioskey().
0088   #include <process.h>       // supports exit().
0089   #include <iostream.h>      // supports cout.
0090   #include <dos.h>           // supports outportb(), inportb().
0091   #elif defined (ZORTECH)
0092   #include <time.h>          // supports clock().
0093   #include <string.h>        // supports strncmp().
0094   #include <bios.h>          // supports bioskey().
0095   #include <stdlib.h>        // supports exit().
0096   #include <stream.hpp>      // supports cout.
0097   #include <dos.h>           // supports outp(), inp().
0098   #elif defined (MICROSOFT)
0099   #include <time.h>          // supports clock().
0100   #include <string.h>        // supports strncmp().
0101   #include <bios.h>          // supports _bios_keybrd().
0102   #include <process.h>       // supports exit().
0103   #include <iostream.h>      // supports cout.
0104   #include <conio.h>         // supports outp(), inp().
0105   #endif
0106
0107   #include "LIB2D.HPP"       // declarations for PhysicalDisplay class.
0108   #include "BLITTER.HPP"            // declarations for Blitter class.
0109   /*
0110
0111   ┌──────────────────────────────────────────────────────────────┐
       │        Prototypes for functions visible throughout this file  │
```

```
0112  |_____|
0113                                                    */
0114  static void zStartup(void);          // initializes a graphics mode.
0115  static void zArguments(int, char far* far*);   // checks arguments.
0116  static void zKeyboard(void);           // checks for a keystroke.
0117  static void zQuit_Pgm(void);          // ends the program gracefully.
0118  static void zPurge(void);          // empties the keyboard buffer.
0119  static void zStubRoutine(void);             // do-nothing stub.
0120  static void zMakeSound(int,double);     // makes a specific sound.
0121  static clock_t zDelay(clock_t,double);    // CPU-independent pause.
0122  static void zInteractiveLoop(Viewport *);        // runtime loop.
0123  /*
0124
0125  |    Declaration of variables visible throughout this file        |
0126
0127                                                    */
0128  static char *StartUpArg[6]={        // legal command-line arguments.
0129        "/M12", "/M10", "/MOE", "/M11", "/M06", "/MHC" };
0130  static int CommandLineArg=zNO;       // indicates if argument exists.
0131  static int CommandLineCompare=0;     // indicates if argument legal.
0132  static int C0=0,C1=1,C2=2,C3=3,C4=4,C5=5,C6=6,
0133   C7=7,C8=8,C9=9,C10=10,C11=11,C12=12,C13=13,
0134   C14=14,C15=15;                          // palette index codes.
0135  static int Mode=0;            // which graphics mode is being used.
0136  static int Result=0;      // captures result of graphics routines.
0137  static int CharWidth=0,CharHeight=0;    // dimensions of character.
0138  static char KeyCode=0;   // token for normal or extended keystroke.
0139  static char KeyNum=0;                 // ASCII number of keystroke.
0140  static char SolidFill[]=
0141              {255,255,255,255,255,255,255,255};   // 100% fill.
0142  static int TextClr=7;              // font color for regular text.
0143  static int PromptClr=7;            // font color for prompt text.
0144  static char Copyright[]=
0145                  "Copyright 1991 Lee Adams.  All rights reserved.";
0146  static char Title[]=
0147   "USING C++ FOR OBJECT-ORIENTED ANIMATION OF MULTIPLE ITEMS.";
0148  static char PressAnyKey[]=
0149    "Press any key to start or stop animation...";
0150  static char RuntimePrompt[]= "Press any key to quit.";
0151  static char StubMessage[]= "The generic stub routine was called.";
0152  static int X_Res=0, Y_Res=0;               // screen resolution.
0153
0154  PhysicalDisplay Display;    // create the physical display object.
0155  Viewport Viewport1(&Display);        // create a viewport object.
0156  /*
0157
0158  |                    Function definitions                         |
0159
0160
0161  |    The executive routine:  program execution begins here         |
0162
0163                                                    */
0164  main(int argc, char *argv[])
0165  {
0166    int NumArgs; char far* far* Arg;
0167
0168  NumArgs= argc;                      // grab number of arguments.
0169  Arg= &argv[0];          // grab address of array of arguments.
0170  zArguments(NumArgs, Arg);     // check the command-line arguments.
0171
0172  zStartup();                      // establish the graphics mode.
0173  Display.Init2D(Mode,0,0,X_Res-1,Y_Res-1);    // set graphics state.
0174  Result= Display.InitUndo();    // create hidden page (unused here).
```

2-3 Continued.

```
0175   if (Result==zFAIL) zQuit_Pgm();          // if hidden page failed.
0176
0177   Display.BlankPage();                      // clear the display.
0178   Display.SetHue(C7);                       // set the drawing color.
0179   Display.SetFill(SolidFill,C7);            // set the fill style.
0180   Viewport1.PutText(2,2,TextClr,Title);     // sign-on notice.
0181   Viewport1.PutText(3,2,TextClr,Copyright); // copyright notice.
0182   Viewport1.DrawBorder(0,0,X_Res-1,Y_Res-1);    // draw a border.
0183   Viewport1.PutText(4,2,PromptClr,PressAnyKey); // display a prompt.
0184   Wait_for_any_key    // this macro was defined earlier at line 0078.
0185
0186   zInteractiveLoop(&Viewport1);             // call the interactive loop.
0187
0188   zQuit_Pgm();            // tidy up and terminate the application.
0189   }
0190   /*
0191
0192   ┌─────────────────────────────────────────────────────────┐
       │        INTERACTIVE CONTROL OF BITBLT OBJECT ON SCREEN    │
0193   └─────────────────────────────────────────────────────────┘
0194                                                            */
0195   static void zInteractiveLoop(Viewport *ViewportObject)
0196   {                // expects to receive the viewport object to be used.
0197     Viewport *ViewPtr;          // uninitialized ptr to a viewport.
0198     int x1= 119, y1= 36, x2= 519, y2= 199;     // background coords.
0199     int ObjBackground= C2;                    // color of background.
0200
0201              // characteristics of actor #1...
0202     int Obj1OffsetX= 1;                       // x offset for movement.
0203     int Obj1OffsetY= 1;                       // y offset for movement.
0204     int Obj1X1= 80, Obj1Y1= 80, Obj1X2= 95, Obj1Y2= 95;    // coords.
0205     int Obj1Color= C4;                        // color of actor.
0206     int Now1X1= 319, Now1Y1= 99; // current position of moving actor.
0207     int Xmin1, Ymin1, Xmax1, Ymax1;           // collision ranges.
0208
0209              // characteristics of actor #2...
0210     int Obj2OffsetX= 1;                       // x offset for movement.
0211     int Obj2OffsetY= -1;                      // y offset for movement.
0212     int Obj2X1= 80, Obj2Y1= 80, Obj2X2= 95, Obj2Y2= 95;    // coords.
0213     int Obj2Color= C3;                        // color of actor.
0214     int Now2X1= 419, Now2Y1= 98; // current position of moving actor.
0215     int Xmin2, Ymin2, Xmax2, Ymax2;           // collision ranges.
0216
0217              // characteristics of actor #3...
0218     int Obj3OffsetX= 2;                       // x offset for movement.
0219     int Obj3OffsetY= -2;                      // y offset for movement.
0220     int Obj3X1= 80, Obj3Y1= 80, Obj3X2= 95, Obj3Y2= 95;    // coords.
0221     int Obj3Color= C5;                        // color of actor.
0222     int Now3X1= 219, Now3Y1= 78; // current position of moving actor.
0223     int Xmin3, Ymin3, Xmax3, Ymax3;           // collision ranges.
0224
0225              // use the appropriate viewport...
0226   ViewPtr= ViewportObject;                    // initialize the pointer.
0227
0228              // create and store actor #1...
0229   Display.SetHue(ObjBackground);              // set the drawing color.
0230   Display.SetFill(SolidFill,ObjBackground);   // set the fill style.
0231   ViewPtr->DrawPanel(Obj1X1,Obj1Y1,Obj1X2,Obj1Y2);    // filled rect.
0232   Display.SetHue(Obj1Color);                  // set the drawing color.
0233   Display.SetFill(SolidFill,Obj1Color);       // set the fill style.
0234   ViewPtr->DrawPanel(Obj1X1+2,Obj1Y1+2,Obj1X2-2,Obj1Y2-2);  // actor.
0235   Display.SetHue(C0);
```

```
0236   ViewPtr->DrawBorder(Obj1X1+2,Obj1Y1+2,Obj1X2-2,Obj1Y2-2);
0237   Blitter *Item1=              // ...and create a new Blitter object.
0238     new Blitter(Obj1X1,Obj1Y1,Obj1X2,Obj1Y2,X_Res,Y_Res,ViewPtr);
0239   Item1->GrabImage();          // grab the actor from the bitmap.
0240   Display.SetHue(C0);                    // set the drawing color.
0241   Display.SetFill(SolidFill,C0);             // set the fill style.
0242   ViewPtr->DrawPanel(Obj1X1,Obj1Y1,Obj1X2,Obj1Y2);    // erase actor.
0243
0244               // create and store actor #2...
0245   Display.SetHue(ObjBackground);            // set the drawing color.
0246   Display.SetFill(SolidFill,ObjBackground);    // set the fill style.
0247   ViewPtr->DrawPanel(Obj2X1,Obj2Y1,Obj2X2,Obj2Y2);   // filled rect.
0248   Display.SetHue(Obj2Color);                // set the drawing color.
0249   Display.SetFill(SolidFill,Obj2Color);        // set the fill style.
0250   ViewPtr->DrawPanel(Obj2X1+2,Obj2Y1+2,Obj2X2-2,Obj2Y2-2); // actor.
0251   Display.SetHue(C0);
0252   ViewPtr->DrawBorder(Obj2X1+2,Obj2Y1+2,Obj2X2-2,Obj2Y2-2);
0253   Blitter *Item2=              // ...and create a new Blitter object.
0254     new Blitter(Obj2X1,Obj2Y1,Obj2X2,Obj2Y2,X_Res,Y_Res,ViewPtr);
0255   Item2->GrabImage();          // grab the actor from the bitmap.
0256   Display.SetHue(C0);                    // set the drawing color.
0257   Display.SetFill(SolidFill,C0);             // set the fill style.
0258   ViewPtr->DrawPanel(Obj2X1,Obj2Y1,Obj2X2,Obj2Y2);    // erase actor.
0259
0260               // create and store actor #3...
0261   Display.SetHue(ObjBackground);            // set the drawing color.
0262   Display.SetFill(SolidFill,ObjBackground);    // set the fill style.
0263   ViewPtr->DrawPanel(Obj3X1,Obj3Y1,Obj3X2,Obj3Y2);   // filled rect.
0264   Display.SetHue(Obj3Color);                // set the drawing color.
0265   Display.SetFill(SolidFill,Obj3Color);        // set the fill style.
0266   ViewPtr->DrawPanel(Obj3X1+2,Obj3Y1+2,Obj3X2-2,Obj3Y2-2); // actor.
0267   Display.SetHue(C0);
0268   ViewPtr->DrawBorder(Obj3X1+2,Obj3Y1+2,Obj3X2-2,Obj3Y2-2);
0269   Blitter *Item3=              // ...and create a new Blitter object.
0270     new Blitter(Obj3X1,Obj3Y1,Obj3X2,Obj3Y2,X_Res,Y_Res,ViewPtr);
0271   Item3->GrabImage();          // grab the actor from the bitmap.
0272   Display.SetHue(C0);                    // set the drawing color.
0273   Display.SetFill(SolidFill,C0);             // set the fill style.
0274   ViewPtr->DrawPanel(Obj3X1,Obj3Y1,Obj3X2,Obj3Y2);    // erase actor.
0275
0276               // create the animation background...
0277   Display.SetHue(ObjBackground);
0278   Display.SetFill(SolidFill,ObjBackground);
0279   ViewPtr->DrawPanel(x1,y1,x2,y2);          // draw the background...
0280   Display.SetHue(C7);
0281   Display.SetFill(SolidFill,C7);
0282   ViewPtr->DrawBorder(x1,y1,x2,y2);    // ...draw a border around it.
0283
0284               // calculate collision points for actor #1...
0285   Xmin1= x1 + 2;                          // left collision boundary.
0286   Ymin1= y1 + 2;                          // top collision boundary.
0287   Xmax1= x2 - ((Obj1X2 - Obj1X1) + 1);   // right collision boundary.
0288   Ymax1= y2 - ((Obj1Y2 - Obj1Y1) + 1);   // bottom collision boundary.
0289
0290               // calculate collision points for actor #2...
0291   Xmin2= x1 + 2;                          // left collision boundary.
0292   Ymin2= y1 + 2;                          // top collision boundary.
0293   Xmax2= x2 - ((Obj2X2 - Obj2X1) + 1);   // right collision boundary.
0294   Ymax2= y2 - ((Obj2Y2 - Obj2Y1) + 2);   // bottom collision boundary.
0295
0296               // calculate collision points for actor #3...
0297   Xmin3= x1 + 4;                          // left collision boundary.
0298   Ymin3= y1 + 2;                          // top collision boundary.
```

```
0299    Xmax3= x2 - ((Obj3X2 - Obj3X1) + 1);   // right collision boundary.
0300    Ymax3= y2 - ((Obj3Y2 - Obj3Y1) + 4);   // bottom collision boundary.
0301
0302          // display a text prompt and begin the animation...
0303    ViewPtr->PutText(24,17,C14,RuntimePrompt);              // prompt.
0304    Item1->DisplayImage(Now1X1,Now1Y1);         // display actor #1.
0305    Item2->DisplayImage(Now2X1,Now2Y1);         // display actor #2.
0306    Item3->DisplayImage(Now3X1,Now3Y1);         // display actor #3.
0307
0308    ANIMATION_LOOP:                                  // loop begins.
0309      zKeyboard();                       // check for user keystroke.
0310      if (KeyCode!=0)
0311        {                                 // if a key was pressed...
0312        delete Item3; delete Item2;
0313        delete Item1; return;            // ...then destroy objects.
0314        }
0315                        // animate actor #1...
0316      Now1X1+= Obj1OffsetX;             // calculate new x coordinate.
0317      if (Now1X1 <= Xmin1) Obj1OffsetX*= -1;         // multiply by -1.
0318      if (Now1X1 >= Xmax1) Obj1OffsetX*= -1;
0319      Now1Y1+= Obj1OffsetY;             // calculate new y coordinate.
0320      if (Now1Y1 <= Ymin1) Obj1OffsetY*= -1;
0321      if (Now1Y1 >= Ymax1) Obj1OffsetY*= -1;
0322      Item1->MoveImage(Obj1OffsetX, Obj1OffsetY);    // move the actor.
0323
0324                        // animate actor #2...
0325      Now2X1+= Obj2OffsetX;             // calculate new x coordinate.
0326      if (Now2X1 <= Xmin2) Obj2OffsetX*= -1;      // =ObjOffsetX*(-1).
0327      if (Now2X1 >= Xmax2) Obj2OffsetX*= -1;
0328      Now2Y1+= Obj2OffsetY;             // calculate new y coordinate.
0329      if (Now2Y1 <= Ymin2) Obj2OffsetY*= -1;
0330      if (Now2Y1 >= Ymax2) Obj2OffsetY*= -1;
0331      Item2->MoveImage(Obj2OffsetX, Obj2OffsetY);    // move the actor.
0332
0333                        // animate actor #3...
0334      Now3X1+= Obj3OffsetX;             // calculate new x coordinate.
0335      if (Now3X1 <= Xmin3) Obj3OffsetX*= -1;      // =ObjOffsetX*(-1).
0336      if (Now3X1 >= Xmax3) Obj3OffsetX*= -1;
0337      Now3Y1+= Obj3OffsetY;             // calculate new y coordinate.
0338      if (Now3Y1 <= Ymin3) Obj3OffsetY*= -1;
0339      if (Now3Y1 >= Ymax3) Obj3OffsetY*= -1;
0340      Item3->MoveImage(Obj3OffsetX, Obj3OffsetY);    // move the actor.
0341
0342    goto ANIMATION_LOOP;                              // loop back.
0343    }
0344    /*
0345
0346    ┌────────────────────────────────────────────────────────────┐
        │                  Terminate the program                       │
0347    └────────────────────────────────────────────────────────────┘
0348                                                                  */
0349    static void zQuit_Pgm(void)
0350    {
0351    Display.ShutDownGraphics();  // graceful shutdown of graphics mode.
0352    exit(0);                 // terminate the program and return OK code.
0353    }
0354    /*
0355
0356    ┌────────────────────────────────────────────────────────────┐
        │         Detect the graphics hardware and set the             │
0357    │   highest mode permitted by the graphics adapter and monitor.│
0358    │   The user can override the autodetect algorithm by providing│
0359    │   an argument on the command-line when the program is started.│
0360    └────────────────────────────────────────────────────────────┘
```

```
0361                                                                          */
0362   static void zStartup(void)
0363   {
0364      int DefaultMode;
0365   DefaultMode= Display.SetupMode();    // get results of autodetect...
0366   switch(DefaultMode)                  // ...and jump to appropriate code.
0367      {
0368      case zFAIL:        goto ABORT_PGM;
0369      case zVGA_12H:     goto VGA_mode;
0370      case zEGA_10H:     goto EGA_ECD_mode;
0371      case zEGA_EH:      goto EGA_SCD_mode;
0372      case zMCGA_11H:    goto MCGA_mode;
0373      case zCGA_6H:      goto CGA_mode;
0374      case zHERC:        goto Hercules_mode;
0375      default:           goto ABORT_PGM;
0376      }
0377   VGA_mode:            // VGA 640x480x16-color, 80x60 character mode.
0378   if(CommandLineArg==zYES)
0379      {                                 // if user has requested a mode.
0380      if((Mode>zVGA_12H)&&(Mode<zHERC)) goto FORCE_USER_MODE;
0381      }
0382   X_Res=640; Y_Res=480; Mode=zVGA_12H; CharWidth=8; CharHeight=8;
0383   return;
0384   EGA_ECD_mode:        // EGA 640x350x16-color, 80x43 character mode.
0385   if(CommandLineArg==zYES)
0386      {
0387      if((Mode==zEGA_EH)||(Mode==zCGA_6H))   // permit only EGA or CGA.
0388      goto FORCE_USER_MODE;
0389      }
0390   X_Res=640; Y_Res=350; Mode=zEGA_10H; CharWidth=8; CharHeight=8;
0391   return;
0392   EGA_SCD_mode:             // EGA 640x200x16-color, 80x25 char mode.
0393   if(CommandLineArg==zYES)
0394      {
0395      if(Mode==zCGA_6H) goto FORCE_USER_MODE;     // only CGA permitted.
0396      }
0397   X_Res=640; Y_Res=200; Mode=zEGA_EH; CharWidth=8; CharHeight=8;
0398   return;
0399   MCGA_mode:                // MCGA 640x480x2-color, 80x60 char mode.
0400   if(CommandLineArg==zYES)
0401      {
0402      if(Mode==zCGA_6H) goto FORCE_USER_MODE;     // only CGA permitted.
0403      }
0404   X_Res=640; Y_Res=480; Mode=zMCGA_11H;
0405   C0=0; C1=1; C2=1; C3=1; C4=0; C5=1; C6=1; C7=1;
0406   C8=1; C9=1; C10=1; C11=1; C12=1; C13=1; C14=0; C15=1;
0407   CharWidth=8; CharHeight=8;
0408   return;
0409   CGA_mode:                 // CGA 640x200x2-color, 80x25 char mode.
0410   X_Res=640; Y_Res=200; Mode=zCGA_6H;
0411   C0=0; C1=1; C2=1; C3=1; C4=0; C5=1; C6=1; C7=1;
0412   C8=1; C9=1; C10=1; C11=1; C12=1; C13=1; C14=0; C15=1;
0413   CharWidth=8; CharHeight=8;
0414   return;
0415   Hercules_mode:            // Hercules 720x348x2-color, 80x25 char mode.
0416   X_Res=720; Y_Res=348; Mode=zHERC;
0417   C0=0; C1=0; C2=1; C3=1; C4=1; C5=1; C6=1; C7=1;
0418   C8=1; C9=1; C10=1; C11=1; C12=1; C13=1; C14=1; C15=1;
0419   CharWidth=9; CharHeight=14;
0420   return;
0421
0422   FORCE_USER_MODE:    // jump to here if command-line argument legal.
0423   CommandLineArg= zNO; // first, reset token to avoid returning here.
```

2-3 Continued.

```
0424  Display.ForceMode(Mode);        // ...then reset the graphics mode.
0425  switch(Mode)                    // ...then jump back to appropriate code.
0426    {
0427    case zEGA_10H:     goto EGA_ECD_mode;
0428    case zEGA_EH:      goto EGA_SCD_mode;
0429    case zMCGA_11H:    goto MCGA_mode;
0430    case zCGA_6H:      goto CGA_mode;
0431    default:           goto ABORT_PGM;
0432    }
0433
0434  ABORT_PGM:        // jump to here if no graphics hardware detected.
0435  cout << "\n\n\rThis C++ graphics programming demo requires a";
0436  cout << "\n\rVGA, EGA, CGA, MCGA, or HGA graphics adapter.\n\r";
0437  exit(-1);                  // terminate, returning an error code.
0438  }
0439  /*
0440
0441 ┌─────────────────────────────────────────────────────────────┐
      │                      Stub routine                           │
0442  └─────────────────────────────────────────────────────────────┘
0443                                                                  */
0444  static void zStubRoutine(void)
0445  {       // this do-nothing routine is a placeholder for future code.
0446  Display.SetHue(C0);                         // set the drawing color.
0447  Display.SetLine(0xffff);                     // set the line style.
0448  Display.SetFill(SolidFill,C0);               // set the fill style.
0449  Viewport1.ClearTextLine();                // clear the dialog line.
0450  Viewport1.PutText(1,2,TextClr,StubMessage);// display text message.
0451  return;
0452  }
0453  /*
0454
0455 ┌─────────────────────────────────────────────────────────────┐
      │            Check the keyboard for a keystroke               │
0456  └─────────────────────────────────────────────────────────────┘
0457                                                                  */
0458  static void zKeyboard(void)
0459  {
0460    union AnyName{int RawCode;char Code[3];}Keystroke;
0461    char TempKey=0;
0462  #if defined (BORLAND)
0463    if (bioskey(1)==zEMPTY) { KeyCode=0; return; }
0464    Keystroke.RawCode= bioskey(0);
0465  #elif defined (ZORTECH)
0466    if (bioskey(1)==zEMPTY) { KeyCode=0; return; }
0467    Keystroke.RawCode= bioskey(0);
0468  #elif defined (MICROSOFT)
0469    if (_bios_keybrd(_KEYBRD_READY)==zEMPTY)
0470      { KeyCode=0; return; }
0471    Keystroke.RawCode= _bios_keybrd(_KEYBRD_READ);
0472  #endif
0473  TempKey= Keystroke.Code[0];
0474  if (TempKey!=0)
0475    {                                      // if a normal keystroke...
0476    KeyCode=1; KeyNum=TempKey; return;
0477    }
0478  if (TempKey==0)
0479    {                                      // if an extended keystroke...
0480    KeyCode=2; KeyNum=Keystroke.Code[1]; return;
0481    }
0482  }
0483  /*
0484 ┌─────────────────────────────────────────────────────────────┐
```

```
0485 |                        Empty the keystroke buffer                        |
0486 |                                                                           |
0487                                                                          */
0488 static void zPurge(void)
0489 {
0490 do zKeyboard();
0491    while (KeyCode!=0);
0492 return;
0493 }
0494 /*
0495
0496 |                             Make a sound                             |
0497
0498                                                                          */
0499 static void zMakeSound(int Hertz,double Duration)
0500 {
0501    static clock_t FormerTime=0;
0502    short Count=0;
0503    int HighByte=0, LowByte=0;
0504    unsigned char OldPort=0, NewPort=0;
0505 FormerTime= clock();
0506 if (Hertz < 40) return;
0507 if (Hertz > 4660) return;
0508 Count= 1193180L/Hertz;
0509 HighByte= Count / 256;
0510 LowByte= Count - (HighByte * 256);
0511 #if defined (BORLAND)
0512    outportb(0x43,0xB6); outportb(0x42,(unsigned char)LowByte);
0513    outportb(0x42,(unsigned char)HighByte); OldPort=inportb(0x61);
0514    NewPort=(OldPort | 0x03); outportb(0x61,NewPort);
0515    zDelay(FormerTime,Duration);
0516    outportb(0x61,OldPort);
0517 #elif defined (ZORTECH)
0518    outp(0x43,0xB6); outp(0x42,LowByte);
0519    outp(0x42,HighByte); OldPort=(unsigned char)inp(0x61);
0520    NewPort=(OldPort | 0x03); outp(0x61,(int)NewPort);
0521    zDelay(FormerTime,Duration);
0522    outp(0x61,(int)OldPort);
0523 #elif defined (MICROSOFT)
0524    outp(0x43,0xB6); outp(0x42,LowByte);
0525    outp(0x42,HighByte); OldPort=(unsigned char)inp(0x61);
0526    NewPort=(OldPort | 0x03); outp(0x61,(int)NewPort);
0527    zDelay(FormerTime,Duration);
0528    outp(0x61,(int)OldPort);
0529 #endif
0530 return;
0531 }
0532 /*
0533
0534 |                                Pause                                |
0535
0536                                                                          */
0537 static clock_t zDelay(clock_t StartTime, double Wait)
0538 {                              // pause for a specified length of time.
0539    clock_t StopTime;
0540    clock_t NewClockTime;
0541 #if defined (BORLAND)
0542    StopTime= StartTime + (Wait * CLK_TCK);
0543 #elif defined (ZORTECH)
0544    StopTime= StartTime + (Wait * CLOCKS_PER_SEC);
0545 #elif defined (MICROSOFT)
0546    StopTime= StartTime + (Wait * CLK_TCK);
0547 #endif
```

```
0548   while ( clock() < StopTime ) {;}
0549   NewClockTime= clock();
0550   return NewClockTime;
0551   }
0552   /*
0553
0554   ┌──────────────────────────────────────────────────────────────┐
       │           Retrieve the command-line arguments, if any          │
0555   └──────────────────────────────────────────────────────────────┘
0556                                                                  */
0557   static void zArguments(int NumArgs, char *Arg[])
0558   {
0559   if(NumArgs==1)
0560     {
0561     CommandLineArg= zNO; return;                      // if no arg.
0562     }
0563   CommandLineCompare= strncmp(StartUpArg[0],Arg[1],5);
0564   if(CommandLineCompare==0)
0565     {
0566     CommandLineArg=zYES; Mode=zVGA_12H; return;       // /M12.
0567     }
0568   CommandLineCompare= strncmp(StartUpArg[1],Arg[1],5);
0569   if(CommandLineCompare==0)
0570     {
0571     CommandLineArg=zYES; Mode=zEGA_10H; return;       // /M10.
0572     }
0573   CommandLineCompare= strncmp(StartUpArg[2],Arg[1],5);
0574   if(CommandLineCompare==0)
0575     {
0576     CommandLineArg=zYES; Mode=zEGA_EH; return;        // /M0E.
0577     }
0578   CommandLineCompare= strncmp(StartUpArg[3],Arg[1],5);
0579   if(CommandLineCompare==0)
0580     {
0581     CommandLineArg=zYES; Mode=zMCGA_11H; return;      // /M11.
0582     }
0583   CommandLineCompare= strncmp(StartUpArg[4],Arg[1],5);
0584   if(CommandLineCompare==0)
0585     {
0586     CommandLineArg=zYES; Mode=zCGA_6H; return;        // /M06.
0587     }
0588   CommandLineCompare= strncmp(StartUpArg[5],Arg[1],5);
0589   if(CommandLineCompare==0)
0590     {
0591     CommandLineArg=zYES; Mode=zHERC; return;          // /MHC.
0592     }
0593   CommandLineArg= zNO;              // if an unrecognized argument.
0594   return;
0595   }
0596   /*
0597
0598   ┌──────────────────────────────────────────────────────────────┐
       │   Supercharged C++ Graphics  --  end of source file BOUNCE.CPP │
0599   └──────────────────────────────────────────────────────────────┘
0600                                                                  */
```

3

Programming a pointing device

Graphics programs that produce graphics output must often also accept graphics input. It is a straightforward task to add a C++ class whose methods will enable your C++ graphics programs to utilize input from a mouse or a digitizing tablet.

Many different mouse products are available in the marketplace. In most cases the software driver provided with the mouse adheres to the Microsoft standard. The driver is the software interface that manages the mouse hardware after receiving instructions from your C++ program. If you limit your code to calling only fundamental functions of the mouse driver, your software will be compatible with almost every mouse and driver it might encounter.

Users also have many digitizing tablets from which to choose. The standard for tablet drivers is less explicit than the mouse standard. Some digitizing tablets offer advanced and specialized features not implemented—or not implemented using the same protocol—on competitors' products. This lack of a definitive software standard means you must often write routines that are dependent upon a particular manufacturer's product. C++ code that works correctly with one brand of tablet might not function at all on another brand.

This chapter provides a working introduction to fundamental mouse programming techniques. A sample program is used to demonstrate a class of methods providing control over a mouse or similar locator device.

Software drivers

Mouse packages are typically provided with bundled software called a *driver*. This software provides a mechanism for your C++ graphics program to communicate with the mouse.

Your program will usually assume that the necessary mouse driver has already been loaded into memory by the user. This resident software is usually accessed through interrupt 33h (33 hex). The driver must be loaded before Turbo C++, Borland C++, or Zortech C++ is started if you are using any of these editors to develop a graphics program that uses mouse input.

Figure 3-1 illustrates a typical memory map of RAM allocation when an .exe program is using a mouse driver. The user first loads the driver software at the operating system prompt and then launches your executable. Your code can easily check for the presence of a driver, allowing appropriate action to be taken if no driver is found.

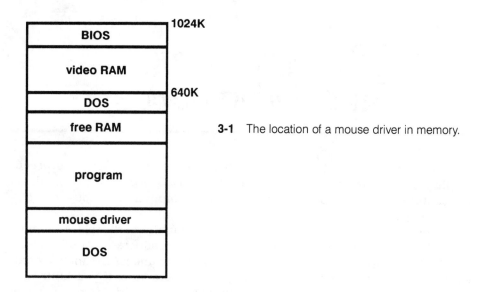

3-1 The location of a mouse driver in memory.

Mouse input devices normally display a cursor in the shape of an arrow icon. The driver software accepts responsibility for ensuring that the cursor is displayed correctly in all VGA, EGA, MCGA, CGA, and Hercules graphics modes.

Mouse compatibility. To correctly display a mouse cursor on a Hercules graphics adapter, you must write a value of 6H to address 40:49H before initializing the driver. This ensures the cursor is displayed on page 0 of the adapter. To display the mouse cursor on page 1, write a value of 5H to address 40:49H.

Programming fundamentals

Creating a C++ class to control a mouse is not difficult, especially if the manufacturer's driver is Microsoft compatible.

Calling the driver involves two or three steps. Whether the driver is a mouse driver or a tablet driver masquerading as a mouse makes no difference to your program's calling protocol.

First, your C++ program primes the CPU registers with appropriate values. Second, your code executes an INT 33H. Third, your routine reads the values returned by the mouse driver in the CPU registers. These return values usually contain the current screen coordinates of the mouse cursor.

Fact *Programming guides.* For a complete listing of mouse functions, see the Microsoft Mouse Programmer's Reference Guide. The user's manuals of many mouse manufacturers contain a brief discussion of fundamental mouse function calls.

Here's How... If you wanted to display the mouse cursor on the screen, you would load a value of 1 into the ax register and execute an INT 33H. To remove the cursor from the screen, you would load a value of 2 into the ax register and execute an INT 33H. In both cases the values of the bx, cx, and dx registers are ignored by the driver. When other mouse functions are called, however, these registers might be needed to pass arguments to the driver.

Typical code to turn on the cursor might look something like this if you are using Turbo C++ or Borland C++.

```
regs.x.ax = 1;
int86(0x33, &regs, &regs);
```

If you are using Zortech C++ or a Microsoft-compatible C++ compiler, the following code will turn on the mouse cursor.

```
inregs.x.ax = 1;
int86(0x33, &inregs, &outregs);
```

In these two examples, the first line of code loads the value 1 into the ax register. The variable named regs (Turbo C++ and Borland C++) or inregs (Zortech C++) is a data structure that stores values the compiler will load into the registers when an interrupt is executed.

The second line of code executes an INT 33H. 0x33 is how C and C++ represent 33 hex. The address of a data structure is also included in the calling arguments, prefaced by the address-of (&) token.

If you are using Turbo C++ or Borland C++ use the regs.x.ax syntax to access the ax register. Use regs.x.bx for the bx register, regs.x.cx for the cx register, and regs.x.dx for the dx register.

If you are using Zortech C++, you access the contents of the ax register by using syntax inregs.x.ax. Use inregs.x.bx to handle the bx register, inregs .x.cx for the cx register, and inregs.x.dx for the dx register.

How to determine mouse coordinates

Here's How... To read the current screen coordinates of the mouse cursor, you must check the CPU registers to find out which values have been returned by call to the driver. The following code fragment shows how to do this with either Turbo C++, Borland C++, or Zortech C++.

```
#if defined (BORLAND)
    regs.x.ax = 3;
    int86(0x33, &regs, &regs);
    MouseButton = regs.x.bx;
```

```
        MouseX = regs.x.cx;
        MouseY = regs.x.dx;
  #elif defined (ZORTECH)
        inregs.x.ax = 3;
        int86(0x33, &inregs, &outregs);
        MouseButton = outregs.x.bx;
        MouseX = outregs.x.cx;
        MouseY = outregs.x.dx;
  #endif
```

The #if defined and #elif defined preprocessor directives are used to advise the compiler which block of source code to compile and which block to ignore. The first executable line in the example loads the ax register with a value of 3. Mouse function 3 tests to see if a mouse button has been pressed and to determine the current position of the mouse cursor.

The second line of source code executes an INT 33H to call the mouse driver.

The third line of code reads the value returned in the cx register. It assigns the value to a variable named MouseButton. The fourth line fetches the cursor's x coordinate from the cx register. The fifth line reads the y coordinate from the dx register.

Your C++ graphics program is now free to use these coordinates for any drawing functions.

Other useful mouse functions

Specialized services are also available. Mouse function 4 resets the position of the cursor. This function works with only a mouse, however. It will not operate correctly with a Microsoft-compatible tablet driver that is posing as a mouse. Because the tablet cursor is logically linked to an explicit location on the physical surface of a tablet, the displayed cursor will immediately jump to a location that represents the actual position of the crosshair on the tablet surface.

Other advanced functions include the ability to fine tune the movement ratio between the on-screen cursor and the pointing device, the ability to increase the speed of movement of the cursor, the ability to set up viewports on the display screen, and the capability to change the shape of the cursor. You can also alter the hot spot token. The *hot spot* is a pixel on the displayed cursor that determines the particular xy coordinates being returned to your program by the mouse hardware.

A sample program: CLICK.CPP

Demo Figure 3-2 depicts typical displays produced by the sample program CLICK.CPP, whose complete source code is provided in FIG. 3-3 at the end of the chapter. The program draws a line to the current mouse position each time you click the left mouse button.

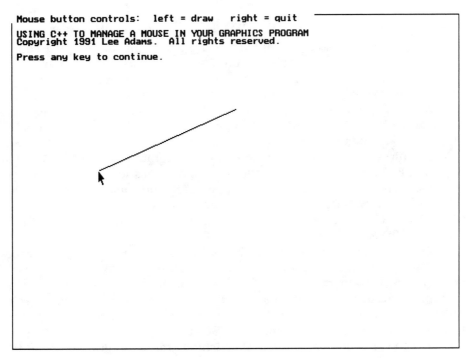

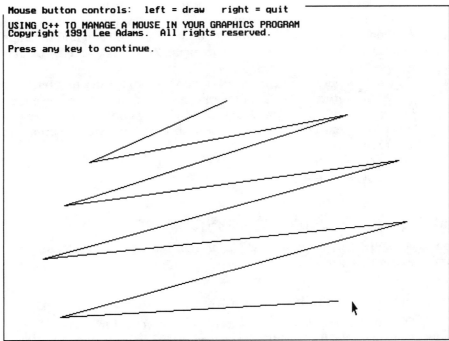

3-2 Graphics output from the sample program CLICK.CPP. Top: pressing the left mouse button causes a line to be drawn from the previous position to the current position. Bottom: the input loop makes it possible to draw polylines and other continuing shapes.

How to compile and link the sample program

The program listing presented in FIG. 3-3 contains the complete source code for the main module of the C++ demonstration program called "Using C++ to Manage a Mouse in Your Graphics Program." If you are using the companion disks to the book, the source code is in the file named CLICK.CPP. Three C++ source files are needed to build the finished .exe file. These are CLICK.CPP from FIG. 3-3 and two of the class libraries in appendix E.

The class library that provides the language bindings and low-level graphics routines for this demonstration program is found in FIG. E-2 in appendix E. This listing contains the implementations for class PhysicalDisplay and class Viewport. If you are using the companion disks to the book, this file is named LIB2D.CPP. The class declarations are presented in FIG. E-1 in appendix E. If you are using the companion disks to the book, this file is named LIB2D.HPP.

The class library that provides the mouse management methods for this demonstration program is found in FIG. E-6 in appendix E. This listing contains the implementations for class PointingDevice. If you are using the companion disks to the book, this file is named MOUSE.CPP. The class declarations are presented in FIG. E-5 in appendix E. If you are using the companion disks to the book, this file is named MOUSE.HPP.

You can compile, link, and run this demonstration program using Turbo C++, Borland C++, or Zortech C++. If you are using Turbo C++, you might wish to read appendix A for guidance in compiling, linking, and running the demonstration program. If you are using Borland C++, you can find the appropriate information in appendix B. If you are using Zortech C++, refer to appendix C.

You must create a Turbo C++ or Borland C++ project list to advise your compiler which source files to bind together to build the finished .exe file. If you are using Zortech C++, you must name the files on the compiler command line field. Refer to the appendices described earlier if you are unfamiliar with this technique.

After a successful compile and link the animated screen should resemble the screen prints shown in FIG. 3-2.

How to run the demonstration program

You need a VGA, EGA, MCGA, CGA, or Hercules graphics adapter and a mouse to run this demo.

Using the editor to run the program

To run the program under the control of your Turbo C++, Borland C++, or Zortech C++ editor, make sure that the finished .exe file is in the default directory. If you used Turbo C++ or Borland C++ to compile the program, the appropriate graphics driver must be in the default directory. If you are using a VGA or EGA, the EGAVGA.BGI file must be present. If you are using an MCGA or CGA, the CGA.BGI file must be located in the default directory. If you are using a Hercules graphics adapter, the HERC.BGI file must be available. If you used Zortech C++ to compile the demonstration program, the appropriate graphics drivers have already been linked into the .exe code.

The built-in autodetect routine will detect the graphics hardware in your computer system and will set up the best graphics mode supported by your computer hardware. To override the autodetect routine use the Turbo C++, Borland C++, or Zortech C++ editor to simulate a command-line argument. The header in FIG. 3-3 provides a set of arguments you can use. See the appendices for guidance applicable to your particular compiler. If you are using a VGA, you can override the autodetect routine and force the demonstration program to run in an EGA, MCGA, or CGA mode. If you are using an EGA, you can force the program to run in a lower-resolution EGA mode or a CGA mode.

Running the program from the operating system prompt

Here's How... To start the program from the operating system prompt, simply enter CLICK. The .exe file and any required graphics drivers must be present in the default directory. If the software finds a VGA present in your system, the program will animate using the 640×480×16-color mode. If an EGA and enhanced monitor are found, the 640×350×16-color mode is used. If an EGA and standard display are present, the program sets up the 640×200×16-color mode. If an MCGA is detected, the 640×480×2-color mode is employed. If a CGA is found, the 640×200×2-color mode is used. If the program detects a Hercules graphics adapter, it starts up in the 720×348×2-color mode.

You can force the program to start up in a different mode by adding a command-line argument when you start the program from the operating system prompt. Enter CLICK /M11 to force the 640×480×2-color mode. Enter CLICK /M10 to force the 640×350×16-color mode. Entering CLICK /M0E forces the program to run in the 640×200×16-color mode. Enter CLICK /M06 to test the demonstration program in the 640×200×2-color mode.

Using the demonstration program

The program uses a mouse polling loop to allow you to draw a polyline. Each time you press the left mouse button (called *clicking* the button), a line will be drawn from the previous position to the current position of the mouse. To exit the program, simply press the right mouse button.

Programmer's Guide to CLICK.CPP

Code The complete listing for the demonstration program CLICK.CPP is presented in FIG. 3-3. The source code consists of an informative header, conditional compilation directives, declaration of constants and macros, file include directives, function prototypes, variable declarations, and the executable functions.

Conditional compilation

Information and source code for conditional compilation is located at lines 0046 through 0063. If you are using Turbo C++ or Borland C++, the program is ready to compile, subject to the instructions in appendix B. If you are using Zortech C++, change line 0062 to #define FG and change line 0063 to #define ZORTECH.

Constants

The C++ const keyword is used to declare and assign values to constant variables at lines 0065 through 0072.

Macros

A macro defined at line 0078 will be expanded by the C++ compiler at line 0182.

Include files

The code at lines 0080 through 0108 loads the appropriate header files and C++ class declaration files. Line 0107 loads LIB2D.HPP, which declares the data members and methods of class PhysicalDisplay and class Viewport. Line 0108 loads MOUSE.HPP, which declares the data members and methods of class PointingDevice.

Function prototypes

Function declarations are provided in lines 0110 through 0121. Functions declared here are visible throughout this source file. They can be called by any other function in the source file. Because each function is declared with the static qualifier, it is not available to functions located in other source files.

Variable declarations

Lines 0123 through 0153 declare global variables visible throughout this source file. These variables have file scope and can be modified by any function in the file.

Object declarations

Note line 0150, which creates an object from class PhysicalDisplay. The object is named Display. The program will later call the methods of this object to help it manage the display. The methods are declared in the class declaration listing LIB2D.HPP and are defined in the class implementation listing LIB2D.CPP in appendix E. The object created at line 0150 is a static object. It has file scope and will remain available until the program terminates.

Line 0151 creates an object from the Viewport class. The object is named Viewport1. The address of Display is passed to this new object. Viewport1 will need to use the methods of Display to generate graphics output. The object created at line 0155 is a static object with file scope. It will remain active until program termination.

Line 0152 creates an object from the PointingDevice class. The object is named "Mouse." The methods of this object provide access to the functions of the memory-resident mouse driver. The pointer that is declared at line 0153 will be used to access a table of data about the mouse state.

main( )

The main( ) function is located at lines 0158 through 0210. After first checking to see if any command line arguments were used to start the program, an appropriate graphics mode is set.

The code at lines 0184 through 0207 manages the mouse. The Detect( ) method of class PointingDevice is used to check if a mouse is present and ready to be used. The code at line 0185 aborts the program if no mouse is found.

The Show( ) method is called at line 0187 to display the mouse cursor.

The mouse polling loop is located at lines 0195 through 0204. The Info( ) method of class PointingDevice is called in order to grab the address of a structure that contains data about the current state of the mouse, including the cursor position and status of the buttons. The MPtr pointer was declared earlier at line 0153.

Line 0197 checks to see if the left mouse button has been pressed. If so, the Hide( ) method is called to remove the mouse cursor before the DrawLine( ) method of class Viewport is called to draw a line. Note how the -> addressing notation is used to fetch the x and y coordinates from the data structure mentioned earlier.

Line 0203 tests to determine if the right button has been pressed. The logic jumps to line 0206 if the user wants to quit the mouse loop. Note how line 0207 calls method Hide( ) of class PointingDevice to erase the mouse cursor before terminating the program.

Terminating the program

The function at lines 0212 through 0220 calls method ShutDownGraphics( ) of class PhysicalDisplay to terminate the graphics state. Line 0219 returns an OK value to the operating system.

The Startup( ) function

The function at lines 0222 through 0305 calls the SetupMode( ) method of class PhysicalDisplay to detect the graphics hardware.

The StubRoutine( ) function

The stub routine at lines 0307 through 0319 is a do-nothing routine. It dis plays a simple message on the dialog line at the top of the display.

The Keyboard( ) function

The function at lines 0321 through 0349 detects and retrieves keystrokes from the keyboard buffer. The function at lines 0351 through 0360 keeps calling the zKeyboard( ) function until the keyboard buffer is empty. This routine purges unwanted keystrokes from the keyboard buffer after a lengthy graphics operation.

The MakeSound( ) function

The function at lines 0362 through 0398 generates a sound from the system speaker.

The Pause( ) function

The function at lines 0400 through 0418 causes the program to pause for a specified period of time. The code uses the value returned by the system clock and multiplies it by the number of CPU cycles per second. If you are using Turbo C++ or Borland C++, this value is the CLK_TCK global variable. If you are using Zortech C++ it is CLOCKS_PER_SEC. The pause function is unused in this demonstration program, but is used in the mouse-driven paint/draw demo in chapter 6, where it is necessary to avoid inadvertent double-clicks.

The Arguments( ) function

The function at lines 0420 through 0462 compares the command line argument with a set of permitted strings. The function assigns an appropriate value to the global variable named "Mode." Mode is used by other functions that generate graphics output.

Programmer's Guide to LIB2D.HPP

Code The complete source code for the declarations for class PhysicalDisplay and class Viewport is found in LIB2D.HPP in appendix E. The source from LIB2D.HPP must be #included at the beginning of any program that wishes to use the methods of class PhysicalDisplay or class Viewport. See the discussion in chapter 1 for further information about LIB2D.HPP.

Programmer's Guide to LIB2D.CPP

Code The source code in LIB2D.CPP, presented in appendix E, provides language bindings that produce low-level graphics. The routines in

LIB2D.CPP call the appropriate runtime library functions in Turbo C++'s graphics.lib, Borland C++'s graphics.lib, Zortech C++'s fg.lib, or Microsoft's graph.lib.

LIB2D.CPP is the class implementation listing for class PhysicalDisplay and class Viewport. Class PhysicalDisplay manages the state of the display. Class Viewport is responsible for maintaining a viewport and producing low-level graphics. These two classes generate nearly all the low-level graphics required by the demonstration programs in the book. See the discussion in chapter 1 for further information about class PhysicalDisplay and class Viewport.

Programmer's Guide to MOUSE.HPP

The complete source code for the declarations for class PointingDevice is found in MOUSE.HPP in appendix E. MOUSE.HPP must be #included at the beginning of any program using the methods of class PointingDevice.

The two preprocessor directives at lines 0049 and 0050 ensure that MOUSE.HPP will not be #included twice. A previous inclusion will define the variable MOUSE_HPP, causing the test at line 0049 to fail, making the C++ compiler jump directly to 0090.

The code at lines 0054 through 0067 declares data members and a method that are not visible to functions or methods outside class PointingDevice.

The code at lines 0069 through 0079 declares methods of class PointingDevice that can be called by any in-scope function or method.

Programmer's Guide to MOUSE.CPP

The complete source code for the implementation for class PointingDevice is found in MOUSE.CPP in appendix E. The methods of class PointingDevice provide interactive control over a mouse (or any locator masquerading as a mouse) at runtime.

Constructor

The constructor for class PointingDevice is located at lines 0070 through 0085. This routine is mainly used to initialize the contents of the data structure that will hold values indicating the runtime status of the mouse. The calling module will use a pointer to access these values.

Method Detect( )

The Detect( ) method at line 0100 and the Init( ) method at line 0148 use mouse function 0 and INT 33H to initialize the mouse driver. The returned value in the ax register is placed into the MouseParams structure field named MouseFlag. Note how MouseFlag is addressed using dot notation.

The caller, method Detect( ), uses MouseFlag to determine if a driver is loaded and ready to be used. If MouseFlag is 0, then no driver is present. If MouseFlag is any value other than 0, then a driver is present. The mouse driver (or tablet driver posing as a mouse driver) must be initialized before any calls are made, otherwise unpredictable and erratic results can occur. Note how the switch( ) statement at line 0104 enables the proper minimum and maximum screen locations to be set, depending upon which graphics mode is in effect.

Method Data( )

The Data( ) method of class PointingDevice at lines 0166 through 0173 simply returns the address of the MouseParams structure. This allows the calling module to directly read the contents of the structure, which contains the current location of the mouse cursor, and so on.

Method Show( )

The Show( ) method of class PointingDevice at lines 0175 through 0192 uses mouse function 1 and INT 33H to display the screen cursor. For most mouse and tablet products, this cursor is usually an arrowhead that points up and to the left.

Method Hide( )

The Hide( ) method of class PointingDevice at lines 0194 through 0211 uses mouse function 2 and INT 33H to remove the cursor from the screen. This method should always be called before any graphics are drawn. If you inadvertently draw over the cursor, it will leave residue on the screen when the driver uses the XOR logical operator to move the cursor to its next location.

Method Info( )

The Info( ) method of class PointingDevice at lines 0213 through 0239 carries out two tasks. It first reports whether or not a mouse button has been pressed. This information is returned in the bx register and is stored in the MouseButton field of the MouseParams structure. Second, method Info( ) fetches the current coordinates of the mouse cursor. These coordinates are called the hot spot, and are located at the tip of the default arrowhead cursor.

Method Pos( )

The Pos( ) method at lines 0245 through 0266 resets the location of the cursor on the screen. The code uses mouse function 4 and passes the xy coordinates in the cx and dx registers.

Trap Setting the position. Mouse hardware uses relative offsets to measure the current position. If you lift the mouse from the desktop and set it down elsewhere, the screen cursor will not move significantly. Conversely, if you lift a crosshair cursor from the surface of a tablet and set it down elsewhere on the tablet, the screen cursor will most definitely move. A tablet uses absolute coordinates. A mouse uses relative coordinates. Your C++ graphics program might be inviting erratic behavior if it resets the position of the cursor without considering that the software user might be using a tablet, not a mouse.

Method HLimit( )

The HLimit( ) method of class PointingDevice at lines 0268 through 0293 uses mouse function 7 and INT 33H to define the maximum and minimum x coordinates permitted for the on-screen cursor. If the user moves the pointing device outside this range, the screen cursor will act as if it has hit a hidden barrier. The minimum x coordinate is passed in the cx register, the maximum x coordinate in the cx register.

Method VLimit( )

The VLimit( ) method at lines 0295 through 0320 sets the minimum and maximum y coordinates allowed for the mouse cursor at runtime. The minimum y coordinate is passed in the cx register. The maximum y coordinate is passed to the driver in the dx register.

Using const for readable code

Note the definition for the constant variable zMOUSE at line 0068. This is defined as 0x33, the number of the interrupt service to be called. Using this convention makes the code easier to understand.

Tips for trouble-free mouse programming

The most important guideline for writing programs that use mouse and tablet input is to keep it simple. Most of the C++ graphics programs you write will need only four functions. Mouse function 0 initializes the driver. Mouse function 1 displays the screen cursor. Mouse function 2 erases the screen cursor. Mouse function 3 reads the current screen coordinates and tests if a button has been pressed.

Other mouse functions can enhance the visual impression your program makes, but they will also increase the possibility of incompatibility with mouse devices that stray from the Microsoft standard.

Mouse programming tips. Your C++ graphics applications will be free of mouse bugs if you follow these two rules:

1. Keep it simple. Use only mouse functions 0, 1, 2, and 3. Use only the left mouse button.
2. Route all mouse and tablet calls through one class object. Use class PointingDevice as a good starting point, and add more methods if you need them.

Modularity is an important principle to keep in mind when writing programs that use mouse input. Use just one class object, or just one method, or just one function as the entry point to the driver. This makes it easier to correct erratic behavior during development and testing.

3-3 Sample program CLICK.CPP. Supports VGA, EGA, MCGA, CGA, and Hercules adapters. This application demonstrates how to use a class of pointing device routines for interactive mouse control.

```
0001   /*
0002
0003            Lee Adams' SUPERCHARGED C++ GRAPHICS
0004       Interactive demo:  using a mouse with your C++ application
0005
0006    SOURCE FILE:   CLICK.CPP
0007           TYPE:   C++ source file for a multimodule application.
0008        PURPOSE:   Demonstrates how to manage a mouse from your
0009                   C++ graphics program.
0010    PROGRAM LIST:  CLICK.CPP, LIB2D.CPP and MOUSE.CPP.
0011       LANGUAGES:  Turbo C++, Borland C++, Zortech C++ and
0012                   all C++ compilers compatible with AT&T C++ 2.0
0013                   specification; and nominal compatibility with
0014                   Microsoft C++ (see the discussion in the book).
0015    MEMORY MODEL:  large.
0016    COMMAND-LINE:  you can specify a graphics mode by using the
0017                   command-line argument /Mnn as shown below:
0018                       /M12  640x480x16-color VGA
0019                       /M11  640x480x2-color VGA, MCGA
0020                       /M10  640x350x16-color VGA, EGA
0021                       /MOE  640x200x16-color VGA, EGA
0022                       /M06  640x200x2-color VGA, MCGA, EGA, CGA
0023                       /MHC  720x348x2-color Hercules
0024                   If no command-line argument is used, hardware
0025                   autodetect is used to select the best mode.
0026    OUTPUT:  Click the left mouse button to draw a polyline.
0027             Click the right button to terminate the demo.
0028    LICENSE:  As purchaser of the book in which this source code
0029       appears you are granted a royalty-free license to reproduce
0030       and distribute executable files generated using this code
0031       provided that you accept the conditions of the License
0032       Agreement and Limited Warranty described in the book.
0033    PUBLICATION: Contains material from Windcrest/McGraw-Hill
0034       book 3489, published by TAB BOOKS.
0035    U.S. GOVERNMENT RESTRICTED RIGHTS:  This software and its
0036       documentation is provided with restricted rights.  The use,
0037       duplication, or disclosure by the Government is subject to
0038       restrictions set forth in subdivision (b)(3)(ii) of The
0039       Rights in Technical Data and Computer Software clause at
0040       252.227-7013.  Contractor/manufacturer is Lee Adams, c/o
0041       TAB BOOKS, 13311 Monterey Ave., Blue Ridge Summit PA 17294.
0042    TRADEMARK:  Lee Adams is a trademark of Lee Adams.
0043
0044       Copyright 1991 Lee Adams.  All rights reserved worldwide.
0045
0046
0047                      CONDITIONAL COMPILATION
0048    To compile only those blocks of code that support the C++
0049    compiler and graphics library that you are using, you should
0050    #define the appropriate tokens on lines 0062 and 0063.
0051            GRAPHICS LIBRARY
```

```
0052        Borland's graphics.lib           #define BGI
0053        Zortech's fg.lib or fgdebug.lib  #define FG
0054        Microsoft's graph.lib            #define MS
0055               COMPILER
0056        Borland Turbo C++ compiler       #define BORLAND
0057        Zortech C++ compiler             #define ZORTECH
0058        AT&T-compatible C++ compilers    #define MICROSOFT
0059     Be sure you define only one compiler and one graphics library.
0060
0061                                                                    */
0062     #define BGI     1 // indicates the graphics library you are using.
0063     #define BORLAND 1 // indicates the C++ compiler you are using.
0064     /*
0065
0066    ┌────────────────────────────────────────────────────────────┐
        │                         Constants                            │
0067    └────────────────────────────────────────────────────────────┘
0068                                                                    */
0069     const int zFAIL=0; const int zEMPTY=0;
0070     const int zYES=1; const int zNO=0;
0071     const int zVGA_12H=1; const int zEGA_10H=2; const int zEGA_EH=3;
0072     const int zMCGA_11H=4; const int zCGA_6H=5; const int zHERC=6;
0073     /*
0074
0075    ┌────────────────────────────────────────────────────────────┐
        │                          Macros                              │
0076    └────────────────────────────────────────────────────────────┘
0077                                                                    */
0078     #define Wait_for_any_key  while(KeyCode==0) zKeyboard(); KeyCode=0;
0079     /*
0080
0081    ┌────────────────────────────────────────────────────────────┐
        │                       Include files                          │
0082    └────────────────────────────────────────────────────────────┘
0083                                                                    */
0084     #if defined (BORLAND)
0085     #include <time.h>        // supports clock().
0086     #include <string.h>      // supports strncmp().
0087     #include <bios.h>        // supports bioskey().
0088     #include <process.h>     // supports exit().
0089     #include <iostream.h>    // supports cout.
0090     #include <dos.h>         // supports outportb(), inportb().
0091     #elif defined (ZORTECH)
0092     #include <time.h>        // supports clock().
0093     #include <string.h>      // supports strncmp().
0094     #include <bios.h>        // supports bioskey().
0095     #include <stdlib.h>      // supports exit().
0096     #include <stream.hpp>    // supports cout.
0097     #include <dos.h>         // supports outp(), inp().
0098     #elif defined (MICROSOFT)
0099     #include <time.h>        // supports clock().
0100     #include <string.h>      // supports strncmp().
0101     #include <bios.h>        // supports _bios_keybrd().
0102     #include <process.h>     // supports exit().
0103     #include <iostream.h>    // supports cout.
0104     #include <conio.h>       // supports outp(), inp().
0105     #endif
0106
0107     #include "LIB2D.HPP"     // declarations for PhysicalDisplay class.
0108     #include "MOUSE.HPP"     // declarations for PointingDevice class.
0109     /*
0110
0111    ┌────────────────────────────────────────────────────────────┐
        │      Prototypes for functions visible throughout this file   │
0112    └────────────────────────────────────────────────────────────┘
0113                                                                    */
0114     static void zStartup(void);          // initializes a graphics mode.
```

```
0115   static void zArguments(int, char far* far*);    // checks arguments.
0116   static void zKeyboard(void);              // checks for a keystroke.
0117   static void zQuit_Pgm(void);         // ends the program gracefully.
0118   static void zPurge(void);          // empties the keyboard buffer.
0119   static void zStubRoutine(void);              // do-nothing stub.
0120   static void zMakeSound(int,double);      // makes a specific sound.
0121   static clock_t zDelay(clock_t,double);   // CPU-independent pause.
0122   /*
0123
0124        ┌──────────────────────────────────────────────────────┐
       │    Declaration of variables visible throughout this file │
0125        └──────────────────────────────────────────────────────┘
0126                                                                  */
0127   static char *StartUpArg[6]={         // legal command-line arguments.
0128          "/M12", "/M10", "/MOE", "/M11", "/M06", "/MHC" };
0129   static int CommandLineArg=zNO;       // indicates if argument exists.
0130   static int CommandLineCompare=0;     // indicates if argument legal.
0131   static int C0=0,C1=1,C2=2,C3=3,C4=4,C5=5,C6=6,
0132    C7=7,C8=8,C9=9,C10=10,C11=11,C12=12,C13=13,
0133    C14=14,C15=15;                            // palette index codes.
0134   static int Mode=0;              // which graphics mode is being used.
0135   static int Result=0;       // captures result of graphics routines.
0136   static int CharWidth=0,CharHeight=0;   // dimensions of character.
0137   static char KeyCode=0;   // token for normal or extended keystroke.
0138   static char KeyNum=0;                 // ASCII number of keystroke.
0139   static char SolidFill[]=
0140                {255,255,255,255,255,255,255,255};   // 100% fill.
0141   static int TextClr=7;              // font color for regular text.
0142   static int PromptClr=7;             // font color for prompt text.
0143   static char Copyright[]=
0144          "Copyright 1991 Lee Adams.  All rights reserved.";
0145   static char Title[]=
0146   "USING C++ TO MANAGE A MOUSE IN YOUR GRAPHICS PROGRAM";
0147   static char PressAnyKey[]= "Press any key to continue.";
0148   static char StubMessage[]= "The generic stub routine was called.";
0149   static int X_Res=0, Y_Res=0;                  // screen resolution.
0150   PhysicalDisplay Display;       // create the physical display object.
0151   Viewport Viewport1(&Display);         // create a viewport object.
0152   PointingDevice Mouse;         // create a pointing-device object.
0153   static mdata *MPtr;     // uninitialized ptr to mouse runtime data.
0154   /*
0155
0156        ┌──────────────────────────────────────────────────────┐
       │                   Function definitions                   │
0157        └──────────────────────────────────────────────────────┘
0158
0159        ┌──────────────────────────────────────────────────────┐
       │    The executive routine:  program execution begins here │
0160        └──────────────────────────────────────────────────────┘
0161                                                                  */
0162   main(int argc, char *argv[])
0163   {
0164      int NumArgs; char far* far* Arg;
0165
0166   NumArgs= argc;                           // grab number of arguments.
0167   Arg= &argv[0];            // grab address of array of arguments.
0168   zArguments(NumArgs, Arg);     // check the command-line arguments.
0169
0170   zStartup();                        // establish the graphics mode.
0171   Display.Init2D(Mode,0,0,X_Res-1,Y_Res-1);   // set graphics state.
0172   Result= Display.InitUndo();   // create hidden page (unused here).
0173   if (Result==zFAIL) zQuit_Pgm();          // if hidden page failed.
0174
0175   Display.BlankPage();                         // clear the display.
```

```
0176  Display.SetHue(C7);                          // set the drawing color.
0177  Display.SetFill(SolidFill,C7);                // set the fill style.
0178  Viewport1.PutText(3,2,TextClr,Title);         // sign-on notice.
0179  Viewport1.PutText(4,2,TextClr,Copyright);     // copyright notice.
0180  Viewport1.DrawBorder(0,0,X_Res-1,Y_Res-1);    // draw a border.
0181  Viewport1.PutText(6,2,PromptClr,PressAnyKey); // display a prompt.
0182  Wait_for_any_key     // this macro was defined earlier in line 0078.
0183
0184  Result= Mouse.Detect(Mode);                   // initialize the mouse.
0185  if (Result== zFAIL) zQuit_Pgm();
0186  MPtr= Mouse.Data();          // grab a pointer to the mouse data.
0187  Mouse.Show();                // display the mouse cursor.
0188  Display.SetHue(C0); Display.SetLine(0xffff);
0189  Display.SetFill(SolidFill,C0); Viewport1.ClearTextLine();
0190  Viewport1.PutText(1,2,C15,
0191    "Mouse button controls:  left = draw   right = quit");
0192  Display.SetHue(C12);                          // set the drawing color.
0193  Viewport1.SetPosition(319,99);
0194
0195  MOUSELOOP:                        // mouse-control loop begins here.
0196    Mouse.Info();                   // fetch mouse status information.
0197    if (MPtr->MouseButton==1)
0198      {                   // if left button pressed, draw a line...
0199      Mouse.Hide();
0200      Viewport1.DrawLine( MPtr->MouseX, MPtr->MouseY );
0201      Mouse.Show();
0202      }
0203    if (MPtr->MouseButton==2) goto MOUSE_DONE;   // if right button.
0204  goto MOUSELOOP;     // otherwise, jump back to start of mouse loop.
0205
0206  MOUSE_DONE:             // jump to here if right mouse button pressed.
0207  Mouse.Hide();                         // remove the mouse cursor.
0208
0209  zQuit_Pgm();               // tidy up and terminate the application.
0210  }
0211  /*
0212
0213  ┌──────────────────────────────────────────────────────────┐
      │                  Terminate the program                     │
0214  └──────────────────────────────────────────────────────────┘
0215                                                            */
0216  static void zQuit_Pgm(void)
0217  {
0218  Display.ShutDownGraphics();  // graceful shutdown of graphics mode.
0219  exit(0);                  // terminate the program and return OK code.
0220  }
0221  /*
0222
0223  ┌──────────────────────────────────────────────────────────┐
      │          Detect the graphics hardware and set the          │
0224  │  highest mode permitted by the graphics adapter and monitor.│
0225  │  The user can override the autodetect algorithm by providing│
0226  │  an argument on the command-line when the program is started.│
0227  └──────────────────────────────────────────────────────────┘
0228                                                            */
0229  static void zStartup(void)
0230  {
0231    int DefaultMode;
0232  DefaultMode= Display.SetupMode();    // get results of autodetect...
0233  switch(DefaultMode)                  // ...and jump to appropriate code.
0234    {
0235    case zFAIL:        goto ABORT_PGM;
0236    case zVGA_12H:     goto VGA_mode;
0237    case zEGA_10H:     goto EGA_ECD_mode;
0238    case zEGA_EH:      goto EGA_SCD_mode;
```

```
0239    case zMCGA_11H:    goto MCGA_mode;
0240    case zCGA_6H:      goto CGA_mode;
0241    case zHERC:        goto Hercules_mode;
0242    default:           goto ABORT_PGM;
0243    }
0244 VGA_mode:             // VGA 640x480x16-color, 80x60 character mode.
0245 if(CommandLineArg==zYES)
0246    {                              // if user has requested a mode.
0247    if((Mode>zVGA_12H)&&(Mode<zHERC)) goto FORCE_USER_MODE;
0248    }
0249 X_Res=640; Y_Res=480; Mode=zVGA_12H; CharWidth=8; CharHeight=8;
0250 return;
0251 EGA_ECD_mode:         // EGA 640x350x16-color, 80x43 character mode.
0252 if(CommandLineArg==zYES)
0253    {
0254    if((Mode==zEGA_EH)||(Mode==zCGA_6H))   // permit only EGA or CGA.
0255    goto FORCE_USER_MODE;
0256    }
0257 X_Res=640; Y_Res=350; Mode=zEGA_10H; CharWidth=8; CharHeight=8;
0258 return;
0259 EGA_SCD_mode:               // EGA 640x200x16-color, 80x25 char mode.
0260 if(CommandLineArg==zYES)
0261    {
0262    if(Mode==zCGA_6H) goto FORCE_USER_MODE;    // only CGA permitted.
0263    }
0264 X_Res=640; Y_Res=200; Mode=zEGA_EH; CharWidth=8; CharHeight=8;
0265 return;
0266 MCGA_mode:                  // MCGA 640x480x2-color, 80x60 char mode.
0267 if(CommandLineArg==zYES)
0268    {
0269    if(Mode==zCGA_6H) goto FORCE_USER_MODE;    // only CGA permitted.
0270    }
0271 X_Res=640; Y_Res=480; Mode=zMCGA_11H;
0272 C0=0; C1=1; C2=1; C3=1; C4=1; C5=1; C6=1; C7=1;
0273 C8=1; C9=1; C10=1; C11=1; C12=1; C13=1; C14=1; C15=1;
0274 CharWidth=8; CharHeight=8;
0275 return;
0276 CGA_mode:                   // CGA 640x200x2-color, 80x25 char mode.
0277 X_Res=640; Y_Res=200; Mode=zCGA_6H;
0278 C0=0; C1=1; C2=1; C3=1; C4=1; C5=1; C6=1; C7=1;
0279 C8=1; C9=1; C10=1; C11=1; C12=1; C13=1; C14=1; C15=1;
0280 CharWidth=8; CharHeight=8;
0281 return;
0282 Hercules_mode:         // Hercules 720x348x2-color, 80x25 char mode.
0283 X_Res=720; Y_Res=348; Mode=zHERC;
0284 C0=0; C1=1; C2=1; C3=1; C4=1; C5=1; C6=1; C7=1;
0285 C8=1; C9=1; C10=1; C11=1; C12=1; C13=1; C14=1; C15=1;
0286 CharWidth=9; CharHeight=14;
0287 return;
0288
0289 FORCE_USER_MODE:    // jump to here if command-line argument legal.
0290 CommandLineArg= zNO; // first, reset token to avoid returning here.
0291 Display.ForceMode(Mode);        // ...then reset the graphics mode.
0292 switch(Mode)            // ...then jump back to appropriate code.
0293    {
0294    case zEGA_10H:     goto EGA_ECD_mode;
0295    case zEGA_EH:      goto EGA_SCD_mode;
0296    case zMCGA_11H:    goto MCGA_mode;
0297    case zCGA_6H:      goto CGA_mode;
0298    default:           goto ABORT_PGM;
0299    }
0300
```

```
0301    ABORT_PGM:          // jump to here if no graphics hardware detected.
0302    cout << "\n\n\rThis C++ graphics programming demo requires a";
0303    cout << "\n\rVGA, EGA, CGA, MCGA, or HGA graphics adapter.\n\r";
0304    exit(-1);                       // terminate, returning an error code.
0305    }
0306    /*
0307
0308    ┌─────────────────────────────────────────────────────────────────┐
        │                        Stub routine                              │
0309    └─────────────────────────────────────────────────────────────────┘
0310                                                                       */
0311    static void zStubRoutine(void)
0312    {       // this do-nothing routine is a placeholder for future code.
0313    Display.SetHue(C0);                     // set the drawing color.
0314    Display.SetLine(0xffff);                // set the line style.
0315    Display.SetFill(SolidFill,C0);          // set the fill style.
0316    Viewport1.ClearTextLine();              // clear the dialog line.
0317    Viewport1.PutText(1,2,TextClr,StubMessage);// display text message.
0318    return;
0319    }
0320    /*
0321
0322    ┌─────────────────────────────────────────────────────────────────┐
        │                Check the keyboard for a keystroke                │
0323    └─────────────────────────────────────────────────────────────────┘
0324                                                                       */
0325    static void zKeyboard(void)
0326    {
0327      union AnyName{int RawCode;char Code[3];}Keystroke;
0328      char TempKey=0;
0329    #if defined (BORLAND)
0330      if (bioskey(1)==zEMPTY) { KeyCode=0; return; }
0331      Keystroke.RawCode= bioskey(0);
0332    #elif defined (ZORTECH)
0333      if (bioskey(1)==zEMPTY) { KeyCode=0; return; }
0334      Keystroke.RawCode= bioskey(0);
0335    #elif defined (MICROSOFT)
0336      if (_bios_keybrd(_KEYBRD_READY)==zEMPTY)
0337        { KeyCode=0; return; }
0338      Keystroke.RawCode= _bios_keybrd(_KEYBRD_READ);
0339    #endif
0340    TempKey= Keystroke.Code[0];
0341    if (TempKey!=0)
0342        {                                   // if a normal keystroke...
0343        KeyCode=1; KeyNum=TempKey; return;
0344        }
0345    if (TempKey==0)
0346        {                                   // if an extended keystroke...
0347        KeyCode=2; KeyNum=Keystroke.Code[1]; return;
0348        }
0349    }
0350    /*
0351
0352    ┌─────────────────────────────────────────────────────────────────┐
        │                  Empty the keystroke buffer                       │
0353    └─────────────────────────────────────────────────────────────────┘
0354                                                                       */
0355    static void zPurge(void)
0356    {
0357    do zKeyboard();
0358      while (KeyCode!=0);
0359    return;
0360    }
0361    /*
0362
0363    ┌─────────────────────────────────────────────────────────────────┐
        │                        Make a sound                               │
```

```
0364  |_____|
0365                                                    */
0366  static void zMakeSound(int Hertz,double Duration)
0367  {
0368    static clock_t FormerTime=0;
0369    short Count=0;
0370    int HighByte=0, LowByte=0;
0371    unsigned char OldPort=0, NewPort=0;
0372  FormerTime= clock();
0373  if (Hertz < 40) return;
0374  if (Hertz > 4660) return;
0375  Count= 1193180L/Hertz;
0376  HighByte= Count / 256;
0377  LowByte= Count - (HighByte * 256);
0378  #if defined (BORLAND)
0379    outportb(0x43,0xB6); outportb(0x42,(unsigned char)LowByte);
0380    outportb(0x42,(unsigned char)HighByte); OldPort=inportb(0x61);
0381    NewPort=(OldPort | 0x03); outportb(0x61,NewPort);
0382    zDelay(FormerTime,Duration);
0383    outportb(0x61,OldPort);
0384  #elif defined (ZORTECH)
0385    outp(0x43,0xB6); outp(0x42,LowByte);
0386    outp(0x42,HighByte); OldPort=(unsigned char)inp(0x61);
0387    NewPort=(OldPort | 0x03); outp(0x61,(int)NewPort);
0388    zDelay(FormerTime,Duration);
0389    outp(0x61,(int)OldPort);
0390  #elif defined (MICROSOFT)
0391    outp(0x43,0xB6); outp(0x42,LowByte);
0392    outp(0x42,HighByte); OldPort=(unsigned char)inp(0x61);
0393    NewPort=(OldPort | 0x03); outp(0x61,(int)NewPort);
0394    zDelay(FormerTime,Duration);
0395    outp(0x61,(int)OldPort);
0396  #endif
0397  return;
0398  }
0399  /*
0400  ┌─────────────────────────────────────────────┐
0401  │                    Pause                      │
0402  │                                               │
0403  └─────────────────────────────────────────────┘*/
0404  static clock_t zDelay(clock_t StartTime, double Wait)
0405  {                        // pause for a specified length of time.
0406    clock_t StopTime;
0407    clock_t NewClockTime;
0408  #if defined (BORLAND)
0409    StopTime= StartTime + (Wait * CLK_TCK);
0410  #elif defined (ZORTECH)
0411    StopTime= StartTime + (Wait * CLOCKS_PER_SEC);
0412  #elif defined (MICROSOFT)
0413    StopTime= StartTime + (Wait * CLK_TCK);
0414  #endif
0415  while ( clock() < StopTime ) {;}
0416  NewClockTime= clock();
0417  return NewClockTime;
0418  }
0419  /*
0420  ┌─────────────────────────────────────────────┐
0421  │        Retrieve the command-line arguments, if any │
0422  │                                               │
0423  └─────────────────────────────────────────────┘*/
0424  static void zArguments(int NumArgs, char *Arg[])
```

```
0425  {
0426  if(NumArgs==1)
0427    {
0428    CommandLineArg= zNO; return;                                // if no arg.
0429    }
0430  CommandLineCompare= strncmp(StartUpArg[0],Arg[1],5);
0431  if(CommandLineCompare==0)
0432    {
0433    CommandLineArg=zYES; Mode=zVGA_12H; return;                 // /M12.
0434    }
0435  CommandLineCompare= strncmp(StartUpArg[1],Arg[1],5);
0436  if(CommandLineCompare==0)
0437    {
0438    CommandLineArg=zYES; Mode=zEGA_10H; return;                 // /M10.
0439    }
0440  CommandLineCompare= strncmp(StartUpArg[2],Arg[1],5);
0441  if(CommandLineCompare==0)
0442    {
0443    CommandLineArg=zYES; Mode=zEGA_EH; return;                  // /MOE.
0444    }
0445  CommandLineCompare= strncmp(StartUpArg[3],Arg[1],5);
0446  if(CommandLineCompare==0)
0447    {
0448    CommandLineArg=zYES; Mode=zMCGA_11H; return;                // /M11.
0449    }
0450  CommandLineCompare= strncmp(StartUpArg[4],Arg[1],5);
0451  if(CommandLineCompare==0)
0452    {
0453    CommandLineArg=zYES; Mode=zCGA_6H; return;                  // /M06.
0454    }
0455  CommandLineCompare= strncmp(StartUpArg[5],Arg[1],5);
0456  if(CommandLineCompare==0)
0457    {
0458    CommandLineArg=zYES; Mode=zHERC; return;                    // /MHC.
0459    }
0460  CommandLineArg= zNO;                        // if an unrecognized argument.
0461  return;
0462  }
0463  /*
0464
0465  ┌──────────────────────────────────────────────────────────────────┐
       │   Supercharged C++ Graphics  --  end of source file CLICK.CPP      │
0466   └──────────────────────────────────────────────────────────────────┘
0467                                                                      */
```

4

Programming for keyboard and disk

Fundamental input/output functions are important even to graphics programs. Being able to detect and manage keystrokes can help make your C++ software more interactive. Being able to read and write disk files can help your C++ software store graphic images for later use.

Programming the keyboard

If you are using Turbo C++, Borland C++, or Zortech C++ the kbhit( ) library function can be called to determine if a key has been pressed while your C++ program is executing.

On each occasion your user strikes a key, either one or two key codes are placed in the keyboard buffer, which is a block of memory maintained in low RAM.

If the keystroke is a normal key like q, w, e, r, t, y, Enter, Esc, and others, then a single key code is written to the keyboard buffer. If the keystroke is an extended key like F2, Alt+X, Ctrl+P, left-arrow, PgDn, and others, then two key codes are written to the keyboard buffer. The first key code is a null value or ASCII 0. In this case the second key code—the extended code—is the code that represents the keystroke. If the user of your software presses the up-arrow key, the two keycodes placed in the keyboard buffer will be null and 72.

The library function kbhit( ) returns a value of type int. If the returned value is nonzero, a key has been pressed and one or more key codes are available in the keyboard buffer. If kbhit( ) returns a value of zero the keyboard buffer is empty.

After determining that one or more key codes are waiting to be fetched from the keyboard buffer, you can call getch( ) to retrieve a key code. The getch( ) library function returns a value of type int. If the value is nonzero, it represents a regular keystroke. If the value returned by getch( ) is zero, you must call getch( ) again to fetch the extended keystroke.

Both the kbhit( ) and the getch( ) library functions are direct calls to DOS. However, Turbo C++, Borland C++, and Zortech C++ each provide a library function that makes a direct call to BIOS interrupt 0x14, the keyboard interrupt. By using bioskey( ) to access the keyboard buffer, you can remove one layer of operating system functions from the keyboard management process.

If you are using Turbo C++, Borland C++, or Zortech C++ the following line will determine if a key code is present in the keyboard buffer.

```
if (bioskey(1) ! = 0)
```

The following function call will fetch the key code(s) from the keyboard buffer.

```
RawCode = bioskey(0);
```

The bioskey(0) runtime library function returns a value of type int. If the keystroke is a regular key, the low byte in the int is the key code char. If the keystroke is an extended key, the low byte is null (zero) and the high byte is the key code char.

In addition to providing a lower level interface to the keyboard, bioskey( ) can return valuable information about whether the shift keys are pressed, whether Num Lock is toggled, whether Caps Lock is toggled, whether Ins is toggled, and so on. Commercial software often uses these advanced features, so the demonstration program later in this chapter provides a working keyboard loop using the bioskey( ) function.

Programming the disk

Graphic images can be saved to disk as binary files—and loaded from disk for later use—after you have grasped a few diskdrive-specific programming skills.

Probably the most useful runtime library function for disk I/O is access( ). This function can—and should—be called before each disk read or write to make certain that the target file either exists or does not exist, as the case may be. A call to access( ) will also ensure that the path is legal. The path is the drive and directory portion of the complete file name. The access( ) function can also be used to verify that the diskdrive is operating correctly.

If you are using Turbo C++ or Borland C++, here is how to check to see if a file already exists.

```
if ((access("filename.ext",00)) = = 0)
```

The following line tests to determine if a file is write-protected (read- only).

```
if ((access("filename.ext",02)) = = − 1)
```

The access( ) function always returns 0 if the requested operation is allowed, − 1 if not. In either instance, if the path or file name is not found, the global variable errno is set to ENOENT.

See appendix G for more information about the global variable errno.

If you are using Zortech C++, the following line checks to determine if a file already exists.

```
if ((access("filename.ext",F_OK)) = = 0)
```

Here is how to ascertain if the file is write-protected.

```
if ((access("filename.ext",W_OK)) = = − 1)
```

After you have used access( ) to prequalify your intended disk operation, you can use the fwrite( ) library function to write your graphics data to disk. The ferror( ) function can be called immediately thereafter to check if any disk errors occurred.

The fread( ) library function can be used to load a graphics image from disk into RAM. The filelength( ) function is a handy way to determine the length of the file beforehand, so you can allocate a properly sized block of memory to hold the incoming data.

The demonstration program in this chapter uses a class whose methods provide bitblt objects capable of saving themselves to disk and loading themselves from disk.

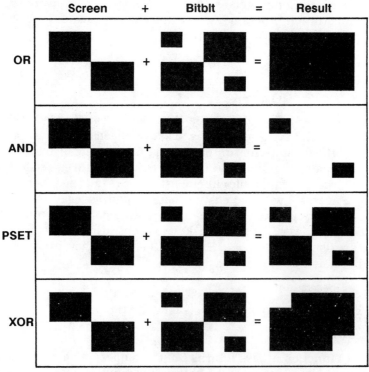

4-1 The effect at bitwise logic on graphic array transfers.

A sample program: BLOCK.CPP

As FIG. 4-1 shows, a number of visually interesting effects can be produced by using different logical operators with bitblts. The demonstration program provided in this chapter moves a bitblt icon across the display without damaging the background graphics.

Demo Figure 4-2 depicts the startup display produced by the sample program BLOCK.CPP, whose complete source code is provided in FIG. 4-5 at the end of the chapter. The program allows you to use the keyboard to interactively control the movement of the bitblt icon, as shown in FIG. 4-3, without interfering with the background image.

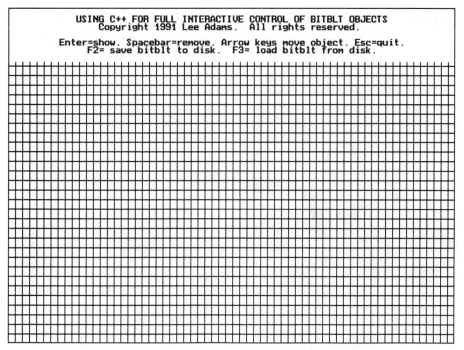

USING C++ FOR FULL INTERACTIVE CONTROL OF BITBLT OBJECTS
Copyright 1991 Lee Adams. All rights reserved.

Enter=show. Spacebar=remove. Arrow keys move object. Esc=quit.
F2= save bitblt to disk. F3= load bitblt from disk.

4-2 Graphics output from the sample program BLOCK.CPP. Shown here is the startup grid over which a multicolor bitblt will be moved.

How to compile and link the sample program

Here's How... The program listing presented in FIG. 4-5 contains the complete source code for the main module of the C++ demonstration program called "Using C++ for Full Interactive Control of Bitblt Objects." If you are using the companion disks to the book, the source code is in the file named

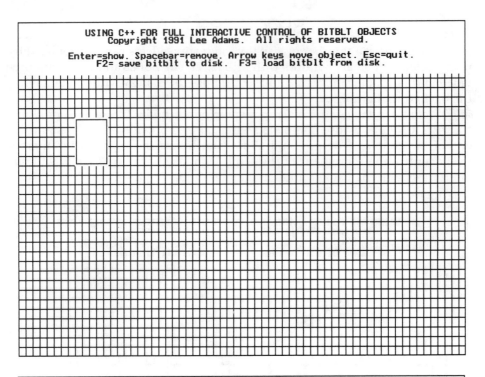

4-3 Graphics output from the sample program BLOCK.CPP. The self-controlling bitblt object can move across the display without disrupting the background image.

BLOCK.CPP. Three C++ source files are needed to build the finished .exe file. These are BLOCK.CPP from FIG. 4-5 and two of the class libraries in appendix E.

Class The class library that provides the language bindings and low-level graphics routines for this demonstration program is found in FIG. E-2 in appendix E. This listing contains the implementations for class PhysicalDisplay and class Viewport. If you are using the companion disks to the book, this file is named LIB2D.CPP. The class declarations are presented in FIG. E-1 in appendix E. If you are using the companion disks to the book, this file is named LIB2D.HPP.

Class The class library that provides the bitblt objects for this demonstration program is found in FIG. E-8 in appendix E. This listing contains the implementations for class Bitblt. If you are using the companion disks to the book, this file is named BITBLT.CPP. The class declarations are presented in FIG. E-7 in appendix E. If you are using the companion disks to the book, this file is named BITBLT.HPP.

You can compile, link, and run this demonstration program using either Turbo C++, Borland C++, or Zortech C++. If you are using Turbo C++, you might want to check appendix A for assistance in compiling, linking, and running the demonstration program. If you are using Borland C++, see appendix B. If you are using Zortech C++, refer to appendix C for discussion.

You must create a Turbo C++ or Borland C++ project list to advise your compiler which source files to bind together to build the finished .exe file. If you are using Zortech C++, name the files on the compiler command line field. Refer to the appendices if you require assistance.

After a successful compile and link the screen should resemble the screen prints shown in FIGS. 4-2 and 4-3.

How to run the demonstration program

You need a VGA, EGA, MCGA, CGA, or Hercules graphics adapter to run this interactive demonstration program.

Using the editor to run the program

Here's How... To run the program under your Turbo C++, Borland C++, or Zortech C++ editor, make sure that the finished .exe file is in the default directory. If you used Turbo C++ or Borland C++ to compile the program, the appropriate graphics driver must be in the default directory. If you are using a VGA or EGA, the EGAVGA.BGI file must be present. If you are using an MCGA or CGA, the CGA.BGI file must be present. If you are using a Hercules graphics adapter, the HERC.BGI file must be present. If you use Zortech C++, the appropriate graphics drivers will be linked into the .exe code and no external driver will be required.

The built-in autodetect routine of the demonstration program detects the graphics hardware in your computer system and sets up the best graphics mode supported by your hardware. To override the autodetect routine use the Turbo C++, Borland C++, or Zortech C++ editor to simulate a command line argument. The header in FIG. 4-5 provides a set of arguments that you can use to specify a graphics mode. See the appendices for further discussion. If you are using a VGA, you can override the autodetect routine and force the demonstration program to run in an EGA, MCGA, or CGA mode. If you are using an EGA, you can force the program to run in a lower-resolution EGA mode or a CGA mode.

Running the program from the operating system prompt

To start the program from the operating system prompt, simply enter BLOCK. The .exe file and any required graphics drivers must be present in the default directory. If the software finds a VGA present in your system, the program will animate using the $640 \times 480 \times 16$-color mode. If an EGA and enhanced monitor are found, the $640 \times 350 \times 16$-color mode is used. If an EGA and standard display are present, the program sets up the $640 \times 200 \times 16$-color mode. If an MCGA is detected, the $640 \times 480 \times 2$-color mode is employed. If a CGA is found, the $640 \times 200 \times 2$-color mode is used. If the program detects a Hercules graphics adapter, it start up in the $720 \times 348 \times 2$-color mode.

You can force the program to start up in a different mode by adding a command line argument when you start the program from the operating system prompt. Enter BLOCK /M11 to force the $640 \times 480 \times 2$-color mode. Enter BLOCK /M10 to force the $640 \times 350 \times 16$-color mode. Entering BLOCK /M0E forces the program to run in the $640 \times 200 \times 16$-color mode. Enter BLOCK /M06 to test the demonstration program in the $640 \times 200 \times 2$-color mode.

Using the demonstration program

After starting the program, press Enter to display the bitblt icon. Then you can use the arrow keys on the numeric keypad to move the bitblt across the display. The left-arrow, right-arrow, up-arrow, and down-arrow keys correspond directly to the bitblt's movement on the screen.

At startup the program saved a different version of the bitblt to disk. You can load this image from disk into memory by pressing F3. When you next move the bitblt the new image will appear, as shown in FIG. 4-4. You can save the current bitblt to disk by pressing F2.

Press the space bar to remove the bitblt from the screen. Press Enter to display it again.

Press either Esc or Alt+X to quit the program.

Programmer's Guide to BLOCK.CPP

The complete listing for the demonstration program BLOCK.CPP is presented in FIG. 4-5. The source code consists of an informative header, conditional compilation directives, declaration of constants and

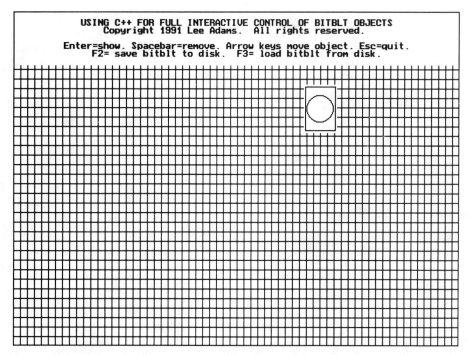

4-4 Graphics output from the sample program BLOCK.CPP. After a successful load from disk, the new bitblt image replaces the default startup bitblt.

macros, file include directives, function prototypes, variable declarations, and the executable functions.

Conditional compilation

Information and source code for conditional compilation is located at lines 0048 through 0065. If you are using Turbo C++ or Borland C++, the program is ready to compile, subject to the instructions provided in appendix B. If you are using Zortech C++, change line 0064 to read #define FG and change line 0065 to read #define ZORTECH.

Constants

The C++ qualifier, const, is used to declare and assign values to constant variables at lines 0067 through 0090. Note how key code values are assigned to variables like zENTER, zLEFT_ARROW, and zF3. These constants will make the source code easier to understand when the interactive loop is encountered.

Include files

The code at lines 0092 through 0120 uses the #include directive to load in the appropriate header files and C++ class declaration files. Line 0119 loads LIB-

2D.HPP, which declares the data members and methods of class PhysicalDisplay and class Viewport. Line 0120 loads BITBLT.HPP, which declares the data members and methods of class Bitblt. Class Bitblt is discussed later in this chapter.

Function prototypes

Function declarations are provided in lines 0122 through 0134. These functions are visible throughout this source file and can be called by any other function in the source file. Because each function is declared with the static qualifier, it is not available to functions located in other source files.

Variable declarations

Lines 0136 through 0169 declare global variables that are visible throughout this source file. These variables have file scope.

Object declarations

Object Note line 0168, which creates an object from class PhysicalDisplay named Display. The program will later call the methods of this object to help it manage the display. The methods are declared in the class declaration listing LIB2D.HPP and are defined in the class implementation listing LIB2D.CPP in appendix E. The object created at line 0168 is a static object that has file scope. It will remain available until the program ends.

Line 0169 creates an object from the Viewport class. The object is named Viewport1. The address of Display is passed to this new object. Viewport1 will need to use the methods of Display to generate graphics output. The object created at line 0169 is a static object with file scope. It will remain active until program termination.

main( )

The main( ) function is located at lines 0174 through 0193. After first checking to see if any command line arguments were used to launch the program, the code switches to an appropriate graphics mode, and then calls the function that manages the interactive control of the bitblt object.

Managing the bitblt icon

Here's How... The function at lines 0195 through 0313 provides interactive control over the bitblt at runtime. Local variables are declared at lines 0201 through 0210. A local pointer is given the address of the viewport object to be used at line 0213. If you had more than one viewport active, each viewport could have its own interactive bitblt.

The source code at lines 0215 through 0233 draws an icon, creates a bitblt object of class Bitblt, stores the image in a graphic array, and uses a method of class Bitblt to save the bitblt to disk. The C++ delete operator is then used to destroy the object. The call to method SaveImageFile( ) at line 0229 writes the disk file.

The code at lines 0235 through 0247 draws another icon. The C++ new operator at line 0242/0243 creates an object named Item1 of class Bitblt. Methods from class PhysicalDisplay and class Viewport are used to draw the image. The GrabImage( ) method of class Bitblt is used at line 0244 to store the image as a graphic array in RAM.

The code at lines 0249 through 0270 draws a grid of lines on the background.

The interactive loop for this demonstration program is located at lines 0278 through 0312. Line 0279 calls a keyboard routine to check for keystrokes. The code at lines 0280 and 0281 determines if the inbound key is a normal key or an extended key. The logic flow then jumps to the appropriate line label, either EXTENDED_KEY or NORMAL_KEY.

The switch( ) block at lines 0283 through 0299 uses the key code to generate an appropriate response. The arrow keys will cause method MoveImage( ) of class Bitblt to be called. F3 will generate a call to method LoadImageFile( ). Alt + X will invoke the C++ delete operator (to destroy the Bitblt object and release the memory and the program will terminate.

Terminating the program

The function at lines 0315 through 0323 calls a method of class PhysicalDisplay to terminate the graphics state. Line 0322 returns an OK code to the operating system.

The Startup( ) function

The function at lines 0325 through 0408 calls the SetupMode( ) method of class PhysicalDisplay to detect the graphics hardware.

The StubRoutine( ) function

The stub routine at lines 0410 through 0422 is a do-nothing routine that displays a simple message on the dialog line at the top of the display. A stub like this is helpful when you are building large programs. By calling the stub, you can avoid taking the time to build specific routines while you are getting your prototype up and running.

The Keyboard( ) function

The function at lines 0424 through 0452 detects and retrieves keystrokes from the keyboard buffer. The principle behind this block of code was discussed earlier in the chapter. The function at lines 0454 through 0463 repeatedly calls the keyboard function until the keyboard buffer is empty. This ensures no unwanted keystrokes remain in the buffer after the program has performed a lengthy graphics operation.

The MakeSound( ) function

The zMakeSound( ) function at lines 0465 through 0501 generates a sound from the system speaker. Appropriate values are sent to the hardware ports, and the function provides direct control over the speaker.

The Pause( ) function

The function at lines 0503 through 0521 pauses program execution for a specified length of time. The code uses the value returned by the system clock and multiplies it by the number of ticks per second. If you are using Turbo C++ or Borland C++, this value is represented by the global variable CLK_TCK. If you are using Zortech C++ it is represented by CLOCKS_PER_SEC. The sleep( ) library function of Turbo C++ and Borland C++ can be used instead of this function.

The Arguments( ) function

The function at lines 0523 through 0565 compares the command line argument with a set of legal strings. The function assigns an appropriate value to the global variable named Mode, which is used by other functions that produce graphics output.

Programmer's Guide to LIB2D.HPP

The complete source code for the declarations for class PhysicalDisplay and class Viewport is found in LIB2D.HPP in appendix E. The source from LIB2D.HPP must be #included at the beginning of any program that wishes to use the methods of class PhysicalDisplay or class Viewport. See the discussion in chapter 1 for more information about LIB2D.HPP.

Programmer's Guide to LIB2D.CPP

The source code in LIB2D.CPP, presented in appendix E, provides language bindings that produce low-level graphics. The routines in LIB2D.CPP call the appropriate runtime library functions in Turbo C++'s graphics.lib, Borland C++'s graphics.lib, Zortech C++'s fg.lib, or Microsoft's graph.lib.

LIB2D.CPP is the class implementation listing for class PhysicalDisplay and class Viewport. Class PhysicalDisplay manages the state of the display. Class Viewport is responsible for maintaining a viewport and producing low-level graphics. These two classes generate nearly all the low-level graphics required by the demonstration programs in the book. See the discussion in chapter 1 for further information about class PhysicalDisplay and class View-port.

Programmer's Guide to BITBLT.HPP

The complete source code for the declarations for class Bitblt is found in BITBLT.HPP in appendix E. The source from BITBLT.HPP must be #included at the beginning of any program that wishes to use the methods of class Bitblt.

Note the directives at lines 0052 and 0053. These two preprocessor directives ensure that BITBLT.HPP will not be #included if it has already been #included. A previous inclusion will have defined the variable BITBLT_HPP, which would cause the test at line 0053 to fail. The compiler would then refrain from compiling the file.

The source code at lines 0056 through 0089 declares data members and a method—all of which are not visible to functions or methods outside class Bitblt. The code at lines 0091 through 0100 declares methods of class Bitblt that can be called by any in-scope function or method.

Programmer's Guide to BITBLT.CPP

The complete source code for the implementation for class Bitblt is found in BITBLT.CPP in appendix E. The methods of class Bitblt provide bitblts capable of displaying, moving, and erasing themselves. Class Bitblt also provides methods that enable a bitblt to save itself to disk and load itself from disk.

Constructor

The constructor for objects of class Bitblt is located at lines 0061 through 0078. The constructor expects to receive in its argument list the diagonal bounding coordinates of the bitblt being created, the horizontal and vertical resolution of the current graphics screen mode, and a pointer to the Viewport object to be used for low-level graphics output to the display.

Much of the constructor's activity is centered around initializing tokens that will indicate the state of the bitblt at runtime. The methods of class Bitblt need to know if memory has been allocated, if a graphic array has already been stored in RAM, if the bitblt is already being displayed, and so on.

Destructor

The destructor for class Bitblt is presented at lines 0080 through 0087. The destructor is automatically called whenever an object of class Bitblt is destroyed. A call to private method FreeBlock( ) ensures that the memory allocated for the graphic array is released back to the C++ free store.

Method GrabImage( )

The method at lines 0089 through 0108 captures the image from the display. Note the -> addressing notation at line 0097, used to send a message to the MemBlock( ) method of an object named Generic. Generic is a pointer to the Viewport object that was passed when the bitblt was activated. A subsequent call to method GetBlock( ) stores the image in the memory allocated by method MemBlock( ).

The code at line 0106 sets a token to indicate that the bitblt is ready to be used. This token will be verified by other methods that want to write a bitblt to the display. This helps avoid generating a runtime error in the event the client program makes an illegal call to a method.

Method DisplayImage( )

The method at lines 0121 through 0146 places the bitblt onto the screen. The test at line 01276 ensures that DisplayImage( ) will not place a second bitblt on the display if the bitblt is already present. The test at line 0128 ensures that a graphic array exists. The tests at lines 0129 through 0132 ensures that the requested location for installation is legal. Lines 0133 and 0134 use variables defined at line 0071 which correspond to the pixel logic to be used for subsequent bitblt write operations.

The switch( ) block at lines 0137 through 0143 writes the bitblt to the display using the appropriate logic. See FIG. 4-1.

Method EraseImage( )

The method at lines 0148 through 0158 erases the bitblt from the display. The background was saved in line 0136 when the bitblt was written to the screen. Line 0155 in method EraseImage( ) writes this background image back to the screen.

Method MoveImage( )

The method at lines 0160 through 0186 can be used to cleanly move an already displayed bitblt to another location on the screen. The method takes care of all the low-level housekeeping chores. It removes the existing bitblt and restores the background. Then it places the bitblt at the desired new location. Note in particular line 0176, which calls method GetBlock( ) in order to save the background before the new location is overwritten. This ensures that any subsequent call to method MoveImage( ) will have the resources it needs to restore the background image.

Method NameImageFile( )

The method at lines 0188 through 0197 uses the strcpy( ) library function to copy a string into the variable that is used as the file name for disk operations.

Method SaveImageFile( )

The method at lines 0199 through 0232 saves the bitblt image to disk using the file name received as an argument. Note how the access( ) function is used to detect if the file already exists and is read-only. Any attempt to write a file of this status would generate a runtime error, of course.

The code that actually writes the file is located at lines 0223 through 0230. An interesting wrinkle is the BlockSize variable used in the call to fwrite( ) at line 0225. This variable indicates the number of bytes to be written to the file. A call to method GetBlockSize( ) of class Viewport at line 0100 provided this value.

Also important is the use of the ferror( ) function at line 0226. This code ensures that the file operation was error-free.

Method LoadImageFile( )

The method at lines 0234 through 0267 loads a binary image file from disk and stores it in the graphic array maintained by the methods of class Bitblt.

The code at lines 0242 through 0248 uses a call to access( ) to ensure that the file exists on disk. Then a call to filelength( ) is used to determine the length of file. If the size is larger than the buffer maintained by class Bitblt, the load operation is cancelled. Writing bytes past the end of the buffer could overwrite other data or executable code, producing unpredictable behavior at runtime.

The fread( ) function at line 0260 uses the result of the filelength( ) call to read the file. Again, the ferror( ) function is used to report any errors resulting from the file operation.

Using and modifying class Bitblt

In its current form class, Bitblt provides a suite of powerful bitblt operations. The methods can be used to manage icons and even menu systems, as a demonstration program later in the book will illustrate. Each instance of class Bitblt acts independently of other bitblts, providing you with a versatile set of imaging tools to manipulate sections of the display.

You might find it useful to add methods to class Bitblt to enable a graceful recovery if the image to be loaded is larger than the available buffer in RAM. Either use the C++ operator new or the malloc( ) function to allocate a buffer of appropriate size.

4-5 Sample program BLOCK.CPP. Supports VGA, EGA, MCGA, CGA, and Hercules adapters. This application demonstrates bitblt objects capable of displaying, moving, erasing, saving, and loading themselves during program execution.

```
0001   /*
0002
0003               Lee Adams' SUPERCHARGED C++ GRAPHICS
0004    | Interactive bitblt demo:  display, movement, and file save/load |
```

```
0005 |─────────────────────────────────────────────────────────────|
0006 |   SOURCE FILE:   BLOCK.CPP                                     |
0007 |          TYPE:   C++ source file for a multimodule application.|
0008 |       PURPOSE:   Demonstrates bitblt objects and operations.   |
0009 | PROGRAM LIST:    BLOCK.CPP, LIB2D.CPP and BITBLT.CPP.          |
0010 |     LANGUAGES:   Turbo C++, Borland C++, Zortech C++, and      |
0011 |                  all C++ compilers compatible with AT&T C++ 2.0 |
0012 |                  specification; and nominal compatibility with  |
0013 |                  Microsoft C++ (see the discussion in the book).|
0014 | MEMORY MODEL:    large.                                         |
0015 | COMMAND-LINE:    you can specify a graphics mode by using the   |
0016 |                  command-line argument /Mnn as shown below:     |
0017 |                       /M12  640x480x16-color VGA                |
0018 |                       /M11  640x480x2-color VGA, MCGA           |
0019 |                       /M10  640x350x16-color VGA, EGA           |
0020 |                       /MOE  640x200x16-color VGA, EGA           |
0021 |                       /M06  640x200x2-color VGA, MCGA, EGA, CGA |
0022 |                       /MHC  720x348x2-color Hercules            |
0023 |                       If no command-line argument is used, hardware|
0024 |                  autodetect is used to select the best mode.   |
0025 | OUTPUT:   You can use the arrow keys to move a bitblt object    |
0026 |           around the display using a non-destructive graphic   |
0027 |           array operation preserving the background.  You can   |
0028 |           also exercise class methods that can save a bitblt    |
0029 |           to disk or load a previously-saved bitblt from disk.  |
0030 | LICENSE:  As purchaser of the book in which this source code    |
0031 |   appears you are granted a royalty-free license to reproduce   |
0032 |   and distribute executable files generated using this code     |
0033 |   provided that you accept the conditions of the License        |
0034 |   Agreement and Limited Warranty described in the book.         |
0035 | PUBLICATION: Contains material from Windcrest/McGraw-Hill       |
0036 |   book 3489, published by TAB BOOKS.                            |
0037 | U.S. GOVERNMENT RESTRICTED RIGHTS:  This software and its       |
0038 |   documentation is provided with restricted rights.  The use,   |
0039 |   duplication, or disclosure by the Government is subject to     |
0040 |   restrictions set forth in subdivision (b)(3)(ii) of The       |
0041 |   Rights in Technical Data and Computer Software clause at       |
0042 |   252.227-7013.  Contractor/manufacturer is Lee Adams, c/o      |
0043 |   TAB BOOKS, 13311 Monterey Ave., Blue Ridge Summit PA 17294.   |
0044 | TRADEMARK:  Lee Adams is a trademark of Lee Adams.              |
0045 |                                                                 |
0046 |      Copyright 1991 Lee Adams.  All rights reserved worldwide.  |
0047 |─────────────────────────────────────────────────────────────|
0048
0049 |─────────────────────────────────────────────────────────────|
0050 |                    CONDITIONAL COMPILATION                      |
0051 | To compile only those blocks of code that support the C++       |
0052 | compiler and graphics library that you are using, you should    |
0053 | #define the appropriate tokens on lines 0064 and 0065.          |
0053 |                    GRAPHICS LIBRARY                             |
0054 |      Borland's graphics.lib               #define BGI          |
0055 |      Zortech's fg.lib or fgdebug.lib      #define FG           |
0056 |      Microsoft's graph.lib                #define MS           |
0057 |                    COMPILER                                     |
0058 |      Borland Turbo C++ compiler           #define BORLAND      |
0059 |      Zortech C++ compiler                 #define ZORTECH      |
0060 |      AT&T-compatible C++ compilers        #define MICROSOFT    |
0061 | Be sure you define only one compiler and one graphics library.  |
0062 |                                                                 |
0063 |                                                              */ |
0064 #define BGI      1  // indicates the graphics library you are using.
0065 #define BORLAND 1  // indicates the C++ compiler you are using.
0066 /*
```

```
0067
0068  ┌─────────────────────────────────────────────────────────────┐
      │                         Constants                           │
0069  └─────────────────────────────────────────────────────────────┘
0070                                                               */
0071   const int zFAIL=  0;                        // boolean tokens...
0072   const int zEMPTY= 0;
0073   const int zYES=   1;
0074   const int zNO=    0;
0075   const int zVGA_12H=   1;                     // display mode tokens...
0076   const int zEGA_10H=   2;
0077   const int zEGA_EH=    3;
0078   const int zMCGA_11H= 4;
0079   const int zCGA_6H=    5;
0080   const int zHERC=      6;
0081   const int zALT_X=        45;                 // keystroke codes...
0082   const int zENTER=        13;
0083   const int zESC=          27;
0084   const int zRT_ARROW=     77;
0085   const int zLEFT_ARROW=   75;
0086   const int zUP_ARROW=     72;
0087   const int zDN_ARROW=     80;
0088   const int zSPACE=        32;
0089   const int zF2=           60;
0090   const int zF3=           61;
0091   /*
0092
0093  ┌─────────────────────────────────────────────────────────────┐
      │                       Include files                         │
0094  └─────────────────────────────────────────────────────────────┘
0095                                                               */
0096   #if defined (BORLAND)
0097   #include <time.h>         // supports clock().
0098   #include <string.h>       // supports strncmp().
0099   #include <bios.h>         // supports bioskey().
0100   #include <process.h>      // supports exit().
0101   #include <iostream.h>     // supports cout.
0102   #include <dos.h>          // supports outportb(), inportb().
0103   #elif defined (ZORTECH)
0104   #include <time.h>         // supports clock().
0105   #include <string.h>       // supports strncmp().
0106   #include <bios.h>         // supports bioskey().
0107   #include <stdlib.h>       // supports exit().
0108   #include <stream.hpp>     // supports cout.
0109   #include <dos.h>          // supports outp(), inp().
0110   #elif defined (MICROSOFT)
0111   #include <time.h>         // supports clock().
0112   #include <string.h>       // supports strncmp().
0113   #include <bios.h>         // supports _bios_keybrd().
0114   #include <process.h>      // supports exit().
0115   #include <iostream.h>     // supports cout.
0116   #include <conio.h>        // supports outp(), inp().
0117   #endif
0118
0119   #include "LIB2D.HPP"      // declarations for PhysicalDisplay class.
0120   #include "BITBLT.HPP"            // declarations for Bitblt class.
0121   /*
0122
0123  ┌─────────────────────────────────────────────────────────────┐
      │     Prototypes for functions visible throughout this file   │
0124  └─────────────────────────────────────────────────────────────┘
0125                                                               */
0126   static void zStartup(void);          // initializes a graphics mode.
0127   static void zArguments(int, char far* far*);   // checks arguments.
0128   static void zKeyboard(void);               // checks for a keystroke.
0129   static void zQuit_Pgm(void);         // ends the program gracefully.
```

4-5 Continued.

```
0130  static void zPurge(void);                // empties the keyboard buffer.
0131  static void zStubRoutine(void);               // do-nothing stub.
0132  static void zMakeSound(int,double);      // makes a specific sound.
0133  static clock_t zDelay(clock_t,double);    // CPU-independent pause.
0134  static void zInteractiveLoop(Viewport *);        // runtime loop.
0135  /*
0136
0137     ┌─────────────────────────────────────────────────────────────┐
        │       Declaration of variables visible throughout this file   │
0138     └─────────────────────────────────────────────────────────────┘
0139                                                                  */
0140  static char *StartUpArg[6]=           // legal command-line arguments.
0141         { "/M12", "/M10", "/MOE", "/M11", "/M06", "/MHC" };
0142  static int CommandLineArg=zNO;       // indicates if argument exists.
0143  static int CommandLineCompare=0;      // indicates if argument legal.
0144  static int C0=0,C1=1,C2=2,C3=3,C4=4,C5=5,C6=6,
0145      C7=7,C8=8,C9=9,C10=10,C11=11,C12=12,C13=13,
0146      C14=14,C15=15;                          // palette index codes.
0147  static int Mode=0;            // which graphics mode is being used.
0148  static int Result=0;       // captures result of graphics routines.
0149  static int CharWidth=0,CharHeight=0;     // dimensions of character.
0150  static char KeyCode=0;    // token for normal or extended keystroke.
0151  static char KeyNum=0;                   // ASCII number of keystroke.
0152  static char SolidFill[]=
0153              {255,255,255,255,255,255,255,255};   // 100% fill.
0154  static int TextClr=7;              // font color for regular text.
0155  static int PromptClr=7;             // font color for prompt text.
0156  static char Copyright[]=
0157                "Copyright 1991 Lee Adams.  All rights reserved.";
0158  static char Title[]=
0159      "USING C++ FOR FULL INTERACTIVE CONTROL OF BITBLT OBJECTS";
0160  static char PressAnyKey[]="Press any key to create bitblt object.";
0161  static char RuntimePrompt1[]=
0162      "Enter=show. Spacebar=remove. Arrow keys move object. Esc=quit.";
0163  static char RuntimePrompt2[]=
0164      "F2= save bitblt to disk.  F3= load bitblt from disk.";
0165  static char StubMessage[]= "The generic stub routine was called.";
0166  static int X_Res=0, Y_Res=0;                  // screen resolution.
0167
0168  PhysicalDisplay Display;       // create the physical display object.
0169  Viewport Viewport1(&Display);          // create a viewport object.
0170  /*
0171
0172     ┌─────────────────────────────────────────────────────────────┐
        │                    Function definitions                        │
0173     └─────────────────────────────────────────────────────────────┘
0174
0175     ┌─────────────────────────────────────────────────────────────┐
        │     The executive routine:  program execution begins here      │
0176     └─────────────────────────────────────────────────────────────┘
0177                                                                  */
0178  main(int argc, char *argv[])
0179  {
0180    int NumArgs; char far* far* Arg;
0181
0182  NumArgs= argc;                        // grab number of arguments.
0183  Arg= &argv[0];               // grab address of array of arguments.
0184  zArguments(NumArgs, Arg);        // check the command-line arguments.
0185
0186  zStartup();                      // establish the graphics mode.
0187  Display.Init2D(Mode,0,0,X_Res-1,Y_Res-1);    // set graphics state.
0188  Result= Display.InitUndo();       // create hidden page (unused here).
0189  if (Result==zFAIL) zQuit_Pgm();           // if hidden page failed.
0190  Display.BlankPage();                      // clear the display.
0191  zInteractiveLoop(&Viewport1);       // call the interactive loop.
```

```
0192   zQuit_Pgm();                    // tidy up and terminate the application.
0193   }
0194   /*
0195
0196   ┌─────────────────────────────────────────────────────────────┐
       │       Interactive control of the bitblt object on the screen  │
0197   └─────────────────────────────────────────────────────────────┘
0198                                                                    */
0199   static void zInteractiveLoop(Viewport *ViewportObject)
0200   {                      // expects to receive the viewport object to be used.
0201     Viewport *ViewPtr;              // uninitialized ptr to a viewport.
0202     int ObjOffsetX= 12;                      // x offset for movement.
0203     int ObjOffsetY= 8;                       // y offset for movement.
0204     int ObjX1= 80, ObjY1= 100,
0205         ObjX2= 127, ObjY2= 150;   // diagonal coords of the bitblt.
0206     int ObjColor= C4;                        // color of object.
0207     int TestColor= C2;        // color of object for testing file I/O.
0208     int ObjMode= 0;                          // write mode.
0209     int x1,y1,x2,y2;                         // line coordinates.
0210     int CenterX, CenterY, Radius;            // circle parameters.
0211
0212     // step one:  pick the viewport ----------------------------------
0213     ViewPtr= ViewportObject;                 // initialize the pointer.
0214
0215     // step two:  create a test image and store it on disk -----------
0216     Display.SetHue(TestColor);               // set the drawing color.
0217     Display.SetFill(SolidFill,TestColor);    // set the fill style.
0218     ViewPtr->DrawPanel(ObjX1,ObjY1,ObjX2,ObjY2);   // filled rectangle.
0219     Display.SetHue(C10);                     // set the drawing color.
0220     Display.SetFill(SolidFill,C7);           // set the fill style.
0221     ViewPtr->DrawBorder(ObjX1+2,ObjY1+2,ObjX2-2,ObjY2-2);  // add trim.
0222     CenterX= ObjX1 + ( (ObjX2 - ObjX1) / 2);
0223     CenterY= ObjY1 + ( (ObjY2 - ObjY1) / 2);
0224     Radius= ( (ObjX2 - ObjX1) / 2) - 4;
0225     ViewPtr->DrawCircle(CenterX,CenterY,Radius);
0226     Bitblt *Item=                 // ...and create a new bitblt object.
0227       new Bitblt(ObjX1,ObjY1,ObjX2,ObjY2,X_Res,Y_Res,ViewPtr);
0228     Item->GrabImage();            // grab the image from the bitmap.
0229     Item->SaveImageFile("DEFAULTS.BLT");    // save the image to disk.
0230     Display.SetHue(C0);                     // reset the drawing color.
0231     Display.SetFill(SolidFill,C0);          // reset the fill style.
0232     ViewPtr->DrawPanel(ObjX1,ObjY1,ObjX2,ObjY2);    // erase the image.
0233     delete Item;                            // destroy the object.
0234
0235     // step three:  create another image and store it in RAM ---------
0236     Display.SetHue(ObjColor);               // set the drawing color.
0237     Display.SetFill(SolidFill,ObjColor);    // set the fill style.
0238     ViewPtr->DrawPanel(ObjX1,ObjY1,ObjX2,ObjY2);    // filled rectangle.
0239     Display.SetHue(C7);                     // set the drawing color.
0240     Display.SetFill(SolidFill.C7):          // set the fill style.
0241     ViewPtr->DrawBorder(ObjX1+2,ObjY1+2,ObjX2-2,ObjY2-2);  // add trim.
0242     Bitblt *Item1=                // ...and create a new bitblt object.
0243       new Bitblt(ObjX1,ObjY1,ObjX2,ObjY2,X_Res,Y_Res,ViewPtr);
0244     Item1->GrabImage();           // grab the image from the bitmap.
0245     Display.SetHue(C0);                     // set the drawing color.
0246     Display.SetFill(SolidFill,C0);          // set the fill style.
0247     ViewPtr->DrawPanel(ObjX1,ObjY1,ObjX2,ObjY2);    // erase the image.
0248
0249     // step four:  create a background -------------------------------
0250     Display.SetHue(C1);                     // restore default drawing color.
0251     Display.SetFill(SolidFill,C1);          // restore default fill style.
0252     ViewPtr->DrawPanel(1,1,X_Res-2,Y_Res-2);        // blue background.
0253     Display.SetHue(C9);                     // intense blue pattern.
0254     x1= 1; y1= 60; x2= X_Res-2; y2= Y_Res-2;
```

```
0255   while (y1 < y2)
0256      {                              // draw a set of horizontal lines...
0257      ViewPtr->SetPosition(x1,y1);
0258      ViewPtr->DrawLine(x2,y1);
0259      y1+= 10;
0260      }
0261   x1= 10; y1=56; x2= X_Res-2; y2= Y_Res-2;
0262   while (x1 < x2)
0263      {                              // draw a set of vertical lines...
0264      ViewPtr->SetPosition(x1,y1);
0265      ViewPtr->DrawLine(x1,y2);
0266      x1+= 10;
0267      }
0268   Display.SetHue(C7);
0269   Display.SetFill(SolidFill,C7);
0270   ViewPtr->DrawBorder(0,0,X_Res-1,Y_Res-1);
0271
0272   // step five: provide interactive controls -----------------------
0273   ViewPtr->PutText(2,13,TextClr,Title);
0274   ViewPtr->PutText(3,17,TextClr,Copyright);
0275   ViewPtr->PutText(5,10,PromptClr,RuntimePrompt1);      // prompts...
0276   ViewPtr->PutText(6,15,PromptClr,RuntimePrompt2);
0277   zMakeSound(420,.2); zMakeSound(400,.2);              // audio cue.
0278   INPUT_LOOP:                         // keyboard loop begins.
0279   zKeyboard();                        // check for user keystroke.
0280   if (KeyCode==0) goto INPUT_LOOP;    // loop back if no keystroke.
0281   if (KeyCode!=2) goto NORMAL_KEY;    // jump if normal keystroke.
0282   EXTENDED_KEY:              // fall through to here if extended key.
0283   switch (KeyNum)            // switcher for extended keystrokes.
0284      {                       // the arrow keys move the bitblt.
0285      case zRT_ARROW:   Item1->MoveImage(ObjOffsetX,0,ObjMode);
0286                        zPurge(); break;
0287      case zLEFT_ARROW: Item1->MoveImage(-ObjOffsetX,0,ObjMode);
0288                        zPurge(); break;
0289      case zUP_ARROW:   Item1->MoveImage(0,-ObjOffsetY,ObjMode);
0290                        break;
0291      case zDN_ARROW:   Item1->MoveImage(0,ObjOffsetY,ObjMode);
0292                        break;
0293      case zF3:         Item1->LoadImageFile("DEFAULTS.BLT");
0294                        break;
0295      case zF2:         Item1->SaveImageFile("DEFAULTS.BLT");
0296                        break;
0297      case zALT_X:      delete Item1; zQuit_Pgm();      // a trapdoor.
0298      default:          zMakeSound(450,.2);      // unsupported key.
0299      }
0300   zPurge();                          // empty the keyboard buffer.
0301   goto INPUT_LOOP;              // force jump back to start of loop.
0302   NORMAL_KEY:                  // jump to here if normal keystroke.
0303   switch (KeyNum)
0304      {
0305      case zESC:     delete Item1; return;      // destroy object.
0306      case zENTER:   Item1->DisplayImage(ObjX1,ObjY1,ObjMode);
0307                     break;                     // show the bitblt.
0308      case zSPACE:   Item1->EraseImage(); break;   // remove bitblt.
0309      default:       zMakeSound(450,.2);      // unsupported key.
0310      }
0311   zPurge();                          // empty the keyboard buffer.
0312   goto INPUT_LOOP;                                  // loop back.
0313   }
0314   /*
0315
0316   ┌──────────────────────────────────────────────────────────────┐
       │                   Terminate the program                        │
```

```
0317 |_____|
0318                                                          */
0319 static void zQuit_Pgm(void)
0320 {
0321 Display.ShutDownGraphics();  // graceful shutdown of graphics mode.
0322 exit(0);                     // terminate the program and return OK code.
0323 }
0324 /*
0325 ┌────────────────────────────────────────────────────────┐
0326 │           Detect the graphics hardware and set the      │
0327 │   highest mode permitted by the graphics adapter and monitor. │
0328 │   The user can override the autodetect algorithm by providing │
0329 │   an argument on the command-line when the program is started. │
0330 └────────────────────────────────────────────────────────┘
0331                                                          */
0332 static void zStartup(void)
0333 {
0334    int DefaultMode;
0335 DefaultMode= Display.SetupMode();   // get results of autodetect...
0336 switch(DefaultMode)                 // ...and jump to appropriate code.
0337    {
0338    case zFAIL:        goto ABORT_PGM;
0339    case zVGA_12H:     goto VGA_mode;
0340    case zEGA_10H:     goto EGA_ECD_mode;
0341    case zEGA_EH:      goto EGA_SCD_mode;
0342    case zMCGA_11H:    goto MCGA_mode;
0343    case zCGA_6H:      goto CGA_mode;
0344    case zHERC:        goto Hercules_mode;
0345    default:           goto ABORT_PGM;
0346    }
0347 VGA_mode:            // VGA 640x480x16-color, 80x60 character mode.
0348 if(CommandLineArg==zYES)
0349    {                              // if user has requested a mode.
0350    if((Mode>zVGA_12H)&&(Mode<zHERC)) goto FORCE_USER_MODE;
0351    }
0352 X_Res=640; Y_Res=480; Mode=zVGA_12H; CharWidth=8; CharHeight=8;
0353 return;
0354 EGA_ECD_mode:        // EGA 640x350x16-color, 80x43 character mode.
0355 if(CommandLineArg==zYES)
0356    {
0357    if((Mode==zEGA_EH)||(Mode==zCGA_6H))   // permit only EGA or CGA.
0358    goto FORCE_USER_MODE;
0359    }
0360 X_Res=640; Y_Res=350; Mode=zEGA_10H; CharWidth=8; CharHeight=8;
0361 return;
0362 EGA_SCD_mode:            // EGA 640x200x16-color, 80x25 char mode.
0363 if(CommandLineArg==zYES)
0364    {
0365    if(Mode==zCGA_6H) goto FORCE_USER_MODE;    // only CGA permitted.
0366    }
0367 X_Res=640; Y_Res=200; Mode=zEGA_EH; CharWidth=8; CharHeight=8;
0368 return;
0369 MCGA_mode:               // MCGA 640x480x2-color, 80x60 char mode.
0370 if(CommandLineArg==zYES)
0371    {
0372    if(Mode==zCGA_6H) goto FORCE_USER_MODE;    // only CGA permitted.
0373    }
0374 X_Res=640; Y_Res=480; Mode=zMCGA_11H;
0375 C0=0; C1=0; C2=1; C3=1; C4=1; C5=1; C6=1; C7=1;
0376 C8=1; C9=1; C10=0; C11=1; C12=1; C13=1; C14=1; C15=1;
0377 CharWidth=8; CharHeight=8;
0378 return;
0379 CGA_mode:                // CGA 640x200x2-color, 80x25 char mode.
```

```
0380  X_Res=640; Y_Res=200; Mode=zCGA_6H;
0381  C0=0; C1=0; C2=1; C3=1; C4=1; C5=1; C6=1; C7=1;
0382  C8=1; C9=1; C10=0; C11=1; C12=1; C13=1; C14=1; C15=1;
0383  CharWidth=8; CharHeight=8;
0384  return;
0385  Hercules_mode:          // Hercules 720x348x2-color, 80x25 char mode.
0386  X_Res=720; Y_Res=348; Mode=zHERC;
0387  C0=0; C1=0; C2=1; C3=1; C4=1; C5=1; C6=1; C7=1;
0388  C8=1; C9=1; C10=0; C11=1; C12=1; C13=1; C14=1; C15=1;
0389  CharWidth=9; CharHeight=14;
0390  return;
0391
0392  FORCE_USER_MODE:    // jump to here if command-line argument legal.
0393  CommandLineArg= zNO; // first, reset token to avoid returning here.
0394  Display.ForceMode(Mode);         // ...then reset the graphics mode.
0395  switch(Mode)            // ...then jump back to appropriate code.
0396    {
0397    case zEGA_10H:     goto EGA_ECD_mode;
0398    case zEGA_EH:      goto EGA_SCD_mode;
0399    case zMCGA_11H:    goto MCGA_mode;
0400    case zCGA_6H:      goto CGA_mode;
0401    default:           goto ABORT_PGM;
0402    }
0403
0404  ABORT_PGM:          // jump to here if no graphics hardware detected.
0405  cout << "\n\n\rThis C++ graphics programming demo requires a";
0406  cout << "\n\rVGA, EGA, CGA, MCGA, or HGA graphics adapter.\n\r";
0407  exit(-1);                   // terminate, returning an error code.
0408  }
0409  /*
0410
0411  ┌──────────────────────────────────────────────────────────────┐
         │                       Stub routine                             │
0412     └──────────────────────────────────────────────────────────────┘
0413                                                                    */
0414  static void zStubRoutine(void)
0415  {        // this do-nothing routine is a placeholder for future code.
0416  Display.SetHue(C0);                      // set the drawing color.
0417  Display.SetLine(0xffff);                 // set the line style.
0418  Display.SetFill(SolidFill,C0);           // set the fill style.
0419  Viewport1.ClearTextLine();               // clear the dialog line.
0420  Viewport1.PutText(1,2,TextClr,StubMessage);// display text message.
0421  return;
0422  }
0423  /*
0424
0425  ┌──────────────────────────────────────────────────────────────┐
         │            Check the keyboard for a keystroke                  │
0426     └──────────────────────────────────────────────────────────────┘
0427                                                                    */
0428  static void zKeyboard(void)
0429  {
0430    union AnyName{int RawCode;char Code[3];}Keystroke;
0431    char TempKey=0;
0432  #if defined (BORLAND)
0433    if (bioskey(1)==zEMPTY) { KeyCode=0; return; }
0434    Keystroke.RawCode= bioskey(0);
0435  #elif defined (ZORTECH)
0436    if (bioskey(1)==zEMPTY) { KeyCode=0; return; }
0437    Keystroke.RawCode= bioskey(0);
0438  #elif defined (MICROSOFT)
0439    if (_bios_keybrd(_KEYBRD_READY)==zEMPTY)
0440      { KeyCode=0; return; }
```

```
0441    Keystroke.RawCode= _bios_keybrd(_KEYBRD_READ);
0442  #endif
0443  TempKey= Keystroke.Code[0];
0444  if (TempKey!=0)
0445    {                                          // if a normal keystroke...
0446    KeyCode=1; KeyNum=TempKey; return;
0447    }
0448  if (TempKey==0)
0449    {                                          // if an extended keystroke...
0450    KeyCode=2; KeyNum=Keystroke.Code[1]; return;
0451    }
0452  }
0453  /*
0454
0455  ┌────────────────────────────────────────────────────────────────┐
        │               Empty the keystroke buffer                        │
0456  └────────────────────────────────────────────────────────────────┘
0457                                                                    */
0458  static void zPurge(void)
0459  {
0460  do zKeyboard();
0461    while (KeyCode!=0);
0462  return;
0463  }
0464  /*
0465
0466  ┌────────────────────────────────────────────────────────────────┐
        │                      Make a sound                               │
0467  └────────────────────────────────────────────────────────────────┘
0468                                                                    */
0469  static void zMakeSound(int Hertz,double Duration)
0470  {
0471    static clock_t FormerTime=0;
0472    short Count=0;
0473    int HighByte=0, LowByte=0;
0474    unsigned char OldPort=0, NewPort=0;
0475  FormerTime= clock();
0476  if (Hertz < 40) return;
0477  if (Hertz > 4660) return;
0478  Count= 1193180L/Hertz;
0479  HighByte= Count / 256;
0480  LowByte= Count - (HighByte * 256);
0481  #if defined (BORLAND)
0482    outportb(0x43,0xB6); outportb(0x42,(unsigned char)LowByte);
0483    outportb(0x42,(unsigned char)HighByte); OldPort=inportb(0x61);
0484    NewPort=(OldPort | 0x03); outportb(0x61,NewPort);
0485    zDelay(FormerTime,Duration);
0486    outportb(0x61,OldPort);
0487  #elif defined (ZORTECH)
0488    outp(0x43,0xB6); outp(0x42,LowByte);
0489    outp(0x42,HighByte); OldPort=(unsigned char)inp(0x61);
0490    NewPort=(OldPort | 0x03); outp(0x61,(int)NewPort);
0491    zDelay(FormerTime,Duration);
0492    outp(0x61,(int)OldPort);
0493  #elif defined (MICROSOFT)
0494    outp(0x43,0xB6); outp(0x42,LowByte);
0495    outp(0x42,HighByte); OldPort=(unsigned char)inp(0x61);
0496    NewPort=(OldPort | 0x03); outp(0x61,(int)NewPort);
0497    zDelay(FormerTime,Duration);
0498    outp(0x61,(int)OldPort);
0499  #endif
0500  return;
0501  }
0502  /*
0503  ┌────────────────────────────────────────────────────────────────┐
```

4-5 Continued.

```
0504                                   Pause
0505   |_____|
0506                                                            */
0507   static clock_t zDelay(clock_t StartTime, double Wait)
0508   {                           // pause for a specified length of time.
0509      clock_t StopTime;
0510      clock_t NewClockTime;
0511   #if defined (BORLAND)
0512      StopTime= StartTime + (Wait * CLK_TCK);
0513   #elif defined (ZORTECH)
0514      StopTime= StartTime + (Wait * CLOCKS_PER_SEC);
0515   #elif defined (MICROSOFT)
0516      StopTime= StartTime + (Wait * CLK_TCK);
0517   #endif
0518   while ( clock() < StopTime ) {;}
0519   NewClockTime= clock();
0520   return NewClockTime;
0521   }
0522   /*
0523   _____
0524   |            Retrieve the command-line arguments, if any     |
0525   |_____|
0526                                                            */
0527   static void zArguments(int NumArgs, char *Arg[])
0528   {
0529   if(NumArgs==1)
0530      {
0531      CommandLineArg= zNO; return;                     // if no arg.
0532      }
0533   CommandLineCompare= strncmp(StartUpArg[0],Arg[1],5);
0534   if(CommandLineCompare==0)
0535      {
0536      CommandLineArg=zYES; Mode=zVGA_12H; return;       // /M12.
0537      }
0538   CommandLineCompare= strncmp(StartUpArg[1],Arg[1],5);
0539   if(CommandLineCompare==0)
0540      {
0541      CommandLineArg=zYES; Mode=zEGA_10H; return;       // /M10.
0542      }
0543   CommandLineCompare= strncmp(StartUpArg[2],Arg[1],5);
0544   if(CommandLineCompare==0)
0545      {
0546      CommandLineArg=zYES; Mode=zEGA_EH; return;        // /MOE.
0547      }
0548   CommandLineCompare= strncmp(StartUpArg[3],Arg[1],5);
0549   if(CommandLineCompare==0)
0550      {
0551      CommandLineArg=zYES; Mode=zMCGA_11H; return;      // /M11.
0552      }
0553   CommandLineCompare= strncmp(StartUpArg[4],Arg[1],5);
0554   if(CommandLineCompare==0)
0555      {
0556      CommandLineArg=zYES; Mode=zCGA_6H; return;        // /M06.
0557      }
0558   CommandLineCompare= strncmp(StartUpArg[5],Arg[1],5);
0559   if(CommandLineCompare==0)
0560      {
0561      CommandLineArg=zYES; Mode=zHERC; return;          // /MHC.
0562      }
0563   CommandLineArg= zNO;              // if an unrecognized argument.
0564   return;
```

```
0565   }
0566   /*
0567
0568        ┌──────────────────────────────────────────────────────────────┐
             │  Supercharged C++ Graphics  --   end of source file BLOCK.CPP │
             └──────────────────────────────────────────────────────────────┘
0569
0570                                                                      */
```

Part Two

Building 2-D graphics applications

5
Interactive GUI menu graphics

The menu system that your graphics program uses to interact with the user is called the *front end*. In addition to pull-down menus, a front end can also use GUI components like icons, dialog boxes, buttons, and so on. *GUI* is an acronym for graphical user interface.

You can easily add pull-down menus to your own C++ graphics programs by using the methods of class Bitblt, introduced in the previous chapter. The methods of this class can provide bitblts capable of displaying, moving, erasing, saving, and loading themselves. The bitblt object looks after all the housekeeping chores, such as carefully saving a copy of the background before writing a graphic array to the display.

This chapter presents a demonstration program that illustrates one way of implementing a pull-down menu system for your C++ graphics programs.

A sample program: GUI.CPP

As FIG. 5-1 shows, graphic arrays can be used to efficiently manage an interactive menu system. The demonstration program provides a menuing shell suitable as a front end to your C++ graphics programs.

Demo Figure 5-2 depicts a typical display produced by the interactive sample program GUI.CPP, whose complete source code is provided in FIG. 5-5 at the end of the chapter. The program allows you to use the keyboard to interactively control a menu bar hightlight bar, a set of pull-down menus, and a menu highlight bar.

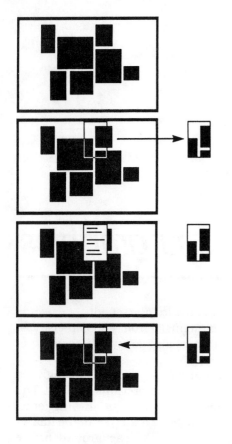

5-1 The fundamental principle underlying a GUI menu system. The background image is stored in a graphic array before the menu is drawn. When the menu is exited, the previously existing background stored in the graphic array is written back to the screen.

How to compile and link the sample program

The program listing presented in FIG. 5-5 contains the complete source code for the main module of the C++ demonstration program called "Using C++ for Menu Systems." If you are using the companion disks to the book, the source code is in the file named GUI.CPP. Three C++ source files are needed to build the finished .exe file. These are GUI.CPP from FIG. 5-5 and two of the class libraries in appendix E.

The class library that provides the language bindings and low-level graphics routines for this demonstration program is found in FIG. E-2 in appendix E. This listing contains the implementations for class PhysicalDisplay and class Viewport. If you are using the companion disks to the book, this file is named LIB2D.CPP. The class declarations are presented in FIG. E-1 in appendix E. If you are using the companion disks to the book, this file is named LIB2D.HPP.

The class library that provides the bitblt objects for this demonstration program is found in FIG. E-8 in appendix E. This listing contains the implementations for class Bitblt. If you are using the companion disks to the

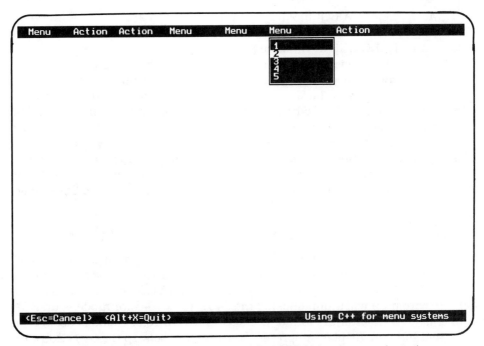

```
   Menu    Action  Action   Menu      Menu    Menu        Action
                                                1
                                                2
                                                3
                                                4
                                                5




   <Esc=Cancel>   <Alt+X=Quit>                      Using C++ for menu systems
```

5-2 Graphics output from the sample program GUI.CPP. Using the arrow keys, the user can navigate through various pull-down menus.

book, this file is named BITBLT.CPP. The class declarations are presented in FIG. E-7 in appendix E. If you are using the companion disks to the book, this file is named BITBLT.HPP.

You can compile, link, and run this demonstration program using either Turbo C++ or Borland C++. If you are using Turbo C++ refer to appendix A for help in compiling, linking, and running the demonstration program. If you are using Borland C++ see appendix B.

You should specify a Turbo C++ or Borland C++ project list to advise your compiler which source files to bind together to build the finished .exe file.

After a successful compile and link the screen will resemble the screen print shown in FIG. 5-2.

How to run the demonstration program

You need a VGA, EGA, MCGA, CGA, or Hercules graphics adapter to run this interactive demonstration program.

Using the editor to run the program

To run the program under your Turbo C++ or Borland C++ editor, ensure the finished .exe file is in the default directory. The appropriate graphics driver must be in the default directory. If you are using a VGA or EGA, the EGAVGA.BGI file must be present. If you are using an MCGA or CGA, the CGA.BGI file must be present. If you are using a Hercules graphics adapter, the HERC.BGI file must be present.

The built-in autodetect routine of the demonstration program detects the graphics hardware in your computer system and sets up the best graphics mode supported by your hardware. To override the autodetect routine use the Turbo C++ or Borland C++ editor to simulate a command line argument. The header in FIG. 5-5 provides a set of arguments that you can use to specify a graphics mode. See the appendices for further discussion. If you are using a VGA, you can override the autodetect routine and force the demonstration program to run in an EGA, MCGA, or CGA mode. If you are using an EGA, you can force the program to run in a lower-resolution EGA mode or a CGA mode.

Running the program from the operating system prompt

To start the program from the operating system prompt, simply enter GUI. The .exe file and any required graphics drivers must be present in the default directory. If the software finds a VGA present in your system, the program will animate using the $640 \times 480 \times 16$-color mode. If an EGA and enhanced monitor are found, the $640 \times 350 \times 16$-color mode is used. If an EGA and standard display are present, the program sets up the $640 \times 200 \times 16$-color mode. If an MCGA is detected, the $640 \times 480 \times 2$-color mode is employed. If a CGA is found, the $640 \times 200 \times 2$-color mode is used. If the program detects a Hercules graphics adapter, it will start up in the $720 \times 348 \times 2$-color mode.

You can force the program to start up in a different mode by adding a command line argument when you start the program from the operating system prompt. Enter GUI /M11 to force the $640 \times 480 \times 2$-color mode. Enter GUI /M10 to force the $640 \times 350 \times 16$-color mode. Entering GUI /M0E forces the program to run in the $640 \times 200 \times 16$-color mode. Entering GUI /M06 tests the demonstration program in the $640 \times 200 \times 2$-color mode.

Using the demonstration program

Use the left-arrow and right-arrow keys to pan the highlight bar to the left or right on the main menu bar. Press Enter to choose the selection currently under the highlight bar. If you have selected an Action item, the dialog line delivers a context-sensitive message, as shown in FIG. 5-3. If you select a pull-down menu, you can now use the down-arrow and up-arrow keys to scroll the highlight bar through the vertical selections in the menu, as shown in FIG. 5-4. All menu selections are inactive. In this implementation of GUI.CPP they are simply routed to a stub routine. The exception is the Quit selection in the first pull-down menu, which will terminate the program if it is selected. Alternatively, you can press Esc when you are in the main menu bar to quit the program. Pressing Esc when you are in a pull-down menu closes the menu and returns the highlight bar to the main menu bar.

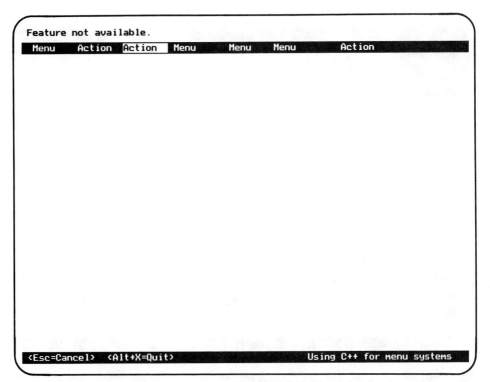

5-3 Graphics output from the sample program GUI.CPP. The dialog line located above the menu bar can be used to provide context-sensitive messages to the user.

Exercising the program

You might find it useful to start the program and work your way through each menu position. GUI.CPP is robust and difficult to crash. Every menu feature is tied to a stub routine. A text message is displayed as you try each core function. The first menu contains the only active feature, Quit.

Try holding down the right-arrow key while you are on the main menu bar. The highlight bar will continue to pan and wrap around until you release the key. Then the cursor will instantly stop, avoiding run-on. The zPurge( ) function makes this possible. The same feature is provided inside each pull-down menu.

Programmer's Guide to GUI.CPP

The complete listing for the demonstration program GUI.CPP is presented in FIG. 5-5. The source code consists of an informative header, conditional compilation directives, declaration of constants and macros, file include directives, function prototypes, variable declarations, and the executable functions.

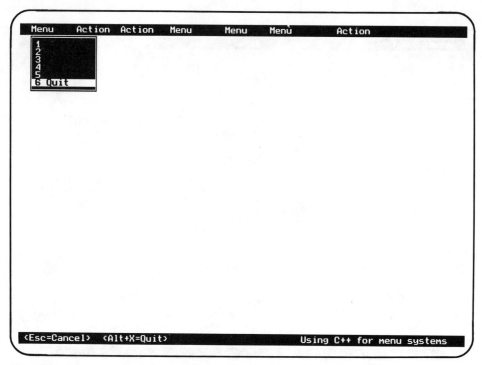

5-4 Graphics output from the sample program GUI.CPP. The Quit selection is enabled in the source code, demonstrating how to add functionality to the menu selections.

Conditional compilation

Code for conditional compilation is located at lines 0051 through 0066. If you are using Turbo C++ or Borland C++ the program is ready to compile, subject to the instructions provided in appendix B. If you are using Zortech C++ you must make substantial changes to the source code, using fg_drawmatrix ( ) to create XORable highlight bars. The source code in the demonstration program does not explicitly support Zortech C++'s Flash Graphics because the program needs to XOR graphic arrays to create the menu bar labels and to operate the highlight bars.

Constants

The C++ qualifier, const, is used to declare and assign values to constant variables at lines 0068 through 0097. The declarations and assignments at lines 0077 through 0079 are tokens that will indicate the kind of action being provided to the user. The declarations and assignments at lines 0081 through 0087 will indicate the current logical position in the menu hierarchy.

Include files

The code at lines 0105 through 0126 uses #include to load in the appropriate header files and C++ class declaration files. Line 0125 loads LIB2D.HPP, which declares the data members and methods of class PhysicalDisplay and class Viewport. Line 0126 loads BITBLT.HPP, which declares the data members and methods of class Bitblt. The methods of class Bitblt are used to display and remove the pull-down menus at runtime.

Function prototypes

Function declarations are provided in lines 0128 through 0155. These functions are visible throughout this source file and can be called by any other function in the source file. Each function is declared with the static qualifier and is not available to functions located in other source files.

Variable declarations

Lines 0157 through 0212 declare global variables that are visible throughout this source file. These variables have file scope.

Object declarations

Object The code at line 0211 creates an object from class PhysicalDisplay named Display. The program will later call the methods of this object to help it manage the display. The methods are declared in the class declaration listing LIB2D.HPP and are defined in the class implementation listing LIB2D.CPP in appendix E. The object created at line 0211 is a static object with file scope. It will remain available until the program ends. Line 0212 creates an object from the Viewport class named Viewport1. The address of Display is passed to this new object because Viewport1 uses the methods of Display to generate graphics output. The object created at line 0212 is a static object with file scope that will remain active until program termination.

main( )

The main( ) function is located at lines 0217 through 0272. The code first checks to see if any command line arguments were used to start the program. Then the code sets to an appropriate graphics mode, creates and stores various images used by the menu system, and finally calls the function that manages the interactive control of menu system.

Setting parameters for the menus

The function zSetParameters( ) at lines 0274 through 0304 defines the colors, image sizes, and other variable values used by functions that draw the menus and the sign-on screen. Note how the Mode variable is used to decide how to define the spacing variables for the panning and scrolling highlight bars.

Creating a menu bar

The function zCreateBars( ) at lines 0306 through 0354 creates the main menu bar with its white reverse labels, the help bar at the bottom of the screen, and some other text labels. The strcpy( ) function is used to load a text string into the variable Text3, which is in turn used to write the text string to the screen. The main menu bar is created by first saving the text labels in an array at line 0333. A filled rectangle is then created on the screen and the text array is XOR'd onto the rectangle at line 0335. The finished image is then saved in an array at line 0336.

Creating the menus

The function zCreateMenus( ) at lines 0356 through 0464 creates and stores the pull-down menus for the program. Each line that begins with the strcpy( ) instruction can be modified to change the selections list of any pull-down menu. To create a menu, the code first saves the text in a graphic array. Then a bordered rectangle is drawn. The graphic array containing the text is XOR'd onto the rectangle and the bitblt object is deleted. The finished image is then saved in a new bitblt object, ready to be used by the menu manager loop later in the source code.

Creating the highlight bars

The function zCreateHiBars( ) at lines 0466 through 0494 creates the panning and scrolling highlight bars used by the menu system. These are filled rectangles which are saved as graphic arrays. The highlight bar that pans horizontally across the main menu bar is named PanBar. The highlight bar that scrolls vertically through the pull-down menus is named ScrollBar.

Creating the sign-on screen

The function zDrawScreen( ) at lines 0496 through 0516 draws the user interface. Note how the graphic arrays that hold the main menu bar and the help bar are written to the screen at lines 0505 and 0512.

Managing the main menu bar

The function at lines 0620 through 0711 in the source code is a loop responsible for managing the highlight bar on the main menu bar. The beginning of this loop is at line 0629. Label LOOP0 is at the start of a loop that manages the pull-down menus.

Moving the highlight bar

The function zPanning( ) at lines 0713 through 0747 moves the highlight bar left and right along the main menu bar. Because this bitblt image is XOR'd onto the screen, the underlying labels on the menu bar remain visible. Note how px1, px2, px3, px4, px5, px6, and px7 are used to update the horizontal position of the panning bar.

Because the switch( ) function at line 0721 uses the PanPosition token to describe the logical position of the highlight bar on the menu bar, this function can pan either left or right. The if( ) statement is used at lines 0719 and 0720 to handle wraparounds at each end of the panning highlight bar.

Installing a pull-down menu

The function zInstallMenu( ) at lines 0749 through 0800 installs a menu on the screen. The variables Selection and PanPosition control which menu is to be used. They also control the coordinate scrolling position of the highlight bar.

The switch( ) statement at line 0757 is used to branch to the appropriate code for each of the supported menu positions. Note how zStubRoutine( ) is used as a placeholder for future code.

Because the methods of class Bitblt are used to write a menu to the display, all the low-level work of saving the background is taken care of by the bitblt object itself.

Removing a pull-down menu

The function zUninstallMenu( ) at lines 0802 through 0815 removes a pull-down menu from the screen by calling method EraseImage( ) of class Bitblt. Refer back to chapter 4 for a thorough discussion of the bitblt capabilities of this class.

Navigating between menus

The function zPanMenu( ) at lines 0818 through 0865 allows you to jump from one menu directly to another by using the left-arrow and right-arrow keys. This is accomplished by using the PanPosition variable to keep track of the active menu.

Scrolling through menu selections

The function zScrolling( ) at lines 0867 through 0903 manages the scrolling highlight bar on the pull-down menus. This routine can handle menus of different sizes because variables and not constants are used to control wraparound situations.

Calling the core functions

The function zMenuChoices( ) at lines 0905 through 0957 calls various core graphics functions. Nested switch( ) functions are used to run this switching operation. At present zMenuChoices( ) repeatedly calls zStubRoutine( ). You can substitute a call to your own graphics functions when you use GUI.C as a front end to your own C++ graphics program.

Terminating the program

The function at lines 0518 through 0533 calls a method of class PhysicalDisplay to terminate the graphics state. Before doing so, however, note how it uses a method of class Viewport to free the memory used by the highlight bar graphic arrays. In lines 0525 through 0528 the C++ delete operator is used to destroy the pull-down menu objects. Finally, line 0532 returns an OK code to the operating system.

The Startup( ) function

The function at lines 0535 through 0618 uses the SetupMode( ) method of class PhysicalDisplay to detect the graphics hardware. Refer back to chapter 1 for a more detailed discussion of this function.

The StubRoutine( ) function

The stub routine at lines 0959 through 0970 is a do-nothing routine that displays a simple message on the dialog line at the top of the display. The stub is called whenever the user chooses a selection that is not implemented. The variable Text4 was defined in line 0208 as ''Feature not available.''

Clearing the dialog line

The function at lines 0972 through 0982 clears the dialog line. It first calls methods of class PhysicalDisplay to set the current drawing color, the current line style, and the current fill style. It then calls method ClearTextLine( ) of class Viewport, which uses a solid rectangle to clear the dialog area.

Displaying the ready prompt

The function at lines 0985 through 0993 uses method PutText( ) of class Viewport to write a string to the dialog line. The variable Text5 was defined earlier at line 0209 as a character string: ''C++ menu system ready for your next command.''

The keystroke loops

The function at lines 0995 through 1019 relies upon the switch( ) statement to handle incoming keystrokes when the program is at the menu bar level. Note the use of the default label at lines 1010 and 1018. These lines ensure that any key not explicitly supported in the switch( ) block will generate an audio cue. The function at lines 1022 through 1045 manages inbound keystrokes when the program is displaying a pull-down menu. Both of these two loop functions are called after the standard navigating keys have been tested for by the menu manager function at lines 0620 through 0711.

The Keyboard( ) function

The function at lines 1047 through 1071 detects and retrieves keystrokes from the keyboard buffer. The function at lines 1074 through 1083 repeatedly calls the keyboard function until the keyboard buffer is empty. This ensures no unwanted keystrokes remain in the buffer after the user has held down an arrow key to rapidly move the highlight bar. When the user releases the key, the highlight bar will stop immediately. The zPurge( ) function is an effective way to avoid cursor run-on.

The MakeSound( ) function

The zMakeSound( ) function at lines 1085 through 1115 generates a sound from the system speaker. This function is called by the stub routine, which is in turn called whenever an unimplemented menu item is selected by the user.

The Pause( ) function

The function at lines 1117 through 1129 pauses program execution. The code uses the value returned by the system clock and multiplies it by the number of ticks per second. If you are using Turbo C++ or Borland C++, this value is represented by the global variable CLK_TCK. If you are using Zortech C++ it is represented by CLOCKS_PER_SEC. The sleep( ) library function of Turbo C++ and Borland C++ can be used instead of this function.

The Arguments( ) function

The function at lines 1131 through 1173 compares the command line argument with a set of legal strings. The function assigns an appropriate value to the global variable named Mode, which is used by other functions that produce graphics output.

Programmer's Guide to LIB2D.HPP

Code The complete source code for the declarations for class PhysicalDisplay and class Viewport is found in LIB2D.HPP in appendix E. The source from LIB2D.HPP must be #included at the beginning of any program that wishes to use the methods of class PhysicalDisplay or class Viewport. See the discussion in chapter 1 for more information about LIB2D.HPP.

Programmer's Guide to LIB2D.CPP

Code The source code in LIB2D.CPP, presented in appendix E, provides language bindings that produce low-level graphics. The routines in LIB2D.CPP call the appropriate runtime library functions in Turbo C++'s graphics.lib, Borland C++'s graphics.lib, Zortech C++'s fg.lib, or Microsoft's graph.lib.

LIB2D.CPP is the class implementation listing for class PhysicalDisplay and class Viewport. Class PhysicalDisplay manages the state of the display. Class Viewport is responsible for maintaining a viewport and producing low-level graphics. These two classes generate nearly all the low-level graphics required by the demonstration programs in the book. See the discussion in chapter 1 for further information about class PhysicalDisplay and class Viewport.

Programmer's Guide to BITBLT.HPP

Code The complete source code for the declarations for class Bitblt is found in BITBLT.HPP in appendix E. The source from BITBLT.HPP must be #included at the beginning of any program that wishes to use the methods of class Bitblt. See the discussion in chapter 4 for more information about BITBLT.HPP.

Programmer's Guide to BITBLT.CPP

Code The source code in BITBLT.CPP, presented in appendix E, provides methods to manage bitblt capable of displaying, moving, erasing, saving, and loading themselves. The routines in BITBLT.CPP call methods of class PhysicalDisplay and class Viewport in LIB2D.CPP. Refer to chapter 4 for a more detailed discussion of the methods of class Bitblt.

5-5 Sample program GUI.CPP. Supports VGA, EGA, MCGA, CGA, and Hercules adapters. This application demonstrates how to use C++ bitblt objects to build an interactive menu system.

```
0001   /*
0002
0003              Lee Adams' SUPERCHARGED C++ GRAPHICS
0004       Interactive demo:  classes and objects for menuing interfaces
0005
0006       SOURCE FILE:  GUI.CPP
0007              TYPE:  C++ source file for a multimodule application.
0008           PURPOSE:  Demonstrates fundamental classes that can
0009                     be used to control a graphical user interface
0010                     (GUI) or menu-driven front end.  This demo
0011                     program can be used as a template to build
0012                     more advanced 2D, 3D, or animated applications.
0013      PROGRAM LIST:  GUI.CPP, BITBLT.CPP, and LIB2D.CPP.
0014         LANGUAGES:  Turbo C++, Borland C++, and all C++ compilers
0015                     compatible with AT&T C++ 2.0 specification;
0016                     and nominal compatibility with Microsoft C++
```

```
0017                        (see the discussion in the book).
0018      MEMORY MODEL:    large.
0019      COMMAND-LINE:    you can specify a graphics mode by using the
0020                        command-line argument /Mnn as shown below:
0021                             /M12  640x480x16-color VGA
0022                             /M11  640x480x2-color VGA, MCGA
0023                             /M10  640x350x16-color VGA, EGA
0024                             /M0E  640x200x16-color VGA, EGA
0025                             /M06  640x200x2-color VGA, MCGA, EGA, CGA
0026                             /MHC  720x348x2-color Hercules
0027                        If no command-line argument is used, hardware
0028                        autodetect is used to select the best mode.
0029      OUTPUT:   You can use the keyboard to navigate through various
0030                pull-down menus in an interactive GUI menuing system.
0031                Context-sensitive messages appear on the dialog line
0032                when you make a selection.
0033      LICENSE:  As purchaser of the book in which this source code
0034         appears you are granted a royalty-free license to reproduce
0035         and distribute executable files generated using this code
0036         provided that you accept the conditions of the License
0037         Agreement and Limited Warranty described in the book.
0038      PUBLICATION: Contains material from Windcrest/McGraw-Hill
0039         book 3489, published by TAB BOOKS.
0040      U.S. GOVERNMENT RESTRICTED RIGHTS:  This software and its
0041         documentation is provided with restricted rights.  The use,
0042         duplication, or disclosure by the Government is subject to
0043         restrictions set forth in subdivision (b)(3)(ii) of The
0044         Rights in Technical Data and Computer Software clause at
0045         252.227-7013.  Contractor/manufacturer is Lee Adams, c/o
0046         TAB BOOKS, 13311 Monterey Ave., Blue Ridge Summit PA 17294.
0047      TRADEMARK:  Lee Adams is a trademark of Lee Adams.
0048
0049      Copyright 1991 Lee Adams.  All rights reserved worldwide.
0050
0051
0052                    CONDITIONAL COMPILATION
0053      To compile only those blocks of code that support the C++
0054      compiler and graphics library that you are using, you should
0055      #define the appropriate tokens on lines 0065 and 0066.
0056            GRAPHICS LIBRARY
0057         Borland's graphics.lib              #define BGI
0058         Microsoft's graph.lib               #define MS
0059                COMPILER
0060         Borland Turbo C++ compiler          #define BORLAND
0061         AT&T-compatible C++ compilers        #define MICROSOFT
0062      Be sure you define only one compiler and one graphics library.
0063
0064                                                                    */
0065   #define BGI     1  // indicates the graphics library you are using.
0066   #define BORLAND 1  // indicates the C++ compiler you are using.
0067   /*
0068
0069                           Constants
0070
0071                                                                    */
0072   const int zFAIL=     0;                   // boolean tokens...
0073   const int zEMPTY=    0;
0074   const int zYES=      1;
0075   const int zNO=       0;
0076
0077   const int zACTIVE=   1;                   // navigation tokens...
0078   const int zBACKOUT=  2;
0079   const int zSTUB=     3;
```

```
0080
0081   const int zMENU1=     1;                   // menu heirarchy tokens...
0082   const int zACTION1=   2;
0083   const int zACTION2=   3;
0084   const int zMENU2=     4;
0085   const int zMENU3=     5;
0086   const int zMENU4=     6;
0087   const int zACTION3=   7;
0088
0089   const int zVGA_12H=   1;                   // graphics mode tokens...
0090   const int zEGA_10H=   2;
0091   const int zEGA_EH=    3;
0092   const int zMCGA_11H=  4;
0093   const int zCGA_6H=    5;
0094   const int zHERC=      6;
0095
0096   const int FILTER=     1;                   // bitblt logic tokens...
0097   const int OVERWRITE= 0;
0098   /*
0099
0100   ┌─────────────────────────────────────────────────────────────┐
       │                         Macros                              │
0101   └─────────────────────────────────────────────────────────────┘
0102                                                               */
0103   #define Wait_for_any_key  while(KeyCode==0) zKeyboard(); KeyCode=0;
0104   /*
0105
0106   ┌─────────────────────────────────────────────────────────────┐
       │                      Include files                          │
0107   └─────────────────────────────────────────────────────────────┘
0108                                                               */
0109   #if defined (BORLAND)
0110   #include <time.h>        // supports clock().
0111   #include <string.h>      // supports strncmp().
0112   #include <bios.h>        // supports bioskey().
0113   #include <process.h>     // supports exit().
0114   #include <iostream.h>    // supports cout.
0115   #include <dos.h>         // supports outportb(), inportb().
0116   #elif defined (MICROSOFT)
0117   #include <time.h>        // supports clock().
0118   #include <string.h>      // supports strncmp().
0119   #include <bios.h>        // supports _bios_keybrd().
0120   #include <process.h>     // supports exit().
0121   #include <iostream.h>    // supports cout.
0122   #include <conio.h>       // supports outp(), inp().
0123   #endif
0124
0125   #include "LIB2D.HPP"     // declarations for PhysicalDisplay class.
0126   #include "BITBLT.HPP"             // declarations for Bitblt class.
0127   /*
0128
0129   ┌─────────────────────────────────────────────────────────────┐
       │        Prototypes for functions visible throughout this file │
0130   └─────────────────────────────────────────────────────────────┘
0131                                                               */
0132   static void zStartup(void);          // initializes a graphics mode.
0133   static void zArguments(int, char far* far*);   // checks arguments.
0134   static void zKeyboard(void);              // checks for a keystroke.
0135   static void zQuit_Pgm(void);          // ends the program gracefully.
0136   static void zSetParameters(void);       // assignments for interface.
0137   static void zDrawScreen(void);  // creates user interface graphics.
0138   static void zCreateBars(void);                // creates menu bars.
0139   static void zCreateMenus(void);      // creates the pull-down menus.
0140   static void zCreateHiBars(void);      // creates the highlight bars.
0141   static void zMenuBarLoop(void); // manages menu system at run-time.
```

```
0142    static void zMenuBarKeys(void);   // manages keys at menu bar level.
0143    static void zPanning(void);        // moves the panning highlight bar.
0144    static void zPurge(void);          // empties the keyboard buffer.
0145    static void zInstallMenu(void);    // installs a menu.
0146    static void zUninstallMenu(void);  // removes a menu.
0147    static void zPanMenu(void);        // manages cross-menu panning.
0148    static void zScrolling(void);      // manages scrolling highlight bar.
0149    static void zDropMenuKeys(void);   // manages keys for menus.
0150    static void zMenuChoices(void);    // calls functions for menus.
0151    static void zStubRoutine(void);    // do-nothing stub.
0152    static void zMenuBarText(void);    // back-out stub for prototyping.
0153    static void zMakeSound(int,double);    // makes a sound.
0154    static clock_t zDelay(clock_t,double);    // CPU-independent pause.
0155    static void zClearTextLine(void);  // blanks the dialog text line.
0156    /*
0157
0158    ┌─────────────────────────────────────────────────────────────┐
        │    Declarations of variables visible throughout this file     │
        └─────────────────────────────────────────────────────────────┘
0159
0160                                                                   */
0161    static char *StartUpArg[6]=        // legal command-line arguments.
0162            { "/M12", "/M10", "/MOE", "/M11", "/MO6", "/MHC" };
0163    static int CommandLineArg=zNO;     // indicates if argument exists.
0164    static int CommandLineCompare=0;   // indicates if argument legal.
0165    static int C0=0,C1=1,C2=2,C3=3,C4=4,C5=5,C6=6,
0166            C7=7,C8=8,C9=9,C10=10,C11=11,C12=12,C13=13,
0167            C14=14,C15=15;             // palette index codes.
0168    static int Mode=0;                 // which graphics mode is being used.
0169    static int Result=0;               // captures result of graphics routines.
0170    static int CharWidth=0, CharHeight=0;    // dimensions of character.
0171    static char KeyCode=0;    // token for normal or extended keystroke.
0172    static char KeyNum=0;              // ASCII number of keystroke.
0173    static char SolidFill[]=
0174                {255,255,255,255,255,255,255,255};    // 100% fill.
0175    static int FontClr=7;              // font color for regular text.
0176    static int PromptClr=7;            // font color for prompt text.
0177    static char Copyright[]=
0178                "Copyright 1991 Lee Adams.  All rights reserved.";
0179    static char Title[]=
0180      "USING C++ TO MANAGE A GUI MENU SYSTEM";
0181    static char PressAnyKey[]= "Press any key to continue.";
0182    static char StubMessage[]= "The generic stub routine was called.";
0183    static int X_Res=0, Y_Res=0;                  // screen resolution.
0184    Bitblt *Menu1;          // uninitialized ptrs to bitblt objects...
0185    Bitblt *Menu2;
0186    Bitblt *Menu3;
0187    Bitblt *Menu4;
0188    int x1=0,y1=0,x2=0,y2=0;           // coords for graphic array saves.
0189    int PanPosition=1;                 // panning bar position indicator.
0190    char far *MenuBarBitBlt;           // menu bar graphic array.
0191    char far *HelpBarBitBlt;           // help bar graphic array.
0192    char far *PanBar;                  // panning highlight bar.
0193    char far *ScrollBar;               // scrolling highlight bar.
0194    int BarClr=7,BgClr=1,TextClr=7,MenuClr=7;    // interface colors.
0195    int p1=0,p2=0;            // install coords for panning highlight bar.
0196    int px1=0,px2=0,px3=0,px4=0,px5=0,px6=0,px7=0;    // pan coords.
0197    int py1=0,py2=0,py3=0,py4=0,py5=0,py6=0;    // scroll coords.
0198    int Selection=0;            // position of scrolling highlight bar.
0199    int MaxSelection=0;         // number of choices in active menu.
0200    int p3=0,p4=0;              // xy install coords for active menu.
0201    int p5=0,p6=0;              // xy coords for scrolling highlight bar.
0202    int Status=0;                      // status of menus logic.
0203    int Choice=0;       // flag to indicate user-selected core function.
0204    int Installed=0;    // flag to indicate which object is displayed.
```

5-5 Continued.

```
0205   char Text1[]= "Copyright 1991 Lee Adams. All rights reserved.";
0206   char Text2[]= "Using C++ for menu systems";
0207   char Text3[]= "                    ";   // empty string for building menus.
0208   char Text4[]= "Feature not available.";
0209   char Text5[]= "C++ menu system ready for your next command.";
0210
0211   PhysicalDisplay Display;              // the physical display object.
0212   Viewport Viewport1(&Display);              // a viewport object.
0213   /*
0214
0215   ┌──────────────────────────────────────────────────────────┐
       │                  Function definitions                      │
0216   └──────────────────────────────────────────────────────────┘
0217
0218   ┌──────────────────────────────────────────────────────────┐
       │     The executive routine:  program execution begins here  │
0219   └──────────────────────────────────────────────────────────┘
0220                                                              */
0221   main(int argc, char *argv[])
0222   {
0223     int NumArgs; char far* far* Arg;
0224
0225   NumArgs= argc;                         // grab number of arguments.
0226   Arg= &argv[0];                  // grab address of array of arguments.
0227   zArguments(NumArgs, Arg);       // check the command-line arguments.
0228
0229   zStartup();                        // establish the graphics mode.
0230   Display.Init2D(Mode,0,0,X_Res-1,Y_Res-1);    // set graphics state.
0231   Result= Display.InitUndo();   // create hidden page (unused here).
0232   if (Result==zFAIL) zQuit_Pgm();        // if hidden page failed.
0233
0234   Display.BlankPage();                     // clear the display.
0235   Display.SetHue(C7);                   // set the drawing color.
0236   Display.SetFill(SolidFill,C7);           // set the fill style.
0237   Viewport1.PutText(3,2,FontClr,Title);        // sign-on notice.
0238   Viewport1.PutText(4,2,FontClr,Copyright);    // copyright notice.
0239   switch (Mode)
0240     {            // notify user which display mode is being used...
0241     case zVGA_12H:  Viewport1.PutText(6,2,FontClr,
0242                     "Using the 640x480x16-color VGA mode.");
0243                     break;
0244     case zEGA_10H:  Viewport1.PutText(6,2,FontClr,
0245                     "Using the 640x350x16-color VGA and EGA mode.");
0246                     break;
0247     case zEGA_EH:   Viewport1.PutText(6,2,FontClr,
0248                     "Using the 640x200x16-color VGA and EGA mode.");
0249                     break;
0250     case zMCGA_11H: Viewport1.PutText(6,2,FontClr,
0251                     "Using the 640x480x2-color VGA and MCGA mode.");
0252                     break;
0253     case zCGA_6H:   Viewport1.PutText(6,2,FontClr,
0254                     "Using the 640x200x2-color CGA mode.");
0255                     break;
0256     case zHERC:     Viewport1.PutText(6,2,FontClr,
0257                     "Using the 720x348x2-color Hercules mode.");
0258     }
0259   Viewport1.DrawBorder(0,0,X_Res-1,Y_Res-1);       // draw a border.
0260   Viewport1.PutText(8,2,PromptClr,PressAnyKey);    // show a prompt.
0261   Wait_for_any_key   // this macro was defined earlier at line 0110.
0262
0263   zSetParameters();        // defines menu system sizes and colors.
0264   zCreateBars();                       // creates the menu bars.
0265   zCreateMenus();              // creates the pull-down menus.
```

```
0266  zCreateHiBars();    // creates panning and scrolling highlight bars.
0267  zDrawScreen();                       // builds the sign-on screen.
0268
0269  zMenuBarLoop();                      // activate the menu system.
0270
0271  zQuit_Pgm();             // tidy up and terminate the application.
0272  }
0273  /*
0274
0275  ┌─────────────────────────────────────────────────────────────┐
      │          Assign sizes and colors for the interface           │
0276  └─────────────────────────────────────────────────────────────┘
0277                                                               */
0278  static void zSetParameters(void)
0279  {
0280  if (Mode==zMCGA_11H) BgClr= C0;
0281  if (Mode==zCGA_6H) BgClr= C0;
0282  if (Mode==zHERC) BgClr= C0;
0283  if (Mode==zHERC)
0284    {                                 // device-dependent pan spacing.
0285    px1= 17; px2= 89; px3= 161; px4= 242;
0286    px5= 332; px6= 405; px7= 512;
0287    }
0288  else
0289    {
0290    px1= 15; px2= 79; px3= 143; px4= 215;
0291    px5= 295; px6= 359; px7= 455;
0292    }
0293  p1= px1; p2= 15;     // initialize coords for panning highlight bar.
0294  if (Mode==zHERC)
0295    {                              // device-dependent scroll spacing.
0296    py1= 38; py2= 52; py3= 66; py4= 80; py5= 94; py6= 108;
0297    }
0298  else
0299    {
0300    py1= 32; py2= 40; py3= 48; py4= 56; py5= 64; py6= 72;
0301    }
0302  p4= py1-6;                    // y coord for level 1 pull-down menus.
0303  return;
0304  }
0305  /*
0306
0307  ┌─────────────────────────────────────────────────────────────┐
      │                 Create various bar graphics                  │
0308  └─────────────────────────────────────────────────────────────┘
0309                                                               */
0310  static void zCreateBars(void)
0311  {
0312  Display.BlankPage();              // step one:  create the menu bar.
0313  Display.SetHue(BarClr);
0314  Display.SetFill(SolidFill,BarClr);
0315  strcpy(Text3,"Menu");
0316  Viewport1.PutText(2,3,TextClr,Text3);
0317  strcpy(Text3,"Action");
0318  Viewport1.PutText(2,11,TextClr,Text3);
0319  strcpy(Text3,"Action");
0320  Viewport1.PutText(2,19,TextClr,Text3);
0321  strcpy(Text3,"Menu");
0322  Viewport1.PutText(2,28,TextClr,Text3);
0323  strcpy(Text3,"Menu");
0324  Viewport1.PutText(2,38,TextClr,Text3);
0325  strcpy(Text3,"Menu");
0326  Viewport1.PutText(2,46,TextClr,Text3);
0327  strcpy(Text3,"Action");
0328  Viewport1.PutText(2,58,TextClr,Text3);
```

5-5 Continued.

```
0329
0330    x1= 0; y1= CharHeight - 2;                        // upper left coords.
0331    x2= X_Res-1; y2= (CharHeight*2)+1;               // lower right coords.
0332    MenuBarBitBlt= Viewport1.MemBlock(x1,y1,x2,y2); // allocate memory.
0333    Viewport1.GetBlock(x1,y1,x2,y2,MenuBarBitBlt);
0334    Viewport1.DrawPanel(x1,y1,x2,y2);
0335    Viewport1.PutXOR(x1,y1,MenuBarBitBlt);
0336    Viewport1.GetBlock(x1,y1,x2,y2,MenuBarBitBlt);    // store menu bar.
0337
0338    Display.BlankPage();                // step two:  create the help bar.
0339    strcpy(Text3,"<Esc=Cancel>");
0340    Viewport1.PutText(4,2,TextClr,Text3);
0341    strcpy(Text3,"<Alt+X=Quit>");
0342    Viewport1.PutText(4,16,TextClr,Text3);
0343    Viewport1.PutText(4,52,TextClr,Text2);
0344    x1= 0; y1= (CharHeight*3)-2;
0345    x2= X_Res-1; y2= (CharHeight*4)+1;
0346    HelpBarBitBlt= Viewport1.MemBlock(x1,y1,x2,y2); // allocate memory.
0347    Viewport1.GetBlock(x1,y1,x2,y2,HelpBarBitBlt);
0348    Viewport1.DrawPanel(x1,y1,x2,y2);
0349    Viewport1.PutXOR(x1,y1,HelpBarBitBlt);
0350    Viewport1.GetBlock(x1,y1,x2,y2,HelpBarBitBlt);    // store help bar.
0351
0352    Display.BlankPage();                    // blank the display and return.
0353    return;
0354    }
0355    /*
0356
0357    ┌─────────────────────────────────────────────────────┐
           │              Create the drop-down menus               │
0358    └─────────────────────────────────────────────────────┘
0359                                                              */
0360    static void zCreateMenus(void){
0361    strcpy(Text3,"1");
0362    Viewport1.PutText(2,4,TextClr,Text3);
0363    strcpy(Text3,"2");
0364    Viewport1.PutText(3,4,TextClr,Text3);
0365    strcpy(Text3,"3");
0366    Viewport1.PutText(4,4,TextClr,Text3);
0367    strcpy(Text3,"4");
0368    Viewport1.PutText(5,4,TextClr,Text3);
0369    strcpy(Text3,"5");
0370    Viewport1.PutText(6,4,TextClr,Text3);
0371    strcpy(Text3,"6 Quit");
0372    Viewport1.PutText(7,4,TextClr,Text3);
0373    x1= CharWidth*2; y1= CharHeight-6;
0374    x2= x1+((CharWidth*12)-1); y2= y1+((CharHeight*6)+11);
0375    Bitblt *MenuTemp1=              // create a temporary bitblt object...
0376       new Bitblt(x1,y1,x2,y2,X_Res,Y_Res,&Viewport1);
0377    MenuTemp1->GrabImage();                   // ...and grab a screen image.
0378    Display.SetHue(MenuClr); Display.SetFill(SolidFill,MenuClr);
0379    Viewport1.DrawPanel(x1,y1,x2,y2);                        // menu panel.
0380    Display.SetHue(C0);
0381    Viewport1.DrawBorder(x1+2,y1+2,x2-2,y2-2);               // rule trim.
0382    Viewport1.DrawBorder(x1,y1,x2,y2);                     // border trim.
0383    MenuTemp1->DisplayImage(x1,y1,FILTER);       // xor text onto menu.
0384    delete MenuTemp1;                   // destroy the temporary object.
0385    Bitblt *MenuA=                          // create menu 1 object...
0386       new Bitblt(x1,y1,x2,y2,X_Res,Y_Res,&Viewport1);
0387    MenuA->GrabImage();              // ...and initialize it with an image.
0388    Menu1= MenuA;                  // initialize the file-scope pointer.
0389    Display.BlankPage();
0390
```

```
0391  strcpy(Text3,"1");
0392  Viewport1.PutText(2,4,TextClr,Text3);
0393  strcpy(Text3,"2");
0394  Viewport1.PutText(3,4,TextClr,Text3);
0395  strcpy(Text3,"3");
0396  Viewport1.PutText(4,4,TextClr,Text3);
0397  strcpy(Text3,"4");
0398  Viewport1.PutText(5,4,TextClr,Text3);
0399  y2= y2-(CharHeight*2);
0400  Bitblt *MenuTemp2= new Bitblt(x1,y1,x2,y2,X_Res,Y_Res,&Viewport1);
0401  MenuTemp2->GrabImage();
0402  Display.SetHue(MenuClr);
0403  Display.SetFill(SolidFill,MenuClr);
0404  Viewport1.DrawPanel(x1,y1,x2,y2);
0405  Display.SetHue(C0);
0406  Viewport1.DrawBorder(x1+2,y1+2,x2-2,y2-2);
0407  Viewport1.DrawBorder(x1,y1,x2,y2);
0408  MenuTemp2->DisplayImage(x1,y1,FILTER);
0409  delete MenuTemp2;
0410  Bitblt *MenuB= new Bitblt(x1,y1,x2,y2,X_Res,Y_Res,&Viewport1);
0411  MenuB->GrabImage();
0412  Menu2= MenuB;
0413  Display.BlankPage();
0414
0415  strcpy(Text3,"1");
0416  Viewport1.PutText(2,4,TextClr,Text3);
0417  strcpy(Text3,"2");
0418  Viewport1.PutText(3,4,TextClr,Text3);
0419  strcpy(Text3,"3");
0420  Viewport1.PutText(4,4,TextClr,Text3);
0421  strcpy(Text3,"4");
0422  Viewport1.PutText(5,4,TextClr,Text3);
0423  Bitblt *MenuTemp3= new Bitblt(x1,y1,x2,y2,X_Res,Y_Res,&Viewport1);
0424  MenuTemp3->GrabImage();
0425  Display.SetHue(MenuClr);
0426  Display.SetFill(SolidFill,MenuClr);
0427  Viewport1.DrawPanel(x1,y1,x2,y2);
0428  Display.SetHue(C0);
0429  Viewport1.DrawBorder(x1+2,y1+2,x2-2,y2-2);
0430  Viewport1.DrawBorder(x1,y1,x2,y2);
0431  MenuTemp3->DisplayImage(x1,y1,FILTER);
0432  delete MenuTemp3;
0433  Bitblt *MenuC= new Bitblt(x1,y1,x2,y2,X_Res,Y_Res,&Viewport1);
0434  MenuC->GrabImage();
0435  Menu3= MenuC;
0436  Display.BlankPage();
0437
0438  strcpy(Text3,"1");
0439  Viewport1.PutText(2,4,TextClr,Text3);
0440  strcpy(Text3,"2");
0441  Viewport1.PutText(3,4,TextClr,Text3);
0442  strcpy(Text3,"3");
0443  Viewport1.PutText(4,4,TextClr,Text3);
0444  strcpy(Text3,"4");
0445  Viewport1.PutText(5,4,TextClr,Text3);
0446  strcpy(Text3,"5");
0447  Viewport1.PutText(6,4,TextClr,Text3);
0448  y2= y2+CharHeight;
0449  Bitblt *MenuTemp4= new Bitblt(x1,y1,x2,y2,X_Res,Y_Res,&Viewport1);
0450  MenuTemp4->GrabImage();
0451  Display.SetHue(MenuClr);
0452  Display.SetFill(SolidFill,MenuClr);
0453  Viewport1.DrawPanel(x1,y1,x2,y2);
```

```
0454   Display.SetHue(C0);
0455   Viewport1.DrawBorder(x1+2,y1+2,x2-2,y2-2);
0456   Viewport1.DrawBorder(x1,y1,x2,y2);
0457   MenuTemp4->DisplayImage(x1,y1,FILTER);
0458   delete MenuTemp4;
0459   Bitblt *MenuD= new Bitblt(x1,y1,x2,y2,X_Res,Y_Res,&Viewport1);
0460   MenuD->GrabImage();
0461   Menu4= MenuD;
0462   Display.BlankPage();
0463   return;
0464   }
0465   /*
0466
0467   ┌──────────────────────────────────────────────────────────────┐
       │              Create the highlight bars                         │
0468   └──────────────────────────────────────────────────────────────┘
0469                                                                  */
0470   static void zCreateHiBars(void)
0471   {
0472   Display.SetHue(BarClr);
0473   Display.SetFill(SolidFill,BarClr);
0474   x1= 0; y1= 0;
0475   x2= (CharWidth*8)-1; y2= CharHeight+1;
0476   Viewport1.DrawPanel(x1,y1,x2,y2);
0477   PanBar= Viewport1.MemBlock(x1,y1,x2,y2);
0478   Viewport1.GetBlock(x1,y1,x2,y2,PanBar);        // store panning bar.
0479   x1= 0; y1= 0;
0480   if (Mode==zHERC)
0481     {
0482     x2= (CharWidth*11)+2;
0483     }
0484   else
0485     {
0486     x2= (CharWidth*11)+1;
0487     }
0488   y2= CharHeight-1;
0489   Viewport1.DrawPanel(x1,y1,x2,y2);
0490   ScrollBar=Viewport1.MemBlock(x1,y1,x2,y2);
0491   Viewport1.GetBlock(x1,y1,x2,y2,ScrollBar);  // store scrolling bar.
0492   Display.BlankPage();
0493   return;
0494   }
0495   /*
0496
0497   ┌──────────────────────────────────────────────────────────────┐
       │              Create the sign-on screen                         │
0498   └──────────────────────────────────────────────────────────────┘
0499                                                                  */
0500   static void zDrawScreen(void)
0501   {
0502   Display.SetHue(BgClr);
0503   Display.SetFill(SolidFill,BgClr);
0504   Viewport1.DrawPanel(0,14,X_Res-1,Y_Res-1);        // active window.
0505   Viewport1.PutPSET(0,14,MenuBarBitBlt);           // install menu bar.
0506   if (Mode==zHERC)
0507     {
0508     Viewport1.PutPSET(0,Y_Res-18,HelpBarBitBlt);
0509     }
0510   else
0511     {
0512     Viewport1.PutPSET(0,Y_Res-12,HelpBarBitBlt); // install help bar.
0513     }
0514   Viewport1.PutText(1,2,TextClr,Text1);             // Menu system ready.
0515   return;
```

```
0516  }
0517  /*
0518  ┌─────────────────────────────────────────────────────────────┐
0519  │                  Terminate the program                       │
0520  │                                                             │
0521  └─────────────────────────────────────────────────────────────┘    */
0522  static void zQuit_Pgm(void){
0523  Viewport1.FreeBlock(ScrollBar);            // deallocate memory...
0524  Viewport1.FreeBlock(PanBar);
0525  delete Menu4;                      // destroy menu objects...
0526  delete Menu3;
0527  delete Menu2;
0528  delete Menu1;
0529  Viewport1.FreeBlock(HelpBarBitBlt);        // deallocate memory...
0530  Viewport1.FreeBlock(MenuBarBitBlt);
0531  Display.ShutDownGraphics();  // graceful shutdown of graphics mode.
0532  exit(0);              // terminate the program and return an OK code.
0533  }
0534  /*
0535  ┌─────────────────────────────────────────────────────────────┐
0536  │         Detect the graphics hardware and set the            │
0537  │ highest most permitted by the graphics adapter and monitor. │
0538  │ The user can override the autodetect algorithm by providing │
0539  │ an argument on the command-line when the program is started. │
0540  │                                                             │
0541  └─────────────────────────────────────────────────────────────┘    */
0542  static void zStartup(void)
0543  {
0544    int DefaultMode;
0545  DefaultMode= Display.SetupMode();   // get results of autodetect...
0546  switch(DefaultMode)             // ...and jump to appropriate code.
0547    {
0548    case zFAIL:        goto ABORT_PGM;
0549    case zVGA_12H:     goto VGA_mode;
0550    case zEGA_10H:     goto EGA_ECD_mode;
0551    case zEGA_EH:      goto EGA_SCD_mode;
0552    case zMCGA_11H:    goto MCGA_mode;
0553    case zCGA_6H:      goto CGA_mode;
0554    case zHERC:        goto Hercules_mode;
0555    default:           goto ABORT_PGM;
0556    }
0557  VGA_mode:            // VGA 640x480x16-color, 80x60 character mode.
0558  if(CommandLineArg==zYES)
0559    {                              // if user has requested a mode.
0560    if((Mode>zVGA_12H)&&(Mode<zHERC)) goto FORCE_USER_MODE;
0561    }
0562  X_Res=640; Y_Res=480; Mode=zVGA_12H; CharWidth=8; CharHeight=8;
0563  return;
0564  EGA_ECD_mode:        // EGA 640x350x16-color, 80x43 character mode.
0565  if(CommandLineArg==zYES)
0566    {
0567    if((Mode==zEGA_EH)||(Mode==zCGA_6H))   // permit only EGA or CGA.
0568    goto FORCE_USER_MODE;
0569    }
0570  X_Res=640; Y_Res=350; Mode=zEGA_10H; CharWidth=8; CharHeight=8;
0571  return;
0572  EGA_SCD_mode:                // EGA 640x200x16-color, 80x25 char mode.
0573  if(CommandLineArg==zYES)
0574    {
0575    if(Mode==zCGA_6H) goto FORCE_USER_MODE;     // only CGA permitted.
0576    }
0577  X_Res=640; Y_Res=200; Mode=zEGA_EH; CharWidth=8; CharHeight=8;
0578  return;
```

```
0579  MCGA_mode:                    // MCGA 640x480x2-color, 80x60 char mode.
0580  if(CommandLineArg==zYES)
0581    {
0582    if(Mode==zCGA_6H) goto FORCE_USER_MODE;     // only CGA permitted.
0583    }
0584  X_Res=640; Y_Res=480; Mode=zMCGA_11H;
0585  C0=0; C1=1; C2=1; C3=1; C4=1; C5=1; C6=1; C7=1;
0586  C8=1; C9=1; C10=1; C11=1; C12=1; C13=1; C14=1; C15=1;
0587  CharWidth=8; CharHeight=8;
0588  return;
0589  CGA_mode:                     // CGA 640x200x2-color, 80x25 char mode.
0590  X_Res=640; Y_Res=200; Mode=zCGA_6H;
0591  C0=0; C1=1; C2=1; C3=1; C4=1; C5=1; C6=1; C7=1;
0592  C8=1; C9=1; C10=1; C11=1; C12=1; C13=1; C14=1; C15=1;
0593  CharWidth=8; CharHeight=8;
0594  return;
0595  Hercules_mode:                // Hercules 720x348x2-color, 80x25 char mode.
0596  X_Res=720; Y_Res=348; Mode=zHERC;
0597  C0=0; C1=1; C2=1; C3=1; C4=1; C5=1; C6=1; C7=1;
0598  C8=1; C9=1; C10=1; C11=1; C12=1; C13=1; C14=1; C15=1;
0599  CharWidth=9; CharHeight=14;
0600  return;
0601
0602  FORCE_USER_MODE:    // jump to here if command-line argument legal.
0603  CommandLineArg= zNO; // first, reset token to avoid returning here.
0604  Display.ForceMode(Mode);         // ...then reset the graphics mode.
0605  switch(Mode)              // ...then jump back to appropriate code.
0606    {
0607    case zEGA_10H:     goto EGA_ECD_mode;
0608    case zEGA_EH:      goto EGA_SCD_mode;
0609    case zMCGA_11H:    goto MCGA_mode;
0610    case zCGA_6H:      goto CGA_mode;
0611    default:           goto ABORT_PGM;
0612    }
0613
0614  ABORT_PGM:         // jump to here if no graphics hardware detected.
0615  cout << "\n\n\rThis C++ graphics programming demo requires a";
0616  cout << "\n\rVGA, EGA, CGA, MCGA, or HGA graphics adapter.\n\r";
0617  exit(-1);                      // terminate, returning an error code.
0618  }
0619  /*
0620
0621  ┌──────────────────────────────────────────────────────────────┐
       │              Manage the menu system at run-time                │
0622   └──────────────────────────────────────────────────────────────┘
0623                                                                   */
0624  static void zMenuBarLoop(void)
0625  {
0626  PanPosition=1;           // initialize panning bar position indicator.
0627  Viewport1.PutXOR(p1,p2,PanBar);       // install panning hilite bar.
0628  zMakeSound(450,.2);zMakeSound(420,.2);               // audio cue.
0629  LOOP0:                                   // menu bar loop begins.
0630  zKeyboard();                           // check for user keystroke.
0631  if (KeyCode!=2) goto LABEL1;        // jump if not an extended key.
0632  switch (KeyNum)
0633    {
0634    case 77: PanPosition=PanPosition+1;zPanning();zPurge();
0635          zClearTextLine();goto LOOP0;               // right arrow.
0636    case 75: PanPosition=PanPosition-1;zPanning();zPurge();
0637          zClearTextLine();goto LOOP0;                // left arrow.
0638    }
0639  LABEL1:
0640  if (KeyCode!=1) goto LABEL2;      // jump past if not a normal key.
```

```
0641  if (KeyNum==13)                                  // if <Enter> key...
0642    {
0643    zInstallMenu(); zPurge();
0644    switch (PanPosition)
0645      {
0646      case zMENU1:    goto MENULOOP;
0647      case zACTION1: goto LOOP0;
0648      case zACTION2: goto LOOP0;
0649      case zMENU2:    goto MENULOOP;
0650      case zMENU3:    goto MENULOOP;
0651      case zMENU4:    goto MENULOOP;
0652      case zACTION3: goto LOOP0;
0653      }
0654    }
0655  LABEL2:
0656  if (KeyCode!=0)                                    // if a key was retrieved.
0657    {                                                // switcher for system keystrokes.
0658    zMenuBarKeys();                                  // empty the keyboard buffer.
0659    zPurge();
0660    }
0661  goto LOOP0;                                        // loop back.
0662  MENULOOP:                                          // menus loop begins.
0663  zKeyboard();                                       // check for user keystroke.
0664  if (KeyCode!=2) goto LABEL3;                       // jump if not an extended key.
0665  switch (KeyNum)
0666    {
0667    case 80: Selection=Selection+1; zScrolling(); zPurge();  // down.
0668             zClearTextLine(); goto MENULOOP;
0669    case 72: Selection=Selection-1; zScrolling(); zPurge();  // up.
0670             zClearTextLine(); goto MENULOOP;
0671    case 77: PanPosition=PanPosition+1;              // right arrow.
0672             if (PanPosition==2) PanPosition=4;      // bypass Action1.
0673             if (PanPosition==3) PanPosition=4;      // bypass Action2.
0674             zPanMenu(); zPurge();
0675             zClearTextLine(); goto MENULOOP;
0676    case 75: PanPosition=PanPosition-1;              // left arrow.
0677             if (PanPosition==2) PanPosition=1;      // bypass Action1.
0678             if (PanPosition==3) PanPosition=1;      // bypass Action2.
0679             zPanMenu(); zPurge();
0680             zClearTextLine(); goto MENULOOP;
0681    }
0682  LABEL3:
0683  if (KeyCode!=1) goto LABEL4;                       // jump past if not a normal key.
0684  if (KeyNum==13)
0685    {                                                // if <Enter> key...
0686    zMenuChoices(); zPurge(); goto LABEL5;           // call core function.
0687    }
0688  if (KeyNum==27)
0689    {                                                // if <Esc> key...
0690    zUninstallMenu(); zPurge();                      // back out of the menu.
0691    Viewport1.PutXOR(p1,p2,PanBar); zMenuBarText();
0692    goto LOOP0;
0693    }
0694  LABEL4:
0695  if (KeyCode!=0)                                    // if a key was retrieved.
0696    {                                                // switcher for menus keystrokes.
0697    zDropMenuKeys();                                 // empty the keyboard buffer.
0698    zPurge();
0699    }
0700  goto MENULOOP;                                     // loop back.
0701  LABEL5:          // decide re-entrant point after core function.
0702  switch (Status)
0703    {
```

5-5 Continued.

```
0704      case zACTIVE:   Status=zBACKOUT;
0705                      Viewport1.PutXOR(p1,p2,PanBar);
0706                      goto LOOP0;
0707      case zBACKOUT: zUninstallMenu();goto LOOP0;
0708      case zSTUB:     Status=zBACKOUT;goto MENULOOP;
0709      }
0710  return;
0711  }
0712  /*
0713
0714  ┌──────────────────────────────────────────────────────────────┐
        │              Move the panning highlight bar                  │
0715  └──────────────────────────────────────────────────────────────┘
0716                                                              */
0717  static void zPanning(void)
0718  {
0719  if (PanPosition>7) PanPosition=1;          // wraparound past right.
0720  if (PanPosition<1) PanPosition=7;          // wraparound past left.
0721  switch (PanPosition)
0722      {                              // determine where to move cursor.
0723      case zMENU1:    Viewport1.PutXOR(p1,p2,PanBar); p1=px1;
0724                      Viewport1.PutXOR(p1,p2,PanBar);
0725                      break;
0726      case zACTION1: Viewport1.PutXOR(p1,p2,PanBar); p1=px2;
0727                      Viewport1.PutXOR(p1,p2,PanBar);
0728                      break;
0729      case zACTION2: Viewport1.PutXOR(p1,p2,PanBar); p1=px3;
0730                      Viewport1.PutXOR(p1,p2,PanBar);
0731                      break;
0732      case zMENU2:    Viewport1.PutXOR(p1,p2,PanBar); p1=px4;
0733                      Viewport1.PutXOR(p1,p2,PanBar);
0734                      break;
0735      case zMENU3:    Viewport1.PutXOR(p1,p2,PanBar); p1=px5;
0736                      Viewport1.PutXOR(p1,p2,PanBar);
0737                      break;
0738      case zMENU4:    Viewport1.PutXOR(p1,p2,PanBar); p1=px6;
0739                      Viewport1.PutXOR(p1,p2,PanBar);
0740                      break;
0741      case zACTION3: Viewport1.PutXOR(p1,p2,PanBar); p1=px7;
0742                      Viewport1.PutXOR(p1,p2,PanBar);
0743                      break;
0744      default:        break;
0745      }
0746  return;
0747  }
0748  /*
0749
0750  ┌──────────────────────────────────────────────────────────────┐
        │              Install a menu on the screen                    │
0751  └──────────────────────────────────────────────────────────────┘
0752                                                              */
0753  static void zInstallMenu(void)
0754  {
0755  Selection=1;                          // reset virtual scroll position.
0756  p6=py1;                               // reset y coord scroll position.
0757  switch (PanPosition)
0758      {
0759      case zMENU1:  p3=px1-1;                    // reset x install coord.
0760                    Viewport1.PutXOR(p1,p2,PanBar);  // remove pan bar.
0761                    Menu1->DisplayImage(p3,p4,OVERWRITE);       // menu.
0762                    p5=px1+2;                 // reset x coord for scroll bar.
0763                    Viewport1.PutXOR(p5,p6,ScrollBar);  // install bar.
0764                    MaxSelection=6;     // reset number of menu choices.
0765                    Installed=zMENU1;                       // set a token.
```

```
0766                       break;                // get out of switch() brancher.
0767     case zACTION1:  zStubRoutine();
0768                     break;
0769     case zACTION2:  zStubRoutine();
0770                     break;
0771     case zMENU2:    p3=px4-1;
0772                     Viewport1.PutXOR(p1,p2,PanBar);
0773                     Menu2->DisplayImage(p3,p4,OVERWRITE);
0774                     p5=px4+2;
0775                     Viewport1.PutXOR(p5,p6,ScrollBar);
0776                     MaxSelection=4;
0777                     Installed=zMENU2;
0778                     break;
0779     case zMENU3:    p3=px5-1;
0780                     Viewport1.PutXOR(p1,p2,PanBar);
0781                     Menu3->DisplayImage(p3,p4,OVERWRITE);
0782                     p5=px5+2;
0783                     Viewport1.PutXOR(p5,p6,ScrollBar);
0784                     MaxSelection=4;
0785                     Installed=zMENU3;
0786                     break;
0787     case zMENU4:    p3=px6-1;
0788                     Viewport1.PutXOR(p1,p2,PanBar);
0789                     Menu4->DisplayImage(p3,p4,OVERWRITE);
0790                     p5=px6+2;
0791                     Viewport1.PutXOR(p5,p6,ScrollBar);
0792                     MaxSelection=5;
0793                     Installed=zMENU4;
0794                     break;
0795     case zACTION3:  zStubRoutine();
0796                     break;
0797     default:        break;
0798     }
0799  return;
0800  }
0801  /*
0802
0803  ┌──────────────────────────────────────────────────────────┐
       │              Remove a menu from the screen               │
0804   └──────────────────────────────────────────────────────────┘
0805                                                               */
0806  static void zUninstallMenu(void)
0807  {
0808  switch(Installed)
0809    {
0810    case zMENU1:   Menu1->EraseImage(); Installed=0; break;
0811    case zMENU2:   Menu2->EraseImage(); Installed=0; break;
0812    case zMENU3:   Menu3->EraseImage(); Installed=0; break;
0813    case zMENU4:   Menu4->EraseImage(); Installed=0; break;
0814    }
0815  return;
0816  }
0817  /*
0818
0819  ┌──────────────────────────────────────────────────────────┐
       │              Pan directly between two menus             │
0820   └──────────────────────────────────────────────────────────┘
0821                                                               */
0822  static void zPanMenu(void)
0823  {
0824  if (PanPosition>6) PanPosition=1;      // wraparound to skip Action3.
0825  if (PanPosition<1) PanPosition=6;                    // wraparound.
0826  Selection=1;                           // reset virtual scroll position.
0827  p6=py1;                                // reset y coord scroll position.
0828  zUninstallMenu();                              // remove existing menu.
```

5-5 Continued.

```
0829    switch (PanPosition)
0830      {
0831      case zMENU1: p1=px1;              // reset x coord for panning bar.
0832                   MaxSelection=6;      // reset number of menu choices.
0833                   p3=px1-1;            // reset x coord for menu.
0834                   p5=px1+2;            // reset x coord for scrolling bar.
0835                   Menu1->DisplayImage(p3,p4,OVERWRITE);     // menu.
0836                   Viewport1.PutXOR(p5,p6,ScrollBar);   // install bar.
0837                   Installed=zMENU1;
0838                   break;              // get out of switch() brancher.
0839      case zMENU2: p1=px4;
0840                   MaxSelection=4;
0841                   p3=px4-1;
0842                   p5=px4+2;
0843                   Menu2->DisplayImage(p3,p4,OVERWRITE);
0844                   Viewport1.PutXOR(p5,p6,ScrollBar);
0845                   Installed=zMENU2;
0846                   break;
0847      case zMENU3: p1=px5;
0848                   MaxSelection=4;
0849                   p3=px5-1;
0850                   p5=px5+2;
0851                   Menu3->DisplayImage(p3,p4,OVERWRITE);
0852                   Viewport1.PutXOR(p5,p6,ScrollBar);
0853                   Installed=zMENU3;
0854                   break;
0855      case zMENU4: p1=px6;
0856                   MaxSelection=5;
0857                   p3=px6-1;
0858                   p5=px6+2;
0859                   Menu4->DisplayImage(p3,p4,OVERWRITE);
0860                   Viewport1.PutXOR(p5,p6,ScrollBar);
0861                   Installed=zMENU4;
0862                   break;
0863      }
0864    return;
0865    }
0866    /*
0867
0868    ┌──────────────────────────────────────────────────────────────┐
        │              Manage the scrolling highlight bar               │
0869    └──────────────────────────────────────────────────────────────┘
0870                                                                  */
0871    static void zScrolling(void)
0872    {
0873    if (Selection>MaxSelection) Selection=1;    // vertical wraparound.
0874    if (Selection<1) Selection=MaxSelection;    // vertical wraparound.
0875    switch (Selection)
0876      {
0877      case 1: Viewport1.PutXOR(p5,p6,ScrollBar);     // remove former.
0878              p6=py1;                              // reset y coord.
0879              Viewport1.PutXOR(p5,p6,ScrollBar);    // install new.
0880              break;                       // get out of switch() brancher.
0881      case 2: Viewport1.PutXOR(p5,p6,ScrollBar);
0882              p6=py2;
0883              Viewport1.PutXOR(p5,p6,ScrollBar);
0884              break;
0885      case 3: Viewport1.PutXOR(p5,p6,ScrollBar);
0886              p6=py3;
0887              Viewport1.PutXOR(p5,p6,ScrollBar);
0888              break;
0889      case 4: Viewport1.PutXOR(p5,p6,ScrollBar);
0890              p6=py4;
```

```
0891            Viewport1.PutXOR(p5,p6,ScrollBar);
0892            break;
0893    case 5: Viewport1.PutXOR(p5,p6,ScrollBar);
0894            p6=py5;
0895            Viewport1.PutXOR(p5,p6,ScrollBar);
0896            break;
0897    case 6: Viewport1.PutXOR(p5,p6,ScrollBar);
0898            p6=py6;
0899            Viewport1.PutXOR(p5,p6,ScrollBar);
0900            break;
0901    }
0902 return;
0903 }
0904 /*
0905 ┌─────────────────────────────────────────────────────────────┐
0906 │                  Call the core functions                    │
0907 └─────────────────────────────────────────────────────────────┘
0908                                                              */
0909 static void zMenuChoices(void)
0910 {
0911 switch (PanPosition)
0912    {                            // determine which menu is being used.
0913    case zMENU1: goto MENU1_CHOICES;
0914    case zMENU2: goto MENU2_CHOICES;
0915    case zMENU3: goto MENU3_CHOICES;
0916    case zMENU4: goto MENU4_CHOICES;
0917    }
0918 MENU1_CHOICES:
0919 switch (Selection)
0920    {
0921    case 1: Choice=1; zStubRoutine(); break;
0922    case 2: Choice=2; zStubRoutine(); break;
0923    case 3: Choice=3; zStubRoutine(); break;
0924    case 4: Choice=4; zStubRoutine(); break;
0925    case 5: Choice=5; zStubRoutine(); break;
0926    case 6: Choice=6; zQuit_Pgm();
0927    }
0928 return;
0929 MENU2_CHOICES:
0930 switch (Selection)
0931    {
0932    case 1: Choice=20; zStubRoutine(); break;
0933    case 2: Choice=21; zStubRoutine(); break;
0934    case 3: Choice=22; zStubRoutine(); break;
0935    case 4: Choice=23; zStubRoutine(); break;
0936    }
0937 return;
0938 MENU3_CHOICES:
0939 switch (Selection)
0940    {
0941    case 1: Choice=24; zStubRoutine(); break;
0942    case 2: Choice=25; zStubRoutine(); break;
0943    case 3: Choice=26; zStubRoutine(); break;
0944    case 4: Choice=27; zStubRoutine(); break;
0945    }
0946 return;
0947 MENU4_CHOICES:
0948 switch (Selection)
0949    {
0950    case 1: Choice=28; zStubRoutine(); break;
0951    case 2: Choice=29; zStubRoutine(); break;
0952    case 3: Choice=30; zStubRoutine(); break;
0953    case 4: Choice=31; zStubRoutine(); break;
```

5-5 Continued.

```
0954    case 5: Choice=32; zStubRoutine(); break;
0955    }
0956  return;
0957  }
0958  /*

0959  ┌─────────────────────────────────────────────────────────┐
0960  │                      Stub routine                       │
0961  └─────────────────────────────────────────────────────────┘
0962                                                          */
0963  static void zStubRoutine(void)
0964  {
0965  Status=zSTUB;                          // set the navigation token.
0966  zClearTextLine();                      // clear the text dialog line.
0967  Viewport1.PutText(1,2,TextClr,Text4);        // display message.
0968  zMakeSound(450,.2);
0969  return;
0970  }
0971  /*

0972  ┌─────────────────────────────────────────────────────────┐
0973  │                Clear the text dialog line               │
0974  └─────────────────────────────────────────────────────────┘
0975                                                          */
0976  static void zClearTextLine(void)
0977  {
0978  Display.SetHue(C0);                       // set the drawing color.
0979  Display.SetLine(0xffff);                  // set the line style.
0980  Display.SetFill(SolidFill,C0);            // set the fill style.
0981  Viewport1.ClearTextLine();             // call the viewport method.
0982  }
0983  /*

0984  ┌─────────────────────────────────────────────────────────┐
0985  │                Display the ready prompt                  │
0986  └─────────────────────────────────────────────────────────┘
0987                                                          */
0988  static void zMenuBarText(void)
0989  {
0990  zClearTextLine();
0991  Viewport1.PutText(1,2,TextClr,Text5);
0992  return;
0993  }
0994  /*

0995  ┌─────────────────────────────────────────────────────────┐
0996  │                Keystroke loop for menu bar              │
0997  └─────────────────────────────────────────────────────────┘
0998                                                          */
0999  static void zMenuBarKeys(void)
1000  {
1001  if (KeyCode==2) goto EXTENDEDKEYS;      // if extended key, jump...
1002  NORMALKEYS:                    // ...else use switcher for normal keys.
1003  switch (KeyNum)
1004    {
1005    case 27:   return;
1006    case 13:   return;
1007    case 8:    return;
1008    case 9:    return;
1009    case 32:   return;
1010    default:   zMakeSound(450,.2); return;
1011    }
1012  EXTENDEDKEYS:                   // switcher for extended keystrokes.
1013  switch (KeyNum)
1014    {
```

```
1015    case 59:   return;
1016    case 60:   return;
1017    case 45:   zQuit_Pgm();
1018    default:   zMakeSound(450,.2); return;
1019    }
1020  }
1021  /*
1022
1023  ┌─────────────────────────────────────────────────────────────┐
      │               Keystroke loop for menus                       │
1024  └─────────────────────────────────────────────────────────────┘
1025                                                               */
1026  static void zDropMenuKeys(void)
1027  {
1028  if (KeyCode==2) goto EXTENDEDKEYS2;     // if extended key, jump...
1029  NORMALKEYS2:                    // ...else use switcher for normal keys.
1030  switch (KeyNum)
1031    {
1032    case 8:    return;
1033    case 9:    return;
1034    case 32:   return;
1035    default:   zMakeSound(450,.2); return;
1036    }
1037  EXTENDEDKEYS2:                     // switcher for extended keystrokes.
1038  switch (KeyNum)
1039    {
1040    case 59:   return;
1041    case 60:   return;
1042    case 45:   zQuit_Pgm();
1043    default:   zMakeSound(450,.2); return;
1044    }
1045  }
1046  /*
1047
1048  ┌─────────────────────────────────────────────────────────────┐
      │            Check the keyboard for a keystroke                │
1049  └─────────────────────────────────────────────────────────────┘
1050                                                               */
1051  static void zKeyboard(void)
1052  {      // can detect keypad keys like PgUp and control keys like F2.
1053    union AnyName{int RawCode;char Code[3];}Keystroke;
1054    char TempKey=0;
1055  #if defined (BORLAND)
1056    if (bioskey(1)==zEMPTY) { KeyCode=0; return; }
1057    Keystroke.RawCode= bioskey(0);
1058  #elif defined (MICROSOFT)
1059    if (_bios_keybrd(_KEYBRD_READY)==zEMPTY)
1060      { KeyCode=0; return; }
1061    Keystroke.RawCode= _bios_keybrd(_KEYBRD_READ);
1062  #endif
1063  TempKey= Keystroke.Code[0];
1064  if (TempKey!=0)
1065    {                                      // if a normal keystroke...
1066    KeyCode=1; KeyNum=TempKey; return;
1067    }
1068  if (TempKey==0)
1069    {                                      // if an extended keystroke...
1070    KeyCode=2; KeyNum=Keystroke.Code[1]; return;
1071    }
1072  }
1073  /*
1074
1075  ┌─────────────────────────────────────────────────────────────┐
      │             Empty the keystroke buffer                       │
1076  └─────────────────────────────────────────────────────────────┘
1077                                                               */
```

```
1078   static void zPurge(void)
1079   {
1080   do zKeyboard();
1081     while (KeyCode!=0);
1082   return;
1083   }
1084   /*
1085
```

```
1086                          Make a sound
```

```
1088                                                              */
1089   static void zMakeSound(int Hertz,double Duration)
1090   {
1091     static clock_t FormerTime=0;
1092     short Count=0;
1093     int HighByte=0, LowByte=0;
1094     unsigned char OldPort=0, NewPort=0;
1095   FormerTime= clock();
1096   if (Hertz < 40) return;
1097   if (Hertz > 4660) return;
1098   Count= 1193180L/Hertz;
1099   HighByte= Count / 256;
1100   LowByte= Count - (HighByte * 256);
1101   #if defined (BORLAND)
1102     outportb(0x43,0xB6); outportb(0x42,(unsigned char)LowByte);
1103     outportb(0x42,(unsigned char)HighByte); OldPort=inportb(0x61);
1104     NewPort=(OldPort | 0x03); outportb(0x61,NewPort);
1105     zDelay(FormerTime,Duration);
1106     outportb(0x61,OldPort);
1107   #elif defined (MICROSOFT)
1108     outp(0x43,0xB6); outp(0x42,LowByte);
1109     outp(0x42,HighByte); OldPort=(unsigned char)inp(0x61);
1110     NewPort=(OldPort | 0x03); outp(0x61,(int)NewPort);
1111     zDelay(FormerTime,Duration);
1112     outp(0x61,(int)OldPort);
1113   #endif
1114   return;
1115   }
1116   /*
1117
```

```
1118                             Pause
```

```
1120                                                              */
1121   static clock_t zDelay(clock_t StartTime, double Wait)
1122   {                        // pause for a specified length of time.
1123     clock_t StopTime;
1124     clock_t NewClockTime;
1125   StopTime= StartTime + (Wait * CLK_TCK);
1126   while ( clock() < StopTime ) {;}
1127   NewClockTime= clock();
1128   return NewClockTime;
1129   }
1130   /*
1131
```

```
1132           Retrieve the command-line arguments, if any
```

```
1134                                                              */
1135   static void zArguments(int NumArgs, char *Arg[])
1136   {
1137   if(NumArgs==1)
1138     {
```

```
1139      CommandLineArg= zNO; return;                              // if no arg.
1140      }
1141   CommandLineCompare= strncmp(StartUpArg[0],Arg[1],5);
1142   if(CommandLineCompare==0)
1143      {
1144      CommandLineArg=zYES; Mode=zVGA_12H; return;              // /M12.
1145      }
1146   CommandLineCompare= strncmp(StartUpArg[1],Arg[1],5);
1147   if(CommandLineCompare==0)
1148      {
1149      CommandLineArg=zYES; Mode=zEGA_10H; return;              // /M10.
1150      }
1151   CommandLineCompare= strncmp(StartUpArg[2],Arg[1],5);
1152   if(CommandLineCompare==0)
1153      {
1154      CommandLineArg=zYES; Mode=zEGA_EH; return;               // /M0E.
1155      }
1156   CommandLineCompare= strncmp(StartUpArg[3],Arg[1],5);
1157   if(CommandLineCompare==0)
1158      {
1159      CommandLineArg=zYES; Mode=zMCGA_11H; return;             // /M11.
1160      }
1161   CommandLineCompare= strncmp(StartUpArg[4],Arg[1],5);
1162   if(CommandLineCompare==0)
1163      {
1164      CommandLineArg=zYES; Mode=zCGA_6H; return;               // /M06.
1165      }
1166   CommandLineCompare= strncmp(StartUpArg[5],Arg[1],5);
1167   if(CommandLineCompare==0)
1168      {
1169      CommandLineArg=zYES; Mode=zHERC; return;                 // /MHC.
1170      }
1171   CommandLineArg= zNO;                        // if an unrecognized argument.
1172   return;
1173   }
1174   /*
1175
1176   ┌──────────────────────────────────────────────────────────────┐
       │    Supercharged C++ Graphics -- end of source file GUI.CPP     │
       └──────────────────────────────────────────────────────────────┘
1177
1178                                                                   */
```

6

Interactive draw/paint graphics

Draw/paint programs are one of the most common forms of interactive graphics software. By using the sketchpad paradigm, the display becomes a drawing surface, the keyboard becomes a toolbox, and the mouse becomes a pencil or brush.

Some of the skill-builders presented in earlier demonstration programs are consolidated in the sample application in this chapter. Keyboard polling loops are used to provide access to an on-screen menu. A mouse polling loop provides pointing capabilities during the interactive drawing portions of the program. The low-level display management methods of class PhysicalDisplay and the low-level graphics output methods of class Viewport provide any easy way to generate graphics for the user. The graphic array methods of class Bitblt provide a means to implement a dynamic swatch for portraying colors and patterns while the user selects pen and brush attributes.

A sample program: SKETCH.CPP

Figure 6-1 depicts typical displays produced by the sample program SKETCH.CPP, whose complete source code is provided in FIG. 6-5 at the end of the chapter. The program provides an interactive environment for sketching and painting using a mouse. Polylines, rectangles, circles, curves, solid fills, dithered fills, patterned fills, and an Undo function are supported.

How to compile and link the sample program

The program listing presented in FIG. 6-5 contains the complete source code for the main module of the C++ demonstration program called "Using C++ to Create Paint/Draw Programs." If you are using the com-

6-1 Graphics output from the interactive sample program SKETCH.CPP. Top: output of the rectangle function. Bottom: the working display provides an on-screen menu of available drawing functions.

panion disks to the book, the source code is in the file named SKETCH.CPP. Four C++ source files are needed to build the finished .exe file. These are SKETCH.CPP from FIG. 6-5 and three class libraries in appendix E.

Class The class library that provides the language bindings and low-level graphics routines for this demonstration program is found in FIG. E-2 in appendix E. This listing contains the implementations for class PhysicalDisplay and class Viewport. If you are using the companion disks to the book, this file is named LIB2D.CPP. The class declarations are presented in FIG. E-1 in appendix E. If you are using the companion disks to the book, this file is named LIB2D.HPP.

Class The class library that provides the mouse management methods for this demonstration program is found in FIG. E-6 in appendix E. This listing contains the implementations for class PointingDevice. If you are using the companion disks to the book, this file is named MOUSE.CPP. The class declarations are presented in FIG. E-5 in appendix E. If you are using the companion disks to the book, this file is named MOUSE.HPP.

Class The class library that provides the bitblt methods for this demonstration program is found in FIG. E-8 in appendix E. This listing contains the implementations for class Bitblt. If you are using the companion disks to the book, this file is named BITBLT.CPP. The class declarations are presented in FIG. E-7 in appendix E. If you are using the companion disks to the book, this file is named BITBLT.HPP.

You can compile, link, and run this demonstration program using either Turbo C++, Borland C++, or Zortech C++. If you are using Turbo C++, read appendix A for help in compiling, linking, and running the demonstration program. If you are using Borland C++, you can find the appropriate information in appendix B. If you are using Zortech C++, refer to appendix C.

You must create a Turbo C++ or Borland C++ project list to advise your compiler which source files to bind together to build the finished .exe file. If you are using Zortech C++, you must name the files on the compiler command line field. Refer to the appendices described earlier if you are unfamiliar with this technique.

After a successful compile and link, the animated screen should resemble the screen prints shown in FIG. 6-5.

How to run the demonstration program

You need a VGA, EGA, MCGA, CGA, or Hercules graphics adapter and a mouse to run this demo.

Using the editor to run the program

Here's How... To run the program under the control of your Turbo C++, Borland C++, or Zortech C++ editor, make sure that the finished .exe file is in the default directory. If you used Turbo C++ or Borland C++ to compile the program, the appropriate graphics driver must be in the default directory. If you are using a VGA or EGA, the EGAVGA.BGI file must be present. If you are using an MCGA or CGA, the CGA.BGI file must be located in the default directory. If you are using a Hercules graphics adapter, the HERC.BGI file must be available. If you used Zortech C++ to compile the demonstration program, the appropriate graphics drivers have already been linked into the .exe code.

The built-in autodetect routine will detect the graphics hardware in your computer system and will set up the best graphics mode supported by your computer hardware. To override the autodetect routine use the Turbo C++, Borland C++, or Zortech C++ editor to simulate a command line argument. The header in FIG. 6-5 provides a set of arguments you can use. See the appendices for guidance applicable to your particular compiler. If you are using a VGA, you can override the autodetect routine and force the demonstration program to run in an EGA, MCGA, or CGA mode. If you are using an EGA, you can force the program to run in a lower-resolution EGA mode or a CGA mode.

Running the program from the operating system prompt

To start the program from the operating system prompt, simply enter SKETCH. The .exe file and any required graphics drivers must be present in the default directory. If the software finds a VGA present in your system, the program will animate using the 640×480×16-color mode. If an EGA and enhanced monitor are found, the 640×350×16-color mode is used. If an EGA and standard display are present, the program sets up the 640×200×16-color mode. If an MCGA is detected, the 640×480×2-color mode is employed. If a CGA is found, the 640×200×2-color mode is used. If the program detects a Hercules graphics adapter, it starts up in the 720×348×2-color mode.

You can force the program to start up in a different mode by adding a command line argument when you start the program from the operating system prompt. Enter SKETCH /M11 to force the 640×480×2-color mode. Enter SKETCH /M10 to force the 640×350×16-color mode. Entering SKETCH /M0E forces the program to run in the 640×200×16-color mode. Entering SKETCH /M06 tests the demonstration program in the 640×200×2-color mode.

Using the demonstration program

Use the keys annotated by the on-screen menu to select a graphics function, then use the mouse to implement the function. Press the Backspace key to undo your most recent graphics. Press Alt+X to end the program.

New Press Ctrl+F1 to blank the drawing surface. See FIG. 6-1. The New command does not affect the current drawing color, fill style, hatch pattern, or dither shade. Press the Backspace key to restore the image using the Undo function.

Line Press Ctrl+F2 to begin drawing a line. Move the mouse cursor to a desired location and click the left mouse button. The polyline will begin at this location. Move the mouse cursor to another location and click the mouse button. A line will be drawn from the previous location to the new location. Continue the line as required. Press the right mouse button to finish the line and return to the on-screen menu level. You can use the Backspace key to undo the polyline.

Curve   Press Ctrl + F3 to begin drawing a parametric curve. Move the mouse cursor to an appropriate location and click the left mouse button to set the start point for the curve. Then move the mouse cursor to a position that identifies a magnetic point and click the left mouse button. Then identify a second magnetic point. Finally, identify and click the left mouse button on the end position for the curve and the program will draw a smooth curve. See FIG. 6- 2. The curve will start at the first location you selected and will end at the fourth location you selected. The second and third positions you selected will act as magnets, drawing the curve close to them as it winds its way towards the end point. You can use the Undo function to remove the curve if you wish.

Rectangle   Press Ctrl + F4 to begin drawing rectangles. Press the left mouse button to select the starting corner for a rectangle. Move the mouse cursor to an appropriate location and click the left mouse button to select the diagonally opposite ending corner for the rectangle. The program will draw a rectangle as shown in FIG. 6-1. Repeat this process to continue drawing more rectangles. The program is smart enough to draw a rectangle no matter where you position your diagonal corners—upper left, upper right, lower left, or lower right. When you are finished, press the right mouse button to return to the on-screen menu. You can use the Backspace key to implement an Undo function to remove the rectangles you have drawn.

Circle   Press Ctrl + F5 to begin drawing circles. Move the mouse cursor to a location corresponding to the center of a circle and press the left mouse button. Move the mouse cursor to a position that corresponds to the horizontal radius of the circle you want to draw. The vertical location of the mouse cursor is ignored by the program. Press the left mouse cursor and the program draws a circle. See FIG. 6-2. Continue drawing circles by moving the mouse cursor and clicking the left mouse button to select another circle center, and so on. The Undo function can be used if desired.

Eraser   Press Ctrl + F6 to use the eraser. Click the left mouse button, or click and drag the left mouse button, to restore a small block of graphics to the background color. When you are finished erasing, click the right mouse button to return to the on-screen menu. The Undo function can be used to restore what you have erased.

Solid fill   Press Ctrl + F7 to use the solid fill function. Move the mouse cursor to a location where you want the fill to start. Click the left mouse button and the area bounded by the current edge color will be filled with the current fill color. Use F2 to set the current fill color. Use F3 to set the current edge color. You can use the Backspace Undo function to undo a fill. When you have finished filling

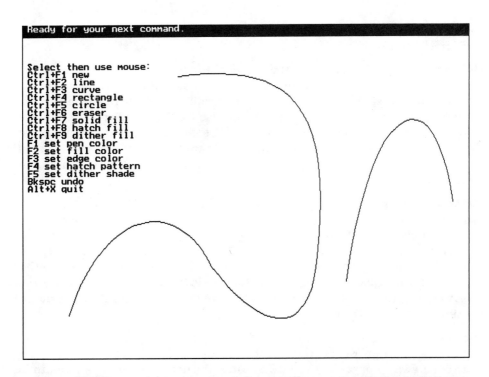

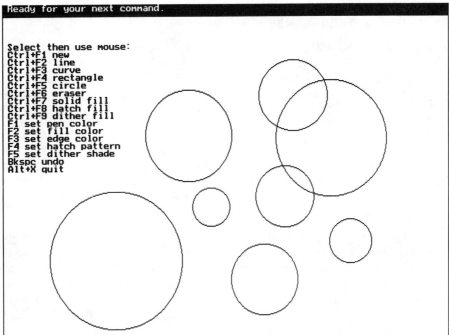

6-2 Graphics output from the interactive sample program SKETCH.CPP. Top: output of the curve function. Bottom: output of the circle function.

all the areas you have selected, press the right mouse button to return to the on-screen menu.

Hatch fill   Press Ctrl + F8 to use the hatch fill function. Move the mouse cursor to a location where you want the fill to start. Click the left mouse button and the area bounded by the current edge color will be filled with the current fill pattern and current fill color. See FIG. 6-3. Use F2 to set the current fill color. Use F3 to set the current edge color. Use F4 to set the current hatch pattern. You can use the Backspace Undo function to undo a fill. When you have finished filling all the areas you have selected, press the right mouse button to return to the on-screen menu.

Dither fill   Press Ctrl + F9 to use the dithered fill function. Move the mouse cursor to a location where you want the fill to start. Click the left mouse button and the area bounded by the current edge color will be filled with the current dither pattern and current fill color. See FIG. 6-3. Use F2 to set the current fill color. Use F3 to set the current edge color. Use F5 to set the current dither shade pattern. You can use the Backspace Undo function to undo a fill. When you have finished filling all the areas you have selected, press the right mouse button to return to the on-screen menu.

Set pen color   Press F1 to set the current drawing color. A rectangular swatch appears on the upper left corner of the drawing surface. The swatch shows the current drawing color. Use the Tab key to see the next available color. Continue to use the Tab key until you find the color you want, then press Enter to activate the color and return to the on-screen menu.

Set fill color   Press F2 to set the current fill color. A rectangular swatch appears on the upper left corner of the drawing surface. The swatch shows the current fill color. Use the Tab key to see the next available color. Continue to use the Tab key until you find the color you want, then press Enter to activate the color and return to the on-screen menu.

Set edge color   Press F3 to set the current edge color. The edge color is the boundary used by the fill routines. A rectangular swatch appears on the upper left corner of the drawing surface. The swatch shows the current edge color. Use the Tab key to see the next available color. Continue to use the Tab key until you find the color you want, then press Enter to activate the color and return to the on-screen menu.

Set hatch pattern   Press F4 to set the current fill pattern. A rectangular swatch appears on the upper left corner of the drawing surface. The swatch shows the current fill pattern. See FIG. 6-3. Use the Tab key to see the next available pattern. Continue to use the Tab key until you find the pattern you want, then press Enter to activate the color and return to the on-screen menu. Note that the pattern is drawn in the current fill color, which can be changed by using F2.

Set dither shade   Press F5 to set the current dither shade. A rectangular swatch appears on the upper left corner of the drawing surface. The swatch

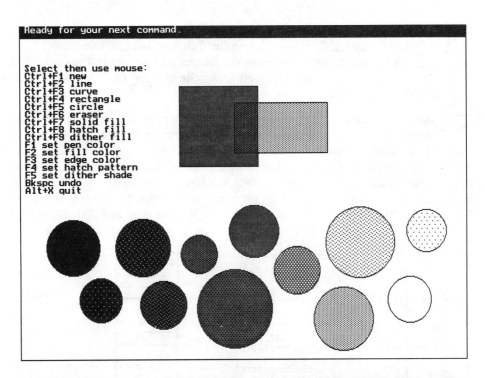

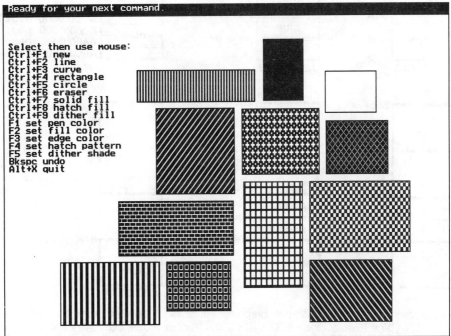

6-3 Graphics output from the interactive sample program SKETCH.CPP. Top: output of the dither fill function. Bottom: output of the hatch fill function.

shows the current dither shade. See FIG. 6-3. Use the Tab key to see the next available shade pattern. Continue to use the Tab key until you find the shade you want, then press Enter to activate the dither and return to the on-screen menu. Note that the shade is generated using the current fill color, which can be changed by using F2.

Undo Press the Backspace key to undo your most recent graphics function. The Undo function relies upon hidden graphics pages, as shown in FIG. 6-4. If you are using the VGA 640×480×16-color mode, the program maintains a simulated hidden page in RAM. If you are using the EGA 640×350×16-color mode or 640×200×16-color mode, the hidden page is located on the display memory of the graphics adapter itself. If you are using the CGA 640×200×2-color mode, the hidden page is located in RAM. If you are

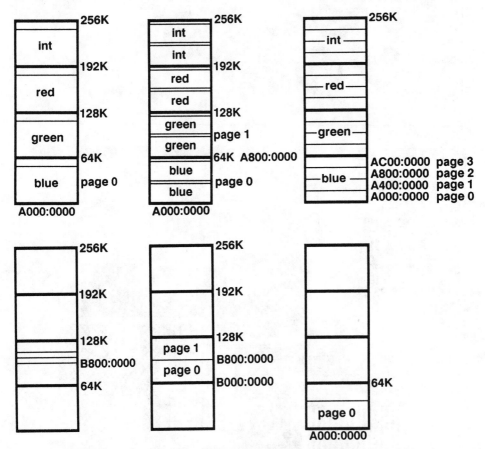

6-4 Display memory on different graphics adapters. Clockwise from top left: VGA 640×480×16-color mode, EGA 640×350×16-color mode, EGA 640×200×16-color mode, MCGA 640×480×2-color mode, Hercules 720×348×2-color mode, and CGA 640×200×2-color mode.

using the Hercules $720 \times 348 \times 2$-color mode, the second page is located on the graphics adapter. The Undo function is supported in only the Turbo C++ and Borland C++ versions of the demonstration program.

Programmer's Guide to SKETCH.CPP

Code The complete listing for the demonstration program SKETCH.CPP is presented in FIG. 6-5. The source code consists of an informative header, conditional compilation directives, declaration of constants and macros, file include directives, function prototypes, variable declarations, and the executable functions.

Conditional compilation

Information and source code for conditional compilation is located at lines 0047 through 0064. If you are using Turbo C++ or Borland C++, the program is ready to compile, subject to the instructions in appendix B. If you are using Zortech C++, change line 0063 to #define FG and change line 0064 to #define ZORTECH.

Constants

The C++ const keyword is used to declare and assign values to constant variables at lines 0066 through 0104. Note in particular how the various keystroke combinations are defined, such as zCTRL_F1, for example.

Macros

A macro defined at line 0110 will be expanded by the C++ compiler at line 0273.

Include files

The code at lines 0112 through 0141 loads the appropriate header files and C++ class declaration files. Line 0139 loads LIB2D.HPP, which declares the data members and methods of class PhysicalDisplay and class Viewport. Line 0140 loads MOUSE.HPP, which declares the data members and methods of class PointingDevice. Line 0141 loads BITBLT.HPP, which declares the data members and methods of class Bitblt.

Function prototypes

Function declarations are provided in lines 0143 through 0164. Functions declared here are visible throughout this source file. They can be called by any other function in the source file. Because each function is declared with the static qualifier, it is not available to functions located in other source files.

Variable declarations

Lines 0166 through 0236 declare global variables visible throughout this source file. These variables have file scope and can be modified by any function in the file.

Object declarations

Object Note line 0233, which creates an object from class PhysicalDisplay. The object is named Display. The program will later call the methods of this object to help it manage the display. The methods are declared in the class declaration listing LIB2D.HPP and are defined in the class implementation listing LIB2D.CPP in appendix E. The object created at line 0233 is a static object. It has file scope and will remain available until the program terminates.

Line 0234 creates an object from the Viewport class. The object is named Viewport1. The address of Display is passed to this new object. Viewport1 will need to use the methods of Display to generate graphics output. The object created at line 0234 is a static object with file scope. It will remain active until program termination.

Line 0235 creates an object from the PointingDevice class. The object is named Mouse. The methods of this object provide access to the functions of the memory-resident mouse driver. The pointer that is declared at line 0236 will be used to access a table of data about the mouse state.

main( )

The main( ) function is located at lines 0241 through 0319. After first checking to see if any command line arguments were used to start the program, an appropriate graphics mode is set. Lines 0275 through 0292 display the on-screen menu. The mouse is initialized at lines 0295 through 0297, as discussed in chapter 3. Lines 0299 through 0311 initialize assorted variables that represent the graphics state, such as current fill color, and so on.

The code at line 0317 calls the function that provides the interactive loop to access the drawing functions provided by the program.

The interactive loop

Here's Why... The function at lines 0321 through 0383 is a keyboard polling loop. After calling the zKeyboard( ) function to fetch an inbound keystroke, the switch( ) block at lines 0332 through 0355 is used to call the appropriate core function by passing a token to zCoreFunction( ).

Note the code at lines 0364 through 0377, which implements the Undo function. After calling method Restore( ) of class Viewport, a context-sensitive message is displayed on the dialog line.

Managing the mouse

The function at lines 0385 through 0481 provides a mouse polling loop. Only when the program is inside this loop is the mouse cursor displayed. As soon as the mouse function processes a button press, the mouse cursor is removed from the display and control returns to the caller, which is one of the core functions.

Viewport compatibility

Because SKETCH.CPP uses a viewport to clip all graphics on the display, the mouse coordinates returned by the mouse polling function must be skewed to match the viewport. The mouse uses physical screen coordinates, not viewport coordinates. For example, the GS_penx variable, which represents the current x coordinate, is derived by simply subtracting the left boundary of the viewport from the current mouse horizontal location.

Core function manager

The function at lines 0435 through 0666 is the switcher that calls the appropriate core function. When zInteractiveLoop( ) calls this function, it passes to it a token representing the desired graphics operation. The switch( ) block at lines 0442 through 0454 uses the token to jump to a target line label. NEW_IMAGE at line 0456 implements the New function. Note how the on-screen menu must be refreshed after the drawing surface is cleared.

DRAW_LINE at line 0484 implements the Line function. Note how it calls zMouseManager( ) at line 0497 to fetch the current mouse coordinates when a button is clicked. Line 0503 calls function zGetViewportCoords( ) to convert these mouse coordinates to viewport coordinates.

DRAW_CURVE at line 0507 implements the Curve function. Line 0531 calls the zDrawCurveFunction( ) function that employs cubic parametric equations to draw the curve from the four sets of coordinates input by the user of SKETCH.CPP.

DRAW_RECT at line 0535 implements the Rectangle function. Note in particular the code at lines 0553 through 0560, which swaps the diagonal coordinates. The DrawBorder( ) method of class Viewport expects the coordinates to be normalized—upper left coordinates first, followed by lower right coordinates.

DRAW_CIRCLE at line 0566 implements the circle function.

ERASER at line 0591 implements the eraser function. Eraser simply calls the DrawPanel( ) method of class Viewport to draw a filled rectangle on the display. The rectangle is the same color as the background color, of course.

SOLID_FILL at line 0610 implements the Solid Fill function. A simple loop allows the user to fill as many objects as desired.

PATTERN_FILL at line 0628 implements the Hatch Fill function.

DITHERED_FILL at line 0646 implements the Dithered Fill function.

Drawing a parametric curve

The function at lines 0668 through 0703 draws a cubic parametric curve. It expects to receive in its argument list the coordinates of the four points selected by the user. The first point is the starting position for the curve. The next two points are magnetic points that attract the curve. The fourth point is the ending position for the curve.

The formulas used in this function can be obtained from any standard mathematics text and have been discussed in previous volumes in the *Applied C Graphics* series from TAB/McGraw-Hill.

Editing the drawing color and pattern

The function at lines 0705 through 0906 allows the user to modify the current drawing color, the current fill color, the current edge color, the current fill pattern, and the current dither shade. The function provides a swatch to illustrate the current selection by using the C++ new operator to create a bitblt object. Lines 0714 and 0715, for example, create an object of class Bitblt named SwatchBackground. A second object named SwatchBlank is created at line 0724.

The primary loop for this function is located at lines 0741 through 0763. Note how the C++ delete operator is used if the switch( ) block necessitates removing the swatch and returning to the caller. You can follow the logic through the switch( ) block to the target line label WHICHCOLOR, which in turn selects the appropriate block of code to manipulate the swatch. This function can be written much more cleverly, of course, but at the expense of readability.

Terminating the program

The function at lines 0908 through 0916 calls method ShutDownGraphics( ) of class PhysicalDisplay to terminate the graphics state. Line 0915 returns an OK value to the operating system.

The Startup( ) function

The function at lines 0918 through 1001 calls the SetupMode( ) method of class PhysicalDisplay to detect the graphics hardware.

The StubRoutine( ) function

The stub routine at lines 1003 through 1013 is a do-nothing routine. It displays a simple message on the dialog line at the top of the display.

Blank the dialog line

The function at lines 1015 through 1026 blanks the dialog line by calling method ClearTextLine( ) of class Viewport.

The Keyboard( ) function

The function at lines 1028 through 1056 detects and retrieves keystrokes from the keyboard buffer. The function at lines 1058 through 1067 keeps calling the zKeyboard( ) function until the keyboard buffer is empty. This routine purges unwanted keystrokes from the keyboard buffer after a lengthy graphics operation like the curve routine.

The MakeSound( ) function

The function at lines 1069 through 1105 generates a sound from the system speaker.

The Pause( ) function

The function at lines 1107 through 1125 causes the program to pause for a specified period of time. The code uses the value returned by the system clock and multiplies it by the number of CPU cycles per second. If you are using Turbo C++ or Borland C++, this value is the CLK_TCK global variable. If you are using Zortech C++, it is CLOCKS_PER_SEC. The pause function is used to avoid inadvertent double-clicks when the demonstration program is run on fast hardware operating at 20 MHz and above.

The Arguments( ) function

The function at lines 1127 through 1169 compares the command line argument with a set of permitted strings. The function assigns an appropriate value to the global variable named Mode.

Programmer's Guide to LIB2D.HPP

The complete source code for the declarations for class PhysicalDisplay and class Viewport is found in LIB2D.HPP in appendix E. The source from LIB2D.HPP must be #included at the beginning of any program that wishes to use the methods of class PhysicalDisplay or class Viewport. See the discussion in chapter 1 for further information about LIB2D.HPP.

Programmer's Guide to LIB2D.CPP

The source code in LIB2D.CPP, presented in appendix E, provides language bindings that produce low-level graphics. The routines in LIB2D.CPP call the appropriate runtime library functions in Turbo C++'s graphics.lib, Borland C++'s graphics.lib, Zortech C++'s fg.lib, or Microsoft's graph.lib.

LIB2D.CPP is the class implementation listing for class PhysicalDisplay and class Viewport. Class PhysicalDisplay manages the state of the display. Class Viewport is responsible for maintaining a viewport and producing low-level graphics. These two classes generate nearly all the low-level graphics required by the demonstration programs in the book. See the discussion in chapter 1 for further information about class PhysicalDisplay and class Viewport.

Programmer's Guide to MOUSE.HPP

Code The complete source code for the declarations for class PointingDevice is found in MOUSE.HPP in appendix E. MOUSE.HPP must be #included at the beginning of any program using the methods of class PointingDevice. Class PointingDevice provides methods that are integral to the operation of this demonstration.

The code at lines 0054 through 0067 declares data members and a method that are not visible to functions or methods outside class PointingDevice.

The code at lines 0069 through 0079 declares methods of class PointingDevice that can be called by any in-scope function.

Programmer's Guide to MOUSE.CPP

Code The complete source code for the implementation for class PointingDevice is found in MOUSE.CPP in appendix E. The methods of class PointingDevice provide interactive control over a mouse at runtime.

Constructor

The constructor for class PointingDevice is located at lines 0070 through 0085. The constructor is used to initialize the contents of the data structure that will hold values indicating the runtime status of the mouse. SKETCH.CPP uses a pointer to access these values.

Method Detect( )

The Detect( ) method at line 0100 and the Init( ) method at line 0148 use mouse function 0 and INT 33H to initialize the mouse driver. The returned value in the ax register is placed into the MouseParams structure field named MouseFlag.

The caller, method Detect( ), uses MouseFlag to determine if a driver is loaded and ready to be used. If MouseFlag is 0, then no driver is present. If MouseFlag is any value other than 0, then a driver is present. The mouse driver must be initialized before any calls are made; otherwise unpredictable results can occur. Note how the switch( ) statement at line 0104 enables the proper minimum and maximum screen locations to be set depending on the graphics mode.

Method Data( )

The Data( ) method of class PointingDevice at lines 0166 through 0173 is a pointer to the MouseParams structure. This allows SKETCH.CPP to read the contents of the structure, which contains the current location of the mouse cursor, and so on.

Method Show( )

The Show( ) method of class PointingDevice at lines 0175 through 0192 uses mouse function 1 and INT 33H to display the screen cursor.

Method Hide( )

The Hide( ) method of class PointingDevice at lines 0194 through 0211 uses mouse function 2 and INT 33H to remove the cursor from the screen. This method is always called before any graphics are drawn.

Method Info( )

The Info( ) method of class PointingDevice at lines 0213 through 0239 carries out two tasks. It first reports whether or not a mouse button has been pressed. This information is returned in the bx register and is stored in the MouseButton field of the MouseParams structure. Method Info( ) also fetches the current coordinates of the mouse cursor.

Method Pos( )

The Pos( ) method at lines 0245 through 0266 resets the location of the cursor on the screen. The code uses mouse function 4 and passes the xy coordinates in the cx and dx registers.

Method HLimit( )

The HLimit( ) method of class PointingDevice at lines 0268 through 0293 uses mouse function 7 and INT 33H to define the maximum and minimum x coordinates permitted for the on-screen cursor. If the user moves the pointing device outside this range, the screen cursor will act as if it has encountered an invisible boundary. The minimum x coordinate is passed in the cx register, the maximum x coordinate in the cx register.

Method VLimit( )

The VLimit( ) method at lines 0295 through 0320 sets the minimum and maximum y coordinates allowed for the mouse cursor at runtime. The minimum y coordinate is passed in the cx register. The maximum y coordinate is passed to the driver in the dx register.

Programmer's Guide to BITBLT.HPP

[Code] The complete source code for the declarations for class Bitblt is found in BITBLT.HPP in appendix E. The source from BITBLT.HPP must be #included at the beginning of any program that wishes to use the methods of class Bitblt. The methods of class Bitblt provide the on-screen swatch that shows the current drawing, fill, edge, and dither selection while you are choosing a new attribute.

The source code at lines 0056 through 0089 declares data members and a method that are not visible to functions or methods outside class Bitblt. The code at lines 0091 through 0100 declares methods of class Bitblt that can be called by any in-scope function or method.

Programmer's Guide to BITBLT.CPP

[Code] The complete source code for the implementation for class Bitblt is found in BITBLT.CPP in appendix E. The methods of class Bitblt provide bitblts capable of displaying, moving, and erasing themselves. Class Bitblt also provides methods that enable a bitblt to save itself to disk and load itself from disk, although those methods are not called by SKETCH.CPP.

Constructor

The constructor for objects of class Bitblt is located at lines 0061 through 0078. The constructor receives as its argument list the diagonal bounding coordinates of the bitblt being created, the horizontal and vertical resolution of the current graphics screen mode, and a pointer to the Viewport object to be used for low-level graphics output to the display.

Destructor

The destructor for class Bitblt is located at lines 0080 through 0087. The destructor is automatically called whenever an object of class Bitblt is destroyed. A call to private method FreeBlock( ) ensures that the memory allocated for the graphic array is released back to the C++ free store.

Method GrabImage( )

The method at lines 0089 through 0108 captures the image from the display. Note the -> addressing notation at line 0097, used to call method MemBlock( ) of object Generic. Generic is a pointer to the Viewport object that was passed when the bitblt was activated. A call to method GetBlock( ) stores the image in the memory allocated by method MemBlock( ).

The code at line 0106 sets a token to indicate that the bitblt is ready to be used. This token will be verified by other methods that want to write a bitblt to the display. This helps avoid runtime errors.

Method DisplayImage( )

The method at lines 0121 through 0146 writes the bitblt to the screen. The test at line 0128 ensures that a graphic array exists. The tests at lines 0129 through 0132 ensures that the requested location for installation is legal. Lines 0133 and 0134 use variables defined at line 0071 which correspond to the pixel logic to be used for subsequent bitblt write operations.

Method EraseImage( )

The method at lines 0148 through 0158 erases the bitblt from the display. The background was saved in line 0136 when the bitblt was written to the screen. Line 0155 in method EraseImage( ) writes this background image back to the screen.

Method MoveImage( )

The method at lines 0160 through 0186 can be used to move a displayed bitblt to another location on the screen. The method takes care of all the low-level housekeeping chores. It removes the existing bitblt and restores the background. Then it places the bitblt at the desired new location. Note in particular line 0176, which calls method GetBlock( ) in order to save the background before the new location is overwritten. SKETCH.CPP does not call method MoveImage( ) of class Bitblt.

6-5 Sample program SKETCH.CPP. Supports VGA, EGA, MCGA, CGA, and Hercules adapters. This interactive application demonstrates how to use low-level C++ classes for the physical display and viewports to build a paint/draw program.

```
0001   /*
0002
0003                 Lee Adams' SUPERCHARGED C++ GRAPHICS
0004             Interactive demo:  typical paint/draw routines
0005
0006      SOURCE FILE:   SKETCH.CPP
0007             TYPE:   C++ source file for a multimodule application.
0008          PURPOSE:   Demonstrates fundamental routines for paint
0009                     and draw applications.
0010     PROGRAM LIST:   SKETCH.CPP, LIB2D.CPP, BITBLT.CPP, MOUSE.CPP.
0011        LANGUAGES:   Turbo C++, Borland C++, Zortech C++ and
0012                     all C++ compilers compatible with AT&T C++ 2.0
0013                     specification; and nominal compatibility with
0014                     Microsoft C++ (see the discussion in the book).
0015     MEMORY MODEL:   large.
0016     COMMAND-LINE:   you can specify a graphics mode by using the
0017                     command-line argument /Mnn as shown below:
0018                         /M12   640x480x16-color VGA
0019                         /M11   640x480x2-color VGA, MCGA
```

6-5 Continued.

```
0020                    /M10   640x350x16-color VGA, EGA
0021                    /M0E   640x200x16-color VGA, EGA
0022                    /M06   640x200x2-color VGA, MCGA, EGA, CGA
0023                    /MHC   720x348x2-color Hercules
0024              If no command-line argument is used, hardware
0025              autodetect is used to select the best mode.
0026    OUTPUT:  You can use the mouse to create and manipulate
0027             various graphics using the paint/draw metaphor.
0028             An undo function is supported.
0029    LICENSE:  As purchaser of the book in which this source code
0030       appears you are granted a royalty-free license to reproduce
0031       and distribute executable files generated using this code
0032       provided that you accept the conditions of the License
0033       Agreement and Limited Warranty described in the book.
0034    PUBLICATION: Contains material from Windcrest/McGraw-Hill
0035       book 3489, published by TAB BOOKS.
0036    U.S. GOVERNMENT RESTRICTED RIGHTS:  This software and its
0037       documentation is provided with restricted rights.  The use,
0038       duplication, or disclosure by the Government is subject to
0039       restrictions set forth in subdivision (b)(3)(ii) of The
0040       Rights in Technical Data and Computer Software clause at
0041       252.227-7013.  Contractor/manufacturer is Lee Adams, c/o
0042       TAB BOOKS, 13311 Monterey Ave., Blue Ridge Summit PA 17294.
0043    TRADEMARK:  Lee Adams is a trademark of Lee Adams.
0044
0045       Copyright 1991 Lee Adams.  All rights reserved worldwide.
0046
0047
0048                    CONDITIONAL COMPILATION
0049    To compile only those blocks of code that support the C++
0050    compiler and graphics library that you are using, you should
0051    #define the appropriate tokens on lines 0063 and 0064.
0052             GRAPHICS LIBRARY
0053       Borland's graphics.lib            #define BGI
0054       Zortech's fg.lib or fgdebug.lib   #define FG
0055       Microsoft's graph.lib             #define MS
0056             COMPILER
0057       Borland Turbo C++ compiler        #define BORLAND
0058       Zortech C++ compiler              #define ZORTECH
0059       AT&T-compatible C++ compilers     #define MICROSOFT
0060    Be sure you define only one compiler and one graphics library.
0061
0062                                                              */
0063    #define BGI     1 // indicates the graphics library you are using.
0064    #define BORLAND 1 // indicates the C++ compiler you are using.
0065    /*
0066
0067                    Constants
0068
0069                                                              */
0070    const int zFAIL=0; const int zEMPTY=0;
0071    const int zYES=1; const int zNO=0;
0072    const int zVGA_12H=1; const int zEGA_10H=2; const int zEGA_EH=3;
0073    const int zMCGA_11H=4; const int zCGA_6H=5; const int zHERC=6;
0074    const int OVERWRITE= 0; const int zNOTHING= 0;
0075    const int zNORMAL=  1; const int zEXTENDED= 2;
0076
0077                    // codes for various keystrokes...
0078    const int zESC=       27;
0079    const int zTAB=        9;
0080    const int zENTER=     13;
0081    const int zBACKSPACE=  8;
```

```
0082   const int zALT_X=        45;
0083
0084   const int zF1=           59;
0085   const int zF2=           60;
0086   const int zF3=           61;
0087   const int zF4=           62;
0088   const int zF5=           63;
0089   const int zF6=           64;
0090   const int zF7=           65;
0091   const int zF8=           66;
0092   const int zF9=           67;
0093   const int zF10=          68;
0094
0095   const int zCTRL_F1=      94;
0096   const int zCTRL_F2=      95;
0097   const int zCTRL_F3=      96;
0098   const int zCTRL_F4=      97;
0099   const int zCTRL_F5=      98;
0100   const int zCTRL_F6=      99;
0101   const int zCTRL_F7=      100;
0102   const int zCTRL_F8=      101;
0103   const int zCTRL_F9=      102;
0104   const int zCTRL_F10=     103;
0105   /*
0106
0107   ┌──────────────────────────── Macros ────────────────────────────┐
0108
0109                                                                   */
0110   #define Wait_for_any_key  while(KeyCode==0) zKeyboard(); KeyCode=0;
0111   /*
0112
0113   ┌────────────────────────── Include files ──────────────────────────┐
0114
0115                                                                   */
0116   #if defined (BORLAND)
0117   #include <time.h>        // supports clock().
0118   #include <string.h>      // supports strncmp().
0119   #include <bios.h>        // supports bioskey().
0120   #include <process.h>     // supports exit().
0121   #include <iostream.h>    // supports cout.
0122   #include <dos.h>         // supports outportb(), inportb().
0123   #elif defined (ZORTECH)
0124   #include <time.h>        // supports clock().
0125   #include <string.h>      // supports strncmp().
0126   #include <bios.h>        // supports bioskey().
0127   #include <stdlib.h>      // supports exit().
0128   #include <stream.hpp>    // supports cout.
0129   #include <dos.h>         // supports outp(), inp().
0130   #elif defined (MICROSOFT)
0131   #include <time.h>        // supports clock().
0132   #include <string.h>      // supports strncmp().
0133   #include <bios.h>        // supports _bios_keybrd().
0134   #include <process.h>     // supports exit().
0135   #include <iostream.h>    // supports cout.
0136   #include <conio.h>       // supports outp(), inp().
0137   #endif
0138
0139   #include "LIB2D.HPP"     // declarations for PhysicalDisplay class.
0140   #include "MOUSE.HPP"     // declarations for PointingDevice class.
0141   #include "BITBLT.HPP"    // declarations for Bitblt class.
0142   /*
0143
0144   ┌──────── Prototypes for functions visible throughout this file ────────┐
```

```
0145
0146                                                            */
0147   static void zStartup(void);           // initializes a graphics mode.
0148   static void zArguments(int, char far* far*);   // checks arguments.
0149   static void zKeyboard(void);           // checks for a keystroke.
0150   static void zQuit_Pgm(void);           // ends the program gracefully.
0151   static void zPurge(void);              // empties the keyboard buffer.
0152   static void zStubRoutine(void);        // do-nothing stub.
0153   static void zMakeSound(int,double);    // makes a specific sound.
0154   static clock_t zDelay(clock_t,double); // CPU-independent pause.
0155   static void zBlankTextLine(void);      // blanks the dialog line.
0156   static void zDrawCurve(int,int,int,int,
0157                   int,int,int,int);         // draws curve.
0158   static void zGetCurvePoint(int,int,int,int,int,int,
0159               int,int,float,float,float);   // point on curve.
0160   static void zEditColor(int);           // alters colors and patterns.
0161   static void zMouseManager(void);       // mouse polling loop.
0162   static void zCoreFunction(int);        // implements user's selections.
0163   static void zGetViewportCoords(int,int);  // converts coordinates.
0164   static void zInteractiveLoop(void);    // master loop.
0165   /*
0166
0167   ┌─────────────────────────────────────────────────────────────┐
        │     Declaration of variables visible throughout this file    │
0168   └─────────────────────────────────────────────────────────────┘
0169                                                            */
0170   static char *StartUpArg[6]={         // legal command-line arguments.
0171           "/M12", "/M10", "/MOE", "/M11", "/M06", "/MHC" };
0172   static int CommandLineArg=zNO;        // indicates if argument exists.
0173   static int CommandLineCompare=0;      // indicates if argument legal.
0174   static int C0=0,C1=1,C2=2,C3=3,C4=4,C5=5,C6=6,
0175   C7=7,C8=8,C9=9,C10=10,C11=11,C12=12,C13=13,
0176   C14=14,C15=15;                        // palette index codes.
0177   static int Mode=0;              // which graphics mode is being used.
0178   static int Result=0;            // captures result of graphics routines.
0179   static int CharWidth=0,CharHeight=0;  // dimensions of character.
0180   static char KeyCode=0;    // token for normal or extended keystroke.
0181   static char KeyNum=0;                 // ASCII number of keystroke.
0182   static char SolidFill[]=
0183              {255,255,255,255,255,255,255,255};  // 100% fill.
0184   static int TextClr=0;                 // color for regular text.
0185   static int PromptClr=7;               // color for prompt text.
0186   static int MenuClr=0;                 // color for menu text.
0187   static char Copyright[]=
0188              "Copyright 1991 Lee Adams.  All rights reserved.";
0189   static char Title[]=
0190   "USING C++ TO CREATE PAINT/DRAW PROGRAMS";
0191   static char PressAnyKey[]= "Press any key to continue.";
0192   static char StubMessage[]= "Inactive function.";
0193   static int X_Res= 0, Y_Res= 0;              // screen resolution.
0194   static int clipx1= 0, clipy1= 0,
0195           clipx2= 0, clipy2= 0;               // clipping coords.
0196   static int sx= 0,sy= 0;               // current pen position.
0197   static int GS_penx= 0, GS_peny= 0;    // current pen position.
0198   static int GS_penclr= 0, GS_fillclr= 0,
0199     GS_boundaryclr= 0;                        // foreground clrs.
0200   static int GS_bgclr= 0;                     // background color.
0201   static char * GS_hatch;                     // hatch pattern.
0202   static char * GS_shade;                     // halftone pattern.
0203   static int hatch_index= 0, shade_index= 0,          // indexers.
0204           penclr_index= 0, fillclr_index= 0,
0205           boundary_index= 0;
0206
```

```
0207                    // assorted patterns for dithered fills...
0208    static char fill_0[]=    {0,0,0,0,0,0,0,0};                    //    0%.
0209    static char fill_3[]=    {0,32,0,0,0,2,0,0};                   //    3%.
0210    static char fill_6[]=    {32,0,2,0,128,0,8,0};                 //    6%.
0211    static char fill_12[]=   {32,2,128,8,32,2,128,8};              //   12%.
0212    static char fill_25[]=   {68,17,68,17,68,17,68,17};            //   25%.
0213    static char fill_37[]=   {170,68,170,17,170,68,170,17};        //   37%.
0214    static char fill_50[]=   {85,170,85,170,85,170,85,170};        //   50%.
0215    static char fill_62[]=   {85,187,85,238,85,187,85,238};        //   62%.
0216    static char fill_75[]=   {187,238,187,238,187,238,187,238};    //   75%.
0217    static char fill_87[]=   {223,253,127,247,223,253,127,247};    //   87%.
0218    static char fill_93[]=   {255,223,255,255,255,253,255,255};    //   93%.
0219    static char fill_100[]=  {255,255,255,255,255,255,255,255};    //  100%.
0220
0221                    // assorted patterns for hatched fills...
0222    static char hatch_1[]=   {204,204,204,204,204,204,204,204};
0223    static char hatch_2[]=   {240,240,240,240,240,240,240,240};
0224    static char hatch_3[]=   {24,48,96,192,129,3,6,12};
0225    static char hatch_4[]=   {24,12,6,3,129,192,96,48};
0226    static char hatch_5[]=   {15,15,15,15,240,240,240,240};
0227    static char hatch_6[]=   {255,1,1,1,255,16,16,16};
0228    static char hatch_7[]=   {0,126,66,66,66,66,126,0};
0229    static char hatch_8[]=   {0,126,126,126,126,126,126,0};
0230    static char hatch_9[]=   {130,68,40,16,40,68,130,1};
0231    static char hatch_10[]=  {129,24,24,126,126,24,24,129};
0232
0233    PhysicalDisplay Display;        // create the physical display object.
0234    Viewport Viewport1(&Display);            // create a viewport object.
0235    PointingDevice Mouse;            // create a pointing-device object.
0236    static mdata *MPtr;     // uninitialized ptr to mouse runtime data.
0237    /*
0238
0239    ┌──────────────────────────────────────────────────────────────┐
         │              Function definitions                              │
0240    └──────────────────────────────────────────────────────────────┘
0241
0242    ┌──────────────────────────────────────────────────────────────┐
         │     The executive routine:  program execution begins here      │
0243    └──────────────────────────────────────────────────────────────┘
0244                                                                       */
0245    main(int argc, char *argv[])
0246    {
0247      int NumArgs; char far* far* Arg;
0248
0249    NumArgs= argc;                          // grab number of arguments.
0250    Arg= &argv[0];              // grab address of array of arguments.
0251    zArguments(NumArgs, Arg);      // check the command-line arguments.
0252
0253                    // initialize the graphics mode...
0254    zStartup();                         // establish the graphics mode.
0255    Display.Init2D(Mode,0,0,X_Res-1,Y_Res-1);    // set graphics state.
0256    Result= Display.InitUndo();        // create hidden page for Undo.
0257    if (Result==zFAIL) zQuit_Pgm();         // if hidden page failed.
0258
0259                    // initialize the display...
0260    Display.BlankPage();                        // clear the display.
0261    clipx1= 1; clipy1= 13;      // set the viewport clipping coords...
0262    clipx2= X_Res-2; clipy2= Y_Res-2;
0263    #if defined (FG)
0264       clipy1= 16;
0265    #endif
0266    Display.SetHue(C15);
0267    Viewport1.DrawBorder(clipx1-1,clipy1-1,X_Res-1,Y_Res-1);
0268    Display.SetHue(C7); Display.SetFill(SolidFill,C7);
0269    Viewport1.DrawPanel(clipx1,clipy1,clipx2,clipy2);
```

```
0270  Viewport1.PutText(3,2,TextClr,Title);              // sign-on notice.
0271  Viewport1.PutText(4,2,TextClr,Copyright);          // copyright notice.
0272  Viewport1.PutText(1,2,PromptClr,PressAnyKey);  // display a prompt.
0273  Wait_for_any_key     // this macro was defined earlier in line 0136.
0274
0275                  // display the paint/draw functions...
0276  Viewport1.PutText(6,2,MenuClr,"Select then use mouse:");
0277  Viewport1.PutText(7,2,MenuClr, "Ctrl+F1 new");
0278  Viewport1.PutText(8,2,MenuClr, "Ctrl+F2 line");
0279  Viewport1.PutText(9,2,MenuClr, "Ctrl+F3 curve");
0280  Viewport1.PutText(10,2,MenuClr,"Ctrl+F4 rectangle");
0281  Viewport1.PutText(11,2,MenuClr,"Ctrl+F5 circle");
0282  Viewport1.PutText(12,2,MenuClr,"Ctrl+F6 eraser");
0283  Viewport1.PutText(13,2,MenuClr,"Ctrl+F7 solid fill");
0284  Viewport1.PutText(14,2,MenuClr,"Ctrl+F8 hatch fill");
0285  Viewport1.PutText(15,2,MenuClr,"Ctrl+F9 dither fill");
0286  Viewport1.PutText(16,2,MenuClr,"F1 set pen color");
0287  Viewport1.PutText(17,2,MenuClr,"F2 set fill color");
0288  Viewport1.PutText(18,2,MenuClr,"F3 set edge color");
0289  Viewport1.PutText(19,2,MenuClr,"F4 set hatch pattern");
0290  Viewport1.PutText(20,2,MenuClr,"F5 set dither shade");
0291  Viewport1.PutText(21,2,MenuClr,"Bkspc undo");
0292  Viewport1.PutText(22,2,MenuClr,"Alt+X quit");
0293
0294                       // initialize the mouse...
0295  Result= Mouse.Detect(Mode);
0296  if (Result== zFAIL) zQuit_Pgm();          // if no mouse, then quit.
0297  MPtr= Mouse.Data();              // grab a pointer to the mouse data.
0298
0299                  // initialize the graphics state...
0300  GS_penx= 20; GS_peny= 20;
0301  GS_penclr= C0; GS_fillclr= C0; GS_boundaryclr= C0; GS_bgclr= C7;
0302  GS_hatch= hatch_1; GS_shade= fill_50;
0303  hatch_index= 1; shade_index= 7;
0304  penclr_index= 0; fillclr_index= 0; boundary_index= 0;
0305  #if defined (BGI)
0306    GS_fillclr= C1; fillclr_index= 1;
0307    if (Mode==zCGA_6H)
0308      {
0309      GS_fillclr= C0; fillclr_index= 0;
0310      }
0311  #endif
0312
0313  zBlankTextLine();
0314  Viewport1.PutText(1,2,PromptClr,"Ready to begin drawing.");
0315  Display.BackUp();          // store the display page for future undo.
0316
0317  zInteractiveLoop();                          // call the master loop.
0318  zQuit_Pgm();                 // tidy up and terminate the application.
0319  }
0320  /*
0321
0322  ┌──────────────────────────────────────────────────────────────────┐
         │                      Interactive loop                          │
0323  └──────────────────────────────────────────────────────────────────┘
0324                                                                    */
0325  static void zInteractiveLoop(void)
0326  {
0327  EXECUTIVELOOP:              // start of the keyboard polling loop.
0328    zKeyboard();                            // poll the keyboard.
0329    if (KeyCode==zNOTHING) goto EXECUTIVELOOP;   // if no keystroke.
0330    if (KeyCode!=zEXTENDED) goto NORMALKEY;  // if not extended key.
0331  EXTENDEDKEY:
```

```
0332    switch (KeyNum)
0333      {             // these are the primary run-time control keys...
0334      case zALT_X:    return;                              // quit.
0335      case zCTRL_F1:  zCoreFunction(1); break;
0336      case zCTRL_F2:  zCoreFunction(2); break;
0337      case zCTRL_F3:  zCoreFunction(3); break;
0338      case zCTRL_F4:  zCoreFunction(4); break;
0339      case zCTRL_F5:  zCoreFunction(5); break;
0340      case zCTRL_F6:  zCoreFunction(6); break;
0341      case zCTRL_F7:  zCoreFunction(7); break;
0342      case zCTRL_F8:  zCoreFunction(8); break;
0343      case zCTRL_F9:  zCoreFunction(9); break;
0344      case zF1:       zEditColor(1); break;
0345      case zF2:       zEditColor(2); break;
0346      case zF3:       zEditColor(3); break;
0347      case zF4:       zEditColor(4); break;
0348      case zF5:       zEditColor(5); break;
0349      case zF6:
0350      case zF7:
0351      case zF8:
0352      case zF9:
0353      case zF10:
0354      default:  zMakeSound(450,.2); zPurge();     // unsupported key.
0355      }
0356    zBlankTextLine();
0357    Viewport1.PutText(1,2,PromptClr,"Ready for your next command.");
0358    zPurge();
0359    goto EXECUTIVELOOP;
0360  NORMALKEY:                          // jump to here if a normal key.
0361    switch (KeyNum)
0362      {
0363      case zESC:  return;                                  // quit.
0364      case zBACKSPACE:                                     // undo.
0365  #if defined (BGI)
0366          Display.Restore(); zBlankTextLine();
0367          Viewport1.PutText(1,2,PromptClr,"Undo completed.");
0368          break;
0369  #elif defined (FG)
0370          zBlankTextLine();
0371          Viewport1.PutText(1,2,PromptClr,
0372            "Undo not supported.  Refer to book.");
0373          zMakeSound(450,.2); break;
0374  #elif defined (MS)
0375          Display.Restore(); zBlankTextLine();
0376          Viewport1.PutText(1,2,PromptClr,"Undo completed.");
0377          break;
0378  #endif
0379      default:    zMakeSound(450,.2);             // unsupported key.
0380      }
0381    zPurge();
0382    goto EXECUTIVELOOP;                           // loop back.
0383  }
0384  /*
0385
0386  ┌────────────────────────────────────────────────────────────┐
       │                    Manage the mouse                          │
       └────────────────────────────────────────────────────────────┘
0387
0388                                                              */
0389  static void zMouseManager(void)
0390  {
0391  #if defined (BORLAND)
0392    delay(1000);          // pause to avoid inadvertent double-clicks.
0393  #elif defined (ZORTECH)
0394      int Delay, Dummy= 0;
```

```
0395      for (Delay=1; Delay<30000; Delay++) Dummy++;
0396      Dummy= 0;
0397      for (Delay=1; Delay<30000; Delay++) Dummy++;
0398  #elif defined (MICROSOFT)
0399        int Delay, Dummy= 0;
0400      for (Delay=1; Delay<30000; Delay++) Dummy++;
0401      Dummy= 0;
0402      for (Delay=1; Delay<30000; Delay++) Dummy++;
0403  #endif
0404  Mouse.Show();                          // display the mouse cursor.
0405  MOUSE_LOOP:                                    // loop begins here.
0406  Mouse.Info();                          // check the mouse's status.
0407  if (MPtr->MouseButton==1)
0408      {                                  // if left button pressed...
0409      sx= MPtr->MouseX;              // update current pen position...
0410      sy= MPtr->MouseY;
0411      Mouse.Hide(); return;      // remove cursor and return to caller.
0412      }
0413  if (MPtr->MouseButton==2)
0414      {                                 // if right button pressed...
0415      Mouse.Hide(); return;      // remove cursor and return to caller.
0416      }
0417  goto MOUSE_LOOP;                                  // infinite loop.
0418  }
0419  /*
0420
0421      ┌─────────────────────────────────────────────────────────────┐
           │  Convert physical coords returned by mouse to viewport coords │
0422       └─────────────────────────────────────────────────────────────┘
0423                                                                      */
0424  static void zGetViewportCoords(int x,int y)
0425  {
0426  #if defined (FG)
0427    GS_penx= x; GS_peny= y; return;
0428  #endif
0429  GS_penx= x - clipx1;
0430  GS_peny= y - clipy1;
0431  return;
0432  }
0433  /*
0434
0435      ┌─────────────────────────────────────────────────────────────┐
           │      Logic manager:  calls the appropriate core functions     │
0436       └─────────────────────────────────────────────────────────────┘
0437                                                                      */
0438  static void zCoreFunction(int Selection)
0439  {
0440      int x1,x2,y1,y2,x3,y3,x4,y4,xrad,yrad;
0441
0442  switch (Selection)
0443      {
0444      case 1:    goto NEW_IMAGE;
0445      case 2:    goto DRAW_LINE;
0446      case 3:    goto DRAW_CURVE;
0447      case 4:    goto DRAW_RECT;
0448      case 5:    goto DRAW_CIRCLE;
0449      case 6:    goto ERASER;
0450      case 7:    goto SOLID_FILL;
0451      case 8:    goto PATTERN_FILL;
0452      case 9:    goto DITHERED_FILL;
0453      default: zMakeSound(450,.2); goto DONE;
0454      }
0455
0456  NEW_IMAGE:
```

```
0457    Display.BackUp();
0458    Viewport1.WindowOpen(clipx1,clipy1,clipx2,clipy2);
0459    Viewport1.WindowClear(GS_bgclr);
0460    Viewport1.WindowClose(X_Res,Y_Res);
0461 #if defined (FG)
0462    Display.SetHue(C7); Display.SetFill(SolidFill,C7);
0463    Viewport1.DrawPanel(clipx1,clipy1,clipx2,clipy2);
0464 #endif
0465    Viewport1.PutText(6,2,MenuClr,"Select then use mouse:");
0466    Viewport1.PutText(7,2,MenuClr, "Ctrl+F1 new");
0467    Viewport1.PutText(8,2,MenuClr, "Ctrl+F2 line");
0468    Viewport1.PutText(9,2,MenuClr, "Ctrl+F3 curve");
0469    Viewport1.PutText(10,2,MenuClr,"Ctrl+F4 rectangle");
0470    Viewport1.PutText(11,2,MenuClr,"Ctrl+F5 circle");
0471    Viewport1.PutText(12,2,MenuClr,"Ctrl+F6 eraser");
0472    Viewport1.PutText(13,2,MenuClr,"Ctrl+F7 solid fill");
0473    Viewport1.PutText(14,2,MenuClr,"Ctrl+F8 hatch fill");
0474    Viewport1.PutText(15,2,MenuClr,"Ctrl+F9 dither fill");
0475    Viewport1.PutText(16,2,MenuClr,"F1 set pen color");
0476    Viewport1.PutText(17,2,MenuClr,"F2 set fill color");
0477    Viewport1.PutText(18,2,MenuClr,"F3 set edge color");
0478    Viewport1.PutText(19,2,MenuClr,"F4 set hatch pattern");
0479    Viewport1.PutText(20,2,MenuClr,"F5 set dither shade");
0480    Viewport1.PutText(21,2,MenuClr,"Bkspc undo");
0481    Viewport1.PutText(22,2,MenuClr,"Alt+X quit");
0482    goto DONE;
0483
0484 DRAW_LINE:
0485    zBlankTextLine();
0486    Viewport1.PutText(1,2,PromptClr,
0487     "Left button: draw line segment.  Right: done.");
0488    Display.SetHue(GS_penclr);
0489    zMouseManager();                        // poll the mouse or tablet.
0490    if (MPtr->MouseButton!=1) goto DONE;    // if right button, stop.
0491    Display.BackUp();
0492    zGetViewportCoords(sx,sy);          // convert to viewport coords.
0493    Viewport1.WindowOpen(clipx1,clipy1,clipx2,clipy2);
0494    Viewport1.SetPosition(GS_penx,GS_peny);
0495    Viewport1.DrawLine(GS_penx,GS_peny);
0496    LINELOOP:                           // enter the line-drawing loop.
0497    zMouseManager();                        // poll the mouse or tablet.
0498    if (MPtr->MouseButton!=1)
0499     {                                      // if not left button...
0500     Viewport1.WindowClose(X_Res,Y_Res);
0501     goto DONE;
0502     }
0503    zGetViewportCoords(sx,sy);          // convert to viewport coords.
0504    Viewport1.DrawLine(GS_penx,GS_peny);    // draw the line segment.
0505    goto LINELOOP;                      // loop until right button pressed.
0506
0507 DRAW_CURVE:
0508    zBlankTextLine();
0509    Viewport1.PutText(1,2,PromptClr,
0510     "Left button: set curve points.  Right: done.");
0511    Display.BackUp();
0512    Display.SetHue(GS_penclr);
0513    CURVELOOP:
0514    zMouseManager();                                // get starting point.
0515    if (MPtr->MouseButton!=1) goto DONE;
0516    zGetViewportCoords(sx,sy);
0517    x1= GS_penx; y1= GS_peny;
0518    zMouseManager();                            // get first magnetic point.
0519    if (MPtr->MouseButton!=1) goto DONE;
```

```
0520    zGetViewportCoords(sx,sy);
0521    x2= GS_penx; y2= GS_peny;
0522    zMouseManager();                        // get second magnetic point.
0523    if (MPtr->MouseButton!=1) goto DONE;
0524    zGetViewportCoords(sx,sy);
0525    x3= GS_penx; y3= GS_peny;
0526    zMouseManager();                        // get ending point.
0527    if (MPtr->MouseButton!=1) goto DONE;
0528    zGetViewportCoords(sx,sy);
0529    x4= GS_penx; y4= GS_peny;
0530    Viewport1.WindowOpen(clipx1,clipy1,clipx2,clipy2);
0531    zDrawCurve(x1,y1,x2,y2,x3,y3,x4,y4);
0532    Viewport1.WindowClose(X_Res,Y_Res);
0533    goto CURVELOOP;
0534
0535  DRAW_RECT:
0536    Display.BackUp();
0537    zBlankTextLine();
0538    Viewport1.PutText(1,2,PromptClr,
0539      "Left button: set diagonal coords.  Right: done.");
0540    Display.SetHue(GS_penclr);
0541    OUTER_RECT_LOOP:
0542    zMouseManager();                        // get upper left vertex.
0543    if (MPtr->MouseButton==2) goto DONE;
0544    zGetViewportCoords(sx,sy);
0545    x1= GS_penx; y1= GS_peny;
0546    RECTANGLE_LOOP:
0547      zMouseManager();                      // get lower right vertex.
0548      if (MPtr->MouseButton==2) goto DONE;
0549      zGetViewportCoords(sx,sy);
0550      x2= GS_penx; y2= GS_peny;
0551      if (x2==x1) goto RECTANGLE_LOOP;
0552      if (y2==y1) goto RECTANGLE_LOOP;
0553    if (x1>x2)
0554      {                                     // if must swap left-right coords...
0555      xrad= x1; x1= x2; x2= xrad;
0556      }
0557    if (y1>y2)
0558      {                                     // if must swap top-bottom coords...
0559      yrad= y1; y1= y2; y2= yrad;
0560      }
0561    Viewport1.WindowOpen(clipx1,clipy1,clipx2,clipy2);
0562    Viewport1.DrawBorder(x1,y1,x2,y2);
0563    Viewport1.WindowClose(X_Res,Y_Res);
0564    goto OUTER_RECT_LOOP;
0565
0566  DRAW_CIRCLE:
0567    Display.BackUp();
0568    zBlankTextLine();
0569    Viewport1.PutText(1,2,PromptClr,
0570      "Left button: set center then radius.  Right: done.");
0571    Display.SetHue(GS_penclr);
0572    OUTER_CIRCLE_LOOP:
0573    zMouseManager();                        // get center coords.
0574    if (MPtr->MouseButton!=1) goto DONE;
0575    zGetViewportCoords(sx,sy);
0576    x1= GS_penx; y1= GS_peny;
0577    INNER_CIRCLE_LOOP:
0578      zMouseManager();                      // get radius size.
0579      if (MPtr->MouseButton!=1) goto DONE;
0580      zGetViewportCoords(sx,sy);
0581      x2= GS_penx;
```

```
0582        if (x2==x1) goto INNER_CIRCLE_LOOP;
0583        if (x2>x1) xrad=x2-x1;
0584        if (x1>x2) xrad=x1-x2;
0585        if (xrad<10) goto INNER_CIRCLE_LOOP;
0586      Viewport1.WindowOpen(clipx1,clipy1,clipx2,clipy2);
0587      Viewport1.DrawCircle(x1,y1,xrad);
0588      Viewport1.WindowClose(X_Res,Y_Res);
0589      goto OUTER_CIRCLE_LOOP;
0590
0591    ERASER:
0592      Display.BackUp();
0593      zBlankTextLine();
0594      Viewport1.PutText(1,2,PromptClr,
0595        "Left button: erase.  Right: done.");
0596      Display.SetHue(GS_bgclr); Display.SetFill(fill_100,GS_bgclr);
0597      ERASER_LOOP:
0598      zMouseManager();
0599      if (MPtr->MouseButton!=1)
0600        {
0601        Display.SetHue(GS_penclr);goto DONE;
0602        }
0603      zGetViewportCoords(sx,sy);
0604      x1= GS_penx; y1= GS_peny; x2= x1+14; y2= y1+8;
0605      Viewport1.WindowOpen(clipx1,clipy1,clipx2,clipy2);
0606      Viewport1.DrawPanel(x1,y1,x2,y2);
0607      Viewport1.WindowClose(X_Res,Y_Res);
0608      goto ERASER_LOOP;
0609
0610    SOLID_FILL:
0611      Display.BackUp();
0612      zBlankTextLine();
0613      Viewport1.PutText(1,2,PromptClr,
0614        "Left button: solid fill.  Right: done.");
0615      Display.SetFill(fill_100,GS_fillclr);
0616      SOLID_FILL_LOOP:
0617      zMouseManager();
0618      if (MPtr->MouseButton!=1)
0619        {
0620        Display.SetHue(GS_penclr); goto DONE;
0621        }
0622      zGetViewportCoords(sx,sy);
0623      Viewport1.WindowOpen(clipx1,clipy1,clipx2,clipy2);
0624      Viewport1.Fill(GS_penx,GS_peny,GS_boundaryclr);
0625      Viewport1.WindowClose(X_Res,Y_Res);
0626      goto SOLID_FILL_LOOP;
0627
0628    PATTERN_FILL:
0629      Display.BackUp();
0630      zBlankTextLine();
0631      Viewport1.PutText(1,2,PromptClr,
0632        "Left button: hatched fill.  Right: done.");
0633      Display.SetFill(GS_hatch,GS_fillclr);
0634      PATTERN_LOOP:
0635      zMouseManager();
0636      if (MPtr->MouseButton!=1)
0637        {
0638        Display.SetHue(GS_penclr); goto DONE;
0639        }
0640      zGetViewportCoords(sx,sy);
0641      Viewport1.WindowOpen(clipx1,clipy1,clipx2,clipy2);
0642      Viewport1.Fill(GS_penx,GS_peny,GS_boundaryclr);
0643      Viewport1.WindowClose(X_Res,Y_Res);
0644      goto PATTERN_LOOP;
```

```
0645
0646  DITHERED_FILL:
0647    Display.BackUp();
0648    zBlankTextLine();
0649    Viewport1.PutText(1,2,PromptClr,
0650      "Left button: dithered fill.  Right: done.");
0651    Display.SetFill(GS_shade,GS_fillclr);
0652  DITHERED_LOOP:
0653    zMouseManager();
0654    if (MPtr->MouseButton!=1)
0655      {
0656      Display.SetHue(GS_penclr); goto DONE;
0657      }
0658    zGetViewportCoords(sx,sy);
0659    Viewport1.WindowOpen(clipx1,clipy1,clipx2,clipy2);
0660    Viewport1.Fill(GS_penx,GS_peny,GS_boundaryclr);
0661    Viewport1.WindowClose(X_Res,Y_Res);
0662    goto DITHERED_LOOP;
0663
0664  DONE:
0665  return;
0666  }
0667  /*
0668
0669  ┌──────────────────────────────────────────────────────┐
      │              Draw a parametric curve                 │
0670  └──────────────────────────────────────────────────────┘
0671                                                        */
0672  static void zDrawCurve(int x1,int y1,int x2,int y2,
0673                         int x3,int y3,int x4,int y4)
0674  {
0675    float t,t2,t3;                    // declare local variables.
0676  t= 0.0; t2= t * t; t3= t * t * t;    // reset control parameters.
0677  zGetCurvePoint(x1,y1,x2,y2,x3,y3,x4,y4,t,t2,t3);    // find start.
0678  Viewport1.SetPosition(GS_penx,GS_peny);
0679  for (t=0.0; t<=1.01; t+=.05)
0680    {                               // find all subsequent points...
0681    t2= t * t; t3= t * t * t;
0682    zGetCurvePoint(x1,y1,x2,y2,x3,y3,x4,y4,t,t2,t3);
0683    Viewport1.DrawLine(GS_penx,GS_peny);
0684    }
0685  return;
0686  }
0687  static void zGetCurvePoint(int x1,int y1,int x2,int y2,
0688                             int x3,int y3,int x4,int y4,
0689                             float t,float t2,float t3)
0690  {                               // calculate next point on curve...
0691    float j1,j2,j3,j4;            // declare local variables.
0692  j1= x1 * (-t3+3*t2-3*t+1);
0693  j2= x2 * (3*t3-6*t2+3*t);
0694  j3= x3 * (-3*t3+3*t2);
0695  j4= x4 * t3;
0696  GS_penx= j1 + j2 + j3 + j4;              // reset x coordinate.
0697  j1= y1 * (-t3+3*t2-3*t+1);
0698  j2= y2 * (3*t3-6*t2+3*t);
0699  j3= y3 * (-3*t3+3*t2);
0700  j4= y4 * t3;
0701  GS_peny= j1 + j2 + j3 + j4;              // reset y coordinate.
0702  return;
0703  }
0704  /*
0705
0706  ┌──────────────────────────────────────────────────────┐
      │  Edit the solid color, dithering pattern, and hatch pattern
      └──────────────────────────────────────────────────────┘
```

```
0707   └──────────────────────────────────────────────────────────┘
0708                                                              */
0709   static void zEditColor(int Choice)
0710   {
0711   zBlankTextLine();
0712   Viewport1.PutText(1,2,PromptClr,
0713     "Tab: select next color.  Enter: done.");
0714   Bitblt *SwatchBackground=                  // create a bitblt object...
0715     new Bitblt(clipx1,clipy1,clipx1+50,clipy1+50,
0716               X_Res,Y_Res,&Viewport1);
0717   SwatchBackground->GrabImage();        // save the existing background.
0718   Display.SetFill(fill_100,GS_bgclr);
0719   Display.SetHue(GS_bgclr);
0720   Display.SetLine(0xffff);
0721   Viewport1.WindowOpen(clipx1,clipy1,clipx2,clipy2);
0722   Viewport1.DrawPanel(0,0,50,50);            // blank the swatch area.
0723   Viewport1.WindowClose(X_Res,Y_Res);
0724   Bitblt *SwatchBlank=                       // create a bitblt object...
0725     new Bitblt(clipx1,clipy1,clipx1+50,clipy1+50,
0726               X_Res,Y_Res,&Viewport1);
0727   SwatchBlank->GrabImage();                  // save the blank swatch area.
0728
0729   switch (Choice)
0730     {                   // set the appropriate current fill variables...
0731     case 1: Display.SetFill(fill_100,GS_penclr); break;
0732     case 2: Display.SetFill(fill_100,GS_fillclr); break;
0733     case 3: Display.SetFill(fill_100,GS_boundaryclr); break;
0734     case 4: Display.SetFill(GS_hatch,GS_fillclr); break;
0735     case 5: Display.SetFill(GS_shade,GS_fillclr); break;
0736     }
0737   Viewport1.WindowOpen(clipx1,clipy1,clipx2,clipy2);
0738   Viewport1.DrawPanel(0,0,50,50);            // draw the swatch.
0739   Viewport1.WindowClose(X_Res,Y_Res);
0740
0741   EDITCOLORLOOP:                             // keyboard loop.
0742   zKeyboard();
0743   if (KeyCode==zNOTHING) goto EDITCOLORLOOP;
0744   if (KeyCode==zEXTENDED)
0745     {
0746     zMakeSound(450,.2); zPurge(); goto EDITCOLORLOOP;
0747     }
0748   switch(KeyNum)
0749     {
0750     case zESC:                              // delete objects and return;
0751           SwatchBackground->DisplayImage(clipx1,clipy1,OVERWRITE);
0752           delete SwatchBlank; delete SwatchBackground;
0753           return;
0754     case zENTER:                            // delete objects and return.
0755           SwatchBackground->DisplayImage(clipx1,clipy1,OVERWRITE);
0756           delete SwatchBlank; delete SwatchBackground;
0757           return;
0758     case zTAB:
0759           goto WHICHCOLOR;                  // if Tab then select next hue.
0760     default: zMakeSound(450,.2); break;
0761     }
0762   zPurge();
0763   goto EDITCOLORLOOP;
0764
0765   WHICHCOLOR:                    // jump to here if a new swatch needed.
0766   switch(Choice)
0767     {                           // jump to appropriate swatch generator.
0768     case 1: goto SETPENCLR;
0769     case 2: goto SETFILLCLR;
```

```
0770    case 3: goto SETBOUNDARYCLR;
0771    case 4: goto SETHATCH;
0772    case 5: goto SETSHADE;
0773    }
0774
0775    SETPENCLR:                          /* display new penclr swatch */
0776    penclr_index= penclr_index + 1;
0777    if (penclr_index>15) penclr_index= 0;
0778    switch (penclr_index)
0779    {
0780    case 0: GS_penclr=C0; break;
0781    case 1: GS_penclr=C1; break;
0782    case 2: GS_penclr=C2; break;
0783    case 3: GS_penclr=C3; break;
0784    case 4: GS_penclr=C4; break;
0785    case 5: GS_penclr=C5; break;
0786    case 6: GS_penclr=C6; break;
0787    case 7: GS_penclr=C7; break;
0788    case 8: GS_penclr=C8; break;
0789    case 9: GS_penclr=C9; break;
0790    case 10: GS_penclr=C10; break;
0791    case 11: GS_penclr=C11; break;
0792    case 12: GS_penclr=C12; break;
0793    case 13: GS_penclr=C13; break;
0794    case 14: GS_penclr=C14; break;
0795    case 15: GS_penclr=C15; break;
0796    }
0797    Display.SetFill(fill_100,GS_penclr);
0798    Viewport1.WindowOpen(clipx1,clipy1,clipx2,clipy2);
0799    Viewport1.DrawPanel(0,0,50,50);
0800    Viewport1.WindowClose(X_Res,Y_Res);
0801    goto EDITCOLORLOOP;
0802
0803    SETFILLCLR:                         /* display new fillclr swatch */
0804    fillclr_index= fillclr_index + 1;
0805    if (fillclr_index>15) fillclr_index= 0;
0806    switch(fillclr_index)
0807    {
0808    case 0: GS_fillclr=C0; break;
0809    case 1: GS_fillclr=C1; break;
0810    case 2: GS_fillclr=C2; break;
0811    case 3: GS_fillclr=C3; break;
0812    case 4: GS_fillclr=C4; break;
0813    case 5: GS_fillclr=C5; break;
0814    case 6: GS_fillclr=C6; break;
0815    case 7: GS_fillclr=C7; break;
0816    case 8: GS_fillclr=C8; break;
0817    case 9: GS_fillclr=C9; break;
0818    case 10: GS_fillclr=C10; break;
0819    case 11: GS_fillclr=C11; break;
0820    case 12: GS_fillclr=C12; break;
0821    case 13: GS_fillclr=C13; break;
0822    case 14: GS_fillclr=C14; break;
0823    case 15: GS_fillclr=C15; break;
0824    }
0825    Display.SetFill(fill_100,GS_fillclr);
0826    Viewport1.WindowOpen(clipx1,clipy1,clipx2,clipy2);
0827    Viewport1.DrawPanel(0,0,50,50);
0828    Viewport1.WindowClose(X_Res,Y_Res);
0829    goto EDITCOLORLOOP;
0830
0831    SETBOUNDARYCLR:                     /* display new boundaryclr swatch */
```

```
0832   boundary_index= boundary_index + 1;
0833   if (boundary_index>15) boundary_index= 0;
0834   switch(boundary_index)
0835     {
0836     case 0: GS_boundaryclr=C0; break;
0837     case 1: GS_boundaryclr=C1; break;
0838     case 2: GS_boundaryclr=C2; break;
0839     case 3: GS_boundaryclr=C3; break;
0840     case 4: GS_boundaryclr=C4; break;
0841     case 5: GS_boundaryclr=C5; break;
0842     case 6: GS_boundaryclr=C6; break;
0843     case 7: GS_boundaryclr=C7; break;
0844     case 8: GS_boundaryclr=C8; break;
0845     case 9: GS_boundaryclr=C9; break;
0846     case 10: GS_boundaryclr=C10; break;
0847     case 11: GS_boundaryclr=C11; break;
0848     case 12: GS_boundaryclr=C12; break;
0849     case 13: GS_boundaryclr=C13; break;
0850     case 14: GS_boundaryclr=C14; break;
0851     case 15: GS_boundaryclr=C15; break;
0852     }
0853   Display.SetFill(fill_100,GS_boundaryclr);
0854   Viewport1.WindowOpen(clipx1,clipy1,clipx2,clipy2);
0855   Viewport1.DrawPanel(0,0,50,50);
0856   Viewport1.WindowClose(X_Res,Y_Res);
0857   goto EDITCOLORLOOP;
0858
0859   SETHATCH:                                /* display new hatch swatch */
0860   hatch_index= hatch_index + 1;
0861   if (hatch_index>10) hatch_index= 1;
0862   switch(hatch_index)
0863     {
0864     case 1: GS_hatch=hatch_1; break;
0865     case 2: GS_hatch=hatch_2; break;
0866     case 3: GS_hatch=hatch_3; break;
0867     case 4: GS_hatch=hatch_4; break;
0868     case 5: GS_hatch=hatch_5; break;
0869     case 6: GS_hatch=hatch_6; break;
0870     case 7: GS_hatch=hatch_7; break;
0871     case 8: GS_hatch=hatch_8; break;
0872     case 9: GS_hatch=hatch_9; break;
0873     case 10: GS_hatch=hatch_10; break;
0874     }
0875   Display.SetFill(GS_hatch,GS_fillclr);
0876   SwatchBlank->DisplayImage(clipx1,clipy1,OVERWRITE);
0877   Viewport1.WindowOpen(clipx1,clipy1,clipx2,clipy2);
0878   Viewport1.DrawPanel(0,0,50,50);
0879   Viewport1.WindowClose(X_Res,Y_Res);
0880   goto EDITCOLORLOOP;
0881
0882   SETSHADE:                                /* display new shade swatch */
0883   shade_index= shade_index + 1;
0884   if (shade_index>12) shade_index= 1;
0885   switch(shade_index)
0886     {
0887     case 1: GS_shade=fill_0; break;
0888     case 2: GS_shade=fill_3; break;
0889     case 3: GS_shade=fill_6; break;
0890     case 4: GS_shade=fill_12; break;
0891     case 5: GS_shade=fill_25; break;
0892     case 6: GS_shade=fill_37; break;
0893     case 7: GS_shade=fill_50; break;
0894     case 8: GS_shade=fill_62; break;
```

```
0895      case 9: GS_shade=fill_75; break;
0896      case 10: GS_shade=fill_87; break;
0897      case 11: GS_shade=fill_93; break;
0898      case 12: GS_shade=fill_100; break;
0899      }
0900    Display.SetFill(GS_shade,GS_fillclr);
0901    SwatchBlank->DisplayImage(clipx1,clipy1,OVERWRITE);
0902    Viewport1.WindowOpen(clipx1,clipy1,clipx2,clipy2);
0903    Viewport1.DrawPanel(0,0,50,50);
0904    Viewport1.WindowClose(X_Res,Y_Res);
0905    goto EDITCOLORLOOP;
0906    }
0907    /*
0908
0909  ┌─────────────────────────────────────────────────────────┐
0910  │                  Terminate the program                  │
0911  └─────────────────────────────────────────────────────────┘
                                                                   */
0912    static void zQuit_Pgm(void)
0913    {
0914    Display.ShutDownGraphics();  // graceful shutdown of graphics mode.
0915    exit(0);                     // terminate the program and return OK code.
0916    }
0917    /*
0918
0919  ┌─────────────────────────────────────────────────────────┐
0920  │        Detect the graphics hardware and set the         │
0921  │  highest mode permitted by the graphics adapter and monitor.  │
0922  │  The user can override the autodetect algorithm by providing  │
0923  │  an argument on the command-line when the program is started.  │
0924  └─────────────────────────────────────────────────────────┘
                                                                   */
0925    static void zStartup(void)
0926    {
0927      int DefaultMode;
0928    DefaultMode= Display.SetupMode();   // get results of autodetect...
0929    switch(DefaultMode)                 // ...and jump to appropriate code.
0930      {
0931      case zFAIL:      goto ABORT_PGM;
0932      case zVGA_12H:   goto VGA_mode;
0933      case zEGA_10H:   goto EGA_ECD_mode;
0934      case zEGA_EH:    goto EGA_SCD_mode;
0935      case zMCGA_11H:  goto MCGA_mode;
0936      case zCGA_6H:    goto CGA_mode;
0937      case zHERC:      goto Hercules_mode;
0938      default:         goto ABORT_PGM;
0939      }
0940    VGA_mode:          // VGA 640x480x16-color, 80x60 character mode.
0941    if(CommandLineArg==zYES)
0942      {                            // if user has requested a mode.
0943      if((Mode>zVGA_12H)&&(Mode<zHERC)) goto FORCE_USER_MODE;
0944      }
0945    X_Res=640; Y_Res=480; Mode=zVGA_12H; CharWidth=8; CharHeight=8;
0946    return;
0947    EGA_ECD_mode:      // EGA 640x350x16-color, 80x43 character mode.
0948    if(CommandLineArg==zYES)
0949      {
0950      if((Mode==zEGA_EH)||(Mode==zCGA_6H))   // permit only EGA or CGA.
0951      goto FORCE_USER_MODE;
0952      }
0953    X_Res=640; Y_Res=350; Mode=zEGA_10H; CharWidth=8; CharHeight=8;
0954    return;
0955    EGA_SCD_mode:              // EGA 640x200x16-color, 80x25 char mode.
0956    if(CommandLineArg==zYES)
```

```
0957    {
0958    if(Mode==zCGA_6H) goto FORCE_USER_MODE;     // only CGA permitted.
0959    }
0960    X_Res=640; Y_Res=200; Mode=zEGA_EH; CharWidth=8; CharHeight=8;
0961    return;
0962    MCGA_mode:                    // MCGA 640x480x2-color, 80x60 char mode.
0963    if(CommandLineArg==zYES)
0964    {
0965    if(Mode==zCGA_6H) goto FORCE_USER_MODE;     // only CGA permitted.
0966    }
0967    X_Res=640; Y_Res=480; Mode=zMCGA_11H;
0968    C0=0; C1=1; C2=1; C3=1; C4=1; C5=1; C6=1; C7=1;
0969    C8=1; C9=1; C10=1; C11=1; C12=1; C13=1; C14=1; C15=1;
0970    CharWidth=8; CharHeight=8;
0971    return;
0972    CGA_mode:                     // CGA 640x200x2-color, 80x25 char mode.
0973    X_Res=640; Y_Res=200; Mode=zCGA_6H;
0974    C0=0; C1=1; C2=1; C3=1; C4=1; C5=1; C6=1; C7=1;
0975    C8=1; C9=1; C10=1; C11=1; C12=1; C13=1; C14=1; C15=1;
0976    CharWidth=8; CharHeight=8;
0977    return;
0978    Hercules_mode:            // Hercules 720x348x2-color, 80x25 char mode.
0979    X_Res=720; Y_Res=348; Mode=zHERC;
0980    C0=0; C1=1; C2=1; C3=1; C4=1; C5=1; C6=1; C7=1;
0981    C8=1; C9=1; C10=1; C11=1; C12=1; C13=1; C14=1; C15=1;
0982    CharWidth=9; CharHeight=14;
0983    return;
0984
0985    FORCE_USER_MODE:    // jump to here if command-line argument legal.
0986    CommandLineArg= zNO; // first, reset token to avoid returning here.
0987    Display.ForceMode(Mode);        // ...then reset the graphics mode.
0988    switch(Mode)            // ...then jump back to appropriate code.
0989    {
0990    case zEGA_10H:     goto EGA_ECD_mode;
0991    case zEGA_EH:      goto EGA_SCD_mode;
0992    case zMCGA_11H:    goto MCGA_mode;
0993    case zCGA_6H:      goto CGA_mode;
0994    default:           goto ABORT_PGM;
0995    }
0996
0997    ABORT_PGM:         // jump to here if no graphics hardware detected.
0998    cout << "\n\n\rThis C++ graphics programming demo requires a";
0999    cout << "\n\rVGA, EGA, CGA, MCGA, or HGA graphics adapter.\n\r";
1000    exit(-1);                    // terminate, returning an error code.
1001    }
1002    /*
1003
1004    ┌─────────────────────────────────────────────────────────────────┐
        │                      Stub routine                                 │
1005    └─────────────────────────────────────────────────────────────────┘
1006                                                                      */
1007    static void zStubRoutine(void)
1008    {
1009    zBlankTextLine();                       // blank the dialog text line.
1010    Viewport1.PutText(1,2,PromptClr,StubMessage); // display a message.
1011    zMakeSound(450,.2);                              // audio cue.
1012    return;
1013    }
1014    /*
1015
1016    ┌─────────────────────────────────────────────────────────────────┐
        │                   Blank the dialog text line                      │
1017    └─────────────────────────────────────────────────────────────────┘
1018                                                                      */
1019    static void zBlankTextLine(void)
```

```
1020  {
1021  Display.SetHue(C0);
1022  Display.SetLine(0xffff);
1023  Display.SetFill(SolidFill,C0);
1024  Viewport1.ClearTextLine();
1025  return;
1026  }
1027  /*
1028
1029      ┌──────────────────────────────────────────────────────────┐
              │          Check the keyboard for a keystroke                │
1030          └──────────────────────────────────────────────────────────┘
1031                                                                    */
1032  static void zKeyboard(void)
1033  {
1034    union AnyName{int RawCode;char Code[3];}Keystroke;
1035    char TempKey=0;
1036  #if defined (BORLAND)
1037    if (bioskey(1)==zEMPTY) { KeyCode=0; return; }
1038    Keystroke.RawCode= bioskey(0);
1039  #elif defined (ZORTECH)
1040    if (bioskey(1)==zEMPTY) { KeyCode=0; return; }
1041    Keystroke.RawCode= bioskey(0);
1042  #elif defined (MICROSOFT)
1043    if (_bios_keybrd(_KEYBRD_READY)==zEMPTY)
1044      { KeyCode=0; return; }
1045    Keystroke.RawCode= _bios_keybrd(_KEYBRD_READ);
1046  #endif
1047  TempKey= Keystroke.Code[0];
1048  if (TempKey!=0)
1049    {                                    // if a normal keystroke...
1050    KeyCode=1; KeyNum=TempKey; return;
1051    }
1052  if (TempKey==0)
1053    {                                    // if an extended keystroke...
1054    KeyCode=2; KeyNum=Keystroke.Code[1]; return;
1055    }
1056  }
1057  /*
1058
1059      ┌──────────────────────────────────────────────────────────┐
              │               Empty the keystroke buffer                   │
1060          └──────────────────────────────────────────────────────────┘
1061                                                                    */
1062  static void zPurge(void)
1063  {
1064  do zKeyboard();
1065    while (KeyCode!=0);
1066  return;
1067  }
1068  /*
1069
1070      ┌──────────────────────────────────────────────────────────┐
              │                     Make a sound                           │
1071          └──────────────────────────────────────────────────────────┘
1072                                                                    */
1073  static void zMakeSound(int Hertz,double Duration)
1074  {
1075    static clock_t FormerTime=0;
1076    short Count=0;
1077    int HighByte=0, LowByte=0;
1078    unsigned char OldPort=0, NewPort=0;
1079  FormerTime= clock();
1080  if (Hertz < 40) return;
1081  if (Hertz > 4660) return;
```

```
1082   Count= 1193180L/Hertz;
1083   HighByte= Count / 256;
1084   LowByte= Count - (HighByte * 256);
1085   #if defined (BORLAND)
1086     outportb(0x43,0xB6); outportb(0x42,(unsigned char)LowByte);
1087     outportb(0x42,(unsigned char)HighByte); OldPort=inportb(0x61);
1088     NewPort=(OldPort | 0x03); outportb(0x61,NewPort);
1089     zDelay(FormerTime,Duration);
1090     outportb(0x61,OldPort);
1091   #elif defined (ZORTECH)
1092     outp(0x43,0xB6); outp(0x42,LowByte);
1093     outp(0x42,HighByte); OldPort=(unsigned char)inp(0x61);
1094     NewPort=(OldPort | 0x03); outp(0x61,(int)NewPort);
1095     zDelay(FormerTime,Duration);
1096     outp(0x61,(int)OldPort);
1097   #elif defined (MICROSOFT)
1098     outp(0x43,0xB6); outp(0x42,LowByte);
1099     outp(0x42,HighByte); OldPort=(unsigned char)inp(0x61);
1100     NewPort=(OldPort | 0x03); outp(0x61,(int)NewPort);
1101     zDelay(FormerTime,Duration);
1102     outp(0x61,(int)OldPort);
1103   #endif
1104   return;
1105   }
1106   /*
1107
1108   ┌─────────────────────────────────────────────────────────────────┐
       │                              Pause                                │
1109   └─────────────────────────────────────────────────────────────────┘
1110                                                                     */
1111   static clock_t zDelay(clock_t StartTime, double Wait)
1112   {                          // pause for a specified length of time.
1113     clock_t StopTime;
1114     clock_t NewClockTime;
1115   #if defined (BORLAND)
1116     StopTime= StartTime + (Wait * CLK_TCK);
1117   #elif defined (ZORTECH)
1118     StopTime= StartTime + (Wait * CLOCKS_PER_SEC);
1119   #elif defined (MICROSOFT)
1120     StopTime= StartTime + (Wait * CLK_TCK);
1121   #endif
1122   while ( clock() < StopTime ) {;}
1123   NewClockTime= clock();
1124   return NewClockTime;
1125   }
1126   /*
1127
1128   ┌─────────────────────────────────────────────────────────────────┐
       │            Retrieve the command-line arguments, if any            │
1129   └─────────────────────────────────────────────────────────────────┘
1130                                                                     */
1131   static void zArguments(int NumArgs, char *Arg[])
1132   {
1133   if(NumArgs==1)
1134     {
1135     CommandLineArg= zNO; return;                         // if no arg.
1136     }
1137   CommandLineCompare= strncmp(StartUpArg[0],Arg[1],5);
1138   if(CommandLineCompare==0)
1139     {
1140     CommandLineArg=zYES; Mode=zVGA_12H; return;          // /M12.
1141     }
1142   CommandLineCompare= strncmp(StartUpArg[1],Arg[1],5);
1143   if(CommandLineCompare==0)
1144     {
```

```
1145     CommandLineArg=zYES; Mode=zEGA_10H; return;              // /M10.
1146     }
1147  CommandLineCompare= strncmp(StartUpArg[2],Arg[1],5);
1148  if(CommandLineCompare==0)
1149     {
1150     CommandLineArg=zYES; Mode=zEGA_EH; return;               // /M0E.
1151     }
1152  CommandLineCompare= strncmp(StartUpArg[3],Arg[1],5);
1153  if(CommandLineCompare==0)
1154     {
1155     CommandLineArg=zYES; Mode=zMCGA_11H; return;             // /M11.
1156     }
1157  CommandLineCompare= strncmp(StartUpArg[4],Arg[1],5);
1158  if(CommandLineCompare==0)
1159     {
1160     CommandLineArg=zYES; Mode=zCGA_6H; return;               // /M06.
1161     }
1162  CommandLineCompare= strncmp(StartUpArg[5],Arg[1],5);
1163  if(CommandLineCompare==0)
1164     {
1165     CommandLineArg=zYES; Mode=zHERC; return;                 // /MHC.
1166     }
1167  CommandLineArg= zNO;                      // if an unrecognized argument.
1168  return;
1169  }
1170  /*
1171
1172      Supercharged C++ Graphics  --  end of source file SKETCH.CPP
1173
1174                                                                      */
```

7
Interactive desktop publishing graphics

Many users are surprised to find that desktop publishing software runs in graphics mode. The headings and subheadings used in page layout software are font output—either stroked or bitmapped. The rules and borders are lines and rectangles. The illustrations are PCX or TIFF images.

Similarly, many programmers are delighted to discover that writing desktop publishing software is not as difficult as they first imagined. Apart from loading in illustrations from image files and sending output to a laser printer—neither of which are trivial exercises—desktop publishing software consists mainly of manipulating rectangles on a logical display. See FIG. 7-1.

Page design components

By using rectangles to represent the components of a page layout, your C++ graphics program can specify size and position for a variety of headings, subheadings, illustrations, folios, and text columns. Inserting a component into its assigned rectangle is called *pouring*. For example, the built-in font capabilities of Turbo C++ and Borland C++ can be used to pour a heading into its assigned rectangle on a page. *Text-pouring* refers to algorithms that fill a column rectangle with a body of text material.

Although learning the vocabulary and the techniques of the publishing, graphic design, and printing trades can take a lifetime, it does not take nearly as long to build the programming skills needed to create desktop publishing software. This chapter presents a demonstration program that pours text onto a page layout. The demo uses the methods of a class designed to support desktop publishing development.

The class methods use an algorithm that can support text-pouring for rectangles of many different shapes and sizes. See FIG. 7-2. You can use the class as a template to build your own methods to place headings and subheadings onto a page layout.

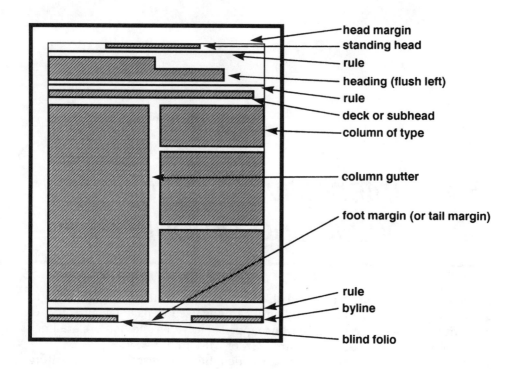

head margin
standing head
rule
heading (flush left)
rule
deck or subhead
column of type
column gutter
foot margin (or tail margin)
rule
byline
blind folio

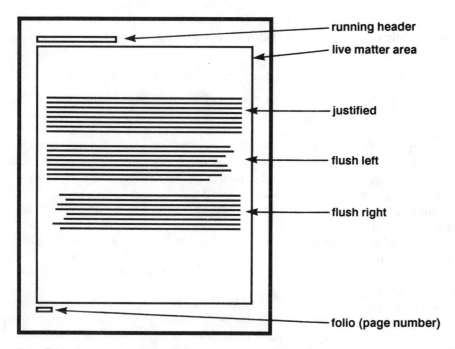

running header
live matter area
justified
flush left
flush right
folio (page number)

7-1 Typical components of a page layout useful for desktop publishing programs.

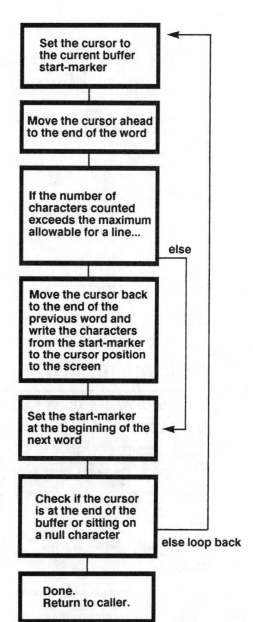

7-2 Logic chart for a typical text-pouring function suitable for use in desktop publishing software.

Set the cursor to the current buffer start-marker

Move the cursor ahead to the end of the word

If the number of characters counted exceeds the maximum allowable for a line...

else

Move the cursor back to the end of the previous word and write the characters from the start-marker to the cursor position to the screen

Set the start-marker at the beginning of the next word

Check if the cursor is at the end of the buffer or sitting on a null character

else loop back

Done.
Return to caller.

A sample program: DESKTOP.CPP

Demo Figure 7-3 depicts typical before-and-after displays produced by the sample program DESKTOP.CPP, whose complete source code is provided in FIG. 7-4 at the end of the chapter. The program reads from a standard ASCII text file and pours characters into a page layout.

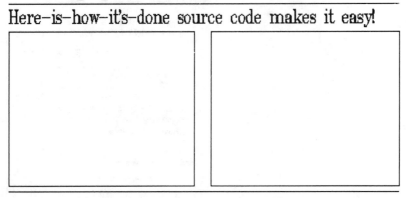

A Windcrest/McGraw-Hill Exclusive!

Using C++ to write your own desktop publishing software

Here–is–how–it's–done source code makes it easy!

A Windcrest/McGraw-Hill Exclusive!

Using C++ to write your own desktop publishing software

Here–is–how–it's–done source code makes it easy!

This is dummy copy. It is being used to test this demo program. The text is taken from a document file that was created with a word processor and saved in ASCII format. This demo program uses an* object of the Layout class to read the text from the disk file into a buffer in RAM. The class methods then calculate the number of characters per line and lines per column for each column on the* page. The Layout class methods are smart enough to strip out any carriage returns, line feeds, and tabs that they find in the text buffer before writing each line of text to the appropriate column* area. You can easily add more instances of the

Layout class to enable your program to handle different sized columns on the same page -- or even to handle advanced layout functions like run arounds!* You can experiment with your own dummy copy if you wish. Simply save a document in ASCII mode with your favorite word processor or text editor. Then tell the demo program the name of the document file* you want to pour onto the page. The algorithm used in this demo program can be easily adapted to handle headings too. This is dummy copy. It is being used to test this demo program. The text is taken* from a document file that was created with a word

7-3 Graphics output from the sample program DESKTOP.CPP. Top: the layout of the page, complete with running head, heading, subhead, and columnar blocks. Bottom: the C++ demonstration program has successfully poured text from an ASCII file into the columnar blocks.

How to compile and link the sample program

The program listing presented in FIG. 7-4 contains the complete source code for the main module of the C++ demonstration program called "Using C++ to Write Your Own Desktop Publishing Software." If you

are using the companion disks to the book, the source code is in the file named DESKTOP.CPP. Three C++ source files are needed to build the finished .exe file. These are DESKTOP.CPP from FIG. 7-4 and two class libraries in appendix E.

[Class] The class library that provides the language bindings and low-level graphics routines for this demonstration program is found in FIG. E-2 in appendix E. This listing contains the implementations for class PhysicalDisplay and class Viewport. If you are using the companion disks to the book, this file is named LIB2D.CPP. The class declarations are presented in FIG. E-1 in appendix E. If you are using the companion disks to the book, this file is named LIB2D.HPP.

[Class] The class library that provides the text-pouring methods for this demonstration program is found in FIG. E-12 in appendix E. This listing contains the implementations for class Layout. If you are using the companion disks to the book, this file is named PUBLISH.CPP. The class declarations are presented in FIG. E-11 in appendix E. If you are using the companion disks to the book, this file is named PUBLISH.HPP.

You can compile, link, and run this demonstration program using either Turbo C++ or Zortech C++. If you are using Turbo C++, read appendix A for help in compiling, linking, and running the demonstration program. If you are using Zortech C++, refer to appendix C. (Although the demonstration program itself is compatible at the source code level with Borland C++, the class library might require a few modifications. If your version of Borland C++ complains when you try to compile the demonstration program, you need to modify class Layout in PUBLISH.HPP and PUBLISH.CPP to remove any static variables. You can use LIB2DBC.HPP and LIB2DBC.CPP as a working guide.)

You must create a Turbo C++ project list to advise your compiler which source files to bind together to build the finished .exe file. If you are using Zortech C++, you must name the files on the compiler command line field. Refer to the appendices described earlier if you are unfamiliar with this technique.

After a successful compile and link, the animated screen should resemble the screen prints shown in FIG. 7-3.

How to run the demonstration program

You need a VGA, EGA, MCGA, CGA, or Hercules graphics adapter and a mouse to run this demo.

Using the editor to run the program

[Here's How...] To run the program under the control of your Turbo C++ or Zortech C++ editor, make sure that the finished .exe file is in the default directory. If you used Turbo C++ to compile the program, the appropriate graphics driver must be in the default directory. If you are using a VGA or EGA, the EGAVGA.BGI file must be present. If you are using an MCGA or CGA, the CGA.BGI file must be located in the default directory. If you are using a Hercules graphics adapter, the HERC.BGI file must be available. If you used

Zortech C++ to compile the demonstration program, the appropriate graphics drivers have already been linked into the .exe code.

The built-in autodetect routine will detect the graphics hardware in your computer system and will set up the best graphics mode supported by your computer hardware. To override the autodetect routine, use the Turbo C++ or Zortech C++ editor to simulate a command line argument. The header in FIG. 7-4 provides a set of arguments you can use. See the appendices for guidance applicable to your particular compiler. If you are using a VGA, you can override the autodetect routine and force the demonstration program to run in an EGA, MCGA, or CGA mode. If you are using an EGA, you can force the program to run in a lower resolution EGA mode or a CGA mode.

Running the program from the operating system prompt

To start the program from the operating system prompt, simply enter DESKTOP. The .exe file and any required graphics drivers must be present in the default directory. If the software finds a VGA present in your system, the program will animate using the 640×480×16-color mode. If an EGA and enhanced monitor are found, the 640×350×16-color mode is used. If an EGA and standard display are present, the program sets up the 640×200×16-color mode. If an MCGA is detected, the 640×480×2-color mode is employed. If a CGA is found, the 640×200×2-color mode is used. If the program detects a Hercules graphics adapter, it starts up in the 720×348×2-color mode.

You can force the program to start up in a different mode by adding a command line argument when you start the program from the operating system prompt. Enter DESKTOP /M11 to force the 640×480×2-color mode. Enter DESKTOP /M10 to force the 640×350×16-color mode. Entering DESKTOP /M0E forces the program to run in the 640×200×16-color mode. Enter DESKTOP /M06 tests the demonstration program in the 640×200×2-color mode.

Using the demonstration program

The program first creates and displays a sample page layout, as shown in the top portion of FIG. 7-3. It then prompts you to press any key. The software then searches the current directory for a file named DUMMY.DOC. If you are using the companion disks to *Lee Adams' Supercharged C++ Graphics*, you will find this file on the disk. If you are typing in the listings from the book, you can use any text file that has been saved in ASCII format.

The demo program uses the methods of class Layout to pour the text from the ASCII file into the appropriate areas in the page layout. The results of a typical text-pouring operation are shown in the lower portion of FIG. 7-3. The program automatically calculates the number of lines that will fit into each column. It also calculates the number of characters that will fit into each line. During the text-pouring function, extraneous characters like tabs, carriage returns, and line feeds are stripped out of the text stream and replaced with an asterisk.

After the text has been poured, press any key to end the demonstration program.

Programmer's Guide to DESKTOP.CPP

Code The complete listing for the demonstration program DESKTOP.CPP is presented in FIG. 7-4. The source code consists of an informative header, conditional compilation directives, declaration of constants and macros, file include directives, function prototypes, variable declarations, and the executable functions.

Conditional compilation

Information and source code for conditional compilation is located at lines 0047 through 0064. If you are using Turbo C++, the program is ready to compile, subject to the instructions in appendix B. If you are using Zortech C++, change line 0063 to #define FG and change line 0064 to #define ZORTECH.

Constants

The C++ const keyword is used to declare and assign values to constant variables at lines 0066 through 0076.

Macros

A macro defined at line 0082 will be expanded by the C++ compiler at numerous locations later in the source code.

Include files

The code at lines 0084 through 0116 loads the appropriate header files and C++ class declaration files. Line 0115 loads LIB2D.HPP, which declares the data members and methods of class PhysicalDisplay and class Viewport. Line 0116 loads DESKTOP.HPP, which declares the data members and methods of class Layout.

Function prototypes

Function declarations are provided in lines 0118 through 0130. Functions declared here are visible throughout this source file. They can be called by any other function in the source file. Because each function is declared with the static qualifier, it is not available to functions located in other source files.

Variable declarations

Lines 0132 through 0167 declare global variables visible throughout this source file. These variables have file scope and can be modified by any function in the file.

Object declarations

Object Line 0165 creates an object from class PhysicalDisplay named Display. The program will later call the methods of this object to help it manage the display. The methods are declared in the class declaration listing LIB-2D.HPP and are defined in the class implementation listing LIB2D.CPP in appendix E. The object created at line 0165 is a static object. It has file scope and will remain available until the program terminates.

Line 0166 creates an object from the Viewport class. The object is named Viewport1. The address of Display is passed to this new object. Viewport1 will need to use the methods of Display to generate graphics output. The object created at line 0166 is a static object with file scope. It will remain active until program termination.

Line 0167 creates an object from the Layout class. The object is named Desktop. The methods of this object provide the text-pouring capabilities required to place the text onto the sample page layout. Note how the address of Viewport1 is passed to this new object. Desktop will call the low-level graphics functions of methods of class Viewport when it writes each line of text to the screen in graphics mode.

main( )

The main( ) function is located at lines 0172 through 0203. After first checking to see if any command line arguments were used to start the program, an appropriate graphics mode is set. The code at line 0200 calls the function that manages the text-pouring demonstration.

Desktop publishing demonstration

The function at lines 0205 through 0333 manages the desktop publishing demonstration.

Local variables used by the function are declared at lines 0211 through 0221. These variables are explicitly assigned meaningful values at lines 0223 through 0231. The code has been organized in this manner to make it more convenient for you to tinker with the program. You can easily change the size, shape, and location of the columnar rectangles by tweaking the values in this block of code.

The page layout shown in the top portion of FIG. 7-3 is created by the code at lines 0233 through 0277. Note in particular the code at lines 0247 through 0265, which writes the heading and subheading using Turbo C++'s triplex font, trip.chr. You can also see how the local variables defined earlier are used to build the page layout.

The text is poured into the rectangles by the code at lines 0279 through 0318. The code calls various methods of class Layout. The value returned by these methods is checked often in order to trap any runtime errors. This is especially important whenever disk files are involved in an operation. Note in particular line 0299, which calls method PourText( ) to actually write the text to the first column. The result returned by PourText( ) is the pointer into the text buffer at the end of the text-pouring operation. This value is passed to method SetCurrentMarker( ) at line 0307 when the program begins work on the second columnar rectangle. As the lower portion of FIG. 7-3 shows, the text runs-on from the bottom of the first column to the start of the second column.

Error management and context-sensitive messages are handled by the code at lines 0321 through 0331. If the VGA 640×480×16-color mode or the MCGA 640×480×2-color mode is used, the entire sample ASCII file will be written to the display. If other modes are used, the rectangles will be filled before the end of the ASCII file is encountered. In either case, the demonstration program is smart enough to advise you of the result.

Terminating the program

The function at lines 0335 through 0343 calls a method of class PhysicalDisplay to shut down the graphics state. Line 0342 returns an OK value to the operating system.

The Startup( ) function

The function at lines 0345 through 0428 calls the SetupMode( ) method of class PhysicalDisplay to detect the graphics hardware and to invoke the best mode for the graphics adapter.

The StubRoutine( ) function

The stub routine at lines 0430 through 0442 is a do-nothing routine that displays a message on the dialog line at the top of the display.

The Keyboard( ) function

The function at lines 0444 through 0472 fetches keystrokes from the keyboard buffer. The function at lines 0474 through 0483 repeatedly calls zKeyboard( ) until the keyboard buffer is empty.

The MakeSound( ) function

The function at lines 0485 through 0521 generates a sound using the system speaker.

The Pause( ) function

The function at lines 0523 through 0541 causes the program to pause. The value returned by the system clock is multiplied by the number of cycles per second in order that the function can operate in real time.

The Arguments( ) function

The function at lines 0543 through 0585 compares the command line argument with a list of recognized strings. The function then assigns a token value to the global variable named Mode.

Programmer's Guide to LIB2D.HPP

Code The complete source code for the declarations for class PhysicalDisplay and class Viewport is found in LIB2D.HPP in appendix E. LIB2D.HPP must be #included in any program that uses the methods of class PhysicalDisplay or class Viewport. See the discussion in chapter 1 for further information.

Programmer's Guide to LIB2D.CPP

Code LIB2D.CPP provides language bindings that produce low-level graphics. The source code for LIB2D.CPP is provided in appendix E. The routines in LIB2D.CPP call the appropriate runtime library functions in Turbo C++'s graphics.lib and Zortech C++'s fg.lib.

LIB2D.CPP is the class implementation listing for class PhysicalDisplay and class Viewport. Class PhysicalDisplay manages the display. Class Viewport controls the viewport and generates low-level graphics. See the discussion in chapter 1 for further information.

Programmer's Guide to PUBLISH.HPP

Code The complete source code for the declarations for class Layout is found in PUBLISH.HPP in appendix E. PUBLISH.HPP must be #included in any program that uses the methods of class Layout. The methods of class Layout provide text-pouring functions useful for desktop publishing software.

The source code at lines 0068 through 0091 declares data members and two methods that are not visible to functions or methods outside class Layout. The code at lines 0093 through 0101 declares methods of class Layout callable by any in-scope function or method.

Programmer's Guide to PUBLISH.CPP

Code The complete source code for the implementation for class Layout is found in PUBLISH.CPP in appendix E. The methods of class Layout provide routines that can calculate the number of lines of text that will fit into a rectangle, the number of characters that will fit into each line of text, and text buffer management operations.

Constructor

The constructor for class Layout is located at lines 0067 through 0080. Line 0073 assigns the address of the viewport that is to be used to a pointer named Generic. The -> addressing notation will be used to call methods of Generic. Otherwise, the constructor is concerned mainly with initializing global variables used by the methods.

Destructor

The destructor for class Layout is located at lines 0082 through 0089. Line 0088 calls method ReleaseBuffer( ) to release the memory used as a text buffer.

Method SetupBuffer( )

The method at lines 0091 through 0115 allocates memory for a buffer to hold the text from the ASCII file. Line 0099 uses the access( ) runtime library function to confirm that the file exists. Then line 0102 uses filelength( ) to determine the length of the file. The C++ new operator is used at line 0104 to allocate a buffer large enough to hold the text. The buffer is set up as a single-dimension array. Note the error-checking code at lines 0105 through 0109, which provides a graceful recovery if the memory allocation fails. Line 0112 sets a token that will be checked by other methods before they try to manipulate the text in the buffer.

Method ReleaseBuffer( )

The method at lines 0117 through 0127 frees the memory that was used to store the text data. The C++ delete operator is used to return the memory to the free store. Lines 0124 and 0125 reset some tokens in order to avoid any runtime errors.

Method LoadText( )

The method at lines 0129 through 0144 reads the text from the ASCII file into the buffer in RAM. The fread( ) library function is used to read the appropriate number of chars into the buffer. The TextReady token set at line 0140 will be checked by other methods before they attempt to write text from the buffer to the display.

Method SetLineLength( )

The method at lines 0146 through 0165 calculates the maximum number of characters that will fit into one line of the column rectangle. The algorithm uses straightforward math, based on the width of the system font, TextWidth. This is 8 pixels in VGA, MCGA, EGA, and CGA modes. It is 9 pixels in Hercules modes.

Method SetNumLines( )

The method at lines 0167 through 0187 calculates the number of text lines that will fit into a column rectangle. The variable TextHeight, belonging to the viewport object, is used to compute this value.

Method SetCurrentMarker( )

The method at lines 0189 through 0197 adjusts the index that points into the array holding the text. This method provides a means for manipulating the index when text must be continued into a second, third, or fourth rectangle. You can run text around an illustration by creating a rectangle at the side of the illustration. The SetCurrentMarker( ) method allows you to continue the text around the illustration.

Method WriteLine( )

The method at lines 0199 through 0231 writes one line of text to the display. See FIG. 7-2 for a visualization of the algorithm used to invoke method WriteLine( ).

Note the code at lines 0212 through 0227, which is responsible for detecting and stripping out carriage returns, line feeds, and tabs. The ASCII code for a line feed is 10. The ASCII code for a carriage return is 13. The ASCII code for a tab is 15. In this block of source code, an arbitrary decision has been made to replace carriage return characters with asterisk characters. This is a handy way to see the result of the stripping operation on the display. If you were writing a commercial software product, however, you would shuffle all following characters in the string one place to the left.

Method PourText( )

The method at lines 0233 through 0297 is the coded version of the algorithm portrayed in FIG. 7-2. The code uses nested loops. The outer loop steps along word by word. The inner loop works on a character by character basis. Between the two of them, they can detect when the next word will exceed the available space on any one line, back up, and then call method WriteLine( ) to write the string to the display. Note the traps at lines 0250 through 0252, which are used to detect an end-of-file condition. Although most ASCII text files will use the Ctrl+Z character to mark the end of the data, occasionally files will be encountered that use the Esc or null character instead.

7-4 Sample program DESKTOP.CPP. Supports VGA, EGA, MCGA, CGA, and Hercules adapters. This application demonstrates a text-pouring class suitable for use in developing desktop publishing software.

```
0001  /*
0002
0003            Lee Adams' SUPERCHARGED C++ GRAPHICS
0004      Interactive demo:  desktop publishing routines for C++
0005
0006    SOURCE FILE:  DESKTOP.CPP
0007           TYPE:  C++ source file for a multimodule application.
0008        PURPOSE:  Demonstrates a fundamental class useful for
0009                  desktop publishing software. Text can be poured
0010                  into column areas on a page layout.
0011  PROGRAM LIST:   DESKTOP.CPP, LIB2D.CPP and PUBLISH.CPP.
0012      LANGUAGES:  Turbo C++, Borland C++, Zortech C++, and
0013                  all C++ compilers compatible with AT&T C++ 2.0
0014                  specification; and nominal compatibility with
0015                  Microsoft C++ (see the discussion in the book).
0016  MEMORY MODEL:   large.
0017  COMMAND-LINE:   you can specify a graphics mode by using the
0018                  command-line argument /Mnn as shown below:
0019                      /M12  640x480x16-color VGA
0020                      /M11  640x480x2-color VGA, MCGA
0021                      /M10  640x350x16-color VGA, EGA
0022                      /M0E  640x200x16-color VGA, EGA
0023                      /M06  640x200x2-color VGA, MCGA, EGA, CGA
0024                      /MHC  720x348x2-color Hercules
0025                  If no command-line argument is used, hardware
0026                  autodetect is used to select the best mode.
0027  OUTPUT:  Text is poured from an ASCII file into two column
0028           blocks on a page layout complete with headings.
0029  LICENSE:  As purchaser of the book in which this source code
0030    appears you are granted a royalty-free license to reproduce
0031    and distribute executable files generated using this code
0032    provided that you accept the conditions of the License
0033    Agreement and Limited Warranty described in the book.
0034  PUBLICATION: Contains material from Windcrest/McGraw-Hill
0035    book 3489, published by TAB BOOKS.
0036  U.S. GOVERNMENT RESTRICTED RIGHTS:  This software and its
0037    documentation is provided with restricted rights.  The use,
0038    duplication, or disclosure by the Government is subject to
0039    restrictions set forth in subdivision (b)(3)(ii) of The
0040    Rights in Technical Data and Computer Software clause at
0041    252.227-7013.  Contractor/manufacturer is Lee Adams, c/o
0042    TAB BOOKS, 13311 Monterey Ave., Blue Ridge Summit PA 17294.
0043  TRADEMARK:  Lee Adams is a trademark of Lee Adams.
0044
0045      Copyright 1991 Lee Adams.  All rights reserved worldwide.
0046
0047
0048                  CONDITIONAL COMPILATION
0049  To compile only those blocks of code that support the C++
0050  compiler and graphics library that you are using, you should
0051  #define the appropriate tokens on lines 0063 and 0064.
0052          GRAPHICS LIBRARY
0053      Borland's graphics.lib              #define BGI
0054      Zortech's fg.lib or fgdebug.lib     #define FG
0055      Microsoft's graph.lib               #define MS
0056              COMPILER
0057      Borland Turbo C++ compiler          #define BORLAND
0058      Zortech C++ compiler                #define ZORTECH
```

7-4 Continued.

```
0059            AT&T-compatible C++ compilers        #define MICROSOFT
0060       Be sure you define only one compiler and one graphics library.
0061
0062                                                                          */
0063   #define BGI     1  // indicates the graphics library you are using.
0064   #define BORLAND 1  // indicates the C++ compiler you are using.
0065   /*
0066
0067   ┌────────────────────────────────────────────────────────────────────┐
        │                           Constants                                │
0068    └────────────────────────────────────────────────────────────────────┘
0069                                                                          */
0070   const int zSUCCESS= 1;
0071   const int zFAIL=    0;
0072   const int zEMPTY=   0;
0073   const int zYES=     1;
0074   const int zNO=      0;
0075   const int zVGA_12H=1; const int zEGA_10H=2; const int zEGA_EH=3;
0076   const int zMCGA_11H=4; const int zCGA_6H=5; const int zHERC=6;
0077   /*
0078
0079   ┌────────────────────────────────────────────────────────────────────┐
        │                            Macros                                  │
0080    └────────────────────────────────────────────────────────────────────┘
0081                                                                          */
0082   #define Wait_for_any_key  while(KeyCode==0) zKeyboard(); KeyCode=0;
0083   /*
0084
0085   ┌────────────────────────────────────────────────────────────────────┐
        │                         Include files                              │
0086    └────────────────────────────────────────────────────────────────────┘
0087                                                                          */
0088   #if defined (BORLAND)
0089   #include <time.h>          // supports clock().
0090   #include <string.h>        // supports strncmp().
0091   #include <bios.h>          // supports bioskey().
0092   #include <process.h>       // supports exit().
0093   #include <iostream.h>      // supports cout.
0094   #include <dos.h>           // supports outportb(), inportb().
0095   #elif defined (ZORTECH)
0096   #include <time.h>          // supports clock().
0097   #include <string.h>        // supports strncmp().
0098   #include <bios.h>          // supports bioskey().
0099   #include <stdlib.h>        // supports exit().
0100   #include <stream.hpp>      // supports cout.
0101   #include <dos.h>           // supports outp(), inp().
0102   #elif defined (MICROSOFT)
0103   #include <time.h>          // supports clock().
0104   #include <string.h>        // supports strncmp().
0105   #include <bios.h>          // supports _bios_keybrd().
0106   #include <process.h>       // supports exit().
0107   #include <iostream.h>      // supports cout.
0108   #include <conio.h>         // supports outp(), inp().
0109   #endif
0110
0111   #if defined (BGI)
0112   #include <graphics.h>      // supports font output.
0113   #endif
0114
0115   #include "LIB2D.HPP"       // declarations for PhysicalDisplay class.
0116   #include "PUBLISH.HPP"             // declarations for Layout class.
0117   /*
0118
0119   ┌────────────────────────────────────────────────────────────────────┐
        │       Prototypes for functions visible throughout this file        │
0120    └────────────────────────────────────────────────────────────────────┘
```

```
0121                                                        */
0122   static void zStartup(void);           // initializes a graphics mode.
0123   static void zArguments(int, char far* far*);   // checks arguments.
0124   static void zKeyboard(void);          // checks for a keystroke.
0125   static void zQuit_Pgm(void);          // ends the program gracefully.
0126   static void zPurge(void);             // empties the keyboard buffer.
0127   static void zStubRoutine(void);             // do-nothing stub.
0128   static void zMakeSound(int,double);      // makes a specific sound.
0129   static clock_t zDelay(clock_t,double);    // CPU-independent pause.
0130   static void zDesktopPublishing(void);              // demo.
0131   /*
0132
0133   ┌─────────────────────────────────────────────────────────────┐
        │   Declaration of variables visible throughout this file     │
0134   └─────────────────────────────────────────────────────────────┘
0135                                                        */
0136   static char *StartUpArg[6]={        // legal command-line arguments.
0137          "/M12", "/M10", "/MOE", "/M11", "/M06", "/MHC" };
0138   static int CommandLineArg=zNO;      // indicates if argument exists.
0139   static int CommandLineCompare=0;    // indicates if argument legal.
0140   static int C0=0,C1=1,C2=2,C3=3,C4=4,C5=5,C6=6,
0141     C7=7,C8=8,C9=9,C10=10,C11=11,C12=12,C13=13,
0142     C14=14,C15=15;                        // palette index codes.
0143   static int Mode=0;             // which graphics mode is being used.
0144   static int Result=0;         // captures result of graphics routines.
0145   static int CharWidth=0,CharHeight=0;     // dimensions of character.
0146   static char KeyCode=0;   // token for normal or extended keystroke.
0147   static char KeyNum=0;                  // ASCII number of keystroke.
0148   static char SolidFill[]=
0149              {255,255,255,255,255,255,255,255};   // 100% fill.
0150   static int TextClr=7;           // font color for regular text.
0151   static int PromptClr=7;              // font color for prompt text.
0152   static char Copyright[]=
0153           "Copyright 1991 Lee Adams.  All rights reserved.";
0154   static char Title[]=
0155   "USING C++ TO CREATE DESKTOP PUBLISHING SOFTWARE";
0156   static char PressAnyKey[]= "Press any key to continue.";
0157   static char StubMessage[]= "The generic stub routine was called.";
0158   static char Prompt1[]= "Press any key to design the page.";
0159   static char Prompt2[]= "Press any key to pour the text.";
0160   static char ErrorMsg1[]= "An error occurred. Press any key.";
0161   static char AllDone[]= "Text poured successfully. Press any key.";
0162   static char MoreToDo[]= "Text remaining in buffer. Press any key.";
0163   static int X_Res=0, Y_Res=0;              // screen resolution.
0164
0165   PhysicalDisplay Display;     // create the physical display object.
0166   Viewport Viewport1(&Display);          // create a viewport object.
0167   Layout Desktop(&Viewport1);          // create a column object.
0168   /*
0169
0170   ┌─────────────────────────────────────────────────────────────┐
        │                   Function definitions                      │
0171   └─────────────────────────────────────────────────────────────┘
0172
0173   ┌─────────────────────────────────────────────────────────────┐
        │   The executive routine:  program execution begins here     │
0174   └─────────────────────────────────────────────────────────────┘
0175                                                        */
0176   main(int argc, char *argv[])
0177   {
0178     int NumArgs; char far* far* Arg;
0179     int LoopX1, LoopY1, LoopX2, LoopY2, LoopColor, LoopMaxHues;
0180     int LoopCount;
0181
0182   NumArgs= argc;                         // grab number of arguments.
0183   Arg= &argv[0];              // grab address of array of arguments.
```

```
0184    zArguments(NumArgs, Arg);         // check the command-line arguments.
0185
0186    zStartup();                              // establish the graphics mode.
0187    Display.Init2D(Mode,0,0,X_Res-1,Y_Res-1);    // set graphics state.
0188    Result= Display.InitUndo();    // create hidden page (unused here).
0189    if (Result==zFAIL) zQuit_Pgm();          // if hidden page failed.
0190
0191    Display.BlankPage();                          // clear the display.
0192    Display.SetHue(C7);                       // set the drawing color.
0193    Display.SetFill(SolidFill,C7);              // set the fill style.
0194    Viewport1.PutText(2,2,TextClr,Title);          // sign-on notice.
0195    Viewport1.PutText(3,2,TextClr,Copyright);     // copyright notice.
0196    Viewport1.DrawBorder(0,0,X_Res-1,Y_Res-1);        // draw a border.
0197    Viewport1.PutText(6,2,PromptClr,Prompt1);     // display a prompt.
0198    Wait_for_any_key     // this macro was defined earlier at line 0082.
0199
0200    zDesktopPublishing();                    // perform the demonstration.
0201
0202    zQuit_Pgm();            // tidy up and terminate the application.
0203    }
0204    /*
0205
0206    ┌──────────────────────────────────────────────────────────────┐
        │           Demonstrate the desktop publishing functions         │
0207    └──────────────────────────────────────────────────────────────┘
0208                                                                   */
0209    static void zDesktopPublishing(void)
0210    {                      // draw a page layout and pour text into it.
0211      int PageX1, PageY1, PageX2, PageY2;          // page dimensions.
0212      int LeftMargin, RightMargin, TopMargin, BottomMargin; // margins.
0213      int Gutter;                            // gutter between columns.
0214      int PageColor;                                // color of page.
0215      int TextColor;                        // color of text on page.
0216      int ColumnWidth;              // width of a column (in pixels).
0217      int RectX1, RectY1, RectX2, RectY2;      // column coordinates.
0218      int Result;                    // result returned by methods.
0219    #if defined (BGI)              // if using Turbo C++ graphics...
0220      struct textsettingstype loadquery;     // use to test font load.
0221    #endif
0222
0223    // step one:  assign some values --------------------------------
0224    PageX1= 0; PageY1= 24;                // upper left corner of page.
0225    PageX2= 639; PageY2= Y_Res-1;        // lower right corner of page.
0226    LeftMargin= 40; RightMargin= 40;          // left right margins.
0227    TopMargin= 24; BottomMargin= 24;          // top bottom margins.
0228    ColumnWidth= 268;                    // column is 268 pixels wide.
0229    Gutter= 24;                          // space between columns.
0230    PageColor= C7;                                  // white page.
0231    TextColor= C0;                    // black text on white page.
0232
0233    // step two:  draw the page layout ------------------------------
0234    Display.BlankPage();                          // blank the display.
0235    Display.SetHue(PageColor);              // set the drawing color.
0236    Display.SetFill(SolidFill,PageColor);      // set the fill color.
0237    Viewport1.DrawPanel(PageX1, PageY1, PageX2, PageY2);  // draw page.
0238    Display.SetHue(TextColor);
0239    Viewport1.PutText(7,24,TextColor,              // standing head.
0240                   "A Windcrest/McGraw-Hill Exclusive!");
0241    Viewport1.SetPosition(PageX1 + LeftMargin,PageY1 + TopMargin + 11);
0242    Viewport1.DrawLine(PageX2 - RightMargin, PageY1 + TopMargin + 11);
0243    Viewport1.SetPosition(PageX1 + LeftMargin,PageY1 + TopMargin + 80);
0244    Viewport1.DrawLine(PageX2 - RightMargin, PageY1 + TopMargin + 80);
0245    Viewport1.SetPosition(PageX1 + LeftMargin, PageY2 - BottomMargin);
```

```
0246 Viewport1.DrawLine(PageX2 - RightMargin, PageY2 - BottomMargin);
0247 #if defined (BGI)                    // if using Turbo C++ graphics...
0248   settextstyle(1, HORIZ_DIR, 0);              // set the typeface.
0249   gettextsettings(&loadquery);             // load the font file.
0250   if (loadquery.font != 1)
0251     {                           // if the font file was not found...
0252     settextstyle(DEFAULT_FONT, HORIZ_DIR, 1);   // restore default,
0253     goto NO_FONT_FILE;            // and jump past font output code.
0254     }
0255   setusercharsize(1,1,1,1);                       // set typesize.
0256   moveto(PageX1 + LeftMargin, PageY1 + TopMargin + 11);
0257   outtext("Using C++ to write your own");
0258   moveto(PageX1 + LeftMargin, PageY1 + TopMargin + 40);
0259   outtext("desktop publishing software");
0260   setusercharsize(11,16,11,16);                   // set typesize.
0261   moveto(PageX1 + LeftMargin, PageY1 + TopMargin + 81);
0262   outtext("Here-is-how-it's-done source code makes it easy!");
0263   settextstyle(DEFAULT_FONT, HORIZ_DIR, 1);     // restore default.
0264 NO_FONT_FILE:            // jump to here if font file not found.
0265 #endif
0266 RectX1= PageX1 + LeftMargin;      // draw the column rectangles...
0267 RectY1= PageY1 + 133;
0268 RectX2= PageX1 + LeftMargin + ColumnWidth;
0269 RectY2= PageY2 - (BottomMargin + 6);
0270 Viewport1.DrawBorder(RectX1, RectY1, RectX2, RectY2);
0271 RectX1= PageX1 + LeftMargin + ColumnWidth + Gutter;
0272 RectY1= PageY1 + 133;
0273 RectX2= PageX1 + LeftMargin + (ColumnWidth * 2) + Gutter;
0274 RectY2= PageY2 - (BottomMargin + 6);
0275 Viewport1.DrawBorder(RectX1, RectY1, RectX2, RectY2);
0276 Viewport1.PutText(1,2,PromptClr,Prompt2);      // display a prompt.
0277 Wait_for_any_key
0278
0279 // step three:  pour text into column rectangles ----------------
0280 Display.SetHue(C0); Display.SetFill(SolidFill,C0);
0281 Viewport1.ClearTextLine();               // clear the dialog line.
0282 Display.SetHue(TextColor);
0283                           // pour text into the first column...
0284 RectX1= PageX1 + LeftMargin;   // reset the bounding coordinates...
0285 RectY1= PageY1 + 133;
0286 RectX2= PageX1 + LeftMargin + ColumnWidth;
0287 RectY2= PageY2 - (BottomMargin + 6);
0288 Result= Desktop.SetupBuffer("DUMMY");      // initialize the object.
0289 if (Result==zFAIL) goto ERROR_OCCURRED;
0290 Result= Desktop.LoadText();              // load in the text file.
0291 if (Result==zFAIL) goto ERROR_OCCURRED;
0292 Result= Desktop.SetLineLength(RectX1, RectX2);
0293 if (Result==zFAIL) goto ERROR_OCCURRED;
0294 Result= Desktop.SetNumLines(RectY1, RectY2);
0295 if (Result==zFAIL) goto ERROR_OCCURRED;
0296 Display.SetHue(PageColor);
0297 Viewport1.DrawBorder(RectX1, RectY1, RectX2, RectY2);
0298 Display.SetHue(TextColor);
0299 Result= Desktop.PourText();         // pour the text into the column.
0300 if (Result==zFAIL) goto ERROR_OCCURRED;
0301 if (Result==zSUCCESS) goto FINISHED;
0302                           // pour text into the next column...
0303 RectX1= PageX1 + LeftMargin + ColumnWidth + Gutter;
0304 RectY1= PageY1 + 133;
0305 RectX2= PageX1 + LeftMargin + (ColumnWidth * 2) + Gutter;
0306 RectY2= PageY2 - (BottomMargin + 6);
0307 Desktop.SetCurrentMarker(Result);
0308 Result= Desktop.SetLineLength(RectX1, RectX2);
```

```
0309   if (Result==zFAIL) goto ERROR_OCCURRED;
0310   Result= Desktop.SetNumLines(RectY1, RectY2);
0311   if (Result==zFAIL) goto ERROR_OCCURRED;
0312   Display.SetHue(PageColor);
0313   Viewport1.DrawBorder(RectX1, RectY1, RectX2, RectY2);
0314   Display.SetHue(TextColor);
0315   Result= Desktop.PourText();                    // pour the text.
0316   if (Result==zFAIL) goto ERROR_OCCURRED;
0317   if (Result==zSUCCESS) goto FINISHED;
0318   goto DEBUGGING;
0319
0320   // step four:  wait for any key ----------------------------------
0321   ERROR_OCCURRED:              // jump to here if an error occurred.
0322     Viewport1.PutText(1,2,PromptClr,ErrorMsg1);
0323     Wait_for_any_key
0324     return;
0325   DEBUGGING:        // jump to here if more text remaining in buffer.
0326     Viewport1.PutText(1,2,PromptClr,MoreToDo);
0327     Wait_for_any_key
0328     return;
0329   FINISHED:              // jump to here when all text has been poured.
0330     Viewport1.PutText(1,2,PromptClr,AllDone);
0331     Wait_for_any_key
0332     return;
0333   }
0334   /*
0335
0336   ┌─────────────────────────────────────────────────────────────┐
         │               Terminate the program                         │
0337     └─────────────────────────────────────────────────────────────┘
0338                                                              */
0339   static void zQuit_Pgm(void)
0340   {
0341   Display.ShutDownGraphics();  // graceful shutdown of graphics mode.
0342   exit(0);                 // terminate the program and return OK code.
0343   }
0344   /*
0345
0346   ┌─────────────────────────────────────────────────────────────┐
         │         Detect the graphics hardware and set the            │
0347     │   highest mode permitted by the graphics adapter and monitor.│
0348     │   The user can override the autodetect algorithm by providing│
0349     │   an argument on the command-line when the program is started.│
0350     └─────────────────────────────────────────────────────────────┘
0351                                                              */
0352   static void zStartup(void)
0353   {
0354     int DefaultMode;
0355   DefaultMode= Display.SetupMode();   // get results of autodetect...
0356   switch(DefaultMode)              // ...and jump to appropriate code.
0357     {
0358     case zFAIL:       goto ABORT_PGM;
0359     case zVGA_12H:    goto VGA_mode;
0360     case zEGA_10H:    goto EGA_ECD_mode;
0361     case zEGA_EH:     goto EGA_SCD_mode;
0362     case zMCGA_11H:   goto MCGA_mode;
0363     case zCGA_6H:     goto CGA_mode;
0364     case zHERC:       goto Hercules_mode;
0365     default:          goto ABORT_PGM;
0366     }
0367   VGA_mode:              // VGA 640x480x16-color, 80x60 character mode.
0368   if(CommandLineArg==zYES)
0369     {                                  // if user has requested a mode.
0370     if((Mode>zVGA_12H)&&(Mode<zHERC)) goto FORCE_USER_MODE;
```

```
0371      }
0372      X_Res=640; Y_Res=480; Mode=zVGA_12H; CharWidth=8; CharHeight=8;
0373      return;
0374      EGA_ECD_mode:              // EGA 640x350x16-color, 80x43 character mode.
0375      if(CommandLineArg==zYES)
0376      {
0377        if((Mode==zEGA_EH)||(Mode==zCGA_6H))   // permit only EGA or CGA.
0378        goto FORCE_USER_MODE;
0379      }
0380      X_Res=640; Y_Res=350; Mode=zEGA_10H; CharWidth=8; CharHeight=8;
0381      return;
0382      EGA_SCD_mode:              // EGA 640x200x16-color, 80x25 char mode.
0383      if(CommandLineArg==zYES)
0384      {
0385        if(Mode==zCGA_6H) goto FORCE_USER_MODE;      // only CGA permitted.
0386      }
0387      X_Res=640; Y_Res=200; Mode=zEGA_EH; CharWidth=8; CharHeight=8;
0388      return;
0389      MCGA_mode:                 // MCGA 640x480x2-color, 80x60 char mode.
0390      if(CommandLineArg==zYES)
0391      {
0392        if(Mode==zCGA_6H) goto FORCE_USER_MODE;      // only CGA permitted.
0393      }
0394      X_Res=640; Y_Res=480; Mode=zMCGA_11H;
0395      C0=0; C1=1; C2=1; C3=1; C4=1; C5=1; C6=1; C7=1;
0396      C8=1; C9=1; C10=1; C11=1; C12=1; C13=1; C14=1; C15=1;
0397      CharWidth=8; CharHeight=8;
0398      return;
0399      CGA_mode:                  // CGA 640x200x2-color, 80x25 char mode.
0400      X_Res=640; Y_Res=200; Mode=zCGA_6H;
0401      C0=0; C1=1; C2=1; C3=1; C4=1; C5=1; C6=1; C7=1;
0402      C8=1; C9=1; C10=1; C11=1; C12=1; C13=1; C14=1; C15=1;
0403      CharWidth=8; CharHeight=8;
0404      return;
0405      Hercules_mode:             // Hercules 720x348x2-color, 80x25 char mode.
0406      X_Res=720; Y_Res=348; Mode=zHERC;
0407      C0=0; C1=1; C2=1; C3=1; C4=1; C5=1; C6=1; C7=1;
0408      C8=1; C9=1; C10=1; C11=1; C12=1; C13=1; C14=1; C15=1;
0409      CharWidth=9; CharHeight=14;
0410      return;
0411
0412      FORCE_USER_MODE:     // jump to here if command-line argument legal.
0413      CommandLineArg= zNO; // first, reset token to avoid returning here.
0414      Display.ForceMode(Mode);        // ...then reset the graphics mode.
0415      switch(Mode)              // ...then jump back to appropriate code.
0416      {
0417        case zEGA_10H:     goto EGA_ECD_mode;
0418        case zEGA_EH:      goto EGA_SCD_mode;
0419        case zMCGA_11H:    goto MCGA_mode;
0420        case zCGA_6H:      goto CGA_mode;
0421        default:           goto ABORT_PGM;
0422      }
0423
0424      ABORT_PGM:         // jump to here if no graphics hardware detected.
0425      cout << "\n\n\rThis C++ graphics programming demo requires a";
0426      cout << "\n\rVGA, EGA, CGA, MCGA, or HGA graphics adapter.\n\r";
0427      exit(-1);                   // terminate, returning an error code.
0428      }
0429      /*
0430      ┌────────────────────────────────────────────────────────────────┐
0431      │                         Stub routine                           │
0432      └────────────────────────────────────────────────────────────────┘
0433                                                                      */
```

```
0434   static void zStubRoutine(void)
0435   {       // this do-nothing routine is a placeholder for future code.
0436   Display.SetHue(C0);                        // set the drawing color.
0437   Display.SetLine(0xffff);                   // set the line style.
0438   Display.SetFill(SolidFill,C0);             // set the fill style.
0439   Viewport1.ClearTextLine();                 // clear the dialog line.
0440   Viewport1.PutText(1,2,TextClr,StubMessage);// display text message.
0441   return;
0442   }
0443   /*
0444
0445   ┌─────────────────────────────────────────────────────────────┐
       │            Check the keyboard for a keystroke                 │
0446   └─────────────────────────────────────────────────────────────┘
0447                                                                   */
0448   static void zKeyboard(void)
0449   {
0450     union AnyName{int RawCode;char Code[3];}Keystroke;
0451     char TempKey=0;
0452   #if defined (BORLAND)
0453     if (bioskey(1)==zEMPTY) { KeyCode=0; return; }
0454     Keystroke.RawCode= bioskey(0);
0455   #elif defined (ZORTECH)
0456     if (bioskey(1)==zEMPTY) { KeyCode=0; return; }
0457     Keystroke.RawCode= bioskey(0);
0458   #elif defined (MICROSOFT)
0459     if (_bios_keybrd(_KEYBRD_READY)==zEMPTY)
0460       { KeyCode=0; return; }
0461     Keystroke.RawCode= _bios_keybrd(_KEYBRD_READ);
0462   #endif
0463   TempKey= Keystroke.Code[0];
0464   if (TempKey!=0)
0465     {                                     // if a normal keystroke...
0466     KeyCode=1; KeyNum=TempKey; return;
0467     }
0468   if (TempKey==0)
0469     {                                     // if an extended keystroke...
0470     KeyCode=2; KeyNum=Keystroke.Code[1]; return;
0471     }
0472   }
0473   /*
0474
0475   ┌─────────────────────────────────────────────────────────────┐
       │                Empty the keystroke buffer                     │
0476   └─────────────────────────────────────────────────────────────┘
0477                                                                   */
0478   static void zPurge(void)
0479   {
0480   do zKeyboard();
0481     while (KeyCode!=0);
0482   return;
0483   }
0484   /*
0485
0486   ┌─────────────────────────────────────────────────────────────┐
       │                      Make a sound                             │
0487   └─────────────────────────────────────────────────────────────┘
0488                                                                   */
0489   static void zMakeSound(int Hertz,double Duration)
0490   {
0491     static clock_t FormerTime=0;
0492     short Count=0;
0493     int HighByte=0, LowByte=0;
0494     unsigned char OldPort=0, NewPort=0;
0495   FormerTime= clock();
```

```
0496  if (Hertz < 40) return;
0497  if (Hertz > 4660) return;
0498  Count= 1193180L/Hertz;
0499  HighByte= Count / 256;
0500  LowByte= Count - (HighByte * 256);
0501  #if defined (BORLAND)
0502    outportb(0x43,0xB6); outportb(0x42,(unsigned char)LowByte);
0503    outportb(0x42,(unsigned char)HighByte); OldPort=inportb(0x61);
0504    NewPort=(OldPort | 0x03); outportb(0x61,NewPort);
0505    zDelay(FormerTime,Duration);
0506    outportb(0x61,OldPort);
0507  #elif defined (ZORTECH)
0508    outp(0x43,0xB6); outp(0x42,LowByte);
0509    outp(0x42,HighByte); OldPort=(unsigned char)inp(0x61);
0510    NewPort=(OldPort | 0x03); outp(0x61,(int)NewPort);
0511    zDelay(FormerTime,Duration);
0512    outp(0x61,(int)OldPort);
0513  #elif defined (MICROSOFT)
0514    outp(0x43,0xB6); outp(0x42,LowByte);
0515    outp(0x42,HighByte); OldPort=(unsigned char)inp(0x61);
0516    NewPort=(OldPort | 0x03); outp(0x61,(int)NewPort);
0517    zDelay(FormerTime,Duration);
0518    outp(0x61,(int)OldPort);
0519  #endif
0520  return;
0521  }
0522  /*
0523
0524  ┌─────────────────────────────────────────────────────────┐
      │                        Pause                            │
0525  └─────────────────────────────────────────────────────────┘
0526                                                            */
0527  static clock_t zDelay(clock_t StartTime, double Wait)
0528  {                           // pause for a specified length of time.
0529    clock_t StopTime;
0530    clock_t NewClockTime;
0531  #if defined (BORLAND)
0532    StopTime= StartTime + (Wait * CLK_TCK);
0533  #elif defined (ZORTECH)
0534    StopTime= StartTime + (Wait * CLOCKS_PER_SEC);
0535  #elif defined (MICROSOFT)
0536    StopTime= StartTime + (Wait * CLK_TCK);
0537  #endif
0538  while ( clock() < StopTime ) {;}
0539  NewClockTime= clock();
0540  return NewClockTime;
0541  }
0542  /*
0543
0544  ┌─────────────────────────────────────────────────────────┐
      │          Retrieve the command-line arguments, if any    │
0545  └─────────────────────────────────────────────────────────┘
0546                                                            */
0547  static void zArguments(int NumArgs, char *Arg[])
0548  {
0549  if(NumArgs==1)
0550    {
0551    CommandLineArg= zNO; return;                          // if no arg.
0552    }
0553  CommandLineCompare= strncmp(StartUpArg[0],Arg[1],5);
0554  if(CommandLineCompare==0)
0555    {
0556    CommandLineArg=zYES; Mode=zVGA_12H; return;           // /M12.
0557    }
0558  CommandLineCompare= strncmp(StartUpArg[1],Arg[1],5);
```

```
0559  if(CommandLineCompare==0)
0560    {
0561    CommandLineArg=zYES; Mode=zEGA_10H; return;              // /M10.
0562    }
0563  CommandLineCompare= strncmp(StartUpArg[2],Arg[1],5);
0564  if(CommandLineCompare==0)
0565    {
0566    CommandLineArg=zYES; Mode=zEGA_EH; return;               // /MOE.
0567    }
0568  CommandLineCompare= strncmp(StartUpArg[3],Arg[1],5);
0569  if(CommandLineCompare==0)
0570    {
0571    CommandLineArg=zYES; Mode=zMCGA_11H; return;             // /M11.
0572    }
0573  CommandLineCompare= strncmp(StartUpArg[4],Arg[1],5);
0574  if(CommandLineCompare==0)
0575    {
0576    CommandLineArg=zYES; Mode=zCGA_6H; return;               // /M06.
0577    }
0578  CommandLineCompare= strncmp(StartUpArg[5],Arg[1],5);
0579  if(CommandLineCompare==0)
0580    {
0581    CommandLineArg=zYES; Mode=zHERC; return;                 // /MHC.
0582    }
0583  CommandLineArg= zNO;                    // if an unrecognized argument.
0584  return;
0585  }
0586  /*
0587
0588    ┌─────────────────────────────────────────────────────────────────┐
        │  Supercharged C++ Graphics  --  end of source file DESKTOP.CPP    │
        └─────────────────────────────────────────────────────────────────┘
0589
0590                                                                    */
```

Part Three

Building 3-D
graphics applications

8
Programming concepts for 3-D images

3-D graphics can add an element of realism to your C++ graphics software that is difficult to achieve with two-dimensional graphics. One of the class libraries provided in appendix E, class Model3D in LIB3D.CPP, provides methods to create and manipulate shaded 3-D solids. The class uses the backplane removal algorithm to eliminate the hidden surfaces of convex three-dimensional objects.

No matter which graphics adapter you are using—VGA, EGA, MCGA, CGA, or Hercules—you can generate shaded 3-D models on your personal computer using C++.

Three-dimensional geometry

Two commonly-used methods used for building 3-D models on personal computers are the B-rep and CSG methods. See FIG. 8-1.

B-rep modeling

B-rep is an acronym for boundary-representation. Only the outer skin—the boundary—of the object is drawn by the 3-D routines. The surfaces of a B-rep model are constructed of facets or polygons. Groups of facets can be joined together to create different shapes, curves, or complex models.

Not only is B-rep modeling easy to implement on a personal computer, but it is fast and it can produce realistic imagery. Hidden surface removal can be accomplished using different algorithms.

The B-rep technique has limitations. It is mathematically difficult to join two models together or to drill a hole through an existing model. The B-rep model algorithm considers only the boundaries of the object, not solid volumes or internal composition.

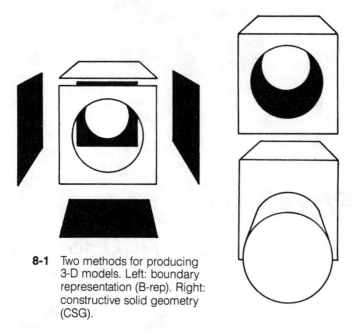

8-1 Two methods for producing 3-D models. Left: boundary representation (B-rep). Right: constructive solid geometry (CSG).

CSG modeling

CSG is an acronym for constructive solid geometry. CSG models are made up of 3-D solids like cubes, parallelepipeds, cylinders, spheres, and others. Because each of these sub-objects is also a 3-D solid, these sub-objects can be combined together to produce more complex objects. CSG considers the volumetric structure of an object, so the software can drill a hole into a model, or perform other operations, if it wants to. A cylinder represents the intended hole and is subtracted mathematically from the model. This type of 3-D logical operation is called a 3-D Boolean operation or Euler operation.

CSG modeling is used in applications where specific gravity, mass, moment of inertia, density, and other engineering-based considerations are important. CSG modeling is true solid modeling, but unlike B-rep modeling, CSG is very time-consuming and memory-intensive.

User input

3-D graphics software often gives the user the ability to interact with the software during the creation of 3-D models. This creative interaction often relies upon extrusion and sub-objects.

Revolve, extrude, and sweep

The 3-D functions revolve, extrude, and sweep are used to build 3-D objects from a 2-D outline. The user specifies a 2-D shape and then indicates which direction to revolve the outline and how many degrees to rotate. The software is responsible for generating the 3-D object. This revolving or revolution function works equally well with both B-rep and CSG models.

The extrude function also takes a 2-D outline and turns it into a 3-D object. The user specifies how far forward to stretch or extrude the shape. The extrude function also works with both B-rep and CSG models.

The sweep function is similar to extrude, except that the stretching occurs along a curve rather than a straight line like the extrude function.

Quadric primitives

Revolve, extrude, and sweep all rely upon input from the user. Some software takes a different approach, providing ready-to-use sub-objects in a 3-D toolkit. The user selects a desired sub-object and then advises the 3-D software where to position the sub-object. Typical sub-objects, also called quadric primitives, include cylinders, cones, spheres, hyperboloids, paraboloids, wedges, parallelepipeds, pyramids, laminas, toruses, and others. The user can manipulate the scale and ratio of each primitive.

Curved surfaces

Smoothly curved surfaces can be constructed by both the B-rep and the CSG modeling systems. A ruled surface is the surface created by constructing a set of straight lines between two curved lines. These two lines are usually parametric curves whose end-points and control points have been specified by the end-user. A cubic patch surface is a curved surface bounded by four curved edges.

Euler operations

Euler operations, also called 3-D Boolean operations, simulate the way the real world works. Euler operations include joining, intersection, and subtraction.

Joining means attaching two solids to each other. Intersection means the solid which results from the common volume when two solids are attached. Subtraction means removing the volume of one solid from another solid.

Coordinate systems

C++ graphics programs that use 3-D images make use of xyz coordinates to describe shapes and environments. The x dimension describes left and right measurements. The y coordinate describes up and down measurements. The z coordinate describes near and far measurements.

Object and world coordinates

Object coordinates are the xyz dimensions that describe the fundamental shape of a 3-D object. World coordinates are the xyz coordinates that would describe the object if it were placed in a specific 3-D environment at a certain location and rotation. They are called world coordinates because the 3-D environment is called the 3-D world.

Camera and image plane coordinates

Camera coordinates are the xyz coordinates that describe how the object would appear to an observer at a specified location in the 3-D environment. The camera location is called the *viewpoint*.

Image plane coordinates refer to the xy coordinates that would be present on a two-dimension image plane (or window) placed between the camera and the 3-D object. See FIG. 8-2.

Screen coordinates

Screen coordinates are the xy coordinates which can be drawn on the computer display screen. Screen coordinates, also called *display* coordinates, are the result of scaling the image plane coordinates to fit the display screen.

Calculating each set of coordinates in this 3-D cycle involves sine and cosine formulas derived from matrix math.

Writing 3-D graphics software

In addition to a solid grounding in fundamental graphics programming techniques, any C programmer wishing to create a 3-D graphics program needs an understanding of 3-D programming concepts.

3-D programming terminology

Like any other discipline within the broad field of visualization graphics, 3-D graphics has its own syntax.

Modeling   Modeling refers to the act of drawing the shape of the 3-D object. Modeling concerns itself with getting the shape and volume right. See FIG. 8-3.

Coordinates are the xyz measurements that represent a specific point on the model. Coordinate system means the xyz axis system used to measure width, height, and depth—the three dimensions of 3-D. A number of contradictory coordinate systems are in use today.

Rendering   Rendering means shading or coloring the 3-D model in a manner appropriate to the light sources in the scene. See FIG. 8-4 and FIG. 8-5. Hidden surface removal and visible surface detection refer to techniques of drawing 3-D objects so that backside surfaces or surfaces hidden by other objects surfaces are correctly drawn or discarded, as the situation requires. See FIG. 8-3.

Solids modeling refers to 3-D algorithms that treat each object as a solid with mass. Constructive solid geometry (CSG) uses solids modeling. B-rep modeling uses facets or polygons to build solids from the skin or boundary of the object.

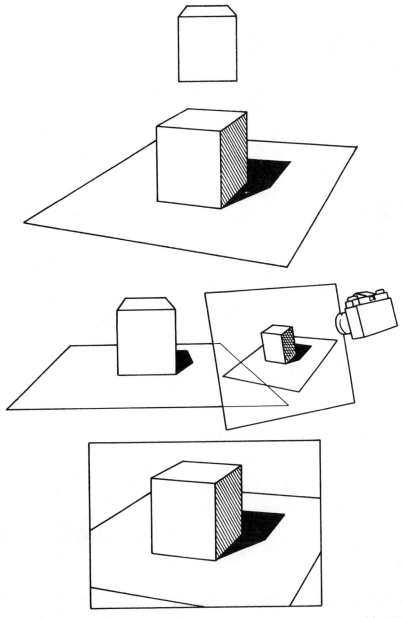

8-2 Typical 3-D modeling transformations. From top: object coordinates, world coordinates, camera coordinates, and display coordinates.

Creating and manipulating 3-D models

3-D graphics programming relies upon xyz coordinates, which are used to describe a unique location in 3-D space. There are different types of 3-D space, however. A model must follow an evolutionary path through each type of 3-D

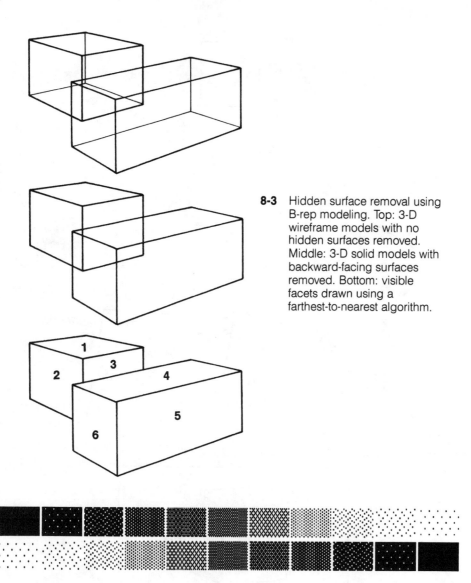

8-3 Hidden surface removal using B-rep modeling. Top: 3-D wireframe models with no hidden surfaces removed. Middle: 3-D solid models with backward-facing surfaces removed. Bottom: visible facets drawn using a farthest-to-nearest algorithm.

8-4 Dithered fill.

space until the finished model can be displayed on the computer screen. See FIG. 8-2.

Step one: Object coordinates

Object coordinates define the fundamental shape of the model. These coordinates describe object space, which is not related to any other environment or to any other object. Object coordinates form the most important part of a 3-D database.

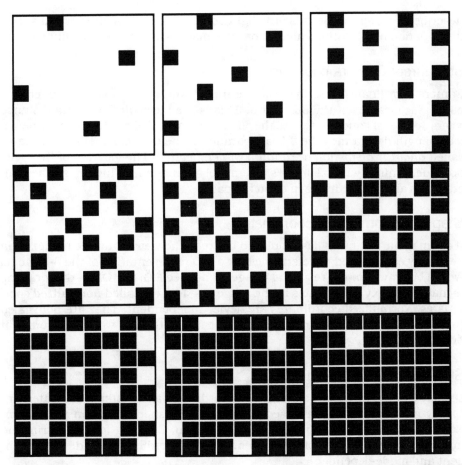

8-5 The 8 × 8 matrices used to create dithered fills suitable for shading 3-D models. (See also Fig. 8-4.)

8-6 The three axis planes used in 3-D modeling and shading.

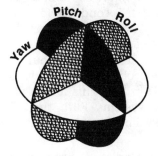

Step two: World coordinates

World coordinates describe the shape of a model at a specific orientation and location in a specific 3-D environment called the *world*. World coordinates describe world space. Because the light source is also present in world space, illumination and lighting calculations are made using world coordinates.

Step three: Camera coordinates

Camera coordinates describe how the model would look to an observer at a particular location in the 3-D world. This is the viewpoint. Viewing distance refers to the distance between the viewpoint and the model. The camera's focal length determines the 3-D appearance of the image. Focal length is also called *angular distortion* or *amount of perspective*. The location of the viewpoint determines which surfaces of a model are hidden, so hidden surface calculations are mainly made in camera space.

Step four: Normalized coordinates

If an imaginary pane of glass is placed between the viewer and the model, then geometry can be used to determine how a 2-D representation of the 3-D model would be drawn on the resulting image plane. See FIG. 8-2. Often this drawing is made using xy coordinates in the range of – 1 to +1, called normalized coordinates. Normalized coordinates are device-independent. They are not scaled to the display screen, but rather are still scaled to the 3-D world environment being used.

Step five: Display coordinates

Display coordinates, also called *screen* coordinates and *raster* coordinates, are the xy coordinates that are used to draw the finished image on the screen. Ratio formulas scale the image to fit the screen. Clipping formulas trim the image at the boundaries of the screen. Display coordinates are device-dependent and mode-dependent.

The transformation sequence

First, object coordinates are used to describe the fundamental shape of the model. Second, world coordinates are used to describe its rotated and translated position in the particular 3-D environment being considered. Third, camera coordinates describe how the model would appear to a viewer located at a specific viewpoint. Fourth, an imaginary image plane is placed between the viewpoint and the model in order to convert the 3-D camera coordinates to a 2-D image. This fourth step is sometimes combined with step five in many 3-D systems. Fifth, the 2-D image is scaled and clipped to create the display coordinates which are used to draw the image on the screen.

Contradictory coordinate systems

A number of contradictory 3-D coordinate systems are used in different applications. These systems are named according to how they can be represented by the human hand.

The standard right-hand coordinate system is the most widely used. It specifies positive z as nearer, positive y as higher, and positive x as right. The ground plane is represented by xz coordinates.

The distinguishing feature of the left-hand system is the use of negative z as nearer. In all other respects, the x and y coordinates mean the same measurements as in the right-hand system. The ground plane is represented by xz coordinates.

Components of 3-D models

3-D models are usually constructed of four-sided polygons or three-sided polygons called *facets*. Each side of a facet is called a *halfedge*. Halfedges do not exist in the real world. This is because real objects have three dimensions: width, depth, and height. Facets possess no thickness.

When a facet shares a halfedge with another facet as part of a 3-D solid, the intersection is called an *edge*. A 3-D model constructed from individual facets is comprised of certain components. A *vertex* is a corner where three or more edges meet. An *edge* is the boundary between two facets. A facet is one small plane on the surface of the model. A *hidden surface* is any facet or portion of a facet which is hidden from view—either because it faces away from the viewer, or because it is obscured by other facets.

Modeling formulas

The mathematical formulas that are needed to manipulate a 3-D model and to produce a set of display coordinates are based on matrix math, using sine and cosine in a traditional algebraic formula format. As the demonstration program in the next chapter shows, the rotation formulas can be broken down into three components: yaw, roll, and pitch. See FIG. 8-6. The translation formulas also can be broken down into three components: near/far, left/right, and up/down. By selectively manipulating these components in the 3-D formulas, the position of the object, the world, and the viewpoint can each be rotated and moved independent of one another.

Rendering methods

Three methods of rendering are available to C graphics programmers. They are wire-frame, solid, and shaded. Shading methods include Lambert or facet shading, Gouraud or smooth shading, Phong shading, ray tracing, and radiosity shading.

Wire-frame models

Wire-frame models are built with only edges. No attempt is made at hidden surface removal. See FIG. 8-3. If a wire-frame model is constructed of facets, the facets are not shaded. They are left transparent.

Solid models

Solid models are built with opaque facets. Hidden surfaces are detected and are removed. The model appears solid like it does in real life. No attempt is made to shade the model according to the existing lighting conditions.

Shaded models

Shaded models are built from facets that have been shaded to represent the intensity of light falling upon each facet. Using either the 16-color modes or the 2-color modes of VGA, EGA, MCGA, CGA, or Hercules graphics adapters, an acceptable range of colors can be generated using bit tiling. See FIG. 8-4. Because bit tiling relies upon setting a mixture of pixels in an area, the human eye sees the resulting overall pattern, not the individual pixels, so different shades can be simulated. See FIG. 8-5.

Techniques of hidden surface removal

There are many different algorithms used for hidden surface removal on personal computers. Some, however, take a lot of computing power. Others are effective only when used in combination with other algorithms in the same program.

Radial sort methods

The radial pre-sort method requires that the programmer use only those coordinates that are visible. A slight variation, the radial standard sort method, uses the software itself to determine which coordinates are visible at runtime. Only visible coordinates are provided to the 3-D modeling and rendering formulas.

Plane equation methods

The plane equation method is also called the *backplane removal* method. In any simple convex 3-D solid, such as a cube, facets that face away from the viewer are hidden from view. The plane equation method uses surface normals perpendicular to the surface and vector cross-products to determine which side of the surface is facing the observer.

The separation plane method places an imaginary plane between two solid 3-D models. Vector math is used to determine on which side of the separation plane each model rests. Further information can be derived, identifying which model is farthest from the viewpoint and hidden from view by the nearer model.

Depth-sort methods

Depth-sort methods compare the z coordinates of different facets to determine which facets are nearer to the viewer. A z buffer is a block of memory that contains color codes for the nearest z coordinate for each pixel on the display screen.

Ray-tracing and radiosity

The ray tracing method uses vector formulas to trace the path of individual light rays. Typical ray tracers follow light rays back from the observer's eye to various objects in the scene.

Radiosity calculates the distribution of light rays in the scene based upon energy distribution, independent of the location of the viewer.

Decomposition and minimax

The *decomposition* method breaks up the scene into small cubic solids. The *minimax* method uses two bounding rectangles to determine if an overlap exists between two images on the display.

Yaw, roll, and pitch

The 3-D world is often based upon a spherical coordinate system. See FIG. 8-6. The angles that a spherical coordinate system provides are used as sine and cosine formulas in the 3-D modeling and rendering calculations.

The viewpoint is always located at position 0,0,0 and is called the *origin* in a spherical coordinate system. Rotation is calculated in yaw, roll, and pitch planes. Translation is a result of moving various object coordinates and world coordinates about the coordinate system.

This book uses x as the left/right axis, y as the up/down axis, and z as the near/far axis.

The light source

The position of the light source is expressed in world coordinates. This means that any calculations of illumination are made after the object coordinates have been transformed into world coordinates.

If the world is rotated, the position of the light source remains constant relative to the position of the world. This means that if the viewpoint changes, the illumination level would change as you move the viewpoint behind the object, for example.

Illumination

The level of illumination falling on a facet is calculated by comparing the incoming light vector to the surface perpendicular. The smaller the angle, the more light rays striking the surface—the brighter the surface will appear. If the angle exceeds 90 degrees, the surface is not lighted by the light source and receives only ambient light reflected from other objects in the scene.

The specific surface normal model: Lambert shading

Lambert shading, named after eighteenth-century mathematician Johann Lambert, is also called facet shading. *Facet shading* uses color interpolation on individual facets to shade the 3-D model. Dithering or bit tiling is used to shade areas on the screen according to the relationship between the angle of the incoming light ray and the surface normal of the facet being considered.

The average surface normal model: Gouraud shading

Gouraud shading, named after French motorcar designer Henri Gouraud, is also called smooth shading. *Gouraud shading* uses color interpolation on individual scan lines to achieve a smooth effect which reduces the harsh edges between facets. Such harsh edges are called *discontinuities* or *mach bands*. Gouraud shading can be used on any 256-color mode or with 16 shades of gray.

The individual normal interpolation model: Phong shading

Phong shading, named after computer science researcher Bui T. Phong, uses color interpolation on individual pixels. Because this method considers each individual pixel, special effects like highlights—called *specular reflections*—can be generated. Surface normals and their relationships to incoming light rays are the basis for this method of shading.

The cosine power specular reflection model: Ray tracing

Ray tracing follows the paths of individual reflected and refracted rays of light as they move through the scene. This method makes it possible to generate effects like reflections, shadows, and so on.

Reflections. Mirrored reflections appearing on the surfaces of models in a 3-D scene are based upon reflection mapping algorithms. The viewpoint is first moved to the surface of the object. A bitmap containing the view from that viewpoint is generated. Next, the viewpoint is relocated back to the original position. Now the bitmap is used to wrap the reflection onto the surface of the mirrored object.

The diffuse illumination model: Radiosity shading

Instead of tracing individual rays of light, the radiosity method considers the overall energy levels from different light sources and different reflective, absorptive, or refractive surfaces in the scene. The radiosity method is better at modeling diffuse light than the ray tracing method.

Surface mapping and texture mapping

Surface mapping and texture mapping can be used with Lambert shading, Gouraud shading, and ray-tracers. Just like ratio math can be used to scale device-independent coordinates to fit a particular screen, 3-D formulas can be used to scale the contents of a bitmap buffer to fit on the surface of a 3-D object. The contents of the map are wrapped onto the surface of the object.

Bump mapping

Bump mapping is used with ray-tracing techniques to simulate rough surfaces like orange peels. By randomly distorting the surface normals on the surface of the 3-D object, slight variations in brightness can be introduced. These variations simulate a rough-surfaced object.

Reflection mapping

Reflection mapping is based upon the translated viewpoint concept. It can be used with either Lambert shading, Gouraud shading, or ray tracers. It is most dramatic when ray tracing is used. By temporarily moving the viewpoint to the surface of the reflective object, you can see how the reflected scene appears. If the 3-D formulas are used to store this scene in a bitmap, the reflection can be mapped onto the surface of the object when the viewpoint is moved back to its original position.

Manipulating the model

Building a 3-D model requires translation, rotation, and extrusion. Translation is movement along the x axis, y axis, or z axis in the 3-D environment. The model is not rotated, but merely moved along these axes. Rotation changes the yaw, roll, or pitch angle of the model. It is not moved to any new location in the 3-D environment, but merely rotated. Extrusion changes the shape of the model. A facet can be deformed along either the x axis, y axis, or z axis. Rotation and translation are performed with world coordinates. Extrusion is performed with object coordinates.

A 3-D class for C++

A class whose methods provide 3-D modeling and shading capabilities is provided in LIB3D.HPP and LIB3D.CPP in appendix E. Class Model3D forms the essential underpinnings for the interactive 3-D modeler, whose complete source code is presented in the next chapter.

Programmer's Guide to LIB3D.HPP

Code The complete source code for the declarations for class Model3D is found in LIB3D.HPP in appendix E. LIB3D.HPP must be #included in any program that uses the methods of class Model3D to build shaded 3-D objects.

Programmer's Guide to LIB3D.CPP

Code LIB3D.CPP is the class implementation listing for class Model3D, providing routines that can create, move, rotate, stretch, and otherwise manipulate a 3-D modeling environment and the 3-D objects that populate the 3-D world.

Constructor

The constructor for class Model3D at lines 0087 through 0201 is responsible for initializing all 3-D and 2-D parameters for whatever graphics mode is currently in effect.

Method Initialize3D( )

The method at lines 0212 through 0246 initializes some parameters used by the 3-D routines, including the camera angle and object angle.

Method Instance( )

The method at lines 0248 through 0317 resets the angle measurements that control the yaw, roll, and pitch orientation of the 3-D cursor. Instance( ) also adjusts the xyz axis measurements that control the movement (translation) of the 3-D cursor and the stretching (extrusion) of the cursor's shape.

Method Camera( )

The method at lines 0319 through 0417 calls methods of class Viewport to draw the volumetric 3-D cursor on the display.

Method Camera( )

The method at lines 0419 through 0487 controls the viewing angle of the camera.

Method DrawGrndPlane( )

The method at lines 0489 through 0535 draws the transparent 3-D ground-plane that is displayed while you are adjusting the camera angle.

Method VisibilityTest( )

The method at lines 0536 through 0550 uses vector math to determine which side of a facet is facing the viewpoint. The result is placed in a variable named visible. If visible is less than 0 the facet is visible. If visible equals 0 the facet is being viewing edge-on. If visible is greater than 0, the facet is hidden.

Method GetNewObjParams( )

The method at lines 0552 through 0581 calculates the angles and distances which other functions will use to draw a sub-object. This function is called each time the 3-D cursor is moved.

Method SetObjAngle( )

The method at lines 0583 through 0598 calculates the new sine and cosine values for a new instance of a sub-object, in this case the 3-D volumetric cursor. These values are used by the 3-D formulas.

Method SetCamAngle( )

The method at lines 0600 through 0615 calculates the new sine and cosine values for a new viewpoint. These values are used by the 3-D formulas.

Method PutObjToScreen( )

The method at lines 0617 through 0629 is like a macro that calls other lower-level 3-D routines to transform a set of coordinates through object coordinates, world coordinates, camera coordinates, image plane coordinates, and display coordinates.

Method PutWorldToScreen( )

The method at lines 0631 through 0642 takes a set of coordinates from world coordinates through to display coordinates.

Method GetWorldCoords( )

The method at lines 0644 through 0657 transforms object coordinates to world coordinates.

Method GetCameraCoords( )

The method at lines 0659 through 0674 converts world coordinates to camera coordinates.

Method GetImageCoords( )

The method at lines 0676 through 0686 converts camera coordinates to image plane coordinates. These coordinates are 2-D device-independent coordinates that are not yet ready to be drawn on the screen.

Method GetScreenCoords( )

The method at lines 0688 through 0700 transforms image plane coordinates to display coordinates, which are scaled and clipped, ready to fit the screen.

Method DrawFacet( )

The method at lines 0702 through 0767 draws a four-sided dithered facet. Note in particular the code at lines 0725 through 0762, which sets the bit tiling pattern.

Method GetBrightness( )

The method at lines 0769 through 0798 uses the cross product of two vectors to determine the amount of illumination falling upon a vector whose three camera coordinates have been provided to the routine.

Method SetshadingColor( )

The method at lines 0800 through 0810 toggles the shading hue between grays, blues, greens, cyans, reds, and magentas.

Method DrawCube( )

The method at lines 0842 through 0937 retrieves appropriate object coordinates from a set of arrays, tests each surface for visibility, and calls method DrawFacet( ) to draw the surface on the display. Method DrawCube( ) relies upon the calculations of method GetCubeCoords( ) at lines 0816 through 0840 to determine the object coordinates of the parallelepiped. A parallelepiped is a six-sided carton-like container used in 3-D modeling and rendering.

Related Material. A more detailed discussion of 3-D modeling and shading can be found in two earlier volumes in the Applied C Graphics series from Windcrest/McGraw-Hill: *High-Performance CAD Graphics In C*, Windcrest book 3059 (published March 1989, ISBN 0-8306-9359-9), and *Lee Adams' Visualization Graphics in C*, Windcrest book 3487 (published February 1991, ISBN 0-8306-3487-8). If you are interesting in building full-length paint, draw, drafting, and 3-D CAD programs, see *Supercharged C Graphics: A Programmer's Source Code Toolbox*, Windcrest book 3289 (published April 1990, ISBN 0-8306-3289-1).

9
Interactive 3-D graphics

The methods of class Model3D, described in the previous chapter, can be used to create an interactive 3-D modeler capable of building complex 3-D shaded solids.

A sample program: OBJECTS.CPP

Demo Figure 9-1 shows typical displays produced by the sample program OBJECTS.CPP, whose complete source code is provided in FIG. 9-6 at the end of the chapter. The program provides an interactive 3-D modeling environment in which you can build 3-D shaded solids.

How to compile and link the sample program

Here's How... The program listing presented in FIG. 9-6 contains the complete source code for the main module of the C++ demonstration program called "Using C++ for Interactive 3-D Modeling and Rendering." If you are using the companion disks to the book, the source code is in the file named OBJECTS.CPP. Three C++ source files are needed to create .exe file. These are OBJECTS.CPP from FIG. 9-6 and two class libraries in appendix E.

Class The class library that provides the language bindings and low-level graphics routines for this demonstration program is found in FIG. E-2 in appendix E. This listing contains the implementations for class PhysicalDisplay and class Viewport. If you are using the companion disks to the book, this file is named LIB2D.CPP. The class declarations are presented in FIG. E-1 in appendix E. If you are using the companion disks to the book, this file is named LIB2D.HPP.

The class library that provides the 3-D routines for this demonstration program is found in FIG. E-4 in appendix E. This listing contains the implementations for class Model3D. If you are using the companion disks to the book, this file is named LIB3D.CPP. The class declarations are presented in FIG. E-3 in appendix E. If you are using the companion disks to the book, this file is named LIB3D.HPP.

You can compile, link, and run this demonstration program using Turbo C++, Borland C++, or Zortech C++. If you are using Turbo C++, see appendix A for help in compiling the demonstration program. If you are using Borland C++ see appendix B. If you are using Zortech C++ see appendix C.

You must create a Turbo C++ or Borland C++ project list to advise your compiler which source files to bind together to build the finished .exe file. If you are using Zortech C++, you must name the files on the compiler command line field.

After a successful compile and link the animated screen should resemble the screen prints shown in FIG. 9-1.

How to run the demonstration program

You need a VGA, EGA, MCGA, CGA, or Hercules graphics adapter to run this sample application.

Using the editor to run the program

To run the program under the control of your Turbo C++, Borland C++, or Zortech C++ editor, make sure that the finished .exe file is in the default directory. If you used Turbo C++ or Borland C++ to compile the program, the appropriate graphics driver must be in the default directory. If you are using a VGA or EGA, the EGAVGA.BGI file must be present. If you are using an MCGA or CGA, the CGA.BGI file must be located in the default directory. If you are using a Hercules graphics adapter, the HERC.BGI file must be available. If you used Zortech C++ to compile the demonstration program, the appropriate graphics drivers have already been linked into the .exe code.

The built-in autodetect routine will detect the graphics hardware in your computer system and will set up the best graphics mode supported by your computer hardware. To override the autodetect routine, use the Turbo C++, Borland C++, or Zortech C++ editor to simulate a command line argument. The header in FIG. 9-6 provides a set of arguments you can use. See the appendices for guidance applicable to your particular compiler. If you are using a VGA, you can override the autodetect routine and force the demonstration program to run in an EGA, MCGA, or CGA mode. If you are using an EGA, you can force the program to run in a low-resolution EGA mode or the $640 \times 200 \times$ 2-color CGA mode.

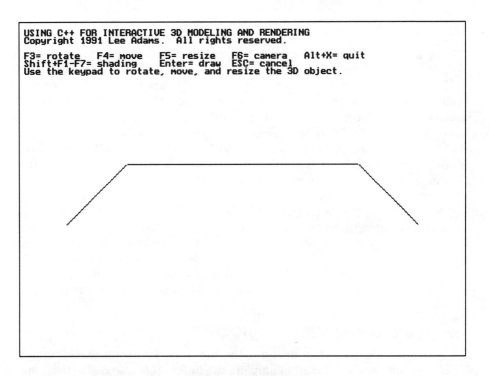

USING C++ FOR INTERACTIVE 3D MODELING AND RENDERING
Copyright 1991 Lee Adams. All rights reserved.

F3= rotate   F4= move   F5= resize   F6= camera   Alt+X= quit
Shift+F1-F7= shading   Enter= draw ESC= cancel
Use the keypad to rotate, move, and resize the 3D object.

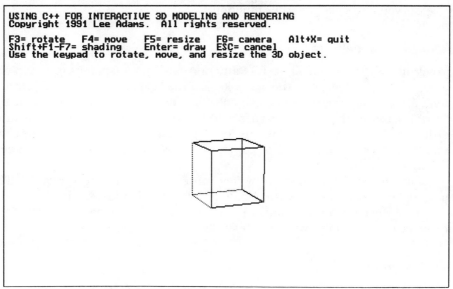

9-1 Graphics output from the sample program OBJECTS.CPP. Top: the groundplane has been pitched forward. Bottom: the 3-D volumetric cursor, ready to be translated, rotated, or extruded.

Running the program from the operating system prompt

To start the program from the operating system prompt, simply enter OBJECTS. The .exe file and any required graphics drivers must be present in the default directory. If the software finds a VGA present in your system, the program will animate using the 640×480×16-color mode. If an EGA and enhanced monitor are found, the 640×350×16-color mode is used. If an EGA and standard display are present, the program sets up the 640×200×16-color mode. If an MCGA is detected, the 640×480×2-color mode is employed. If a CGA is found, the 640×200×2-color mode is used. If the program detects a Hercules graphics adapter, it starts up in the 720×348×2-color mode.

You can force the program to start up in a different mode by adding a command line argument when you start the program from the operating system prompt. Enter OBJECTS /M11 to force the 640×480×2-color mode. Enter OBJECTS /M10 to set up the 640×350×16-color mode. Entering OBJECTS /M0E causes the program to run in the 640×200×16-color mode. Entering OBJECTS / M06 runs the demonstration program in the 640×200×2-color mode.

Using the demonstration program

All controls are activated from the main screen. After selecting a 3-D function, you must either complete the function or use Esc to back out of it before you can select another function.

Adjusting the camera

To set the viewing angle, press F6 Camera Angle. A transparent groundplane appears on the screen. Use the arrow keys of the keypad to adjust the yaw and pitch of the groundplane. See the top portion of FIG. 9-1. Holding down the up-arrow key moves the camera higher, and the groundplane is pitched forward, letting you look down on it. Holding down the down-arrow key moves the camera lower. You can rotate the groundplane a full 90 degrees in the pitch plane if you wish.

Holding down the right-arrow key moves the camera to the right. The groundplane rotates clockwise. Holding down the left-arrow key moves the camera to the left. You can rotate the scene a full 360 degrees in the yaw plane if you wish. Press Enter when you have finished positioning the groundplane.

Moving an object

Now press F4 Move Object to put the 3-D cursor on the screen. This volumetric transparent cursor represents a 3-D bounding box for the solid that you will eventually draw. Use the arrow keys of the keypad to move the object in the 3-D environment. See the bottom portion of FIG. 9-1. The left-arrow key and right-arrow key move the object along the x axis, usually left to right. The PgUp and PgDn keys move the object along the z axis, usually near to far. The up-arrow and down-arrow keys move the object higher or lower in the scene, affecting its elevation.

At this stage, you can press Enter to draw the solid at the current location, or you can press Esc to leave the cursor at its present location and select another function.

Rotating an object

Whichever you choose, you can now select F3 Rotate Object to adjust the yaw, roll, or pitch angle of the object in the scene. If you have already drawn the object, you might wish to select F4 Move Object first to move the cursor off the object to a new location. Holding down the right-arrow key rotates the cursor counterclockwise in the yaw plane. Holding down the left-arrow key rotates the cursor clockwise in the yaw plane. Holding down the up-arrow key pitches the object back. Pressing the down-arrow key pitches the object forward. Press the PgUp key to tilt the object clockwise in the roll plane. Holding down the Home key rolls the object counterclockwise. No matter which rotation keys you use, you can turn the object a full 360 degrees in any or all of the yaw, roll, and pitch planes. When you are finished rotating, press Enter to draw the object at that orientation, or press Esc to leave the cursor at that position and return to the main command level.

Changing the shading color

The 3-D visualization editor will render solids in either blue, green, cyan, red, magenta, or gray shades. Press Shift+F1 to activate blue shades. Press Shift+F2 to select green shading. Press Shift+F3 to choose cyan shading. Use Shift+F4 to select red shades. Press Shift+F5 to use magenta shades. Use Shift+F6 to select gray shading. The default condition is blue. When you toggle between different shading colors, no effect is seen on the screen until the next solid you draw. You can use solids of different colors in the same 3-D scene.

Changing the size of an object

The demonstration program provides you with full control over extrusion—you can stretch the 3-D cursor, making it longer, wider, or taller. The resulting 3-D object drawn will adopt the shape of the volumetric 3-D cursor. Use F5 Resize Object to put the 3-D cursor on the screen. Hold down the right-arrow key to extrude the object along the x axis, making it longer. Press the left-arrow key to make it smaller along the x axis. Press the up-arrow key to make the object taller. Hold down the down-arrow key to make it shorter. Pressing the PgDn key makes the object wider in the z plane, towards you. Holding down the PgUp key makes the object thinner in the z plane. Experiment with the keypad keys until you achieve an extruded size that is appropriate, then press Enter to draw the solid.

Building complex models from different objects

OBJECTS.CPP uses backplane removal to implement hidden surface removal. This means that backward-facing planes on the surfaces of the parallelepipeds and cylinders are not drawn. Only forward-facing facets are drawn. If you use multiple objects in the same scene, you must be careful to draw the farthest objects first. See FIG. 9-2. By creating nearer objects later, you can ensure that their facets correctly obscure the facets of objects farther away.

The demonstration program is also capable of drawing composite images used for business presentation graphics, engineering, and design work, as shown in FIG. 9-3, FIG. 9-4, and FIG. 9-5.

Programmer's Guide to OBJECTS.CPP

The complete listing for the demonstration program OBJECTS.CPP is presented in FIG. 9-6. The source code consists of an informative header, conditional compilation directives, declaration of constants and macros, file include directives, function prototypes, variable declarations, and the executable functions.

Conditional compilation

Information and source code for conditional compilation is located at lines 0047 through 0064. If you are using Turbo C++ or Borland C++, the program is ready to compile, subject to the instructions in appendix B. If you are using Zortech C++, change line 0063 to #define FG and change line 0064 to #define ZORTECH.

Constants

The C++ const keyword is used to declare and assign values to constant variables at lines 0066 through 0112.

Include files

The code at lines 0120 through 0148 loads the appropriate header files and C++ class declaration files. Line 0147 loads LIB2D.HPP, which declares the data members and methods of class PhysicalDisplay and class Viewport. Line 0148 loads LIB3D.HPP, which declares the data members and methods of class Model3D.

Function prototypes

Function declarations are provided in lines 0153 through 0162. Functions declared here are visible throughout this source file. They can be called by any other function in the source file. Because each function is declared with the static qualifier, it is not available to functions located in other source files.

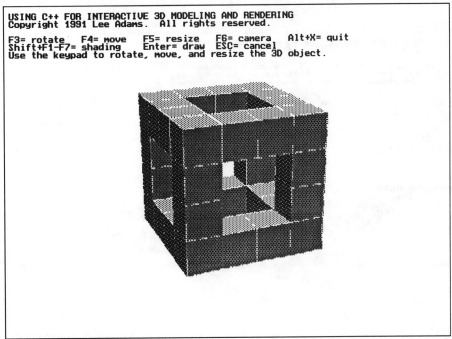

USING C++ FOR INTERACTIVE 3D MODELING AND RENDERING
Copyright 1991 Lee Adams. All rights reserved.

F3= rotate   F4= move   F5= resize   F6= camera   Alt+X= quit
Shift+F1-F7= shading   Enter= draw ESC= cancel
Use the keypad to rotate, move, and resize the 3D object.

9-2   Graphics output from the sample program OBJECTS.CPP. Shown here is a typical inter-active session with the demonstration program. Complex models are constructed of numerous subobjects using a farthest-to-nearest methodology. (See also Fig. 8-3.)

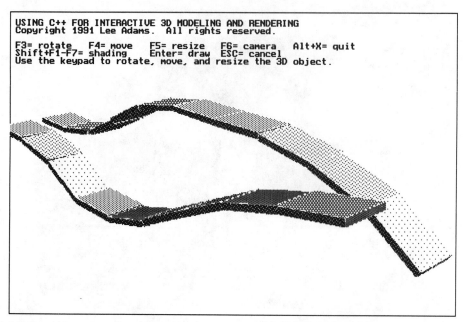

9-3 Graphics output from the sample program OBJECTS.CPP. Business presentation graphics like 3-D ribbon charts can be created using the demonstration program.

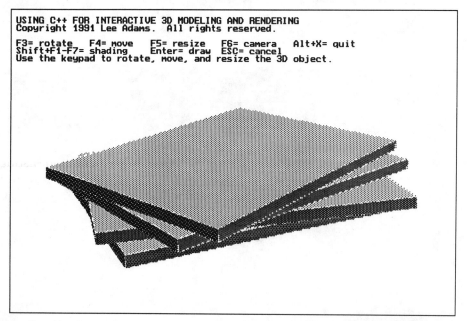

9-4 Graphics output from the sample program OBJECTS.CPP. The 3-D volumetric cursor can be extruded (stretched or squeezed) to create parallelepipeds (boxes) at any desired configuration. Rotation and translation is then used to position the resulting solids.

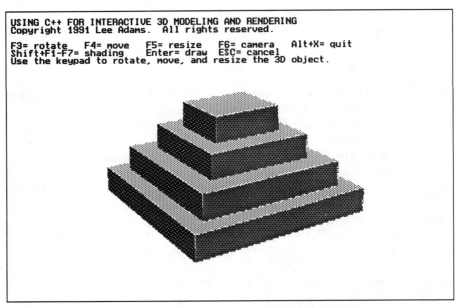

USING C++ FOR INTERACTIVE 3D MODELING AND RENDERING
Copyright 1991 Lee Adams.   All rights reserved.

F3= rotate   F4= move   F5= resize   F6= camera   Alt+X= quit
Shift+F1-F7= shading   Enter= draw   ESC= cancel
Use the keypad to rotate, move, and resize the 3D object.

9-5 Graphics output from the sample program OBJECTS.CPP. Structured, symmetrical solids can be created by extrusion and translation of the 3-D volumetric cursor.

Variable declarations

Lines 0164 through 0198 declare global variables visible throughout this source file. These variables have file scope and can be modified by any function in the file.

Object declarations

Note line 0197, which creates an object from class PhysicalDisplay, named Display. The program will later call the methods of this object to help it manage the display. The methods are declared in the class declaration listing LIB2D.HPP and are defined in the class implementation listing LIB2D.CPP in appendix E. The object created at line 0197 is a static object. It has file scope and will remain available until the program terminates.

Line 0198 creates an object from the Viewport class. The object is named Viewport1. The address of Display is passed to this new object. Viewport1 will need to use the methods of Display to generate graphics output. The object created at line 0198 is a static object with file scope. It will remain active until program termination.

main( )

The main( ) function is located at lines 0203 through 0234. The code first checks to see if any command line arguments were used to start the program. It then sets an appropriate graphics mode.

The code at line 0231 calls the function that provides the interactive loop to control the 3-D modeler.

Interactive 3-D modeling

The function at lines 0236 through 0414 lets the user manipulate the yaw and pitch of the 3-D world and build 3-D solids inside the world.

Note line 0247, when the C++ new operator is used to create an instance of class Model3D named Model. Line 0248 calls method Initialize3D( ) of this object to prepare the 3-D modeling and rendering environment.

The block at lines 0249 through 0287 is a keyboard polling loop that lets the user choose a 3-D modeling function from the on-screen menu. Note line 0265, for example, where the code makes a call to method Camera( ) of class Model3D to rotate the camera.

The loop at lines 0289 through 0413 is a series of switch( ) blocks that interpret incoming keystrokes for the various 3-D functions supported by this demonstration program. The variables named WhichPlane, WhichDir, and WhichTask are used as arguments when calls are made to the appropriate methods of class Model3D.

Note also line 0275, which uses the C++ delete operator to destroy the object before returning control to the caller.

Terminating the program

The function at lines 0416 through 0424 calls method ShutDownGraphics( ) of class PhysicalDisplay to terminate the graphics state. Line 0423 returns an OK token.

The Startup( ) function

The function at lines 0426 through 0509 calls the SetupMode( ) method of class PhysicalDisplay to detect the graphics hardware.

The StubRoutine( ) function

The stub routine at lines 0511 through 0523 is a do-nothing routine. It displays a message at the top of the display.

The Keyboard( ) function

The function at lines 0525 through 0552 fetches keystrokes from the keyboard buffer. The function at lines 0555 through 0564 keeps calling the zKeyboard( ) function until the keyboard buffer is empty. This routine purges unwanted keystrokes from the keyboard buffer after a lengthy graphics operation like drawing a 3-D cube.

The MakeSound( ) function

The function at lines 0566 through 0602 generates a sound from the system speaker.

The Pause( ) function

The function at lines 0604 through 0622 causes the program to pause for a specified period of time.

The Arguments( ) function

The function at lines 0624 through 0666 compares the command line argument with a list of expected strings. The function assigns an appropriate value to the global variable named Mode.

Programmer's Guide to LIB2D.HPP

Code The complete source code for the declarations for class PhysicalDisplay and class Viewport is found in LIB2D.HPP in appendix E. The source from LIB2D.HPP must be #included at the beginning of any program that wishes to use the methods of class PhysicalDisplay or class Viewport. See the discussion in chapter 1 for further information about LIB2D.HPP.

Programmer's Guide to LIB2D.CPP

Code The source code in LIB2D.CPP, presented in appendix E, provides language bindings that produce low-level graphics. The routines in LIB2D.CPP call the appropriate runtime library functions in Turbo C++'s graphics.lib, Borland C++'s graphics.lib, Zortech C++'s fg.lib, or Microsoft's graph.lib.

LIB2D.CPP is the class implementation listing for class PhysicalDisplay and class Viewport. Class PhysicalDisplay manages the state of the display. Class Viewport is responsible for viewports and low-level graphics. These two classes generate most low-level graphics used by the demonstration programs in the book. See the discussion in chapter 1 for further information about class PhysicalDisplay and class Viewport.

Programmer's Guide to LIB3D.HPP

Code The complete source code for the declarations for class Model3D is found in LIB3D.HPP in appendix E. LIB3D.HPP must be #included in any program that uses the methods of class Model3D.

Programmer's Guide to LIB3D.CPP

Code LIB3D.CPP is the class implementation listing for class Model3D. The methods of class Model3D provide routines that can be used to build shaded 3-D solids with automatic hidden surface removal. Refer to chapter 8 for a more detailed discussion of LIB3D.CPP.

9-6 Sample program OBJECTS.CPP. Supports VGA, EGA, MCGA, CGA, and Hercules adapters. This application demonstrates a C++ class suitable for building interactive 3-D modeling and shading software.

```
0001   /*
0002
0003              Lee Adams' SUPERCHARGED C++ GRAPHICS
0004          Interactive demo:  3D modeling and rendering class
0005
0006     SOURCE FILE:  OBJECTS.CPP
0007            TYPE:  C++ source file for a multimodule application.
0008         PURPOSE:  Demonstrates fundamental classes useful for
0009                   creating objects capable of displaying 3D
0010                   shaded models with hidden surfaces removed.
0011    PROGRAM LIST:  OBJECTS.CPP, LIB2D.CPP and LIB3D.CPP.
0012       LANGUAGES:  Turbo C++, Borland C++, Zortech C++, and
0013                   all C++ compilers compatible with AT&T C++ 2.0
0014                   specification; and nominal compatibility with
0015                   Microsoft C++ (see the discussion in the book).
0016    MEMORY MODEL:  large.
0017    COMMAND-LINE:  you can specify a graphics mode by using the
0018                   command-line argument /Mnn as shown below:
0019                        /M12  640x480x16-color VGA
0020                        /M11  640x480x2-color VGA, MCGA
0021                        /M10  640x350x16-color VGA, EGA
0022                        /M0E  640x200x16-color VGA, EGA
0023                        /M06  640x200x2-color VGA, MCGA, EGA, CGA
0024                        /MHC  720x348x2-color Hercules
0025                   If no command-line argument is used, hardware
0026                   autodetect is used to select the best mode.
0027     OUTPUT:  Draws solid boxes (cubes and parallelepipeds) with
0028                   shaded surfaces.  Hidden surfaces are removed.
0029     LICENSE:  As purchaser of the book in which this source code
0030       appears you are granted a royalty-free license to reproduce
0031       and distribute executable files generated using this code
0032       provided that you accept the conditions of the License
0033       Agreement and Limited Warranty described in the book.
0034     PUBLICATION: Contains material from Windcrest/McGraw-Hill
0035       book 3489, published by TAB BOOKS.
0036     U.S. GOVERNMENT RESTRICTED RIGHTS:  This software and its
0037       documentation is provided with restricted rights.  The use,
0038       duplication, or disclosure by the Government is subject to
0039       restrictions set forth in subdivision (b)(3)(ii) of The
0040       Rights in Technical Data and Computer Software clause at
0041       252.227-7013.  Contractor/manufacturer is Lee Adams, c/o
0042       TAB BOOKS, 13311 Monterey Ave., Blue Ridge Summit PA 17294.
0043     TRADEMARK:  Lee Adams is a trademark of Lee Adams.
0044
0045        Copyright 1991 Lee Adams.  All rights reserved worldwide.
0046
0047
0048                        CONDITIONAL COMPILATION
```

```
0049        To compile only those blocks of code that support the C++
0050        compiler and graphics library that you are using, you should
0051        #define the appropriate tokens on lines 0063 and 0064.
0052              GRAPHICS LIBRARY
0053          Borland's graphics.lib              #define BGI
0054          Zortech's fg.lib or fgdebug.lib     #define FG
0055          Microsoft's graph.lib               #define MS
0056                COMPILER
0057          Borland Turbo C++ compiler          #define BORLAND
0058          Zortech C++ compiler                #define ZORTECH
0059          AT&T-compatible C++ compilers       #define MICROSOFT
0060        Be sure you define only one compiler and one graphics library.
0061
0062                                                                   */
0063    #define BGI     1 // indicates the graphics library you are using.
0064    #define BORLAND 1 // indicates the C++ compiler you are using.
0065    /*
0066
0067    ┌──────────────────────────────────────────────────────────────┐
           │                          Constants                           │
           └──────────────────────────────────────────────────────────────┘
0068
0069                                                                   */
0070    const int zFAIL=0; const int zEMPTY=0;        // boolean tokens...
0071    const int zYES=1; const int zNO=0;
0072    const int zVGA_12H=1;                          // display mode tokens...
0073    const int zEGA_10H=2;
0074    const int zEGA_EH=3;
0075    const int zMCGA_11H=4;
0076    const int zCGA_6H=5;
0077    const int zHERC=6;
0078    const int zLEFT_ARROW= 75;                     // codes for extended keys...
0079    const int zRT_ARROW=   77;
0080    const int zDN_ARROW=   80;
0081    const int zUP_ARROW=   72;
0082    const int zPGUP=       73;
0083    const int zPGDN=       81;
0084    const int zHOME=       71;
0085    const int zALT_X=      45;
0086    const int zF3=         61;
0087    const int zF4=         62;
0088    const int zF5=         63;
0089    const int zF6=         64;
0090    const int zF7=         65;
0091    const int zSHIFT_F1=   84;
0092    const int zSHIFT_F2=   85;
0093    const int zSHIFT_F3=   86;
0094    const int zSHIFT_F4=   87;
0095    const int zSHIFT_F5=   88;
0096    const int zSHIFT_F6=   89;
0097    const int zSHIFT_F7=   90;
0098    const int zENTER=      13;                      // codes for normal keys...
0099    const int zESC=        27;
0100    const int zYAW=             1;    // for 3D modeling and shading...
0101    const int zROLL=           2;
0102    const int zPITCH=          3;
0103    const int zPLUS=           1;
0104    const int zMINUS=          2;
0105    const int zX=              2;
0106    const int zY=              1;
0107    const int zZ=              3;
0108    const int zRotateCursor=   1;
0109    const int zMoveCursor=     2;
0110    const int zSizeCursor=     3;
0111    const int zRotateCamera=   4;
```

```
0112   const int zNoTask=          0;
0113   /*
0114
0115   ╔══════════════════════════════════════════════════════════╗
0116   ║                          Macros                          ║
0117   ╚══════════════════════════════════════════════════════════╝  */
0118   #define Wait_for_any_key  while(KeyCode==0) zKeyboard(); KeyCode=0;
0119   /*
0120
0121   ╔══════════════════════════════════════════════════════════╗
0122   ║                      Include files                       ║
0123   ╚══════════════════════════════════════════════════════════╝  */
0124   #if defined (BORLAND)
0125   #include <time.h>          // supports clock().
0126   #include <string.h>        // supports strncmp().
0127   #include <bios.h>          // supports bioskey().
0128   #include <process.h>       // supports exit().
0129   #include <iostream.h>      // supports cout.
0130   #include <dos.h>           // supports outportb(), inportb().
0131   #elif defined (ZORTECH)
0132   #include <time.h>          // supports clock().
0133   #include <string.h>        // supports strncmp().
0134   #include <bios.h>          // supports bioskey().
0135   #include <stdlib.h>        // supports exit().
0136   #include <stream.hpp>      // supports cout.
0137   #include <dos.h>           // supports outp(), inp().
0138   #elif defined (MICROSOFT)
0139   #include <time.h>          // supports clock().
0140   #include <string.h>        // supports strncmp().
0141   #include <bios.h>          // supports _bios_keybrd().
0142   #include <process.h>       // supports exit().
0143   #include <iostream.h>      // supports cout.
0144   #include <conio.h>         // supports outp(), inp().
0145   #endif
0146
0147   #include "LIB2D.HPP"       // declarations for PhysicalDisplay class.
0148   #include "LIB3D.HPP"       // declarations for Model3D class.
0149   /*
0150
0151   ╔══════════════════════════════════════════════════════════╗
0152   ║     Prototypes for functions visible throughout this file ║
0153   ╚══════════════════════════════════════════════════════════╝  */
0154   static void zStartup(void);              // initializes a graphics mode.
0155   static void zArguments(int, char far* far*);   // checks arguments.
0156   static void zKeyboard(void);             // checks for a keystroke.
0157   static void zQuit_Pgm(void);             // ends the program gracefully.
0158   static void zPurge(void);                // empties the keyboard buffer.
0159   static void zStubRoutine(void);          // do-nothing stub.
0160   static void zMakeSound(int,double);      // makes a specific sound.
0161   static clock_t zDelay(clock_t,double);   // CPU-independent pause.
0162   static void zInteractive3DLoop(Viewport *);            // 3D loop.
0163   /*
0164
0165   ╔══════════════════════════════════════════════════════════╗
0166   ║     Declaration of variables visible throughout this file ║
0167   ╚══════════════════════════════════════════════════════════╝  */
0168   static char *StartUpArg[6]={        // legal command-line arguments.
0169        "/M12", "/M10", "/MOE", "/M11", "/M06", "/MHC" };
0170   static int CommandLineArg=zNO;      // indicates if argument exists.
0171   static int CommandLineCompare=0;    // indicates if argument legal.
0172   static int C0=0,C1=1,C2=2,C3=3,C4=4,C5=5,C6=6,
0173    C7=7,C8=8,C9=9,C10=10,C11=11,C12=12,C13=13,
```

```
0174       C14=14,C15=15;                              // palette index codes.
0175   static int Mode=0;                    // which graphics mode is being used.
0176   static int Result=0;               // captures result of graphics routines.
0177   static int CharWidth=0,CharHeight=0;        // dimensions of character.
0178   static char KeyCode=0;     // token for normal or extended keystroke.
0179   static char KeyNum=0;                    // ASCII number of keystroke.
0180   static char SolidFill[]=
0181               {255,255,255,255,255,255,255,255};    // 100% fill.
0182   static int TextClr=0;                 // font color for regular text.
0183   static int PromptClr=0;                // font color for prompt text.
0184   static char Copyright[]=
0185               "Copyright 1991 Lee Adams.  All rights reserved.";
0186   static char Title[]=
0187   "USING C++ FOR INTERACTIVE 3D MODELING AND RENDERING";
0188   static char Prompt1[]=
0189   "F3= rotate   F4= move   F5= resize   F6= camera   Alt+X= quit";
0190   static char Prompt2[]=
0191   "Shift+F1-F7= shading    Enter= draw  ESC= cancel";
0192   static char Prompt3[]=
0193   "Use the keypad to rotate, move, and resize the 3D object.";
0194   static char StubMessage[]= "The generic stub routine was called.";
0195   static int X_Res=0, Y_Res=0;                 // screen resolution.
0196
0197   PhysicalDisplay Display;      // create the physical display object.
0198   Viewport Viewport1(&Display);          // create a viewport object.
0199   /*
0200
0201   ┌─────────────────────────────────────────────────────────┐
0202   │                   Function definitions                    │
0203   └─────────────────────────────────────────────────────────┘
0204   ┌─────────────────────────────────────────────────────────┐
       │   The executive routine:  program execution begins here   │
0205   └─────────────────────────────────────────────────────────┘
0206                                                              */
0207   main(int argc, char *argv[])
0208   {
0209       int NumArgs; char far* far* Arg;
0210   NumArgs= argc;                          // grab number of arguments.
0211   Arg= &argv[0];              // grab address of array of arguments.
0212   zArguments(NumArgs, Arg);       // check the command-line arguments.
0213
0214   zStartup();                          // establish the graphics mode.
0215   Display.Init2D(Mode,0,0,X_Res-1,Y_Res-1);    // set graphics state.
0216   Result= Display.InitUndo();    // create hidden page (unused here).
0217   if (Result==zFAIL) zQuit_Pgm();          // if hidden page failed.
0218
0219   Display.SetHue(C7);                       // set the drawing color.
0220   Display.SetFill(SolidFill,C7);              // set the fill style.
0221   Viewport1.DrawPanel(0,0,X_Res-1,Y_Res-1);   // clear the display.
0222   Viewport1.PutText(2,2,TextClr,Title);          // sign-on notice.
0223   Viewport1.PutText(3,2,TextClr,Copyright);     // copyright notice.
0224   Display.SetHue(C15);
0225   Viewport1.DrawBorder(0,0,X_Res-1,Y_Res-1);        // draw a border.
0226   Display.SetHue(C7);
0227   Viewport1.PutText(5,2,PromptClr,Prompt1);   // show key commands...
0228   Viewport1.PutText(6,2,PromptClr,Prompt2);
0229   Viewport1.PutText(7,2,PromptClr,Prompt3);
0230
0231   zInteractive3DLoop(&Viewport1);               // call the 3D loop.
0232
0233   zQuit_Pgm();                // tidy up and terminate the application.
0234   }
0235   /*
0236   ┌─────────────────────────────────────────────────────────┐
```

```
0237                    Keyboard loop for 3D modeling and shading
0238
0239                                                                        */
0240   static void zInteractive3DLoop(Viewport *ViewportObject)
0241   {
0242     int WhichTask= 0;           // indicates which 3D task being used.
0243     int WhichPlane= 0;              // arg passed to 3D cursor routine.
0244     int WhichDir= 0;                // arg passed to 3D cursor routine.
0245
0246   Model3D *Model= new Model3D(&Display);           // create object.
0247   Model->Initialize3D(0,0,X_Res-1,Y_Res-1,ViewportObject);
0248
0249   PRIMARY_3D_LOOP:
0250     zKeyboard();                               // check for a keystroke.
0251     if (KeyCode==0) goto PRIMARY_3D_LOOP;          // if no keystroke.
0252     if (KeyCode!=2) goto NORMAL_3DKEY1;  // jump if not extended key.
0253     EXTENDED_3DKEY1:      // fall through to here if an extended key.
0254       switch(KeyNum)
0255         {
0256         case zF3:         WhichTask= zRotateCursor;
0257                           Model->DrawCursor(zINSTALL);
0258                           goto SECONDARY_3D_LOOP;
0259         case zF4:         WhichTask= zMoveCursor;
0260                           Model->DrawCursor(zINSTALL);
0261                           goto SECONDARY_3D_LOOP;
0262         case zF5:         WhichTask= zSizeCursor;
0263                           Model->DrawCursor(zINSTALL);
0264                           goto SECONDARY_3D_LOOP;
0265         case zF6:         WhichTask= zRotateCamera;
0266                           Model->Camera(6);
0267                           goto SECONDARY_3D_LOOP;
0268         case zSHIFT_F1:   Model->SetShadingColor(1); break;
0269         case zSHIFT_F2:   Model->SetShadingColor(2); break;
0270         case zSHIFT_F3:   Model->SetShadingColor(3); break;
0271         case zSHIFT_F4:   Model->SetShadingColor(4); break;
0272         case zSHIFT_F5:   Model->SetShadingColor(5); break;
0273         case zSHIFT_F6:   Model->SetShadingColor(6); break;
0274         case zSHIFT_F7:   Model->SetShadingColor(7); break;
0275         case zALT_X:  delete Model; return;
0276         default:          zMakeSound(300,.2);
0277         }
0278     zPurge();
0279     goto PRIMARY_3D_LOOP;                                // loop back.
0280   NORMAL_3DKEY1:         // jump to here if a normal keystroke.
0281     switch(KeyNum)
0282       {
0283       case zESC:  delete Model; return;
0284       default:    zMakeSound(300,.2);
0285       }
0286     zPurge();
0287     goto PRIMARY_3D_LOOP;                                // loop back.
0288
0289   SECONDARY_3D_LOOP:  // jump to here after a task has been invoked.
0290     zKeyboard();                            // check for a keystroke.
0291     if (KeyCode==0) goto SECONDARY_3D_LOOP;        // if no keystroke.
0292     if (KeyCode!=2) goto NORMAL_3DKEY2;  // jump if not extended key.
0293     EXTENDED_3DKEY2:      // fall through to here if an extended key.
0294       if (WhichTask==zRotateCursor)
0295         {
0296         switch(KeyNum)
0297           {
```

```
0298        case zLEFT_ARROW:   WhichPlane= zYAW; WhichDir= zPLUS;
0299                            break;
0300        case zRT_ARROW:     WhichPlane= zYAW; WhichDir= zMINUS;
0301                            break;
0302        case zUP_ARROW:     WhichPlane= zPITCH; WhichDir= zPLUS;
0303                            break;
0304        case zDN_ARROW:     WhichPlane= zPITCH; WhichDir= zMINUS;
0305                            break;
0306        case zHOME:         WhichPlane= zROLL; WhichDir= zMINUS;
0307                            break;
0308        case zPGUP:         WhichPlane= zROLL; WhichDir= zPLUS;
0309                            break;
0310        default:  zMakeSound(300,.2); zPurge();
0311                        goto SECONDARY_3D_LOOP;
0312        }
0313      Model->Instance(0,0,0);
0314      Model->Instance(WhichTask, WhichPlane, WhichDir);
0315      Model->GetNewObjParams();
0316      Model->DrawCursor(zUPDATE);
0317      zPurge(); goto SECONDARY_3D_LOOP;
0318      }
0319    if (WhichTask==zMoveCursor)
0320      {
0321      switch(KeyNum)
0322        {
0323        case zLEFT_ARROW:   WhichPlane= zX; WhichDir= zPLUS;
0324                            break;
0325        case zRT_ARROW:     WhichPlane= zX; WhichDir= zMINUS;
0326                            break;
0327        case zUP_ARROW:     WhichPlane= zY; WhichDir= zMINUS;
0328                            break;
0329        case zDN_ARROW:     WhichPlane= zY; WhichDir= zPLUS;
0330                            break;
0331        case zPGUP:         WhichPlane= zZ; WhichDir= zPLUS;
0332                            break;
0333        case zPGDN:         WhichPlane= zZ; WhichDir= zMINUS;
0334                            break;
0335        default:  zMakeSound(300,.2); zPurge();
0336                        goto SECONDARY_3D_LOOP;
0337        }
0338      Model->Instance(0,0,0);
0339      Model->Instance(WhichTask, WhichPlane, WhichDir);
0340      Model->GetNewObjParams();
0341      Model->DrawCursor(zUPDATE);
0342      zPurge(); goto SECONDARY_3D_LOOP;
0343      }
0344    if (WhichTask==zSizeCursor)
0345      {
0346      switch(KeyNum)
0347        {
0348        case zLEFT_ARROW:   WhichPlane= zX; WhichDir= zMINUS;
0349                            break;
0350        case zRT_ARROW:     WhichPlane= zX; WhichDir= zPLUS;
0351                            break;
0352        case zUP_ARROW:     WhichPlane= zY; WhichDir= zPLUS;
0353                            break;
0354        case zDN_ARROW:     WhichPlane= zY; WhichDir= zMINUS;
0355                            break;
0356        case zPGUP:         WhichPlane= zZ; WhichDir= zMINUS;
0357                            break;
0358        case zPGDN:         WhichPlane= zZ; WhichDir= zPLUS;
0359                            break;
0360        default:  zMakeSound(300,.2); zPurge();
```

```
0361                    goto SECONDARY_3D_LOOP;
0362            }
0363        Model->Instance(0,0,0);
0364        Model->Instance(WhichTask, WhichPlane, WhichDir);
0365        Model->GetNewObjParams();
0366        Model->DrawCursor(zUPDATE);
0367        zPurge(); goto SECONDARY_3D_LOOP;
0368        }
0369     if (WhichTask==zRotateCamera)
0370       {
0371       switch(KeyNum)
0372         {
0373         case zLEFT_ARROW:  Model->Camera(1); break;
0374         case zRT_ARROW:    Model->Camera(2); break;
0375         case zDN_ARROW:    Model->Camera(3); break;
0376         case zUP_ARROW:    Model->Camera(4); break;
0377         default:  zMakeSound(300,.2); zPurge();
0378                   goto SECONDARY_3D_LOOP;
0379         }
0380       zPurge(); goto SECONDARY_3D_LOOP;
0381       }
0382     zMakeSound(300,.2);
0383     zPurge();
0384     goto SECONDARY2_3D_LOOP;
0385   NORMAL_3DKEY2:              // jump to here if a normal keystroke.
0386     if (KeyNum==zENTER)
0387       {
0388       switch(WhichTask)
0389         {
0390         case zRotateCursor:  Model->DrawCursor(zREMOVE);
0391                              Model->DrawCube(); break;
0392         case zMoveCursor:    Model->DrawCursor(zREMOVE);
0393                              Model->DrawCube(); break;
0394         case zSizeCursor:    Model->DrawCursor(zREMOVE);
0395                              Model->DrawCube(); break;
0396         case zRotateCamera:  Model->Camera(5); break;
0397         }
0398       WhichTask= zNoTask;
0399       zPurge(); goto PRIMARY_3D_LOOP;
0400       }
0401     if (KeyNum==zESC)
0402       {
0403       switch(WhichTask)
0404         {
0405         case zRotateCursor:  Model->DrawCursor(zREMOVE); break;
0406         case zMoveCursor:    Model->DrawCursor(zREMOVE); break;
0407         case zSizeCursor:    Model->DrawCursor(zREMOVE); break;
0408         case zRotateCamera:  Model->Camera(5); break;
0409         }
0410       WhichTask= zNoTask;
0411       zPurge(); goto PRIMARY_3D_LOOP;
0412       }
0413     zMakeSound(300,.2); zPurge(); goto SECONDARY_3D_LOOP;
0414   }
0415   /*
0416
0417   ┌─────────────────────────────────────────────────────┐
        │                 Terminate the program               │
0418   └─────────────────────────────────────────────────────┘
0419                                                       */
0420   static void zQuit_Pgm(void)
0421   {
0422   Display.ShutDownGraphics();  // graceful shutdown of graphics mode.
```

```
0423   exit(0);                    // terminate the program and return OK code.
0424   }
0425   /*
0426
0427   ┌─────────────────────────────────────────────────────────────┐
       │              Detect the graphics hardware and set the         │
0428   │   highest mode permitted by the graphics adapter and monitor. │
0429   │   The user can override the autodetect algorithm by providing │
0430   │   an argument on the command-line when the program is started.│
0431   └─────────────────────────────────────────────────────────────┘
0432                                                                  */
0433   static void zStartup(void)
0434   {
0435     int DefaultMode;
0436   DefaultMode= Display.SetupMode();   // get results of autodetect...
0437   switch(DefaultMode)               // ...and jump to appropriate code.
0438     {
0439     case zFAIL:      goto ABORT_PGM;
0440     case zVGA_12H:   goto VGA_mode;
0441     case zEGA_10H:   goto EGA_ECD_mode;
0442     case zEGA_EH:    goto EGA_SCD_mode;
0443     case zMCGA_11H:  goto MCGA_mode;
0444     case zCGA_6H:    goto CGA_mode;
0445     case zHERC:      goto Hercules_mode;
0446     default:         goto ABORT_PGM;
0447     }
0448   VGA_mode:              // VGA 640x480x16-color, 80x60 character mode.
0449   if(CommandLineArg==zYES)
0450     {                                // if user has requested a mode.
0451     if((Mode>zVGA_12H)&&(Mode<zHERC)) goto FORCE_USER_MODE;
0452     }
0453   X_Res=640; Y_Res=480; Mode=zVGA_12H; CharWidth=8; CharHeight=8;
0454   return;
0455   EGA_ECD_mode:          // EGA 640x350x16-color, 80x43 character mode.
0456   if(CommandLineArg==zYES)
0457     {
0458     if((Mode==zEGA_EH)||(Mode==zCGA_6H))   // permit only EGA or CGA.
0459     goto FORCE_USER_MODE;
0460     }
0461   X_Res=640; Y_Res=350; Mode=zEGA_10H; CharWidth=8; CharHeight=8;
0462   return;
0463   EGA_SCD_mode:              // EGA 640x200x16-color, 80x25 char mode.
0464   if(CommandLineArg==zYES)
0465     {
0466     if(Mode==zCGA_6H) goto FORCE_USER_MODE;     // only CGA permitted.
0467     }
0468   X_Res=640; Y_Res=200; Mode=zEGA_EH; CharWidth=8; CharHeight=8;
0469   return;
0470   MCGA_mode:                 // MCGA 640x480x2-color, 80x60 char mode.
0471   if(CommandLineArg==zYES)
0472     {
0473     if(Mode==zCGA_6H) goto FORCE_USER_MODE;     // only CGA permitted.
0474     }
0475   X_Res=640; Y_Res=480; Mode=zMCGA_11H;
0476   C0=0; C1=1; C2=1; C3=1; C4=1; C5=1; C6=1; C7=1;
0477   C8=1; C9=1; C10=1; C11=1; C12=1; C13=1; C14=1; C15=1;
0478   CharWidth=8; CharHeight=8;
0479   return;
0480   CGA_mode:                   // CGA 640x200x2-color, 80x25 char mode.
0481   X_Res=640; Y_Res=200; Mode=zCGA_6H;
0482   C0=0; C1=1; C2=1; C3=1; C4=1; C5=1; C6=1; C7=1;
0483   C8=1; C9=1; C10=1; C11=1; C12=1; C13=1; C14=1; C15=1;
0484   CharWidth=8; CharHeight=8;
0485   return;
```

```
0486  Hercules_mode:          // Hercules 720x348x2-color, 80x25 char mode.
0487  X_Res=720; Y_Res=348; Mode=zHERC;
0488  C0=0; C1=1; C2=1; C3=1; C4=1; C5=1; C6=1; C7=1;
0489  C8=1; C9=1; C10=1; C11=1; C12=1; C13=1; C14=1; C15=1;
0490  CharWidth=9; CharHeight=14;
0491  return;
0492
0493  FORCE_USER_MODE:     // jump to here if command-line argument legal.
0494  CommandLineArg= zNO; // first, reset token to avoid returning here.
0495  Display.ForceMode(Mode);           // ...then reset the graphics mode.
0496  switch(Mode)                // ...then jump back to appropriate code.
0497    {
0498    case zEGA_10H:      goto EGA_ECD_mode;
0499    case zEGA_EH:       goto EGA_SCD_mode;
0500    case zMCGA_11H:     goto MCGA_mode;
0501    case zCGA_6H:       goto CGA_mode;
0502    default:            goto ABORT_PGM;
0503    }
0504
0505  ABORT_PGM:          // jump to here if no graphics hardware detected.
0506  cout << "\n\n\rThis C++ graphics programming demo requires a";
0507  cout << "\n\rVGA, EGA, CGA, MCGA, or HGA graphics adapter.\n\r";
0508  exit(-1);                    // terminate, returning an error code.
0509  }
0510  /*
0511
0512  ┌──────────────────────────────────────────────────────────────┐
                              Stub routine
0513  └──────────────────────────────────────────────────────────────┘
0514                                                                    */
0515  static void zStubRoutine(void)
0516  {       // this do-nothing routine is a placeholder for future code.
0517  Display.SetHue(C0);                          // set the drawing color.
0518  Display.SetLine(0xffff);                      // set the line style.
0519  Display.SetFill(SolidFill,C0);                // set the fill style.
0520  Viewport1.ClearTextLine();                   // clear the dialog line.
0521  Viewport1.PutText(1,2,TextClr,StubMessage);// display text message.
0522  return;
0523  }
0524  /*
0525
0526  ┌──────────────────────────────────────────────────────────────┐
                    Check the keyboard for a keystroke
0527  └──────────────────────────────────────────────────────────────┘
0528                                                                    */
0529  static void zKeyboard(void)
0530  {
0531    union AnyName{int RawCode;char Code[3];}Keystroke;
0532    char TempKey=0;
0533  #if defined (BORLAND)
0534    if (bioskey(1)==zEMPTY) { KeyCode=0; return; }
0535    Keystroke.RawCode= bioskey(0);
0536  #elif defined (ZORTECH)
0537    if (bioskey(1)==zEMPTY) { KeyCode=0; return; }
0538    Keystroke.RawCode= bioskey(0);
0539  #elif defined (MICROSOFT)
0540    if (_bios_keybrd(_KEYBRD_READY)==zEMPTY)
0541      { KeyCode=0; return; }
0542    Keystroke.RawCode= _bios_keybrd(_KEYBRD_READ);
0543  #endif
0544  TempKey= Keystroke.Code[0];
0545  if (TempKey!=0)
0546    {                                      // if a normal keystroke...
0547    KeyCode=1; KeyNum=TempKey; return;
```

```
0548    }
0549  if (TempKey==0)
0550    {                                              // if an extended keystroke...
0551    KeyCode=2; KeyNum=Keystroke.Code[1]; return;
0552    }
0553  }
0554  /*
0555
0556  ┌──────────────────────────────────────────────────────────────────┐
0556  │                  Empty the keystroke buffer                        │
0557  └──────────────────────────────────────────────────────────────────┘
0558                                                                        */
0559  static void zPurge(void)
0560  {
0561  do zKeyboard();
0562    while (KeyCode!=0);
0563  return;
0564  }
0565  /*
0566
0567  ┌──────────────────────────────────────────────────────────────────┐
0567  │                        Make a sound                                │
0568  └──────────────────────────────────────────────────────────────────┘
0569                                                                        */
0570  static void zMakeSound(int Hertz,double Duration)
0571  {
0572    static clock_t FormerTime=0;
0573    short Count=0;
0574    int HighByte=0, LowByte=0;
0575    unsigned char OldPort=0, NewPort=0;
0576  FormerTime= clock();
0577  if (Hertz < 40) return;
0578  if (Hertz > 4660) return;
0579  Count= 1193180L/Hertz;
0580  HighByte= Count / 256;
0581  LowByte= Count - (HighByte * 256);
0582  #if defined (BORLAND)
0583    outportb(0x43,0xB6); outportb(0x42,(unsigned char)LowByte);
0584    outportb(0x42,(unsigned char)HighByte); OldPort=inportb(0x61);
0585    NewPort=(OldPort | 0x03); outportb(0x61,NewPort);
0586    zDelay(FormerTime,Duration);
0587    outportb(0x61,OldPort);
0588  #elif defined (ZORTECH)
0589    outp(0x43,0xB6); outp(0x42,LowByte);
0590    outp(0x42,HighByte); OldPort=(unsigned char)inp(0x61);
0591    NewPort=(OldPort | 0x03); outp(0x61,(int)NewPort);
0592    zDelay(FormerTime,Duration);
0593    outp(0x61,(int)OldPort);
0594  #elif defined (MICROSOFT)
0595    outp(0x43,0xB6); outp(0x42,LowByte);
0596    outp(0x42,HighByte); OldPort=(unsigned char)inp(0x61);
0597    NewPort=(OldPort | 0x03); outp(0x61,(int)NewPort);
0598    zDelay(FormerTime,Duration);
0599    outp(0x61,(int)OldPort);
0600  #endif
0601  return;
0602  }
0603  /*
0604
0605  ┌──────────────────────────────────────────────────────────────────┐
0605  │                          Pause                                     │
0606  └──────────────────────────────────────────────────────────────────┘
0607                                                                        */
0608  static clock_t zDelay(clock_t StartTime, double Wait)
0609  {                                // pause for a specified length of time.
0610    clock_t StopTime;
```

```
0611    clock_t NewClockTime;
0612 #if defined (BORLAND)
0613    StopTime= StartTime + (Wait * CLK_TCK);
0614 #elif defined (ZORTECH)
0615    StopTime= StartTime + (Wait * CLOCKS_PER_SEC);
0616 #elif defined (MICROSOFT)
0617    StopTime= StartTime + (Wait * CLK_TCK);
0618 #endif
0619 while ( clock() < StopTime ) {;}
0620 NewClockTime= clock();
0621 return NewClockTime;
0622 }
0623 /*
0624
0625 ┌─────────────────────────────────────────────────────────────┐
0626 │              Retrieve the command-line arguments, if any      │
0627 └─────────────────────────────────────────────────────────────┘   */
0628 static void zArguments(int NumArgs, char *Arg[])
0629 {
0630 if(NumArgs==1)
0631   {
0632   CommandLineArg= zNO; return;                          // if no arg.
0633   }
0634 CommandLineCompare= strncmp(StartUpArg[0],Arg[1],5);
0635 if(CommandLineCompare==0)
0636   {
0637   CommandLineArg=zYES; Mode=zVGA_12H; return;           // /M12.
0638   }
0639 CommandLineCompare= strncmp(StartUpArg[1],Arg[1],5);
0640 if(CommandLineCompare==0)
0641   {
0642   CommandLineArg=zYES; Mode=zEGA_10H; return;           // /M10.
0643   }
0644 CommandLineCompare= strncmp(StartUpArg[2],Arg[1],5);
0645 if(CommandLineCompare==0)
0646   {
0647   CommandLineArg=zYES; Mode=zEGA_EH; return;            // /MOE.
0648   }
0649 CommandLineCompare= strncmp(StartUpArg[3],Arg[1],5);
0650 if(CommandLineCompare==0)
0651   {
0652   CommandLineArg=zYES; Mode=zMCGA_11H; return;          // /M11.
0653   }
0654 CommandLineCompare= strncmp(StartUpArg[4],Arg[1],5);
0655 if(CommandLineCompare==0)
0656   {
0657   CommandLineArg=zYES; Mode=zCGA_6H; return;            // /M06.
0658   }
0659 CommandLineCompare= strncmp(StartUpArg[5],Arg[1],5);
0660 if(CommandLineCompare==0)
0661   {
0662   CommandLineArg=zYES; Mode=zHERC; return;              // /MHC.
0663   }
0664 CommandLineArg= zNO;                    // if an unrecognized argument.
0665 return;
0666 }
0667 /*
0668
0669 ┌─────────────────────────────────────────────────────────────┐
0670 │   Supercharged C++ Graphics  --  end of source file OBJECTS.CPP │
0671 └─────────────────────────────────────────────────────────────┘   */
```

Part Four

Animation

10
Display animation

The class libraries provided in appendix E can be used to produce profes-
sional-quality animation sequences. In particular, the methods of class Blitter
can provide a platform for building advanced cel animation.

The demonstration program in this chapter uses anatomical exaggeration
to animate a running cartoon character, as shown in FIG. 10-1. Seven versions
of the character are used to produce the animation sequence, called a walk
cycle or a run cycle by professional animators.

The walk cycle

The complete walk cycle used by the demonstration program is shown in FIG.
10-2. The character undergoes considerable vertical movement, as illustrated
by the relative positions of the head. Note also the extreme positions of the
limbs. This is a powerful technique used by professional animators to add a
sense of urgency and pizazz to their work.

A walk cycle is a vital element in cel animation. It provides a template you
can use to animate a variety of characters. The character itself seldom moves
across the screen when a walk cycle is used, but rather a background is panned
behind the character to provide the illusion of movement.

Here's Why... Probably the most important component of the seven keyframes used
in FIG. 10-2 is the bounce. When the character's foot strikes the ground,
the head and neck tilt forward in response to the impact. Note also
how the torso is shortened as the spine compresses. It is little tricks like this
that professional animators use to turn good animation into great animation.

Keyframes and tweens

The sample animation presented in this chapter is based upon four keyframes. These are positions 1, 3, 5, and 7 in FIG. 10-2. Positions 2, 4, and 6 are

10-1 Graphics output from the sample program STRIDES.CPP. The silhouette character runs in an anatomically exaggerated sequence of animated bitblt frames.

10-2 The seven frames that comprise the animation sequence in the demonstration program STRIDES.CPP.

in-betweens (tweens) that are derived from the keyframes using visual interpolation. Although all the images in this demo were drawn by hand, it is not unreasonably difficult to build a software program to generate tweens automatically. The demo in the next chapter shows you how.

The professional touch

The demonstration program in this chapter produces a dramatic animation sequence that you can adapt for your own purposes. The impressive graphics are not so much a result of the animation routines as from the quality of drawings used. Indeed, it is quality—not quantity—that makes the difference here. If you have aspirations of writing first-class animation software, you must take the time to thoroughly research the field.

The computer algorithm

The animation process is a simple one, thanks to the power of C++ objects. First, a set of seven drawings were produced by a combination of freehand sketching and tracing. During this creative process, the drawings were often positioned over one another to ensure that the difference between each frame was visually pleasing. Next, each drawing was superimposed over a quarter-inch grid. This allowed important vertices to be quantified using x and y coordinates. These coordinates were stored in the arrays at the beginning of the demonstration program in this chapter. Then, source code was created to read the coordinates and draw the cartoon character. Each version of the character is stored as a graphic array in RAM using the methods of class Blitter. Finally, the seven versions of characters are written to the display in sequence, creating the animation sequence. Of course, like all explanations this is a simplification. The author spent the better part of an hour tweaking the x and y coordinates to get the characters to the finished stage you see in the demo. But because of the standard methodology used by the data arrays, it was not a difficult task to identify the two or three coordinates that had been mistakenly entered when the drawings were over the quarter-inch grid.

A sample program: STRIDES.CPP

Figure 10-1 depicts one frame from the animated sample program STRIDES.CPP, whose complete source code is provided in FIG. 10-3 at the end of the chapter. The program uses professional keyframes to animate a running cartoon character.

How to compile and link the sample program

The program listing presented in FIG. 10-3 contains the complete source code for the main module of the C++ demonstration program called "Using C++ for Advanced Cel Animation Effects." If you are using the companion disks to the book, the source code is in the file named STRIDES.CPP. Three C++ source files are needed to build the finished .exe file. These are STRIDES.CPP from FIG. 10-3 and two of the class libraries in appendix E.

The class library that provides the language bindings and low-level graphics routines for this demonstration program is found in FIG. E-2 in appendix E. This listing contains the implementations for class PhysicalDisplay and class Viewport. If you are using the companion disks to the book, this file is named LIB2D.CPP. The class declarations are presented in FIG. E-1 in appendix E. If you are using the companion disks to the book, this file is named LIB2D.HPP.

Class The class library that provides the bitblt animation methods for this demonstration program is found in FIG. E-10 in appendix E. This listing contains the implementations for class Blitter. If you are using the companion disks to the book, this file is named BLITTER.CPP. The class declarations are presented in FIG. E-9 in appendix E. If you are using the companion disks to the book, this file is named BLITTER.HPP.

You can compile, link, and run this demonstration program using Turbo C++, Borland C++, or Zortech C++. If you are using Turbo C++, read appendix A for guidance in compiling, linking, and running the demonstration program. If you are using Borland C++, you can find the appropriate information in appendix B. If you are using Zortech C++, refer to appendix C.

You must create a Turbo C++ or Borland C++ project list to advise your compiler which source files to bind together to build the finished .exe file. If you are using Zortech C++, you must name the files on the compiler command line field. Refer to the appendices described earlier if you are unfamiliar with this technique.

After a successful compile and link, the animated screen should resemble the screen print shown in FIG. 10-1.

How to run the demonstration program

You need a VGA, EGA, MCGA, CGA, or Hercules graphics adapter to run this demonstration program.

Using the editor to run the program

Here's How... To run the program under the control of your Turbo C++, Borland C++, or Zortech C++ editor, make sure that the finished .exe file is in the default directory. If you used Turbo C++ or Borland C++ to compile the program, the appropriate graphics driver must be in the default directory. If you are using a VGA or EGA, the EGAVGA.BGI file must be present. If you are using an MCGA or CGA, the CGA.BGI file must be located in the default directory. If you are using a Hercules graphics adapter, the HERC.BGI file must be available. These graphics drivers are installed on your hard disk by the Turbo C++ and Borland C++ installation utilities. If you used Zortech C++ to compile the demonstration program, the appropriate graphics drivers have already been linked into the finished executable code by the Zortech linker.

You need a VGA, EGA, MCGA, CGA, or Hercules graphics adapter to run the demonstration program BOUNCE.CPP. The built-in autodetect routine will detect the graphics hardware in your computer system and will set up the best graphics mode supported by your computer hardware. To override the autodetect routine use the Turbo C++, Borland C++, or Zortech C++ editor to simulate a command line argument. The source code in FIG. 10-3 provides a set of recognized arguments you can use. If you are using a VGA, you can override the autodetect routine and force the demonstration program to run in an EGA, MCGA, or CGA mode. If you are using an EGA, you can force the program to run in a low-resolution EGA mode or a CGA mode.

Running the program from the operating system prompt

Here's How... To start the program from the operating system prompt, simply enter STRIDES. The .exe file and any required graphics drivers must be present in the default directory. If the software finds a VGA present in your system, the program will animate using the 640×480×16-color mode. If an EGA and enhanced monitor are found, the 640×350×16-color mode is used. If an EGA and standard display are present, the program sets up the 640×200×16-color mode. If an MCGA is detected, the 640×480×2-color mode is employed. If a CGA is found, the 640×200×2-color mode is used. If the program detects a Hercules graphics adapter, it will use the 720×348×2-color mode.

You can force the program to start up in a different mode by adding a command line argument when you start the program from the operating system prompt. Enter STRIDES /M11 to force the 640×480×2-color mode. Enter STRIDES /M10 to force the 640×350×16-color mode. Entering STRIDES /M0E forces the program to run in the 640×200×16-color mode. Entering STRIDES /M06 tests the demonstration program in the 640×200×2-color mode.

Using the demonstration program

The demonstration program uses high-speed bitblt overwrite technology to create an animation sequence of a running cartoon character. See FIG. 10-2. The keyframes that make up the sequence are based on professional animation techniques which exaggerate the movement of the limbs.

The program produces satisfactory results on a 16 MHz or 20 MHz personal computer using the 640×480×16-color mode or the 640×350×16-color mode. If a 4.77 MHz or 8 MHz computer is used, the demonstration program should be forced to run in the 640×480×2-color MCGA mode or the 640×200×2-color CGA mode. The two-color modes require fewer pixels to be written for each new frame, thereby producing much faster refresh rates.

You can stop the demonstration program by pressing any key.

Programmer's Guide to STRIDES.CPP

Code The complete listing for the demonstration program STRIDES.CPP is presented in FIG. 10-3. The source code consists of an informative header, conditional compilation directives, declaration of constants and macros, file include directives, function prototypes, variable declarations, and the executable functions.

Conditional compilation

Information and source code for conditional compilation is located at lines 0050 through 0067. If you are using Turbo C++ or Borland C++, the program is ready to compile, subject to the instructions provided in appendix B. If you are using Zortech C++, change line 0066 to read #define FG and change line 0067 to read #define ZORTECH.

Constants

The C++ qualifier, const, is used to declare and assign values to constant variables at lines 0069 through 0082.

Include files

The code at lines 0084 through 0112 uses the #include directive to load in the appropriate header files and C++ class declaration files. Line 0111 loads LIB-2D.HPP, which declares the data members and methods of class PhysicalDisplay and class Viewport. Line 0112 loads BLITTER.HPP, which declares the data members and methods of class Blitter.

Function prototypes

Function declarations are provided in lines 0114 through 0127. These functions are visible throughout this source file and can be called by any other function in the source file. Because each function is declared with the static qualifier, it is not available to functions located in other source files.

Variable declarations

Lines 0129 through 0304 declare global variables that are visible throughout this source file. These variables have file scope. Note the set of seven arrays defined at lines 0161 through 0293. These arrays contain the xy coordinates needed to draw each frame of the animation sequence. The // comments describe the body part referenced by each group of coordinates.

The pointer declarations at lines 0295 through 0301 will be used later to call the methods of the seven instances of class Blitter.

Object declarations

Object Note line 0303, which creates an object from class PhysicalDisplay. The object is named Display. The program will later call the methods of this object to help it manage the display. The methods are declared in the class declaration listing LIB2D.HPP and are defined in the class implementation listing LIB2D.CPP in appendix E. The object created at line 0303 is a static object. It has file scope and will remain available until the program terminates.

Line 0304 creates an object from the Viewport class. The object is named Viewport1. The address of Display is passed to this new object. Viewport1 will need to use the methods of Display to generate graphics output. The object created at line 0155 is a static object with file scope. It will remain active until program termination.

main( )

The main( ) function is located at lines 0309 through 0359. After first checking to see if any command line arguments were used to start the demonstration program, the code switches to an appropriate graphics mode, and then calls the functions that draw the frames and manage the animation sequence.

Creating the individual frames

The function at lines 0361 through 0442 draws seven versions of the running cartoon character using the xy coordinates of the arrays defined at lines 0161 through 0293. The code at lines 0367 through 0371 is remarked so you can understand how a single frame is drawn. The code at lines 0373 through 0391 uses the same algorithm for each of the six remaining frames.

Note how the C++ new operator is used to dynamically create seven instances of class Blitter. The address of each object is assigned to a global pointer variable, making it possible for other functions in this source file to call the methods of each object.

The function at lines 0398 through 0441 draws one frame. Each component of the cartoon character is a polygon, except for the head, which is a circle. This regime greatly simplifies the drawing process, making it possible to use the arrays defined earlier. The function repeatedly calls the DrawPolygon ( ) method of class Viewport to help it get the job done.

Managing the animation sequence

Here's How... The function at lines 0444 through 0474 manages the animation sequence. The code at lines 0450 through 0456 uses the Display-Image( ) method of class Blitter to display each frame in rapid sequence. Then the loop at lines 0458 through 0473 uses the MoveImage( ) method of class Blitter to continue displaying each frame in proper order. Note how an offset value of 0,0 is passed to MoveImage( ), ensuring that each new frame is written directly over the previous frame. As FIG. 10-2 shows, the effect of animation is produced by the images themselves, not by moving the frames that hold the images.

Line 0459 checks for a keystroke. If one is found, the code at lines 0462 through 0464 uses the C++ delete operator to destroy all the instances of class Blitter before returning to the caller.

Terminating the program

The function at lines 0476 through 0484 calls a method of class PhysicalDisplay to terminate the graphics state. Line 0483 returns an OK code to the operating system.

The Startup( ) function

The function at lines 0483 through 0569 calls the SetupMode( ) method of class PhysicalDisplay to detect the graphics hardware.

The Keyboard( ) function

The function at lines 0571 through 0599 detects and retrieves keystrokes from the keyboard buffer. The function at lines 0601 through 0610 can be used to repeatedly call the keyboard function until the keyboard buffer is empty.

The MakeSound( ) function

The zMakeSound( ) function at lines 0612 through 0648 generates a sound from the system speaker. Appropriate values are sent to the hardware ports to provide direct control over the speaker.

The Pause( ) function

The function at lines 0650 through 0668 pauses the program. The code uses the value returned by the system clock and multiplies it by the number of ticks per second. If you are using Turbo C++ or Borland C++, this value is stored in the global variable CLK_TCK. If you are using Zortech C++ it is stored in CLOCKS_PER_SEC.

The Arguments( ) function

The function at lines 0670 through 0712 compares the command line argument with a set of permitted strings. The function assigns an appropriate value to the global variable named Mode. This function makes it possible to run the animation sequence in a variety of different graphics modes if you have a VGA or EGA.

Programmer's Guide to LIB2D.HPP

Code The complete source code for the declarations for class PhysicalDisplay and class Viewport is found in LIB2D.HPP in appendix E. LIB2D.HPP must be #included at the beginning of any program that uses the methods of class PhysicalDisplay or class Viewport.

The header

The informative header for the class declaration listing is located at lines 0001 through 0040.

Cross-compiler development

The preprocessor directives at lines 0046 through 0052 are used to inform the compiler which compiler-dependent blocks of code to compile.

Declaring class PhysicalDisplay

The code that declares class PhysicalDisplay is located at lines 0054 through 0115. The private qualifier at line 0057 identifies the beginning of a set of declarations for variables and member functions that are visible only to the class itself. Outside functions will not be able to access these data members and methods. The public qualifier at line 0095 identifies member functions that can be called by any in-scope function. The constructor is declared at line 0096. Line 0097 uses the tilde character to declare the destructor.

This block of code declares class PhysicalDisplay, but does not provide the executable code to implement the methods of class PhysicalDisplay. Functionality will be added later in LIB2D.CPP, which contains the class implementation.

Declaring class Viewport

The code at lines 0117 through 0165 declares the data members and methods of class Viewport. Note the directives at lines 0137 through 0158, which cause the compiler to compile only those blocks of code supporting Turbo C++, Borland C++, Zortech C++, or Microsoft. Also of interest is the code at lines 0160 through 0162, which uses function overloading to declare three variants of a method named WindowOpen( ).

Programmer's Guide to LIB2D.CPP

Code The source code in LIB2D.CPP, presented in appendix E, provides the graphics library language bindings that produce the low-level graphics used by most of the demonstration programs in the book. The source code calls the appropriate runtime library functions in Turbo C++'s graphics.lib, Borland C++'s graphics.lib, Zortech C++'s fg.lib, or Microsoft's graph.lib.

LIB2D.CPP is the class implementation listing for class PhysicalDisplay and class Viewport. Class PhysicalDisplay is generally responsible for managing the state of the overall display. Class Viewport is responsible for maintaining a viewport and producing low-level graphics like lines, rectangles, fills, bitblts, and so forth. Between them, these two classes form the underpinnings for almost all graphics generated by the demonstration programs in *Lee Adams' Supercharged C++ Graphics*.

The header

The informative header for LIB2D.CPP is located at lines 0001 through 0040. In addition to other information, the header describes a list of graphics adapters and graphics modes explicitly supported by the language bindings.

Conditional compilation

The code at lines 0041 through 0059 supports conditional compilation. If you are using Turbo C++ or Borland C++ the source listing is ready to compile, subject to the instructions provided in appendix B for Borland C++. If you are using Zortech C++, change line 0058 to #define FG and change line 0059 to #define ZORTECH.

Constants

The constants declared and initialized at lines 0061 through 0073 are used as decision-makers for the if( ) statements and the switch( ) blocks later in the listing.

The PhysicalDisplay class

The methods of class PhysicalDisplay are responsible for managing the display, setting the mode, blanking the screen, setting the current color, setting the fill style, and setting the active or display page.

The constructor

The constructor for class PhysicalDisplay is located at lines 0094 through 0112. A number of variables are initialized by this block of code.

The destructor

The destructor for class PhysicalDisplay is located at lines 0114 through 0121. The destructor is called automatically whenever an object of class PhysicalDisplay is destroyed.

Method SetupMode( )

The implementation for the SetupMode method of class PhysicalDisplay is located at lines 0123 through 0196. This block of code contains the autodetect routine used by each demonstration program. If you are using Turbo C++ or Borland C++, the detectgraph( ) library function is used to identify the graphics adapter. If you are using Zortech C++, the fg_get_type( ) library function is used.

Method ForceMode( )

The method at lines 0199 through 0256 can be used if the user wants to override the autodetect routine by using a command line argument when the program is started.

Method Init2D( )

The method at lines 0259 through 0295 sets the current graphics state. It uses a variable named token to help it initialize variables that will be required for graphics operations.

Method ShutDownGraphics( )

The method at lines 0298 through 0323 cleans up the graphics state and switches back to the default text mode. The block of code at lines 0300 through 0311 frees memory that might have been used by a hidden graphics page in RAM.

Setting attributes

The code at lines 0325 through 0404 sets attributes for pens and brushes. Method SetHue( ) at line 0329 sets the current drawing color. Method SetWriteMode( ) at line 0342 sets the overwrite or exclusive-or drawing mode. Method SetLine( ) at line 0358 sets the line style—solid or pattern. Method SetFill( ) at line 0371 sets the fill pattern, either solid or dithered. Method SetRGB( ) at line 0388 sets the hardware color by adjusting the red, green, and blue guns of the monitor.

Graphics page operations

The code at lines 0406 through 0446 controls page operations. Method SetWritePage( ) at line 0410 controls the page to which graphics will be written. Method SetDisplayPage( ) at line 0423 controls which page is being displayed. Method BlankPage( ) at line 0436 blanks the active page.

Hidden page operations

The code at lines 1028 through 1379 provides hidden page operations. Method InitUndo( ) at line 1032 initializes a hidden graphics page either on the display adapter or in RAM. If the hidden page must be simulated in RAM, InitUndo( ) calls method InitHiddenPage( ) at line 1081. In that event, method FreeMemory( ) at line 1095 will be called when the graphics are shut down, in order to free the memory allocated in RAM.

Method BackUp( ) at line 1108 copies the contents of page 0 to the hidden page. Method Restore( ) at line 1245 copies the contents of the hidden page back to page 0.

The Viewport class

The methods of class Viewport provide low-level graphics output, including lines, viewports, rectangles, polygons, facets, circles, bitblts, and text output. Class Viewport relies on the methods of class PhysicalDisplay.

The constructor

The constructor for class Viewport is located at lines 0449 through 0457. A pointer named GenericDisplay is used to capture the address of the PhysicalDisplay object passed to the constructor. The methods of class Viewport need to call the methods of class PhysicalDisplay to generate graphics output.

The destructor

The destructor for class Viewport is located at lines 0459 through 0466.

Graphics viewport operations

The code at lines 0468 through 0571 provides viewports for graphics output. A viewport is a subset of the display screen.

Low-level drawing functions

The code at lines 0573 through 0787 provides a set of low-level drawing functions. Method SetPosition( ) at line 0577 sets the current position of the graphics cursor. Method Drawline( ) at line 0590 draws a line from the current position to the specified coordinates using the current color and line style. Method DrawBorder( ) at line 0611 draws a hollow rectangle. Method Draw-Panel( ) at line 0631 draws a filled rectangle using the current fill style. Method DrawPolygon( ) at line 0649 draws a filled polygon of three or more sides. Method DrawFacet( ) at line 0691 draws a hollow polygon of three, four, five, six, or more sides. Method Drawcircle( ) at line 0729 draws a circle. Method Fill( ) at line 0776 performs a standard floodfill function.

Graphic array operations

The code at lines 0789 through 0935 provides bitblt functionality, used by class Bitblt and class Blitter.

Method MemBlock( ) at line 0793 allocates memory in RAM to hold the graphic array. Method GetBlockSize( ) at line 0827 can be used to calculate the number of bytes required to store the graphic array in memory. Method FreeBlock( ) frees the memory.

Method GetBlock( ) captures the image from the display and stores it as a graphic array in RAM. Method PutXOR( ) writes the graphic array back to the screen using exclusive-or logic. Method PutAND( ) and PutPSET( ) can also be used to write the graphic array to the screen.

Text operations

The code at lines 0937 through 1026 manages text output while in a graphics mode. Method PutText( ) writes a string of text to the display at a specified position. Method SetTextRowCol( ) can be used to set the starting position for the text operation. Method ClearTextLine( ) clears the dialog line.

Programmer's Guide to BLITTER.HPP

[Code] The complete source code for the declarations for class Blitter is found in BLITTER.HPP in appendix E. BLITTER.HPP must be #included at the beginning of any program that uses the methods of class Blitter.

The source code at lines 0050 through 0071 declares data members and a method that are not visible to functions or methods outside class Blitter. The code at lines 0073 through 0078 declares methods of class Blitter that can be called by any in-scope function or method.

Programmer's Guide to BLITTER.CPP

[Code] The complete source code for the implementation for class Blitter is found in BLITTER.CPP in appendix E. The methods of class Blitter provide bitblt operations that are optimized for high-speed overwrite animation sequences.

Constructor

The constructor for objects of class Blitter is located at lines 0058 through 0072. The constructor expects to receive the diagonal bounding coordinates of the bitblt being created, the horizontal and vertical resolution of the current graphics screen mode, and a pointer to the Viewport object to be used for low-level graphics output to the display.

The constructor initializes tokens that will indicate the state of the bitblt at runtime. The methods of class Blitter need to know if memory has been allocated, if a graphic array has already been stored in RAM, if the bitblt is already being displayed, and so forth.

Destructor

The destructor for class Blitter is presented at lines 0075 through 0082. The destructor is automatically called whenever an object of class Blitter is destroyed. A call to method FreeBlock( ) ensures that the memory allocated for the graphic array is released back to the free store.

Method GrabImage( )

The method at lines 0084 through 0098 captures the image from the display. The -> addressing notation is used to send a message to the MemBlock( ) method of an object named Generic. Generic is a pointer to the Viewport object that was passed when the bitblt was activated. A subsequent call to method GetBlock( ) stores the image in the memory allocated by method MemBlock( ).

Line 0096 sets a token, indicating that the bitblt is ready to be used. This token will be inspected by other methods that want to write a bitblt to the display, in order to avoid generating a runtime error.

Method DisplayImage( )

The method at lines 0110 through 0126 places the bitblt onto the screen. The test at line 0116 ensures that DisplayImage( ) will not place a second bitblt on the display if the bitblt is already being displayed. The test at line 0117 ensures that a graphic array exists. The tests at lines 0119 through 0122 ensures that the requested location is legal.

The PutPSET method of class Viewport is called to write the bitblt to the display.

Method MoveImage( )

The method at lines 0128 through 0142 will move an already-displayed bitblt a specified distance from its current location and redisplay it. The distance to be moved is passed to the method in its argument list. The code at line 0135 increments the current location of the bitblt. The call to method PutPSET of class Viewport at line 0140 writes the bitblt to the new location.

10-3 Sample program STRIDES.CPP. Supports VGA, EGA, MCGA, CGA, and Hercules adapters. This application demonstrates a specialized bitblt class suitable for building display animation sequences.

```
0001   /*
0002
0003   ┌──────────────────────────────────────────────────────────┐
       │            Lee Adams' SUPERCHARGED C++ GRAPHICS           │
0004   │   Interactive demo:  cel animation of running cartoon character │
0005   │
0006   │   SOURCE FILE:   STRIDES.CPP
0007   │          TYPE:   C++ source file for a multimodule application.
0008   │       PURPOSE:   Demonstrates a fundamental bitblt class that
0009   │                  can be used to produce sophisticated cel
0010   │                  animation.  This demo program can be used as a
0011   │                  template to build more advanced applications.
0012   │  PROGRAM LIST:   STRIDES.CPP, BLITTER.CPP, and LIB2D.CPP.
0013   │     LANGUAGES:   Turbo C++, Borland C++, Zortech C++, and
0014   │                  all C++ compilers compatible with AT&T C++ 2.0
0015   │                  specification; and nominal compatibility with
0016   │                  Microsoft C++ (see the discussion in the book).
0017   │  MEMORY MODEL:   large.
0018   │  COMMAND-LINE:   you can specify a graphics mode by using the
```

```
0019                    command-line argument /Mnn as shown below:
0020                      /M12  640x480x16-color VGA
0021                      /M11  640x480x2-color VGA, MCGA
0022                      /M10  640x350x16-color VGA, EGA
0023                      /M0E  640x200x16-color VGA, EGA
0024                      /M06  640x200x2-color VGA, MCGA, EGA, CGA
0025                      /MHC  720x348x2-color Hercules
0026                    If no command-line argument is used, hardware
0027                    autodetect is used to select the best mode.
0028      OUTPUT:  After creating and storing in memory seven keyframes,
0029               the software uses high-speed overwrite bitblt methods
0030               to animate a running cartoon character in silhouette.
0031               The figure's movements are anatomically exaggerated.
0032      LICENSE:  As purchaser of the book in which this source code
0033         appears you are granted a royalty-free license to reproduce
0034         and distribute executable files generated using this code
0035         provided that you accept the conditions of the License
0036         Agreement and Limited Warranty described in the book.
0037      PUBLICATION: Contains material from Windcrest/McGraw-Hill
0038         book 3489, published by TAB BOOKS.
0039      U.S. GOVERNMENT RESTRICTED RIGHTS:  This software and its
0040         documentation is provided with restricted rights.  The use,
0041         duplication, or disclosure by the Government is subject to
0042         restrictions set forth in subdivision (b)(3)(ii) of The
0043         Rights in Technical Data and Computer Software clause at
0044         252.227-7013.  Contractor/manufacturer is Lee Adams, c/o
0045         TAB BOOKS, 13311 Monterey Ave., Blue Ridge Summit PA 17294.
0046      TRADEMARK:  Lee Adams is a trademark of Lee Adams.
0047
0048         Copyright 1991 Lee Adams.  All rights reserved worldwide.
0049
0050
0051                         CONDITIONAL COMPILATION
0052      To compile only those blocks of code that support the C++
0053      compiler and graphics library that you are using, you should
0054      #define the appropriate tokens on lines 0066 and 0067.
0055            GRAPHICS LIBRARY
0056         Borland's graphics.lib              #define BGI
0057         Zortech's fg.lib or fgdebug.lib     #define FG
0058         Microsoft's graph.lib               #define MS
0059            COMPILER
0060         Borland Turbo C++ compiler          #define BORLAND
0061         Zortech C++ compiler                #define ZORTECH
0062         AT&T-compatible C++ compilers       #define MICROSOFT
0063      Be sure you define only one compiler and one graphics library.
0064
0065                                                                  */
0066      #define BGI     1  // indicates the graphics library you are using.
0067      #define BORLAND 1  // indicates the C++ compiler you are using.
0068      /*
0069
0070                              Constants
0071
0072                                                                  */
0073      const int zFAIL=0;
0074      const int zEMPTY=0;
0075      const int zYES=1;
0076      const int zNO=0;
0077      const int zVGA_12H=1;
0078      const int zEGA_10H=2;
0079      const int zEGA_EH=3;
0080      const int zMCGA_11H=4;
0081      const int zCGA_6H=5;
```

10-3 Continued.

```
0082   const int zHERC=6;
0083   /*
0084
0085   ┌─────────────────────────────────────────────────────────────┐
       │                      Include files                          │
0086   └─────────────────────────────────────────────────────────────┘
0087                                                               */
0088   #if defined (BORLAND)
0089   #include <time.h>        // supports clock().
0090   #include <string.h>      // supports strncmp().
0091   #include <bios.h>        // supports bioskey().
0092   #include <process.h>     // supports exit().
0093   #include <iostream.h>    // supports cout.
0094   #include <dos.h>         // supports outportb(), inportb().
0095   #elif defined (ZORTECH)
0096   #include <time.h>        // supports clock().
0097   #include <string.h>      // supports strncmp().
0098   #include <bios.h>        // supports bioskey().
0099   #include <stdlib.h>      // supports exit().
0100   #include <stream.hpp>    // supports cout.
0101   #include <dos.h>         // supports outp(), inp().
0102   #elif defined (MICROSOFT)
0103   #include <time.h>        // supports clock().
0104   #include <string.h>      // supports strncmp().
0105   #include <bios.h>        // supports _bios_keybrd().
0106   #include <process.h>     // supports exit().
0107   #include <iostream.h>    // supports cout.
0108   #include <conio.h>       // supports outp(), inp().
0109   #endif
0110
0111   #include "LIB2D.HPP"     // declarations for PhysicalDisplay class.
0112   #include "BLITTER.HPP"   // declarations for the Blitter class.
0113   /*
0114
0115   ┌─────────────────────────────────────────────────────────────┐
       │    Prototypes for functions visible throughout this file    │
0116   └─────────────────────────────────────────────────────────────┘
0117                                                               */
0118   static void zStartup(void);          // initializes a graphics mode.
0119   static void zArguments(int, char far* far*);   // checks arguments.
0120   static void zKeyboard(void);          // checks for a keystroke.
0121   static void zQuit_Pgm(void);          // ends the program gracefully.
0122   static void zPurge(void);             // empties the keyboard buffer.
0123   static void zMakeSound(int,double);   // makes a specific sound.
0124   static clock_t zDelay(clock_t,double);   // CPU-independent pause.
0125   static void zDrawCels(void);          // creates the individual cels.
0126   static void zDrawOneCartoon(void);             // draws one cel.
0127   static void zAnimateCels(void);       // runs the animation.
0128   /*
0129
0130   ┌─────────────────────────────────────────────────────────────┐
       │    Declaration of variables visible throughout this file    │
0131   └─────────────────────────────────────────────────────────────┘
0132                                                               */
0133   static char *StartUpArg[6]=           // legal command-line arguments.
0134       { "/M12", "/M10", "/MOE", "/M11", "/M06", "/MHC" };
0135   static int CommandLineArg=zNO;        // indicates if argument exists.
0136   static int CommandLineCompare=0;      // indicates if argument legal.
0137   static int C0=0,C1=1,C2=2,C3=3,C4=4,C5=5,C6=6,
0138           C7=7,C8=8,C9=9,C10=10,C11=11,C12=12,C13=13,
0139           C14=14,C15=15;                // palette index codes.
0140   static int Mode=0;                    // which graphics mode is being used.
0141   static int Result=0;           // captures result of graphics routines.
0142   static int CharWidth=0, CharHeight=0;   // dimensions of character.
0143   static char KeyCode=0;   // token for normal or extended keystroke.
```

```
0144    static char KeyNum=0;                       // ASCII number of keystroke.
0145    static char SolidFill[]=
0146                    {255,255,255,255,255,255,255,255};   // 100% fill.
0147    static int TextClr=0;                       // color for regular text.
0148    static int PromptClr=7;                     // color for prompt text.
0149    static char Copyright[]=
0150        "Copyright 1991 Lee Adams.  All rights reserved.";
0151    static char Title[]=
0152        "USING C++ FOR ADVANCED CEL ANIMATION EFFECTS.";
0153    static char PressAnyKey[]= "Press any key to continue.";
0154    static char StubMessage[]= "The generic stub routine was called.";
0155    static int X_Res=0, Y_Res=0;                // screen resolution.
0156    int DrawPtr, TempPtr;               // indexes into array of coords.
0157    int * ArrayPtr;                     // points to any array of coords.
0158    int Count, Repeat;                          // loop counters.
0159
0160            // database of xy coordinates for the cel images...
0161    int keyframe1[]=
0162    {
0163    36,16,                                      // circle
0164    45,23,49,27,47,28,42,25,                    // neck
0165    54,26,78,54,76,60,57,57,42,30,              // torso
0166    15,25,24,27,23,33,12,32,                    // leading fist
0167    22,32,30,44,26,46,20,35,                    // leading forearm
0168    45,35,48,38,25,46,23,44,                    // leading upper arm
0169    55,28,69,20,70,23,58,31,                    // trailing upper arm
0170    68,20,91,20,91,23,70,23,                    // trailing forearm
0171    91,20,100,15,100,18,91,23,                  // trailing hand
0172    31,52,65,55,71,60,35,55,                    // leading thigh
0173    40,57,51,75,41,74,31,52,                    // leading calf
0174    46,68,51,75,22,72,40,68,                    // leading foot
0175    76,60,106,92,101,94,69,60,                  // trailing thigh
0176    76,60,106,92,101,94,69,60,                  // trailing calf
0177    104,92,111,92,111,108,104,106,              // trailing foot
0178    111,108,105,115,100,115,104,107             // trailing toe
0179    };
0180    int keyframe2[]=
0181    {
0182    36,13,                                      // circle
0183    44,20,48,24,43,24,41,21,                    // neck
0184    51,22,77,55,71,58,54,56,40,25,              // torso
0185    20,31,20,39,12,40,10,33,                    // leading fist
0186    20,36,34,43,35,45,20,39,                    // leading forearm
0187    44,32,46,36,35,45,34,42,                    // leading upper arm
0188    54,25,76,25,76,28,54,28,                    // trailing upper arm
0189    78,25,95,33,95,37,74,28,                    // trailing forearm
0190    95,33,105,30,104,35,95,37,                  // trailing hand
0191    52,52,54,55,32,60,28,59,                    // leading thigh
0192    28,59,32,60,32,85,28,78,                    // leading calf
0193    32,78,32,85,10,75,28,78,                    // leading foot
0194    75,56,92,73,88,76,70,57,                    // trailing thigh
0195    92,74,116,86,112,90,88,76,                  // trailing calf
0196    116,86,120,85,120,108,112,90,               // trailing foot
0197    116,86,120,85,120,108,112,90                //trailing toe
0198    };
0199    int keyframe3[]=
0200    {
0201    38,10,                                      // circle
0202    45,16,48,21,44,22,41,17,                    // neck
0203    52,20,75,55,70,56,53,54,40,22,              // torso
0204    20,36,24,44,17,47,13,40,                    // leading fist
0205    22,40,40,43,40,47,22,44,                    // leading forearm
0206    37,43,44,31,47,36,40,47,                    // leading upper arm
```

```
0207  55,25,76,29,74,31,55,29,              // trailing upper arm
0208  76,29,90,45,85,48,74,31,              // trailing forearm
0209  90,45,100,45,95,49,85,49,             // trailing hand
0210  53,54,55,58,35,72,30,69,              // leading thigh
0211  35,72,16,96,17,85,30,69,              // leading calf
0212  17,85,20,90,17,96,0,80,               // leading foot
0213  75,55,92,70,88,74,70,57,              // trailing thigh
0214  92,70,121,77,122,81,87,73,            // trailing calf
0215  121,77,126,75,139,95,122,81,          // trailing foot
0216  121,77,126,75,139,95,122,81           // trailing toe
0217  };
0218  int keyframe4[]=
0219  {
0220  38,13,                                // circle
0221  45,19,48,23,44,25,41,20,              // neck
0222  52,22,70,56,64,60,46,60,40,26,        // torso
0223  32,43,36,46,34,51,27,48,              // leading fist
0224  36,46,50,44,50,48,36,49,              // leading forearm
0225  36,46,50,44,50,48,36,49,              // leading upper arm
0226  55,35,69,45,62,50,55,40,              // trailing upper arm
0227  55,35,69,45,62,50,55,40,              // trailing forearm
0228  55,35,69,45,62,50,55,40,              // trailing hand
0229  46,59,51,60,31,75,26,73,              // leading thigh
0230  26,73,31,76,25,105,22,97,             // leading calf
0231  22,97,26,99,25,105,0,95,              // leading foot
0232  58,60,64,60,58,78,50,78,              // trailing thigh
0233  58,78,75,85,74,89,50,78,              // trailing calf
0234  75,85,80,85,80,103,74,88,             // trailing foot
0235  75,85,80,85,80,103,74,88              // trailing toe
0236  };
0237  int keyframe5[]=
0238  {
0239  38,18,                                // circle
0240  45,25,49,28,43,30,42,26,              // neck
0241  54,28,56,64,45,66,34,64,40,31,        // torso
0242  27,58,26,63,18,58,21,55,              // leading fist
0243  28,58,40,56,40,60,25,63,              // leading forearm
0244  28,58,40,56,40,60,25,63,              // leading upper arm
0245  54,28,57,48,60,46,54,38,              // trailing upper arm
0246  60,48,66,48,52,53,50,50,              // trailing forearm
0247  60,48,66,48,52,53,50,50,              // trailing hand
0248  34,65,40,66,14,76,12,74,              // leading thigh
0249  22,74,40,78,38,82,12,76,              // leading calf
0250  40,78,46,76,45,96,38,82,              // leading foot
0251  40,68,45,66,27,85,20,84,              // trailing thigh
0252  27,85,33,114,25,107,20,84,            // trailing calf
0253  25,107,31,107,32,115,5,115,           // trailing foot
0254  25,107,31,107,32,115,5,115            // trailing toe
0255  };
0256  int keyframe6[]=
0257  {
0258  38,22,                                // circle
0259  41,29,45,35,39,35,39,30,              // neck
0260  38,36,49,33,60,68,52,70,39,70,        // torso
0261  12,48,16,54,11,59,5,51,               // leading fist
0262  15,52,34,55,38,59,15,56,              // leading forearm
0263  33,55,40,40,40,50,38,60,              // leading upper arm
0264  50,38,65,50,60,50,50,43,              // trailing upper arm
0265  60,50,65,50,60,67,58,63,              // trailing forearm
0266  60,50,65,50,60,67,58,63,              // trailing hand
0267  38,66,39,70,16,80,15,76,              // leading thigh
0268  22,77,49,85,36,85,16,80,              // leading calf
```

```
0269   40,83,49,86,32,102,36,86,                         // leading foot
0270   45,72,52,70,43,91,38,90,                         // trailing thigh
0271   41,89,62,104,54,103,38,92,                        // trailing calf
0272   53,104,63,104,54,115,49,112,                      // trailing foot
0273   52,112,53,115,43,115,49,112                       // trailing toe
0274   };
0275   int keyframe7[]=
0276   {
0277   38,19,                                                 // circle
0278   45,25,48,30,43,31,42,26,                                // neck
0279   51,30,69,62,60,65,49,61,40,32,                         // torso
0280   14,33,15,41,6,42,4,34,                           // leading fist
0281   15,38,30,45,30,50,15,41,                      // leading forearm
0282   30,45,41,38,42,42,30,50,                    // leading upper arm
0283   53,32,73,36,71,39,55,36,                    // trailing upper arm
0284   73,37,83,53,80,55,71,40,                     // trailing forearm
0285   83,53,93,55,89,57,80,55,                        // trailing hand
0286   49,61,60,65,22,65,23,61,                         // leading thigh
0287   31,65,53,81,40,80,23,65,                          // leading calf
0288   48,77,53,81,27,89,40,79,                          // leading foot
0289   61,65,67,63,68,84,63,85,                         // trailing thigh
0290   68,83,84,99,80,101,63,85,                         // trailing calf
0291   81,98,89,98,85,113,80,111,                        // trailing foot
0292   89,111,85,112,80,115,76,115                       // trailing toe
0293   };
0294   static int Facet[12];                           // array of coords.
0295   Blitter * Cel1;          // file-scope pointers to Blitter objects...
0296   Blitter * Cel2;
0297   Blitter * Cel3;
0298   Blitter * Cel4;
0299   Blitter * Cel5;
0300   Blitter * Cel6;
0301   Blitter * Cel7;
0302
0303   PhysicalDisplay Display;              // the physical display object.
0304   Viewport Viewport1(&Display);                 // a viewport object.
0305   /*
0306
0307   ┌──────────────────────────────────────────────────────────┐
       │                    Function definitions                    │
0308   └──────────────────────────────────────────────────────────┘
0309
0310   ┌──────────────────────────────────────────────────────────┐
       │      The executive routine:  program execution begins here  │
0311   └──────────────────────────────────────────────────────────┘
0312                                                                */
0313   main(int argc, char *argv[])
0314   {
0315     int NumArgs; char far* far* Arg;
0316
0317   NumArgs= argc;                          // grab number of arguments.
0318   Arg= &argv[0];                   // grab address of array of arguments.
0319   zArguments(NumArgs, Arg);          // check the command-line arguments.
0320
0321   zStartup();                           // establish the graphics mode.
0322   Display.Init2D(Mode,0,0,X_Res-1,Y_Res-1);    // set graphics state.
0323   Result= Display.InitUndo();      // create hidden page (unused here).
0324   if (Result==zFAIL) zQuit_Pgm();          // if hidden page failed.
0325
0326   Display.BlankPage();                        // clear the display.
0327   Display.SetHue(C7);                    // set the drawing color.
0328   Display.SetFill(SolidFill,C7);            // set the fill style.
0329   Viewport1.DrawPanel(0,0,X_Res-1,Y_Res-1);            // draw bg.
0330   zDrawCels();                              // create all the cels.
0331
```

```
0332   Viewport1.PutText(2,2,TextClr,Title);              // sign-on notice.
0333   Viewport1.PutText(3,2,TextClr,Copyright);        // copyright notice.
0334   switch (Mode)
0335     {              // notify user which display mode is being used...
0336     case zVGA_12H:  Viewport1.PutText(5,2,TextClr,
0337                       "Using the 640x480x16-color VGA mode.");
0338                     break;
0339     case zEGA_10H:  Viewport1.PutText(5,2,TextClr,
0340                       "Using the 640x350x16-color VGA and EGA mode.");
0341                     break;
0342     case zEGA_EH:   Viewport1.PutText(5,2,TextClr,
0343                       "Using the 640x200x16-color VGA and EGA mode.");
0344                     break;
0345     case zMCGA_11H: Viewport1.PutText(5,2,TextClr,
0346                       "Using the 640x480x2-color VGA and MCGA mode.");
0347                     break;
0348     case zCGA_6H:   Viewport1.PutText(5,2,TextClr,
0349                       "Using the 640x200x2-color CGA mode.");
0350                     break;
0351     case zHERC:     Viewport1.PutText(5,2,TextClr,
0352                       "Using the 720x348x2-color Hercules mode.");
0353     }
0354   Viewport1.PutText(6,2,TextClr,"Press any key to quit.");
0355
0356   zAnimateCels();
0357
0358   zQuit_Pgm();               // tidy up and terminate the application.
0359   }
0360   /*
0361
0362   ┌─────────────────────────────────────────────────────────────┐
        │                  Draw the individual cels                     │
0363   └─────────────────────────────────────────────────────────────┘
0364                                                                    */
0365   static void zDrawCels(void)
0366   {
0367   ArrayPtr= keyframe1;                        // point to the first array.
0368   zDrawOneCartoon();                                      // draw the cel.
0369   Blitter *Item1= new Blitter(0,0,143,115,X_Res,Y_Res,&Viewport1);
0370   Item1->GrabImage();        // store the image in a graphic array.
0371   Cel1= Item1;   // assign object pointer to a pointer of file scope.
0372
0373        // use the same sequence to draw the remaining cels...
0374   ArrayPtr= keyframe2; zDrawOneCartoon();
0375   Blitter *Item2= new Blitter(0,0,143,115,X_Res,Y_Res,&Viewport1);
0376   Item2->GrabImage(); Cel2= Item2;
0377   ArrayPtr= keyframe3; zDrawOneCartoon();
0378   Blitter *Item3= new Blitter(0,0,143,115,X_Res,Y_Res,&Viewport1);
0379   Item3->GrabImage(); Cel3= Item3;
0380   ArrayPtr= keyframe4; zDrawOneCartoon();
0381   Blitter *Item4= new Blitter(0,0,143,115,X_Res,Y_Res,&Viewport1);
0382   Item4->GrabImage(); Cel4= Item4;
0383   ArrayPtr= keyframe5; zDrawOneCartoon();
0384   Blitter *Item5= new Blitter(0,0,143,115,X_Res,Y_Res,&Viewport1);
0385   Item5->GrabImage(); Cel5= Item5;
0386   ArrayPtr= keyframe6; zDrawOneCartoon();
0387   Blitter *Item6= new Blitter(0,0,143,115,X_Res,Y_Res,&Viewport1);
0388   Item6->GrabImage(); Cel6= Item6;
0389   ArrayPtr= keyframe7; zDrawOneCartoon();
0390   Blitter *Item7= new Blitter(0,0,143,115,X_Res,Y_Res,&Viewport1);
0391   Item7->GrabImage(); Cel7= Item7;
0392   Display.SetHue(C7);                            // set the drawing color.
0393   Display.SetFill(SolidFill,C7);                     // set the fill style.
```

```
0394   Viewport1.DrawPanel(0,0,150,120);                        // clear bg.
0395   return;
0396   }
0397
0398   static void zDrawOneCartoon(void)
0399   {                              // this function is called by zDrawCels().
0400   Display.SetHue(C7);                              // set the drawing color.
0401   Display.SetFill(SolidFill,C7);                      // set the fill style.
0402   Viewport1.DrawPanel(0,0,150,120);                        // clear bg.
0403   Display.SetHue(C0);                          // reset the drawing color...
0404   Display.SetFill(SolidFill,C0);                    // ...and the fill style.
0405   Viewport1.DrawCircle(ArrayPtr[0],ArrayPtr[1],10); // draw the head.
0406   Viewport1.Fill(ArrayPtr[0],ArrayPtr[1],C0);         // fill the head.
0407   DrawPtr= 2;                              // index into database array.
0408   TempPtr= DrawPtr;                      // remember the starting element.
0409   for (Count= 0; Count <=7; Count++)
0410     {
0411     Facet[Count]= ArrayPtr[DrawPtr]; DrawPtr++;
0412     }
0413   Facet[Count]= ArrayPtr[TempPtr];
0414   TempPtr++;
0415   Count++;
0416   Facet[Count]= ArrayPtr[TempPtr];
0417   Viewport1.DrawPolygon(5,Facet);                      // draw the neck.
0418   TempPtr=DrawPtr;                  // reset to the next starting element.
0419   for (Count= 0; Count <=9; Count++)
0420     {
0421     Facet[Count]= ArrayPtr[DrawPtr]; DrawPtr++;
0422     }
0423   Facet[Count]= ArrayPtr[TempPtr];
0424   TempPtr++;
0425   Count++;
0426   Facet[Count]= ArrayPtr[TempPtr];
0427   Viewport1.DrawPolygon(6,Facet);                      // draw the torso.
0428   for (Repeat= 1; Repeat<= 13; Repeat++)
0429     {                      // for each of the remaining body parts...
0430     TempPtr=DrawPtr;                // reset to the next starting element.
0431     for (Count= 0; Count <=7; Count++)
0432       {
0433       Facet[Count]= ArrayPtr[DrawPtr]; DrawPtr++;
0434       }
0435     Facet[Count]= ArrayPtr[TempPtr];
0436     TempPtr++;
0437     Count++;
0438     Facet[Count]= ArrayPtr[TempPtr];
0439     Viewport1.DrawPolygon(5,Facet);                // draw a filled polygon.
0440     }
0441   return;
0442   }
0443   /*
0444
0445   ┌──────────────────────────────────────────────────────────────┐
       │               Manage the animation sequence                  │
0446   └──────────────────────────────────────────────────────────────┘
0447                                                                  */
0448   static void zAnimateCels(void)
0449   {
0450   Cel1->DisplayImage(319,60);
0451   Cel2->DisplayImage(319,60);
0452   Cel3->DisplayImage(319,60);
0453   Cel4->DisplayImage(319,60);
0454   Cel5->DisplayImage(319,60);
0455   Cel6->DisplayImage(319,60);
0456   Cel7->DisplayImage(319,60);
```

```
0457
0458   ANIMATION_LOOP:
0459     zKeyboard();                          // check for a user keystroke.
0460     if (KeyCode!= 0)                      // if the user pressed any key.
0461       {
0462       delete Cel7; delete Cel6; delete Cel5; delete Cel4;
0463       delete Cel3; delete Cel2; delete Cel1;
0464       return;
0465       }
0466     Cel1->MoveImage(0,0);
0467     Cel2->MoveImage(0,0);
0468     Cel3->MoveImage(0,0);
0469     Cel4->MoveImage(0,0);
0470     Cel5->MoveImage(0,0);
0471     Cel6->MoveImage(0,0);
0472     Cel7->MoveImage(0,0);
0473   goto ANIMATION_LOOP;
0474   }
0475   /*
0476
0477   ┌──────────────────────────────────────────────────────────────┐
         │                  Terminate the program                         │
0478   └──────────────────────────────────────────────────────────────┘
0479                                                                  */
0480   static void zQuit_Pgm(void)
0481   {
0482   Display.ShutDownGraphics();  // graceful shutdown of graphics mode.
0483   exit(0);                 // terminate the program and return an OK code.
0484   }
0485   /*
0486
0487   ┌──────────────────────────────────────────────────────────────┐
         │          Detect the graphics hardware and set the              │
0488     │     highest mode permitted by the graphics adapter and monitor.│
0489     │     The user can override the autodetect algorithm by providing│
0490     │     an argument on the command-line when the program is started.│
0491   └──────────────────────────────────────────────────────────────┘
0492                                                                  */
0493   static void zStartup(void)
0494   {
0495     int DefaultMode;
0496   DefaultMode= Display.SetupMode();   // get results of autodetect...
0497   switch(DefaultMode)                 // ...and jump to appropriate code.
0498     {
0499     case zFAIL:        goto ABORT_PGM;
0500     case zVGA_12H:     goto VGA_mode;
0501     case zEGA_10H:     goto EGA_ECD_mode;
0502     case zEGA_EH:      goto EGA_SCD_mode;
0503     case zMCGA_11H:    goto MCGA_mode;
0504     case zCGA_6H:      goto CGA_mode;
0505     case zHERC:        goto Hercules_mode;
0506     default:           goto ABORT_PGM;
0507     }
0508   VGA_mode:            // VGA 640x480x16-color, 80x60 character mode.
0509   if(CommandLineArg==zYES)
0510     {                                  // if user has requested a mode.
0511     if((Mode>zVGA_12H)&&(Mode<zHERC)) goto FORCE_USER_MODE;
0512     }
0513   X_Res=640; Y_Res=480; Mode=zVGA_12H; CharWidth=8; CharHeight=8;
0514   return;
0515   EGA_ECD_mode:        // EGA 640x350x16-color, 80x43 character mode.
0516   if(CommandLineArg==zYES)
0517     {
0518     if((Mode==zEGA_EH)||(Mode==zCGA_6H))   // permit only EGA or CGA.
```

```
0519    goto FORCE_USER_MODE;
0520    }
0521  X_Res=640; Y_Res=350; Mode=zEGA_10H; CharWidth=8; CharHeight=8;
0522  return;
0523  EGA_SCD_mode:              // EGA 640x200x16-color, 80x25 char mode.
0524  if(CommandLineArg==zYES)
0525    {
0526    if(Mode==zCGA_6H) goto FORCE_USER_MODE;     // only CGA permitted.
0527    }
0528  X_Res=640; Y_Res=200; Mode=zEGA_EH; CharWidth=8; CharHeight=8;
0529  return;
0530  MCGA_mode:                  // MCGA 640x480x2-color, 80x60 char mode.
0531  if(CommandLineArg==zYES)
0532    {
0533    if(Mode==zCGA_6H) goto FORCE_USER_MODE;     // only CGA permitted.
0534    }
0535  X_Res=640; Y_Res=480; Mode=zMCGA_11H;
0536  C0=0; C1=1; C2=1; C3=1; C4=1; C5=1; C6=1; C7=1;
0537  C8=1; C9=1; C10=1; C11=1; C12=1; C13=1; C14=1; C15=1;
0538  CharWidth=8; CharHeight=8;
0539  return;
0540  CGA_mode:                   // CGA 640x200x2-color, 80x25 char mode.
0541  X_Res=640; Y_Res=200; Mode=zCGA_6H;
0542  C0=0; C1=1; C2=1; C3=1; C4=1; C5=1; C6=1; C7=1;
0543  C8=1; C9=1; C10=1; C11=1; C12=1; C13=1; C14=1; C15=1;
0544  CharWidth=8; CharHeight=8;
0545  return;
0546  Hercules_mode:           // Hercules 720x348x2-color, 80x25 char mode.
0547  X_Res=720; Y_Res=348; Mode=zHERC;
0548  C0=0; C1=1; C2=1; C3=1; C4=1; C5=1; C6=1; C7=1;
0549  C8=1; C9=1; C10=1; C11=1; C12=1; C13=1; C14=1; C15=1;
0550  CharWidth=9; CharHeight=14;
0551  return;
0552
0553  FORCE_USER_MODE:    // jump to here if command-line argument legal.
0554  CommandLineArg= zNO; // first, reset token to avoid returning here.
0555  Display.ForceMode(Mode);          // ...then reset the graphics mode.
0556  switch(Mode)                 // ...then jump back to appropriate code.
0557    {
0558    case zEGA_10H:    goto EGA_ECD_mode;
0559    case zEGA_EH:     goto EGA_SCD_mode;
0560    case zMCGA_11H:   goto MCGA_mode;
0561    case zCGA_6H:     goto CGA_mode;
0562    default:          goto ABORT_PGM;
0563    }
0564
0565  ABORT_PGM:       // jump to here if no graphics hardware detected.
0566  cout << "\n\n\rThis C++ graphics programming demo requires a";
0567  cout << "\n\rVGA, EGA, CGA, MCGA, or HGA graphics adapter.\n\r";
0568  exit(-1);                    // terminate, returning an error code.
0569  }
0570  /*
0571
0572  ┌─────────────────────────────────────────────────────────────────┐
       │            Check the keyboard for a keystroke                     │
       └─────────────────────────────────────────────────────────────────┘
0573
0574                                                                      */
0575  static void zKeyboard(void)
0576  {    // can detect keypad keys like PgUp and control keys like F2.
0577    union AnyName{int RawCode;char Code[3];}Keystroke;
0578    char TempKey=0;
0579  #if defined (BORLAND)
0580    if (bioskey(1)==zEMPTY) { KeyCode=0; return; }
0581    Keystroke.RawCode= bioskey(0);
```

```
0582  #elif defined (ZORTECH)
0583     if (bioskey(1)==zEMPTY) { KeyCode=0; return; }
0584     Keystroke.RawCode= bioskey(0);
0585  #elif defined (MICROSOFT)
0586     if (_bios_keybrd(_KEYBRD_READY)==zEMPTY)
0587       { KeyCode=0; return; }
0588     Keystroke.RawCode= _bios_keybrd(_KEYBRD_READ);
0589  #endif
0590  TempKey= Keystroke.Code[0];
0591  if (TempKey!=0)
0592     {                                  // if a normal keystroke...
0593     KeyCode=1; KeyNum=TempKey; return;
0594     }
0595  if (TempKey==0)
0596     {                                  // if an extended keystroke...
0597     KeyCode=2; KeyNum=Keystroke.Code[1]; return;
0598     }
0599  }
0600  /*
0601
0602  ┌──────────────────────────────────────────────────────────────┐
        │                 Empty the keystroke buffer                   │
0603  └──────────────────────────────────────────────────────────────┘
0604                                                                  */
0605  static void zPurge(void)
0606  {
0607  do zKeyboard();
0608     while (KeyCode!=0);
0609  return;
0610  }
0611  /*
0612
0613  ┌──────────────────────────────────────────────────────────────┐
        │                       Make a sound                           │
0614  └──────────────────────────────────────────────────────────────┘
0615                                                                  */
0616  static void zMakeSound(int Hertz,double Duration)
0617  {
0618     static clock_t FormerTime=0;
0619     short Count=0;
0620     int HighByte=0, LowByte=0;
0621     unsigned char OldPort=0, NewPort=0;
0622  FormerTime= clock();
0623  if (Hertz < 40) return;
0624  if (Hertz > 4660) return;
0625  Count= 1193180L/Hertz;
0626  HighByte= Count / 256;
0627  LowByte= Count - (HighByte * 256);
0628  #if defined (BORLAND)
0629     outportb(0x43,0xB6); outportb(0x42,(unsigned char)LowByte);
0630     outportb(0x42,(unsigned char)HighByte); OldPort=inportb(0x61);
0631     NewPort=(OldPort | 0x03); outportb(0x61,NewPort);
0632     zDelay(FormerTime,Duration);
0633     outportb(0x61,OldPort);
0634  #elif defined (ZORTECH)
0635     outp(0x43,0xB6); outp(0x42,LowByte);
0636     outp(0x42,HighByte); OldPort=(unsigned char)inp(0x61);
0637     NewPort=(OldPort | 0x03); outp(0x61,(int)NewPort);
0638     zDelay(FormerTime,Duration);
0639     outp(0x61,(int)OldPort);
0640  #elif defined (MICROSOFT)
0641     outp(0x43,0xB6); outp(0x42,LowByte);
0642     outp(0x42,HighByte); OldPort=(unsigned char)inp(0x61);
0643     NewPort=(OldPort | 0x03); outp(0x61,(int)NewPort);
```

```
0644      zDelay(FormerTime,Duration);
0645      outp(0x61,(int)OldPort);
0646   #endif
0647   return;
0648   }
0649   /*
0650
0651   ┌──────────────────────────────────────────────────────────────────┐
          │                            Pause                                   │
0652      └──────────────────────────────────────────────────────────────────┘
0653                                                                        */
0654   static clock_t zDelay(clock_t StartTime, double Wait)
0655   {                             // pause for a specified length of time.
0656      clock_t StopTime;
0657      clock_t NewClockTime;
0658   #if defined (BORLAND)
0659      StopTime= StartTime + (Wait * CLK_TCK);
0660   #elif defined (ZORTECH)
0661      StopTime= StartTime + (Wait * CLOCKS_PER_SEC);
0662   #elif defined (MICROSOFT)
0663      StopTime= StartTime + (Wait * CLK_TCK);
0664   #endif
0665   while ( clock() < StopTime ) {;}
0666   NewClockTime= clock();
0667   return NewClockTime;
0668   }
0669   /*
0670
0671   ┌──────────────────────────────────────────────────────────────────┐
          │              Retrieve the command-line arguments, if any           │
0672      └──────────────────────────────────────────────────────────────────┘
0673                                                                        */
0674   static void zArguments(int NumArgs, char *Arg[])
0675   {
0676   if(NumArgs==1)
0677      {
0678      CommandLineArg= zNO; return;                          // if no arg.
0679      }
0680   CommandLineCompare= strncmp(StartUpArg[0],Arg[1],5);
0681   if(CommandLineCompare==0)
0682      {
0683      CommandLineArg=zYES; Mode=zVGA_12H; return;           // /M12.
0684      }
0685   CommandLineCompare= strncmp(StartUpArg[1],Arg[1],5);
0686   if(CommandLineCompare==0)
0687      {
0688      CommandLineArg=zYES; Mode=zEGA_10H; return;           // /M10.
0689      }
0690   CommandLineCompare= strncmp(StartUpArg[2],Arg[1],5);
0691   if(CommandLineCompare==0)
0692      {
0693      CommandLineArg=zYES; Mode=zEGA_EH; return;            // /M0E.
0694      }
0695   CommandLineCompare= strncmp(StartUpArg[3],Arg[1],5);
0696   if(CommandLineCompare==0)
0697      {
0698      CommandLineArg=zYES; Mode=zMCGA_11H; return;          // /M11.
0699      }
0700   CommandLineCompare= strncmp(StartUpArg[4],Arg[1],5);
0701   if(CommandLineCompare==0)
0702      {
0703      CommandLineArg=zYES; Mode=zCGA_6H; return;            // /M06.
0704      }
0705   CommandLineCompare= strncmp(StartUpArg[5],Arg[1],5);
0706   if(CommandLineCompare==0)
```

```
0707     {
0708     CommandLineArg=zYES; Mode=zHERC; return;                      // /MHC.
0709     }
0710  CommandLineArg= zNO;                      // if an unrecognized argument.
0711  return;
0712  }
0713  /*
0714
0715  ┌─────────────────────────────────────────────────────────────────┐
      │   Supercharged C++ Graphics  --   end of source file STRIDES.CPP  │
0716  └─────────────────────────────────────────────────────────────────┘
0717                                                                     */
```

11
Cel animation

Cel animation is named after the transparent acetate cels that professional cartoonists use to manipulate different versions of cartoon characters appearing in front of a background. Cel animation has traditionally been very labor intensive because of the huge number of cels required to produce even short sequences of animation. Using the industry standard rate of 30 frames per second, a 30-second television commercial requires 900 individual images. A typical Saturday morning half-hour cartoon show needs more than 40,000 frames.

Morphing and tweening are two techniques that are used to help automate the process of cel animation on personal computers, cutting production time and labor. *Morphing* means transforming a shape into a different shape. *Tweening* refers to the series of images that occur between a beginning image and an ending image. The beginning and ending images are called *keyframes*.

Tweening is useful for a variety of specialized applications. Cartooning is the most obvious use. Tweening capabilities can make your program smart enough to complete the task started by the user.

Keyframes

Keyframes are the starting image and the ending image used by the software to produce the in-between images. Serious computer animators often use a series of keyframes at critical points throughout an animation sequence, as demonstrated in the previous chapter. These keyframes provide touchstones for the software, ensuring that the tweening routines do not stray from the script. The tweening routines are responsible for generating images that show a smooth transition from one keyframe to the next.

The tweening algorithm can simply follow a linear path between the xy coordinates (registration points) in each keyframe, or it can use fitted curves to

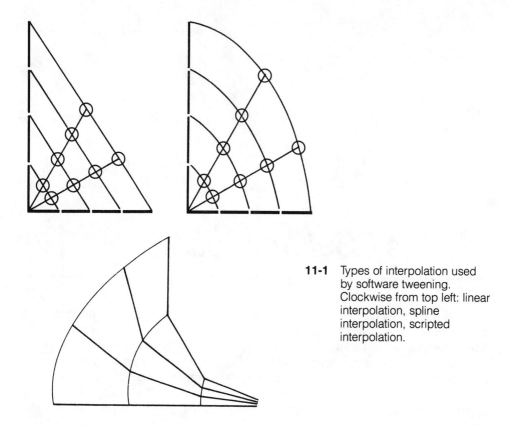

11-1 Types of interpolation used by software tweening. Clockwise from top left: linear interpolation, spline interpolation, scripted interpolation.

create a customized path. See FIG. 11-1. Spline curves are often used, as well as random curves defined by the user. Simulations of robot arms and humanoid characters require combination methods.

A sample program: CEL.CPP

[*Code*] Figure 11-2 depicts typical displays produced by the sample program CEL.CPP, whose complete source code is provided in FIG. 11-4 at the end of the chapter. The program provides an interactive environment for creating in-between images from two keyframes that you draw with a mouse.

How to compile and link the sample program

[*Here's How...*] The program listing presented in FIG. 11-4 contains the complete source code for the main module of the C++ demonstration program called "Using C++ to Generate Inbetween Images for Cel Animation." If you are using the companion disks to the book, the source code is in the file named CEL.CPP. Three C++ source files are needed to build the finished .exe file. These are CEL.CPP from FIG. 11-4 and two class libraries in appendix E.

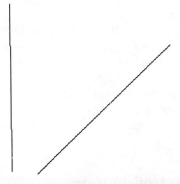

<F1=Create Keyframe 1>   <F2=Create Keyframe 2>

USING C++ TO GENERATE INBETWEEN IMAGES FOR CEL ANIMATION
Copyright 1991 Lee Adams. All rights reserved.

<F3= generates tweens from keyframes>   <Alt+X= quit>

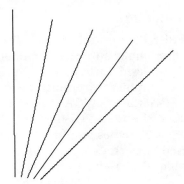

In-between keyframes complete. Press a key.

USING C++ TO GENERATE INBETWEEN IMAGES FOR CEL ANIMATION
Copyright 1991 Lee Adams. All rights reserved.

<F3= generates tweens from keyframes>   <Alt+X= quit>

11-2   Graphics output from the sample program CEL.CPP. Top: each line represents a key frame. Bottom: the software has used linear interpolation to generate tweens (in-between images).

Class The class library that provides the language bindings and low-level graphics routines for this demonstration program is found in FIG. E-2 in appendix E. This listing contains the implementations for class PhysicalDisplay and class Viewport. If you are using the companion disks to the book, this file is named LIB2D.CPP. The class declarations are presented in FIG. E-1 in appendix E. If you are using the companion disks to the book, this file is named LIB2D.HPP.

Class The class library that provides the mouse management methods for this demonstration program is found in FIG. E-6 in appendix E. This listing contains the implementations for class PointingDevice. If you are using the companion disks to the book, this file is named MOUSE.CPP. The class declarations are presented in FIG. E-5 in appendix E. If you are using the companion disks to the book, this file is named MOUSE.HPP.

You can compile, link, and run this demonstration program using Turbo C++, Borland C++, or Zortech C++. If you are using Turbo C++, read appendix A for help in compiling, linking, and running the demonstration program. If you are using Borland C++, you can find the appropriate information in appendix B. If you are using Zortech C++, refer to appendix C.

You must create a Turbo C++ or Borland C++ project list to advise your compiler which source files to bind together to build the finished .exe file. If you are using Zortech C++, you must name the files on the compiler command line field. Refer to the appendices for help.

After a successful compile and link the screen should resemble the screen prints shown in FIG. 11-1.

How to run the demonstration program

You need a VGA, EGA, MCGA, CGA, or Hercules graphics adapter and a mouse to run this demo.

Using the editor to run the program

Here's How... To run the program under the control of your Turbo C++, Borland C++, or Zortech C++ editor, make sure that the finished .exe file is in the default directory. If you used Turbo C++ or Borland C++ to compile the program, the appropriate graphics driver must be in the default directory. If you are using a VGA or EGA, the EGAVGA.BGI file must be present. If you are using an MCGA or CGA, the CGA.BGI file must be located in the default directory. If you are using a Hercules graphics adapter, the HERC.BGI file must be available. If you used Zortech C++ to compile the demonstration program, the appropriate graphics drivers have already been linked into the .exe code.

The built-in autodetect routine will detect the graphics hardware in your computer system and will set up the best graphics mode supported by your computer hardware. To override the autodetect routine use the Turbo C++, Borland C++, or Zortech C++ editor to simulate a command line argument. The header in FIG. 11-4 provides a set of arguments you can use. See the appendices for guidance applicable to your particular compiler. If you are using a VGA, you can override the autodetect routine and force the demonstration program to run in an EGA, MCGA, or CGA mode. If you are using an EGA, you can force the program to run in a lower-resolution EGA mode or a CGA mode.

Running the program from the operating system prompt

To start the program from the operating system prompt, simply enter CEL. The .exe file and any required graphics drivers must be present in the default directory. If the software finds a VGA present in your system, the program will animate using the 640×480×16-color mode. If an EGA and enhanced monitor are found, the 640×350×16-color mode is used. If an EGA and standard display are present, the program sets up the 640×200×16-color mode. If an MCGA is detected, the 640×480×2-color mode is employed. If a CGA is found, the 640×200×2-color mode is used. If the program detects a Hercules graphics adapter, it starts up in the 720×348×2-color mode.

You can force the program to start up in a different mode by adding a command line argument when you start the program from the operating system prompt. Enter CEL /M11 to force the 640×480×2-color mode. Enter CEL /M10 to force the 640×350×16-color mode. Entering CEL /M0E forces the program to run in the 640×200×16-color mode. Entering CEL /M06 runs the program in the 640×200×2-color mode.

Using the demonstration program

Using the demonstration program and a mouse, you can create sets of in-between images from two keyframes that you draw. In its present form the program generates three tweens between two keyframes, yielding a total of five images. You can customize the source code to produce more in-betweens or fewer in-betweens, depending upon your requirements.

All controls are activated from the main screen. You must either complete a selected function or use the right mouse button to back out of it before you can select another function.

Creating the first keyframe

Press F1 at the main command level to activate the editor for the first keyframe. The mouse cursor appears. Using the left mouse button to specify end points, draw a shape. Use the right mouse button to return to the main command level.

Creating the second keyframe

Then press F2 to activate the editor for the second keyframe. The mouse cursor will appear on the screen. Use the left mouse button to draw a shape. The sequence of points you enter is important. The software matches the fourth point of keyframe 1 with the fourth point of keyframe 2, and so on. It is also important to use the same number of points in both keyframes, otherwise the program will return an error message when you try to generate in-between images.

Press the right button to return to the main command level. If you have made a mistake, you can use F1 or F2 to redraw the first keyframe or the second keyframe.

Tweening

Press F3 to instruct the demonstration program to generate a set of three images interpolated from keyframe 1 and keyframe 2. As FIG. 11-3 shows, this demonstration program can be used to create some interesting tweening effects.

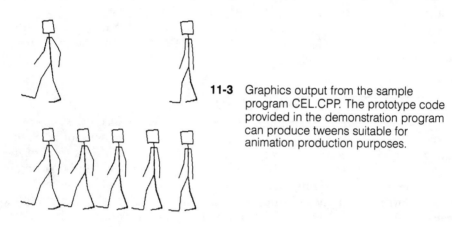

11-3 Graphics output from the sample program CEL.CPP. The prototype code provided in the demonstration program can produce tweens suitable for animation production purposes.

Programmer's Guide to CEL.CPP

Code The complete listing for the demonstration program CEL.CPP is presented in FIG. 11-4. The source code consists of an informative header, conditional compilation directives, declaration of constants and macros, file include directives, function prototypes, variable declarations, and the executable functions.

Conditional compilation

Information and source code for conditional compilation is located at lines 0049 through 0066. If you are using Turbo C++ or Borland C++, the program is ready to compile, subject to the instructions in appendix B. If you are using Zortech C++, change line 0065 to #define FG and change line 0066 to #define ZORTECH.

Constants

The C++ const keyword is used to declare and assign values to constant variables at lines 0068 through 0086.

Macros

A macro defined at line 0092 will be expanded by the C++ compiler at line 0236.

Include files

The code at lines 0094 through 0124 loads the appropriate header files and C++ class declaration files. Line 0123 loads LIB2D.HPP, which declares the data members and methods of class PhysicalDisplay and class Viewport. Line 0124 loads MOUSE.HPP, which declares the data members and methods of class PointingDevice.

Function prototypes

Function declarations are provided in lines 0126 through 0144. Functions declared here are visible throughout this source file. They can be called by any other function in the source file. Because each function is declared with the static qualifier, it is not available to functions located in other source files.

Variable declarations

Lines 0146 through 0206 declare global variables visible throughout this source file. These variables have file scope and can be modified by any function in the file.

Object declarations

Object Line 0203 creates an object from class PhysicalDisplay named Display. The program will later call the methods of this object to help it manage the display. The methods are declared in the class declaration listing LIB-2D.HPP and are defined in the class implementation listing LIB2D.CPP in appendix E. The object created at line 0203 is a static object. It has file scope and will remain available until the program terminates.

Line 0204 creates an object from the Viewport class named Viewport1. The address of Display is passed to this new object. Viewport1 uses the methods of Display to generate graphics output. The object created at line 0205 is a static object with file scope that will remain active until program termination.

Line 0205 creates an object from the PointingDevice class named Mouse. The methods of this object provide access to the functions of the memory-resident mouse driver. The pointer that is declared at line 0206 is used to read a table of data that describes the mouse state at runtime.

main( )

The main( ) function is located at lines 0211 through 0245. After first checking to see if any command line arguments were used to start the program, an appropriate graphics mode is set.

The mouse is initialized at lines 0238 through 0240. See chapter 3 for a discussion of mouse techniques.

The code at line 0242 calls a function to manage the interactive loop that forms the core of the program.

Terminating the program

The function at lines 0247 through 0255 calls method ShutDownGraphics( ) of class PhysicalDisplay to terminate the graphics state. Line 0254 returns an OK token.

The keyboard loop

The function at lines 0257 through 0285 interprets in-bound keystrokes and calls the appropriate core function. The switch( ) block at lines 0270 through 0280 does most of the work with F1, F2, and F3.

The mouse manager

The function at lines 0287 through 0335 is a typical mouse loop. Note how the for( ) statement is used to avoid inadvertent double-clicks of the mouse button. Also note the call to zStorePts( ) at line 0316, whereby the x and y coordinates are stored in an array of points that will be used for the tweening function.

Draw the first keyframe

The function at lines 0337 through 0352 provides high-level management of the first keyframe creation process. The code at line 0346 calls the mouse manager.

Draw the second keyframe

The function at lines 0354 through 0369 manages the drawing of the second keyframe. Tokens like Frame2Done and WhichFrame are reset.

Managing the database

The function at lines 0371 through 0414 stores the incoming x and y coordinates into one of two arrays. Line 0377 ensures that duplicate sets of coordinates are not mistakenly entered. The if( ) statements at line 0385 and 0397 determine whether the first or second keyframe is being built by the user.

The tweening function

The function at lines 0416 through 0528 generates the in-between images. Of particular importance is the code at lines 0424 through 0447. These blocks of code trap some runtime errors, as indicated by the // comments in the source code.

Lines 0466 through 0468 provide a good working example of how this function operates. Line 0466 adds half the difference between two keyframes to the first keyframe. Line 0467 adds one quarter the difference between two keyframes to the first keyframe. Finally, line 0468 adds three quarters of the difference between two keyframes to the first keyframe. If you needed to use curved interpolation instead of linear interpolation, this is the section of code where you would focus your efforts.

The Startup( ) function

The function at lines 0530 through 0613 calls the SetupMode( ) method of class PhysicalDisplay to detect the graphics hardware.

The StubRoutine( ) function

The stub routine at lines 0615 through 0624 is a do-nothing routine. It displays a simple message on the dialog line at the top of the display.

Blank the dialog line

The function at lines 0626 through 0637 calls the ClearTextLine( ) method of class Viewport to clear the dialog text line at the top of the display.

The Keyboard( ) function

The function at lines 0639 through 0667 detects and retrieves keystrokes from the keyboard buffer. The function at lines 0669 through 0678 keeps calling the zKeyboard( ) function until the keyboard buffer is empty. This routine purges unwanted keystrokes from the keyboard buffer after a lengthy graphics operation.

The MakeSound( ) function

The function at lines 0680 through 0716 generates a sound from the system speaker.

The Pause( ) function

The function at lines 0718 through 0736 causes the program to pause for a specified period of time. The code uses the value returned by the system clock and multiplies it by the number of CPU cycles per second. If you are using Turbo C++ or Borland C++, this value is the CLK_TCK global variable. If you are using Zortech C++ it is CLOCKS_PER_SEC. The pause function could have been used to avoid inadvertent double-clicks.

The Arguments( ) function

The function at lines 0738 through 0780 compares the command line argument with a set of recognized arguments.

Programmer's Guide to LIB2D.HPP

Code The complete source code for the declarations for class PhysicalDisplay and class Viewport is found in LIB2D.HPP in appendix E. The source from LIB2D.HPP must be #included at the beginning of any program that wishes to use the methods of class PhysicalDisplay or class Viewport. See the discussion in chapter 1 for further information about LIB2D.HPP.

Programmer's Guide to LIB2D.CPP

Code The source code in LIB2D.CPP, presented in appendix E, provides language bindings that produce low-level graphics. The routines in LIB2D.CPP call the appropriate runtime library functions in Turbo C++'s graphics.lib, Borland C++'s graphics.lib, Zortech C++'s fg.lib, or Microsoft's graph.lib.

LIB2D.CPP is the class implementation listing for class PhysicalDisplay and class Viewport. Class PhysicalDisplay manages the state of the display. Class Viewport is responsible for maintaining a viewport and producing low-level graphics. These two classes generate nearly all the low-level graphics required by the demonstration programs in the book. See the discussion in chapter 1 for further information about class PhysicalDisplay and class Viewport.

Programmer's Guide to MOUSE.HPP

Code The complete source code for the declarations for class PointingDevice is found in MOUSE.HPP in appendix E. MOUSE.HPP must be #included at the beginning of any program that uses the methods of class PointingDevice. See the discussion in chapter 3 for further information about MOUSE.HPP.

Programmer's Guide to MOUSE.CPP

Code The source code in MOUSE.CPP, presented in appendix E, provides low-level control over a mouse. MOUSE.CPP is the class implementation listing for class PointingDevice. See the discussion in chapter 3 for further information about mouse methods.

11-4 Sample program CEL.CPP. Supports VGA, EGA, MCGA, CGA, and Hercules adapters. This application demonstrates keyframe in-betweening techniques useful for building cel animation sequences.

```
0001  /*
0002
0003              Lee Adams' SUPERCHARGED C++ GRAPHICS
0004        Interactive demo:  using tweening to build animation cels
0005
0006    SOURCE FILE:  CEL.CPP
0007           TYPE:  C++ source file for a multimodule application.
0008        PURPOSE:  Demonstrates how to create inbetween images
0009                  from two keyframe images.
0010   PROGRAM LIST:  CEL.CPP, LIB2D.CPP and MOUSE.CPP.
0011      LANGUAGES:  Turbo C++, Borland C++, Zortech C++ and
0012                  all C++ compilers compatible with AT&T C++ 2.0
0013                  specification; and nominal compatibility with
0014                  Microsoft C++ (see the discussion in the book).
0015   MEMORY MODEL:  large.
0016   COMMAND-LINE:  you can specify a graphics mode by using the
0017                  command-line argument /Mnn as shown below:
0018                       /M12  640x480x16-color VGA
0019                       /M11  640x480x2-color VGA, MCGA
0020                       /M10  640x350x16-color VGA, EGA
0021                       /MOE  640x200x16-color VGA, EGA
0022                       /M06  640x200x2-color VGA, MCGA, EGA, CGA
0023                       /MHC  720x348x2-color Hercules
0024                  If no command-line argument is used, hardware
0025                  autodetect is used to select the best mode.
0026   OUTPUT:  You can use a mouse to draw two images which
0027     represent keyframes:  a before image and an after image.
0028     The software will then generate a series of in-between
0029     images (tweens) that provide a smooth transition from the
0030     before image to the after image.
0031   LICENSE:  As purchaser of the book in which this source code
0032     appears you are granted a royalty-free license to reproduce
0033     and distribute executable files generated using this code
0034     provided that you accept the conditions of the License
0035     Agreement and Limited Warranty described in the book.
0036   PUBLICATION: Contains material from Windcrest/McGraw-Hill
0037     book 3489, published by TAB BOOKS.
0038   U.S. GOVERNMENT RESTRICTED RIGHTS:  This software and its
0039     documentation is provided with restricted rights.  The use,
0040     duplication, or disclosure by the Government is subject to
0041     restrictions set forth in subdivision (b)(3)(ii) of The
0042     Rights in Technical Data and Computer Software clause at
0043     252.227-7013.  Contractor/manufacturer is Lee Adams, c/o
0044     TAB BOOKS, 13311 Monterey Ave., Blue Ridge Summit PA 17294.
0045   TRADEMARK:  Lee Adams is a trademark of Lee Adams.
0046
0047     Copyright 1991 Lee Adams.  All rights reserved worldwide.
0048
0049
0050                      CONDITIONAL COMPILATION
0051   To compile only those blocks of code that support the C++
0052   compiler and graphics library that you are using, you should
0053   #define the appropriate tokens on lines 0062 and 0063.
0054             GRAPHICS LIBRARY
0055       Borland's graphics.lib                  #define BGI
0056       Zortech's fg.lib or fgdebug.lib         #define FG
0057       Microsoft's graph.lib                   #define MS
0058               COMPILER
```

11-4 Continued.

```
0059          Borland Turbo C++ compiler          #define BORLAND
0060          Zortech C++ compiler                #define ZORTECH
0061          AT&T-compatible C++ compilers       #define MICROSOFT
0062     Be sure you define only one compiler and one graphics library.
0063
0064                                                                       */
0065     #define BGI    1 // indicates the graphics library you are using.
0066     #define BORLAND 1  // indicates the C++ compiler you are using.
0067     /*
0068
0069     ┌─────────────────────────────────────────────────────────────┐
         │                        Constants                              │
0070     └─────────────────────────────────────────────────────────────┘
0071                                                                       */
0072     const int zFAIL=        0;                      // boolean tokens...
0073     const int zEMPTY=       0;
0074     const int zYES=         1;
0075     const int zNO=          0;
0076     const int zVGA_12H=     1;                      // graphics mode tokens...
0077     const int zEGA_10H=     2;
0078     const int zEGA_EH=      3;
0079     const int zMCGA_11H=    4;
0080     const int zCGA_6H=      5;
0081     const int zHERC=        6;
0082     const int zNUMPOINTS= 100;   // max allowable number of user points.
0083     const int zALT_X=      45;               // command-key codes...
0084     const int zF1=         59;
0085     const int zF2=         60;
0086     const int zF3=         61;
0087     /*
0088
0089     ┌─────────────────────────────────────────────────────────────┐
         │                         Macros                                │
0090     └─────────────────────────────────────────────────────────────┘
0091                                                                       */
0092     #define Wait_for_any_key  while(KeyCode==0) zKeyboard(); KeyCode=0;
0093     /*
0094
0095     ┌─────────────────────────────────────────────────────────────┐
         │                      Include files                            │
0096     └─────────────────────────────────────────────────────────────┘
0097                                                                       */
0098     #if defined (BORLAND)
0099     #include <time.h>          // supports clock().
0100     #include <string.h>        // supports strncmp().
0101     #include <bios.h>          // supports bioskey().
0102     #include <process.h>       // supports exit().
0103     #include <iostream.h>      // supports cout.
0104     #include <dos.h>           // supports outportb(), inportb().
0105     #include <math.h>          // supports abs().
0106     #elif defined (ZORTECH)
0107     #include <time.h>          // supports clock().
0108     #include <string.h>        // supports strncmp().
0109     #include <bios.h>          // supports bioskey().
0110     #include <stdlib.h>        // supports exit() and abs().
0111     #include <stream.hpp>      // supports cout.
0112     #include <dos.h>           // supports outp(), inp().
0113     #elif defined (MICROSOFT)
0114     #include <time.h>          // supports clock().
0115     #include <string.h>        // supports strncmp().
0116     #include <bios.h>          // supports _bios_keybrd().
0117     #include <process.h>       // supports exit().
0118     #include <iostream.h>      // supports cout.
0119     #include <conio.h>         // supports outp(), inp().
0120     #include <math.h>          // supports abs().
```

```
0121    #endif
0122
0123    #include "LIB2D.HPP"        // declarations for PhysicalDisplay class.
0124    #include "MOUSE.HPP"        // declarations for PointingDevice class.
0125    /*
0126
0127    ┌─────────────────────────────────────────────────────────────┐
        │      Prototypes for functions visible throughout this file    │
0128    └─────────────────────────────────────────────────────────────┘
0129                                                                    */
0130    static void zStartup(void);            // initializes a graphics mode.
0131    static void zArguments(int, char far* far*);    // checks arguments.
0132    static void zKeyboard(void);               // checks for a keystroke.
0133    static void zQuit_Pgm(void);           // ends the program gracefully.
0134    static void zPurge(void);           // empties the keyboard buffer.
0135    static void zStubRoutine(void);                   // do-nothing stub.
0136    static void zMakeSound(int,double);      // makes a specific sound.
0137    static clock_t zDelay(clock_t,double);   // CPU-independent pause.
0138    static void zInputLoop(void);                     // user input loop.
0139    static void zMouseLoop(void);            // user control of mouse.
0140    static void zMakeFrame1(void);               // draw keyframe #1.
0141    static void zMakeFrame2(void);               // draw keyframe #2.
0142    static void zTweening(void);         // create in-between frames.
0143    static void zStorePts(void);         // store user-defined points.
0144    static void zBlankTextLine(void);        // blanks the dialog line.
0145    /*
0146
0147    ┌─────────────────────────────────────────────────────────────┐
        │      Declaration of variables visible throughout this file    │
0148    └─────────────────────────────────────────────────────────────┘
0149                                                                    */
0150    static char *StartUpArg[6]={        // legal command-line arguments.
0151          "/M12", "/M10", "/MOE", "/M11", "/M06", "/MHC" };
0152    static int CommandLineArg=zNO;       // indicates if argument exists.
0153    static int CommandLineCompare=0;     // indicates if argument legal.
0154    static int C0=0,C1=1,C2=2,C3=3,C4=4,C5=5,C6=6,
0155    C7=7,C8=8,C9=9,C10=10,C11=11,C12=12,C13=13,
0156    C14=14,C15=15;                       // palette index codes.
0157    static int Mode=0;            // which graphics mode is being used.
0158    static int Result=0;        // captures result of graphics routines.
0159    static int CharWidth=0,CharHeight=0;    // dimensions of character.
0160    static char KeyCode=0;    // token for normal or extended keystroke.
0161    static char KeyNum=0;                    // ASCII number of keystroke.
0162    static char SolidFill[]=
0163                    {255,255,255,255,255,255,255,255};    // 100% fill.
0164    static int TextClr=0;                    // color for regular text.
0165    static int PromptClr=7;                  // color for prompt text.
0166    static char Copyright[]=
0167            "Copyright 1991 Lee Adams.  All rights reserved.";
0168    static char Title[]=
0169    "USING C++ TO GENERATE INBETWEEN IMAGES FOR CEL ANIMATION";
0170    static char PressAnyKey[]= "Press any key to continue.";
0171    static char StubMessage[]= "The generic stub routine was called.";
0172    static int X_Res=0, Y_Res=0;                 // screen resolution.
0173    static int sx=320, sy=99;           // mouse drawing coordinates.
0174    static int Oldsx=319, Oldsy=98;     // duplication-avoidance coords.
0175    static int Frame1Done=zNO, Frame2Done=zNO;        // status tokens.
0176    static int WhichFrame=0;             // keyframe being analyzed.
0177    static int PtNum=0;                  // point being analyzed.
0178    static int TotalPts1=0, TotalPts2=0;         // num pts entered.
0179    static int KeyFrame1[zNUMPOINTS][2];     // arrays to store pts...
0180    static int KeyFrame2[zNUMPOINTS][2];
0181    static int Tween1[zNUMPOINTS][2];
0182    static int Tween2[zNUMPOINTS][2];
0183    static int Tween3[zNUMPOINTS][2];
```

```
0184  static char Text3[]=
0185              "<F3= generates tweens from keyframes>   <Alt+X= quit>";
0186  static char Text4[]=
0187              "<F1=Create Keyframe 1>   <F2=Create Keyframe 2>";
0188  static char Error1[]=
0189              "Keyframes have unequal number of points. Press a key.";
0190  static char Error2[]=     "No points in keyframe(s). Press a key.";
0191  static char Error3[]=     "Nonexistant keyframe(s). Press a key.";
0192  static char Error4[]=
0193              "Max allowable points already entered. Press a key.";
0194  static char Error5[]=
0195              "Press right mouse button to return to main menu.";
0196  static char Status[]=
0197              "In-between keyframes complete. Press a key.";
0198  static char Status1[]=
0199              "<Left= points for keyframe 1> <Right= done>";
0200  static char Status2[]=
0201              "<Left= points for keyframe 2> <Right= done>";
0202
0203  PhysicalDisplay Display;      // create the physical display object.
0204  Viewport Viewport1(&Display);          // create a viewport object.
0205  PointingDevice Mouse;          // create a pointing-device object.
0206  static mdata *MPtr;    // uninitialized ptr to mouse runtime data.
0207  /*
0208
0209  ┌────────────────────────────────────────────────────────────────┐
         │                    Function definitions                         │
0210     └────────────────────────────────────────────────────────────────┘
0211
0212  ┌────────────────────────────────────────────────────────────────┐
         │     The executive routine:  program execution begins here       │
0213     └────────────────────────────────────────────────────────────────┘
0214                                                                    */
0215  main(int argc, char *argv[])
0216  {
0217     int NumArgs; char far* far* Arg;
0218
0219  NumArgs= argc;                          // grab number of arguments.
0220  Arg= &argv[0];           // grab address of array of arguments.
0221  zArguments(NumArgs, Arg);      // check the command-line arguments.
0222
0223  zStartup();                         // establish the graphics mode.
0224  Display.Init2D(Mode,0,0,X_Res-1,Y_Res-1);   // set graphics state.
0225  Result= Display.InitUndo();    // create hidden page (unused here).
0226  if (Result==zFAIL) zQuit_Pgm();            // if hidden page failed.
0227
0228  Display.BlankPage();                          // clear the display.
0229  Display.SetHue(C7);                      // set the drawing color.
0230  Display.SetFill(SolidFill,C7);            // set the fill style.
0231  Viewport1.DrawPanel(0,15,X_Res-1,Y_Res-1);      // use white bg.
0232  Viewport1.PutText(4,2,TextClr,Title);          // sign-on notice.
0233  Viewport1.PutText(5,2,TextClr,Copyright);      // copyright notice.
0234  Viewport1.PutText(7,2,TextClr,Text3);          // start-stop keys.
0235  Viewport1.PutText(1,2,PromptClr,PressAnyKey);  // display a prompt.
0236  Wait_for_any_key     // this macro was defined earlier in line 0078.
0237
0238  Result= Mouse.Detect(Mode);                // initialize the mouse.
0239  if (Result== zFAIL) zQuit_Pgm();
0240  MPtr= Mouse.Data();         // grab a pointer to the mouse data.
0241
0242  zInputLoop();                        // interactive run-time loop.
0243
0244  zQuit_Pgm();            // tidy up and terminate the application.
0245  }
```

```
0246  /*
0247
0248  ┌─────────────────────────────────────────────────────────┐
      │                  Terminate the program                  │
0249  │                                                         │
0250  └─────────────────────────────────────────────────────────┘  */
0251  static void zQuit_Pgm(void)
0252  {
0253  Display.ShutDownGraphics();  // graceful shutdown of graphics mode.
0254  exit(0);                     // terminate the program and return OK code.
0255  }
0256  /*
0257
0258  ┌─────────────────────────────────────────────────────────┐
      │                   User keyboard loop                    │
0259  │                                                         │
0260  └─────────────────────────────────────────────────────────┘  */
0261  static void zInputLoop(void)
0262  {
0263  zBlankTextLine();
0264  Viewport1.PutText(1,2,PromptClr,Text4);
0265  EXECUTIVELOOP:                       // start of keyboard polling loop.
0266    zKeyboard();                               // poll the keyboard.
0267    if (KeyCode==0) goto EXECUTIVELOOP;        // if no keystroke.
0268    if (KeyCode!=2) goto NORMALKEY;   // jump if not an extended key.
0269  EXTENDEDKEY:
0270    switch (KeyNum)
0271      {                              // switcher for extended keys.
0272      case zALT_X:  zQuit_Pgm();                        // quit.
0273      case zF1: zMakeFrame1();             // create keyframe #1.
0274            zPurge(); break;
0275      case zF2: zMakeFrame2();             // create keyframe #2.
0276            zPurge(); break;
0277      case zF3: zTweening();          // generate in-between frames.
0278            zPurge(); break;
0279      default:  zMakeSound(450,.2); zPurge();
0280      }
0281  goto EXECUTIVELOOP;                      // ...and then loop back.
0282  NORMALKEY:                           // jump to here if a normal key.
0283    zMakeSound(400,.1); zPurge();
0284  goto EXECUTIVELOOP;                      // ...and then loop back.
0285  }
0286  /*
0287
0288  ┌─────────────────────────────────────────────────────────┐
      │                Interactive control of mouse             │
0289  │                                                         │
0290  └─────────────────────────────────────────────────────────┘  */
0291  static void zMouseLoop(void)
0292  {
0293    unsigned char Start= zYES;        // indicates start of a line.
0294  #if defined (ZORTECH)
0295    int Delay, Dummy= 0;
0296  #elif defined (MICROSOFT)
0297    int Delay, Dummy= 0;
0298  #endif
0299  Display.SetHue(C0);                 // set drawing color to index.
0300  Display.SetLine(0xffff);            // set line style to solid.
0301  Viewport1.SetPosition(sx,sy);  // set current position for drawing.
0302  Mouse.Show();                       // show the mouse cursor.
0303  MOUSE_LOOP:                         // interactive loop begins...
0304    Mouse.Info();                     // check the status of the mouse.
0305    if (MPtr->MouseButton==1)
0306      {                               // if left button...
0307      sx= MPtr->MouseX;               // grab new coordinates...
0308      sy= MPtr->MouseY;
```

```
0309      Mouse.Hide();                           // remove the cursor...
0310      if (Start==zNO) Viewport1.DrawLine(sx,sy);  // and draw a line.
0311      else                       // otherwise, set a start-point...
0312        {
0313        Start= zNO;
0314        Viewport1.SetPosition(sx,sy);
0315        }
0316      zStorePts();                  // store coords in keyframe array.
0317 #if defined (BORLAND)
0318      delay(1000);       // pause to avoid inadvertent double-clicks.
0319 #elif defined (ZORTECH)
0320      for (Delay=1; Delay<30000; Delay++) Dummy++;
0321      Dummy= 0;
0322      for (Delay=1; Delay<30000; Delay++) Dummy++;
0323 #elif defined (MICROSOFT)
0324      for (Delay=1; Delay<30000; Delay++) Dummy++;
0325      Dummy= 0;
0326      for (Delay=1; Delay<30000; Delay++) Dummy++;
0327 #endif
0328      Mouse.Show();                        // restore the mouse cursor.
0329      }
0330    if (MPtr->MouseButton==2)
0331      {                              // else if right button...
0332      Mouse.Hide(); return;         // ...remove cursor and return.
0333      }
0334 goto MOUSE_LOOP;                          // otherwise loop back.
0335 }
0336 /*
0337
0338 ┌────────────────────────────────────────────────────────────┐
     │                  Draw the first keyframe                     │
0339 └────────────────────────────────────────────────────────────┘
0340                                                              */
0341 static void zMakeFrame1(void)
0342 {
0343 TotalPts1= 0; WhichFrame= 1;
0344 zBlankTextLine();
0345 Viewport1.PutText(1,2,PromptClr,Status1);
0346 zMouseLoop();
0347 Frame1Done= zYES;
0348 WhichFrame= 0;
0349 zBlankTextLine();
0350 Viewport1.PutText(1,2,PromptClr,Text4);
0351 return;
0352 }
0353 /*
0354
0355 ┌────────────────────────────────────────────────────────────┐
     │                  Draw the second keyframe                    │
0356 └────────────────────────────────────────────────────────────┘
0357                                                              */
0358 static void zMakeFrame2(void)
0359 {
0360 TotalPts2= 0; WhichFrame= 2;
0361 zBlankTextLine();
0362 Viewport1.PutText(1,2,PromptClr,Status2);
0363 zMouseLoop();
0364 Frame2Done= zYES;
0365 WhichFrame= 0;
0366 zBlankTextLine();
0367 Viewport1.PutText(1,2,PromptClr,Text4);
0368 return;
0369 }
0370 /*
```

```
0371
0372   ┌──────────────────────────────────────────────────────────────┐
       │                 Store the user-defined points                │
0373   └──────────────────────────────────────────────────────────────┘
0374                                                                 */
0375   static void zStorePts(void)
0376   {
0377   if ((sx==Oldsx)&&(sy==Oldsy))
0378     {                                     // if mouse has not moved...
0379     zMakeSound(450,.2); return;                       // do nothing.
0380     }
0381   else
0382     {                                         // ...otherwise...
0383     Oldsx= sx; Oldsy= sy;         // update the redundance-avoiders.
0384     }
0385   if (WhichFrame==1)
0386     {                                     // if building keyframe 1...
0387     if (TotalPts1>zNUMPOINTS-1)
0388       {                            // if exceeded max pts allowed...
0389       zBlankTextLine();
0390       Viewport1.PutText(1,2,PromptClr,Error4);
0391       zMakeSound(450,.2); goto MAX_LOOP;
0392       }
0393     KeyFrame1[TotalPts1][0]= sx;
0394     KeyFrame1[TotalPts1][1]= sy;
0395     TotalPts1++; return;
0396     }
0397   if (WhichFrame==2)
0398     {                                     // if building keyframe 2...
0399     if (TotalPts2>zNUMPOINTS-1)
0400       {                            // if exceeded max pts allowed...
0401       zBlankTextLine();
0402       Viewport1.PutText(1,2,PromptClr,Error4);
0403       zMakeSound(450,.2); goto MAX_LOOP;
0404       }
0405     KeyFrame2[TotalPts2][0]= sx;
0406     KeyFrame2[TotalPts2][1]= sy;
0407     TotalPts2++; return;
0408     }
0409   MAX_LOOP:  KeyCode= 0;
0410   Wait_for_any_key
0411   zBlankTextLine();
0412   Viewport1.PutText(1,2,PromptClr,Error5);
0413   return;
0414   }
0415   /*
0416
0417   ┌──────────────────────────────────────────────────────────────┐
       │                 Create the inbetween frames                  │
0418   └──────────────────────────────────────────────────────────────┘
0419                                                                 */
0420   static void zTweening(void)
0421   {
0422     int xKF1,yKF1,xKF2,yKF2,xDiff,yDiff;         // local variables.
0423     int Ct=0;                                    // loop counter.
0424   if ((Frame1Done==zNO)||(Frame2Done==zNO))
0425     {                                         // if no keyframes...
0426     zBlankTextLine();
0427     Viewport1.PutText(1,2,PromptClr,Error3);
0428     zMakeSound(450,.2); KeyCode= 0;
0429     Wait_for_any_key
0430     goto ERROR_LOOP;
0431     }
0432   if ((TotalPts1==0)||(TotalPts2==0))
0433     {                                         // if no points...
```

```
0434    zBlankTextLine();
0435    Viewport1.PutText(1,2,PromptClr,Error2);
0436    zMakeSound(450,.2); KeyCode= 0;
0437    Wait_for_any_key
0438    goto ERROR_LOOP;
0439    }
0440 if (TotalPts1!=TotalPts2)
0441    {                        // if keyframes sizes do not match...
0442    zBlankTextLine();
0443    Viewport1.PutText(1,2,PromptClr,Error1);
0444    zMakeSound(450,.2); KeyCode= 0;
0445    Wait_for_any_key
0446    goto ERROR_LOOP;
0447    }
0448 goto POINTS_OK;               // jump past error-handler if all OK.
0449
0450 ERROR_LOOP:
0451 zBlankTextLine();
0452 Viewport1.PutText(1,2,PromptClr,Text4);
0453 return;
0454
0455 POINTS_OK:
0456 for (Ct=0; Ct<TotalPts1; Ct++)
0457    {                        // for each user-defined point...
0458    xKF1= KeyFrame1[Ct][0];        // retrieve the coordinates...
0459    yKF1= KeyFrame1[Ct][1];
0460    xKF2= KeyFrame2[Ct][0];
0461    yKF2= KeyFrame2[Ct][1];
0462    xDiff= abs(xKF1-xKF2);   // calculate the absolute differences...
0463    yDiff= abs(yKF1-yKF2);
0464    if(xKF1<xKF2)
0465      {                      // calculate the in-between x-coords.
0466      Tween2[Ct][0]= xKF1+(xDiff/2);
0467      Tween1[Ct][0]= xKF1+(xDiff/4);
0468      Tween3[Ct][0]= xKF1+(xDiff*3/4);
0469      }
0470    else if (xKF1>xKF2)
0471      {
0472      Tween2[Ct][0]= xKF1-(xDiff/2);
0473      Tween1[Ct][0]= xKF1-(xDiff/4);
0474      Tween3[Ct][0]= xKF1-(xDiff*3/4);
0475      }
0476    else
0477      {
0478      Tween2[Ct][0]= xKF1;
0479      Tween1[Ct][0]= xKF1;
0480      Tween3[Ct][0]= xKF1;
0481      }
0482    if (yKF1<yKF2)
0483      {                      // calculate the in-between y-coords.
0484      Tween2[Ct][1]= yKF1+(yDiff/2);
0485      Tween1[Ct][1]= yKF1+(yDiff/4);
0486      Tween3[Ct][1]= yKF1+(yDiff*3/4);
0487      }
0488    else if (yKF1>yKF2)
0489      {
0490      Tween2[Ct][1]= yKF1-(yDiff/2);
0491      Tween1[Ct][1]= yKF1-(yDiff/4);
0492      Tween3[Ct][1]= yKF1-(yDiff*3/4);
0493      }
0494    else
0495      {
```

```
0496        Tween2[Ct][1]= yKF1;
0497        Tween1[Ct][1]= yKF1;
0498        Tween3[Ct][1]= yKF1;
0499        }
0500    }                                       // end of for...loop.
0501  Display.SetHue(C1);
0502  Viewport1.SetPosition(Tween1[0][0],Tween1[0][1]);
0503  for (Ct=1;Ct<TotalPts1;Ct++)
0504    {                                       // draw first in-between frame.
0505    Viewport1.DrawLine(Tween1[Ct][0],Tween1[Ct][1]);
0506    }
0507  Display.SetHue(C2);
0508  Viewport1.SetPosition(Tween2[0][0],Tween2[0][1]);
0509  for (Ct=1;Ct<TotalPts1;Ct++)
0510    {                                       // draw next in-between frame.
0511    Viewport1.DrawLine(Tween2[Ct][0],Tween2[Ct][1]);
0512    }
0513  Display.SetHue(C4);
0514  Viewport1.SetPosition(Tween3[0][0],Tween3[0][1]);
0515  for (Ct=1;Ct<TotalPts1;Ct++)
0516    {                                       // draw next in-between frame.
0517    Viewport1.DrawLine(Tween3[Ct][0],Tween3[Ct][1]);
0518    }
0519  Display.SetHue(C0);
0520
0521  zBlankTextLine();
0522  Viewport1.PutText(1,2,PromptClr,Status);
0523  KeyCode= 0;
0524  Wait_for_any_key
0525  zBlankTextLine();
0526  Viewport1.PutText(1,2,PromptClr,Text4);
0527  return;
0528  }
0529  /*
0530
0531  ┌────────────────────────────────────────────────────────┐
0531          Detect the graphics hardware and set the
0532      highest mode permitted by the graphics adapter and monitor.
0533      The user can override the autodetect algorithm by providing
0534      an argument on the command-line when the program is started.
0535  └────────────────────────────────────────────────────────┘
0536                                                            */
0537  static void zStartup(void)
0538  {
0539    int DefaultMode;
0540  DefaultMode= Display.SetupMode();   // get results of autodetect...
0541  switch(DefaultMode)                 // ...and jump to appropriate code.
0542    {
0543    case zFAIL:         goto ABORT_PGM;
0544    case zVGA_12H:      goto VGA_mode;
0545    case zEGA_10H:      goto EGA_ECD_mode;
0546    case zEGA_EH:       goto EGA_SCD_mode;
0547    case zMCGA_11H:     goto MCGA_mode;
0548    case zCGA_6H:       goto CGA_mode;
0549    case zHERC:         goto Hercules_mode;
0550    default:            goto ABORT_PGM;
0551    }
0552  VGA_mode:                 // VGA 640x480x16-color, 80x60 character mode.
0553  if(CommandLineArg==zYES)
0554    {                                         // if user has requested a mode.
0555    if((Mode>zVGA_12H)&&(Mode<zHERC)) goto FORCE_USER_MODE;
0556    }
0557  X_Res=640; Y_Res=480; Mode=zVGA_12H; CharWidth=8; CharHeight=8;
0558  return;
```

```
0559   EGA_ECD_mode:           // EGA 640x350x16-color, 80x43 character mode.
0560   if(CommandLineArg==zYES)
0561     {
0562     if((Mode==zEGA_EH)||(Mode==zCGA_6H))   // permit only EGA or CGA.
0563     goto FORCE_USER_MODE;
0564     }
0565   X_Res=640; Y_Res=350; Mode=zEGA_10H; CharWidth=8; CharHeight=8;
0566   return;
0567   EGA_SCD_mode:           // EGA 640x200x16-color, 80x25 char mode.
0568   if(CommandLineArg==zYES)
0569     {
0570     if(Mode==zCGA_6H) goto FORCE_USER_MODE;     // only CGA permitted.
0571     }
0572   X_Res=640; Y_Res=200; Mode=zEGA_EH; CharWidth=8; CharHeight=8;
0573   return;
0574   MCGA_mode:              // MCGA 640x480x2-color, 80x60 char mode.
0575   if(CommandLineArg==zYES)
0576     {
0577     if(Mode==zCGA_6H) goto FORCE_USER_MODE;     // only CGA permitted.
0578     }
0579   X_Res=640; Y_Res=480; Mode=zMCGA_11H;
0580   C0=0; C1=0; C2=0; C3=1; C4=0; C5=1; C6=1; C7=1;
0581   C8=1; C9=1; C10=1; C11=1; C12=1; C13=1; C14=1; C15=1;
0582   CharWidth=8; CharHeight=8;
0583   return;
0584   CGA_mode:                   // CGA 640x200x2-color, 80x25 char mode.
0585   X_Res=640; Y_Res=200; Mode=zCGA_6H;
0586   C0=0; C1=0; C2=0; C3=1; C4=0; C5=1; C6=1; C7=1;
0587   C8=1; C9=1; C10=1; C11=1; C12=1; C13=1; C14=1; C15=1;
0588   CharWidth=8; CharHeight=8;
0589   return;
0590   Hercules_mode:          // Hercules 720x348x2-color, 80x25 char mode.
0591   X_Res=720; Y_Res=348; Mode=zHERC;
0592   C0=0; C1=0; C2=0; C3=1; C4=0; C5=1; C6=1; C7=1;
0593   C8=1; C9=1; C10=1; C11=1; C12=1; C13=1; C14=1; C15=1;
0594   CharWidth=9; CharHeight=14;
0595   return;
0596
0597   FORCE_USER_MODE:    // jump to here if command-line argument legal.
0598   CommandLineArg= zNO; // first, reset token to avoid returning here.
0599   Display.ForceMode(Mode);       // ...then reset the graphics mode.
0600   switch(Mode)                // ...then jump back to appropriate code.
0601     {
0602     case zEGA_10H:      goto EGA_ECD_mode;
0603     case zEGA_EH:       goto EGA_SCD_mode;
0604     case zMCGA_11H:     goto MCGA_mode;
0605     case zCGA_6H:       goto CGA_mode;
0606     default:            goto ABORT_PGM;
0607     }
0608
0609   ABORT_PGM:       // jump to here if no graphics hardware detected.
0610   cout << "\n\n\rThis C++ graphics programming demo requires a";
0611   cout << "\n\rVGA, EGA, CGA, MCGA, or HGA graphics adapter.\n\r";
0612   exit(-1);                    // terminate, returning an error code.
0613   }
0614   /*
0615
0616   ┌──────────────────────────────────────────────────────────────┐
         │                     Stub routine                               │
0617   └──────────────────────────────────────────────────────────────┘
0618                                                                   */
0619   static void zStubRoutine(void)
0620   {
```

```
0621  zBlankTextLine();
0622  Viewport1.PutText(1,2,TextClr,StubMessage);
0623  return;
0624  }
0625  /*
0626
0627  ┌─────────────────────────────────────────────────────────────────┐
      │              Blank the dialog text line                         │
0628  └─────────────────────────────────────────────────────────────────┘
0629                                                                     */
0630  static void zBlankTextLine(void)
0631  {
0632  Display.SetHue(C0);
0633  Display.SetLine(0xffff);
0634  Display.SetFill(SolidFill,C0);
0635  Viewport1.ClearTextLine();
0636  return;
0637  }
0638  /*
0639
0640  ┌─────────────────────────────────────────────────────────────────┐
      │           Check the keyboard for a keystroke                    │
0641  └─────────────────────────────────────────────────────────────────┘
0642                                                                     */
0643  static void zKeyboard(void)
0644  {
0645    union AnyName{int RawCode;char Code[3];}Keystroke;
0646    char TempKey=0;
0647  #if defined (BORLAND)
0648    if (bioskey(1)==zEMPTY) { KeyCode=0; return; }
0649    Keystroke.RawCode= bioskey(0);
0650  #elif defined (ZORTECH)
0651    if (bioskey(1)==zEMPTY) { KeyCode=0; return; }
0652    Keystroke.RawCode= bioskey(0);
0653  #elif defined (MICROSOFT)
0654    if (_bios_keybrd(_KEYBRD_READY)==zEMPTY)
0655      { KeyCode=0; return; }
0656    Keystroke.RawCode= _bios_keybrd(_KEYBRD_READ);
0657  #endif
0658  TempKey= Keystroke.Code[0];
0659  if (TempKey!=0)
0660    {                                      // if a normal keystroke...
0661    KeyCode=1; KeyNum=TempKey; return;
0662    }
0663  if (TempKey==0)
0664    {                                      // if an extended keystroke...
0665    KeyCode=2; KeyNum=Keystroke.Code[1]; return;
0666    }
0667  }
0668  /*
0669
0670  ┌─────────────────────────────────────────────────────────────────┐
      │              Empty the keystroke buffer                         │
0671  └─────────────────────────────────────────────────────────────────┘
0672                                                                     */
0673  static void zPurge(void)
0674  {
0675  do zKeyboard();
0676    while (KeyCode!=0);
0677  return;
0678  }
0679  /*
0680
0681  ┌─────────────────────────────────────────────────────────────────┐
      │                    Make a sound                                 │
0682  └─────────────────────────────────────────────────────────────────┘
0683                                                                     */
```

```
0684  static void zMakeSound(int Hertz,double Duration)
0685  {
0686     static clock_t FormerTime=0;
0687     short Count=0;
0688     int HighByte=0, LowByte=0;
0689     unsigned char OldPort=0, NewPort=0;
0690  FormerTime= clock();
0691  if (Hertz < 40) return;
0692  if (Hertz > 4660) return;
0693  Count= 1193180L/Hertz;
0694  HighByte= Count / 256;
0695  LowByte= Count - (HighByte * 256);
0696  #if defined (BORLAND)
0697     outportb(0x43,0xB6); outportb(0x42,(unsigned char)LowByte);
0698     outportb(0x42,(unsigned char)HighByte); OldPort=inportb(0x61);
0699     NewPort=(OldPort | 0x03); outportb(0x61,NewPort);
0700     zDelay(FormerTime,Duration);
0701     outportb(0x61,OldPort);
0702  #elif defined (ZORTECH)
0703     outp(0x43,0xB6); outp(0x42,LowByte);
0704     outp(0x42,HighByte); OldPort=(unsigned char)inp(0x61);
0705     NewPort=(OldPort | 0x03); outp(0x61,(int)NewPort);
0706     zDelay(FormerTime,Duration);
0707     outp(0x61,(int)OldPort);
0708  #elif defined (MICROSOFT)
0709     outp(0x43,0xB6); outp(0x42,LowByte);
0710     outp(0x42,HighByte); OldPort=(unsigned char)inp(0x61);
0711     NewPort=(OldPort | 0x03); outp(0x61,(int)NewPort);
0712     zDelay(FormerTime,Duration);
0713     outp(0x61,(int)OldPort);
0714  #endif
0715  return;
0716  }
0717  /*
0718
0719  ┌────────────────────────────────────────────────────────────┐
       │                          Pause                             │
0720  └────────────────────────────────────────────────────────────┘
0721                                                              */
0722  static clock_t zDelay(clock_t StartTime, double Wait)
0723  {                         // pause for a specified length of time.
0724     clock_t StopTime;
0725     clock_t NewClockTime;
0726  #if defined (BORLAND)
0727     StopTime= StartTime + (Wait * CLK_TCK);
0728  #elif defined (ZORTECH)
0729     StopTime= StartTime + (Wait * CLOCKS_PER_SEC);
0730  #elif defined (MICROSOFT)
0731     StopTime= StartTime + (Wait * CLK_TCK);
0732  #endif
0733  while ( clock() < StopTime ) {;}
0734  NewClockTime= clock();
0735  return NewClockTime;
0736  }
0737  /*
0738
0739  ┌────────────────────────────────────────────────────────────┐
       │         Retrieve the command-line arguments, if any        │
0740  └────────────────────────────────────────────────────────────┘
0741                                                              */
0742  static void zArguments(int NumArgs, char *Arg[])
0743  {
0744  if(NumArgs==1)
0745     {
```

```
0746      CommandLineArg= zNO; return;                              // if no arg.
0747    }
0748  CommandLineCompare= strncmp(StartUpArg[0],Arg[1],5);
0749  if(CommandLineCompare==0)
0750    {
0751      CommandLineArg=zYES; Mode=zVGA_12H; return;                // /M12.
0752    }
0753  CommandLineCompare= strncmp(StartUpArg[1],Arg[1],5);
0754  if(CommandLineCompare==0)
0755    {
0756      CommandLineArg=zYES; Mode=zEGA_10H; return;                // /M10.
0757    }
0758  CommandLineCompare= strncmp(StartUpArg[2],Arg[1],5);
0759  if(CommandLineCompare==0)
0760    {
0761      CommandLineArg=zYES; Mode=zEGA_EH; return;                 // /MOE.
0762    }
0763  CommandLineCompare= strncmp(StartUpArg[3],Arg[1],5);
0764  if(CommandLineCompare==0)
0765    {
0766      CommandLineArg=zYES; Mode=zMCGA_11H; return;               // /M11.
0767    }
0768  CommandLineCompare= strncmp(StartUpArg[4],Arg[1],5);
0769  if(CommandLineCompare==0)
0770    {
0771      CommandLineArg=zYES; Mode=zCGA_6H; return;                 // /M06.
0772    }
0773  CommandLineCompare= strncmp(StartUpArg[5],Arg[1],5);
0774  if(CommandLineCompare==0)
0775    {
0776      CommandLineArg=zYES; Mode=zHERC; return;                   // /MHC.
0777    }
0778  CommandLineArg= zNO;                      // if an unrecognized argument.
0779  return;
0780  }
0781  /*

0782
0783  ┌─────────────────────────────────────────────────────────────────┐
      │    Supercharged C++ Graphics  --   end of source file CEL.CPP    │
      └─────────────────────────────────────────────────────────────────┘
0784
0785                                                                    */
```

12

Kinetic animation

Procedural animation uses a plan of motion provided by the programmer to animate moving objects. Kinetic animation uses the laws of physics.

This chapter provides a demonstration program that shows how to implement kinetic animation on your personal computer using simplified laws of physics. The source code presented in this chapter can be used to build applications using the formulas, reactions, and forces relevant to your field of work.

Using geometry to study motion

Using geometry to study motion is called *kinematics*. Computer programmers use kinetics to mean the same thing. The study of motion in general is called *dynamics*. Computer animators attempting to simulate natural motion use the term *forward dynamics*. Dynamics refers to the movement involved in the process. Forward refers to the calculation of what is going to happen next. Any study of natural motion that adheres to the laws of physics is founded upon Newton's so-called three laws of motion.

Newton's three laws of motion

The first law   A body at rest will continue to remain at rest until some outside force acts upon it. A body that is moving at uniform velocity will continue to move at uniform velocity until some outside force acts upon it.

The second law   When a force is applied to a body, the body accelerates in the direction the force is acting. The body accelerates at a proportional rate to the size of the force.

The third law   For every force there is an equal and opposite reacting force.

By taking these three principles into account—along with considerations like gravity, friction, mass, momentum, velocity, conservation of energy, work, inertia, and torque—you can accurately model the real world.

Dynamics

The study of motion requires an understanding of the principles that affect things in our everyday lives. Force is a push or pull which produces a change of motion. Mass is a measure of inertia or resistance to change of motion. Velocity is the rate of change of position of an object. Acceleration is the rate of change of velocity. Momentum is the product of mass and velocity.

Forward dynamics

The field of forward dynamics, or kinetic animation, makes heavy use of the principle of constraints, especially geometric constraints and force constraints.

Geometric constraints

Geometric constraints are things like the plasticity or rigidity of the object, the shape of the object, the mass and position of the wall with which the object is about to collide, and other constraints. (See FIG. 12-1.)

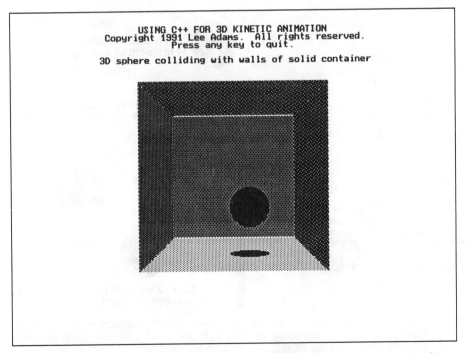

12-1 Graphics output from the sample program HIT.CPP. A shadow is thrown on the floor as the 3-D sphere ricochets off the six walls of the container.

Force constraints

Force constraints are things like inertia, torque, field force, kinetic force, and velocity. Force constraints produce effects like acceleration or deceleration. Force constraints are resisted by an object's inertia or mass. By manipulating these constraints in a 3-D scene, your C++ software can simulate the actions of real objects in the real world.

The fourth dimension of time

A physicist defines time as a measure of duration. The passage of time, and change, often means motion. The display of motion on personal computers is called *computer animation*. Time adds a fourth dimension to the three dimensions of width, depth, and height. Just as length is a measure of distance between two points, time is a measure of duration between two moments.

Collision detection

An important part of kinetic animation is collision detection. See FIG. 12-2. You can use different algorithms to test if one object has collided with another. These methods include the radius method, the bounding box method, and the standard equation for a plane.

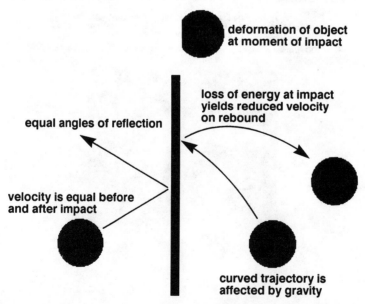

12-2   Left: the paradigm used by the demonstration program assumes zero-gravity and the absence of model deformation at impact. Right: a more realistic paradigm would adhere to the laws of physics.

The radius method of collision detection

Here's How... You can easily detect collisions between spheres. The surface of the sphere is always a fixed distance from its center. This distance is the radius. If the distance between an object and a sphere is less than the radius of the sphere, then a collision has occurred. If the distance between the centers of two spheres is less than twice the radii of the spheres, a collision has occurred.

The bounding box method of collision detection

Here's How... If the object is non-spherical you can use the bounding box method to detect collisions. By constructing a 3-D bounding box around each object in the scene, you can reduce the number of calculations you must make to detect collisions. By building a 2-D bounding box around each object's image on the display screen, you can quickly detect if a potential for collision exists. If the bounding boxes interfere with each other, you can then check the various vertices of each object to see if one object has collided with another.

Standard equation for a plane

Here's How... The standard equation for a plane uses vector math to determine on which side of a plane a particular point is located. If the point is the camera position, then the plane equation will determine if the plane being considered is hidden from view or not. If you consider the relationship between a point on the surface of one object with a facet on the surface of another object, you can use the standard equation for a plane to determine whether that point is on the outside of the facet or the inside. If the point is inside the object, then a collision has occurred.

Different types of collisions

Collisions can occur between *dynamic* objects—two moving objects. The resulting vector for each object is a function of each object's mass, linear velocity, angular velocity (spin), and point of impact. These are not trivial calculations.

A collision between a moving object and a nondynamic object, like a fixed wall, is much easier to control. The demonstration program presented later in this chapter uses simple rebounds and ricochets, ignoring the effect of friction and deformation. In the real world, a collision often involves destruction of matter, converting it into heat through friction and crushing of both objects.

Collision response involves a careful consideration of the rigidity or plasticity of the involved objects. It might also involve such concepts as morphing, where one object is transformed into a new shape as a result of the collision, or where two objects are fused together into a new mass.

A sample program: HIT.CPP

Demo Figure 12-1 depicts a typical display produced by the sample program HIT.CPP, whose complete source code is provided in FIG. 12-3 at the end of the chapter. The program provides an animated simulation of a 3-D sphere bouncing off the walls of a 3-D container.

How to compile and link the sample program

Here's How... The program listing presented in FIG. 12-3 contains the complete source code for the main module of the C++ demonstration program called "Using C++ for 3-D Kinetic Animation." If you are using the companion disks to the book, the source code is in the file named HIT.CPP. Four C++ source files are needed to build the finished .exe file. These are HIT.CPP from FIG. 12-3 and three class libraries in appendix E.

Class The class library that provides the language bindings and low-level graphics routines for this demonstration program is found in FIG. E-2 in appendix E. This listing contains the implementations for class PhysicalDisplay and class Viewport. If you are using the companion disks to the book, this file is named LIB2D.CPP. The class declarations are presented in FIG. E-1 in appendix E. If you are using the companion disks to the book, this file is named LIB2D.HPP.

Class The class library that provides the 3-D routines for this demonstration program is found in FIG. E-14 in appendix E. This listing contains the implementations for class Kinetic3D. If you are using the companion disks to the book, this file is named KINETIC.CPP. The class declarations are presented in FIG. E-13 in appendix E. If you are using the companion disks to the book, this file is named KINETIC.HPP.

You can compile, link, and run this demonstration program using either Turbo C++ or Borland C++. If you are using Turbo C++, see appendix A. If you are using Borland C++, see appendix B.

You must create a Turbo C++ or Borland C++ project list to advise your compiler which source files to bind together to build the finished .exe file.

After a successful compile and link, the screen should resemble the screen print shown in FIG. 12-1.

How to run the demonstration program

You need a VGA or EGA graphics adapter to run this animated demo.

Using the editor to run the program

Here's How... To run the program under the control of your Turbo C++ or Borland C++ editor make sure that the finished .exe file is in the default directory. The appropriate graphics driver must also be in the default directory. If you are using a VGA or EGA, the EGAVGA.BGI file must be present.

The built-in autodetect routine will detect the graphics hardware in your computer system and will set up the best graphics mode supported by your computer hardware. To override the autodetect, routine use the Turbo C++ or Borland C++ editor to simulate a command line argument. The header in FIG. 12-3 provides a set of arguments you can use. See the appendices for guidance applicable to your particular compiler. You can override the autodetect routine and force the demonstration program to run in 640×200×16-color mode instead of the 640×350×16-color mode.

Running the program from the operating system prompt

To start the program from the operating system prompt, simply enter HIT. The .exe file and any required graphics drivers must be present in the default directory. If the software finds a VGA present in your system, the program will animate using the 640×350×16-color mode. If an EGA and enhanced monitor are found, the 640×350×16-color mode is used. If an EGA and standard display are present, the program sets up the 640×200×16-color mode.

You can force the program into a different mode by using a command line argument when you start the program from the operating system prompt. Entering HIT /MOE forces the program to run in the 640×200×16-color mode.

Using the demonstration program

The program uses a combination of real-time hidden page animation and bitblt animation to simulate a 3-D sphere rebounding from the walls of a 3-D container. The wall of the container nearest you is transparent. As the sphere gets nearer, it gets larger. The shadow of the sphere appears at the correct location on the bottom of the container and acts as a visual cue during the animation display.

Press any key to stop the program.

Programmer's Guide to HIT.CPP

The complete listing for the demonstration program HIT.CPP is presented in FIG. 12-3. The source code consists of an informative header, conditional compilation directives, declaration of constants and macros, file include directives, function prototypes, variable declarations, and the executable functions.

Conditional compilation

Information and source code for conditional compilation is located at lines 0043 through 0058. If you are using Turbo C++ or Borland C++, the program is ready to compile, subject to the instructions in appendix B.

Constants

The C++ const keyword is used to declare and assign values to constant variables at lines 0060 through 0088.

Include files

The code at lines 0096 through 0120 loads the appropriate header files and C++ class declaration files. Line 0118 loads LIB2D.HPP, which declares the data members and methods of class PhysicalDisplay and class Viewport. Line 0120 loads KINETIC.HPP, which declares the data members and methods of class Kinetic3D.

Function prototypes

Function declarations are provided in lines 0122 through 0138. Functions declared here are visible throughout this source file. They can be called by any other function in the source file. Because each function is declared with the static qualifier, it is not available to functions located in other source files.

Variable declarations

Lines 0140 through 0189 declare global variables visible throughout this source file. These variables have file scope and can be modified by any function in the file.

Object declarations

Object Line 0187 creates an object from class PhysicalDisplay named Display. The program will later call the methods of this object to help it manage the display. The methods are declared in the class declaration listing LIB-2D.HPP and are defined in the class implementation listing LIB2D.CPP in appendix E. The object created at line 0187 is a static object. It has file scope and will remain available until the program terminates.

Line 0188 creates an object from the Viewport class named Viewport1. The address of Display is passed to this new object. Viewport1 uses the methods of Display to generate graphics output. The object created at line 0188 is a static object with file scope that will remain active until program termination.

Line 0189 creates an object from the Kinetic3D class named Sphere. The methods of this class provide 3-D routines that assist the program in moving the sphere and detecting collisions with the boundaries of the container.

main( )

The main( ) function is located at lines 0194 through 0251. After first checking to see if any command line arguments were used to start the program, an appropriate graphics mode is set. The code at lines 0230 through 0246 prepares the environment for the kinetic animation. The 3-D container is drawn, and the image is saved to a hidden page. Some pointers are initialized. The graphics driver is reset to write to the hidden page. The starting position of the sphere in 3-D space is defined. Finally, the code at line 0248 calls the function that manages the animation.

Drawing the sphere

The function at lines 0253 through 0281 draws the sphere on the hidden graphics page during the animation sequence. Line 0259 calls a method of class Viewport to erase the previous sphere by writing the background image back to the screen. The code at line 0260 calls another function to draw the shadow. The block of code at lines 0261 through 0278 calculates the size and location of the new sphere, saves the background, and draws the new sphere. Line 0279 then calls a method of class PhysicalDisplay to copy the contents of the hidden page to the display page.

Drawing the shadow

The function at lines 0283 through 0317 draws the shadow of the sphere on the bottom of the 3-D container. Line 0303 saves the background before the shadow is drawn, in order that the next time zDrawShadow( ) is called line 0289 can restore the background.

Controlling the movement

The function at lines 0319 through 0335 manages the kinetics. The code at lines 0327 through 0329 adjusts the position of the sphere on each pass through the animation loop. Line 0330 calls a function to determine if the sphere has collided with the container. Line 0331 calls a function to draw the sphere at the new position in the 3-D environment. Lines 0332 and 0333 check for incoming keystrokes which would terminate the animation.

Detecting a collision

The function at lines 0337 through 0371 determines if the sphere has collided with the container. Note line 0344, for example, where the sphere's radius of 10 is subtracted from the position of the right wall of the container in order to determine the point at which a collision would occur.

Drawing the container

The function at lines 0373 through 0403 draws the 3-D container. The location of a wall is set by calling method SetLaminaPosition( ) of class Kinetic3D. The orientation of a wall is determined by a call to method SetLaminaAngle( ) of class Kinetic3D. The shading color is controlled by a call to method Set-ShadingColor( ) of class Kinetic3D.

Managing the bitblts

The function at lines 0405 through 0448 manages the graphic arrays used by the demonstration program. The block of code that begins at line 0411 creates and stores the sphere array. The extreme 2-D dimensions of the sphere are calculated and an appropriately sized rectangle is saved in order to be able to restore the background during the animation sequence. The block of code beginning at line 0429 sets up and stores the shadow array.

Terminating the program

The function at lines 0450 through 0458 calls method ShutDownGraphics( ) of class PhysicalDisplay to terminate the graphics state. Line 0457 returns an OK value.

The Startup( ) function

The function at lines 0460 through 0501 calls the SetupMode( ) method of class PhysicalDisplay to detect the graphics hardware.

The Keyboard( ) function

The function at lines 0503 through 0531 detects and retrieves keystrokes from the keyboard buffer. The function at lines 0533 through 0542 keeps calling the zKeyboard( ) function until the keyboard buffer is empty.

The MakeSound( ) function

The function at lines 0544 through 0580 generates a sound from the system speaker.

The Pause( ) function

The function at lines 0582 through 0600 causes the program to pause.

The Arguments( ) function

The function at lines 0602 through 0644 compares the command line argument with a set of recognized arguments.

Programmer's Guide to LIB2D.HPP

Code The complete source code for the declarations for class PhysicalDisplay and class Viewport is found in LIB2D.HPP in appendix E. The source from LIB2D.HPP must be #included at the beginning of any program that wishes to use the methods of class PhysicalDisplay or class Viewport. See the discussion in chapter 1 for further information about LIB2D.HPP.

Programmer's Guide to LIB2D.CPP

Code The source code in LIB2D.CPP, presented in appendix E, provides language bindings that produce low-level graphics. The routines in LIB2D.CPP call the appropriate runtime library functions in Turbo C++'s graphics.lib or Borland C++'s graphics.lib.

LIB2D.CPP is the class implementation listing for class PhysicalDisplay and class Viewport. Class PhysicalDisplay manages the state of the display. Class Viewport is responsible for maintaining a viewport and producing low-level graphics. These two classes generate nearly all the low-level graphics required by the demonstration programs in the book. See the discussion in chapter 1 for further information about class PhysicalDisplay and class Viewport.

Programmer's Guide to KINETIC.HPP

Code The complete source code for the declarations for class Kinetic3D is found in KINETIC.HPP in appendix E. KINETIC.HPP must be #included in any program that uses the methods of class Kinetic3D to help manage 3-D animation sequences.

Programmer's Guide to KINETIC.CPP

Code KINETIC.CPP is the class implementation listing for class Kinetic3D, providing routines that can calculate the position and orientation of a 3-D facet.

Constructor

The constructor for class Kinetic3D at lines 0087 through 0187 is responsible for initializing all 3-D and 2-D parameters for whatever graphics mode is currently in effect.

Method Initialize3D( )

The method at lines 0199 through 0232 initializes some parameters used by the 3-D routines, including the camera angle, object angle, dimensions of the image plane, and so on.

Method SetLaminaAngle( )

The method at lines 0234 through 0246 resets the orientation of a lamina (one-sided polygon) in the 3-D world. This method is used to draw the walls of the 3-D container.

Method SetLaminaPosition( )

The method at lines 0248 through 0259 resets the position (translation) of a lamina in the 3-D world. This method is used to draw the walls of the 3-D container.

Method DrawLamina( )

The method at lines 0261 through 0306 draws a lamina at the orientation and position set by method SetLaminaAngle( ) and method SetLaminaPosition( ).

Method GetDisplayCoords( )

The method at lines 0308 through 0323 returns pointers to the xy display coordinates for a specific point in 3-D space. This method is called by the demonstration program to get the extreme limits of the sphere during the animation.

Method VisibilityTest( )

The method at lines 0325 through 0339 uses vector math to determine which side of a facet is facing the viewpoint. The result is placed in a variable named visible. If visible is less than 0 the facet is visible. If visible equals 0 the facet is being viewing edge-on. If visible is greater than 0, the facet is hidden.

Method SetObjAngle( )

The method at lines 0341 through 0356 calculates the new sine and cosine values for a new instance of a 3-D object.

Method SetCamAngle( )

The method at lines 0358 through 0373 calculates the new sine and cosine values for a new viewpoint. These values are used by the 3-D formulas.

Method PutObjToScreen( )

The method at lines 0375 through 0387 calls other lower-level 3-D routines to transform a set of coordinates through object coordinates, world coordinates, camera coordinates, image plane coordinates, and display coordinates.

Method GetWorldCoords( )

The method at lines 0389 through 0402 transforms object coordinates to world coordinates.

Method GetCameraCoords( )

The method at lines 0404 through 0419 converts world coordinates to camera coordinates.

Method GetImageCoords( )

The method at lines 0421 through 0431 converts camera coordinates to image plane coordinates. These coordinates are 2-D device-independent coordinates not yet ready to be drawn.

Method GetScreenCoords( )

The method at lines 0433 through 0445 transforms image plane coordinates to display coordinates, which are scaled and clipped, ready to fit the screen.

Method DrawFacet( )

The method at lines 0447 through 0512 draws a four-sided dithered facet.

Method GetBrightness( )

The method at lines 0514 through 0543 uses the cross product of two vectors to determine the amount of illumination falling upon a vector whose three camera coordinates have been provided to the routine.

Method SetshadingColor( )

The method at lines 0545 through 0555 toggles the shading hue between grays, blues, greens, cyans, reds, and magentas.

12-3 Sample program HIT.CPP. Supports VGA and EGA adapters. This application demonstrates a specialized C++ class useful for building 3-D kinetic animation sequences approximating the laws of physics.

```
0001   /*
0002
0003                  Lee Adams' SUPERCHARGED C++ GRAPHICS
0004       Animated demo:   3D kinetic animation and collision detection
0005
0006       SOURCE FILE:   HIT.CPP
0007             TYPE:    C++ source file for a multimodule application.
0008          PURPOSE:    Demonstrates methods from a class useful for
0009                      kinetic animation of 3D solids and for
0010                      collision detection.
0011     PROGRAM LIST:    HIT.CPP, LIB2D.CPP, BITBLT.CPP and KINETIC.CPP.
0012        LANGUAGES:    Turbo C++, Borland C++,  and all C++ compilers
0013                      compatible with AT&T C++ 2.0 specification;
0014                      and nominal compatibility with Microsoft C++
0015                      (see the discussion in the book).
0016     MEMORY MODEL:    large.
```

12-3 Continued.

```
0017    COMMAND-LINE:  you can specify a graphics mode by using the
0018                   command-line argument /Mnn as shown below:
0019                        /M10  640x350x16-color VGA, EGA
0020                        /MOE  640x200x16-color VGA, EGA
0021                   If no command-line argument is used, hardware
0022                   autodetect is used to select the best mode.
0023    OUTPUT:  Animates the movement of a 3D sphere inside a closed
0024             container.  Detects collisions and rebounds.
0025    LICENSE:  As purchaser of the book in which this source code
0026      appears you are granted a royalty-free license to reproduce
0027      and distribute executable files generated using this code
0028      provided that you accept the conditions of the License
0029      Agreement and Limited Warranty described in the book.
0030    PUBLICATION: Contains material from Windcrest/McGraw-Hill
0031      book 3489, published by TAB BOOKS.
0032    U.S. GOVERNMENT RESTRICTED RIGHTS:  This software and its
0033      documentation is provided with restricted rights.  The use,
0034      duplication, or disclosure by the Government is subject to
0035      restrictions set forth in subdivision (b)(3)(ii) of The
0036      Rights in Technical Data and Computer Software clause at
0037      252.227-7013.  Contractor/manufacturer is Lee Adams, c/o
0038      TAB BOOKS, 13311 Monterey Ave., Blue Ridge Summit PA 17294.
0039    TRADEMARK:  Lee Adams is a trademark of Lee Adams.
0040
0041       Copyright 1991 Lee Adams.  All rights reserved worldwide.
0042
0043
0044                   CONDITIONAL COMPILATION
0045    To compile only those blocks of code that support the C++
0046    compiler and graphics library that you are using, you should
0047    #define the appropriate tokens on lines 0057 and 0058.
0048            GRAPHICS LIBRARY
0049        Borland's graphics.lib              #define BGI
0050        Microsoft's graph.lib               #define MS
0051              COMPILER
0052        Borland Turbo C++ compiler          #define BORLAND
0053        AT&T-compatible C++ compilers       #define MICROSOFT
0054    Be sure you define only one compiler and one graphics library.
0055
0056                                                               */
0057    #define BGI     1  // indicates the graphics library you are using.
0058    #define BORLAND 1  // indicates the C++ compiler you are using.
0059    /*
0060
0061                          Constants
0062
0063                                                               */
0064    const int zFAIL=0; const int zEMPTY=0;     // boolean tokens...
0065    const int zYES=1; const int zNO=0;
0066
0067    const int zVGA_12H=   1;                    // display mode tokens...
0068    const int zEGA_10H=   2;
0069    const int zEGA_EH=    3;
0070    const int zMCGA_11H=  4;
0071    const int zCGA_6H=    5;
0072    const int zHERC=      6;
0073
0074    const int zTOP=        40;                  // dimensions of container...
0075    const int zBOTTOM=    -40;
0076    const int zLEFT=      -40;
0077    const int zRIGHT=      40;
0078    const int zNEAR=       80;
```

```
0079   const int zFAR=          -80;
0080
0081   const int zTOPCLR=        1;                    // colors of container...
0082   const int zBOTTOMCLR=     1;
0083   const int zLEFTCLR=       1;
0084   const int zRIGHTCLR=      1;
0085   const int zNEARCLR=       1;
0086   const int zFARCLR=        1;
0087
0088   const int OVERWRITE=      0;
0089   /*
0090
0091   ┌─────────────────────────────────────────────────────────────────┐
       │                            Macros                                 │
0092   └─────────────────────────────────────────────────────────────────┘
0093                                                                     */
0094   #define Wait_for_any_key  while(KeyCode==0) zKeyboard(); KeyCode=0;
0095   /*
0096
0097   ┌─────────────────────────────────────────────────────────────────┐
       │                         Include files                             │
0098   └─────────────────────────────────────────────────────────────────┘
0099                                                                     */
0100   #if defined (BORLAND)
0101   #include <time.h>          // supports clock().
0102   #include <string.h>        // supports strncmp().
0103   #include <bios.h>          // supports bioskey().
0104   #include <process.h>       // supports exit().
0105   #include <iostream.h>      // supports cout.
0106   #include <dos.h>           // supports outportb(), inportb().
0107   #include <graphics.h>      // supports fillellipse().
0108   #elif defined (MICROSOFT)
0109   #include <time.h>          // supports clock().
0110   #include <string.h>        // supports strncmp().
0111   #include <bios.h>          // supports _bios_keybrd().
0112   #include <process.h>       // supports exit().
0113   #include <iostream.h>      // supports cout.
0114   #include <conio.h>         // supports outp(), inp().
0115   #include <graph.h>         // supports _ellipse().
0116   #endif
0117
0118   #include "LIB2D.HPP"       // declarations for PhysicalDisplay class.
0119   #include "BITBLT.HPP"      // declarations for Bitblt class.
0120   #include "KINETIC.HPP"     // declarations for Kinetic3D class.
0121   /*
0122
0123   ┌─────────────────────────────────────────────────────────────────┐
       │        Prototypes for functions visible throughout this file      │
0124   └─────────────────────────────────────────────────────────────────┘
0125                                                                     */
0126   static void zStartup(void);              // initializes a graphics mode.
0127   static void zArguments(int, char far* far*);    // checks arguments.
0128   static void zKeyboard(void);                 // checks for a keystroke.
0129   static void zQuit_Pgm(void);             // ends the program gracefully.
0130   static void zPurge(void);                // empties the keyboard buffer.
0131   static void zMakeSound(int,double);          // makes a specific sound.
0132   static clock_t zDelay(clock_t,double);     // CPU-independent pause.
0133   static void zDrawSphere(void);            // draws the simulated sphere.
0134   static void zDrawShadow(void);               // draws sphere's shadow.
0135   static void zDrawContainer(void);               // draws the container.
0136   static void zKinetic(void);           // manages the kinetic movement.
0137   static void zCollisionCheck(void);          // checks for 3D collision.
0138   static void zSetUpArray(void);           // sets up hidden page arrays.
0139   /*
0140
0141   ┌─────────────────────────────────────────────────────────────────┐
       │       Declaration of variables visible throughout this file       │
       └─────────────────────────────────────────────────────────────────┘
```

12-3 Continued.

```
0142
0143                                                                      */
0144    static char *StartUpArg[6]={        // legal command-line arguments.
0145          "/M12", "/M10", "/MOE", "/M11", "/M06", "/MHC" };
0146    static int CommandLineArg=zNO;       // indicates if argument exists.
0147    static int CommandLineCompare=0;     // indicates if argument legal.
0148    static int C0=0,C1=1,C2=2,C3=3,C4=4,C5=5,C6=6,
0149      C7=7,C8=8,C9=9,C10=10,C11=11,C12=12,C13=13,
0150      C14=14,C15=15;                     // palette index codes.
0151    static int Mode=0;                   // which graphics mode is being used.
0152    static int Result=0;              // captures result of graphics routines.
0153    static int CharWidth=0,CharHeight=0;    // dimensions of character.
0154    static char KeyCode=0;     // token for normal or extended keystroke.
0155    static char KeyNum=0;                // ASCII number of keystroke.
0156    static char SolidFill[]=
0157              {255,255,255,255,255,255,255,255};  // 100% fill.
0158    static int TextClr=0;                // color for regular text.
0159    static int PromptClr=0;              // color for prompt text.
0160    static char Copyright[]=
0161              "Copyright 1991 Lee Adams.  All rights reserved.";
0162    static char Title[]= "USING C++ FOR 3D KINETIC ANIMATION";
0163    static char Caption[]=
0164              "3D sphere colliding with walls of solid container";
0165    static char Prompt[]= "Press any key to quit.";
0166    static int X_Res=0, Y_Res=0;                 // screen resolution.
0167    static float xSphereCenter,ySphereCenter,zSphereCenter;
0168    static float xObj=0,yObj=0,zObj=0;    // object instancing coords.
0169    static int xDisplay=0,yDisplay=0;     // physical screen coords.
0170    static char far * SphereArray;
0171    static char far * ShadowArray;
0172    static int *xDisplayPtr;                          // pointers...
0173    static int *yDisplayPtr;
0174    static int xA,yA,xB,yB,xC,yC,xD,yD,xE,yE;    // sphere's block.
0175    static int SphereColor=0;                    // color of sphere.
0176    static float xMove=2.5,yMove=2.5,zMove=5;            // vectors.
0177    static float xShadowCenter,yShadowCenter,zShadowCenter;
0178    static int xSA,ySA,xSB,ySB,xSC,ySC,
0179          xSD,ySD,xSE,ySE;               // shadow's block.
0180    #if defined (BGI)
0181       static int ShadowColor=0;
0182    #elif defined (MS)
0183       static int ShadowPrepColor=8;
0184       static int ShadowColor=4;
0185    #endif
0186
0187    PhysicalDisplay Display;      // create the physical display object.
0188    Viewport Viewport1(&Display);          // create a viewport object.
0189    Kinetic3D Sphere(&Display);       // create a 3D kinetics object.
0190    /*
0191
0192    ┌─────────────────────────────────────────────────────────────┐
         │              Function definitions                             │
0193    └─────────────────────────────────────────────────────────────┘
0194
0195    ┌─────────────────────────────────────────────────────────────┐
         │   The executive routine:  program execution begins here       │
0196    └─────────────────────────────────────────────────────────────┘
0197                                                                      */
0198    main(int argc, char *argv[])
0199    {
0200       int NumArgs; char far* far* Arg;
0201    NumArgs= argc;                       // grab number of arguments.
0202    Arg= &argv[0];              // grab address of array of arguments.
0203    zArguments(NumArgs, Arg);       // check the command-line arguments.
```

```
0204
0205                    // set the graphics environment...
0206   zStartup();                              // establish the graphics mode.
0207   Display.Init2D(Mode,0,0,X_Res-1,Y_Res-1);     // set graphics state.
0208   Result= Display.InitUndo();      // create hidden page (unused here).
0209   if (Result==zFAIL) zQuit_Pgm();          // if hidden page failed.
0210
0211                    // set up the graphics display...
0212   Display.SetHue(C7);                       // set the drawing color.
0213   Display.SetFill(SolidFill,C7);             // set the fill style.
0214   Viewport1.DrawPanel(0,0,X_Res-1,Y_Res-1);     // clear the display.
0215   Viewport1.PutText(3,24,TextClr,Title);         // sign-on notice.
0216   Viewport1.PutText(4,18,TextClr,Copyright);    // copyright notice.
0217   if (Mode==zEGA_10H)
0218     {                              // if using 640x350x16-color mode...
0219     Viewport1.PutText(7,17,TextClr,Caption);          // caption.
0220     }
0221   if (Mode==zEGA_EH)
0222     {                              // if using 640x200x16-color mode...
0223     Viewport1.PutText(21,17,TextClr,Caption);
0224     }
0225   Viewport1.PutText(5,30,TextClr,Prompt);    // press any key to quit.
0226   Display.SetHue(C15);
0227   Viewport1.DrawBorder(0,0,X_Res-1,Y_Res-1);        // draw a border.
0228   Display.SetHue(C7);
0229
0230                    // prepare for the kinetic animation...
0231   Sphere.Initialize3D(0,0,X_Res-1,Y_Res-1,
0232              &Viewport1);       // initialize the 3D kinetics routines.
0233   zDrawContainer();                             // draw the container.
0234   Display.BackUp();                          // save to hidden page.
0235   xDisplayPtr=&xDisplay;            // point to xDisplay variable.
0236   yDisplayPtr=&yDisplay;            // point to yDisplay variable.
0237   Display.SetWritePage(1);                   // write to hidden page.
0238   Display.SetDisplayPage(0);             // set the displaying page.
0239   Display.SetHue(SphereColor);       // set the active drawing state...
0240   Display.SetLine(0xffff);
0241   Display.SetFill(SolidFill,SphereColor);
0242   zSetUpArray();                             // initialize the arrays.
0243   xSphereCenter= -10;    // initialize starting position of sphere...
0244   ySphereCenter= 20;
0245   zSphereCenter= 60;
0246   xMove= 1; yMove= -2; zMove= -2.5;        // set the movement factors.
0247
0248   zKinetic();                      // run the animated visualization loop.
0249
0250   zQuit_Pgm();                     // tidy up and terminate the application.
0251   }
0252   /*
0253
0254   ┌────────────────────────────────────────────────────────────┐
        │                    DRAW THE SPHERE                           │
        └────────────────────────────────────────────────────────────┘
0255
0256                                                                  */
0257   static void zDrawSphere(void)
0258   {
0259   Viewport1.PutPSET(xE,yE,SphereArray);         // erase prev sphere.
0260   zDrawShadow();                                // draw new shadow.
0261   xObj=xSphereCenter; yObj=ySphereCenter; zObj=zSphereCenter;
0262   Sphere.GetDisplayCoords(xObj,yObj,zObj,xDisplayPtr,yDisplayPtr);
0263   xA=xDisplay; yA=yDisplay;
0264   xObj=xSphereCenter+10; yObj=ySphereCenter; zObj=zSphereCenter;
0265   Sphere.GetDisplayCoords(xObj,yObj,zObj,xDisplayPtr,yDisplayPtr);
0266   xB=xDisplay; yB=yDisplay;
```

```
0267  xObj=xSphereCenter; yObj=ySphereCenter-10; zObj=zSphereCenter;
0268  Sphere.GetDisplayCoords(xObj,yObj,zObj,xDisplayPtr,yDisplayPtr);
0269  xC=xDisplay; yC=yDisplay;
0270  xD=xB-xA; yD=yC-yA; xE=xA-xD; yE=yA-yD;
0271  Viewport1.GetBlock(xE,yE,xB,yC,SphereArray);          // save bg.
0272  Display.SetHue(SphereColor);
0273  Display.SetFill(SolidFill,SphereColor);
0274  #if defined (BGI)
0275    fillellipse(xA,yA,xD,yD);
0276  #elif defined (MS)
0277    _ellipse(_GFILLINTERIOR,xE,yE,xB,yC);
0278  #endif
0279  Display.Restore();              // copy hidden page to visible page.
0280  return;
0281  }
0282  /*
0283
0284  ┌─────────────────────────────────────────────────────────────────┐
0285  │                      DRAW SPHERE'S SHADOW                         │
0286  └─────────────────────────────────────────────────────────────────┘  */
0287  static void zDrawShadow(void)
0288  {
0289  Viewport1.PutPSET(xSE,ySE,ShadowArray);    // erase previous shadow.
0290  xShadowCenter=xSphereCenter;
0291  yShadowCenter=zBOTTOM;
0292  zShadowCenter=zSphereCenter;
0293  xObj=xShadowCenter; yObj=yShadowCenter; zObj=zShadowCenter;
0294  Sphere.GetDisplayCoords(xObj,yObj,zObj,xDisplayPtr,yDisplayPtr);
0295  xSA=xDisplay; ySA=yDisplay;
0296  xObj=xShadowCenter+10; yObj=yShadowCenter; zObj=zShadowCenter;
0297  Sphere.GetDisplayCoords(xObj,yObj,zObj,xDisplayPtr,yDisplayPtr);
0298  xSB=xDisplay; ySB=yDisplay;
0299  xObj=xShadowCenter; yObj=yShadowCenter; zObj=zShadowCenter+10;
0300  Sphere.GetDisplayCoords(xObj,yObj,zObj,xDisplayPtr,yDisplayPtr);
0301  xSC=xDisplay; ySC=yDisplay;
0302  xSD=xSB-xSA; ySD=ySC-ySA; xSE=xSA-xSD; ySE=ySA-ySD;
0303  Viewport1.GetBlock(xSE,ySE,xSB,ySC,ShadowArray);// save background.
0304  #if defined (BGI)
0305    Display.SetHue(ShadowColor);
0306    Display.SetFill(SolidFill,ShadowColor);
0307    fillellipse(xSA,ySA,xSD,ySD);
0308  #elif defined (MS)
0309    Display.SetHue(ShadowPrepColor);
0310    Display.SetFill(FullFill,ShadowPrepColor);
0311    _ellipse(_GFILLINTERIOR,xSE,ySE,xSB,ySC);
0312    Display.SetHue(ShadowColor);
0313    Display.SetFill(FullFill,ShadowColor);
0314    _ellipse(_GFILLINTERIOR,xSE,ySE,xSB,ySC);
0315  #endif
0316  return;
0317  }
0318  /*
0319
0320  ┌─────────────────────────────────────────────────────────────────┐
0321  │                    KINETIC MOVEMENT CONTROLLER                    │
0322  └─────────────────────────────────────────────────────────────────┘  */
0323  static void zKinetic(void)
0324  {
0325  zDrawSphere();   // draw on hidden page, then copy to visible page.
0326  KINETIC_LOOP:
0327    xSphereCenter= xSphereCenter+xMove;               // x displacement.
```

```
0328    ySphereCenter= ySphereCenter+yMove;              // y displacement.
0329    zSphereCenter= zSphereCenter+zMove;              // z displacement.
0330    zCollisionCheck();                               // collision detection.
0331    zDrawSphere();         // draw on hidden page, copy to visible page.
0332    zKeyboard();                              // check for a keystroke...
0333    if (KeyCode==0) goto KINETIC_LOOP;      // ...loop if no keystroke.
0334    return;                              // otherwise return to caller.
0335    }
0336    /*
0337
0338    ┌──────────────────────────────────────────────────────────────┐
        │          COLLISION DETECTION IN 3D ENVIRONMENT                 │
0339    └──────────────────────────────────────────────────────────────┘
0340                                                                   */
0341    static void zCollisionCheck(void)
0342    {
0343    LEFT_RIGHT_TEST:
0344      if( xSphereCenter >= (zRIGHT-10) )
0345        {
0346        xMove= xMove*(-1); goto TOP_BOTTOM_TEST;
0347        }
0348      if( xSphereCenter <= (zLEFT+10) )
0349        {
0350        xMove= xMove*(-1);
0351        }
0352    TOP_BOTTOM_TEST:
0353      if( ySphereCenter >= (zTOP-10) )
0354        {
0355        yMove= yMove*(-1); goto NEAR_FAR_TEST;
0356        }
0357      if( ySphereCenter <= (zBOTTOM+10) )
0358        {
0359        yMove= yMove*(-1);
0360        }
0361    NEAR_FAR_TEST:
0362      if( zSphereCenter >= (zNEAR-10) )
0363        {
0364        zMove= zMove*(-1); return;
0365        }
0366      if( zSphereCenter <= (zFAR+10) )
0367        {
0368        zMove= zMove*(-1);
0369        }
0370    return;
0371    }
0372    /*
0373
0374    ┌──────────────────────────────────────────────────────────────┐
        │                    DRAW THE CONTAINER                          │
0375    └──────────────────────────────────────────────────────────────┘
0376                                                                   */
0377    static void zDrawContainer(void)
0378    {
0379    Sphere.SetLaminaAngle(0,0,0);
0380    Sphere.SetLaminaPosition(0,0,zFAR);
0381    Sphere.SetShadingColor(zFARCLR);
0382    Sphere.DrawLamina(40,40);                              // far panel.
0383    Sphere.SetLaminaAngle(0,0,1.57079);
0384    Sphere.SetLaminaPosition(0,zBOTTOM,0);
0385    Sphere.SetShadingColor(zBOTTOMCLR);
0386    Sphere.DrawLamina(40,80);                           // bottom panel.
0387    Sphere.SetLaminaAngle(-1.57079,0,0);
0388    Sphere.SetLaminaPosition(zLEFT,0,0);
0389    Sphere.SetShadingColor(zLEFTCLR);
0390    Sphere.DrawLamina(80,40);                             // left panel.
```

```
0391    Sphere.SetLaminaAngle(1.57079,0,0);
0392    Sphere.SetLaminaPosition(zRIGHT,0,0);
0393    Sphere.SetShadingColor(zRIGHTCLR);
0394    Sphere.DrawLamina(80,40);                        // right panel.
0395    Sphere.SetLaminaAngle(0,0,-1.57079);
0396    Sphere.SetLaminaPosition(0,zTOP,0);
0397    Sphere.SetShadingColor(zTOPCLR);
0398    Sphere.DrawLamina(40,80);                        // top panel.
0399
0400    Sphere.SetLaminaAngle(0,0,0);
0401    Sphere.SetLaminaPosition(0,0,0);                 // restore!
0402    return;
0403    }
0404    /*
0405
0406    ┌──────────────────────────────────────────────────────────────┐
        │           INITIALIZE MEMORY FOR THE GRAPHIC ARRAYS            │
0407    └──────────────────────────────────────────────────────────────┘
0408                                                                  */
0409    static void zSetUpArray(void)
0410    {
0411    CREATE_SPHERE_ARRAY:
0412      xSphereCenter=0; ySphereCenter=0; zSphereCenter=(zNEAR);
0413      xObj=xSphereCenter; yObj=ySphereCenter; zObj=zSphereCenter;
0414      Sphere.GetDisplayCoords(xObj,yObj,zObj,xDisplayPtr,yDisplayPtr);
0415      xA=xDisplay; yA=yDisplay;
0416      xObj=xSphereCenter+10; yObj=ySphereCenter; zObj=zSphereCenter;
0417      Sphere.GetDisplayCoords(xObj,yObj,zObj,xDisplayPtr,yDisplayPtr);
0418      xB=xDisplay; yB=yDisplay;
0419      xObj=xSphereCenter; yObj=ySphereCenter-10; zObj=zSphereCenter;
0420      Sphere.GetDisplayCoords(xObj,yObj,zObj,xDisplayPtr,yDisplayPtr);
0421      xC=xDisplay; yC=yDisplay;
0422      xD=xB-xA; yD=yC-yA; xE=xA-xD; yE=yA-yD;
0423      SphereArray=Viewport1.MemBlock(xE,yE,xB,yC);  // allocate memory.
0424      if (SphereArray==NULL)
0425        {                              // if memory allocation failed...
0426        zQuit_Pgm();
0427        }
0428      Viewport1.GetBlock(xE,yE,xB,yC,SphereArray); // initialize array.
0429    CREATE_SHADOW_ARRAY:
0430      xShadowCenter=0; yShadowCenter=zBOTTOM; zShadowCenter=zNEAR;
0431      xObj=xShadowCenter; yObj=yShadowCenter; zObj=zShadowCenter;
0432      Sphere.GetDisplayCoords(xObj,yObj,zObj,xDisplayPtr,yDisplayPtr);
0433      xSA=xDisplay; ySA=yDisplay;
0434      xObj=xShadowCenter+10; yObj=yShadowCenter; zObj=zShadowCenter;
0435      Sphere.GetDisplayCoords(xObj,yObj,zObj,xDisplayPtr,yDisplayPtr);
0436      xSB=xDisplay; ySB=yDisplay;
0437      xObj=xShadowCenter; yObj=yShadowCenter; zObj=zShadowCenter+10;
0438      Sphere.GetDisplayCoords(xObj,yObj,zObj,xDisplayPtr,yDisplayPtr);
0439      xSC=xDisplay; ySC=yDisplay;
0440      xSD=xSB-xSA; ySD=ySC-ySA; xSE=xSA-xSD; ySE=ySA-ySD;
0441      ShadowArray=Viewport1.MemBlock(xSE,ySE,xSB,ySC); // allocate mem.
0442      if (ShadowArray==NULL)
0443        {                              // if memory allocation failed...
0444        zQuit_Pgm();
0445        }
0446      Viewport1.GetBlock(xSE,ySE,xSB,ySC,ShadowArray);   // init array.
0447    return;
0448    }
0449    /*
0450
0451    ┌──────────────────────────────────────────────────────────────┐
        │                   Terminate the program                      │
0452    └──────────────────────────────────────────────────────────────┘
```

```
0453                                                                    */
0454    static void zQuit_Pgm(void)
0455    {
0456    Display.ShutDownGraphics();  // graceful shutdown of graphics mode.
0457    exit(0);                     // terminate the program and return OK code.
0458    }
0459    /*
0460
0461    ┌────────────────────────────────────────────────────────────────┐
0461    │           Detect the graphics hardware and set the               │
0462    │    highest mode permitted by the graphics adapter and monitor,   │
0463    │    either the 640x350x16-color or VGA and EGA mode, or the       │
0464    │    640x200x16-color EGA mode.                                    │
0465    │                                                                  │
0465    └────────────────────────────────────────────────────────────────┘
0466                                                                    */
0467    static void zStartup(void)
0468    {
0469       int DefaultMode;
0470    DefaultMode= Display.SetupMode();
0471    switch (DefaultMode)
0472       {
0473       case zVGA_12H:    Display.ForceMode(zEGA_10H);
0474                         goto EGA_ECD_mode;
0475       case zEGA_10H:    goto EGA_ECD_mode;
0476       case zEGA_EH:     goto EGA_SCD_mode;
0477       default:          goto ABORT_PGM;
0478       }
0479
0480    EGA_ECD_mode:    // VGA/EGA 640x350x16-color, 80x43 character mode.
0481    if(CommandLineArg==zYES)
0482       {
0483       if (Mode==zEGA_EH)
0484         {
0485         CommandLineArg= zNO;
0486         Display.ForceMode(Mode);
0487         goto EGA_SCD_mode;
0488         }
0489       }
0490    X_Res=640; Y_Res=350; Mode=zEGA_10H; CharWidth=8; CharHeight=8;
0491    return;
0492
0493    EGA_SCD_mode:               // EGA 640x200x16-color, 80x25 char mode.
0494    X_Res=640; Y_Res=200; Mode=zEGA_EH; CharWidth=8; CharHeight=8;
0495    return;
0496
0497    ABORT_PGM:       // jump to here if no graphics hardware detected.
0498    cout << "\n\n\rThis animated C++ graphics programming demo";
0499    cout << "\n\rrequires a VGA or EGA graphics adapter.\n\r";
0500    exit(-1);                    // terminate, returning an error code.
0501    }
0502    /*
0503
0504    ┌────────────────────────────────────────────────────────────────┐
0504    │              Check the keyboard for a keystroke                  │
0505    └────────────────────────────────────────────────────────────────┘
0506                                                                    */
0507    static void zKeyboard(void)
0508    {
0509       union AnyName{int RawCode;char Code[3];}Keystroke;
0510       char TempKey=0;
0511    #if defined (BORLAND)
0512       if (bioskey(1)==zEMPTY) { KeyCode=0; return; }
0513       Keystroke.RawCode= bioskey(0);
0514    #elif defined (ZORTECH)
0515       if (bioskey(1)==zEMPTY) { KeyCode=0; return; }
```

```
0516    Keystroke.RawCode= bioskey(0);
0517  #elif defined (MICROSOFT)
0518    if (_bios_keybrd(_KEYBRD_READY)==zEMPTY)
0519      { KeyCode=0; return; }
0520    Keystroke.RawCode= _bios_keybrd(_KEYBRD_READ);
0521  #endif
0522  TempKey= Keystroke.Code[0];
0523  if (TempKey!=0)
0524    {                                      // if a normal keystroke...
0525    KeyCode=1; KeyNum=TempKey; return;
0526    }
0527  if (TempKey==0)
0528    {                                      // if an extended keystroke...
0529    KeyCode=2; KeyNum=Keystroke.Code[1]; return;
0530    }
0531  }
0532  /*
0533
0534  ┌────────────────────────────────────────────────────────┐
        │                Empty the keystroke buffer                │
0535  └────────────────────────────────────────────────────────┘
0536                                                              */
0537  static void zPurge(void)
0538  {
0539  do zKeyboard();
0540    while (KeyCode!=0);
0541  return;
0542  }
0543  /*
0544
0545  ┌────────────────────────────────────────────────────────┐
        │                     Make a sound                         │
0546  └────────────────────────────────────────────────────────┘
0547                                                              */
0548  static void zMakeSound(int Hertz,double Duration)
0549  {
0550    static clock_t FormerTime=0;
0551    short Count=0;
0552    int HighByte=0, LowByte=0;
0553    unsigned char OldPort=0, NewPort=0;
0554  FormerTime= clock();
0555  if (Hertz < 40) return;
0556  if (Hertz > 4660) return;
0557  Count= 1193180L/Hertz;
0558  HighByte= Count / 256;
0559  LowByte= Count - (HighByte * 256);
0560  #if defined (BORLAND)
0561    outportb(0x43,0xB6); outportb(0x42,(unsigned char)LowByte);
0562    outportb(0x42,(unsigned char)HighByte); OldPort=inportb(0x61);
0563    NewPort=(OldPort | 0x03); outportb(0x61,NewPort);
0564    zDelay(FormerTime,Duration);
0565    outportb(0x61,OldPort);
0566  #elif defined (ZORTECH)
0567    outp(0x43,0xB6); outp(0x42,LowByte);
0568    outp(0x42,HighByte); OldPort=(unsigned char)inp(0x61);
0569    NewPort=(OldPort | 0x03); outp(0x61,(int)NewPort);
0570    zDelay(FormerTime,Duration);
0571    outp(0x61,(int)OldPort);
0572  #elif defined (MICROSOFT)
0573    outp(0x43,0xB6); outp(0x42,LowByte);
0574    outp(0x42,HighByte); OldPort=(unsigned char)inp(0x61);
0575    NewPort=(OldPort | 0x03); outp(0x61,(int)NewPort);
0576    zDelay(FormerTime,Duration);
0577    outp(0x61,(int)OldPort);
```

```
0578  #endif
0579  return;
0580  }
0581  /*
0582
0583  ┌─────────────────────────────────────────────────────────────────┐
      │                             Pause                               │
0584  └─────────────────────────────────────────────────────────────────┘
0585                                                                    */
0586  static clock_t zDelay(clock_t StartTime, double Wait)
0587  {                              // pause for a specified length of time.
0588    clock_t StopTime;
0589    clock_t NewClockTime;
0590  #if defined (BORLAND)
0591    StopTime= StartTime + (Wait * CLK_TCK);
0592  #elif defined (ZORTECH)
0593    StopTime= StartTime + (Wait * CLOCKS_PER_SEC);
0594  #elif defined (MICROSOFT)
0595    StopTime= StartTime + (Wait * CLK_TCK);
0596  #endif
0597  while ( clock() < StopTime ) {;}
0598  NewClockTime= clock();
0599  return NewClockTime;
0600  }
0601  /*
0602
0603  ┌─────────────────────────────────────────────────────────────────┐
      │            Retrieve the command-line arguments, if any           │
0604  └─────────────────────────────────────────────────────────────────┘
0605                                                                    */
0606  static void zArguments(int NumArgs, char *Arg[])
0607  {
0608  if(NumArgs==1)
0609    {
0610    CommandLineArg= zNO; return;                        // if no arg.
0611    }
0612  CommandLineCompare= strncmp(StartUpArg[0],Arg[1],5);
0613  if(CommandLineCompare==0)
0614    {
0615    CommandLineArg=zYES; Mode=zVGA_12H; return;          // /M12.
0616    }
0617  CommandLineCompare= strncmp(StartUpArg[1],Arg[1],5);
0618  if(CommandLineCompare==0)
0619    {
0620    CommandLineArg=zYES; Mode=zEGA_10H; return;          // /M10.
0621    }
0622  CommandLineCompare= strncmp(StartUpArg[2],Arg[1],5);
0623  if(CommandLineCompare==0)
0624    {
0625    CommandLineArg=zYES; Mode=zEGA_EH; return;           // /MOE.
0626    }
0627  CommandLineCompare= strncmp(StartUpArg[3],Arg[1],5);
0628  if(CommandLineCompare==0)
0629    {
0630    CommandLineArg=zYES; Mode=zMCGA_11H; return;         // /M11.
0631    }
0632  CommandLineCompare= strncmp(StartUpArg[4],Arg[1],5);
0633  if(CommandLineCompare==0)
0634    {
0635    CommandLineArg=zYES; Mode=zCGA_6H; return;           // /M06.
0636    }
0637  CommandLineCompare= strncmp(StartUpArg[5],Arg[1],5);
0638  if(CommandLineCompare==0)
0639    {
0640    CommandLineArg=zYES; Mode=zHERC; return;             // /MHC.
```

12-3 Continued.

```
0641    }
0642    CommandLineArg= zNO;                    // if an unrecognized argument.
0643    return;
0644    }
0645    /*
0646
0647    ┌─────────────────────────────────────────────────────────────────────┐
        │   Supercharged C++ Graphics  --  end of source file HIT.CPP         │
        └─────────────────────────────────────────────────────────────────────┘
0648
0649                                                                        */
```

Appendices

A
Compiling the sample programs with Turbo C++

The sample programs in the book were developed and tested using Turbo C++ 1.2 and the BGI graphics library that is bundled with the compiler, graphics.lib. This appendix provides a step-by-step guide to compiling, linking, and running the demonstration programs using Turbo C++ 1.2.

Installation

First, install Turbo C++ onto your hard disk by following the installation instructions in the "Getting Started" guide. If you want your development setup to match my platform, use C:\TURBOCPP as the target directory.

Second, after installation is complete, you might wish to create two new specialized subdirectories to help organize your programming sessions. These two directories, named C:\TURBOCPP\SOURCE and C:\TURBOCPP \OUTPUT, are used to store your source files and your output files.

Use DOS's MD command to make these two new subdirectories. Enter:

```
MD C:\TURBOCPP\SOURCE
MD C:\TURBOCPP\OUTPUT
```

During a programming session your source files will be stored in C:\TUR-BOCPP\SOURCE and will include .hpp class declaration files, .cpp class implementation files, and .cpp program files. If you adhere to the suggestions provided in this appendix, C:\TURBOCPP\SOURCE will also contain the .prj and .dsk files used by the Turbo C++ editor to store the project list and desktop configuration for your programming sessions.

During a programming session, your output files will be stored in C: \TURBOCPP\OUTPUT and will include .obj object files and .exe executable files.

Next, copy the appropriate graphics drivers and font files from C:\TURBOCPP\BGI to your working subdirectories. During a typical programming session, you will be running your programs under the control of the Turbo C++ editor. The current directory, as explained later in this appendix, will be C:\TURBOCPP\SOURCE. Turbo C++ will expect to find any graphics drivers or font files that it needs in the current directory. If you are using a VGA or EGA graphics adapter, copy EGAVGA.BGI from C:\TURBOCPP\BGI to C:\TURBOCPP\SOURCE. If you are using an MCGA or CGA adapter, copy CGA.BGI. If you are using a Hercules graphics adapter, copy HERC.BGI to C:\TURBOCPP\SOURCE. Because one of the demonstration programs uses fonts, you will also need to copy the font file TRIP.CHR from C:\TURBOCPP\BGI to C:\TURBOCPP\SOURCE.

During your programming sessions, the executable files you create will be written to the output directory, C:\TURBOCPP\OUTPUT. The Turbo C++ editor is intelligent enough to know where to find the executable file during a programming session. You might, however, occasionally want to execute these files directly from the operating system command line. At startup, the executable file will expect to find the graphics drivers and font files it needs in the current directory. The simplest way to fill this requirement is to copy the appropriate graphics drivers and font files into C:\TURBOCPP\OUTPUT and make that directory the current directory before running the .exe file from the command-line. Note that not all .exe files created by Turbo C++ need to load a graphics driver or font file at runtime, although this is the default condition. See the discussion later in this appendix for guidance on binding the graphics driver and font file right into the finished executable to make a stand-alone file.

Tip You might want to configure your Turbo C++ editor to match the platform that was used to prepare the demonstration programs in the book. This eliminates many variables from the programming paradigm and will help you track down any discrepancies if you encounter difficulties compiling, linking, and running the sample applications.

The demonstration programs

If you have the companion disks to the book, copy all the source files from the disks to C:\TURBOCPP\SOURCE. If you are typing the source code from the listings in the book, you can use any text editor or word processor that you prefer, provided that you store the resulting file in ASCII format.

The program listings in the book are identical to the source code provided on the companion disks. The files on the companion disk are direct copies of the files on the author's hard disk. The program listings in the book are direct laser prints of the files on the author's hard disk. Whether you are using the companion disk or typing the listings from the book, you are using a first-generation copy of the source code used throughout the text.

Starting Turbo C++

To begin a programming session, you must first make C:\TURBOCPP \SOURCE the current directory and then start the Turbo C++ integrated programming environment (IDE). The IDE is also called the Turbo C++ editor.

Here's How... To reset the current directory, enter the following line at the operating system prompt:

    CD C:\TURBOCPP\SOURCE

Then, to start the Turbo C++ editor, enter the following line at the operating system prompt.

    C:\TURBOCPP\BIN\TC /x /p

For convenience, you can place these two lines in a batch file and simply run the batch file to start a programming session, of course. My batch file is named TURBOCPP.BAT.

If you are using a VGA or EGA graphics adapter, you should include the /p argument on the command-line that starts the Turbo C++ editor. This argument instructs the editor to restore the default color palette for the VGA or EGA on each occasion you return to the editor after running a program. Without this argument, any palette changes that you make during your graphics programming session will remain in effect when you return to the Turbo C++ editor.

The /x argument in the command-line shown above instructs Turbo C++ to use extended memory for the temporary files it requires while building the executable file from your source and object files. If you are not using extended memory with your computer, then delete the /x argument from the command-line used to invoke the Turbo C++ editor.

Configuring your C++ programming environment

The Turbo C++ editor was configured in the following manner during development and testing of the demonstration programs in the book. You might find it helpful to configure your platform in a similar manner—at least until you have successfully compiled and run a few of the sample applications.

Navigating the Turbo C++ menu system

For the purposes of this discussion, the following syntax is used. Run/Arguments is intended to mean that you select the Run menu from the menu bar, and choose the Arguments selection from the Run menu. Or, stated another way, Run/Arguments means the Arguments selection from the Run menu.

A working configuration

First, set the Run/Arguments option to /M10. This will ensure that each demonstration program you compile will run in the 640×350×16-color mode. If you are using a VGA graphics adapter, you can easily change this to /M12 after you have verified the program compiles, links, and runs correctly. If you are using an MCGA, CGA, or Hercules adapter, the Run/Arguments option will have no effect. The demonstration program will use the built-in autodetect function to start up in the best graphics mode for the particular adapter you are using.

The Run/Arguments option is used by the Turbo C++ editor to simulate a command-line argument when you are testing a program under the control of the editor. Refer to the heading that accompanies each source listing for the legal command-line arguments. If you are using a VGA or EGA adapter, for example, you can run any of the demonstration programs in the 640×200×2-color CGA mode by using the command-line argument /M06, which represents mode 06 hex.

Next, set Options/Full menus to ON.

The following options were selected in the "Options/Compiler/Code Generation" menu. "Options" was set to standard stack frame. The large model was chosen. Floating point emulation was activated. The 8088/8086 instruction set was requested. The C calling convention was enabled. The following "Options" flags were activated: generate underbars, debug info in OBJS, treat enums as ints, and fast floating point. Some of these selections are arbitrary, but you might find it helpful to mimic my platform until you have successfully compiled, linked, and run a few of the demonstration programs.

Next, select the following items from "Options/Compiler/C++" options. Choose smart C++ virtual tables. Instruct Turbo C++ to use the C++ compiler always. Set the out-of-line inline functions to ON.

From the "Options/Compiler/Optimizations" menu set "Register Variables" to automatic. Instruct the compiler to optimize for speed.

Choose the following from the "Options/Compiler/Source" menu. Use Turbo C++ keywords. Set the identifier length to 32.

Activate the following options in the "Options/Compiler/Messages" menu. Stop after ten errors. Stop after ten warnings. Set "Display Warnings" to ON. Finally, make no changes to the default settings for Portability, ANSI violations, C++ warnings, and Frequent Errors.

Use the default settings for the "Options/Transfer" menu.

Enable the following switches in the "Options/Make" menu. Instruct the compiler to break on errors. Set the "Check Auto-dependences" option to ON.

In the Options/Linker menu the map file selection should be set to OFF. Set to ON the default libraries, graphic library, no stack warning, and case-sensitive link.

Set source debugging to "none" in the "Options/Debugger" menu. Set display swapping to smart and use the default settings for all the other options in this menu.

Name the following working directories in the "Options/Directories" menu. Set C:\TURBOCPP\INCLUDE as the include directory. Name C: \TURBOCPP\LIB as the library directory. Type in C:\TURBOCPP\OUTPUT as the output directory.

Next, set the items in the "Options/Environment/Preferences" menu. Select 25-line screen size. Enable new window for source tracking. Disable all auto save functions.

In the "Options/Environment/Editor" menu, activate insert mode and autoindent mode. Set tab size to two and name .cpp as the default extension.

In the "Options/Environment/Mouse" menu use the existing defaults.

Storing the editor configuration

After you are satisfied with the editor configurations, you can save these settings in a configuration file. When you next start the editor, it reads the configuration file and resets its internal flags for your customized working environment.

 To save the startup configuration, select the "Options/Save" menu. Be sure that "Environment," "Desktop," and "Project" are enabled when you save.

Testing a sample program

To compile, link, and run a sample program you must first provide to the Turbo C++ editor a list of the source files required to build the finished executable file. Select the "Project/Open Project" menu. Enter STARTUP when prompted for a project file name. The Project window will appear. Next, press Ins to tell the Turbo C++ editor that you want to add some file names to the project list. The Add Item to Project List window will appear.

Type STARTUP.CPP or use the Tab key and arrow keys to select STARTUP.CPP from the available files. The file name STARTUP.CPP will appear in the "Project" window.

Next, type LIB2D.CPP or use the Tab and arrow keys to select LIB2D.CPP from the available files. The file name LIB2D.CPP will appear in the Project window.

Press Esc to remove the "Add" window from the display.

Activate the "File/Open" menu. Type or select STARTUP.CPP. Turbo C++ will load the file STARTUP.CPP into the editing buffer. Use the "File/Open" menu again to load LIB2D.CPP and LIB2D.HPP into memory.

Press F6 to make the Project window active. Press Alt+F3 to remove it from the display. Press F6 followed by F5 to make the STARTUP.CPP window full-screen. Press F6 then F5 to make the LIB2D.CPP window full-screen. Use F6 followed by F5 to make the LIB2D.HPP window full-screen. Finally, press F6 again to make the STARTUP.CPP window the active window.

You now have all required source files in the text-editing buffers, as well as an up-to-date project list. To save the project list use the "Options/Save" menu and be sure all the switches are selected when you select OK. The next time you want to load the STARTUP.CPP demonstration program, you simply select STARTUP.PRJ and the Turbo C++ editor will load in all the necessary source files for you.

To compile, link, and run the demonstration program, press Ctrl + F9.

Trap **Turbo C++ graphics drivers**. Your finished program will appear to load correctly but will do nothing meaningful at runtime if the required graphics driver cannot be found. The program will search the current directory for EGAVGA.BGI if you are using a VGA or EGA graphics adapter. It will look for CGA.BGI if you are using an MCGA or CGA graphics adapter. It will attempt to load HERC.BGI if you are using a Hercules graphics adapter. You should ensure that the appropriate graphics driver is in the current directory.

Running other demonstration programs

Each demonstration program listing contains a header that provides a list of required source files. To run a demonstration program, use the instructions provided above to create a project list consisting of the source files named in the header of the source code listing.

How to prepare a program for distribution

In its default configuration, the Turbo C++ editor will not instruct the compiler and linker to bind the BGI graphics drivers and font files into the finished executable file. For graphics programs, at least one BGI graphics driver is required at program startup. You can use the following instructions to bind one or more graphics drivers and font files into your finished program.

Step one   Convert the appropriate .BGI and .CHR files to .OBJ object file format. Your Turbo C++ compiler package provides a special utility program called BGIOBJ.EXE that does the job. Assuming that BGIOBJ.EXE and the appropriate graphics driver file or font file are both located in the same directory, you can use the following command line to make the conversion. Enter:

    BGIOBJ EGAVGA.BGI

This command line will create an object file named EGAVGA.OBJ that can be linked into your finished .exe file.

To convert a font file, you might use the following syntax.

    BGIOBJ TRIP.CHR

This command line will create an object file named TRIP.OBJ that can be linked into your finished .exe file.

Step two   Add the newly created object file(s) to Turbo C++'s graphics library, graphics.lib. Assuming that the Turbo C++ library manager, TLIB.EXE, and the work files are all located in the same directory, you can use the following command line to add the graphics driver object file and font object file to the compiler's graphics library.

```
TLIB GRAPHICS + EGAVGA + TRIP
```

This command line invokes TLIB.EXE and adds EGAVGA.OBJ and TRIP.OBJ to GRAPHICS.LIB.

If you do not add the newly created object files to graphics.lib, you will need to specify the object files in the project file for the program you are building when you are using the Turbo C++ editor. Your programming environment is kept simpler if you add the object files to graphics.lib—and a simpler programming session usually makes for fewer mistakes and program bugs.

Step three   Add custom code to your source file to force the Turbo C++ linker to use the newly created object files when building your executable file. For example, to use the EGAVGA graphics driver routines, add the following statement to your code.

```
if (registerbgidriver(EGAVGA_driver) < 0) exit(-1);
```

To use the font characters from TRIP.CHR, add the following statement to your source code.

```
if (registerbgidriver(triplex_font) < 0) exit(-1);
```

In the first example, you would use CGA_driver to bind the routines from CGA.BGI into your finished program. You would use Herc_driver to bind the routines from HERC.BGI into your finished executable. The fundamental principle is to use the function registerbgidriver( ) before using any other BGI graphics function in your program.

For further help in binding .BGI graphics drivers and .CHR font files into your finished executable file, consult the text file UTIL.DOC that was installed onto your hard disk when you installed your Turbo C++ compiler.

B
Compiling
the sample programs
with Borland C++

The sample programs in the book were tested using Borland C++ 2.0 and the BGI graphics library that is shipped with the compiler, graphics.lib. This appendix provides a step-by-step guide to compiling, linking, and running the demonstration programs using Borland C++ 2.0.

Installation

First, install Borland C++ on your hard disk by following the installation instructions in the "Getting Started" guide. If you want your development environment to match my platform, use C:\BORLANDC as the target directory.

Second, after installation has been completed, you might wish to create two additional subdirectories to help organize your programming sessions. These two directories are named C:\BORLANDC\SOURCE and C:\BORLANDC\OUTPUT. They are used to store your source files and your output files.

Use the DOS MD command to make these two new subdirectories:

```
MD C:\BORLANDC\SOURCE
MD C:\BORLANDC\OUTPUT
```

During a programming session your source files will be stored in C:\BORLANDC\SOURCE. Source files include .hpp class declaration files, .cpp class implementation files, and .cpp program files. If you follow the suggestions provided in this appendix, C:\BORLANDC\SOURCE will also contain the .prj and .dsk files used by the Borland C++ editor to store the project list and desktop configuration for your C++ programming sessions.

During a programming session your output files will be stored in C:\BORLANDC\OUTPUT. Output files include .obj object files and .exe executable files.

Next, copy the appropriate graphics drivers and font files from C:\ BORLANDC\BGI to your working subdirectories. During a typical programming session, you will be running your programs under the control of the Borland C++ editor. The current directory will be C:\BORLANDC\SOURCE. Borland C++ will expect to find any graphics drivers or font files that it needs in the current directory. If you are using a VGA or EGA graphics adapter, copy EGAVGA.BGI from C:\BORLANDC\BGI to C:\BORLANDC\SOURCE. If you are using an MCGA or CGA adapter, copy CGA.BGI. If you are using a Hercules graphics adapter, copy HERC.BGI to C:\BORLANDC\SOURCE.

During your programming sessions, the executable files you create will be written to the output directory, C:\BORLANDC\OUTPUT. The Borland C++ editor is bright enough to know where to find the executable file during a programming session. You might, however, occasionally want to execute these files directly from the operating system command line. At program startup, the executable file will expect to find the graphics drivers and font files it needs in the current directory. The simplest way to meet this requirement is to copy the appropriate graphics drivers and font files into C:\BORLANDC\OUTPUT. Then make that directory the current directory before running the .exe file from the command line. Not all .exe files created by Borland C++ need to load a graphics driver or font file at runtime, although this is the default condition. See the discussion later in this appendix for guidance on binding the graphics driver and font file right into the finished executable file.

You might want to configure your Borland C++ editor to match the platform that was used to prepare the demonstration programs in the book. This eliminates many variables from the programming paradigm and will help you track down any discrepancies if you encounter difficulties compiling, linking, and running the sample applications.

The demonstration programs

If you have the companion disks to the book, copy all the source files from the disks to C:\BORLANDC\SOURCE. If you are typing the source code from the listings in the book, you can use any text editor or word processor that you prefer, provided that you store the resulting file in ASCII format.

The program listings in the book are identical to the source code provided on the companion disks. The files on the companion disk are direct copies of the files on my hard disk. The program listings in the book are direct laser prints of the files on my hard disk. Whether you are using the companion disk or typing the listings from the book, you are using a first-generation copy of the source code used to build and verify the demonstration programs discussed in the text.

Starting Borland C++

To begin a programming session, you must first make C:\BORLANDC \SOURCE the current directory and then start the Borland C++ integrated programming environment (IDE). The IDE is also called the Borland C++ editor.

 To reset the current directory, type the following line at the operating system prompt.

CD C:\BORLANDC\SOURCE

Then, to start the Borland C++ editor, type the following line at the operating system prompt.

C:\BORLANDC\BIN\BC /x /p

For convenience you can place these two lines in a batch file and simply run the batch file to start a programming session, of course. The batch file I use is named BORLANDC.BAT.

If you are using a VGA or EGA graphics adapter, you should include the /p argument on the command-line when you start the Borland C++ editor. This argument instructs the editor to restore the default color palette for the VGA or EGA on each occasion you return to the editor after running a program. Without this argument, any palette changes that you make during your graphics programming session will remain in effect when you return to the Borland C++ editor.

The /x argument in the command-line shown above instructs Borland C++ to use extended memory for the temporary files it requires while building the executable file from your source and object files. If you are not using extended memory with your computer, then delete the /x argument from the command-line when you invoke the Borland C++ editor.

Configuring your C++ programming environment

The Borland C++ editor was configured in the following manner during development and testing of the demonstration programs in the book. You might find it helpful to configure your platform in a similar manner, at least until you have successfully compiled and run a few of the sample applications.

Navigating the Borland C++ menu system

For the purposes of this discussion, the following syntax is used. Run/Arguments is intended to mean that you select the Run menu from the menu bar, and then choose the Arguments selection from the Run menu. As used here, Run/Arguments means the Arguments selection from the Run menu.

A working configuration

First, set the Run/Arguments option to /M10. This will ensure that each demonstration program you compile will run in the 640×350×16-color mode. If you are using a VGA graphics adapter, you can easily change this to /M12 after you have verified the program compiles, links, and runs correctly. If you are using an MCGA, CGA, or Hercules adapter, the Run/Arguments option will have no effect. The demonstration program will use its built-in autodetect function to start up in the best graphics mode for the particular adapter you are using.

The Run/Arguments option is used by the Borland C++ editor to simulate a command line argument when you are testing a program under the control of the editor. Refer to the heading that accompanies each source listing for a list of legal command line arguments. If you are using a VGA or EGA adapter, for example, you can run any of the demonstration programs in the 640×200×2-color CGA mode by using the command-line argument /M06, which represents mode 06 hex.

The following options were selected in the Options/Compiler/Code Generation menu. The large model was chosen. Treat enums as ints was enabled. Assume SS equals DS was set to Default for memory model. Floating point emulation was activated. The 8088/8086 instruction set was requested. The following Options flags were activated: generate underbars, debug info in OBJS, and fast floating point. Some of these selections are arbitrary, although you might find it helpful to emulate the author's platform until you have successfully compiled, linked, and run some of the demonstration programs.

Next, Options/Compiler/Entry-Exit Code was configured as follows. DOS standard was selected as the Prolog-Epilog Code Generation mode. The calling convention was set to C. Stack options was set to standard stack frame.

Select the following items from Options/Compiler/C++ options. Choose smart C++ virtual tables. Instruct Borland C++ to use the C++ compiler always. Set the out-of-line inline functions to ON.

From the Options/Compiler/Optimizations menu set Register Variables to automatic. Instruct the compiler to optimize for speed.

Choose the following from the Options/Compiler/Source menu. Use Borland C++ keywords. Set the identifier length to 32.

Activate the following options in the Options/Compiler/Messages menu. Stop after ten errors. Stop after ten warnings. Set Display Warnings to on. Finally, make no changes to the default settings for Portability, ANSI violations, C++ warnings, and Frequent Errors.

Use the default settings for the Options/Transfer menu.

Enable the following switches in the Options/Make menu. Instruct the compiler to break on errors. Set Generate Import Library to ON. Set the Check Auto-dependences option to ON.

In the Options/Linker menu the map file selection should be set to OFF. Set to ON the default libraries, graphic library, no stack warning, and case-sensitive link. Standard DOS EXE was activated as the output selection. Code Pack Size was set to 8192. Segment alignment was defined as 512.

In the Options/Application menu use the existing default settings.

Set source debugging to none in the Options/Debugger menu. Set display swapping to smart and use the default settings for all the other options in this menu.

Name the following working directories in the Options/Directories menu. Set C:\BORLANDC\INCLUDE as the include directory. Name C:\BORLANDC\LIB as the library directory. Type in C:\BORLANDC\OUTPUT as the output directory.

Next, select the appropriate items in the Options/Environment/Preferences menu. Choose 25-line screen size. Enable new window for source tracking. Disable all auto save functions.

In the Options/Environment/Editor menu, activate insert mode and autoindent mode. Set tab size to two and name .cpp as the default extension.

In the Options/Environment/Mouse menu use the existing defaults.

In the Options/Environment/Desktop menu the following selections were activated: History Lists and Clipboard.

Storing the editor configuration

After you are satisfied with the editor configurations, you should save these settings in a configuration file. When you next start the editor, it reads the configuration file and resets its internal flags for your customized working environment.

 To save the startup configuration, select the Options/Save menu. Be sure that Environment, Desktop, and Project are enabled when you save.

Testing a sample program

To compile, link, and run a sample program, you must first specify a list of the source files required to build the finished executable file. Select the Project /Open Project menu. Enter STARTUP when prompted for a project file name. The Project window will appear. Next, press Ins to tell the Borland C++ editor that you want to add some file names to the project list. The Add Item to Project List window will appear.

Enter STARTUP.CPP or use the Tab key and arrow keys to select STARTUP.CPP from the available files. The file name STARTUP.CPP will appear in the Project window.

Next, type LIB2DBC.CPP or use the Tab and arrow keys to select LIB2DBC .CPP from the available files. The file name LIB2DBC.CPP will appear in the Project window.

Press Esc to remove the Add window from the display.

Activate the File/Open menu. Type or select STARTUP.CPP. Borland C++ will load the file STARTUP.CPP into the editing buffer. Use the File/Open menu again to load LIB2DBC.CPP and LIB2DBC.HPP into memory.

Press F6 to make the Project window active. Press Alt+F3 to remove it from the display. Press F6 followed by F5 to make the STARTUP.CPP window full-screen. Press F6 then F5 to make the LIB2DBC.CPP window full-screen. Use F6 followed by F5 to make the LIB2DBC.HPP window full-screen. Finally, press F6 again to make the STARTUP.CPP window the active window.

You now have all required source files in the text-editing buffers, as well as an up-to-date project list. To save the project list use the Options/Save menu. Be sure all the switches are selected when you select OK. The next time you want to load the STARTUP.CPP demonstration program, you can simply select STARTUP.PRJ and the Borland C++ editor will load in all the necessary source files for you.

Because the demonstration programs are explicitly formatted for use with Turbo C++, you must alter one line of code before compilation. Simply change line 0112 in STARTUP.CPP as follows. Delete #include "LIB2D.HPP" and insert instead #include "LIB2DBC.HPP." Then press F2 to save the modified file to your hard disk.

To compile, link, and run the demonstration program, press Ctrl+F9.

Borland C++ graphics drivers. Your finished program will appear to load correctly, but it will do nothing meaningful at runtime if the required graphics driver cannot be found. The program will search the current directory for EGAVGA.BGI if you are using a VGA or EGA graphics adapter. It will look for CGA.BGI if you are using an MCGA or CGA graphics adapter. It will attempt to load HERC.BGI if you are using a Hercules graphics adapter. You should ensure that the appropriate graphics driver is in the current directory.

Running other demonstration programs

Each demonstration program listing contains a header that provides a list of required source files. To run a demonstration program, use the instructions provided above to create a project list consisting of the source files named in the header of the source code listing.

Because of subtle differences between the Turbo C++ and Borland C++ parsers, some of the class libraries in appendix E have been customized for use with Borland C++. See the discussion in appendix E for more on this. To run the demonstration programs with your Borland C++ compiler, be sure to use the LIB2DBC.HPP class declaration file instead of the LIB2D.HPP class declaration file. Use the LIB2DBC.CPP class implementation file instead of the LIB2D.CPP class implementation file. Use the MOUSEBC.HPP class declaration file instead of the MOUSE.HPP class declaration file. All other declaration files and implementation files in appendix E can be used without modification with your Borland C++ compiler. Whenever you are working with a demonstration program that #includes LIB2D.HPP, be sure to change the line to #include "LIB2DBC.HPP." If the demonstration program #includes MOUSE.HPP, change the line to read #include "MOUSEBC.HPP" instead.

How to prepare a program for distribution

In its default configuration, Borland C++ will not bind the BGI graphics drivers and font files into the finished executable file. For graphics programs, at least one BGI graphics driver is required at program startup. You can use the following instructions to bind one or more graphics driver and font file into your finished program.

Step one Convert the appropriate .BGI and .CHR files to .obj object file format. Your Borland C++ compiler package provides a special utility program called BGIOBJ.EXE that does the job. Assuming that BGIOBJ.EXE and the appropriate graphics driver file or font file are both located in the same directory, you can use the following command line to make the conversion. Enter:

```
BGIOBJ EGAVGA.BGI
```

This command line will create an object file named EGAVGA.OBJ that can be linked into your finished .exe file.

To convert a font file, you might use the following syntax. Enter:

```
BGIOBJ TRIP.CHR
```

This command line will create an object file named TRIP.OBJ that can be linked into your finished .exe file.

Step two Add the newly created object file(s) to Borland C++'s graphics library, graphics.lib. Assuming that the Borland C++ library manager T-LIB.EXE and the work files are located in the same subdirectory, you can use the following command line to add the graphics driver object file and font object file to the Borland C++ graphics library. Enter:

```
TLIB GRAPHICS + EGAVGA + TRIP
```

This command line invokes TLIB.EXE and adds EGAVGA.OBJ and TRIP.OBJ to GRAPHICS.LIB.

If you do not add the newly created object files to graphics.lib, you will be required to specify the object files in the project list for the program you are building.

Step three Add explicit code to your source file to force the Borland C++ linker to use the newly created object files when building your executable file. For example, to use the EGAVGA graphics driver routines, add the following statement to your code.

```
if (registerbgidriver(EGAVGA_driver) < 0) exit(-1);
```

To use the font characters from TRIP.CHR, add the following statement to your source code.

```
if (registerbgidriver(triplex_font) > 0) exit(-1);
```

In the first example, you would use CGA_driver to bind the routines from CGA.BGI into your finished program. You would use Herc_driver to bind the routines from HERC.BGI into your finished executable. The fundamental principle is to use the function registerbgidriver() before using any other BGI graphics function in your program.

For further help in binding .BGI graphics drivers and .CHR font files into your finished executable file, consult the text file UTIL.DOC that is written to your hard disk when you installed Borland C++.

C

Compiling the sample programs with Zortech C++

The sample programs in the book were tested using Zortech C++ 2.12 and the Flash Graphics graphics library shipped with the compiler, fg.lib. This appendix provides a step-by-step guide to compiling, linking, and running the demonstration programs using Zortech C++ version 2.12.

Installation

First, install Zortech C++ on your hard disk by following the installation instructions in the Zortech "MS-DOS Installation Guide." If you want your development environment to match my platform, use C:\ZORTECH as the target directory.

Second, after installation has been completed, you might wish to create an additional subdirectory to help organize your programming session. This new directory is named C:\ZORTECH\SOURCE. It is used to store your source files and your output files.

Use the DOS MD command to make this new subdirectory. Enter:

```
MD C:\ZORTECH\SOURCE
```

During a programming session, your source files will be stored in C:\ZORTECH\SOURCE. Source files include .hpp class declaration files, .cpp class implementation files, and .cpp program files. Your output files will also be stored in C:\ZORTECH\SOURCE. Output files include .obj object files and .exe executable files.

Tip You might want to configure your Zortech C++ editor to match the platform that was used to prepare the demonstration programs in the book. This eliminates many variables from the programming paradigm and will help you track down any discrepancies if you encounter difficulties compiling, linking, and running the sample applications.

335

The demonstration programs

If you have the companion disks to the book, copy all the source files from the disks to C:\ZORTECH\SOURCE. If you are typing the source code from the listings in the book, you can use any text editor or word processor that you prefer, providing that you store the resulting file in ASCII format.

The program listings in the book are identical to the source code provided on the companion disks. The files on the companion disk are direct copies of the files on my hard disk. The program listings in the book are direct laser prints of the files on my hard disk. Whether you are using the companion disk or typing the listings from the book, you are using a first-generation copy of the source code used to build and verify the demonstration programs discussed in the text.

Starting Zortech C++

To begin a programming session, you must first make C:\ZORTECH \SOURCE the current directory and then start the Zortech C++ editor. The editor is also called the Zortech C++ workbench.

 To reset the current directory, enter the following line at the operating system prompt.

    CD C:\ZORTECH\SOURCE

Then, to start the Zortech C++ editor, enter the following line at the operating system prompt.

    C:\ZORTECH\BIN\ZWB

For convenience you can place these two lines in a batch file and simply run the batch file to start a programming session. The batch file I use is named ZORTECH.BAT.

Configuring your C++ programming environment

The Zortech C++ editor was configured in the following manner during development and testing of the demonstration programs in the book. You might find it helpful to configure your platform in a similar manner, at least until you have successfully compiled and run a few of the sample applications.

Navigating the Zortech C++ menu system

For the purposes of this discussion, the following syntax is used. F10/Options /Configuration is intended to mean that you select the Options menu from the menu bar, and then choose the Configuration selection from the Options menu. In other words, F10/Options/Configuration means the Configuration selection from the Options menu.

A working configuration

First, select the F10/Option/Configuration menu and set Tab Size to 2.

Next, choose the F10/Compile/Compile Options menu. Set the Memory Model to large. Source should be set to Assume C++. Use the default settings for Object Code, Link Options, and Debug Options. Under the Options selection, enable Warnings and Verbose Compile.

In the F10/Compile/Debug Options menu, use the default settings.

Storing the editor configuration

The Zortech C++ 2.12 editor automatically saves the condition of the editing environment in a special configuration file in the C:\ZORTECH\BIN subdirectory whenever you exit a programming session. The next time you start the Zortech C++ editor, the configuration you were using in your previous work session will be in effect.

Testing a sample program

First, start Zortech C++ as described above. When the editor prompts you for a Read File, enter LIB2D.CPP. The Zortech C++ editor will load LIB2D.CPP into the editing buffer.

Next, scroll down to line 0058 and change #define BGI to #define FG. At line 0059 change #define BORLAND to #define ZORTECH. By altering these two lines you are ensuring that only blocks of code that are compatible with Zortech C++ will be compiled.

After making these two changes, select the F10/File/Save menu to save the revised source file to your hard disk. Then choose F10/File/Exit to leave the editor and return to the operating system.

Restart the Zortech C++ editor. When prompted for the name of a Read File, enter STARTUP.CPP. Change line 0067 to #define FG. Change line 0068 to #define ZORTECH. Then choose F10/File/Save to save the revised source file to your hard disk.

In the F10/Compile/Compiler Command Line menu enter LIB2D FG.LIB. This tells the compiler that the files LIB2D.CPP and FG.LIB will be required in addition to the primary file STARTUP.CPP when building the finished executable.

Next, choose F10/Compile/Program Command Line and enter STARTUP /M10. This tells the Zortech C++ editor the command line argument you wish it to invoke when you are testing your program under the control of the editor. The /M10 argument specifies the 640×350×16-color mode of the VGA and EGA. If you are using a VGA, you can later change this to /M12 after you have the demonstration program up and running. If you are using an MCGA, type /M11 instead. If you are using a CGA, you can use /M06. If a Hercules graphics adapter is installed in your computer system, you can use /MHC. The autodetect routine in the LIB2D.CPP class implementation file will override any illegal arguments.

Finally, choose F10/Compile/Compile to compile and link your program. Zortech C++ will compile STARTUP.CPP and LIB2D.CPP to .obj format. It will then link STARTUP.OBJ and LIB2D.OBJ with the Zortech C++ Flash Graphics module FG.LIB to create the finished executable file, STARTUP.EXE.

When you see the Compiled Successfully message, select F10/Compile/Run Program to run the executable file.

Alternatively, you can use the command line version of the Zortech C++ compiler to build an .exe file. Provided that all necessary paths have been defined in your autoexec.bat file or all required files are in the current directory, you can use the following command line with Zortech C++ version 2.12. Enter:

    ZTC -ml -cpp -p -C -v STARTUP LIB2D FG.LIB

Running other demonstration programs

To compile, link, and run other demonstration programs from the book, refer to the header in each source file for a list of files that make up the project list. After you become familiar with the Zortech C++ menu system, you can load more than one source file into the editor during a programming session. Although the Zortech C++ editor lets you switch between the source files on the display, it is important that the primary source file is in the current window when you begin a compile sequence. Zortech C++ compiles the current window first and then checks your F10/Compiler/Compiler Command Line to see if other modules must be added in order to build the finished executable.

When you are testing the other demonstration programs, be sure to change the two preprocessor directives in each demonstration listing and in each class implementation listing. Change #define BGI to #define FG, and change #define BORLAND to #define ZORTECH.

Note that when you use Zortech C++ to compile demonstration programs that need to be linked with the LIB3D.CPP class implementation listing in appendix B, you must explicitly enlarge your program stack. For example, if you are building OBJECTS.CPP, the 3-D interactive modeling and shading demo, you should choose the F10/Compiler/Compiler Command Line menu item and enter:

    =20000 -b LIB3D LIB2D FG.LIB

This sets the stack size to 20000 bytes. The -b switch invokes a special version of the Zortech C++ compiler that can handle large programs. The command line ensures LIB3D.CPP and LIB2D.CPP will be linked with OBJECTS .CPP and FG.LIB when building the finished .exe file.

Alternatively, you can compile OBJECTS.CPP with the command line version of the Zortech C++ 2.12 compiler by using the following line at the operating system prompt. Enter:

    ZTC -ml -cpp -p -C -v OBJECTS =20000 -b LIB3D LIB2D FG.LIB

Zortech C++ programmer's notes

Zortech C++ 2.12 and the graphics library that comes bundled with it, Flash Graphics, were used to test and verify the demonstration programs in the book. If you use Zortech C++ version 2.12 and follow the instructions in this appendix, you can compile, link, and run all the demonstration programs except HIT.CPP and GUI.CPP, which rely upon XOR graphic arrays.

If you are using Zortech C++, the 3-D images produced by the demonstration program OBJECTS.CPP are not shaded or dithered. The 3-D solids are drawn as black-edged facets whose hues can be set interactively.

By carefully inspecting the class implementation listing LIB2D.CPP in appendix E, you can identify the blocks of code that explicitly support the capabilities of the Flash Graphics fg.lib graphics library. For example, Zortech C++ uses the lower left corner of the display as the origin 0,0. LIB2D.CPP also provides significant support for the graphic array functions of Flash Graphics, keeping track of the width and depth of a bitblt, accommodating the fg_color_t type, and performing other low-level maintenance chores.

LIB2D.CPP uses a simple stub routine in place of any calls that attempt to use viewports. You can, however, readily create code to support viewports by using Zortech C++'s fg_box_t ClipBox function.

Using different versions of Zortech C++

To ensure that you are using the same version of Flash Graphics that was used to test the demonstration programs, you might wish to check the Zortech C++ header file fg.h for the following statement.

```
fg_version_sync_June_6_1990 = 0;
```

If you are using a different version of Zortech C++ and Flash Graphics, you might find it helpful to make some minor modifications to the demonstration programs.

If you are using Zortech C++ 2.18 and the companion version of Flash Graphics that is shipped with it, make the following edits.

First, add the following line as the final statement in main() in each demonstration listing.

```
return (EXIT_SUCCESS);
```

Next, instead of using the return value to detect the presence of a graphics adapter at startup, make the following changes to LIB2D.CPP in appendix E.

Delete lines 0175 through 0186 inclusive in method PhysicalDisplay::SetupMode( ). Insert instead the following statement.

```
fg_init();
```

Then, depending on which graphics adapter you are using, add a second statement immediately following fg_init().

If you are using a VGA graphics adapter, add

```
return zVGA_12H;
```

If you are using an EGA graphics adapter with an EGA display, type:

```
return zEGA_10H;
```

If you are using an EGA graphics adapter with a standard color display, use:

```
return zEGA_EH;
```

If you are using an MCGA graphics adapter, type:

```
return zMCGA_11H;
```

If you are using a CGA graphics adapter, type:

```
return zCGA_6H;
```

If you have a Hercules graphics adapter installed in your computer system, type:

```
return zHERC;
```

These changes will provide a manual method for selecting a graphics mode when each demonstration program starts. You can build an autodetect routine by inspecting the various fields in the Flash Graphics structure fg after a call to fg_init( ).

Also note that the editor menu system for Zortech C++ version 2.18 provides a slightly different hierarchy of menus than version 2.12.

D

Compiling
the sample programs
with Microsoft C++

The demonstration programs in the book were developed and tested using Turbo C++ 1.2, Borland C++ 2.0, and Zortech C++ 2.12. However, the source code was carefully designed to provide a smooth migration to Microsoft's anticipated C++ compiler, which was still under development as this book went to press.

Fortunately, Microsoft has traditionally maintained a consistent upgrade path for its C graphics library, graph.lib. The graphics library provided with QuickC 2.00 was a slightly enhanced version of the graphics library provided with the earlier Microsoft C 5.10. Most, if not all, C graphics programs could be compiled without source code changes under both QuickC 2.00 and Microsoft C 5.10. Next to be released were the Microsoft C Professional Development System 6.00 and the QuickC 2.50 compiler, which included binary-compatible graphics libraries that were a further enhancement of the familiar Microsoft graphics library, graph.lib.

Using past performance as a guide, industry analysts have predicted that the graphics library that Microsoft will bundle with its anticipated C++ compiler is likely to be an upwardly compatible version of its traditional graphics library, graph.lib.

The source code for the class libraries in appendix E is nominally compatible with Microsoft's traditional graphics library, graph.lib. The C++ syntax used in the demonstration programs throughout the book adheres to the AT&T C++ 2.0 specification, which is likely to be supported by Microsoft's C++ compiler. The graphics library language bindings used in the LIB2D.CPP class implementation listing in appendix E are compatible with the graphics library distributed with Microsoft QuickC 2.50 and the Microsoft C Professional Development System 6.00.

If you want to compile, link, and run the demonstration programs using Microsoft's anticipated C++ compiler, two types of hand-coding might be required. First, you might encounter a few discrepancies when text is written to the display while in a graphics mode. The background of each character cel might be black. You might be required to change the color being used for text display in each demonstration program. Second, you might need to write new code to support the font displays used in the desktop publishing demonstration program, DESKTOP.CPP.

E

Source code for
the class libraries

This appendix contains the complete source code for the class libraries used by the demonstration programs in the main body of the book. The listings include .hpp class declaration files and .cpp class implementation files. In aggregate, the class libraries provide a working set of language bindings, mapping all graphics calls to Turbo C++ 1.2 graphics.lib, Borland C++ 2.0 graphics.lib, Zortech C++ 2.12 fg.lib, and Microsoft's graph.lib.

If you are using Turbo C++ 1.2 to compile, link, and run the demonstration programs, the class libraries provided in this appendix are ready for you to use with your compiler. You might also find it helpful to read appendix A, "Compiling the sample programs with Turbo C++."

If you are using Borland C++ 2.0 to compile, link, and run the demonstration programs, you might find it helpful to read appendix B, "Compiling the sample programs with Borland C++."

If you are using Zortech C++ 2.12 to compile, link, and run the demonstration programs, you might find it helpful to read appendix C, "Compiling the sample programs with Zortech C++."

License You can use these class libraries in your own C++ graphics software projects, subject to the License Agreement and Limited Warranty described in FIG. 8 in the introduction to the book.

E-1 Source code for LIB2D.HPP, the declaration file for class PhysicalDisplay and class Viewport, providing a set of graphics language bindings for Turbo C++ and Zortech C++. (For Borland C++ language bindings see Fig. E-15.)

```
0001    /*
0002
0003              Lee Adams' SUPERCHARGED C++ GRAPHICS
0004         Header file for graphics library language bindings
0005
```

E-1 Continued.

```
0006       SOURCE FILE:  LIB2D.HPP
0007       TYPE:  declarations for classes PhysicalDisplay and Viewport
0008
0009                DEVELOPER'S GUIDE TO THE INTERFACE
0010     Before using graphics, you must create objects of the classes
0011     PhysicalDisplay and Viewport, and call methods of each object
0012     to switch the display to a graphics mode and setup various
0013     graphics parameters.  To create graphics output, call the
0014     appropriate methods of your objects.  Refer to any of the
0015     demonstration programs in the book for examples of here-is-
0016     how-it's-done source code.
0017     Class declarations are located in LIB2D.HPP (which must be
0018        used in your program as #include "LIB2D.HPP").
0019     Function definitions are located in LIB2D.CPP.
0020        Either LIB2D.CPP or LIB2D.OBJ must be named in the project
0021        list for your program.
0022
0023     LICENSE:  As purchaser of the book in which this source code
0024        appears you are granted a royalty-free license to reproduce
0025        and distribute executable files generated using this code
0026        provided that you accept the conditions of the License
0027        Agreement and Limited Warranty described in the book.
0028     PUBLICATION: Contains material from Windcrest/McGraw-Hill
0029        book 3489, published by TAB BOOKS.
0030     U.S. GOVERNMENT RESTRICTED RIGHTS:  This software and its
0031        documentation is provided with restricted rights.  The use,
0032        duplication, or disclosure by the Government is subject to
0033        restrictions set forth in subdivision (b)(3)(ii) of The
0034        Rights in Technical Data and Computer Software clause at
0035        252.227-7013.  Contractor/manufacturer is Lee Adams, c/o
0036        TAB BOOKS, 13311 Monterey Ave., Blue Ridge Summit PA 17294.
0037     TRADEMARK:  Lee Adams is a trademark of Lee Adams.
0038
0039        Copyright 1991 Lee Adams.  All rights reserved worldwide.
0040
0041                                                              */
0042     #if !defined (__LARGE__)
0043     #error Must use large memory model.
0044     #endif
0045
0046     #if defined (BGI)        // include the appropriate header file...
0047     #include <graphics.h>
0048     #elif defined (FG)
0049     #include <fg.h>
0050     #elif defined (MS)
0051     #include <graph.h>
0052     #endif
0053
0054     class PhysicalDisplay     // physical display (adapter and monitor).
0055     {                // pen color, pen style, brush color, brush style, etc.
0056        // uses the physical coordinates of the current graphics mode.
0057     private:           // accessable by member functions and friends only.
0058        static int ObjectReady;        // indicates if object initialized.
0059        static int RAMpage;            // indicates if hidden page in RAM.
0060        static int ScreenMode;              // current graphics mode.
0061        static int TextWidth;                   // character matrix...
0062        static int TextHeight;
0063        static int ClipLeft;                 // viewport clipping coords...
0064        static int ClipTop;
0065        static int ClipRight;
0066        static int ClipBottom;
0067        static char SolidFill[8];                 // 100% fill pattern.
```

```
0068    static unsigned int Plane_Length;          // length of bitplane.
0069    static char far * BitMap0;      // storage of hidden page in RAM...
0070    static char far * BitMap1;
0071    static char far * BitMap2;
0072    static char far * BitMap3;
0073    union{struct {unsigned int A1; unsigned int A2;} Address;
0074        char far * FarAddress;} U1;  // union to calculate addresses.
0075    static unsigned int Seg1;   // hidden bitplane segment address...
0076    static unsigned int Seg2;
0077    static unsigned int Seg3;
0078    static unsigned int Seg4;
0079    static unsigned int Off1;    // hidden bitplane offset address...
0080    static unsigned int Off2;
0081    static unsigned int Off3;
0082    static unsigned int Off4;
0083    static int CurrentClr;                    // for Zortech's fg.lib...
0084    static int WriteMode;
0085    static int CurrentX;
0086    static int CurrentY;
0087    static int FGmaxY;
0088    static int CurrentFill;
0089    static int CurrentTextX;
0090    static int CurrentTextY;
0091    static int ArrayWidth;
0092    static int ArrayDepth;
0093    char far * InitHiddenPage(void);     // initialize hidden bitmap.
0094    void FreeMemory(char far *);      // releases a block of memory.
0095    public:   // data and methods accessable by any in-scope function.
0096    PhysicalDisplay();                          // constructor.
0097    ~PhysicalDisplay();                          // destructor.
0098    friend class Viewport;      // Viewport objects have full access.
0099    friend class Layout;          // Layout objects have full access.
0100    void Init2D(int,int,int,int,int);     // sets 2D graphics state.
0101    int SetupMode(void);     // detect and set up best graphics mode.
0102    void ForceMode(int);      // forces a particular graphics mode.
0103    void ShutDownGraphics(void);       // return to text mode.
0104    void SetHue(int);          // sets the current drawing color.
0105    void SetWriteMode(int);        // sets PSET or XOR write mode.
0106    void SetRGB(int,int,int,int);    // sets RGB values for a color.
0107    void SetLine(int);            // sets the current line style.
0108    void SetFill(char *, int);      // sets the area zFill style.
0109    void BackUp(void);          // copies page 0 to hidden page.
0110    void Restore(void);          // copies hidden page to page 0.
0111    int InitUndo(void);                    // sets up undo page.
0112    void SetWritePage(int);               // sets the active page.
0113    void SetDisplayPage(int);           // sets the displayed page.
0114    void BlankPage(void);        // blanks the current active page.
0115    };
0116
0117    class Viewport              // a viewport on the physical display.
0118    {              // has access to all members of class PhysicalDisplay.
0119        // is a virtual display using its own local coordinate system.
0120    private:   // data and methods accessable by member functions only.
0121    int ViewportReady;          // indicates if object initialized.
0122    PhysicalDisplay *GenericDisplay;              // backward pointer.
0123    public:   // data and methods accessable by any in-scope function.
0124    Viewport(PhysicalDisplay *);                  // constructor.
0125    ~Viewport();                                  // destructor.
0126    void SetPosition(int,int);      // sets the current xy position.
0127    void DrawLine(int,int);   // draws line from current xy position.
0128    void DrawBorder(int,int,int,int);          // draws rectangle.
0129    void DrawPanel(int,int,int,int);      // draws solid rectangle.
0130    void DrawPolygon(int, int far *);        // draws solid polygon.
```

```
0131    void DrawFacet(int, int far *);      // draws transparent polygon.
0132    void DrawCircle(int,int,int);                      // draws circle.
0133    void PutText(int,int,int,char *);                  // display text.
0134    void SetTextRowCol(int,int);              // set text position.
0135    void ClearTextLine(void);         // blanks the dialog text line.
0136    void Fill(int,int,int);                               // area fill.
0137 #if defined (BGI)              // if using Borland's graphics.lib...
0138    char far * MemBlock(int,int,int,int);        // allocate memory.
0139    void FreeBlock(char far *);               // deallocate memory.
0140    void GetBlock(int,int,int,int,char far *);       // save array.
0141    void PutXOR(int,int,char far *);             // show XOR array.
0142    void PutPSET(int,int,char far *);           // show PSET array.
0143    void PutAND(int,int,char far *);             // show AND array.
0144 #elif defined (FG)                // if using Zortech's fg.lib...
0145    fg_color_t far * MemBlock(int,int,int,int);
0146    void FreeBlock(fg_color_t far *);
0147    void GetBlock(int,int,int,int,fg_color_t far *);
0148    void PutXOR(int,int,fg_color_t far *);
0149    void PutPSET(int,int,fg_color_t far *);
0150    void PutAND(int,int,fg_color_t far *);
0151 #elif defined (MS)           // if using Microsoft's graph.lib...
0152    char far * MemBlock(int,int,int,int);
0153    void FreeBlock(char far *);
0154    void GetBlock(int,int,int,int,char far *);
0155    void PutXOR(int,int,char far *);
0156    void PutPSET(int,int,char far *);
0157    void PutAND(int,int,char far *);
0158 #endif
0159    unsigned long GetBlockSize(int,int,int,int);    // size of array.
0160    void WindowOpen(int,int,int,int); // open a viewport, overloaded.
0161    void WindowOpen(int,int,int,int,int);           //...plus border.
0162    void WindowOpen(int,int,int,int,int,int);      //...plus repaint.
0163    void WindowClose(int,int);               // shuts down viewport.
0164    void WindowClear(int bgclr= 0);   // clear viewport, default 0.
0165 };
0166 /*
0167
0168 ┌──────────────────────────────────────────────────────────────┐
       │            End of LIB2D.HPP header file.                       │
0169   └──────────────────────────────────────────────────────────────┘
0170                                                                   */
```

E-2 Source code for LIB2D.CPP, the implementation file for class PhysicalDisplay and class Viewport, providing low-level graphics methods for Turbo C++ and Zortech C++. (For Borland C++ routines see Fig. E-16.)

```
0001 /*
0002
0003 ┌──────────────────────────────────────────────────────────────┐
       │          Lee Adams' SUPERCHARGED C++ GRAPHICS                  │
0004   │          Graphics library language bindings for C++            │
0005   ├──────────────────────────────────────────────────────────────┤
0006   │      Implementation file for low-level graphics routines       │
0007   ├──────────────────────────────────────────────────────────────┤
0008   │  Source file:  LIB2D.CPP                                       │
0009   │  Type:   implementation file for class methods.                │
0010   │  Include file:  LIB2D.HPP                                      │
0011   │  Graphics libraries:  Borland graphics library (graphics.lib)  │
0012   │                       Zortech graphics library (fg.lib)        │
0013   │                       Microsoft graphics library (graph.lib)   │
```

```
0014          Languages:  Turbo C++, Zortech C++, and all C++ compilers
0015                      compatible with AT&T C++ specification 2.0.
0016          Memory model:  large.
0017          Graphics:  supports 640x480x16 VGA, 640x350x16 EGA, 640x200x16
0018            EGA, 640x480x2 MCGA, 640x200x2 CGA, and 720x348x2 Hercules.
0019          Output:  contains class methods that provide bindings to a
0020                   variety of different retail C++ graphics libraries.
0021          Usage:  refer to the header file LIB2D.HPP for a guide to
0022                  using the methods of PhysicalDisplay and Viewport.
0023          License:  As purchaser of the book in which this module
0024            appears you are granted a royalty-free license to reproduce
0025            and distribute executable files generated using this code,
0026            provided that you accept the conditions of the License
0027            Agreement and Limited Warranty described in the book.
0028          Publication: Contains material from Windcrest/McGraw-Hill
0029            book 3489, published by TAB BOOKS.
0030          U.S. Government Restricted Rights:  This software and its
0031            documentation is provided with restricted rights.  The use,
0032            duplication, or disclosure by the Government is subject to
0033            restrictions set forth in subdivision (b)(3)(ii) of The
0034            Rights in Technical Data and Computer Software clause at
0035            252.227-7013.  Contractor/manufacturer is Lee Adams and TAB
0036            BOOKS, 13311 Monterey Ave., Blue Ridge Summit PA 17214.
0037          Trademarks:  Lee Adams is a trademark of Lee Adams.
0038
0039                   Copyright 1991 Lee Adams.  All rights reserved.
0040
0041
0042                           CONDITIONAL COMPILATION
0043          To compile only those blocks of code that support the C++
0044          compiler and graphics library that you are using, you should
0045          #define the appropriate tokens in the following preprocessor
0046          directives.  Use the following table as your guide:
0047                  GRAPHICS LIBRARY
0048              Borland's graphics.lib                #define BGI
0049              Zortech's fg.lib or fgdebug.lib       #define FG
0050              Microsoft's graph.lib                 #define MS
0051                  COMPILER
0052              Borland Turbo C++ compiler            #define BORLAND
0053              Zortech C++ compiler                  #define ZORTECH
0054              AT&T-compatible C++ compilers         #define MICROSOFT
0055          Be sure you define only one compiler and one graphics library.
0056
0057                                                                        */
0058          #define BGI      1  // indicates the graphics library you are using.
0059          #define BORLAND 1  // indicates the C++ compiler you are using.
0060          /*
0061
0062                                CONSTANTS
0063
0064                                                                        */
0065          const int zFAIL=      0;                    // boolean token.
0066          const int zVGA_12H=   1;              // VGA 640x480x16/256.
0067          const int zEGA_10H=   2;               // EGA 640x350x16/64.
0068          const int zEGA_EH=    3;                  // EGA 640x200x16.
0069          const int zMCGA_11H=  4;                   // MCGA 640x480x2.
0070          const int zCGA_6H=    5;             // CGA 640x200x2-color.
0071          const int zHERC=      6;         // Hercules 720x348x2-color.
0072          const int zYES=       1;                    // boolean token.
0073          const int zNO=        0;                    // boolean token.
0074          /*
0075
0076                                INCLUDE FILES
```

```
0077 |_____|
0078                                                                  */
0079 #include "LIB2D.HPP"       // class declarations.
0080                            // include compiler-dependent header files...
0081 #if defined (BORLAND)
0082 #include <dos.h>            // outportb().
0083 #include <alloc.h>          // farmalloc(), farfree().
0084 #include <mem.h>            // movedata().
0085 #elif defined (ZORTECH)
0086 #include <dos.h>            // outp(), farmalloc(), farfree().
0087 #include <string.h>         // movedata().
0088 #elif defined (MICROSOFT)
0089 #include <conio.h>          // outp().
0090 #include <malloc.h>         // _fmalloc(), _ffree().
0091 #include <string.h>         // movedata().
0092 #endif
0093 /*
0094
0095  ┌─────────────────────────────────────────────────────────────────┐
         Class PhysicalDisplay:   CONSTRUCTOR
0096  └─────────────────────────────────────────────────────────────────┘
0097                                                                  */
0098 PhysicalDisplay::PhysicalDisplay()
0099 {
0100 ObjectReady= zYES;
0101 RAMpage= zNO;
0102 ScreenMode= 0;
0103 TextWidth= 0; TextHeight= 0;
0104 ClipLeft= 0; ClipTop= 0; ClipRight= 0; ClipBottom= 0;
0105 SolidFill[0]= 255; SolidFill[1]= 255; SolidFill[2]= 255;
0106 SolidFill[3]= 255; SolidFill[4]= 255; SolidFill[5]= 255;
0107 SolidFill[6]= 255; SolidFill[7]= 255;
0108 Plane_Length= 0; WriteMode= 0;
0109 #if defined (FG)
0110    fg_version_sync();                // ensure correct fg.lib version.
0111 #endif
0112 }
0113 /*
0114
0115  ┌─────────────────────────────────────────────────────────────────┐
         Class PhysicalDisplay:   DESTRUCTOR
0116  └─────────────────────────────────────────────────────────────────┘
0117                                                                  */
0118 PhysicalDisplay::~PhysicalDisplay()
0119 {
0120 ObjectReady= zNO;
0121 }
0122 /*
0123
0124  ┌─────────────────────────────────────────────────────────────────┐
         STARTUP AND SHUTDOWN OF THE GRAPHICS STATE
0125  └─────────────────────────────────────────────────────────────────┘
0126                                                                  */
0127 int PhysicalDisplay::SetupMode(void)
0128 {                              // detect and set up best graphics mode.
0129 #if defined (BGI)                          // if using graphics.lib...
0130    int graphics_adapter, graphics_mode;
0131   detectgraph(&graphics_adapter,&graphics_mode);
0132    if (graphics_adapter==VGA)
0133    {
0134    graphics_adapter=VGA; graphics_mode=VGAHI;
0135    initgraph(&graphics_adapter,&graphics_mode,"");
0136    settextstyle(0,0,1);
0137    return zVGA_12H;
0138    }
```

```
0139      if (graphics_mode==EGAHI)
0140        {
0141        graphics_adapter=EGA; graphics_mode=EGAHI;
0142        initgraph(&graphics_adapter,&graphics_mode,"");
0143        settextstyle(0,0,1);
0144        return zEGA_10H;
0145        }
0146      if (graphics_mode==EGALO)
0147        {
0148        graphics_adapter=EGA; graphics_mode=EGALO;
0149        initgraph(&graphics_adapter,&graphics_mode,"");
0150        settextstyle(0,0,1);
0151        return zEGA_EH;
0152        }
0153      if (graphics_adapter==MCGA)
0154        {
0155        graphics_adapter=MCGA; graphics_mode=MCGAHI;
0156        initgraph(&graphics_adapter,&graphics_mode,"");
0157        settextstyle(0,0,1);
0158        return zMCGA_11H;
0159        }
0160      if (graphics_adapter==CGA)
0161        {
0162        graphics_adapter=CGA; graphics_mode=CGAHI;
0163        initgraph(&graphics_adapter,&graphics_mode,"");
0164        settextstyle(0,0,1);
0165        return zCGA_6H;
0166        }
0167      if (graphics_adapter==HERCMONO)
0168        {
0169        graphics_adapter=HERCMONO; graphics_mode=HERCMONOHI;
0170        initgraph(&graphics_adapter,&graphics_mode,"");
0171        return zHERC;
0172        }
0173      return zFAIL;
0174  #elif defined (FG)                            // if using fg.lib...
0175        int graphics_adapter;
0176      graphics_adapter= fg_get_type();              // detect hardware.
0177      switch(graphics_adapter)
0178        {
0179        case FG_VGA12:     fg_init_vga12(); return zVGA_12H;
0180        case FG_EGAECD:    fg_init_egaecd(); return zEGA_10H;
0181        case FG_EGACOLOR:  fg_init_egacolor(); return zEGA_EH;
0182        case FG_VGA11:     fg_init_vga11(); return zMCGA_11H;
0183        case FG_CGAHIRES:  fg_init_cga(); return zCGA_6H;
0184        case FG_HERCFULL:  fg_init_herc(); return zHERC;
0185        default: return zFAIL;
0186        }
0187  #elif defined (MS)                        // if using graph.lib...
0188      if (_setvideomoderows(_VRES16COLOR,60)!=zFAIL) return zVGA_12H;
0189      if (_setvideomoderows(_ERESCOLOR,43)!=zFAIL) return zEGA_10H;
0190      if (_setvideomoderows(_HRES16COLOR,25)!=zFAIL) return zEGA_EH;
0191      if (_setvideomoderows(_VRES2COLOR,60)!=zFAIL) return zMCGA_11H;
0192      if (_setvideomoderows(_HRESBW,25)!=zFAIL) return zCGA_6H;
0193      if (_setvideomoderows(_HERCMONO,25)!=zFAIL) return zHERC;
0194      return zFAIL;
0195  #endif
0196  }
0197
0198
0199  void PhysicalDisplay::ForceMode(int NewMode)
0200  {        // force graphics adapter into a downward-compatible mode.
0201    int graphics_adapter, graphics_mode;
```

E-2 Continued.

```
0202   switch(NewMode)
0203   {
0204   #if defined (BGI)                      // if using graphics.lib...
0205     case zEGA_10H:                              // 640x350x16 mode.
0206       graphics_adapter=EGA; graphics_mode=EGAHI;
0207       initgraph(&graphics_adapter,&graphics_mode,"");
0208       settextstyle(0,0,1);
0209       break;
0210     case zEGA_EH:                              // 640x200x16 mode.
0211       graphics_adapter=EGA; graphics_mode=EGALO;
0212       initgraph(&graphics_adapter,&graphics_mode,"");
0213       settextstyle(0,0,1);
0214       break;
0215     case zMCGA_11H:                            // 640x480x2 mode.
0216       ShutDownGraphics();          // unload previous BGI driver.
0217       graphics_adapter=MCGA; graphics_mode=MCGAHI;
0218       initgraph(&graphics_adapter,&graphics_mode,"");
0219       settextstyle(0,0,1);
0220       break;
0221     case zCGA_6H:                              // 640x200x2 mode.
0222       ShutDownGraphics();          // unload previous BGI driver.
0223       graphics_adapter=CGA; graphics_mode=CGAHI;
0224       initgraph(&graphics_adapter,&graphics_mode,"");
0225       settextstyle(0,0,1);
0226       break;
0227   #elif defined (FG)                     // if using fg.lib...
0228     case zEGA_10H:                          // 640x350x16 mode.
0229       fg_term(); fg_init_egaecd();
0230       break;
0231     case zEGA_EH:                           // 640x200x16 mode.
0232       fg_term(); fg_init_egacolor();
0233       break;
0234     case zMCGA_11H:                         // 640x480x2 mode.
0235       fg_term(); fg_init_vga11();
0236       break;
0237     case zCGA_6H:                           // 640x200x2 mode.
0238       fg_term(); fg_init_cga();
0239       break;
0240   #elif defined (MS)                     // if using graph.lib...
0241     case zEGA_10H:                          // 640x350x16 mode.
0242       _setvideomoderows(_ERESCOLOR,43);
0243       break;
0244     case zEGA_EH:                           // 640x200x16 mode.
0245       _setvideomoderows(_HRES16COLOR,25);
0246       break;
0247     case zMCGA_11H:                         // 640x480x2 mode.
0248       _setvideomoderows(_VRES2COLOR,60);
0249       break;
0250     case zCGA_6H:                           // 640x200x2 mode.
0251       _setvideomoderows(_HRESBW,25);
0252       break;
0253   #endif
0254   }
0255   return;
0256   }
0257
0258
0259   void PhysicalDisplay::Init2D(int token,int x1,int yf1,int x2,int y2)
0260   {                              // initialize various parameters.
0261   ClipLeft= x1; ClipTop= yf1; ClipRight= x2; ClipBottom= y2;
0262   FGmaxY= y2; CurrentX= 0; CurrentY= 0;     // used by fg.lib only.
0263   CurrentFill= 7; CurrentClr= 7;            // ...
```

```
0264  CurrentTextX= 0; CurrentTextY= 100;          // ...
0265  ArrayWidth= 0; ArrayDepth= 0;                // ...
0266  #if defined (FG)                             // if using Flash Graphics...
0267    fg_setlinepattern(FG_LINE_USER_DEFINED, 0xffff);
0268    WriteMode= FG_MODE_SET;
0269  #endif
0270  switch (token)
0271    {
0272    case zVGA_12H: Plane_Length=38400;ScreenMode=zVGA_12H;
0273                   #if defined (FG)
0274                      TextWidth=8;TextHeight=14;break;
0275                   #endif
0276                      TextWidth=8;TextHeight=8;break;
0277    case zEGA_10H: Plane_Length=28000;ScreenMode=zEGA_10H;
0278                   #if defined (FG)
0279                      TextWidth=8;TextHeight=14;break;
0280                   #endif
0281                      TextWidth=8;TextHeight=8;break;
0282    case zEGA_EH: Plane_Length=16000;ScreenMode=zEGA_EH;
0283               TextWidth=8;TextHeight=8;break;
0284    case zMCGA_11H: Plane_Length=38400;ScreenMode=zMCGA_11H;
0285                    #if defined (FG)
0286                       TextWidth=8;TextHeight=14;break;
0287                    #endif
0288                       TextWidth=8;TextHeight=8;break;
0289    case zCGA_6H: Plane_Length=16384;ScreenMode=zCGA_6H;
0290               TextWidth=8;TextHeight=8;break;
0291    case zHERC: Plane_Length=32406;ScreenMode=zHERC;
0292             TextWidth=9;TextHeight=14;break;
0293    }
0294  return;
0295  }
0296
0297
0298  void PhysicalDisplay::ShutDownGraphics(void)
0299  {                                   // graceful shutdown of graphics mode.
0300  if (RAMpage==zYES)                         // if a hidden page in RAM...
0301    {                               // then release the appropriate memory...
0302    switch(ScreenMode)
0303      {
0304      case zVGA_12H:    FreeMemory(BitMap3); FreeMemory(BitMap2);
0305                        FreeMemory(BitMap1); FreeMemory(BitMap0);
0306                        break;
0307      case zMCGA_11H:   FreeMemory(BitMap0); break;
0308      case zCGA_6H:     FreeMemory(BitMap0); break;
0309      }
0310    RAMpage= zNO;
0311    }
0312  #if defined (BGI)
0313    cleardevice();                                     // clear the screen.
0314    closegraph();           // shut down graphics, restore original mode.
0315  #elif defined (FG)
0316    fg_fillbox(FG_BLACK, FG_MODE_SET, ~0, fg.displaybox);
0317    fg_term();                                    // restore original mode.
0318  #elif defined (MS)
0319    _clearscreen(_GCLEARSCREEN);                        // clear the screen.
0320    _setvideomode(_DEFAULTMODE);                   // restore original mode.
0321  #endif
0322  return;
0323  }
0324  /*
0325
0326  ┌─────────────────────────────────────────────────────────────────┐
      │               SET ATTRIBUTES FOR PENS AND BRUSHES                 │
```

```
0327  |_____|
0328                                                                      */
0329  void PhysicalDisplay::SetHue(int hueclr)
0330  {                                                 // set the pen color.
0331  #if defined (BGI)
0332    setcolor(hueclr);
0333  #elif defined (FG)
0334    CurrentClr= hueclr;
0335  #elif defined (MS)
0336    _setcolor(hueclr);
0337  #endif
0338  return;
0339  }
0340
0341
0342  void PhysicalDisplay::SetWriteMode(int WMode)
0343  {                                     // set PSET or XOR writing mode.
0344  #if defined (BGI)
0345    if (WMode==1) setwritemode(XOR_PUT);
0346    else setwritemode(COPY_PUT);
0347  #elif defined (FG)
0348    if (WMode==1) WriteMode= FG_MODE_XOR;
0349    else WriteMode= FG_MODE_SET;
0350  #elif defined (MS)
0351    if (WMode==1) _setwritemode(_GXOR);
0352    else _setwritemode(_GPSET);
0353  #endif
0354  return;
0355  }
0356
0357
0358  void PhysicalDisplay::SetLine(int style)
0359  {                                                 // set the pen style.
0360  #if defined (BGI)
0361    setlinestyle(USERBIT_LINE,style,NORM_WIDTH);
0362  #elif defined (FG)
0363    fg_setlinepattern(FG_LINE_USER_DEFINED, style);
0364  #elif defined (MS)
0365    _setlinestyle(style);
0366  #endif
0367  return;
0368  }
0369
0370
0371  void PhysicalDisplay::SetFill(char *pattern,int hueclr)
0372  {                                 // set the brush color and pattern.
0373  #if defined (BGI)
0374    if(ScreenMode>zEGA_EH) {if(hueclr!=0) hueclr=1;}
0375    setfillpattern(pattern,hueclr);
0376    pattern++;
0377    if (*pattern==SolidFill[1]) setfillstyle(SOLID_FILL,hueclr);
0378  #elif defined (FG)
0379    CurrentFill= hueclr;
0380  #elif defined (MS)
0381    _setcolor(hueclr);
0382    _setfillmask(pattern);
0383  #endif
0384  return;
0385  }
0386
0387
0388  void PhysicalDisplay::SetRGB(int Clr,int Red,int Green,int Blue)
```

```
0389  {                          // set the hardware RGB values for a color index.
0390  #if defined (BGI)
0391    setrgbpalette(Clr,Red,Green,Blue);
0392  #elif defined (FG)
0393    fg_setpalette(Clr,Red,Green,Blue);
0394  #elif defined (MS)
0395      long int VGAcode=0;
0396      long int Rv1=0,Gv1=0,Bv1=0;
0397    Rv1=(long)RedVolts;                      // convert to long int...
0398    Gv1=(long)GrnVolts;
0399    Bv1=(long)BluVolts;
0400    VGAcode=(Bv1*65536)+(Gv1*256)+Rv1;       // calculate analog code.
0401    _remappalette(clr,VGAcode);                         // write it.
0402  #endif
0403  return;
0404  }
0405  /*
0406
0407  ┌─────────────────────────────────────────────────────────────────────┐
       │                        PAGE OPERATIONS                                │
0408  └─────────────────────────────────────────────────────────────────────┘
0409                                                                        */
0410  void PhysicalDisplay::SetWritePage(int Page)
0411  {                                          // set the active page.
0412  #if defined (BGI)
0413    setactivepage(Page);
0414  #elif defined (FG)
0415    fg_setactivepage(Page);
0416  #elif defined (MS)
0417    _setactivepage(Page);
0418  #endif
0419  return;
0420  }
0421
0422
0423  void PhysicalDisplay::SetDisplayPage(int Page)
0424  {                                          // set the displayed page.
0425  #if defined (BGI)
0426    setvisualpage(Page);
0427  #elif defined (FG)
0428    fg_setdisplaypage(Page);
0429  #elif defined (MS)
0430    _setvisualpage(Page);
0431  #endif
0432  return;
0433  }
0434
0435
0436  void PhysicalDisplay::BlankPage(void)
0437  {                                          // blank the active page.
0438  #if defined (BGI)
0439    cleardevice();
0440  #elif defined (FG)
0441    fg_fillbox(FG_BLACK, FG_MODE_SET, ~0, fg.displaybox);
0442  #elif defined (MS)
0443    _clearscreen(_GCLEARSCREEN);
0444  #endif
0445  return;
0446  }
0447
0448  /*
0449
0450  ┌─────────────────────────────────────────────────────────────────────┐
       │                  Class Viewport:  CONSTRUCTOR                         │
0451  └─────────────────────────────────────────────────────────────────────┘
```

```
0452                                                                    */
0453    Viewport::Viewport(PhysicalDisplay *Caller)
0454    {      // use physical display object referenced by pointer Caller.
0455    GenericDisplay= Caller; // GenericDisplay points to display object.
0456    ViewportReady= zYES;
0457    }
0458    /*
0459
0460    ┌─────────────────────────────────────────────────────────────────┐
        │              Class Viewport:   DESTRUCTOR                         │
0461    └─────────────────────────────────────────────────────────────────┘
0462                                                                    */
0463    Viewport::~Viewport()
0464    {
0465    ViewportReady= zNO;
0466    }
0467    /*
0468
0469    ┌─────────────────────────────────────────────────────────────────┐
        │                    VIEWPORT OPERATIONS                           │
0470    └─────────────────────────────────────────────────────────────────┘
0471                                                                    */
0472    void Viewport::WindowOpen(int x1,int yf1,int x2,int y2)
0473    {          // open a viewport -- overloaded function has 3 variants.
0474    #if defined (BGI)
0475       setviewport(x1,yf1,x2,y2,1);
0476    #elif defined (FG)
0477       return;
0478    #elif defined (MS)
0479       _setviewport(x1,yf1,x2,y2);
0480    #endif
0481    PhysicalDisplay::ClipLeft= x1;
0482    PhysicalDisplay::ClipTop= yf1;
0483    PhysicalDisplay::ClipRight= x2;
0484    PhysicalDisplay::ClipBottom= y2;
0485    return;
0486    }
0487
0488
0489    void Viewport::WindowOpen(int x1,int yf1,int x2,int y2,
0490                              int borderclr)
0491    {                              // open a viewport with a border.
0492    #if defined (BGI)
0493       GenericDisplay->SetHue(borderclr);
0494       DrawBorder(x1,yf1,x2,y2);
0495       setviewport(x1+1,yf1+1,x2-1,y2-1,1);
0496    #elif defined (FG)
0497       return;
0498    #elif defined (MS)
0499       GenericDisplay->SetHue(borderclr);
0500       DrawBorder(x1,yf1,x2,y2);
0501       _setviewport(x1+1,yf1+1,x2-1,y2-1);
0502    #endif
0503    PhysicalDisplay::ClipLeft= x1 + 1;
0504    PhysicalDisplay::ClipTop= yf1 + 1;
0505    PhysicalDisplay::ClipRight= x2 - 1;
0506    PhysicalDisplay::ClipBottom= y2 - 1;
0507    return;
0508    }
0509
0510
0511    void Viewport::WindowOpen(int x1,int yf1,int x2,int y2,
0512                              int borderclr, int paintclr)
0513    {  // open a viewport with a border and clear the drawing area.
```

```
0514  #if defined (BGI)
0515    GenericDisplay->SetLine(0xffff);
0516    GenericDisplay->SetHue(paintclr);
0517    GenericDisplay->SetFill(PhysicalDisplay::SolidFill, paintclr);
0518    DrawPanel(x1,yf1,x2,y2);
0519    GenericDisplay->SetHue(borderclr);
0520    DrawBorder(x1,yf1,x2,y2);
0521    setviewport(x1+1,yf1+1,x2-1,y2-1,1);
0522  #elif defined (FG)
0523    return;
0524  #elif defined (MS)
0525    GenericDisplay->SetLine(0xffff);
0526    GenericDisplay->SetHue(paintclr);
0527    GenericDisplay->SetFill(PhysicalDisplay::SolidFill, paintclr);
0528    DrawPanel(x1,yf1,x2,y2);
0529    GenericDisplay->SetHue(borderclr);
0530    DrawBorder(x1,yf1,x2,y2);
0531    _setviewport(x1+1,yf1+1,x2-1,y2-1);
0532  #endif
0533  PhysicalDisplay::ClipLeft= x1 + 1;
0534  PhysicalDisplay::ClipTop= yf1 + 1;
0535  PhysicalDisplay::ClipRight= x2 - 1;
0536  PhysicalDisplay::ClipBottom= y2 - 1;
0537  return;
0538  }
0539
0540
0541  void Viewport::WindowClose(int xres,int yres)
0542  {                                                  // close a viewport.
0543  #if defined (BGI)
0544    setviewport(0,0,xres-1,yres-1,1);
0545  #elif defined (FG)
0546    return;
0547  #elif defined (MS)
0548    _setviewport(0,0,xres-1,yres-1);
0549  #endif
0550  PhysicalDisplay::ClipLeft= 0;
0551  PhysicalDisplay::ClipTop= 0;
0552  PhysicalDisplay::ClipRight= xres - 1;
0553  PhysicalDisplay::ClipBottom= yres - 1;
0554  return;
0555  }
0556
0557
0558  void Viewport::WindowClear(int bgclr)
0559  {                                                  // blank a viewport.
0560  #if defined (BGI)
0561    setfillstyle(SOLID_FILL,bgclr);
0562  #elif defined (FG)
0563    return;
0564  #elif defined (MS)
0565    zSetFill(PhysicalDisplay::SolidFill,bgclr);
0566  #endif
0567  DrawPanel(0,0,
0568    (PhysicalDisplay::ClipRight - PhysicalDisplay::ClipLeft),
0569    (PhysicalDisplay::ClipBottom - PhysicalDisplay::ClipTop));
0570  return;
0571  }
0572  /*
0573
0574  +------------------------------------------------------------+
       |              LOW-LEVEL DRAWING FUNCTIONS                   |
       +------------------------------------------------------------+
0575
0576                                                               */
```

```
0577  void Viewport::SetPosition(int x,int y)
0578  {                                        // set the current position.
0579  #if defined (BGI)
0580    moveto(x,y);
0581  #elif defined (FG)
0582    PhysicalDisplay::CurrentX= x; PhysicalDisplay::CurrentY= y;
0583  #elif defined (MS)
0584    _moveto(x,y);
0585  #endif
0586  return;
0587  }
0588
0589
0590  void Viewport::DrawLine(int x,int y)
0591  { // draw a line from the current position using PSET or XOR logic.
0592  #if defined (BGI)
0593    lineto(x,y);
0594  #elif defined (FG)
0595      fg_line_t Line;
0596    Line [FG_X1]= PhysicalDisplay::CurrentX;
0597    Line [FG_Y1]= PhysicalDisplay::FGmaxY - PhysicalDisplay::CurrentY;
0598    Line [FG_X2]= x;
0599    Line [FG_Y2]= PhysicalDisplay::FGmaxY - y;
0600    PhysicalDisplay::CurrentX= x; PhysicalDisplay::CurrentY= y;
0601    fg_drawline(PhysicalDisplay::CurrentClr,
0602                PhysicalDisplay::WriteMode, ~0,
0603                FG_LINE_USER_DEFINED, Line);
0604  #elif defined (MS)
0605    _lineto(x,y);
0606  #endif
0607  return;
0608  }
0609
0610
0611  void Viewport::DrawBorder(int x1,int yf1,int x2,int y2)
0612  {                        // draw a rectangle using PSET or XOR logic.
0613  #if defined (BGI)
0614    rectangle(x1,yf1,x2,y2);
0615  #elif defined (FG)
0616      fg_box_t Box;
0617    Box [FG_X1]= x1;
0618    Box [FG_Y1]= PhysicalDisplay::FGmaxY - y2;
0619    Box [FG_X2]= x2;
0620    Box [FG_Y2]= PhysicalDisplay::FGmaxY - yf1;
0621    fg_drawbox(PhysicalDisplay::CurrentClr,
0622                PhysicalDisplay::WriteMode, ~0,
0623                FG_LINE_USER_DEFINED, Box, fg.displaybox);
0624  #elif defined (MS)
0625    _rectangle(_GBORDER,x1,yf1,x2,y2);
0626  #endif
0627  return;
0628  }
0629
0630
0631  void Viewport::DrawPanel(int x1,int yf1,int x2,int y2)
0632  {                                        // draw a filled rectangle.
0633  #if defined (BGI)
0634    bar(x1,yf1,x2,y2);
0635  #elif defined (FG)
0636      fg_box_t Box;
0637    Box [FG_X1]= x1;
0638    Box [FG_Y1]= PhysicalDisplay::FGmaxY - y2;
```

```
0639      Box [FG_X2]= x2;
0640      Box [FG_Y2]= PhysicalDisplay::FGmaxY - yf1;
0641      fg_fillbox(PhysicalDisplay::CurrentFill, FG_MODE_SET, ~0, Box);
0642 #elif defined (MS)
0643     _rectangle(_GFILLINTERIOR,x1,yf1,x2,y2);
0644 #endif
0645 return;
0646 }
0647
0648
0649 void Viewport::DrawPolygon(int NumVertices,int far *Vertices)
0650 {                                          // draw a filled polygon.
0651 #if defined (FG)
0652     int Count= 1;                           // will be used by fg.lib.
0653 #endif
0654 if (NumVertices < 4) return;            // must have at least 3 sides.
0655 #if defined (BGI)
0656     fillpoly(NumVertices, Vertices);
0657 #elif defined (FG)
0658    if (NumVertices==5)                  // if a four-sided polygon...
0659    {
0660    Vertices[1]= PhysicalDisplay::FGmaxY - Vertices[1];
0661    Vertices[3]= PhysicalDisplay::FGmaxY - Vertices[3];
0662    Vertices[5]= PhysicalDisplay::FGmaxY - Vertices[5];
0663    Vertices[7]= PhysicalDisplay::FGmaxY - Vertices[7];
0664    Vertices[9]= PhysicalDisplay::FGmaxY - Vertices[9];
0665    fg_fillpolygon(PhysicalDisplay::CurrentFill, FG_MODE_SET, ~0,
0666                   NumVertices-1, Vertices, fg.displaybox);
0667    fg_drawpolygon(PhysicalDisplay::CurrentClr, FG_MODE_SET, ~0,
0668                   FG_LINE_USER_DEFINED,
0669                   NumVertices-1, Vertices, fg.displaybox);
0670    }
0671    if (NumVertices!=5)               // if not a four-sided polygon...
0672    {
0673    while (Count < NumVertices*2)        // for each y coordinate...
0674       {            // ...convert to Flash Graphic's coordinate system.
0675      Vertices[Count]= PhysicalDisplay::FGmaxY - Vertices[Count];
0676      Count+= 2;
0677       }
0678    fg_fillpolygon(PhysicalDisplay::CurrentFill, FG_MODE_SET, ~0,
0679                   NumVertices-1, Vertices, fg.displaybox);
0680    fg_drawpolygon(PhysicalDisplay::CurrentClr, FG_MODE_SET, ~0,
0681                   FG_LINE_USER_DEFINED,
0682                   NumVertices-1, Vertices, fg.displaybox);
0683    }
0684 #elif defined (MS)
0685    _polygon(_GFILLINTERIOR, Vertices, NumVertices);
0686 #endif
0687 return;
0688 }
0689
0690
0691 void Viewport::DrawFacet(int NumVertices,int far *Vertices)
0692 {                                          // draw a transparent polygon.
0693 #if defined (FG)
0694     int Count= 1;                           // will be used by fg.lib.
0695 #endif
0696 if (NumVertices < 4) return;            // must have at least 3 sides.
0697 #if defined (BGI)
0698    drawpoly(NumVertices, Vertices);
0699 #elif defined (FG)
0700    if (NumVertices==5)                  // if a four-sided polygon.
0701    {
```

```
0702     Vertices[1]= PhysicalDisplay::FGmaxY - Vertices[1];
0703     Vertices[3]= PhysicalDisplay::FGmaxY - Vertices[3];
0704     Vertices[5]= PhysicalDisplay::FGmaxY - Vertices[5];
0705     Vertices[7]= PhysicalDisplay::FGmaxY - Vertices[7];
0706     Vertices[9]= PhysicalDisplay::FGmaxY - Vertices[9];
0707     fg_drawpolygon(PhysicalDisplay::CurrentClr, FG_MODE_SET, ~0,
0708                    FG_LINE_USER_DEFINED,
0709                    NumVertices-1, Vertices, fg.displaybox);
0710     }
0711     if (NumVertices!=5)              // if not a four-sided polygon...
0712     {
0713     while (Count < NumVertices*2)        // for each y coordinate...
0714        {          // ...convert to Flash Graphic's coordinate system.
0715        Vertices[Count]= PhysicalDisplay::FGmaxY - Vertices[Count];
0716        Count+= 2;
0717        }
0718     fg_drawpolygon(PhysicalDisplay::CurrentClr, FG_MODE_SET, ~0,
0719                    FG_LINE_USER_DEFINED,
0720                    NumVertices-1, Vertices, fg.displaybox);
0721     }
0722  #elif defined (MS)
0723     _polygon(_GBORDER, Vertices, NumVertices);
0724  #endif
0725  return;
0726  }
0727
0728
0729  void Viewport::DrawCircle(int CenterX, int CenterY, int Radius)
0730  {                                      // draw a circle.
0731  #if defined (BGI)
0732     circle(CenterX,CenterY,Radius);
0733  #elif defined (FG)
0734     fg_coord_t xradius, yradius;
0735     float Temp;
0736   xradius= Radius;
0737   CenterY= PhysicalDisplay::FGmaxY - CenterY;
0738   switch(PhysicalDisplay::ScreenMode)
0739     {            // adjust y radius to fit display aspect ratio...
0740     case zVGA_12H:  yradius= (fg_coord_t) Radius; break;
0741     case zEGA_10H:  Temp= ((float) Radius * .729);
0742                     yradius= (fg_coord_t) Temp; break;
0743     case zEGA_EH:   Temp= ((float) Radius * .417);
0744                     yradius= (fg_coord_t) Temp; break;
0745     case zMCGA_11H: yradius= (fg_coord_t) Radius; break;
0746     case zCGA_6H:   Temp= ((float) Radius * .417);
0747                     yradius= (fg_coord_t) Temp; break;
0748     case zHERC:     Temp= ((float) Radius * .64);
0749                     yradius= (fg_coord_t) Temp; break;
0750     }
0751     fg_drawellipse(PhysicalDisplay::CurrentClr, FG_MODE_SET, ~0,
0752                    CenterX, CenterY, xradius, yradius,
0753                    0, 3600, fg.displaybox);
0754  #elif defined (MS)
0755     int xradius;
0756     float yradius;
0757     int x1,yf1,x2,y2;
0758   xradius= Radius;
0759   switch(PhysicalDisplay::ScreenMode)
0760     {            // adjust y radius to fit display aspect ratio...
0761     case zVGA_12H:  yradius= (float) Radius; break;
0762     case zEGA_10H:  yradius= ((float) Radius) * .729; break;
0763     case zEGA_EH:   yradius= ((float) Radius) * .417; break;
```

```
0764        case zMCGA_11H: yradius= (float) Radius; break;
0765        case zCGA_6H:   yradius= ((float) Radius) * .417; break;
0766        case zHERC:     yradius= ((float) Radius) * .64; break;
0767      }
0768    x1= CenterX - xradius; yf1= CenterY - ((int) yradius);
0769    x2= CenterX + xradius; y2= CenterY + ((int) yradius);
0770    _ellipse(_GBORDER,x1,yf1,x2,y2);
0771  #endif
0772  return;
0773  }
0774
0775
0776  void Viewport::Fill(int x,int y,int edgeclr)
0777  {                                       // perform a flood fill.
0778  #if defined (BGI)
0779    floodfill(x,y,edgeclr);
0780  #elif defined (FG)
0781    y= PhysicalDisplay::FGmaxY - y;
0782    fg_fill(x,y,PhysicalDisplay::CurrentFill,edgeclr);
0783  #elif defined (MS)
0784    _floodfill(x,y,edgeclr);
0785  #endif
0786  return;
0787  }
0788  /*
0789
0790  ┌──────────────────────────────────────────────────────────┐
      │                GRAPHIC ARRAY OPERATIONS                  │
0791  └──────────────────────────────────────────────────────────┘
0792                                                            */
0793  #if defined (BGI)              // if using Borland's graphics.lib...
0794    char far * Viewport::MemBlock(int x1,int yf1,int x2,int y2)
0795  #elif defined (FG)                   // if using Zortech's fg.lib...
0796    fg_color_t far * Viewport::MemBlock(int x1,
0797                                        int yf1,int x2,int y2)
0798  #elif defined (MS)            // if using Microsoft's graph.lib...
0799    char far * Viewport::MemBlock(int x1,int yf1,int x2,int y2)
0800  #endif
0801  {     // allocate a block of far heap memory for a graphic array.
0802  #if defined (BGI)
0803    unsigned long blocksize;
0804    char far *blk;
0805    blocksize=(unsigned long)imagesize(x1,yf1,x2,y2);     // get size.
0806    if (blocksize==0xffff) return (char far *)zFAIL;      // if >64K.
0807    blk=(char far*)farmalloc(blocksize);         // allocate memory.
0808  #elif defined (FG)
0809    unsigned long blocksize;
0810    fg_color_t far *blk;
0811    fg_box_t Array;
0812    Array[FG_X1]= x1; Array[FG_Y1]= PhysicalDisplay::FGmaxY - y2;
0813    Array[FG_X2]= x2; Array[FG_Y2]= PhysicalDisplay::FGmaxY - yf1;
0814    blocksize=(unsigned long)(sizeof(fg_color_t)*fg_box_area(Array));
0815    blk= (fg_color_t far *) farmalloc(blocksize);
0816  #elif defined (MS)
0817    unsigned long blocksize;
0818    char far *blk;
0819    blocksize=(unsigned long)_imagesize(x1,yf1,x2,y2);   // get size.
0820    if (blocksize==0xffff) return (char far *)zFAIL;      // if >64K.
0821    blk=(char far*)_fmalloc(blocksize);          // allocate memory.
0822  #endif
0823  return blk;
0824  }
0825
0826
```

```
0827   unsigned long Viewport::GetBlockSize(int x1,int yf1,
0828                                             int x2,int y2)
0829   {              // determine storage requirements of a graphic array.
0830     unsigned long blocksize;
0831   #if defined (BGI)
0832     blocksize=(unsigned long)imagesize(x1,yf1,x2,y2);
0833   #elif defined (FG)
0834       fg_box_t Array;
0835     Array[FG_X1]= x1; Array[FG_Y1]= PhysicalDisplay::FGmaxY - y2;
0836     Array[FG_X2]= x2; Array[FG_Y2]= PhysicalDisplay::FGmaxY - yf1;
0837     blocksize=(unsigned long)(sizeof(fg_color_t)*fg_box_area(Array));
0838   #elif defined (MS)
0839     blocksize=(unsigned long)_imagesize(x1,yf1,x2,y2);    // get size.
0840   #endif
0841   return blocksize;
0842   }
0843
0844
0845   #if defined (BGI)                // if using Borland's graphics.lib...
0846     void Viewport::FreeBlock(char far *blk)
0847     {                        // deallocate a block of far heap memory.
0848     farfree(blk);
0849     return;
0850     }
0851     void Viewport::GetBlock(int x1,int yf1,int x2,
0852                                   int y2,char far *blk)
0853     {                  // save graphic array in a memory block.
0854     getimage(x1,yf1,x2,y2,blk);
0855     return;
0856     }
0857     void Viewport::PutXOR(int x,int y,char far *blk)
0858     {                            // XOR array on screen.
0859     putimage(x,y,blk,XOR_PUT);
0860     return;
0861     }
0862     void Viewport::PutPSET(int x,int y,char far *blk)
0863     {                            // PSET array on screen.
0864     putimage(x,y,blk,COPY_PUT);
0865     return;
0866     }
0867     void Viewport::PutAND(int x,int y,char far *blk)
0868     {                            // AND array on screen.
0869     putimage(x,y,blk,AND_PUT);
0870     return;
0871     }
0872   #elif defined (FG)                    // if using Zortech's fg.lib...
0873     void Viewport::FreeBlock(fg_color_t far *blk)
0874     {                        // deallocate a block of far heap memory.
0875     farfree(blk);
0876     return;
0877     }
0878     void Viewport::GetBlock(int x1,int yf1,int x2,
0879                                   int y2,fg_color_t far *blk)
0880     {                        // save graphic array in a memory block.
0881       fg_box_t Array;
0882     PhysicalDisplay::ArrayWidth= x2 - x1;      // save width, depth...
0883     PhysicalDisplay::ArrayDepth= y2 - yf1;
0884     Array[FG_X1]= x1; Array[FG_Y1]= PhysicalDisplay::FGmaxY - y2;
0885     Array[FG_X2]= x2; Array[FG_Y2]= PhysicalDisplay::FGmaxY - yf1;
0886     fg_readbox(Array, blk);
0887     return;
0888     }
```

```
0889    void Viewport::PutXOR(int x,int y,fg_color_t far *blk)
0890    {                                    // XOR array on screen.
0891    return;
0892    }
0893    void Viewport::PutPSET(int x,int y,fg_color_t far *blk)
0894    {                                    // PSET array on screen.
0895      fg_box_t Array;
0896    Array[FG_X1]= x;
0897    Array[FG_Y1]= (PhysicalDisplay::FGmaxY - y)
0898                    - PhysicalDisplay::ArrayDepth;
0899    Array[FG_X2]= x + PhysicalDisplay::ArrayWidth;
0900    Array[FG_Y2]= Array[FG_Y1] + PhysicalDisplay::ArrayDepth;
0901    fg_writebox(Array, blk);
0902    return;
0903    }
0904    void Viewport::PutAND(int x,int y,fg_color_t far *blk)
0905    {                                    // AND array on screen.
0906    return;
0907    }
0908    #elif defined (MS)              // if using Microsoft's graph.lib...
0909    void Viewport::FreeBlock(char far *blk)
0910    {                              // deallocate a block of far heap memory.
0911    _ffree(blk);
0912    return;
0913    }
0914    void Viewport::GetBlock(int x1,int yf1,int x2,
0915                            int y2,char far *blk)
0916    {                              // save graphic array in a memory block.
0917    _getimage(x1,yf1,x2,y2,blk);
0918    return;
0919    }
0920    void Viewport::PutXOR(int x,int y,char far *blk)
0921    {                                    // XOR array on screen.
0922    _putimage(x,y,blk,_GXOR);
0923    return;
0924    }
0925    void Viewport::PutPSET(int x,int y,char far *blk)
0926    {                                    // PSET array on screen.
0927    _putimage(x,y,blk,_GPSET);
0928    return;
0929    }
0930    void Viewport::PutAND(int x,int y,char far *blk)
0931    {                                    // AND array on screen.
0932    _putimage(x,y,blk,_GAND);
0933    return;
0934    }
0935    #endif
0936    /*
0937
0938    ┌─────────────────────────────────────────────────────────┐
        │        TEXT OPERATIONS USING THE DEFAULT FONT             │
0939    └─────────────────────────────────────────────────────────┘
0940                                                              */
0941    void Viewport::PutText(int row,int col,int clr,char * tptr)
0942    {                     // write a string of text at a specified position.
0943    #if defined (BGI)
0944        int TCrow,TCcol,tempclr;
0945    TCcol= (col * PhysicalDisplay::TextWidth)
0946            - PhysicalDisplay::TextWidth;            // convert col to x.
0947    TCrow= (row * PhysicalDisplay::TextHeight)
0948            - PhysicalDisplay::TextHeight;           // convert row to y.
0949    tempclr=getcolor();setcolor(clr);       // save, set active color.
0950    outtextxy(TCcol,TCrow,tptr);             // display the text.
0951    setcolor(tempclr);                   // Restore previous active color.
```

```
0952    #elif defined (FG)
0953        int FGrow,FGcol;
0954      FGcol= (col * PhysicalDisplay::TextWidth)
0955            - PhysicalDisplay::TextWidth;
0956      FGrow= row * PhysicalDisplay::TextHeight;
0957      FGrow= PhysicalDisplay::FGmaxY - FGrow;
0958      fg_puts(clr, FG_MODE_SET, ~0, FG_ROTO, FGcol, FGrow,
0959            tptr, fg.displaybox);
0960    #elif defined (MS)
0961      _settextposition(row,col);_settextcolor(clr);_outtext(tptr);
0962    #endif
0963    return;
0964    }
0965
0966
0967    void Viewport::SetTextRowCol(int row,int col)
0968    {   // set current text starting position, using rows and columns.
0969    #if defined (BGI)
0970        int TCrow,TCcol;
0971      TCcol= (col * PhysicalDisplay::TextWidth)
0972            - PhysicalDisplay::TextWidth;
0973      TCrow= (row * PhysicalDisplay::TextHeight)
0974            - PhysicalDisplay::TextHeight;
0975      moveto(TCcol,TCrow);
0976    #elif defined (FG)
0977        int FGrow,FGcol;
0978      FGcol= (col * PhysicalDisplay::TextWidth)
0979            - PhysicalDisplay::TextWidth;
0980      FGrow= row * PhysicalDisplay::TextHeight;
0981      FGrow= PhysicalDisplay::FGmaxY - FGrow;
0982      PhysicalDisplay::CurrentTextX= FGcol;
0983      PhysicalDisplay::CurrentTextY= FGrow;
0984    #elif defined (MS)
0985      _settextposition(row,col);
0986    #endif
0987    return;
0988    }
0989
0990
0991    void Viewport::ClearTextLine(void)
0992    {              // blank the first text line on the graphics screen.
0993    #if defined (BGI)
0994      setfillstyle(SOLID_FILL,0);              // this is BGI-specific!
0995      if (PhysicalDisplay::ScreenMode==zHERC)              // if Hercules.
0996        {
0997        DrawPanel(0,0,486,13);
0998        }
0999      else DrawPanel(0,0,431,7);              // if 8x8 characters.
1000    #elif defined (FG)
1001        fg_box_t Box;
1002      if (PhysicalDisplay::ScreenMode==zHERC)
1003        {
1004        Box [FG_X1]= 0;
1005        Box [FG_Y1]= PhysicalDisplay::FGmaxY
1006                    - PhysicalDisplay::TextHeight;
1007        Box [FG_X2]= 486; Box [FG_Y2]= PhysicalDisplay::FGmaxY;
1008        }
1009      else
1010        {
1011        Box [FG_X1]= 0;
1012        Box [FG_Y1]= PhysicalDisplay::FGmaxY
1013                    - PhysicalDisplay::TextHeight;
```

```
1014        Box [FG_X2]= 431; Box [FG_Y2]= PhysicalDisplay::FGmaxY;
1015      }
1016    fg_fillbox(0, FG_MODE_SET, ~0, Box);
1017  #elif defined (MS)
1018    _setcolor(0); _setfillmask(PhysicalDisplay::SolidFill);
1019    if (PhysicalDisplay::ScreenMode==zHERC)            // if Hercules.
1020      {
1021      DrawPanel(0,0,486,13);
1022      }
1023    else DrawPanel(0,0,431,7);                     // if 8x8 characters.
1024  #endif
1025  return;
1026  }
1027  /*
1028  ┌──────────────────────────────────────────────────────────────┐
1029  │                     HIDDEN PAGE OPERATIONS                     │
1030  └──────────────────────────────────────────────────────────────┘
1031                                                                 */
1032  int PhysicalDisplay::InitUndo(void)
1033  {             // initialize a hidden page in RAM or in video memory.
1034  switch(ScreenMode)
1035    {
1036    case zVGA_12H: BitMap0=InitHiddenPage();            // 640x480x16.
1037        if(!BitMap0) return zFAIL;
1038        U1.FarAddress=BitMap0;
1039        Seg1=U1.Address.A2;Off1=U1.Address.A1;
1040        BitMap1=InitHiddenPage();
1041        if(BitMap1==0)
1042          {
1043          FreeMemory(BitMap0); return zFAIL;
1044          }
1045        U1.FarAddress=BitMap1;
1046        Seg2=U1.Address.A2;Off2=U1.Address.A1;
1047        BitMap2=InitHiddenPage();
1048        if(BitMap2==0)
1049          {
1050          FreeMemory(BitMap1); FreeMemory(BitMap0); return zFAIL;
1051          }
1052        U1.FarAddress=BitMap2;
1053        Seg3=U1.Address.A2;Off3=U1.Address.A1;
1054        BitMap3=InitHiddenPage();
1055        if(BitMap3==0)
1056          {
1057          FreeMemory(BitMap2); FreeMemory(BitMap1);
1058          FreeMemory(BitMap0); return zFAIL;
1059          }
1060        U1.FarAddress=BitMap3;
1061        Seg4=U1.Address.A2;Off4=U1.Address.A1;
1062        RAMpage= zYES; break;
1063    case zEGA_10H: break;                               // 640x350x16.
1064    case zEGA_EH: break;                                // 640x200x16.
1065    case zMCGA_11H: BitMap0=InitHiddenPage();           // 640x480x2.
1066        if(BitMap0==0) return zFAIL;
1067        U1.FarAddress=BitMap0;
1068        Seg1=U1.Address.A2;Off1=U1.Address.A1;
1069        RAMpage= zYES; break;
1070    case zCGA_6H: BitMap0=InitHiddenPage();             // 640x200x2.
1071        if(BitMap0==0) return zFAIL;
1072        U1.FarAddress=BitMap0;
1073        Seg1=U1.Address.A2;Off1=U1.Address.A1;
1074        RAMpage= zYES; break;
1075    case zHERC: break;                                  // 720x348x2.
1076    }
```

```
1077  return zYES;
1078  }
1079
1080
1081  char far * PhysicalDisplay::InitHiddenPage(void)
1082  {                          // allocate memory for a hidden RAM bitmap.
1083    char far * vptr;         // buffer address to be returned to caller.
1084  #if defined (BORLAND)
1085    vptr=(char far *)farmalloc(Plane_Length);
1086  #elif defined (MICROSOFT)
1087    vptr=(char far *)_fmalloc(Plane_Length);
1088  #elif defined (ZORTECH)
1089    vptr=(char far *)farmalloc(Plane_Length);
1090  #endif
1091  return vptr;                       // return buffer address to caller.
1092  }
1093
1094
1095  void PhysicalDisplay::FreeMemory(char far *blk)
1096  {                                    // release a block of memory.
1097  #if defined (BGI)
1098    farfree(blk);
1099  #elif defined (FG)
1100    farfree(blk);
1101  #elif defined (MS)
1102    _ffree(blk);
1103  #endif
1104  return;
1105  }
1106
1107
1108  void PhysicalDisplay::BackUp(void)
1109  {                          // copy graphics page 0 to the hidden page.
1110  switch(ScreenMode)
1111  {
1112  case zVGA_12H:                          // VGA 640x480x16-color.
1113      #if defined (MICROSOFT)
1114        outp(0x3ce,4);outp(0x3cf,0);
1115      #elif defined (ZORTECH)
1116        outp(0x3ce,4);outp(0x3cf,0);
1117      #elif defined (BORLAND)
1118        outportb(0x03ce,(unsigned char)4);
1119        outportb(0x03cf,(unsigned char)0);
1120      #endif
1121      movedata(0xa000,0x0000,Seg1,Off1,Plane_Length);
1122      #if defined (MICROSOFT)
1123        outp(0x3ce,4);outp(0x3cf,1);
1124      #elif defined (ZORTECH)
1125        outp(0x3ce,4);outp(0x3cf,1);
1126      #elif defined (BORLAND)
1127        outportb(0x03ce,(unsigned char)4);
1128        outportb(0x03cf,(unsigned char)1);
1129      #endif
1130      movedata(0xa000,0x0000,Seg2,Off2,Plane_Length);
1131      #if defined (MICROSOFT)
1132        outp(0x3ce,4);outp(0x3cf,2);
1133      #elif defined (ZORTECH)
1134        outp(0x3ce,4);outp(0x3cf,2);
1135      #elif defined (BORLAND)
1136        outportb(0x03ce,(unsigned char)4);
1137        outportb(0x03cf,(unsigned char)2);
1138      #endif
```

```
1139        movedata(0xa000,0x0000,Seg3,Off3,Plane_Length);
1140        #if defined (MICROSOFT)
1141          outp(0x3ce,4);outp(0x3cf,3);
1142        #elif defined (ZORTECH)
1143          outp(0x3ce,4);outp(0x3cf,3);
1144        #elif defined (BORLAND)
1145          outportb(0x03ce,(unsigned char)4);
1146          outportb(0x03cf,(unsigned char)3);
1147        #endif
1148        movedata(0xa000,0x0000,Seg4,Off4,Plane_Length);
1149        #if defined (MICROSOFT)
1150          outp(0x3ce,4);outp(0x3cf,0);
1151        #elif defined (ZORTECH)
1152          outp(0x3ce,4);outp(0x3cf,0);
1153        #elif defined (BORLAND)
1154          outportb(0x03ce,(unsigned char)4);
1155          outportb(0x03cf,(unsigned char)0);
1156        #endif
1157        break;
1158    case zEGA_10H:                              // EGA 640x350x16-color.
1159        #if defined (MICROSOFT)
1160          outp(0x03ce,0x08);outp(0x03cf,0xff);outp(0x03c4,0x02);
1161          outp(0x03c5,0x0f);outp(0x03ce,0x05);outp(0x03cf,0x01);
1162          movedata(0xa000,0x0000,0xa800,0x0000,Plane_Length);
1163          outp(0x03ce,0x05);outp(0x03cf,0x00);
1164        #elif defined (ZORTECH)
1165          outp(0x03ce,0x08);outp(0x03cf,0xff);outp(0x03c4,0x02);
1166          outp(0x03c5,0x0f);outp(0x03ce,0x05);outp(0x03cf,0x01);
1167          movedata(0xa000,0x0000,0xa800,0x0000,Plane_Length);
1168          outp(0x03ce,0x05);outp(0x03cf,0x00);
1169        #elif defined (BORLAND)
1170          outportb(0x03ce,(unsigned char)4);
1171          outportb(0x03cf,(unsigned char)0);
1172          outportb(0x03c4,(unsigned char)2);
1173          outportb(0x03c5,(unsigned char)1);
1174          movedata(0xa000,0x0000,0xa800,0x0000,Plane_Length);
1175          outportb(0x03ce,(unsigned char)4);
1176          outportb(0x03cf,(unsigned char)1);
1177          outportb(0x03c4,(unsigned char)2);
1178          outportb(0x03c5,(unsigned char)2);
1179          movedata(0xa000,0x0000,0xa800,0x0000,Plane_Length);
1180          outportb(0x03ce,(unsigned char)4);
1181          outportb(0x03cf,(unsigned char)2);
1182          outportb(0x03c4,(unsigned char)2);
1183          outportb(0x03c5,(unsigned char)4);
1184          movedata(0xa000,0x0000,0xa800,0x0000,Plane_Length);
1185          outportb(0x03ce,(unsigned char)4);
1186          outportb(0x03cf,(unsigned char)3);
1187          outportb(0x03c4,(unsigned char)2);
1188          outportb(0x03c5,(unsigned char)8);
1189          movedata(0xa000,0x0000,0xa800,0x0000,Plane_Length);
1190          outportb(0x03ce,(unsigned char)4);
1191          outportb(0x03cf,(unsigned char)0);
1192          outportb(0x03c4,(unsigned char)2);
1193          outportb(0x03c5,(unsigned char)15);
1194        #endif
1195        break;
1196    case zEGA_EH:                               // EGA 640x200x16-color.
1197        #if defined (MICROSOFT)
1198          outp(0x03ce,0x08);outp(0x03cf,0xff);outp(0x03c4,0x02);
1199          outp(0x03c5,0x0f);outp(0x03ce,0x05);outp(0x03cf,0x01);
1200          movedata(0xa000,0x0000,0xa400,0x0000,Plane_Length);
1201          outp(0x03ce,0x05);outp(0x03cf,0x00);
```

```
1202        #elif defined (ZORTECH)
1203          outp(0x03ce,0x08);outp(0x03cf,0xff);outp(0x03c4,0x02);
1204          outp(0x03c5,0x0f);outp(0x03ce,0x05);outp(0x03cf,0x01);
1205          movedata(0xa000,0x0000,0xa400,0x0000,Plane_Length);
1206          outp(0x03ce,0x05);outp(0x03cf,0x00);
1207        #elif defined (BORLAND)
1208          outportb(0x03ce,(unsigned char)4);
1209          outportb(0x03cf,(unsigned char)0);
1210          outportb(0x03c4,(unsigned char)2);
1211          outportb(0x03c5,(unsigned char)1);
1212          movedata(0xa000,0x0000,0xa400,0x0000,Plane_Length);
1213          outportb(0x03ce,(unsigned char)4);
1214          outportb(0x03cf,(unsigned char)1);
1215          outportb(0x03c4,(unsigned char)2);
1216          outportb(0x03c5,(unsigned char)2);
1217          movedata(0xa000,0x0000,0xa400,0x0000,Plane_Length);
1218          outportb(0x03ce,(unsigned char)4);
1219          outportb(0x03cf,(unsigned char)2);
1220          outportb(0x03c4,(unsigned char)2);
1221          outportb(0x03c5,(unsigned char)4);
1222          movedata(0xa000,0x0000,0xa400,0x0000,Plane_Length);
1223          outportb(0x03ce,(unsigned char)4);
1224          outportb(0x03cf,(unsigned char)3);
1225          outportb(0x03c4,(unsigned char)2);
1226          outportb(0x03c5,(unsigned char)8);
1227          movedata(0xa000,0x0000,0xa400,0x0000,Plane_Length);
1228          outportb(0x03ce,(unsigned char)4);
1229          outportb(0x03cf,(unsigned char)0);
1230          outportb(0x03c4,(unsigned char)2);
1231          outportb(0x03c5,(unsigned char)15);
1232        #endif
1233        break;
1234    case zMCGA_11H: movedata(0xa000,0x0000,Seg1,Off1,Plane_Length);
1235                break;                      // MCGA 640x480x2-color.
1236    case zCGA_6H: movedata(0xb800,0x0000,Seg1,Off1,Plane_Length);
1237                break;                      // CGA 640x200x2-color.
1238    case zHERC: movedata(0xb000,0x0000,0xb800,0x0000,Plane_Length);
1239            break;                          // Herc 720x348x2-color.
1240    }
1241    return;
1242    }
1243
1244
1245    void PhysicalDisplay::Restore(void)
1246    {                       // copy the hidden page to graphics page 0.
1247    switch(ScreenMode)
1248    {
1249    case zVGA_12H:                          // VGA 640x480x16-color.
1250        #if defined (MICROSOFT)
1251          outp(0x3c4,2);outp(0x3c5,1);
1252        #elif defined (ZORTECH)
1253          outp(0x3c4,2);outp(0x3c5,1);
1254        #elif defined (BORLAND)
1255          outportb(0x03c4,(unsigned char)2);
1256          outportb(0x03c5,(unsigned char)1);
1257        #endif
1258        movedata(Seg1,Off1,0xa000,0x0000,Plane_Length);
1259        #if defined (MICROSOFT)
1260          outp(0x3c4,2);outp(0x3c5,2);
1261        #elif defined (ZORTECH)
1262          outp(0x3c4,2);outp(0x3c5,2);
1263        #elif defined (BORLAND)
```

```
1264        outportb(0x03c4,(unsigned char)2);
1265        outportb(0x03c5,(unsigned char)2);
1266     #endif
1267     movedata(Seg2,Off2,0xa000,0x0000,Plane_Length);
1268     #if defined (MICROSOFT)
1269        outp(0x3c4,2);outp(0x3c5,4);
1270     #elif defined (ZORTECH)
1271        outp(0x3c4,2);outp(0x3c5,4);
1272     #elif defined (BORLAND)
1273        outportb(0x03c4,(unsigned char)2);
1274        outportb(0x03c5,(unsigned char)4);
1275     #endif
1276     movedata(Seg3,Off3,0xa000,0x0000,Plane_Length);
1277     #if defined (MICROSOFT)
1278        outp(0x3c4,2);outp(0x3c5,8);
1279     #elif defined (ZORTECH)
1280        outp(0x3c4,2);outp(0x3c5,8);
1281     #elif defined (BORLAND)
1282        outportb(0x03c4,(unsigned char)2);
1283        outportb(0x03c5,(unsigned char)8);
1284     #endif
1285     movedata(Seg4,Off4,0xa000,0x0000,Plane_Length);
1286     #if defined (MICROSOFT)
1287        outp(0x3c4,2);outp(0x3c5,0xf);
1288     #elif defined (ZORTECH)
1289        outp(0x3c4,2);outp(0x3c5,0xf);
1290     #elif defined (BORLAND)
1291        outportb(0x03c4,(unsigned char)2);
1292        outportb(0x03c5,(unsigned char)15);
1293     #endif
1294     break;
1295  case zEGA_10H:                               // 640x350x16-color.
1296     #if defined (MICROSOFT)
1297        outp(0x03ce,0x08);outp(0x03cf,0xff);outp(0x03c4,0x02);
1298        outp(0x03c5,0x0f);outp(0x03ce,0x05);outp(0x03cf,0x01);
1299        movedata(0xa800,0x0000,0xa000,0x0000,Plane_Length);
1300        outp(0x03ce,0x05);outp(0x03cf,0x00);
1301     #elif defined (ZORTECH)
1302        outp(0x03ce,0x08);outp(0x03cf,0xff);outp(0x03c4,0x02);
1303        outp(0x03c5,0x0f);outp(0x03ce,0x05);outp(0x03cf,0x01);
1304        movedata(0xa800,0x0000,0xa000,0x0000,Plane_Length);
1305        outp(0x03ce,0x05);outp(0x03cf,0x00);
1306     #elif defined (BORLAND)
1307        outportb(0x03ce,(unsigned char)4);
1308        outportb(0x03cf,(unsigned char)0);
1309        outportb(0x03c4,(unsigned char)2);
1310        outportb(0x03c5,(unsigned char)1);
1311        movedata(0xa800,0x0000,0xa000,0x0000,Plane_Length);
1312        outportb(0x03ce,(unsigned char)4);
1313        outportb(0x03cf,(unsigned char)1);
1314        outportb(0x03c4,(unsigned char)2);
1315        outportb(0x03c5,(unsigned char)2);
1316        movedata(0xa800,0x0000,0xa000,0x0000,Plane_Length);
1317        outportb(0x03ce,(unsigned char)4);
1318        outportb(0x03cf,(unsigned char)2);
1319        outportb(0x03c4,(unsigned char)2);
1320        outportb(0x03c5,(unsigned char)4);
1321        movedata(0xa800,0x0000,0xa000,0x0000,Plane_Length);
1322        outportb(0x03ce,(unsigned char)4);
1323        outportb(0x03cf,(unsigned char)3);
1324        outportb(0x03c4,(unsigned char)2);
1325        outportb(0x03c5,(unsigned char)8);
1326        movedata(0xa800,0x0000,0xa000,0x0000,Plane_Length);
```

```
1327            outportb(0x03ce,(unsigned char)4);
1328            outportb(0x03cf,(unsigned char)0);
1329            outportb(0x03c4,(unsigned char)2);
1330            outportb(0x03c5,(unsigned char)15);
1331         #endif
1332         break;
1333      case zEGA_EH:                                    // 640x200x16-color.
1334         #if defined (MICROSOFT)
1335            outp(0x03ce,0x08);outp(0x03cf,0xff);outp(0x03c4,0x02);
1336            outp(0x03c5,0x0f);outp(0x03ce,0x05);outp(0x03cf,0x01);
1337            movedata(0xa400,0x0000,0xa000,0x0000,Plane_Length);
1338            outp(0x03ce,0x05);outp(0x03cf,0x00);
1339         #elif defined (ZORTECH)
1340            outp(0x03ce,0x08);outp(0x03cf,0xff);outp(0x03c4,0x02);
1341            outp(0x03c5,0x0f);outp(0x03ce,0x05);outp(0x03cf,0x01);
1342            movedata(0xa400,0x0000,0xa000,0x0000,Plane_Length);
1343            outp(0x03ce,0x05);outp(0x03cf,0x00);
1344         #elif defined (BORLAND)
1345            outportb(0x03ce,(unsigned char)4);
1346            outportb(0x03cf,(unsigned char)0);
1347            outportb(0x03c4,(unsigned char)2);
1348            outportb(0x03c5,(unsigned char)1);
1349            movedata(0xa400,0x0000,0xa000,0x0000,Plane_Length);
1350            outportb(0x03ce,(unsigned char)4);
1351            outportb(0x03cf,(unsigned char)1);
1352            outportb(0x03c4,(unsigned char)2);
1353            outportb(0x03c5,(unsigned char)2);
1354            movedata(0xa400,0x0000,0xa000,0x0000,Plane_Length);
1355            outportb(0x03ce,(unsigned char)4);
1356            outportb(0x03cf,(unsigned char)2);
1357            outportb(0x03c4,(unsigned char)2);
1358            outportb(0x03c5,(unsigned char)4);
1359            movedata(0xa400,0x0000,0xa000,0x0000,Plane_Length);
1360            outportb(0x03ce,(unsigned char)4);
1361            outportb(0x03cf,(unsigned char)3);
1362            outportb(0x03c4,(unsigned char)2);
1363            outportb(0x03c5,(unsigned char)8);
1364            movedata(0xa400,0x0000,0xa000,0x0000,Plane_Length);
1365            outportb(0x03ce,(unsigned char)4);
1366            outportb(0x03cf,(unsigned char)0);
1367            outportb(0x03c4,(unsigned char)2);
1368            outportb(0x03c5,(unsigned char)15);
1369         #endif
1370         break;
1371      case zMCGA_11H: movedata(Seg1,Off1,0xa000,0x0000,Plane_Length);
1372                  break;                          // MCGA 640x480x2-color.
1373      case zCGA_6H: movedata(Seg1,Off1,0xb800,0x0000,Plane_Length);
1374                  break;                          // CGA 640x200x2-color.
1375      case zHERC: movedata(0xb800,0x0000,0xb000,0x0000,Plane_Length);
1376                  break;                          // Herc 720x348x2-color.
1377      }
1378   return;
1379   }
1380   /*
1381
1382      ┌─────────────────────────────────────────────────────────────┐
1383      │       End of LIB2D.CPP graphics library language bindings.     │
1384      └─────────────────────────────────────────────────────────────┘
                                                                      */
```

E-3 Source code for LIB3D.HPP, the declaration file for class Model3D, providing methods for creating fully-shaded solid 3-D models with backplane hidden surface removal.

```
0001  /*
0002
0003           Lee Adams' SUPERCHARGED C++ GRAPHICS
0004              Header file for 3D routines
0005
0006      SOURCE FILE:  LIB3D.HPP
0007      TYPE:  declarations for 3D classes
0008
0009           DEVELOPER'S GUIDE TO THE INTERFACE
0010      Before using 3D graphics, you must create an object of the
0011      class Model3D.  Then call methods of the object to draw the
0012      3D solid and shade it.  Refer to the 3D demonstration
0013      programs in the book for examples of here-is-how-it's-done
0014      source code.
0015      Class declarations are located in LIB3D.HPP (which must be
0016        used in your program as #include "LIB3D.HPP").
0017      Function definitions are located in LIB3D.CPP.  Either
0018        LIB3D.CPP or LIB3D.OBJ must be named in the project list
0019        for your program.
0020
0021      LICENSE:  As purchaser of the book in which this source code
0022        appears you are granted a royalty-free license to reproduce
0023        and distribute executable files generated using this code
0024        provided that you accept the conditions of the License
0025        Agreement and Limited Warranty described in the book.
0026      PUBLICATION: Contains material from Windcrest/McGraw-Hill
0027        book 3489, published by TAB BOOKS.
0028      U.S. GOVERNMENT RESTRICTED RIGHTS:  This software and its
0029        documentation is provided with restricted rights.  The use,
0030        duplication, or disclosure by the Government is subject to
0031        restrictions set forth in subdivision (b)(3)(ii) of The
0032        Rights in Technical Data and Computer Software clause at
0033        252.227-7013.  Contractor/manufacturer is Lee Adams, c/o
0034        TAB BOOKS, 13311 Monterey Ave., Blue Ridge Summit PA 17294.
0035      TRADEMARK:  Lee Adams is a trademark of Lee Adams.
0036
0037        Copyright 1991 Lee Adams.  All rights reserved worldwide.
0038
0039                                                              */
0040  #ifndef LIB3D_HPP              // if file not already included...
0041  #define LIB3D_HPP              // set token to show it has been used.
0042
0043  const int zUPDATE=  0;              // constants used by the methods...
0044  const int zREMOVE=  1;
0045  const int zINSTALL= 6;
0046  const int zRED=     1;
0047  const int zGREEN=   2;
0048  const int zBROWN=   3;
0049  const int zBLUE=    4;
0050  const int zMAGENTA= 5;
0051  const int zCYAN=    6;
0052  const int zGRAY=    7;
0053
0054  class Model3D
0055  {
0056  private:          // accessable by member functions and friends only.
0057    Viewport *Generic;                 // points to a viewport object.
0058    PhysicalDisplay *Ds;               // points to a display object.
0059    void GetCameraCoords(void);        // wrld coords to cam coords.
0060    void GetImageCoords(void);         // cam coords to imge coords.
```

```
0061     void GetScreenCoords(void);          // maps imge plane to screen.
0062     void GetWorldCoords(void);           // obj coords to wrld coords.
0063     void VisibilityTest(void);           // back-plane visibility.
0064     void GetBrightness(void);            // finds brightness of a facet.
0065     void GetCubeCoords(void);            // cam coords & display coords.
0066     void SetObjAngle(void);              // sine, cosine rotation factors.
0067     void SetCamAngle(void);              // sine, cosine rotation factors.
0068     void PutObjToScreen(void);           // object to screen coords.
0069     void PutWorldToScreen(void);         // world to screen coords.
0070     void DrawFacet(void);                          // draws facet.
0071     float DomainWidth, DomainDepth;                    // 3D domain.
0072     float x,y,z;                 // wrld coords in, cam coords out.
0073     float xc1,xc2,xc3,xc4,xc5,xc6,xc7,yc1,yc2,yc3,
0074           yc4,yc5,yc6,yc7,zc1,zc2,zc3,zc4,zc5,zc6,
0075           zc7;                           // camera coords of facet.
0076     float sx1,sx2,sx3,sx4,sx5,sy1,sy2,sy3,
0077           sy4,sy5;                       // display coords of facet.
0078     float xw1,xw2,xw3,yw1,yw2,yw3,
0079           zw1,zw2,zw3;          // raw world coords for brightness.
0080     float sx3D,sy3D;                     // output of 3D formulas.
0081     float cursorx,cursory,cursorz;       // volume of 3D cursor.
0082     float xa,ya,za;                      // temporary in 3D formulas.
0083     float focal_length;                  // angular perspective factor.
0084     double ObjYaw,ObjRoll,ObjPitch;      // object rotation angles.
0085     double sOYaw,cOYaw;
0086     double sORoll,cORoll;
0087     double sOPitch,cOPitch;
0088     float xObj,yObj,zObj;                          // obj trans values.
0089     double ObjYawChg,ObjRollChg,
0090            ObjPitchChg;             // instancing rotation change.
0091     float xObjChg,yObjChg,zObjChg;  // instancing translation change.
0092     double CamYaw,CamRoll,CamPitch;                    // camera.
0093     double sCYaw,sCRoll,sCPitch;
0094     double cCYaw,cCRoll,cCPitch;
0095     float xCam,yCam,zCam;                // world translation values.
0096     float rx,ry;                         // ratios used in windowing.
0097     float hcenter,vcenter;               // center of viewport.
0098     float viewheight;            // viewer's height 0 ft above ground.
0099     float dist;                  // viewer's virtual distance from scene.
0100     float yawdist;               // viewer's actual distance from scene.
0101     int pitchheading,yawheading;           // cam angle, degrees.
0102     int viewchg;                 // degrees to change camera angle.
0103     double yawdelta,pitchdelta;          // current absolute change.
0104     float planex,planey,planez;          // volume of groundplane.
0105     float cursorxchg,cursorychg,
0106           cursorzchg;                    // extrude cursor and object.
0107     float signmx,signmy,signmz;          // coord system tweaking.
0108     float cubeObj[8][3];                 // cube xyz object coords.
0109     float cubeWorld[8][3];         // xw1,yw1,zw1 vertex world coords.
0110     float camcoords[8][3];         // xc1,yc1,zc1 vertex camera coords.
0111     float displaycoords[8][2];        // sx1,sy1 vertex disp coords.
0112     // variables for rendering and backplane removal...
0113     float visible;                       // visibility factor.
0114     float sp1,sp2,sp3;                   // temp values of sp.
0115     float xLight,yLight,zLight;
0116     float illum_range;                   // adapter-dependent range.
0117     float normalized_illum;              // illum factor 0 to 1 range.
0118     float xu,yu,zu;                      // vector vertex 1 to 2.
0119     float xv,yv,zv;                      // vector vertex 1 to 3.
0120     float x_surf_normal,y_surf_normal,z_surf_normal;
0121     float v1,v2;                     // length, surface perp vector.
0122     float v3;                    // ratio, surf perp to unit vector.
```

```
0123        float x_unit_vector,y_unit_vector,z_unit_vector;
0124        int zDeviceIllum;              // adapter-dependent brightness.
0125        int zShadingColor;                        // dithering hue.
0126        int Points[10];                    // array of facet vertices.
0127                   // pixel-based variables...
0128        int clipx1, clipy1;                    // client area coords.
0129        int clipx2, clipy2;                    // client area coords.
0130        int ViewportWidth;                     // width of viewport.
0131        int ViewportDepth;                     // depth of viewport.
0132        int CursorExist;                    // indicates if displayed.
0133        int PlaneExist;                     // indicates if displayed.
0134        int Model3DReady;        // indicates if class object initialized.
0135        int cx1,cy1,cx2,cy2,              // coords for next 3D cursor...
0136            cx3,cy3,cx4,cy4,
0137            cx5,cy5,cx6,cy6,
0138            cx7,cy7,cx8,cy8;
0139        int pcx1,pcy1,pcx2,pcy2,       // coords for previous 3D cursor...
0140            pcx3,pcy3,pcx4,pcy4,
0141            pcx5,pcy5,pcx6,pcy6,
0142            pcx7,pcy7,pcx8,pcy8;
0143        int gcx1,gcy1,gcx2,gcy2,gcx3,gcy3,gcx4,gcy4;      // groundplane...
0144        int gpcx1,gpcy1,gpcx2,gpcy2,gpcx3,gpcy3,gpcx4,gpcy4;
0145             // dither patterns for the shading methods...
0146        char Fill_0[8], Fill_3[8], Fill_6[8];
0147        char Fill_12[8], Fill_25[8], Fill_37[8];
0148        char Fill_50[8], Fill_62[8], Fill_75[8];
0149        char Fill_87[8], Fill_93[8], Fill_100[8];
0150
0151   public:     // data and methods accessable by any in-scope function.
0152        Model3D(PhysicalDisplay *);                     // constructor.
0153        ~Model3D();                                      // destructor.
0154        void Initialize3D(int,int,int,int,Viewport *);   // initialize.
0155        void Instance(int,int,int);            // instancing of object.
0156        void Camera(int);                      // instancing of camera.
0157        void DrawGrndPlane(int);         // draws 3D xz ground plane.
0158        void DrawCursor(int);                     // draws 3D cursor.
0159        void DrawCube(void);                         // draw 3D cube.
0160        void GetNewObjParams(void);     // new object instancing params.
0161        void SetShadingColor(int);                    // dithering hue.
0162   };
0163   #endif
0164   /*
0165
0166   ┌─────────────────────────────────────────────────────────┐
       │                End of LIB3D.HPP header file.            │
0167   └─────────────────────────────────────────────────────────┘
0168                                                              */
```

E-4 Source code for LIB3D.CPP, the implementation file for class Model3D, providing methods for creating fully shaded solid 3-D models with backplane hidden surface removal.

```
0001   /*
0002
0003   ┌─────────────────────────────────────────────────────────┐
       │           Lee Adams' SUPERCHARGED C++ GRAPHICS          │
0004   │           3D modeling and shading routines for C++      │
0005   │                                                         │
0006   │        Implementation file for 3D graphics routines     │
0007   ├─────────────────────────────────────────────────────────┤
0008   │  Source file:  LIB3D.CPP                                │
0009   │  Type:  implementation file for class methods.          │
0010   │  Include file:  LIB3D.HPP                               │
```

E-4 Continued.

```
0011        Graphics libraries:  Borland graphics library (graphics.lib)
0012                             Zortech graphics library (fg.lib)
0013                             Microsoft graphics library (graph.lib)
0014     Languages:  Turbo C++, Zortech C++, and all C++ compilers
0015              compatible with AT&T C++ specification 2.0.
0016     Memory model:  large.
0017     Graphics:  supports 640x480x16 VGA, 640x350x16 EGA, 640x200x16
0018       EGA, 640x480x2 MCGA, 640x200x2 CGA, and 720x348x2 Hercules.
0019     Output:  contains class methods that provide 3D modeling and
0020              shading routines with hidden surface removal.
0021     Usage:  refer to the header file LIB3D.HPP for a guide to
0022              using the methods of class Model3D.
0023     License:  As purchaser of the book in which this module
0024        appears you are granted a royalty-free license to reproduce
0025        and distribute executable files generated using this code,
0026        provided that you accept the conditions of the License
0027        Agreement and Limited Warranty described in the book.
0028     Publication: Contains material from Windcrest/McGraw-Hill
0029        book 3489, published by TAB BOOKS.
0030     U.S. Government Restricted Rights:  This software and its
0031        documentation is provided with restricted rights.  The use,
0032        duplication, or disclosure by the Government is subject to
0033        restrictions set forth in subdivision (b)(3)(ii) of The
0034        Rights in Technical Data and Computer Software clause at
0035        252.227-7013.  Contractor/manufacturer is Lee Adams and TAB
0036        BOOKS, 13311 Monterey Ave., Blue Ridge Summit PA 17214.
0037     Trademarks:  Lee Adams is a trademark of Lee Adams.
0038
0039             Copyright 1991 Lee Adams.  All rights reserved.
0040
0041
0042                     CONDITIONAL COMPILATION
0043     To compile only those blocks of code that support the C++
0044     compiler and graphics library that you are using, you should
0045     #define the appropriate tokens in the following preprocessor
0046     directives.  Use the following table as your guide:
0047              GRAPHICS LIBRARY
0048        Borland's graphics.lib              #define BGI
0049        Zortech's fg.lib or fgdebug.lib     #define FG
0050        Microsoft's graph.lib              #define MS
0051              COMPILER
0052        Borland Turbo C++ compiler          #define BORLAND
0053        Zortech C++ compiler                #define ZORTECH
0054        AT&T C++ 2.0 compatible compilers   #define MICROSOFT
0055     Be sure you define only one compiler and one graphics library.
0056
0057                                                                  */
0058     #define BGI     1 // indicates the graphics library you are using.
0059     #define BORLAND 1 // indicates the C++ compiler you are using.
0060     /*
0061
0062                        CONSTANTS
0063
0064                                                                  */
0065     const int zFAIL=     0;                 // boolean token.
0066     const int zVGA_12H=  1;                 // VGA 640x480x16/256.
0067     const int zEGA_10H=  2;                 // EGA 640x350x16/64.
0068     const int zEGA_EH=   3;                 // EGA 640x200x16.
0069     const int zMCGA_11H= 4;                 // MCGA 640x480x2.
0070     const int zCGA_6H=   5;                 // CGA 640x200x2-color.
0071     const int zHERC=     6;                 // Hercules 720x348x2-color.
0072     const int zFALSE=    0;                 // boolean tokens...
```

```
0073    const int zTRUE=      1;
0074    const int zYES=       1;
0075    const int zNO=        0;
0076    const int zOVERWRITE=    0;                        // writing modes...
0077    const int zTRANSPARENT= 1;
0078    /*
0079
0080    ┌─────────────────────────────────────────────────────────────┐
        │                      INCLUDE FILES                          │
0081    └─────────────────────────────────────────────────────────────┘
0082                                                                  */
0083    #include "LIB2D.HPP"
0084    #include "LIB3D.HPP"                         // class declarations.
0085    #include <math.h>                      // supports sine and cosine.
0086    /*
0087
0088    ┌─────────────────────────────────────────────────────────────┐
        │              Class Model3D:   CONSTRUCTOR                   │
0089    └─────────────────────────────────────────────────────────────┘
0090                                                                  */
0091    Model3D::Model3D(PhysicalDisplay * Disp)
0092    {             // expects to receive a pointer to the physical display.
0093    Ds= Disp;                          // point to physical display object.
0094    DomainWidth= 800; DomainDepth= 600;
0095    x= 0.0; y= 0.0; z= 0.0;
0096    xc1= 0.0; xc2= 0.0; xc3= 0.0; xc4= 0.0; xc5= 0.0;
0097    xc6= 0.0; xc7= 0.0;
0098    yc1= 0.0; yc2= 0.0; yc3= 0.0; yc4= 0.0; yc5= 0.0;
0099    yc6= 0.0; yc7= 0.0;
0100    zc1= 0.0; zc2= 0.0; zc3= 0.0; zc4= 0.0; zc5= 0.0;
0101    zc6= 0.0; zc7= 0.0;
0102    sx1= 0.0; sx2= 0.0; sx3= 0.0; sx4= 0.0; sx5= 0.0;
0103    sy1= 0.0; sy2= 0.0; sy3= 0.0; sy4= 0.0; sy5= 0.0;
0104    xw1= 0; xw2= 0; xw3= 0;
0105    yw1= 0; yw2= 0; yw3= 0;
0106    zw1= 0; zw2= 0; zw3= 0;
0107    sx3D= 0.0; sy3D= 0.0;
0108    cursorx= 10; cursory= 10; cursorz= 10;
0109    xa= 0.0; ya= 0.0; za= 0.0;
0110    focal_length= 1200.0;
0111    ObjYaw= 6.28319; ObjRoll= 6.28319; ObjPitch= 6.28319;
0112    sOYaw= 0.0; cOYaw= 0.0;
0113    sORoll= 0.0; cORoll= 0.0;
0114    sOPitch= 0.0; cOPitch= 0.0;
0115    xObj= 0.0; yObj= 0.0; zObj= 0.0;
0116    ObjYawChg= 0.0; ObjRollChg= 0.0; ObjPitchChg= 0.0;
0117    xObjChg= 0.0; yObjChg= 0.0; zObjChg= 0.0;
0118    CamYaw= 6.28319; CamRoll= 6.28319; CamPitch= 6.28319;
0119    sCYaw= 0.0; sCRoll= 0.0; sCPitch= 0.0;
0120    cCYaw= 0.0; cCRoll= 0.0; cCPitch= 0.0;
0121    xCam= 0.0; yCam= 0.0; zCam= -360.0;
0122    rx= 0.0; ry= 0.0;
0123    hcenter= 0.0; vcenter= 0.0;
0124    viewheight= 0; dist= 360; yawdist= 360;
0125    pitchheading= 360; yawheading= 0;
0126    viewchg= 2; yawdelta= 0; pitchdelta= 0;
0127    planex= 60; planey= 0; planez= 60;
0128    cursorxchg= 0; cursorychg= 0; cursorzchg= 0;
0129    signmx= 1; signmy= -1; signmz= -1;
0130            // vertices for a virtual cube...
0131    cubeObj[0][0]= 10;  cubeObj[0][1]= -10; cubeObj[0][2]= 10;
0132    cubeObj[1][0]= 10;  cubeObj[1][1]=  10; cubeObj[1][2]= 10;
0133    cubeObj[2][0]= -10; cubeObj[2][1]= 10;  cubeObj[2][2]= 10;
0134    cubeObj[3][0]= -10; cubeObj[3][1]= -10; cubeObj[3][2]= 10;
0135    cubeObj[4][0]= 10;  cubeObj[4][1]= 10;  cubeObj[4][2]= -10;
```

```
0136    cubeObj[5][0]= -10; cubeObj[5][1]= 10;  cubeObj[5][2]= -10;
0137    cubeObj[6][0]= -10; cubeObj[6][1]= -10; cubeObj[6][2]= -10;
0138    cubeObj[7][0]= 10;  cubeObj[7][1]= -10; cubeObj[7][2]= -10;
0139              // dither patterns for the shading methods...
0140    Fill_0[0]= 0; Fill_0[1]= 0; Fill_0[2]= 0;
0141    Fill_0[3]= 0; Fill_0[4]= 0; Fill_0[5]= 0;
0142    Fill_0[6]= 0; Fill_0[7]= 0;
0143
0144    Fill_3[0]= 0; Fill_3[1]= 32; Fill_3[2]= 0;
0145    Fill_3[3]= 0; Fill_3[4]= 0; Fill_3[5]= 2;
0146    Fill_3[6]= 0; Fill_3[7]= 0;
0147
0148    Fill_6[0]= 32; Fill_6[1]= 0; Fill_6[2]= 2;
0149    Fill_6[3]= 0; Fill_6[4]= 128; Fill_6[5]= 0;
0150    Fill_6[6]= 8; Fill_6[7]= 0;
0151
0152    Fill_12[0]= 32; Fill_12[1]= 2; Fill_12[2]= 128;
0153    Fill_12[3]= 8; Fill_12[4]= 32; Fill_12[5]= 2;
0154    Fill_12[6]= 128; Fill_12[7]= 8;
0155
0156    Fill_25[0]= 68; Fill_25[1]= 17; Fill_25[2]= 68;
0157    Fill_25[3]= 17; Fill_25[4]= 68; Fill_25[5]= 17;
0158    Fill_25[6]= 68; Fill_25[7]= 17;
0159
0160    Fill_37[0]= 170; Fill_37[1]= 68; Fill_37[2]= 170;
0161    Fill_37[3]= 17; Fill_37[4]= 170; Fill_37[5]= 68;
0162    Fill_37[6]= 170; Fill_37[7]= 17;
0163
0164    Fill_50[0]= 85; Fill_50[1]= 170; Fill_50[2]= 85;
0165    Fill_50[3]= 170; Fill_50[4]= 85; Fill_50[5]= 170;
0166    Fill_50[6]= 85; Fill_50[7]= 170;
0167
0168    Fill_62[0]= 85; Fill_62[1]= 187; Fill_62[2]= 85;
0169    Fill_62[3]= 238; Fill_62[4]= 85; Fill_62[5]= 187;
0170    Fill_62[6]= 85; Fill_62[7]= 238;
0171
0172    Fill_75[0]= 187; Fill_75[1]= 238; Fill_75[2]= 187;
0173    Fill_75[3]= 238; Fill_75[4]= 187; Fill_75[5]= 238;
0174    Fill_75[6]= 187; Fill_75[7]= 238;
0175
0176    Fill_87[0]= 223; Fill_87[1]= 253; Fill_87[2]= 127;
0177    Fill_87[3]= 247; Fill_87[4]= 223; Fill_87[5]= 253;
0178    Fill_87[6]= 127; Fill_87[7]= 247;
0179
0180    Fill_93[0]= 255; Fill_93[1]= 223; Fill_93[2]= 255;
0181    Fill_93[3]= 255; Fill_93[4]= 255; Fill_93[5]= 253;
0182    Fill_93[6]= 255; Fill_93[7]= 255;
0183
0184    Fill_100[0]= 255; Fill_100[1]= 255; Fill_100[2]= 255;
0185    Fill_100[3]= 255; Fill_100[4]= 255; Fill_100[5]= 255;
0186    Fill_100[6]= 255; Fill_100[7]= 255;
0187
0188    visible= 0.0; sp1= 0.0; sp2= 0.0; sp3= 0.0;
0189    xLight= -.1294089; yLight= .8660256; zLight= .4829627;
0190    illum_range= 11; normalized_illum= 0.0;
0191    xu= 0.0; yu= 0.0; zu= 0.0;
0192    xv= 0.0; yv= 0.0; zv= 0.0;
0193    x_surf_normal= 0.0; y_surf_normal= 0.0; z_surf_normal= 0.0;
0194    v1= 0.0; v2= 0.0; v3= 0.0;
0195    x_unit_vector= 0.0; y_unit_vector= 0.0; z_unit_vector= 0.0;
0196    zDeviceIllum= 0; zShadingColor= 4;
0197    clipx1= 0; clipy1= 0; clipx2= 639; clipy2= 479;
```

```
0198  ViewportWidth= 640; ViewportDepth= 480;
0199  CursorExist= zFALSE; PlaneExist= zFALSE;
0200  Model3DReady= zYES;
0201  }
0202  /*
0203
0204  ┌─────────────────────────────────────────────────────────────┐
       │              Class Model3D:  DESTRUCTOR                     │
0205   └─────────────────────────────────────────────────────────────┘
0206                                                              */
0207  Model3D::~Model3D()
0208  {
0209  Model3DReady= zNO;
0210  }
0211  /*
0212
0213  ┌─────────────────────────────────────────────────────────────┐
       │        Initialize and configure the 3D environment         │
0214   └─────────────────────────────────────────────────────────────┘
0215                                                              */
0216  void Model3D::Initialize3D(int kx1,int ky1,int kx2,int ky2,
0217                             Viewport *ViewportPtr)
0218  {      // expects clipping box, display mode, and viewport object.
0219     // NOTE: scaling calculations expect viewport to be full screen,
0220     //       otherwise you must pass a screen mode token to this
0221     //       method so it can calculate the scaling ratio from the
0222     //       aspect ratio of the physical display.
0223  Generic= ViewportPtr;                      // point to viewport object.
0224  clipx1= kx1; clipy1= ky1; clipx2= kx2; clipy2= ky2;
0225  ViewportWidth= clipx2 - clipx1 + 1;              // width of viewport.
0226  ViewportDepth= clipy2 - clipy1 + 1;              // depth of viewport.
0227  rx= ((float)ViewportWidth / DomainWidth);  // horiz scaling factor.
0228  ry= ((float)ViewportDepth / DomainDepth);   // vert scaling factor.
0229  hcenter= ((float)(ViewportWidth - 1)) / 2;   // center of viewport.
0230  vcenter= ((float)(ViewportDepth - 1)) / 2;   // center of viewport.
0231  focal_length= 1200.0; viewheight= 0; dist= 360;
0232  xLight= -.38729; yLight= .77459; zLight= .50000;
0233  CamYaw= 0.0; CamRoll= 0.0; CamPitch= 6.28319;
0234  pitchheading= 360; yawheading= 0; viewchg= 2;
0235  yawdelta= 0; pitchdelta= 0;
0236  SetCamAngle();                              // initialize the camera.
0237  xCam= 0.0; yCam= 0.0; zCam= -360.0;
0238  ObjYaw= 0.0; ObjRoll= 0.0; ObjPitch= 0.0;
0239  SetObjAngle();                          // initialize the 3D cursor.
0240  xObj= 0.0; yObj= 0.0; zObj= 0.0;
0241  ObjYawChg= 0; ObjRollChg= 0; ObjPitchChg= 0;
0242  xObjChg= 0; yObjChg= 0; zObjChg= 0;
0243  cursorx= 15; cursory= 15; cursorz= 15;
0244  planex= 75; planey= 0; planez= 75;
0245  illum_range= 11;     // nominal dithered shade intensities 1 to 12.
0246  return;
0247  }
0248  /*
0249
0250  ┌─────────────────────────────────────────────────────────────┐
       │                  Instance the 3D cursor                     │
0251   └─────────────────────────────────────────────────────────────┘
0252                                                              */
0253  void Model3D::Instance(int param1,int param2,int param3)
0254  {
0255     // If param1==0 then a complete reset is wanted.  If param1==1
0256     // then rotation is wanted.  If param1==2 then translation is
0257     // wanted.  If param1==3 then extrusion is wanted.  In all cases,
0258     // param2 indicates whether x,y,z or yaw, roll, pitch is being
0259     // adjusted.  Param3 indicates whether negative or positive
0260     // adjustment is required.
```

```
0261   if (param1==0)                        // if general reset requested.
0262     {
0263     ObjYawChg=0;ObjRollChg=0;ObjPitchChg=0;        // reset rot chge.
0264     xObjChg=0;yObjChg=0;zObjChg=0;                 // reset trans chge.
0265     cursorxchg=0;cursorychg=0;cursorzchg=0;        // reset ext chge.
0266     return;
0267     }
0268   if (param1==1)                        // if rotation requested.
0269     {
0270     switch (param2)
0271       {
0272       case 1:  if (param3==1){ObjYawChg=.087267;break;}
0273                if (param3==2){ObjYawChg=-.087267;break;}
0274       case 2:  if (param3==2){ObjRollChg=-.087267;break;}
0275                if (param3==1){ObjRollChg=.087267;break;}
0276       case 3:  if (param3==1){ObjPitchChg=.087267;break;}
0277                if (param3==2){ObjPitchChg=-.087267;break;}
0278       default: ObjYawChg=0;ObjRollChg=0;ObjPitchChg=0;
0279                xObjChg=0;yObjChg=0;zObjChg=0;
0280                cursorxchg=0;cursorychg=0;cursorzchg=0;break;
0281       }
0282     return;
0283     }
0284   if (param1==2)                        // if translation requested.
0285     {
0286     switch (param2)
0287       {
0288       case 1:  if (param3==1){yObjChg=2;break;}
0289                if (param3==2){yObjChg=-2;break;}
0290       case 2:  if (param3==1){xObjChg=2;break;}
0291                if (param3==2){xObjChg=-2;break;}
0292       case 3:  if (param3==1){zObjChg=2;break;}
0293                if (param3==2){zObjChg=-2;break;}
0294       default: ObjYawChg=0;ObjRollChg=0;ObjPitchChg=0;
0295                xObjChg=0;yObjChg=0;zObjChg=0;
0296                cursorxchg=0;cursorychg=0;cursorzchg=0;break;
0297       }
0298     return;
0299     }
0300   if (param1==3)                        // if extrusion requested.
0301     {
0302     switch (param2)
0303       {
0304       case 1:  if (param3==2){cursorychg=-2;break;}
0305                if (param3==1){cursorychg=2;break;}
0306       case 2:  if (param3==2){cursorxchg=-2;break;}
0307                if (param3==1){cursorxchg=2;break;}
0308       case 3:  if (param3==2){cursorzchg=-2;break;}
0309                if (param3==1){cursorzchg=2;break;}
0310       default: ObjYawChg=0;ObjRollChg=0;ObjPitchChg=0;
0311                xObjChg=0;yObjChg=0;zObjChg=0;
0312                cursorxchg=0;cursorychg=0;cursorzchg=0;break;
0313       }
0314     return;
0315     }
0316   return;
0317   }
0318   /*
0319
0320   ┌─────────────────────────────────────────────────────────┐
                          Draw the 3D cursor
0321   └─────────────────────────────────────────────────────────┘
0322                                                               */
```

```
0323    void Model3D::DrawCursor(int Option)
0324    {
0325    if (Option==zREMOVE)
0326        {
0327        Ds->SetHue(7); Ds->SetLine(0xaaaa);
0328        Ds->SetWriteMode(zTRANSPARENT);
0329        Generic->SetPosition(pcx6,pcy6);
0330        Generic->DrawLine(pcx1,pcy1);
0331        Generic->DrawLine(pcx4,pcy4);
0332        Generic->SetPosition(pcx1,pcy1);
0333        Generic->DrawLine(pcx2,pcy2);
0334        Ds->SetLine(0xffff);
0335        Generic->SetPosition(pcx5,pcy5);
0336        Generic->DrawLine(pcx6,pcy6);
0337        Generic->DrawLine(pcx7,pcy7);
0338        Generic->DrawLine(pcx8,pcy8);
0339        Generic->SetPosition(pcx3,pcy3);
0340        Generic->DrawLine(pcx8,pcy8);
0341        Generic->DrawLine(pcx5,pcy5);
0342        Generic->DrawLine(pcx4,pcy4);
0343        Generic->DrawLine(pcx3,pcy3);
0344        Generic->DrawLine(pcx2,pcy2);
0345        Generic->DrawLine(pcx7,pcy7);
0346        CursorExist= zFALSE;
0347        Ds->SetWriteMode(zOVERWRITE);
0348        return;
0349        }
0350    x=(-1)*cursorx;y=(-1)*cursory;z=(-1)*cursorz;
0351    PutObjToScreen();cx1=(int)sx3D;cy1=(int)sy3D;
0352    x=cursorx;y=(-1)*cursory;z=(-1)*cursorz;
0353    PutObjToScreen();cx2=(int)sx3D;cy2=(int)sy3D;
0354    x=cursorx;y=(-1)*cursory;z=cursorz;
0355    PutObjToScreen();cx3=(int)sx3D;cy3=(int)sy3D;
0356    x=(-1)*cursorx;y=(-1)*cursory;z=cursorz;
0357    PutObjToScreen();cx4=(int)sx3D;cy4=(int)sy3D;
0358    x=(-1)*cursorx;y=cursory;z=cursorz;
0359    PutObjToScreen();cx5=(int)sx3D;cy5=(int)sy3D;
0360    x=(-1)*cursorx;y=cursory;z=(-1)*cursorz;
0361    PutObjToScreen();cx6=(int)sx3D;cy6=(int)sy3D;
0362    x=cursorx;y=cursory;z=(-1)*cursorz;
0363    PutObjToScreen();cx7=(int)sx3D;cy7=(int)sy3D;
0364    x=cursorx;y=cursory;z=cursorz;
0365    PutObjToScreen();cx8=(int)sx3D;cy8=(int)sy3D;
0366    if (CursorExist==zTRUE)
0367        {                              // if cursor already being displayed...
0368        Ds->SetHue(7); Ds->SetLine(0xaaaa);
0369        Ds->SetWriteMode(zTRANSPARENT);
0370        Generic->SetPosition(pcx6,pcy6);
0371        Generic->DrawLine(pcx1,pcy1);
0372        Generic->DrawLine(pcx4,pcy4);
0373        Generic->SetPosition(pcx1,pcy1);
0374        Generic->DrawLine(pcx2,pcy2);
0375        Ds->SetLine(0xffff);
0376        Generic->SetPosition(pcx5,pcy5);
0377        Generic->DrawLine(pcx6,pcy6);
0378        Generic->DrawLine(pcx7,pcy7);
0379        Generic->DrawLine(pcx8,pcy8);
0380        Generic->SetPosition(pcx3,pcy3);
0381        Generic->DrawLine(pcx8,pcy8);
0382        Generic->DrawLine(pcx5,pcy5);
0383        Generic->DrawLine(pcx4,pcy4);
0384        Generic->DrawLine(pcx3,pcy3);
0385        Generic->DrawLine(pcx2,pcy2);
```

```
0386     Generic->DrawLine(pcx7,pcy7);
0387     }
0388   if (CursorExist==zFALSE)
0389     {                              // if cursor not yet being displayed...
0390     CursorExist= zTRUE;                        // reset the token...
0391     }
0392   Ds->SetHue(7); Ds->SetLine(0xaaaa);
0393   Ds->SetWriteMode(zTRANSPARENT);
0394   Generic->SetPosition(cx6,cy6);
0395   Generic->DrawLine(cx1,cy1);
0396   Generic->DrawLine(cx4,cy4);
0397   Generic->SetPosition(cx1,cy1);
0398   Generic->DrawLine(cx2,cy2);
0399   Ds->SetLine(0xffff);
0400   Generic->SetPosition(cx5,cy5);
0401   Generic->DrawLine(cx6,cy6);
0402   Generic->DrawLine(cx7,cy7);
0403   Generic->DrawLine(cx8,cy8);
0404   Generic->SetPosition(cx3,cy3);
0405   Generic->DrawLine(cx8,cy8);
0406   Generic->DrawLine(cx5,cy5);
0407   Generic->DrawLine(cx4,cy4);
0408   Generic->DrawLine(cx3,cy3);
0409   Generic->DrawLine(cx2,cy2);
0410   Generic->DrawLine(cx7,cy7);
0411   pcx1= cx1; pcy1= cy1; pcx2= cx2; pcy2= cy2;    // remember coords...
0412   pcx3= cx3; pcy3= cy3; pcx4= cx4; pcy4= cy4;
0413   pcx5= cx5; pcy5= cy5; pcx6= cx6; pcy6= cy6;
0414   pcx7= cx7; pcy7= cy7; pcx8= cx8; pcy8= cy8;
0415   Ds->SetWriteMode(zOVERWRITE);
0416   return;
0417   }
0418   /*
0419
0420   ┌──────────────────────────────────────────────────────────────────┐
       │                       Instance the camera                        │
0421   └──────────────────────────────────────────────────────────────────┘
0422                                                              */
0423   void Model3D::Camera(int param)
0424   {
0425   switch (param)
0426     {
0427     case 1:  yawheading=yawheading+viewchg;             // left arrow.
0428              if (yawheading>360) yawheading=yawheading-360;
0429              goto calccamyaw;
0430     case 2:  yawheading=yawheading-viewchg;             // right arrow.
0431              if (yawheading<0) yawheading=yawheading+360;
0432              goto calccamyaw;
0433     case 3:  pitchheading=pitchheading+viewchg;         // down arrow.
0434              if (pitchheading>360)      // keep above groundlevel.
0435                 pitchheading=360;
0436              goto calccampitch;
0437     case 4:  pitchheading=pitchheading-viewchg;            // up arrow.
0438              if (pitchheading<270)         // do not exceed vertical.
0439                 pitchheading=270;
0440              goto calccampitch;
0441     case 5:  DrawGrndPlane(zREMOVE); return;         // remove plane.
0442     case 6:  DrawGrndPlane(zUPDATE); return;        // install plane.
0443     default:  return;            // take no action if illegal param.
0444     }
0445   calccampitch:                        // jump to here if pitch change.
0446     CamPitch=((double)pitchheading)*.0174533;  // convert to radians.
0447     if (pitchheading==360) CamPitch=6.28319;
```

```
0448    if (pitchheading==0) CamPitch=0.0;
0449    SetCamAngle();
0450    pitchdelta=6.28319-CamPitch;      // change in pitch from start-up.
0451    yCam=sin(pitchdelta)*dist*signmy;    // new y Camera translation.
0452    yawdist=sqrt((dist*dist)-(yCam*yCam));       // find hypotenuse.
0453    xCam=sin(yawdelta)*yawdist*signmx;   // new x Camera translation.
0454    zCam=sqrt((yawdist*yawdist)-(xCam*xCam))*signmz;  // new z trans.
0455    DrawGrndPlane(zUPDATE);              // show new world orientation.
0456    return;
0457  calccamyaw:                            // jump to here if yaw change.
0458    CamYaw=((double)yawheading)*.0175433;
0459    if (yawheading==360) CamYaw=6.28319;
0460    if (yawheading==0) CamYaw=0.0;
0461    SetCamAngle();
0462    if ((CamYaw>=4.71239)&&(CamYaw<=6.28319))
0463      {
0464      signmx=-1; signmz=-1; yawdelta=6.28319-CamYaw;
0465      goto calccamyaw1;
0466      }
0467    if ((CamYaw>=0)&&(CamYaw<1.57079))
0468      {
0469      signmx=1;signmz=-1;yawdelta=CamYaw;
0470      goto calccamyaw1;
0471      }
0472    if ((CamYaw>=1.57079)&&(CamYaw<3.14159))
0473      {
0474      signmx=1;signmz=1;yawdelta=3.14159-CamYaw;
0475      goto calccamyaw1;
0476      }
0477    if ((CamYaw>=3.14159)&&(CamYaw<4.71239))
0478      {
0479      signmx=-1;signmz=1;yawdelta=CamYaw-3.14159;
0480      goto calccamyaw1;
0481      }
0482  calccamyaw1:
0483    xCam=sin(yawdelta)*yawdist*signmx;
0484    zCam=cos(yawdelta)*yawdist*signmz;
0485    DrawGrndPlane(zUPDATE);
0486  return;
0487  }
0488  /*
0489
0490  ┌─────────────────────────────────────────────────────────────┐
       │              Draw the 3D groundplane                          │
0491  └─────────────────────────────────────────────────────────────┘
0492                                                              */
0493  void Model3D::DrawGrndPlane(int Option)
0494  {
0495  Ds->SetHue(7); Ds->SetLine(0xffff);
0496  Ds->SetWriteMode(zTRANSPARENT);
0497  if (Option==zREMOVE)
0498    {                    // if user is finished with the groundplane...
0499    Generic->SetPosition(gpcx1,gpcy1);                 // ...remove it.
0500    Generic->DrawLine(gpcx2,gpcy2);
0501    Generic->DrawLine(gpcx3,gpcy3);
0502    Generic->DrawLine(gpcx4,gpcy4);
0503    PlaneExist= zFALSE;
0504    Ds->SetWriteMode(zOVERWRITE);
0505    return;
0506    }
0507  x=planex;y=planey;z=planez;
0508  PutWorldToScreen();gcx1=(int)sx3D;gcy1=(int)sy3D;
0509  x=planex;y=planey;z=(-1)*planez;
0510  PutWorldToScreen();gcx2=(int)sx3D;gcy2=(int)sy3D;
```

```
0511  x=(-1)*planex;y=planey;z=(-1)*planez;
0512  PutWorldToScreen();gcx3=(int)sx3D;gcy3=(int)sy3D;
0513  x=(-1)*planex;y=planey;z=planez;
0514  PutWorldToScreen();gcx4=(int)sx3D;gcy4=(int)sy3D;
0515  if (PlaneExist==zTRUE)
0516     {                               // if plane already being displayed...
0517     Generic->SetPosition(gpcx1,gpcy1);    // remove previous plane...
0518     Generic->DrawLine(gpcx2,gpcy2);
0519     Generic->DrawLine(gpcx3,gpcy3);
0520     Generic->DrawLine(gpcx4,gpcy4);
0521     }
0522  if (PlaneExist==zFALSE)
0523     {                               // if plane not yet being displayed...
0524     PlaneExist= zTRUE;                      // reset the token...
0525     }
0526  Generic->SetPosition(gcx1,gcy1);            // draw the next plane...
0527  Generic->DrawLine(gcx2,gcy2);
0528  Generic->DrawLine(gcx3,gcy3);
0529  Generic->DrawLine(gcx4,gcy4);
0530  gpcx1= gcx1; gpcy1= gcy1; gpcx2= gcx2; gpcy2= gcy2;     // store...
0531  gpcx3= gcx3; gpcy3= gcy3; gpcx4= gcx4; gpcy4= gcy4;
0532  Ds->SetWriteMode(zOVERWRITE);
0533  return;
0534  }
0535  /*
0536
0537  ┌─────────────────────────────────────────────────────────────────┐
       │            Perform the backplane visibility test                  │
0538   └─────────────────────────────────────────────────────────────────┘
0539                                                                      */
0540  void Model3D::VisibilityTest(void)
0541  {
0542     // Enter with 3 vertices as camera coords.
0543     // Exit with visibility token.
0544  sp1= xc1 * ( yc2 * zc3 - yc3 * zc2 );
0545  sp1= (-1) * sp1;
0546  sp2= xc2 * ( yc3 * zc1 - yc1 * zc3 );
0547  sp3= xc3 * ( yc1 * zc2 - yc2 * zc1);
0548  visible= sp1 - sp2 - sp3;
0549  return;
0550  }
0551  /*
0552
0553  ┌─────────────────────────────────────────────────────────────────┐
       │         Calculate object yaw, roll, pitch, translation            │
0554   └─────────────────────────────────────────────────────────────────┘
0555                                                                      */
0556  void Model3D::GetNewObjParams(void)
0557  {
0558     // Enter with the desired change in instancing rotation and
0559     // translation.  Exit with the new object yaw, roll, pitch,
0560     // and translation parameters.
0561  ObjYaw=ObjYaw+ObjYawChg;                         // new object yaw.
0562  if (ObjYaw<=0) ObjYaw=ObjYaw+6.28319;
0563  if (ObjYaw>6.28319) ObjYaw=ObjYaw-6.28319;
0564  ObjRoll=ObjRoll+ObjRollChg;                      // new object roll.
0565  if (ObjRoll<=0) ObjRoll=ObjRoll+6.28319;
0566  if (ObjRoll>6.28319) ObjRoll=ObjRoll-6.28319;
0567  ObjPitch=ObjPitch+ObjPitchChg;                   // new object pitch.
0568  if (ObjPitch<=0) ObjPitch=ObjPitch+6.28319;
0569  if (ObjPitch>6.28319) ObjPitch=ObjPitch-6.28319;
0570  SetObjAngle();     // get new object sine, cosine rotation factors.
0571  xObj=xObj-xObjChg;                   // new object left-right position.
0572  yObj=yObj-yObjChg;                   // new object high-low position.
```

```
0573   zObj=zObj-zObjChg;                          // new object near-far position.
0574   cursorx=cursorx+cursorxchg;                    // new extrusion width.
0575   if (cursorx<2) cursorx=2;
0576   cursory=cursory+cursorychg;                  // new extrusion height.
0577   if (cursory<2) cursory=2;
0578   cursorz=cursorz+cursorzchg;                   // new extrusion depth.
0579   if (cursorz<2) cursorz=2;
0580   return;
0581   }
0582   /*
0583
0584   ┌─────────────────────────────────────────────────────────────────────┐
       │        Calculate object sine and cosine rotation factors            │
0585   │                                                                     │
0586   └─────────────────────────────────────────────────────────────────────┘  */
0587   void Model3D::SetObjAngle(void)
0588   {
0589     // Enter with ObjYaw,ObjRoll,ObjPitch object rotation angles.
0590     // Exit with sine, cosine object rotation factors.
0591   sOYaw= sin(ObjYaw);
0592   cOYaw= cos(ObjYaw);
0593   sORoll= sin(ObjRoll);
0594   cORoll= cos(ObjRoll);
0595   sOPitch= sin(ObjPitch);
0596   cOPitch= cos(ObjPitch);
0597   return;
0598   }
0599   /*
0600
0601   ┌─────────────────────────────────────────────────────────────────────┐
       │        Calculate camera sine and cosine rotation factors            │
0602   │                                                                     │
0603   └─────────────────────────────────────────────────────────────────────┘  */
0604   void Model3D::SetCamAngle(void)
0605   {
0606     // Enter with Yaw,Roll,Pitch world rotation angles.
0607     // Exit with sine, cosine world rotation factors.
0608   sCYaw= sin(CamYaw);
0609   sCRoll= sin(CamRoll);
0610   sCPitch= sin(CamPitch);
0611   cCYaw= cos(CamYaw);
0612   cCRoll= cos(CamRoll);
0613   cCPitch= cos(CamPitch);
0614   return;
0615   }
0616   /*
0617
0618   ┌─────────────────────────────────────────────────────────────────────┐
       │            Transform object coords to screen coords                 │
0619   │                                                                     │
0620   └─────────────────────────────────────────────────────────────────────┘  */
0621   void Model3D::PutObjToScreen(void)
0622   {
0623     // Enter with xyz object coordinates.  This routine transforms
0624     // the obj coords to world coords to image plane coords to
0625     // sx3D,sy3D physical screen coords.
0626   GetWorldCoords(); GetCameraCoords(); GetImageCoords();
0627   GetScreenCoords();
0628   return;
0629   }
0630   /*
0631
0632   ┌─────────────────────────────────────────────────────────────────────┐
       │            Transform world coords to screen coords                  │
0633   │                                                                     │
0634   └─────────────────────────────────────────────────────────────────────┘  */
0635   void Model3D::PutWorldToScreen(void)
```

```
0636  {
0637      // Enter with xyz world coordinates.  This routine transforms
0638      // the world coords to image plane coords to sx3D,sy3D physical
0639      // screen coords.
0640  GetCameraCoords(); GetImageCoords(); GetScreenCoords();
0641  return;
0642  }
0643  /*
0644
0645  ┌─────────────────────────────────────────────────────────────────┐
0646  │          Calculate world coords from object coords              │
0647  └─────────────────────────────────────────────────────────────────┘  */
0648  void Model3D::GetWorldCoords(void)
0649  {
0650      // Enter with xyz unclipped object coordinates.
0651      // Exit with unclipped xyz world coordinates.
0652  xa= cORoll*x+sORoll*y; ya= cORoll*y-sORoll*x;        // roll rotate.
0653  x= cOYaw*xa-sOYaw*z; za= sOYaw*xa+cOYaw*z;            // yaw rotate.
0654  z= cOPitch*za-sOPitch*ya; y= sOPitch*za+cOPitch*ya;     // pitch.
0655  x= x+xObj; y= y+yObj; z= z+zObj;             // lateral movement.
0656  return;
0657  }
0658  /*
0659
0660  ┌─────────────────────────────────────────────────────────────────┐
0661  │          Calculate camera coords from world coords              │
0662  └─────────────────────────────────────────────────────────────────┘  */
0663  void Model3D::GetCameraCoords(void)
0664  {
0665      // Enter with unclipped xyz world coordinates.
0666      // Exit with unclipped xyz camera coordinates.
0667  x=(-1)*x;              // adjust for cartesian coords of 2D screen.
0668  y=y-viewheight;        // adjust world coords to height of viewer.
0669  x=x-xCam;y=y+yCam;z=z+zCam;                    // lateral movement.
0670  xa=cCYaw*x-sCYaw*z;za=sCYaw*x+cCYaw*z;              // yaw rotate.
0671  z=cCPitch*za-sCPitch*y;ya=sCPitch*za+cCPitch*y;    // pitch rotate.
0672  x=cCRoll*xa+sCRoll*ya;y=cCRoll*ya-sCRoll*xa;       // roll rotate.
0673  return;
0674  }
0675  /*
0676
0677  ┌─────────────────────────────────────────────────────────────────┐
0678  │          Calculate dipslay coords from camera coords            │
0679  └─────────────────────────────────────────────────────────────────┘  */
0680  void Model3D::GetImageCoords(void)
0681  {
0682      // Enter with clipped xyz camera coordinates.
0683      // Exit with unclipped sx3D,sy3D display coordinates.
0684  sx3D= focal_length * (x/z); sy3D= focal_length * (y/z);
0685  return;
0686  }
0687  /*
0688
0689  ┌─────────────────────────────────────────────────────────────────┐
0690  │          Calculate screen coords from display coords            │
0691  └─────────────────────────────────────────────────────────────────┘  */
0692  void Model3D::GetScreenCoords(void)
0693  {
0694      // Enter with unclipped sx3D,sy3D display coordinates.
0695      // Exit with sx3D,sy3D device-dependent display coordinates
0696      // scaled to the world range with correct aspect ratio.
0697  sx3D= sx3D * rx; sy3D= sy3D * ry;
```

```
0698    sx3D= sx3D + hcenter; sy3D= sy3D + vcenter;
0699    return;
0700    }
0701    /*
0702
0703    ┌─────────────────────────────────────────────────────────────┐
        │                   Draw a four-sided polygon                   │
0704    └─────────────────────────────────────────────────────────────┘
0705                                                                 */
0706    void Model3D::DrawFacet(void)
0707    {
0708    Points[0]= (int) sx1;            // initialize the array of vertices...
0709    Points[1]= (int) sy1;
0710    Points[2]= (int) sx2;
0711    Points[3]= (int) sy2;
0712    Points[4]= (int) sx3;
0713    Points[5]= (int) sy3;
0714    Points[6]= (int) sx4;
0715    Points[7]= (int) sy4;
0716    Points[8]= (int) sx1;
0717    Points[9]= (int) sy1;
0718    GetBrightness();                      // get brightness factor of facet.
0719    #if defined (FG)                                // if using fg.lib...
0720      Ds->SetHue(0);                            // set edge hue to black.
0721      Ds->SetFill(Fill_100, zShadingColor);   // set solid facet hue.
0722      Ds->SetLine(0xffff);                     // set line style to solid.
0723    #else                    // else if using graphics.lib or graph.lib...
0724      Ds->SetHue(zShadingColor);                 // set the shading hue.
0725      switch (zDeviceIllum)
0726        {                    // set the dither pattern and line style...
0727        case 1:  Ds->SetFill(Fill_6, zShadingColor);
0728                 Ds->SetLine(0x1010);
0729                 break;
0730        case 2:  Ds->SetFill(Fill_6,zShadingColor);
0731                 Ds->SetLine(0x1010);
0732                 break;
0733        case 3:  Ds->SetFill(Fill_6,zShadingColor);
0734                 Ds->SetLine(0x1010);
0735                 break;
0736        case 4:  Ds->SetFill(Fill_12,zShadingColor);
0737                 Ds->SetLine(0x2020);
0738                 break;
0739        case 5:  Ds->SetFill(Fill_25,zShadingColor);
0740                 Ds->SetLine(0x2222);
0741                 break;
0742        case 6:  Ds->SetFill(Fill_37,zShadingColor);
0743                 Ds->SetLine(0xaaaa);
0744                 break;
0745        case 7:  Ds->SetFill(Fill_50,zShadingColor);
0746                 Ds->SetLine(0xaaaa);
0747                 break;
0748        case 8:  Ds->SetFill(Fill_62,zShadingColor);
0749                 Ds->SetLine(0xaaaa);
0750                 break;
0751        case 9:  Ds->SetFill(Fill_75,zShadingColor);
0752                 Ds->SetLine(0xbbbb);
0753                 break;
0754        case 10: Ds->SetFill(Fill_87,zShadingColor);
0755                 Ds->SetLine(0xdddd);
0756                 break;
0757        case 11: Ds->SetFill(Fill_93,zShadingColor);
0758                 Ds->SetLine(0xefef);
0759                 break;
0760        case 12: Ds->SetFill(Fill_100,zShadingColor);
```

```
0761                Ds->SetLine(0xffff);
0762                break;
0763        }
0764 #endif
0765 Generic->DrawPolygon(5,Points);              // draw the shaded facet.
0766 return;
0767 }
0768 /*
0769
0770 ┌──────────────────────────────────────────────────────────────┐
0771 │            Calculate the brightness level of a facet            │
0772 └──────────────────────────────────────────────────────────────┘  */
0773 void Model3D::GetBrightness(void)
0774 {
0775    // Enter with facet world coordinates.
0776    // Exit with illumination level token.
0777 xu=xw2-xw1;yu=yw2-yw1;zu=zw2-zw1;    // vector vertex 1 to vertex 2.
0778 xv=xw3-xw1;yv=yw3-yw1;zv=zw3-zw1;    // vector vertex 1 to vertex 3.
0779 x_surf_normal=(yu*zv)-(zu*yv);
0780 y_surf_normal=(zu*xv)-(xu*zv);
0781 z_surf_normal=(xu*yv)-(yu*xv);
0782 y_surf_normal=y_surf_normal*(-1);
0783 z_surf_normal=z_surf_normal*(-1);    // convert to cartesian system.
0784 v1=(x_surf_normal*x_surf_normal)+(y_surf_normal*y_surf_normal)
0785    +(z_surf_normal*z_surf_normal);
0786 v2=sqrt(v1);          // magnitude of surface perpendicular vector.
0787 v3=1/v2;              // ratio of magnitude to length of unit vector.
0788 x_unit_vector=v3*x_surf_normal;
0789 y_unit_vector=v3*y_surf_normal;
0790 z_unit_vector=v3*z_surf_normal;  // surf perpendicular unit vector.
0791 normalized_illum=(x_unit_vector*xLight)+(y_unit_vector*yLight)
0792    +(z_unit_vector*zLight);              // illumination factor 0 to 1.
0793 normalized_illum=normalized_illum*illum_range;   // expand 0 to 11.
0794 zDeviceIllum= (int) normalized_illum;            // cast to int.
0795 zDeviceIllum++;                           // adjust to range 1 to 12.
0796 if (zDeviceIllum < 4) zDeviceIllum= 4;      // ambient light = 4.
0797 return;
0798 }
0799 /*
0800
0801 ┌──────────────────────────────────────────────────────────────┐
0802 │            Set the current shading color for facets             │
0803 └──────────────────────────────────────────────────────────────┘  */
0804 void Model3D::SetShadingColor(int iHue)
0805 {
0806 if (iHue < 1) return;                     // validate the argument...
0807 if (iHue > 7) return;
0808 zShadingColor= iHue;                      // ...and set the global token.
0809 return;
0810 }
0811 /*
0812
0813 ┌──────────────────────────────────────────────────────────────┐
0814 │            Draw an instance of a parallelepiped                 │
0815 └──────────────────────────────────────────────────────────────┘  */
0816 void Model3D::GetCubeCoords(void)            // called by DrawCube().
0817 {
0818    int t= 0;
0819    float negx,negy,negz;
0820 negx=(-1)*(cursorx);negy=(-1)*(cursory);negz=(-1)*(cursorz);
0821 cubeObj[0][0]=cursorx;cubeObj[0][1]=negy;cubeObj[0][2]=cursorz;
0822 cubeObj[1][0]=cursorx;cubeObj[1][1]=cursory;cubeObj[1][2]=cursorz;
```

```
0823    cubeObj[2][0]=negx;cubeObj[2][1]=cursory;cubeObj[2][2]=cursorz;
0824    cubeObj[3][0]=negx;cubeObj[3][1]=negy;cubeObj[3][2]=cursorz;
0825    cubeObj[4][0]=cursorx;cubeObj[4][1]=cursory;cubeObj[4][2]=negz;
0826    cubeObj[5][0]=negx;cubeObj[5][1]=cursory;cubeObj[5][2]=negz;
0827    cubeObj[6][0]=negx;cubeObj[6][1]=negy;cubeObj[6][2]=negz;
0828    cubeObj[7][0]=cursorx;cubeObj[7][1]=negy;cubeObj[7][2]=negz;
0829    for (t=0;t<=7;t++)
0830      {
0831      x=cubeObj[t][0];y=cubeObj[t][1];z=cubeObj[t][2];
0832      GetWorldCoords();
0833      cubeWorld[t][0]=x;cubeWorld[t][1]=y;cubeWorld[t][2]=z;
0834      GetCameraCoords();
0835      camcoords[t][0]=x;camcoords[t][1]=y;camcoords[t][2]=z;
0836      GetImageCoords();GetScreenCoords();
0837      displaycoords[t][0]=sx3D;displaycoords[t][1]=sy3D;
0838      }
0839    return;
0840    }
0841
0842    void Model3D::DrawCube(void)      // draw cube at 3D cursor position.
0843    {
0844    GetCubeCoords();                 // get camera coords and display coords.
0845    surface0:
0846      xc1=camcoords[7][0];yc1=camcoords[7][1];zc1=camcoords[7][2];
0847      xc2=camcoords[0][0];yc2=camcoords[0][1];zc2=camcoords[0][2];
0848      xc3=camcoords[3][0];yc3=camcoords[3][1];zc3=camcoords[3][2];
0849      xc4=camcoords[6][0];yc4=camcoords[6][1];zc4=camcoords[6][2];
0850      VisibilityTest();
0851      if (visible > 0) goto surface1;
0852      sx1=displaycoords[7][0];sy1=displaycoords[7][1];
0853      sx2=displaycoords[0][0];sy2=displaycoords[0][1];
0854      sx3=displaycoords[3][0];sy3=displaycoords[3][1];
0855      sx4=displaycoords[6][0];sy4=displaycoords[6][1];
0856      xw3=cubeWorld[7][0];yw3=cubeWorld[7][1];zw3=cubeWorld[7][2];
0857      xw2=cubeWorld[0][0];yw2=cubeWorld[0][1];zw2=cubeWorld[0][2];
0858      xw1=cubeWorld[3][0];yw1=cubeWorld[3][1];zw1=cubeWorld[3][2];
0859      DrawFacet();
0860    surface1:
0861      xc1=camcoords[6][0];yc1=camcoords[6][1];zc1=camcoords[6][2];
0862      xc2=camcoords[5][0];yc2=camcoords[5][1];zc2=camcoords[5][2];
0863      xc3=camcoords[4][0];yc3=camcoords[4][1];zc3=camcoords[4][2];
0864      xc4=camcoords[7][0];yc4=camcoords[7][1];zc4=camcoords[7][2];
0865      VisibilityTest();
0866      if (visible > 0) goto surface2;
0867      sx1=displaycoords[6][0];sy1=displaycoords[6][1];
0868      sx2=displaycoords[5][0];sy2=displaycoords[5][1];
0869      sx3=displaycoords[4][0];sy3=displaycoords[4][1];
0870      sx4=displaycoords[7][0];sy4=displaycoords[7][1];
0871      xw3=cubeWorld[6][0];yw3=cubeWorld[6][1];zw3=cubeWorld[6][2];
0872      xw2=cubeWorld[5][0];yw2=cubeWorld[5][1];zw2=cubeWorld[5][2];
0873      xw1=cubeWorld[4][0];yw1=cubeWorld[4][1];zw1=cubeWorld[4][2];
0874      DrawFacet();
0875    surface2:
0876      xc1=camcoords[3][0];yc1=camcoords[3][1];zc1=camcoords[3][2];
0877      xc2=camcoords[2][0];yc2=camcoords[2][1];zc2=camcoords[2][2];
0878      xc3=camcoords[5][0];yc3=camcoords[5][1];zc3=camcoords[5][2];
0879      xc4=camcoords[6][0];yc4=camcoords[6][1];zc4=camcoords[6][2];
0880      VisibilityTest();
0881      if (visible > 0) goto surface3;
0882      sx1=displaycoords[3][0];sy1=displaycoords[3][1];
0883      sx2=displaycoords[2][0];sy2=displaycoords[2][1];
0884      sx3=displaycoords[5][0];sy3=displaycoords[5][1];
0885      sx4=displaycoords[6][0];sy4=displaycoords[6][1];
```

```
0886    xw3=cubeWorld[3][0];yw3=cubeWorld[3][1];zw3=cubeWorld[3][2];
0887    xw2=cubeWorld[2][0];yw2=cubeWorld[2][1];zw2=cubeWorld[2][2];
0888    xw1=cubeWorld[5][0];yw1=cubeWorld[5][1];zw1=cubeWorld[5][2];
0889    DrawFacet();
0890  surface3:
0891    xc1=camcoords[0][0];yc1=camcoords[0][1];zc1=camcoords[0][2];
0892    xc2=camcoords[1][0];yc2=camcoords[1][1];zc2=camcoords[1][2];
0893    xc3=camcoords[2][0];yc3=camcoords[2][1];zc3=camcoords[2][2];
0894    xc4=camcoords[3][0];yc4=camcoords[3][1];zc4=camcoords[3][2];
0895    VisibilityTest();
0896    if (visible > 0) goto surface4;
0897    sx1=displaycoords[0][0];sy1=displaycoords[0][1];
0898    sx2=displaycoords[1][0];sy2=displaycoords[1][1];
0899    sx3=displaycoords[2][0];sy3=displaycoords[2][1];
0900    sx4=displaycoords[3][0];sy4=displaycoords[3][1];
0901    xw3=cubeWorld[0][0];yw3=cubeWorld[0][1];zw3=cubeWorld[0][2];
0902    xw2=cubeWorld[1][0];yw2=cubeWorld[1][1];zw2=cubeWorld[1][2];
0903    xw1=cubeWorld[2][0];yw1=cubeWorld[2][1];zw1=cubeWorld[2][2];
0904    DrawFacet();
0905  surface4:
0906    xc1=camcoords[7][0];yc1=camcoords[7][1];zc1=camcoords[7][2];
0907    xc2=camcoords[4][0];yc2=camcoords[4][1];zc2=camcoords[4][2];
0908    xc3=camcoords[1][0];yc3=camcoords[1][1];zc3=camcoords[1][2];
0909    xc4=camcoords[0][0];yc4=camcoords[0][1];zc4=camcoords[0][2];
0910    VisibilityTest();
0911    if (visible > 0) goto surface5;
0912    sx1=displaycoords[7][0];sy1=displaycoords[7][1];
0913    sx2=displaycoords[4][0];sy2=displaycoords[4][1];
0914    sx3=displaycoords[1][0];sy3=displaycoords[1][1];
0915    sx4=displaycoords[0][0];sy4=displaycoords[0][1];
0916    xw3=cubeWorld[7][0];yw3=cubeWorld[7][1];zw3=cubeWorld[7][2];
0917    xw2=cubeWorld[4][0];yw2=cubeWorld[4][1];zw2=cubeWorld[4][2];
0918    xw1=cubeWorld[1][0];yw1=cubeWorld[1][1];zw1=cubeWorld[1][2];
0919    DrawFacet();
0920  surface5:
0921    xc1=camcoords[1][0];yc1=camcoords[1][1];zc1=camcoords[1][2];
0922    xc2=camcoords[4][0];yc2=camcoords[4][1];zc2=camcoords[4][2];
0923    xc3=camcoords[5][0];yc3=camcoords[5][1];zc3=camcoords[5][2];
0924    xc4=camcoords[2][0];yc4=camcoords[2][1];zc4=camcoords[2][2];
0925    VisibilityTest();
0926    if (visible > 0) goto surfaces_done;
0927    sx1=displaycoords[1][0];sy1=displaycoords[1][1];
0928    sx2=displaycoords[4][0];sy2=displaycoords[4][1];
0929    sx3=displaycoords[5][0];sy3=displaycoords[5][1];
0930    sx4=displaycoords[2][0];sy4=displaycoords[2][1];
0931    xw3=cubeWorld[1][0];yw3=cubeWorld[1][1];zw3=cubeWorld[1][2];
0932    xw2=cubeWorld[4][0];yw2=cubeWorld[4][1];zw2=cubeWorld[4][2];
0933    xw1=cubeWorld[5][0];yw1=cubeWorld[5][1];zw1=cubeWorld[5][2];
0934    DrawFacet();
0935  surfaces_done:
0936  return;
0937  }
0938  /*
0939
0940  ┌─────────────────────────────────────────────────────────┐
       │         End of LIB3D.CPP 3D graphics routines for C++         │
0941   └─────────────────────────────────────────────────────────┘
0942                                                             */
```

E-5 Source code for MOUSE.HPP, the declaration file for class PointingDevice, providing low-level input control for a mouse.

```
0001  /*
0002
0003              Lee Adams' SUPERCHARGED C++ GRAPHICS
0004              Header file for class PointingDevice
0005
0006     SOURCE FILE:  MOUSE.HPP
0007           TYPE:  include file for class PointingDevice.
0008
0009     PointingDevice class:  PROGRAMMER'S GUIDE TO THE INTERFACE
0010     Detect()........ determines if a mouse is present and
0011                             initializes it if present.
0012     Data()......... returns a pointer to the struct that
0013                             holds runtime data about the mouse.
0014     Show()......... displays the mouse cursor.
0015     Hide()......... hides the mouse cursor.
0016     Pos()......... resets the xy location of the mouse.
0017     Info()......... fetches information about the status
0018                             of the mouse button and the current
0019                             xy coordinates of the mouse cursor.
0020     HLimit()....... sets the minimum and maximum horizontal
0021                             range of the mouse cursor.
0022     VLimit()....... sets the minimum and maximum vertical
0023                             range of the mouse cursor.
0024     Class declarations are located in MOUSE.HPP (which must be
0025         used in your program as #include "MOUSE.HPP").
0026     Function definitions are located in MOUSE.CPP (which uses
0027         the #include file dos.h).  Either MOUSE.CPP or MOUSE.OBJ
0028         must be named in the project list for your program.
0029
0030     LICENSE:  As purchaser of the book in which this source code
0031         appears you are granted a royalty-free license to reproduce
0032         and distribute executable files generated using this code
0033         provided that you accept the conditions of the License
0034         Agreement and Limited Warranty described in the book.
0035     PUBLICATION: Contains material from Windcrest/McGraw-Hill
0036         book 3489, published by TAB BOOKS.
0037     U.S. GOVERNMENT RESTRICTED RIGHTS:  This software and its
0038         documentation is provided with restricted rights.  The use,
0039         duplication, or disclosure by the Government is subject to
0040         restrictions set forth in subdivision (b)(3)(ii) of The
0041         Rights in Technical Data and Computer Software clause at
0042         252.227-7013.  Contractor/manufacturer is Lee Adams, c/o
0043         TAB BOOKS, 13311 Monterey Ave., Blue Ridge Summit PA 17294.
0044     TRADEMARK:  Lee Adams is a trademark of Lee Adams.
0045
0046        Copyright 1991 Lee Adams.  All rights reserved worldwide.
0047
0048                                                                 */
0049  #ifndef MOUSE_HPP          // ensure this file is included only once.
0050  #define MOUSE_HPP
0051
0052  class PointingDevice                      // class declarations.
0053  {
0054  private:                    // can be accessed by member functions only.
0055    static struct mdata      // will contain runtime info about mouse.
0056      {
0057          int MouseFlag;       // indicates if a mouse is installed.
0058          int MouseButton;     // indicates if mouse button pressed.
0059          int MouseX;                     // current x coordinate.
```

```
0060          int MouseY;                              // current y coordinate.
0061          int MouseMinX;              // minimum allowable x coordinate.
0062          int MouseMaxX;              // maximum allowable x coordinate.
0063          int MouseMinY;              // minimum allowable y coordinate.
0064          int MouseMaxY;              // maximum allowable y coordinate.
0065        } MouseParams;                // the name of the struct variable.
0066      int MouseObjectReady;           // indicates if object initialized.
0067      void Init(void);                // low-level initialization of driver.
0068
0069   public:                   // can be accessed by any in-scope function.
0070      PointingDevice();                             // constructor.
0071      ~PointingDevice();                             // destructor.
0072      int Detect(int);                    // initialize if found.
0073      mdata * Data(void);                 // returns ptr to struct.
0074      void Show(void);                    // displays cursor.
0075      void Hide(void);                     // hides cursor.
0076      void Pos(int,int);                  // sets xy coords.
0077      void Info(void);        // checks button status and xy position.
0078      void HLimit(int,int);                 // sets horiz range.
0079      void VLimit(int,int);                  // sets vert range.
0080
0081      #if defined (BORLAND)
0082        static union REGS regs;              // for register contents.
0083      #elif defined (ZORTECH)
0084        static union REGS inregs,outregs;
0085      #elif defined (MICROSOFT)
0086        static union REGS inregs,outregs;
0087      #endif
0088   };
0089
0090   #endif                                          // MOUSE_HPP.
0091   /*
0092
0093   |   Supercharged C++ Graphics  --  end of source file MOUSE.HPP   |
0094
0095                                                                */
```

E-6 Source code for MOUSE.CPP, the implementation file for class PointingDevice, providing low-level input control for a mouse.

```
0001   /*
0002
0003   |          Lee Adams' SUPERCHARGED C++ GRAPHICS              |
0004   |          Implementation file for class PointingDevice      |
0005
0006      SOURCE FILE:  MOUSE.CPP
0007             TYPE:  Implementation file for a class.  Name this
0008                    file or the resulting OBJ file in the project list.
0009        LANGUAGES:  Turbo C++, Zortech C++, and all C++ compilers
0010                    compatible with the AT&T C++ 2.0 specification.
0011            USAGE:  Refer to the header file MOUSE.HPP for a guide
0012                    to using the methods of PointingDevice class objects.
0013          LICENSE:  As purchaser of the book in which this source code
0014             appears you are granted a royalty-free license to reproduce
0015             and distribute executable files generated using this code
0016             provided that you accept the conditions of the License
0017             Agreement and Limited Warranty described in the book.
0018      PUBLICATION: Contains material from Windcrest/McGraw-Hill
0019             book 3489, published by TAB BOOKS.
```

```
0020    U.S. GOVERNMENT RESTRICTED RIGHTS:  This software and its
0021       documentation is provided with restricted rights.  The use,
0022       duplication, or disclosure by the Government is subject to
0023       restrictions set forth in subdivision (b)(3)(ii) of The
0024       Rights in Technical Data and Computer Software clause at
0025       252.227-7013.  Contractor/manufacturer is Lee Adams, c/o
0026       TAB BOOKS, 13311 Monterey Ave., Blue Ridge Summit PA 17294.
0027    TRADEMARK:  Lee Adams is a trademark of Lee Adams.
0028
0029       Copyright 1991 Lee Adams.  All rights reserved worldwide.
0030
0031
0032                        CONDITIONAL COMPILATION
0033    To compile only those blocks of code that support the C++
0034    compiler and graphics library that you are using, you should
0035    #define the appropriate tokens in the following preprocessor
0036    directives.  Use the following table as your guide:
0037              GRAPHICS LIBRARY
0038       Borland's graphics.lib                 #define BGI
0039       Zortech's fg.lib or fgdebug.lib        #define FG
0040       Microsoft's graph.lib                  #define MS
0041              COMPILER
0042       Borland Turbo C++ compiler             #define BORLAND
0043       Zortech C++ compiler                   #define ZORTECH
0044       AT&T-compatible C++ compilers          #define MICROSOFT
0045    Be sure you define only one compiler and one graphics library.
0046
0047                                                                  */
0048    #define BGI      1 // indicates the graphics library you are using.
0049    #define BORLAND  1     // indicates the C++ compiler you are using.
0050
0051    const int zYES=      1;                    // boolean tokens...
0052    const int zNO=       0;
0053    const int zFAIL=     0;
0054    const int zVGA_12H=  1;                    // VGA 640x480x16.
0055    const int zEGA_10H=  2;                    // EGA 640x350x16.
0056    const int zEGA_EH=   3;                    // EGA 640x200x16.
0057    const int zMCGA_11H= 4;                    // MCGA 640x480x2.
0058    const int zCGA_6H=   5;                    // CGA 640x200x2.
0059    const int zHERC=     6;                    // Hercules 720x348x2.
0060    /*
0061
0062                        INCLUDE FILES
0063
0064                                                                  */
0065    #include <dos.h>             // supports int 33h for mouse routines.
0066    #include "LIB2D.HPP"         // graphics library language bindings.
0067    #include "MOUSE.HPP"                      // class declarations.
0068    #define zMOUSE  0x33         // DOS interrupt number for mouse driver.
0069    /*
0070
0071              Class PointingDevice:  CONSTRUCTOR
0072
0073                                                                  */
0074    PointingDevice::PointingDevice(void)
0075    {
0076    MouseParams.MouseFlag= 0;           // initialize struct contents...
0077    MouseParams.MouseButton= 0;
0078    MouseParams.MouseX= 0;
0079    MouseParams.MouseY= 0;
0080    MouseParams.MouseMinX= 0;
0081    MouseParams.MouseMaxX= 0;
0082    MouseParams.MouseMinY= 0;
```

```
0083  MouseParams.MouseMaxY= 0;
0084  MouseObjectReady= zYES;                        // set the status token.
0085  }
0086  /*
0087
0088  ┌──────────────────────────────────────────────────────────────────┐
      │                 Class PointingDevice:   DESTRUCTOR                 │
0089  └──────────────────────────────────────────────────────────────────┘
0090                                                                     */
0091  PointingDevice::~PointingDevice()
0092  {
0093  MouseObjectReady= zNO;                         // reset the status token.
0094  }
0095  /*
0096
0097  ┌──────────────────────────────────────────────────────────────────┐
      │              Initialize a mouse if present in system               │
0098  └──────────────────────────────────────────────────────────────────┘
0099                                                                     */
0100  int PointingDevice::Detect(int GraphicsMode)
0101  {
0102  Init();                              // attempt to initialize the mouse.
0103  if (MouseParams.MouseFlag==0) return zFAIL;  // cancel if no mouse.
0104  switch (GraphicsMode)                // initialize some parameters...
0105    {
0106    case zVGA_12H:  MouseParams.MouseMinX= 0;
0107                    MouseParams.MouseMaxX= 639;
0108                    MouseParams.MouseMinY= 0;
0109                    MouseParams.MouseMaxY= 479;
0110                    break;
0111    case zEGA_10H:  MouseParams.MouseMinX= 0;
0112                    MouseParams.MouseMaxX= 639;
0113                    MouseParams.MouseMinY= 0;
0114                    MouseParams.MouseMaxY= 349;
0115                    break;
0116    case zEGA_EH:   MouseParams.MouseMinX= 0;
0117                    MouseParams.MouseMaxX= 639;
0118                    MouseParams.MouseMinY= 0;
0119                    MouseParams.MouseMaxY= 199;
0120                    break;
0121    case zMCGA_11H: MouseParams.MouseMinX= 0;
0122                    MouseParams.MouseMaxX= 639;
0123                    MouseParams.MouseMinY= 0;
0124                    MouseParams.MouseMaxY= 479;
0125                    break;
0126    case zCGA_6H:   MouseParams.MouseMinX= 0;
0127                    MouseParams.MouseMaxX= 639;
0128                    MouseParams.MouseMinY= 0;
0129                    MouseParams.MouseMaxY= 199;
0130                    break;
0131    case zHERC:     MouseParams.MouseMinX= 0;
0132                    MouseParams.MouseMaxX= 719;
0133                    MouseParams.MouseMinY= 0;
0134                    MouseParams.MouseMaxY= 347;
0135                    break;
0136    default:        return zFAIL;
0137    }
0138  HLimit(MouseParams.MouseMinX, MouseParams.MouseMaxX);
0139  VLimit(MouseParams.MouseMinY, MouseParams.MouseMaxY);
0140  Pos(319,99);
0141  return zYES;
0142  }
0143  /*
0144  ┌────────────────────────────────────────────────────────────────────┐
```

```
0145 |                Low-level initialization of mouse                |
0146
0147                                                                   */
0148 void PointingDevice::Init(void)
0149 {   // is a private member called by PointingDevice::Detect().
0150 #if defined (BORLAND)
0151   regs.x.ax=0;
0152   int86(zMOUSE,&regs,&regs);
0153   MouseParams.MouseFlag=regs.x.ax;
0154 #elif defined (ZORTECH)
0155   inregs.x.ax=0;                              // mouse function #0.
0156   int86(zMOUSE,&inregs,&outregs);      // call interrupt 33 hex.
0157   MouseParams.MouseFlag=outregs.x.ax;    // equals 0 if no mouse.
0158 #elif defined (MICROSOFT)
0159   inregs.x.ax=0;
0160   int86(zMOUSE,&inregs,&outregs);
0161   MouseParams.MouseFlag=outregs.x.ax;
0162 #endif
0163 return;
0164 }
0165 /*
0166
0167 |        Return a pointer to the mouse's runtime data struct        |
0168
0169                                                                   */
0170 mdata * PointingDevice::Data(void)
0171 {
0172 return &MouseParams;
0173 }
0174 /*
0175
0176 |                  Turn on the mouse cursor                         |
0177
0178                                                                   */
0179 void PointingDevice::Show(void)
0180 {
0181 #if defined (BORLAND)
0182   regs.x.ax=1;
0183   int86(zMOUSE,&regs,&regs);
0184 #elif defined (ZORTECH)
0185   inregs.x.ax=1;                              // mouse function #1.
0186   int86(zMOUSE,&inregs,&outregs);      // call interrupt 33 hex.
0187 #elif defined (MICROSOFT)
0188   inregs.x.ax=1;
0189   int86(zMOUSE,&inregs,&outregs);
0190 #endif
0191 return;
0192 }
0193 /*
0194
0195 |                  Turn off the mouse cursor                        |
0196
0197                                                                   */
0198 void PointingDevice::Hide(void)
0199 {
0200 #if defined (BORLAND)
0201   regs.x.ax=2;
0202   int86(zMOUSE,&regs,&regs);
0203 #elif defined (ZORTECH)
0204   inregs.x.ax=2;                              // mouse function #2.
0205   int86(zMOUSE,&inregs,&outregs);      // call interrupt 33 hex.
0206 #elif defined (MICROSOFT)
0207   inregs.x.ax=2;
```

```
0208      int86(zMOUSE,&inregs,&outregs);
0209   #endif
0210   return;
0211   }
0212   /*
0213
0214   ┌─────────────────────────────────────────────────────────────────┐
        │          Determine mouse location and status of buttons         │
0215   └─────────────────────────────────────────────────────────────────┘
0216                                                                     */
0217   void PointingDevice::Info(void)
0218   {
0219   #if defined (BORLAND)
0220      regs.x.ax=3;
0221      int86(zMOUSE,&regs,&regs);
0222      MouseParams.MouseButton=regs.x.bx;
0223      MouseParams.MouseX=regs.x.cx;
0224      MouseParams.MouseY=regs.x.dx;
0225   #elif defined (ZORTECH)
0226      inregs.x.ax=3;
0227      int86(zMOUSE,&inregs,&outregs);
0228      MouseParams.MouseButton=outregs.x.bx;
0229      MouseParams.MouseX=outregs.x.cx;
0230      MouseParams.MouseY=outregs.x.dx;
0231   #elif defined (MICROSOFT)
0232      inregs.x.ax=3;                              // mouse function #3.
0233      int86(zMOUSE,&inregs,&outregs);       // call interrupt 33 hex.
0234      MouseParams.MouseButton=outregs.x.bx;  // 1 (left) or 2 (right).
0235      MouseParams.MouseX=outregs.x.cx;            // get x coordinate.
0236      MouseParams.MouseY=outregs.x.dx;            // get y coordinate.
0237   #endif
0238   return;
0239   }
0240   /*
0241
0242   ┌─────────────────────────────────────────────────────────────────┐
        │              Reset the location of the mouse cursor              │
0243   └─────────────────────────────────────────────────────────────────┘
0244                                                                     */
0245   void PointingDevice::Pos(int Xpos, int Ypos)
0246   {
0247   MouseParams.MouseX= Xpos;
0248   MouseParams.MouseY= Ypos;
0249   #if defined (BORLAND)
0250      regs.x.ax=4;                                // mouse function #4.
0251      regs.x.cx=MouseParams.MouseX;           // set the x coordinate.
0252      regs.x.dx=MouseParams.MouseY;           // set the y coordinate.
0253      int86(zMOUSE,&regs,&regs);            // call interrupt 33 hex.
0254   #elif defined (ZORTECH)
0255      inregs.x.ax=4;
0256      inregs.x.cx=MouseParams.MouseX;
0257      inregs.x.dx=MouseParams.MouseY;
0258      int86(zMOUSE,&inregs,&outregs);
0259   #elif defined (MICROSOFT)
0260      inregs.x.ax=4;
0261      inregs.x.cx=MouseParams.MouseX;
0262      inregs.x.dx=MouseParams.MouseY;
0263      int86(zMOUSE,&inregs,&outregs);
0264   #endif
0265   return;
0266   }
0267   /*
0268
0269   ┌─────────────────────────────────────────────────────────────────┐
        │          Set the minimum and maximum horizontal range           │
       └
```

```
0270  |_____|
0271                                                          */
0272  void PointingDevice::HLimit(int Left,int Right)
0273  {
0274  MouseParams.MouseMinX= Left;
0275  MouseParams.MouseMaxX= Right;
0276  #if defined (BORLAND)
0277    regs.x.ax=7;
0278    regs.x.cx=MouseParams.MouseMinX;
0279    regs.x.dx=MouseParams.MouseMaxX;
0280    int86(zMOUSE,&regs,&regs);
0281  #elif defined (ZORTECH)
0282    inregs.x.ax=7;                              // mouse function #7.
0283    inregs.x.cx=MouseParams.MouseMinX;    // set the minimum x coord.
0284    inregs.x.dx=MouseParams.MouseMaxX;    // set the maximum x coord.
0285    int86(zMOUSE,&inregs,&outregs);         // call interrupt 33 hex.
0286  #elif defined (MICROSOFT)
0287    inregs.x.ax=7;                              // mouse function #7.
0288    inregs.x.cx=MouseParams.MouseMinX;    // set the minimum x coord.
0289    inregs.x.dx=MouseParams.MouseMaxX;    // set the maximum x coord.
0290    int86(zMOUSE,&inregs,&outregs);         // call interrupt 33 hex.
0291  #endif
0292  return;
0293  }
0294  /*
0295
0296  ┌──────────────────────────────────────────────────────┐
      │       Set the minimum and maximum vertical range       │
0297  │                                                        │
0298  └──────────────────────────────────────────────────────┘  */
0299  void PointingDevice::VLimit(int Top ,int Bottom)
0300  {
0301  MouseParams.MouseMinY= Top;
0302  MouseParams.MouseMaxY= Bottom;
0303  #if defined (BORLAND)
0304    regs.x.ax=8;
0305    regs.x.cx=MouseParams.MouseMinY;
0306    regs.x.dx=MouseParams.MouseMaxY;
0307    int86(zMOUSE,&regs,&regs);
0308  #elif defined (ZORTECH)
0309    inregs.x.ax=8;                              // mouse function #8.
0310    inregs.x.cx=MouseParams.MouseMinY;    // set the minimum y coord.
0311    inregs.x.dx=MouseParams.MouseMaxY;    // set the maximum y coord.
0312    int86(zMOUSE,&inregs,&outregs);         // call interrupt 33 hex.
0313  #elif defined (MICROSOFT)
0314    inregs.x.ax=8;
0315    inregs.x.cx=MouseParams.MouseMinY;
0316    inregs.x.dx=MouseParams.MouseMaxY;
0317    int86(zMOUSE,&inregs,&outregs);
0318  #endif
0319  return;
0320  }
0321  /*
0322
0323  ┌──────────────────────────────────────────────────────┐
      │    Supercharged C++ Graphics  --  end of source file MOUSE.CPP │
0324  │                                                        │
0325  └──────────────────────────────────────────────────────┘  */
```

E-7 Source code for BITBLT.HPP, the declaration file for class Bitblt, providing bitblt objects capable of displaying, moving, erasing, saving, and loading themselves.

```
0001  /*
0002
0003              Lee Adams' SUPERCHARGED C++ GRAPHICS
0004                   Header file for class Bitblt
0005
0006    SOURCE FILE:  BITBLT.HPP
0007          TYPE:   include file for class Bitblt.
0008
0009        Bitblt class:  PROGRAMMER'S GUIDE TO THE INTERFACE
0010    Each instance of the Bitblt class can manipulate one copy of
0011    a graphic array image in the bitmap buffer.  Use multiple
0012    instances of the Bitblt class to control multiple images or
0013    copies of the same image.
0014    GrabImage()......allocates memory, grabs the image from the
0015                          bitmap and stores it in a graphic array.
0016    DisplayImage()...displays the bitblt if not already displayed.
0017    EraseImage().....restores the previous background.
0018    MoveImage()......moves the currently-displayed bitblt to
0019                          another location.
0020    NameImageFile()..specifies the filename for disk IO.
0021    SaveImageFile()..saves the graphic array to disk using the
0022                          current filename.
0023    LoadImageFile()..loads a graphic array from disk using the
0024                          current filename.
0025    Class declarations are located in BITBLT.HPP (which must be
0026       used in your program as #include "BITBLT.HPP").
0027    Function definitions are located in BITBLT.CPP (which uses
0028       #include files alloc.h, graphics.h, io.h, stdio.h, and
0029       string.h).  Either BITBLT.CPP or BITBLT.OBJ must be named
0030       in the make file project list for your program.
0031    Each function returns 1 if successful, -1 if error.
0032
0033    LICENSE:  As purchaser of the book in which this source code
0034       appears you are granted a royalty-free license to reproduce
0035       and distribute executable files generated using this code
0036       provided that you accept the conditions of the License
0037       Agreement and Limited Warranty described in the book.
0038    PUBLICATION: Contains material from Windcrest/McGraw-Hill
0039       book 3489, published by TAB BOOKS.
0040    U.S. GOVERNMENT RESTRICTED RIGHTS:  This software and its
0041       documentation is provided with restricted rights.  The use,
0042       duplication, or disclosure by the Government is subject to
0043       restrictions set forth in subdivision (b)(3)(ii) of The
0044       Rights in Technical Data and Computer Software clause at
0045       252.227-7013.  Contractor/manufacturer is Lee Adams, c/o
0046       TAB BOOKS, 13311 Monterey Ave., Blue Ridge Summit PA 17294.
0047    TRADEMARK:  Lee Adams is a trademark of Lee Adams.
0048
0049       Copyright 1991 Lee Adams.  All rights reserved worldwide.
0050
0051                                                              */
0052  #ifndef BITBLT_HPP
0053  #define BITBLT_HPP
0054
0055  class Bitblt                                // class declarations.
0056  {
0057  private:                  // can be accessed by member functions only.
0058    Viewport *Generic;                  // points to a viewport object.
0059    #if defined (BGI)
```

```
0060        char far * Block;          // points to memory block for image.
0061        char far * BgBlock;   // points to memory block for background.
0062    #elif defined (FG)
0063        fg_color_t far * Block;
0064        fg_color_t far * BgBlock;
0065    #elif defined (MS)
0066        char far * Block;
0067        char far * BgBlock;
0068    #endif
0069    unsigned long BlockSize;        // size in bytes of graphic array.
0070    int YES,NO,ERROR,SUCCESS;                          // tokens.
0071    int OVERWRITE;                        // copy as original form.
0072    int NEGATIVE;                         // copy as reverse form.
0073    int SUPERIMPOSE;                 // OR: superimpose as opaque.
0074    int FILTER;           // XOR: superimpose as semi-transparent.
0075    int STENCIL;                        // AND: common areas.
0076    int MAXIMUM_X, MAXIMUM_Y;            // screen dimensions.
0077    int X1,Y1,X2,Y2;                          // bounding box.
0078    int Width, Depth;                     // dimensions of box.
0079    int OldX1,OldY1;                 // previous origin coords.
0080    int Logic;                           // current write mode.
0081    int DefaultLogic;                    // default write mode.
0082    char FileName[13];                              // filename.
0083    int Ready;                    // indicates if saved in memory.
0084    int Displayed;                     // indicates if displayed.
0085    int MemAllocated;          // indicates if memory allocated.
0086    int BgMemAllocated;        // indicates if memory allocated.
0087    int GraphicsError;            // result of library function.
0088    int MaxX, MaxY;               // max legal origin coords.
0089    void FreeBlock(void);             // deallocates memory.
0090
0091    public:          // can be accessed by any function in source file.
0092      Bitblt(int,int,int,int,int,int,Viewport *);
0093      ~Bitblt();                                    // destructor.
0094      int GrabImage(void);
0095      int DisplayImage(int Xa,int Ya,int Mode);
0096      int EraseImage(void);
0097      int MoveImage(int XOffset,int YOffset,int Mode);
0098      int NameImageFile(char * Name);
0099      int SaveImageFile(char * Name="UNTITLED.BLK");
0100      int LoadImageFile(char * Name="UNTITLED.BLK");
0101    };
0102
0103    #endif
0104    /*
0105
0106    ┌─────────────────────────────────────────────────────────────┐
        │  Supercharged C++ Graphics  --  end of source file BITBLT.HPP │
0107    │                                                               │
0108    └─────────────────────────────────────────────────────────────┘  */
```

E-8 Source code for BITBLT.CPP, the declaration file for class Bitblt, providing bitblt objects capable of displaying, moving, erasing, saving, and loading themselves.

```
0001    /*
0002
0003    ┌─────────────────────────────────────────────────────────────┐
        │            Lee Adams' SUPERCHARGED C++ GRAPHICS               │
0004    │              Implementation file for class Bitblt             │
0005    │                                                               │
0006    │    SOURCE FILE:  BITBLT.CPP                                    │
0007    │            TYPE:  Implementation file for a class.  Name this  │
0008    │                  file or the resulting OBJ file in the project list. │
        └─────────────────────────────────────────────────────────────┘
```

```
0009              LANGUAGES:  Turbo C++, Zortech C++, and all C++ compilers
0010                          compatible with AT&T C++ 2.0 specification.
0011                  USAGE:  Refer to the header file BITBLT.HPP for a guide
0012                          to using the methods of Bitblt class objects.
0013          LICENSE:  As purchaser of the book in which this source code
0014            appears you are granted a royalty-free license to reproduce
0015            and distribute executable files generated using this code
0016            provided that you accept the conditions of the License
0017            Agreement and Limited Warranty described in the book.
0018          PUBLICATION: Contains material from Windcrest/McGraw-Hill
0019            book 3489, published by TAB BOOKS.
0020          U.S. GOVERNMENT RESTRICTED RIGHTS:  This software and its
0021            documentation is provided with restricted rights.  The use,
0022            duplication, or disclosure by the Government is subject to
0023            restrictions set forth in subdivision (b)(3)(ii) of The
0024            Rights in Technical Data and Computer Software clause at
0025            252.227-7013.  Contractor/manufacturer is Lee Adams, c/o
0026            TAB BOOKS, 13311 Monterey Ave., Blue Ridge Summit PA 17294.
0027          TRADEMARK:  Lee Adams is a trademark of Lee Adams.
0028
0029          Copyright 1991 Lee Adams.  All rights reserved worldwide.
0030
0031
0032                        CONDITIONAL COMPILATION
0033          To compile only those blocks of code that support the C++
0034          compiler and graphics library that you are using, you should
0035          #define the appropriate tokens in the following preprocessor
0036          directives.  Use the following table as your guide:
0037                  GRAPHICS LIBRARY
0038              Borland's graphics.lib              #define BGI
0039              Zortech's fg.lib or fgdebug.lib     #define FG
0040              Microsoft's graph.lib               #define MS
0041                  COMPILER
0042              Borland Turbo C++ compiler          #define BORLAND
0043              Zortech C++ compiler                #define ZORTECH
0044              AT&T-compatible C++ compilers       #define MICROSOFT
0045          Be sure you define only one compiler and one graphics library.
0046
0047                                                                       */
0048  #define BGI     1  // indicates the graphics library you are using.
0049  #define BORLAND 1  // indicates the C++ compiler you are using.
0050  /*
0051
0052                        INCLUDE FILES
0053
0054                                                                       */
0055  #include <string.h>       // strcpy(), strlen().
0056  #include <io.h>           // access().
0057  #include <stdio.h>        // fread(), fwrite().
0058  #include "LIB2D.HPP"      // declarations for graphics classes.
0059  #include "BITBLT.HPP"     // declarations for Bitblt class.
0060  /*
0061
0062                    Class Bitblt:  CONSTRUCTOR
0063
0064                                                                       */
0065  Bitblt::Bitblt(int Xa,int Ya,int Xb,int Yb,int X_Res,int Y_Res,
0066                 Viewport *ViewportPtr)
0067  {             // use viewport object referenced by pointer Viewport.
0068  Generic= ViewportPtr;        // Generic points to viewport object.
0069  X1= Xa; Y1= Ya; X2= Xb; Y2= Yb; OldX1= X1; OldY1= Y1;
0070  YES= 1; NO= 0; ERROR= -1; SUCCESS= 1;
```

```
0071   OVERWRITE= 0; NEGATIVE= 4; SUPERIMPOSE= 2; FILTER= 1; STENCIL= 3;
0072   MAXIMUM_X= X_Res; MAXIMUM_Y= Y_Res;
0073   GraphicsError= 0; strcpy(FileName,"UNTITLED.BLK");
0074   Logic= OVERWRITE; DefaultLogic= OVERWRITE;
0075   Ready= NO; Displayed= NO; MemAllocated= NO; BgMemAllocated= NO;
0076   Width= X2 - X1; Depth= Y2 - Y1;                    // offsets from origin.
0077   MaxX= MAXIMUM_X - (Width + 1); MaxY= MAXIMUM_Y - (Depth + 1);
0078   }
0079   /*
0080
0081   ┌─────────────────────────────────────────────────────────────┐
       │                  Class Bitblt:  DESTRUCTOR                    │
0082   └─────────────────────────────────────────────────────────────┘
0083                                                                  */
0084   Bitblt::~Bitblt()
0085   {
0086   FreeBlock();
0087   }
0088   /*
0089
0090   ┌─────────────────────────────────────────────────────────────┐
       │              Class Bitblt:  method GrabImage()                │
0091   └─────────────────────────────────────────────────────────────┘
0092                                                                  */
0093   int Bitblt::GrabImage(void)                         // public.
0094   {
0095   if (MemAllocated==YES) return ERROR;
0096   if (BgMemAllocated==YES) return ERROR;
0097   Block= Generic->MemBlock(X1,Y1,X2,Y2);// allocate memory for image.
0098   if (Block==0) return ERROR;           // if memory allocation failed.
0099   MemAllocated= YES;
0100   BlockSize= Generic->GetBlockSize(X1,Y1,X2,Y2);      // get size.
0101   Generic->GetBlock(X1,Y1,X2,Y2,Block);     // store image in memory.
0102   BgBlock= Generic->MemBlock(X1,Y1,X2,Y2); // allocate memory for bg.
0103   if (BgBlock==0) return ERROR;         // if memory allocation failed.
0104   BgMemAllocated=YES;
0105   Generic->GetBlock(X1,Y1,X2,Y2,BgBlock);       // store bg in array.
0106   Ready= YES;
0107   return SUCCESS;
0108   }
0109   /*
0110
0111   ┌─────────────────────────────────────────────────────────────┐
       │              Class Bitblt:  method FreeBlock()                │
0112   └─────────────────────────────────────────────────────────────┘
0113                                                                  */
0114   void Bitblt::FreeBlock(void)                        // private.
0115   {
0116   if (BgMemAllocated==YES) Generic->FreeBlock(BgBlock);
0117   if (MemAllocated==YES) Generic->FreeBlock(Block);
0118   return;
0119   }
0120   /*
0121
0122   ┌─────────────────────────────────────────────────────────────┐
       │              Class Bitblt:  method DisplayImage()             │
0123   └─────────────────────────────────────────────────────────────┘
0124                                                                  */
0125   int Bitblt::DisplayImage(int Xa,int Ya,int Mode)    // public.
0126   {
0127   if (Displayed==YES) return ERROR;
0128   if (Ready==NO) return ERROR;
0129   if (Xa < 0) return ERROR;
0130   if (Ya < 0) return ERROR;
0131   if (Xa > MaxX) return ERROR;
0132   if (Ya > MaxY) return ERROR;
0133   if (Mode < OVERWRITE) return ERROR;
```

```
0134   if (Mode > NEGATIVE) return ERROR;
0135   X1= Xa; Y1= Ya; Logic= Mode;
0136   Generic->GetBlock(X1,Y1,X1+Width,Y1+Depth,BgBlock);      // store bg.
0137   switch(Logic)
0138      {                      // display bitblt using appropriate logic.
0139      case 0:  Generic->PutPSET(X1,Y1,Block); break;
0140      case 1:  Generic->PutXOR(X1,Y1,Block); break;
0141      case 3:  Generic->PutAND(X1,Y1,Block); break;
0142      default: Generic->PutPSET(X1,Y1,Block); break;
0143      }
0144   Displayed= YES; OldX1= X1; OldY1= Y1;
0145   return SUCCESS;
0146   }
0147   /*
0148
0149   ┌─────────────────────────────────────────────────────────────────┐
       │                                                                   │
       │               Class Bitblt:  method EraseImage()                 │
0150   │                                                                   │
       └─────────────────────────────────────────────────────────────────┘
0151                                                                      */
0152   int Bitblt::EraseImage(void)                          // public.
0153   {
0154   if (Displayed==NO) return ERROR;
0155   Generic->PutPSET(OldX1,OldY1,BgBlock);
0156   Displayed= NO;
0157   return SUCCESS;
0158   }
0159   /*
0160
0161   ┌─────────────────────────────────────────────────────────────────┐
       │                                                                   │
       │               Class Bitblt:  method MoveImage()                  │
0162   │                                                                   │
       └─────────────────────────────────────────────────────────────────┘
0163                                                                      */
0164   int Bitblt::MoveImage(int XOffset,int YOffset,int Mode)  // public.
0165   {
0166   if (Displayed==NO) return ERROR;          // if not already displayed.
0167   X1= OldX1 + XOffset; Y1= OldY1 + YOffset;        // calc new coords.
0168   if (X1 < 0) return ERROR;
0169   if (Y1 < 0) return ERROR;
0170   if (X1 > MaxX) return ERROR;
0171   if (Y1 > MaxY) return ERROR;
0172   if (Mode < OVERWRITE) return ERROR;
0173   if (Mode > NEGATIVE) return ERROR;
0174   Logic= Mode;
0175   Generic->PutPSET(OldX1,OldY1,BgBlock);                // restore old bg.
0176   Generic->GetBlock(X1,Y1,X1+Width,Y1+Depth,BgBlock);// store new bg.
0177   switch(Logic)
0178      {    // display bitblt at new location using appropriate logic.
0179      case 0:  Generic->PutPSET(X1,Y1,Block); break;
0180      case 1:  Generic->PutXOR(X1,Y1,Block); break;
0181      case 3:  Generic->PutAND(X1,Y1,Block); break;
0182      default: Generic->PutPSET(X1,Y1,Block); break;
0183      }
0184   OldX1= X1; OldY1= Y1;
0185   return SUCCESS;
0186   }
0187   /*
0188
0189   ┌─────────────────────────────────────────────────────────────────┐
       │                                                                   │
       │               Class Bitblt:  method NameImageFile()              │
0190   │                                                                   │
       └─────────────────────────────────────────────────────────────────┘
0191                                                                      */
0192   int Bitblt::NameImageFile(char * Name)                // public.
0193   {
0194   if (strlen(Name)!=12) return ERROR;
0195   strcpy(FileName,Name);
```

```
0196   return SUCCESS;
0197   }
0198   /*
0199
0200   ┌─────────────────────────────────────────────────────────────┐
       │              Class Bitblt:  method SaveImageFile()            │
0201   └─────────────────────────────────────────────────────────────┘
0202                                                               */
0203   int Bitblt::SaveImageFile(char * Name)              // public.
0204   {
0205   if (strlen(Name)!=12) return ERROR;            // if illegal name.
0206   strcpy(FileName,Name);                         // grab new name.
0207   #if defined (BORLAND)
0208     if ((access(FileName,00))==0)        // if file already exists.
0209       {
0210       if ((access(FileName,02))==-1) return ERROR;   // if read-only.
0211       }
0212   #elif defined (ZORTECH)
0213     if ((access(FileName,F_OK))==0)      // if file already exists.
0214       {
0215       if ((access(FileName,W_OK))==-1) return ERROR; // if read-only.
0216       }
0217   #elif defined (MICROSOFT)
0218     if ((access(FileName,00))==0)        // if file already exists.
0219       {
0220       if ((access(FileName,02))==-1) return ERROR;   // if read-only.
0221       }
0222   #endif
0223   FILE * FileStream;                       // data stream for disk IO.
0224   FileStream= fopen(FileName,"wb");            // open the stream.
0225   fwrite((char *)Block,1,BlockSize,FileStream);    // write to disk.
0226   if ferror(FileStream)                    // if IO error occurred.
0227     {
0228     fclose(FileStream); return ERROR;
0229     }
0230   fclose(FileStream);                          // close the stream.
0231   return SUCCESS;
0232   }
0233   /*
0234
0235   ┌─────────────────────────────────────────────────────────────┐
       │              Class Bitblt:  method LoadImageFile()            │
0236   └─────────────────────────────────────────────────────────────┘
0237                                                               */
0238   int Bitblt::LoadImageFile(char * Name)              // public.
0239   {
0240   if (strlen(Name)!=12) return ERROR;            // illegal filename.
0241   strcpy(FileName,Name);                         // grab new name.
0242   #if defined (BORLAND)
0243     if ((access(FileName,00))==-1) return ERROR;   // does not exist.
0244   #elif defined (ZORTECH)
0245     if ((access(FileName,F_OK))==-1) return ERROR; // does not exist.
0246   #elif defined (MICROSOFT)
0247     if ((access(FileName,00))==-1) return ERROR;   // does not exist.
0248   #endif
0249   FILE * FileStream;                       // data stream for disk IO.
0250   FileStream= fopen(FileName,"rb");    // open stream for binary read.
0251   unsigned long HowLong=filelength(fileno(FileStream));
0252   if (HowLong>BlockSize)                   // if too large to fit.
0253     {
0254     fclose(FileStream); return ERROR;
0255     }
0256   if (HowLong==0xffff)                     // if returned -1 error.
0257     {
0258     fclose(FileStream); return ERROR;
```

```
0259    }
0260    fread(Block,1,HowLong,FileStream);    // read in the file from disk.
0261    if ferror(FileStream)                 // if IO error occurred.
0262    {
0263    fclose(FileStream); return ERROR;
0264    }
0265    fclose(FileStream);                    // close the stream.
0266    return SUCCESS;
0267    }
0268    /*
0269
0270    ┌────────────────────────────────────────────────────────────────┐
        │   Supercharged C++ Graphics  --  end of source file BITBLT.CPP   │
0271    └────────────────────────────────────────────────────────────────┘
0272                                                                    */
```

E-9 Source code for BLITTER.HPP, the declaration file for class Blitter, specializing in high-speed graphic array animation.

```
0001    /*
0002
0003    ┌──────────────────────────────────────────────────────────────┐
        │             Lee Adams' SUPERCHARGED C++ GRAPHICS               │
0004    │                  Header file for class Blitter                 │
0005    │                                                                │
0006    │   SOURCE FILE:  BLITTER.HPP                                    │
0007    │          TYPE:  include file for class Blitter.                │
0008    │                                                                │
0009    │       Blitter class:  PROGRAMMER'S GUIDE TO THE INTERFACE      │
0010    │   Each instance of the Blitter class can manipulate one copy of │
0011    │   a graphic array image in the bitmap buffer.  Use multiple    │
0012    │   instances of the Blitter class to control multiple images or  │
0013    │   copies of the same image using overwrite logic.              │
0014    │   GrabImage()......allocates memory, grabs the image from the  │
0015    │                    bitmap and stores it in a graphic array.    │
0016    │   DisplayImage()...displays the bitblt if not already displayed. │
0017    │   MoveImage()......moves the currently-displayed bitblt to     │
0018    │                    another location using overwrite logic.     │
0019    │   Class declarations are located in BLITTER.HPP (which must be  │
0020    │     used in your program as #include "BLITTER.HPP").           │
0021    │   Function definitions are located in BLITTER.CPP (which uses  │
0022    │     #include file alloc.h.  Either BLITTER.CPP or BLITTER.OBJ   │
0023    │     must be named in the project list for your program.        │
0024    │   Each function returns 1 if successful, -1 if error.          │
0025    │                                                                │
0026    │   LICENSE:  As purchaser of the book in which this source code  │
0027    │     appears you are granted a royalty-free license to reproduce │
0028    │     and distribute executable files generated using this code  │
0029    │     provided that you accept the conditions of the License     │
0030    │     Agreement and Limited Warranty described in the book.      │
0031    │   PUBLICATION: Contains material from Windcrest/McGraw-Hill    │
0032    │     book 3489, published by TAB BOOKS.                         │
0033    │   U.S. GOVERNMENT RESTRICTED RIGHTS:  This software and its     │
0034    │     documentation is provided with restricted rights.  The use, │
0035    │     duplication, or disclosure by the Government is subject to  │
0036    │     restrictions set forth in subdivision (b)(3)(ii) of The    │
0037    │     Rights in Technical Data and Computer Software clause at    │
0038    │     252.227-7013.  Contractor/manufacturer is Lee Adams, c/o   │
0039    │     TAB BOOKS, 13311 Monterey Ave., Blue Ridge Summit PA 17294. │
0040    │   TRADEMARK:  Lee Adams is a trademark of Lee Adams.           │
0041    └──────────────────────────────────────────────────────────────┘
```

```
0042        Copyright 1991 Lee Adams.  All rights reserved worldwide.
0043
0044                                                                       */
0045   #ifndef BLITTER_HPP
0046   #define BLITTER_HPP
0047
0048   class Blitter                              // class declarations.
0049   {
0050   private:              // can be accessed by member functions only.
0051     Viewport *Generic;                  // points to a viewport object.
0052     #if defined (BGI)
0053       char far * Block;              // points to memory block for image.
0054     #elif defined (FG)
0055       fg_color_t far * Block;
0056     #elif defined (MS)
0057       char far * Block;
0058     #endif
0059     unsigned long BlockSize;         // size in bytes of graphic array.
0060     int YES,NO,ERROR,SUCCESS;                              // tokens.
0061     int OVERWRITE;                         // copy as original form.
0062     int MAXIMUM_X, MAXIMUM_Y;              // screen dimensions.
0063     int X1,Y1,X2,Y2;                            // bounding box.
0064     int Width, Depth;                      // dimensions of box.
0065     int Logic;                             // current write mode.
0066     int Ready;                       // indicates if saved in memory.
0067     int Displayed;                        // indicates if displayed.
0068     int MemAllocated;                // indicates if memory allocated.
0069     int GraphicsError;               // result of library function.
0070     int MaxX, MaxY;                      // max legal origin coords.
0071     void FreeBlock(void);                  // deallocates memory.
0072
0073   public:                // can be accessed by any in-scope function.
0074     Blitter(int,int,int,int,int,int,Viewport *);
0075     ~Blitter();                              // destructor.
0076     int GrabImage(void);
0077     int DisplayImage(int xCoord,int yCoord);
0078     int MoveImage(int XOffset,int YOffset);
0079   };
0080
0081   #endif
0082   /*
0083
0084      Supercharged C++ Graphics  --  end of source file BLITTER.HPP
0085
0086                                                                       */
```

E-10 Source code for BLITTER.CPP, the implementation file for class Blitter, providing specialized methods for high-speed graphic array animation.

```
0001   /*
0002
0003            Lee Adams' SUPERCHARGED C++ GRAPHICS
0004            Implementation file for class Blitter
0005
0006      SOURCE FILE:  BLITTER.CPP
0007             TYPE:  Implementation file for a class.  Name this
0008                    file or the resulting OBJ file in the project list.
0009        LANGUAGES:  Turbo C++, Zortech C++, and all C++ compilers
0010                    compatible with AT&T C++ 2.0 specification.
0011            USAGE:  Refer to header file BLITTER.HPP for a guide
0012                    to using the methods of Blitter class objects.
```

```
0013      LICENSE:  As purchaser of the book in which this source code
0014        appears you are granted a royalty-free license to reproduce
0015        and distribute executable files generated using this code
0016        provided that you accept the conditions of the License
0017        Agreement and Limited Warranty described in the book.
0018      PUBLICATION: Contains material from Windcrest/McGraw-Hill
0019        book 3489, published by TAB BOOKS.
0020      U.S. GOVERNMENT RESTRICTED RIGHTS:  This software and its
0021        documentation is provided with restricted rights.  The use,
0022        duplication, or disclosure by the Government is subject to
0023        restrictions set forth in subdivision (b)(3)(ii) of The
0024        Rights in Technical Data and Computer Software clause at
0025        252.227-7013.  Contractor/manufacturer is Lee Adams, c/o
0026        TAB BOOKS, 13311 Monterey Ave., Blue Ridge Summit PA 17294.
0027      TRADEMARK:  Lee Adams is a trademark of Lee Adams.
0028
0029        Copyright 1991 Lee Adams.  All rights reserved worldwide.
0030
0031
0032                      CONDITIONAL COMPILATION
0033      To compile only those blocks of code that support the C++
0034      compiler and graphics library that you are using, you should
0035      #define the appropriate tokens in the following preprocessor
0036      directives.  Use the following table as your guide:
0037                GRAPHICS LIBRARY
0038          Borland's graphics.lib                #define BGI
0039          Zortech's fg.lib or fgdebug.lib       #define FG
0040          Microsoft's graph.lib                 #define MS
0041                COMPILER
0042          Borland Turbo C++ compiler            #define BORLAND
0043          Zortech C++ compiler                  #define ZORTECH
0044          AT&T-compatible C++ compilers         #define MICROSOFT
0045      Be sure you define only one compiler and one graphics library.
0046
0047                                                                   */
0048  #define BGI     1  // indicates the graphics library you are using.
0049  #define BORLAND 1  // indicates the C++ compiler you are using.
0050  /*
0051
0052                         INCLUDE FILES
0053
0054                                                                   */
0055  #include "LIB2D.HPP"      // declarations for graphics classes.
0056  #include "BLITTER.HPP"    // declarations for Blitter class.
0057  /*
0058
0059                   Class Blitter:  CONSTRUCTOR
0060
0061                                                                   */
0062  Blitter::Blitter(int Xa,int Ya,int Xb,int Yb,int X_Res,int Y_Res,
0063                   Viewport *ViewportPtr)
0064  {             // use viewport object referenced by pointer Viewport.
0065  Generic= ViewportPtr;          // Generic points to viewport object.
0066  X1= Xa; Y1= Ya; X2= Xb; Y2= Yb;
0067  YES= 1; NO= 0; ERROR= -1; SUCCESS= 1;
0068  OVERWRITE= 0; MAXIMUM_X= X_Res; MAXIMUM_Y= Y_Res;
0069  GraphicsError= 0; Logic= OVERWRITE;
0070  Ready= NO; Displayed= NO; MemAllocated= NO;
0071  Width= X2 - X1; Depth= Y2 - Y1;              // offsets from origin.
0072  MaxX= MAXIMUM_X - (Width + 1); MaxY= MAXIMUM_Y - (Depth + 1);
0073  }
0074  /*
```

```
0075
0076    ┌──────────────────────────────────────────────────────────┐
        │              Class Blitter:  DESTRUCTOR                  │
0077    │                                                          │
0078    └──────────────────────────────────────────────────────────┘          */
0079    Blitter::~Blitter()
0080    {
0081    FreeBlock();
0082    }
0083    /*
0084
0085    ┌──────────────────────────────────────────────────────────┐
        │              Class Bitblt:  method GrabImage()           │
0086    │                                                          │
0087    └──────────────────────────────────────────────────────────┘          */
0088    int Blitter::GrabImage(void)
0089    {
0090    if (MemAllocated==YES) return ERROR;
0091    Block= Generic->MemBlock(X1,Y1,X2,Y2);// allocate memory for image.
0092    if (Block==0) return ERROR;              // if memory allocation failed.
0093    MemAllocated= YES;
0094    BlockSize= Generic->GetBlockSize(X1,Y1,X2,Y2);         // get size.
0095    Generic->GetBlock(X1,Y1,X2,Y2,Block);     // store image in memory.
0096    Ready= YES;
0097    return SUCCESS;
0098    }
0099    /*
0100
0101    ┌──────────────────────────────────────────────────────────┐
        │              Class Blitter:  method FreeBlock()          │
0102    │                                                          │
0103    └──────────────────────────────────────────────────────────┘          */
0104    void Blitter::FreeBlock(void)                            // private.
0105    {
0106    if (MemAllocated==YES) Generic->FreeBlock(Block);
0107    return;
0108    }
0109    /*
0110
0111    ┌──────────────────────────────────────────────────────────┐
        │              Class Blitter:  method DisplayImage()       │
0112    │                                                          │
0113    └──────────────────────────────────────────────────────────┘          */
0114    int Blitter::DisplayImage(int Xa,int Ya)
0115    {
0116    if (Displayed==YES) return ERROR;
0117    if (Ready==NO) return ERROR;
0118    X1= Xa; Y1= Ya;
0119    if (X1 < 0) return ERROR;
0120    if (Y1 < 0) return ERROR;
0121    if (X1 > MaxX) return ERROR;
0122    if (Y1 > MaxY) return ERROR;
0123    Generic->PutPSET(X1,Y1,Block);
0124    Displayed= YES;
0125    return SUCCESS;
0126    }
0127    /*
0128
0129    ┌──────────────────────────────────────────────────────────┐
        │              Class Blitter:  method MoveImage()          │
0130    │                                                          │
0131    └──────────────────────────────────────────────────────────┘          */
0132    int Blitter::MoveImage(int XOffset,int YOffset)
0133    {
0134    if (Displayed==NO) return ERROR;           // if not already displayed.
0135    X1= X1 + XOffset; Y1= Y1 + YOffset;        // calculate new coords.
0136    if (X1 < 0) return ERROR;
0137    if (Y1 < 0) return ERROR;
```

E-10 Continued.

```
0138  if (X1 > MaxX) return ERROR;
0139  if (Y1 > MaxY) return ERROR;
0140  Generic->PutPSET(X1,Y1,Block);
0141  return SUCCESS;
0142  }
0143  /*
0144
0145  ┌─────────────────────────────────────────────────────────────┐
      │   Supercharged C++ Graphics  --   end of source file BLITTER.CPP │
0146  └─────────────────────────────────────────────────────────────┘
0147                                                              */
```

E-11 Source code for PUBLISH.HPP, the declaration file for class Layout, providing text-pouring methods for desktop publishing functions.

```
0001  /*
0002
0003  ┌─────────────────────────────────────────────────────────────┐
      │              Lee Adams' SUPERCHARGED C++ GRAPHICS             │
0004  │                   Header file for class Layout                │
0005  │                                                               │
0006  │    SOURCE FILE:  PUBLISH.HPP                                  │
0007  │           TYPE:  include file for class Layout.               │
0008  │                                                               │
0009  │      Layout class:  PROGRAMMER'S GUIDE TO THE INTERFACE       │
0010  │  Each instance of the Layout class can manipulate one copy of │
0011  │  a block of text being read from an ASCII file and poured into│
0012  │  a column rectangle on the display.  Page layouts can be built│
0013  │  from numerous columns by using numerous instances of Layout. │
0014  │  SetupBuffer()....validates the ASCII file, determines its    │
0015  │                   length, and allocates memory for a buffer.  │
0016  │  LoadText().......loads the text file into the RAM buffer.    │
0017  │  SetLineLength()..calculates the number of characters per line│
0018  │                   for a specified column rectangle.           │
0019  │  SetNumLines()....calculates the number of lines for a        │
0020  │                   specified column rectangle.                 │
0021  │  PourText().......pours text from the ASCII file in the RAM   │
0022  │                   buffer into the specified column rectangle. │
0023  │                   When finished, returns the cursor position  │
0024  │                   indicating how much text was used.          │
0025  │  SetCurrentMarker()...sets the start position in a buffer for │
0026  │                       text pouring.  This is useful when a    │
0027  │                       text file is to be poured into a number │
0028  │                       of rectangles to make up a page design. │
0029  │  The methods call two private methods.  WriteLine() writes a  │
0030  │  single line of text to a rectangle.  ReleaseBuffer() is      │
0031  │  called by the destructor to free the memory allocated for    │
0032  │  the text.                                                    │
0033  │  Class declarations are located in PUBLISH.HPP (which must be │
0034  │    used in your program as #include "PUBLISH.HPP").           │
0035  │  Function definitions are located in PUBLISH.CPP (which uses  │
0036  │  #include files string.h, stdio.h, and io.h.  Either          │
0037  │  PUBLISH.CPP or PUBLISH.OBJ must be named in the project       │
0038  │  list for your program.  Each function returns -1 if error.   │
0039  │                                                               │
0040  │  LICENSE:  As purchaser of the book in which this source code │
0041  │     appears you are granted a royalty-free license to reproduce│
0042  │     and distribute executable files generated using this code │
0043  │     provided that you accept the conditions of the License    │
0044  │     Agreement and Limited Warranty described in the book.     │
0045  │  PUBLICATION: Contains material from Windcrest/McGraw-Hill    │
0046  │     book 3489, published by TAB BOOKS.                        │
0047  │  U.S. GOVERNMENT RESTRICTED RIGHTS:  This software and its    │
```

```
0048        documentation is provided with restricted rights.  The use,
0049        duplication, or disclosure by the Government is subject to
0050        restrictions set forth in subdivision (b)(3)(ii) of The
0051        Rights in Technical Data and Computer Software clause at
0052        252.227-7013.  Contractor/manufacturer is Lee Adams, c/o
0053        TAB BOOKS, 13311 Monterey Ave., Blue Ridge Summit PA 17294.
0054        TRADEMARK:  Lee Adams is a trademark of Lee Adams.
0055
0056        Copyright 1991 Lee Adams.  All rights reserved worldwide.
0057
0058                                                                    */
0059   #ifndef PUBLISH_HPP
0060   #define PUBLISH_HPP
0061
0062   #include <string.h>    // supports strcpy(), strncpy() and strcat().
0063   #include <stdio.h>          // supports fopen(), fwrite(), fclose().
0064   #include <io.h>              // supports filelength() and access().
0065
0066   class Layout                              // class declarations.
0067   {
0068   private:            // can be accessed by member functions only.
0069     Viewport *Generic;                 // points to a viewport object.
0070     char TextFileName[13];                        // name of file.
0071     char Extension[5];                              // extension.
0072     FILE *text_file;                               // file handle.
0073     long text_file_length;                       // length of file.
0074     char *Article;               // will point to the text buffer.
0075     int BufferReady;              // indicates if buffer allocated.
0076     int TextReady;            // indicates if text loaded into buffer.
0077     int NumLinesDone;       // indicates if number of lines calculated.
0078     int NumCharsDone; // indicates of number of chars/line calculated.
0079     int NumCharacters;        // number of characters per line allowed.
0080     int NumLines;                       // number of lines allowed.
0081     int FirstPosition, LastPosition;    // first, last char position.
0082     int FirstLine, LastLine;           // first and last line allowed.
0083     int MaxCursor;            // max number of characters in buffer.
0084     char TempString[80];        // will hold current string to write.
0085     int Buffer_Marker_1;// start of current string segment in buffer.
0086     int Buffer_Marker_2;  // end of current string segment in buffer.
0087     int Cursor;                   // current cursor position in buffer.
0088     int Current_Line;                    // current line on display.
0089     int TempLength;    // running total of characters being analyzed.
0090     void WriteLine(void);
0091     void ReleaseBuffer(void);
0092
0093   public:               // can be accessed by any in-scope function.
0094     Layout(Viewport *);                            // constructor.
0095     ~Layout();                                     // destructor.
0096     int SetupBuffer(char * Name);
0097     int LoadText(void);
0098     int SetLineLength(int, int);
0099     int SetNumLines(int, int);
0100     void SetCurrentMarker(int);
0101     int PourText(void);
0102   };
0103
0104   #endif
0105   /*
0106
0107        Supercharged C++ Graphics  --  end of source file PUBLISH.HPP
0108
0109                                                                    */
```

E-12 Source code for PUBLISH.CPP, the implementation file for class Layout, providing text-pouring methods for desktop publishing functions.

```
0001  /*
0002
0003          ┌─────────────────────────────────────────────────────────┐
             │           Lee Adams' SUPERCHARGED C++ GRAPHICS            │
0004          │           Implementation file for class Layout           │
0005          ├─────────────────────────────────────────────────────────┤
0006          │  SOURCE FILE:  PUBLISH.CPP                                │
0007          │         TYPE:  Implementation file for a class.  Name this│
0008          │                file or the resulting OBJ file in the project list.│
0009          │    LANGUAGES:  Turbo C++, Zortech C++, and all C++ compilers│
0010          │                compatible with AT&T C++ 2.0 specification.│
0011          │        USAGE:  Refer to header file PUBLISH.HPP for a guide│
0012          │                to using the methods of Layout class objects.│
0013          │  LICENSE:  As purchaser of the book in which this source code│
0014          │    appears you are granted a royalty-free license to reproduce│
0015          │    and distribute executable files generated using this code│
0016          │    provided that you accept the conditions of the License │
0017          │    Agreement and Limited Warranty described in the book.  │
0018          │  PUBLICATION: Contains material from Windcrest/McGraw-Hill│
0019          │    book 3489, published by TAB BOOKS.                     │
0020          │  U.S. GOVERNMENT RESTRICTED RIGHTS:  This software and its│
0021          │    documentation is provided with restricted rights.  The use,│
0022          │    duplication, or disclosure by the Government is subject to│
0023          │    restrictions set forth in subdivision (b)(3)(ii) of The│
0024          │    Rights in Technical Data and Computer Software clause at│
0025          │    252.227-7013.  Contractor/manufacturer is Lee Adams, c/o│
0026          │    TAB BOOKS, 13311 Monterey Ave., Blue Ridge Summit PA 17294.│
0027          │  TRADEMARK: Lee Adams is a trademark of Lee Adams.        │
0028          ├─────────────────────────────────────────────────────────┤
0029          │     Copyright 1991 Lee Adams.  All rights reserved worldwide.│
0030          └─────────────────────────────────────────────────────────┘
0031
0032          ┌─────────────────────────────────────────────────────────┐
             │                  CONDITIONAL COMPILATION                  │
0033          │  To compile only those blocks of code that support the C++│
0034          │  compiler and graphics library that you are using, you should│
0035          │  #define the appropriate tokens in the following preprocessor│
0036          │  directives.  Use the following table as your guide:      │
0037          │          GRAPHICS LIBRARY                                 │
0038          │      Borland's graphics.lib              #define BGI      │
0039          │      Zortech's fg.lib or fgdebug.lib     #define FG       │
0040          │      Microsoft's graph.lib               #define MS       │
0041          │          COMPILER                                         │
0042          │      Borland Turbo C++ compiler          #define BORLAND  │
0043          │      Zortech C++ compiler                #define ZORTECH  │
0044          │      AT&T-compatible C++ compilers       #define MICROSOFT│
0045          │  Be sure you define only one compiler and one graphics library.│
0046          └─────────────────────────────────────────────────────────┘
0047                                                                    */
0048  #define BGI      1  // indicates the graphics library you are using.
0049  #define BORLAND 1  // indicates the C++ compiler you are using.
0050  /*
0051          ┌─────────────────────────────────────────────────────────┐
0052          │                    INCLUDE FILES                          │
0053          └─────────────────────────────────────────────────────────┘
0054                                                                    */
0055  #include "LIB2D.HPP"          // declarations for graphics classes.
0056  #include "PUBLISH.HPP"            // declarations for Layout class.
0057  /*
0058          ┌─────────────────────────────────────────────────────────┐
0059          │                    CONSTANTS                              │
0060          └─────────────────────────────────────────────────────────┘
```

```
0061                                                                    */
0062   const int zYES=     1;
0063   const int zNO=      0;
0064   const int zSUCCESS= 1;
0065   const int zFAIL=    0;
0066   /*

0068   ┌─────────────────────────────────────────────────────────────┐
       │              Class Layout:   CONSTRUCTOR                     │
0069   └─────────────────────────────────────────────────────────────┘
0070                                                                    */
0071   Layout::Layout(Viewport *ViewportPtr)
0072   {         // use the viewport object referenced by pointer Viewport.
0073   Generic= ViewportPtr;            // Generic points to viewport object.
0074   strcpy(TextFileName, "DEFAULT.DOC");
0075   strcpy(Extension, ".DOC");
0076   BufferReady= zNO; TextReady= zNO;
0077   NumLinesDone= zNO; NumCharsDone= zNO;
0078   Buffer_Marker_1= 0; Buffer_Marker_2= 0;
0079   Cursor= 0; Current_Line=0;
0080   }
0081   /*

0083   ┌─────────────────────────────────────────────────────────────┐
       │              Class Layout:   DESTRUCTOR                      │
0084   └─────────────────────────────────────────────────────────────┘
0085                                                                    */
0086   Layout::~Layout()
0087   {
0088   ReleaseBuffer();                  // free the memory used by the buffer.
0089   }
0090   /*

0092   ┌─────────────────────────────────────────────────────────────┐
       │              Class Layout:   method SetupBuffer()           │
0093   └─────────────────────────────────────────────────────────────┘
0094                                                                    */
0095   int Layout::SetupBuffer(char * Name)
0096   {                     // validate the filename and set up a RAM buffer.
0097   strcpy(TextFileName, Name);                       // grab the name.
0098   strcat(TextFileName, Extension);             // append an extension.
0099   if (access(TextFileName,0) == 0)
0100     {                                         // if the file exists...
0101     text_file= fopen(TextFileName, "rb");      // open the file and...
0102     text_file_length= filelength(fileno(text_file));//get its length.
0103     MaxCursor= text_file_length - 1; // set max allowable cursor pos.
0104     Article= new char[text_file_length];        // memory allocation.
0105     if (Article == 0)
0106       {                                      // if allocation failed...
0107       fclose(text_file);                      // close the file and...
0108       return zFAIL;                           // advise the caller.
0109       }
0110     fclose(text_file);                    // otherwise, close the file...
0111     BufferReady= zYES;                      // set an internal token...
0112     return zSUCCESS;                        // and advise the caller.
0113     }
0114   return zFAIL;   // otherwise advise caller filename does not exist.
0115   }
0116   /*

0118   ┌─────────────────────────────────────────────────────────────┐
       │              Class Layout:   method ReleaseBuffer()         │
0119   └─────────────────────────────────────────────────────────────┘
0120                                                                    */
0121   void Layout::ReleaseBuffer(void)
0122   {                       // free the memory allocated to the buffer.
0123   delete(Article);                        // delete the memory object.
```

```
0124  TextReady= zNO;                   // and reset some internal tokens...
0125  BufferReady= zNO; NumLinesDone= zNO; NumCharsDone= zNO;
0126  return;
0127  }
0128  /*
0129
0130  ┌─────────────────────────────────────────────────────────────┐
      │              Class Layout:  method LoadText()                 │
0131  └─────────────────────────────────────────────────────────────┘
0132                                                                */
0133  int Layout::LoadText(void)
0134  {                      // load the ASCII text file into the RAM buffer.
0135  if (BufferReady == zYES)
0136    {                    // if memory has been allocated for the buffer...
0137    text_file= fopen(TextFileName, "rb");           // open the file.
0138    fread((char *)Article, 1, text_file_length, text_file);  // read.
0139    fclose(text_file);                              // close the file.
0140    TextReady= zYES;                       // set an internal token.
0141    return zSUCCESS;                       // advise caller of success.
0142    }
0143  return zFAIL;               // otherwise advise caller of failure.
0144  }
0145  /*
0146
0147  ┌─────────────────────────────────────────────────────────────┐
      │             Class Layout:  method SetLineLength()             │
0148  └─────────────────────────────────────────────────────────────┘
0149                                                                */
0150  int Layout::SetLineLength(int XLeft, int XRight)
0151  {          // calculate number of chars that will fit onto one line,
0152             // and starting and ending column positions.
0153  if (XLeft < PhysicalDisplay::ClipLeft) return zFAIL;
0154  if (XRight > PhysicalDisplay::ClipRight) return zFAIL;
0155  FirstPosition=                          // calculate column position.
0156    (XLeft + (PhysicalDisplay::TextWidth - 1)) /
0157    PhysicalDisplay::TextWidth;
0158  FirstPosition++;
0159  LastPosition=                           // calculate column position.
0160    (XRight + (PhysicalDisplay::TextWidth - 1)) /
0161    PhysicalDisplay::TextWidth;
0162  NumCharacters= (LastPosition - FirstPosition) + 1;
0163  NumCharsDone= zYES;                      // set an internal token.
0164  return zSUCCESS;
0165  }
0166  /*
0167
0168  ┌─────────────────────────────────────────────────────────────┐
      │             Class Layout:  method SetNumLines()               │
0169  └─────────────────────────────────────────────────────────────┘
0170                                                                */
0171  int Layout::SetNumLines(int YTop, int YBottom)
0172  {   // calculate number of lines that will fit into vertical space,
0173      // and starting and ending row position.
0174  if (YTop < PhysicalDisplay::ClipTop) return zFAIL;
0175  if (YBottom > PhysicalDisplay::ClipBottom) return zFAIL;
0176  FirstLine=                              // calculate row position.
0177    (YTop + (PhysicalDisplay::TextHeight - 1)) /
0178    PhysicalDisplay::TextHeight;
0179  FirstLine++;
0180  LastLine=                               // calculate row position.
0181    (YBottom + (PhysicalDisplay::TextHeight - 1)) /
0182    PhysicalDisplay::TextHeight;
0183  NumLines= (LastLine - FirstLine) + 1;   // number of lines allowed.
0184  Current_Line= FirstLine;                // set the current line.
0185  NumLinesDone= zYES;                     // set an internal token.
```

```
0186   return zSUCCESS;
0187   }
0188   /*
0189
0190   ┌─────────────────────────────────────────────────────────┐
0190   │         Class Layout:  method SetCurrentMarker()        │
0191   │                                                         │
0192   └─────────────────────────────────────────────────────────┘ */
0193   void Layout::SetCurrentMarker(int Index)
0194   {        // sets the start position for next text-pouring operation.
0195   Buffer_Marker_1= Index;
0196   return;
0197   }
0198   /*
0199
0200   ┌─────────────────────────────────────────────────────────┐
0200   │         Class Layout:   method WriteLine()              │
0201   │                                                         │
0202   └─────────────────────────────────────────────────────────┘ */
0203   void Layout::WriteLine(void)
0204   {          // writes current string segment from buffer to screen.
0205     int StringLength;
0206     int CharPtr= 0;
0207   StringLength=        // calculate the length of the string segment.
0208     (Buffer_Marker_2 - Buffer_Marker_1) + 1;
0209   strncpy(TempString,      // copy it to a temporary string buffer...
0210           &Article[Buffer_Marker_1],StringLength);
0211   TempString[StringLength]= '\0';     // and append a NULL character.
0212   while (TempString[CharPtr] != '\0')
0213     {                              // for each character in the string...
0214     if (TempString[CharPtr] == 10)
0215       {                    // if a line feed character is detected...
0216       TempString[CharPtr]= 32;        // ...replace it with a space.
0217       }
0218     if (TempString[CharPtr] == 13)
0219       {            // if a carriage return character is detected...
0220       TempString[CharPtr]= 42;    // ...replace it with an asterisk.
0221       }
0222     if (TempString[CharPtr] == 15)
0223       {                        // if a tab character is detected...
0224       TempString[CharPtr]= 32;            // replace it with a space.
0225       }
0226     CharPtr++;                         // point to the next character.
0227     }
0228   Generic->PutText(Current_Line,  // write the string to the display.
0229           FirstPosition,0,TempString);
0230   return;
0231   }
0232   /*
0233
0234   ┌─────────────────────────────────────────────────────────┐
0234   │         Class Layout:  method PourText()                │
0235   │                                                         │
0236   └─────────────────────────────────────────────────────────┘ */
0237   int Layout::PourText(void)
0238   {                             // pour text into the column rectangle.
0239   if (BufferReady!= zYES) return zFAIL;   // is the buffer available?
0240   if (TextReady!= zYES) return zFAIL;   // is buffer loaded with text?
0241   if (NumLinesDone!= zYES) return zFAIL;   // vert calculations done?
0242   if (NumCharsDone!= zYES) return zFAIL;  // horiz calculations done?
0243   Cursor= Buffer_Marker_1;    // set cursor to start of text segment.
0244
0245   CURSOR_LOOP:                 // beginning of word-by-word outer loop.
0246   WORD_LOOP:                   // beginning of char-by-char inner loop.
0247     if ((Cursor < MaxCursor) && (Article[Cursor] != ' '))
0248       {                              // move ahead past current word.
```

```
0249      Cursor++;
0250      if (Article[Cursor] == 26) goto END_OF_TEXT;      // if Ctrl+Z.
0251      if (Article[Cursor] == 27) goto END_OF_TEXT;      // if Esc.
0252      if (Article[Cursor] == '\0') goto END_OF_TEXT;    // if NULL.
0253      goto WORD_LOOP;
0254      }
0255    if (Cursor == MaxCursor) goto END_OF_TEXT;   // if end of buffer.
0256    Cursor--;            // move back to last character of current word.
0257    TempLength=             // calculate length of current text segment.
0258      (Cursor - Buffer_Marker_1) + 1;
0259
0260    if (TempLength >= NumCharacters)
0261      {           // if current length exceeds the allowable length...
0262      while (Article[Cursor] != ' ')
0263        {                 // ...then move back to before current word...
0264        Cursor--;
0265        }
0266      while (Article[Cursor] == ' ')
0267        {    // ...and move back to last character of previous word.
0268        Cursor--;
0269        }
0270      Buffer_Marker_2= Cursor; // set marker for end of text segment.
0271      WriteLine();             // write text segment to the display...
0272      Cursor++;           // move ahead off the last character of word.
0273      while ((Cursor < MaxCursor) && (Article[Cursor] == ' '))
0274        {        // ...and move ahead to first character of next word.
0275        Cursor++;
0276        }
0277      Current_Line++;     // set line marker to the next display line.
0278      if (Current_Line > LastLine)
0279        {             // if at the bottom of the column rectangle...
0280        return Cursor;   // ...then return cursor position to caller.
0281        }
0282      Buffer_Marker_1= Cursor;// reset marker for text segment start.
0283      goto CURSOR_LOOP;                          // ...and loop back.
0284      }
0285    Cursor++;            // move ahead off last character of word.
0286    while ((Cursor < MaxCursor) && (Article[Cursor] == ' '))
0287      {              // move ahead to first character of next word.
0288      Cursor++;
0289      }
0290    goto CURSOR_LOOP;
0291
0292  END_OF_TEXT:             // jump to here if end-of-file suspected.
0293  Cursor--;
0294  Buffer_Marker_2= Cursor;
0295  WriteLine();
0296  return zSUCCESS;        // advise caller all available text used.
0297  }
0298  /*
0299
0300  ┌─────────────────────────────────────────────────────────────────┐
       │  Supercharged C++ Graphics  --  end of source file PUBLISH.CPP  │
       └─────────────────────────────────────────────────────────────────┘
0301
0302                                                                   */
```

E-13 Source code for KINETIC.HPP, the declaration file for class Kinetic3D, providing support for 3-D kinetic animation sequences.

```
0001   /*
0002
0003            Lee Adams' SUPERCHARGED C++ GRAPHICS
0004                 Header file for 3D routines
0005
0006       SOURCE FILE:  KINETIC.HPP
0007       TYPE:   declarations for 3D kinetic animation class
0008
0009              DEVELOPER'S GUIDE TO THE INTERFACE
0010       Before using 3D kinetic animation, you must create an object
0011       of class Kinetic3D.  Then call methods of the object to
0012       animate the 3D solid and to detect collisions.  Refer to the
0013       demonstration program in the book for an example of
0014       here-is-how-it's-done source code.
0015       Class declarations are located in KINETIC.HPP (which must be
0016          used in your program as #include "KINETIC.HPP").
0017       Function definitions are located in KINETIC.CPP.  Either
0018          KINETIC.CPP or KINETIC.OBJ must be named in the project
0019          list for your program.
0020
0021       LICENSE:  As purchaser of the book in which this source code
0022          appears you are granted a royalty-free license to reproduce
0023          and distribute executable files generated using this code
0024          provided that you accept the conditions of the License
0025          Agreement and Limited Warranty described in the book.
0026       PUBLICATION: Contains material from Windcrest/McGraw-Hill
0027          book 3489, published by TAB BOOKS.
0028       U.S. GOVERNMENT RESTRICTED RIGHTS:  This software and its
0029          documentation is provided with restricted rights.  The use,
0030          duplication, or disclosure by the Government is subject to
0031          restrictions set forth in subdivision (b)(3)(ii) of The
0032          Rights in Technical Data and Computer Software clause at
0033          252.227-7013.  Contractor/manufacturer is Lee Adams, c/o
0034          TAB BOOKS, 13311 Monterey Ave., Blue Ridge Summit PA 17294.
0035       TRADEMARK:  Lee Adams is a trademark of Lee Adams.
0036
0037          Copyright 1991 Lee Adams.  All rights reserved worldwide.
0038
0039                                                              */
0040   #ifndef KINETIC_HPP              // if file not already included...
0041   #define KINETIC_HPP              // set token to show it has been used.
0042
0043   const int zUPDATE=  0;           // constants used by the methods...
0044   const int zREMOVE=  1;
0045   const int zINSTALL= 6;
0046   const int zRED=     1;
0047   const int zGREEN=   2;
0048   const int zBROWN=   3;
0049   const int zBLUE=    4;
0050   const int zMAGENTA= 5;
0051   const int zCYAN=    6;
0052   const int zGRAY=    7;
0053
0054   class Kinetic3D
0055   {
0056   private:          // accessible by member functions and friends only.
0057      Viewport *Generic;            // points to a viewport object.
0058      PhysicalDisplay *Ds;          // points to a display object.
0059      void GetCameraCoords(void);      // wrld coords to cam coords.
```

E-13 Continued.

```
0060    void GetImageCoords(void);              // cam coords to imge coords.
0061    void GetScreenCoords(void);             // maps imge plane to screen.
0062    void GetWorldCoords(void);              // obj coords to wrld coords.
0063    void VisibilityTest(void);               // back-plane visibility.
0064    void GetBrightness(void);               // finds brightness of a facet.
0065    void SetObjAngle(void);             // sine, cosine rotation factors.
0066    void SetCamAngle(void);             // sine, cosine rotation factors.
0067    void PutObjToScreen(void);              // object to screen coords.
0068    void DrawFacet(void);                            // draws facet.
0069    float DomainWidth, DomainDepth;                      // 3D domain.
0070    float x,y,z;                     // wrld coords in, cam coords out.
0071    float xc1,xc2,xc3,xc4,xc5,xc6,xc7,yc1,yc2,yc3,
0072          yc4,yc5,yc6,yc7,zc1,zc2,zc3,zc4,zc5,zc6,
0073          zc7;                              // camera coords of facet.
0074    float sx1,sx2,sx3,sx4,sx5,sy1,sy2,sy3,
0075          sy4,sy5;                          // display coords of facet.
0076    float xw1,xw2,xw3,yw1,yw2,yw3,
0077          zw1,zw2,zw3;               // raw world coords for brightness.
0078    float sx3D,sy3D;                       // output of 3D formulas.
0079    float xa,ya,za;                      // temporary in 3D formulas.
0080    float focal_length;                 // angular perspective factor.
0081    double ObjYaw,ObjRoll,ObjPitch;         // object rotation angles.
0082    double sOYaw,cOYaw;
0083    double sORoll,cORoll;
0084    double sOPitch,cOPitch;
0085    float xObj,yObj,zObj;                         // obj trans values.
0086    double ObjYawChg,ObjRollChg,
0087           ObjPitchChg;               // instancing rotation change.
0088    float xObjChg,yObjChg,zObjChg;  // instancing translation change.
0089    double CamYaw,CamRoll,CamPitch;                      // camera.
0090    double sCYaw,sCRoll,sCPitch;
0091    double cCYaw,cCRoll,cCPitch;
0092    float xCam,yCam,zCam;                // world translation values.
0093    float rx,ry;                         // ratios used in windowing.
0094    float hcenter,vcenter;                    // center of viewport.
0095    float viewheight;            // viewer's height 0 ft above ground.
0096    float dist;               // viewer's virtual distance from scene.
0097    float yawdist;             // viewer's actual distance from scene.
0098    int pitchheading,yawheading;            // cam angle, degrees.
0099    int viewchg;                 // degrees to change camera angle.
0100    double yawdelta,pitchdelta;          // current absolute change.
0101    float signmx,signmy,signmz;            // coord system tweaking.
0102    float LaminaObj[4][3];                    // facet object coords.
0103    float LaminaWorld[4][3];                   // facet world coords.
0104    float LaminaCam[4][3];                     // facet camera coords.
0105    float LaminaDisplay[4][2];                  // facet disp coords.
0106          // variables for rendering and backplane removal...
0107    float visible;                             // visibility factor.
0108    float sp1,sp2,sp3;                          // temp values of sp.
0109    float xLight,yLight,zLight;
0110    float illum_range;                  // adapter-dependent range.
0111    float normalized_illum;             // illum factor 0 to 1 range.
0112    float xu,yu,zu;                        // vector vertex 1 to 2.
0113    float xv,yv,zv;                        // vector vertex 1 to 3.
0114    float x_surf_normal,y_surf_normal,z_surf_normal;
0115    float v1,v2;                   // length, surface perp vector.
0116    float v3;                      // ratio, surf perp to unit vector.
0117    float x_unit_vector,y_unit_vector,z_unit_vector;
0118    int zDeviceIllum;               // adapter-dependent brightness.
0119    int zShadingColor;                           // dithering hue.
0120    int Points[10];                     // array of facet vertices.
0121          // pixel-based variables...
```

```
0122    int clipx1, clipy1;                          // client area coords.
0123    int clipx2, clipy2;                          // client area coords.
0124    int ViewportWidth;                            // width of viewport.
0125    int ViewportDepth;                            // depth of viewport.
0126    int Model3DReady;        // indicates if class object initialized.
0127    int cx1,cy1,cx2,cy2,              // coords for next 3D cursor...
0128        cx3,cy3,cx4,cy4,
0129        cx5,cy5,cx6,cy6,
0130        cx7,cy7,cx8,cy8;
0131    int pcx1,pcy1,pcx2,pcy2,          // coords for previous 3D cursor...
0132        pcx3,pcy3,pcx4,pcy4,
0133        pcx5,pcy5,pcx6,pcy6,
0134        pcx7,pcy7,pcx8,pcy8;
0135    int gcx1,gcy1,gcx2,gcy2,gcx3,gcy3,gcx4,gcy4;      // groundplane...
0136    int gpcx1,gpcy1,gpcx2,gpcy2,gpcx3,gpcy3,gpcx4,gpcy4;
0137        // dither patterns for the shading methods...
0138    char Fill_0[8], Fill_3[8], Fill_6[8];
0139    char Fill_12[8], Fill_25[8], Fill_37[8];
0140    char Fill_50[8], Fill_62[8], Fill_75[8];
0141    char Fill_87[8], Fill_93[8], Fill_100[8];
0142
0143    public:    // data and methods accessable by any in-scope function.
0144    Kinetic3D(PhysicalDisplay *);                      // constructor.
0145    ~Kinetic3D();                                      // destructor.
0146    void Initialize3D(int,int,int,int,Viewport *);    // initialize.
0147    void SetShadingColor(int);                     // dithering hue.
0148    void SetLaminaAngle(double,double,double);      // lamina angle.
0149    void SetLaminaPosition(float,float,float);    // lamina position.
0150    void DrawLamina(float,float);            // draws shaded lamina.
0151    void GetDisplayCoords(float,float,float,int *,int *);
0152    };
0153    #endif
0154    /*
0155
0156    ┌─────────────────────────────────────────────────────────────┐
        │            End of KINETIC.HPP header file.                   │
0157    └─────────────────────────────────────────────────────────────┘
0158                                                                  */
```

E-14 Source code for KINETIC.CPP, the implementation file for class Kinetic3D, providing support for 3-D kinetic animation sequences.

```
0001    /*
0002
0003    ┌─────────────────────────────────────────────────────────────┐
        │            Lee Adams' SUPERCHARGED C++ GRAPHICS              │
0004    │            3D kinetic animation routines for C++             │
0005    ├─────────────────────────────────────────────────────────────┤
0006    │     Implementation file for 3D kinetic animation routines    │
0007    ├─────────────────────────────────────────────────────────────┤
0008    │   Source file:  KINETIC.CPP                                  │
0009    │   Type:  implementation file for class methods.              │
0010    │   Include file:  KINETIC.HPP                                 │
0011    │   Graphics libraries:  Borland graphics library (graphics.lib)│
0012    │                        Zortech graphics library (fg.lib)      │
0013    │                        Microsoft graphics library (graph.lib) │
0014    │   Languages:  Turbo C++, Zortech C++, and all C++ compilers  │
0015    │               compatible with AT&T C++ specification 2.0.     │
0016    │   Memory model:  large.                                      │
0017    │   Graphics:  supports 640x480x16 VGA, 640x350x16 EGA, 640x200x16 │
0018    │     EGA, 640x480x2 MCGA, 640x200x2 CGA, and 720x348x2 Hercules.  │
0019    │   Output:  contains class methods that provide 3D kinetic     │
0020    │            animation capabilities.                           │
```

```
0021        Usage:  refer to the header file KINETIC.HPP for a guide to
0022               using the methods of class Kinetic3D.
0023        License:  As purchaser of the book in which this module
0024          appears you are granted a royalty-free license to reproduce
0025          and distribute executable files generated using this code,
0026          provided that you accept the conditions of the License
0027          Agreement and Limited Warranty described in the book.
0028        Publication: Contains material from Windcrest/McGraw-Hill
0029          book 3489, published by TAB BOOKS.
0030        U.S. Government Restricted Rights:  This software and its
0031          documentation is provided with restricted rights.  The use,
0032          duplication, or disclosure by the Government is subject to
0033          restrictions set forth in subdivision (b)(3)(ii) of The
0034          Rights in Technical Data and Computer Software clause at
0035          252.227-7013.  Contractor/manufacturer is Lee Adams and TAB
0036          BOOKS, 13311 Monterey Ave., Blue Ridge Summit PA 17214.
0037        Trademarks:  Lee Adams is a trademark of Lee Adams.
0038
0039              Copyright 1991 Lee Adams.  All rights reserved.
0040
0041
0042                     CONDITIONAL COMPILATION
0043        To compile only those blocks of code that support the C++
0044        compiler and graphics library that you are using, you should
0045        #define the appropriate tokens in the following preprocessor
0046        directives.  Use the following table as your guide:
0047               GRAPHICS LIBRARY
0048          Borland's graphics.lib              #define BGI
0049          Zortech's fg.lib or fgdebug.lib     #define FG
0050          Microsoft's graph.lib               #define MS
0051               COMPILER
0052          Borland Turbo C++ compiler          #define BORLAND
0053          Zortech C++ compiler                #define ZORTECH
0054          AT&T C++ 2.0 compatible compilers   #define MICROSOFT
0055        Be sure you define only one compiler and one graphics library.
0056
0057                                                                   */
0058  #define BGI     1 // indicates the graphics library you are using.
0059  #define BORLAND 1 // indicates the C++ compiler you are using.
0060  /*
0061
0062                          CONSTANTS
0063
0064                                                                   */
0065  const int zFAIL=      0;                    // boolean token.
0066  const int zVGA_12H=   1;              // VGA 640x480x16/256.
0067  const int zEGA_10H=   2;               // EGA 640x350x16/64.
0068  const int zEGA_EH=    3;                  // EGA 640x200x16.
0069  const int zMCGA_11H=  4;                  // MCGA 640x480x2.
0070  const int zCGA_6H=    5;             // CGA 640x200x2-color.
0071  const int zHERC=      6;         // Hercules 720x348x2-color.
0072  const int zFALSE=     0;              // boolean tokens...
0073  const int zTRUE=      1;
0074  const int zYES=       1;
0075  const int zNO=        0;
0076  const int zOVERWRITE=  0;                   // writing modes...
0077  const int zTRANSPARENT= 1;
0078  /*
0079
0080                          INCLUDE FILES
0081
0082                                                                   */
```

```
0083   #include "LIB2D.HPP"
0084   #include "KINETIC.HPP"                        // class declarations.
0085   #include <math.h>                             // supports sine and cosine.
0086   /*
0087
0088   ┌─────────────────────────────────────────────────────────────────┐
       │                 Class Kinetic3D:   CONSTRUCTOR                    │
0089   └─────────────────────────────────────────────────────────────────┘
0090                                                                    */
0091   Kinetic3D::Kinetic3D(PhysicalDisplay * Disp)
0092   {              // expects to receive a pointer to the physical display.
0093   Ds= Disp;                          // point to physical display object.
0094   DomainWidth= 800; DomainDepth= 600;
0095   x= 0.0; y= 0.0; z= 0.0;
0096   xc1= 0.0; xc2= 0.0; xc3= 0.0; xc4= 0.0; xc5= 0.0;
0097   xc6= 0.0; xc7= 0.0;
0098   yc1= 0.0; yc2= 0.0; yc3= 0.0; yc4= 0.0; yc5= 0.0;
0099   yc6= 0.0; yc7= 0.0;
0100   zc1= 0.0; zc2= 0.0; zc3= 0.0; zc4= 0.0; zc5= 0.0;
0101   zc6= 0.0; zc7= 0.0;
0102   sx1= 0.0; sx2= 0.0; sx3= 0.0; sx4= 0.0; sx5= 0.0;
0103   sy1= 0.0; sy2= 0.0; sy3= 0.0; sy4= 0.0; sy5= 0.0;
0104   xw1= 0; xw2= 0; xw3= 0;
0105   yw1= 0; yw2= 0; yw3= 0;
0106   zw1= 0; zw2= 0; zw3= 0;
0107   sx3D= 0.0; sy3D= 0.0;
0108   xa= 0.0; ya= 0.0; za= 0.0;
0109   focal_length= 1200.0;
0110   ObjYaw= 6.28319; ObjRoll= 6.28319; ObjPitch= 6.28319;
0111   sOYaw= 0.0; cOYaw= 0.0;
0112   sORoll= 0.0; cORoll= 0.0;
0113   sOPitch= 0.0; cOPitch= 0.0;
0114   xObj= 0.0; yObj= 0.0; zObj= 0.0;
0115   ObjYawChg= 0.0; ObjRollChg= 0.0; ObjPitchChg= 0.0;
0116   xObjChg= 0.0; yObjChg= 0.0; zObjChg= 0.0;
0117   CamYaw= 6.28319; CamRoll= 6.28319; CamPitch= 6.28319;
0118   sCYaw= 0.0; sCRoll= 0.0; sCPitch= 0.0;
0119   cCYaw= 0.0; cCRoll= 0.0; cCPitch= 0.0;
0120   xCam= 0.0; yCam= 0.0; zCam= -360.0;
0121   rx= 0.0; ry= 0.0;
0122   hcenter= 0.0; vcenter= 0.0;
0123   viewheight= 0; dist= 360; yawdist= 360;
0124   pitchheading= 360; yawheading= 0;
0125   viewchg= 2; yawdelta= 0; pitchdelta= 0;
0126   signmx= 1; signmy= -1; signmz= -1;
0127            // dither patterns for the shading methods...
0128   Fill_0[0]= 0; Fill_0[1]= 0; Fill_0[2]= 0;
0129   Fill_0[3]= 0; Fill_0[4]= 0; Fill_0[5]= 0;
0130   Fill_0[6]= 0; Fill_0[7]= 0;
0131
0132   Fill_3[0]= 0; Fill_3[1]= 32; Fill_3[2]= 0;
0133   Fill_3[3]= 0; Fill_3[4]= 0; Fill_3[5]= 2;
0134   Fill_3[6]= 0; Fill_3[7]= 0;
0135
0136   Fill_6[0]= 32; Fill_6[1]= 0; Fill_6[2]= 2;
0137   Fill_6[3]= 0; Fill_6[4]= 128; Fill_6[5]= 0;
0138   Fill_6[6]= 8; Fill_6[7]= 0;
0139
0140   Fill_12[0]= 32; Fill_12[1]= 2; Fill_12[2]= 128;
0141   Fill_12[3]= 8; Fill_12[4]= 32; Fill_12[5]= 2;
0142   Fill_12[6]= 128; Fill_12[7]= 8;
0143
0144   Fill_25[0]= 68; Fill_25[1]= 17; Fill_25[2]= 68;
0145   Fill_25[3]= 17; Fill_25[4]= 68; Fill_25[5]= 17;
```

```
0146   Fill_25[6]= 68; Fill_25[7]= 17;
0147
0148   Fill_37[0]= 170; Fill_37[1]= 68; Fill_37[2]= 170;
0149   Fill_37[3]= 17; Fill_37[4]= 170; Fill_37[5]= 68;
0150   Fill_37[6]= 170; Fill_37[7]= 17;
0151
0152   Fill_50[0]= 85; Fill_50[1]= 170; Fill_50[2]= 85;
0153   Fill_50[3]= 170; Fill_50[4]= 85; Fill_50[5]= 170;
0154   Fill_50[6]= 85; Fill_50[7]= 170;
0155
0156   Fill_62[0]= 85; Fill_62[1]= 187; Fill_62[2]= 85;
0157   Fill_62[3]= 238; Fill_62[4]= 85; Fill_62[5]= 187;
0158   Fill_62[6]= 85; Fill_62[7]= 238;
0159
0160   Fill_75[0]= 187; Fill_75[1]= 238; Fill_75[2]= 187;
0161   Fill_75[3]= 238; Fill_75[4]= 187; Fill_75[5]= 238;
0162   Fill_75[6]= 187; Fill_75[7]= 238;
0163
0164   Fill_87[0]= 223; Fill_87[1]= 253; Fill_87[2]= 127;
0165   Fill_87[3]= 247; Fill_87[4]= 223; Fill_87[5]= 253;
0166   Fill_87[6]= 127; Fill_87[7]= 247;
0167
0168   Fill_93[0]= 255; Fill_93[1]= 223; Fill_93[2]= 255;
0169   Fill_93[3]= 255; Fill_93[4]= 255; Fill_93[5]= 253;
0170   Fill_93[6]= 255; Fill_93[7]= 255;
0171
0172   Fill_100[0]= 255; Fill_100[1]= 255; Fill_100[2]= 255;
0173   Fill_100[3]= 255; Fill_100[4]= 255; Fill_100[5]= 255;
0174   Fill_100[6]= 255; Fill_100[7]= 255;
0175
0176   visible= 0.0; sp1= 0.0; sp2= 0.0; sp3= 0.0;
0177   xLight= -.1294089; yLight= .8660256; zLight= .4829627;
0178   illum_range= 11; normalized_illum= 0.0;
0179   xu= 0.0; yu= 0.0; zu= 0.0;
0180   xv= 0.0; yv= 0.0; zv= 0.0;
0181   x_surf_normal= 0.0; y_surf_normal= 0.0; z_surf_normal= 0.0;
0182   v1= 0.0; v2= 0.0; v3= 0.0;
0183   x_unit_vector= 0.0; y_unit_vector= 0.0; z_unit_vector= 0.0;
0184   zDeviceIllum= 0; zShadingColor= 4;
0185   clipx1= 0; clipy1= 0; clipx2= 639; clipy2= 479;
0186   ViewportWidth= 640; ViewportDepth= 480;
0187   Model3DReady= zYES;
0188   }
0189   /*
0190
0191   ┌─────────────────────────────────────────────────────────┐
       │              Class Kinetic3D:   DESTRUCTOR              │
0192   └─────────────────────────────────────────────────────────┘
0193                                                           */
0194   Kinetic3D::~Kinetic3D()
0195   {
0196   Model3DReady= zNO;
0197   }
0198   /*
0199
0200   ┌─────────────────────────────────────────────────────────┐
       │          Initialize and configure the 3D environment    │
0201   └─────────────────────────────────────────────────────────┘
0202                                                           */
0203   void Kinetic3D::Initialize3D(int kx1,int ky1,int kx2,int ky2,
0204                            Viewport *ViewportPtr)
0205   {      // expects clipping box, display mode, and viewport object.
0206      // NOTE: scaling calculations expect viewport to be full screen,
0207      //       otherwise you must pass a screen mode token to this
```

```
0208     //        method so it can calculate the scaling ratio from the
0209     //        aspect ratio of the physical display.
0210   Generic= ViewportPtr;                    // point to viewport object.
0211   clipx1= kx1; clipy1= ky1; clipx2= kx2; clipy2= ky2;
0212   ViewportWidth= clipx2 - clipx1 + 1;              // width of viewport.
0213   ViewportDepth= clipy2 - clipy1 + 1;              // depth of viewport.
0214   rx= ((float)ViewportWidth / DomainWidth);  // horiz scaling factor.
0215   ry= ((float)ViewportDepth / DomainDepth);   // vert scaling factor.
0216   hcenter= ((float)(ViewportWidth - 1)) / 2;   // center of viewport.
0217   vcenter= ((float)(ViewportDepth - 1)) / 2;   // center of viewport.
0218   focal_length= 1200.0; viewheight= 0; dist= 360;
0219   xLight= -.38729; yLight= .77459; zLight= .50000;
0220   CamYaw= 0.0; CamRoll= 0.0; CamPitch= 6.28319;
0221   pitchheading= 360; yawheading= 0; viewchg= 2;
0222   yawdelta= 0; pitchdelta= 0;
0223   SetCamAngle();                               // initialize the camera.
0224   xCam= 0.0; yCam= 0.0; zCam= -360.0;
0225   ObjYaw= 0.0; ObjRoll= 0.0; ObjPitch= 0.0;
0226   SetObjAngle();                          // initialize the 3D cursor.
0227   xObj= 0.0; yObj= 0.0; zObj= 0.0;
0228   ObjYawChg= 0; ObjRollChg= 0; ObjPitchChg= 0;
0229   xObjChg= 0; yObjChg= 0; zObjChg= 0;
0230   illum_range= 11;     // nominal dithered shade intensities 1 to 12.
0231   return;
0232   }
0233   /*
0234
0235   ┌─────────────────────────────────────────────────────────────────┐
         │             Set the subject rotation angle                      │
0236   └─────────────────────────────────────────────────────────────────┘
0237                                                                      */
0238   void Kinetic3D::SetLaminaAngle(
0239                   double SubjYaw,double SubjRoll,double SubjPitch)
0240   {
0241   ObjYaw= SubjYaw;
0242   ObjRoll= SubjRoll;
0243   ObjPitch= SubjPitch;
0244   SetObjAngle();
0245   return;
0246   }
0247   /*
0248
0249   ┌─────────────────────────────────────────────────────────────────┐
         │           Set the subject translation offset                    │
0250   └─────────────────────────────────────────────────────────────────┘
0251                                                                      */
0252   void Kinetic3D::SetLaminaPosition(float SubjX,
0253                                  float SubjY, float SubjZ)
0254   {
0255   xObj= SubjX;
0256   yObj= SubjY;
0257   zObj= SubjZ;
0258   return;
0259   }
0260   /*
0261
0262   ┌─────────────────────────────────────────────────────────────────┐
         │     Draw a shaded facet at current rotation/translation         │
0263   └─────────────────────────────────────────────────────────────────┘
0264                                                                      */
0265   void Kinetic3D::DrawLamina(float Lat,float Vert)
0266   {
0267     int C1=0;float negLat,negVert;
0268   negLat=(-1)*(Lat);negVert=(-1)*(Vert);
0269   LaminaObj[0][0]=Lat;LaminaObj[0][1]=negVert;LaminaObj[0][2]=0;
0270   LaminaObj[1][0]=Lat;LaminaObj[1][1]=Vert;LaminaObj[1][2]=0;
```

```
0271    LaminaObj[2][0]=negLat;LaminaObj[2][1]=Vert;LaminaObj[2][2]=0;
0272    LaminaObj[3][0]=negLat;LaminaObj[3][1]=negVert;LaminaObj[3][2]=0;
0273    for (C1=0; C1<=3; C1++)
0274      {
0275      x= LaminaObj[C1][0];
0276      y= LaminaObj[C1][1];
0277      z= LaminaObj[C1][2];
0278      GetWorldCoords();
0279      LaminaWorld[C1][0]= x;
0280      LaminaWorld[C1][1]= y;
0281      LaminaWorld[C1][2]= z;
0282      GetCameraCoords();
0283      LaminaCam[C1][0]= x;
0284      LaminaCam[C1][1]= y;
0285      LaminaCam[C1][2]= z;
0286      GetImageCoords();
0287      GetScreenCoords();
0288      LaminaDisplay[C1][0]= sx3D;
0289      LaminaDisplay[C1][1]= sy3D;
0290      }
0291    xc1=LaminaCam[0][0];yc1=LaminaCam[0][1];zc1=LaminaCam[0][2];
0292    xc2=LaminaCam[1][0];yc2=LaminaCam[1][1];zc2=LaminaCam[1][2];
0293    xc3=LaminaCam[2][0];yc3=LaminaCam[2][1];zc3=LaminaCam[2][2];
0294    xc4=LaminaCam[3][0];yc4=LaminaCam[3][1];zc4=LaminaCam[3][2];
0295    VisibilityTest();
0296    if (visible > 0) return;
0297    sx1=LaminaDisplay[0][0];sy1=LaminaDisplay[0][1];
0298    sx2=LaminaDisplay[1][0];sy2=LaminaDisplay[1][1];
0299    sx3=LaminaDisplay[2][0];sy3=LaminaDisplay[2][1];
0300    sx4=LaminaDisplay[3][0];sy4=LaminaDisplay[3][1];
0301    xw3=LaminaWorld[0][0];yw3=LaminaWorld[0][1];zw3=LaminaWorld[0][2];
0302    xw2=LaminaWorld[1][0];yw2=LaminaWorld[1][1];zw2=LaminaWorld[1][2];
0303    xw1=LaminaWorld[2][0];yw1=LaminaWorld[2][1];zw1=LaminaWorld[2][2];
0304    DrawFacet();
0305    return;
0306    }
0307    /*
0308
0309    ┌─────────────────────────────────────────────────────────────┐
           Get the physical display coords for a 3D point
0310
0311                                                                  */
0312    void Kinetic3D::GetDisplayCoords(float xParam,
0313                              float yParam, float zParam,
0314                              int *xDisplayPtr, int *yDisplayPtr)
0315    {
0316    x= xParam;
0317    y= yParam;
0318    z= zParam;
0319    PutObjToScreen();
0320    *xDisplayPtr= (int)sx3D;
0321    *yDisplayPtr= (int)sy3D;
0322    return;
0323    }
0324    /*
0325
0326    ┌─────────────────────────────────────────────────────────────┐
           Perform the backplane visibility test
0327
0328                                                                  */
0329    void Kinetic3D::VisibilityTest(void)
0330    {
0331      // Enter with 3 vertices as camera coords.
0332      // Exit with visibility token.
```

```
0333  sp1= xc1 * ( yc2 * zc3 - yc3 * zc2 );
0334  sp1= (-1) * sp1;
0335  sp2= xc2 * ( yc3 * zc1 - yc1 * zc3 );
0336  sp3= xc3 * ( yc1 * zc2 - yc2 * zc1);
0337  visible= sp1 - sp2 - sp3;
0338  return;
0339  }
0340  /*
0341
0342  ┌──────────────────────────────────────────────────────────┐
       │      Calculate object sine and cosine rotation factors     │
0343  └──────────────────────────────────────────────────────────┘
0344                                                              */
0345  void Kinetic3D::SetObjAngle(void)
0346  {
0347    // Enter with ObjYaw,ObjRoll,ObjPitch object rotation angles.
0348    // Exit with sine, cosine object rotation factors.
0349  sOYaw= sin(ObjYaw);
0350  cOYaw= cos(ObjYaw);
0351  sORoll= sin(ObjRoll);
0352  cORoll= cos(ObjRoll);
0353  sOPitch= sin(ObjPitch);
0354  cOPitch= cos(ObjPitch);
0355  return;
0356  }
0357  /*
0358
0359  ┌──────────────────────────────────────────────────────────┐
       │      Calculate camera sine and cosine rotation factors     │
0360  └──────────────────────────────────────────────────────────┘
0361                                                              */
0362  void Kinetic3D::SetCamAngle(void)
0363  {
0364    // Enter with Yaw,Roll,Pitch world rotation angles.
0365    // Exit with sine, cosine world rotation factors.
0366  sCYaw= sin(CamYaw);
0367  sCRoll= sin(CamRoll);
0368  sCPitch= sin(CamPitch);
0369  cCYaw= cos(CamYaw);
0370  cCRoll= cos(CamRoll);
0371  cCPitch= cos(CamPitch);
0372  return;
0373  }
0374  /*
0375
0376  ┌──────────────────────────────────────────────────────────┐
       │          Transform object coords to screen coords          │
0377  └──────────────────────────────────────────────────────────┘
0378                                                              */
0379  void Kinetic3D::PutObjToScreen(void)
0380  {
0381    // Enter with xyz object coordinates.  This routine transforms
0382    // the obj coords to world coords to image plane coords to
0383    // sx3D,sy3D physical screen coords.
0384  GetWorldCoords(); GetCameraCoords(); GetImageCoords();
0385  GetScreenCoords();
0386  return;
0387  }
0388  /*
0389
0390  ┌──────────────────────────────────────────────────────────┐
       │          Calculate world coords from object coords         │
0391  └──────────────────────────────────────────────────────────┘
0392                                                              */
0393  void Kinetic3D::GetWorldCoords(void)
0394  {
0395    // Enter with xyz unclipped object coordinates.
```

E-14 Continued.

```
0396      // Exit with unclipped xyz world coordinates.
0397    xa= cORoll*x+sORoll*y; ya= cORoll*y-sORoll*x;        // roll rotate.
0398    x= cOYaw*xa-sOYaw*z; za= sOYaw*xa+cOYaw*z;             // yaw rotate.
0399    z= cOPitch*za-sOPitch*ya; y= sOPitch*za+cOPitch*ya;      // pitch.
0400    x= x+xObj; y= y+yObj; z= z+zObj;              // lateral movement.
0401    return;
0402    }
0403    /*
0404
0405  ┌────────────────────────────────────────────────────────────────┐
      │           Calculate camera coords from world coords            │
0406  └────────────────────────────────────────────────────────────────┘
0407                                                                  */
0408    void Kinetic3D::GetCameraCoords(void)
0409    {
0410      // Enter with unclipped xyz world coordinates.
0411      // Exit with unclipped xyz camera coordinates.
0412    x=(-1)*x;                 // adjust for cartesian coords of 2D screen.
0413    y=y-viewheight;           // adjust world coords to height of viewer.
0414    x=x-xCam;y=y+yCam;z=z+zCam;                     // lateral movement.
0415    xa=cCYaw*x-sCYaw*z;za=sCYaw*x+cCYaw*z;               // yaw rotate.
0416    z=cCPitch*za-sCPitch*y;ya=sCPitch*za+cCPitch*y;    // pitch rotate.
0417    x=cCRoll*xa+sCRoll*ya;y=cCRoll*ya-sCRoll*xa;        // roll rotate.
0418    return;
0419    }
0420    /*
0421
0422  ┌────────────────────────────────────────────────────────────────┐
      │          Calculate dipslay coords from camera coords           │
0423  └────────────────────────────────────────────────────────────────┘
0424                                                                  */
0425    void Kinetic3D::GetImageCoords(void)
0426    {
0427      // Enter with clipped xyz camera coordinates.
0428      // Exit with unclipped sx3D,sy3D display coordinates.
0429    sx3D= focal_length * (x/z); sy3D= focal_length * (y/z);
0430    return;
0431    }
0432    /*
0433
0434  ┌────────────────────────────────────────────────────────────────┐
      │          Calculate screen coords from display coords           │
0435  └────────────────────────────────────────────────────────────────┘
0436                                                                  */
0437    void Kinetic3D::GetScreenCoords(void)
0438    {
0439      // Enter with unclipped sx3D,sy3D display coordinates.
0440      // Exit with sx3D,sy3D device-dependent display coordinates
0441      // scaled to the world range with correct aspect ratio.
0442    sx3D= sx3D * rx; sy3D= sy3D * ry;
0443    sx3D= sx3D + hcenter; sy3D= sy3D + vcenter;
0444    return;
0445    }
0446    /*
0447
0448  ┌────────────────────────────────────────────────────────────────┐
      │                  Draw a four-sided polygon                     │
0449  └────────────────────────────────────────────────────────────────┘
0450                                                                  */
0451    void Kinetic3D::DrawFacet(void)
0452    {
0453    Points[0]= (int) sx1;          // initialize the array of vertices...
0454    Points[1]= (int) sy1;
0455    Points[2]= (int) sx2;
0456    Points[3]= (int) sy2;
0457    Points[4]= (int) sx3;
```

```
0458    Points[5]= (int) sy3;
0459    Points[6]= (int) sx4;
0460    Points[7]= (int) sy4;
0461    Points[8]= (int) sx1;
0462    Points[9]= (int) sy1;
0463    GetBrightness();                        // get brightness factor of facet.
0464    #if defined (FG)                                   // if using fg.lib...
0465      Ds->SetHue(0);                         // set edge hue to black.
0466      Ds->SetFill(Fill_100, zShadingColor);     // set solid facet hue.
0467      Ds->SetLine(0xffff);                  // set line style to solid.
0468    #else                   // else if using graphics.lib or graph.lib...
0469      Ds->SetHue(zShadingColor);                  // set the shading hue.
0470      switch (zDeviceIllum)
0471        {                       // set the dither pattern and line style...
0472        case 1:  Ds->SetFill(Fill_6, zShadingColor);
0473                 Ds->SetLine(0x1010);
0474                 break;
0475        case 2:  Ds->SetFill(Fill_6,zShadingColor);
0476                 Ds->SetLine(0x1010);
0477                 break;
0478        case 3:  Ds->SetFill(Fill_6,zShadingColor);
0479                 Ds->SetLine(0x1010);
0480                 break;
0481        case 4:  Ds->SetFill(Fill_12,zShadingColor);
0482                 Ds->SetLine(0x2020);
0483                 break;
0484        case 5:  Ds->SetFill(Fill_25,zShadingColor);
0485                 Ds->SetLine(0x2222);
0486                 break;
0487        case 6:  Ds->SetFill(Fill_37,zShadingColor);
0488                 Ds->SetLine(0xaaaa);
0489                 break;
0490        case 7:  Ds->SetFill(Fill_50,zShadingColor);
0491                 Ds->SetLine(0xaaaa);
0492                 break;
0493        case 8:  Ds->SetFill(Fill_62,zShadingColor);
0494                 Ds->SetLine(0xaaaa);
0495                 break;
0496        case 9:  Ds->SetFill(Fill_75,zShadingColor);
0497                 Ds->SetLine(0xbbbb);
0498                 break;
0499        case 10: Ds->SetFill(Fill_87,zShadingColor);
0500                 Ds->SetLine(0xdddd);
0501                 break;
0502        case 11: Ds->SetFill(Fill_93,zShadingColor);
0503                 Ds->SetLine(0xefef);
0504                 break;
0505        case 12: Ds->SetFill(Fill_100,zShadingColor);
0506                 Ds->SetLine(0xffff);
0507                 break;
0508        }
0509    #endif
0510    Generic->DrawPolygon(5,Points);           // draw the shaded facet.
0511    return;
0512    }
0513    /*
0514
0515    ┌────────────────────────────────────────────────────────────┐
         │        Calculate the brightness level of a facet           │
0516     └────────────────────────────────────────────────────────────┘
0517                                                                  */
0518    void Kinetic3D::GetBrightness(void)
0519    {
0520      // Enter with facet world coordinates.
```

```
0521     // Exit with illumination level token.
0522 xu=xw2-xw1;yu=yw2-yw1;zu=zw2-zw1;      // vector vertex 1 to vertex 2.
0523 xv=xw3-xw1;yv=yw3-yw1;zv=zw3-zw1;      // vector vertex 1 to vertex 3.
0524 x_surf_normal=(yu*zv)-(zu*yv);
0525 y_surf_normal=(zu*xv)-(xu*zv);
0526 z_surf_normal=(xu*yv)-(yu*xv);
0527 y_surf_normal=y_surf_normal*(-1);
0528 z_surf_normal=z_surf_normal*(-1);      // convert to cartesian system.
0529 v1=(x_surf_normal*x_surf_normal)+(y_surf_normal*y_surf_normal)
0530    +(z_surf_normal*z_surf_normal);
0531 v2=sqrt(v1);            // magnitude of surface perpendicular vector.
0532 v3=1/v2;               // ratio of magnitude to length of unit vector.
0533 x_unit_vector=v3*x_surf_normal;
0534 y_unit_vector=v3*y_surf_normal;
0535 z_unit_vector=v3*z_surf_normal;  // surf perpendicular unit vector.
0536 normalized_illum=(x_unit_vector*xLight)+(y_unit_vector*yLight)
0537    +(z_unit_vector*zLight);         // illumination factor 0 to 1.
0538 normalized_illum=normalized_illum*illum_range;   // expand 0 to 11.
0539 zDeviceIllum= (int) normalized_illum;             // cast to int.
0540 zDeviceIllum++;                      // adjust to range 1 to 12.
0541 if (zDeviceIllum < 4) zDeviceIllum= 4;      // ambient light = 4.
0542 return;
0543 }
0544 /*
0545
0546 ┌──────────────────────────────────────────────────────────┐
         Set the current shading color for facets
0547
0548                                                            */
0549 void Kinetic3D::SetShadingColor(int iHue)
0550 {
0551 if (iHue < 1) return;                  // validate the argument...
0552 if (iHue > 7) return;
0553 zShadingColor= iHue;               // ...and set the global token.
0554 return;
0555 }
0556 /*
0557
0558 ┌──────────────────────────────────────────────────────────┐
          End of KINETIC.CPP 3D graphics routines for C++
0559
0560                                                            */
```

E-15 Source code for LIB2DBC.HPP, the declaration file for class PhysicalDisplay and class Viewport, providing a set of graphics language bindings for Borland C++. (For Turbo C++ and Zortech C++ language bindings, see Fig. E-1.)

```
0001 /*
0002
0003 ┌──────────────────────────────────────────────────────────┐
           Lee Adams' SUPERCHARGED C++ GRAPHICS
0004       Header file for graphics library language bindings
0005
0006     SOURCE FILE:  LIB2DBC.HPP        For use with Borland C++ 2.0
0007     TYPE:  declarations for classes PhysicalDisplay and Viewport
0008
0009          DEVELOPER'S GUIDE TO THE INTERFACE
0010     Before using graphics, you must create objects of the classes
0011     PhysicalDisplay and Viewport, and call methods of each object
0012     to switch the display to a graphics mode and setup various
0013     graphics parameters.  To create graphics output, call the
0014     appropriate methods of your objects.  Refer to any of the
```

```
0015     demonstration programs in the book for examples of here-is-
0016     how-it's-done source code.
0017     Class declarations are located in LIB2DBC.HPP (which must be
0018       used in your program as #include "LIB2DBC.HPP").
0019     Function definitions are located in LIB2DBC.CPP.
0020       Either LIB2DBC.CPP or LIB2DBC.OBJ must be named in the
0021       project list for your program.
0022
0023     LICENSE:  As purchaser of the book in which this source code
0024       appears you are granted a royalty-free license to reproduce
0025       and distribute executable files generated using this code
0026       provided that you accept the conditions of the License
0027       Agreement and Limited Warranty described in the book.
0028     PUBLICATION: Contains material from Windcrest/McGraw-Hill
0029       book 3489, published by TAB BOOKS.
0030     U.S. GOVERNMENT RESTRICTED RIGHTS:  This software and its
0031       documentation is provided with restricted rights.  The use,
0032       duplication, or disclosure by the Government is subject to
0033       restrictions set forth in subdivision (b)(3)(ii) of The
0034       Rights in Technical Data and Computer Software clause at
0035       252.227-7013.  Contractor/manufacturer is Lee Adams, c/o
0036       TAB BOOKS, 13311 Monterey Ave., Blue Ridge Summit PA 17294.
0037     TRADEMARK:  Lee Adams is a trademark of Lee Adams.
0038
0039         Copyright 1991 Lee Adams.  All rights reserved worldwide.
0040
0041                                                                  */
0042  #if !defined (__LARGE__)
0043  #error Must use large memory model.
0044  #endif
0045
0046  #if defined (BGI)          // include the appropriate header file...
0047  #include <graphics.h>
0048  #elif defined (FG)
0049  #include <fg.h>
0050  #elif defined (MS)
0051  #include <graph.h>
0052  #endif
0053
0054  class PhysicalDisplay     // physical display (adapter and monitor).
0055  {             // pen color, pen style, brush color, brush style, etc.
0056        // uses the physical coordinates of the current graphics mode.
0057  private:        // accessable by member functions and friends only.
0058    int ObjectReady;             // indicates if object initialized.
0059    int RAMpage;                 // indicates if hidden page in RAM.
0060    int ScreenMode;                     // current graphics mode.
0061    int TextWidth;                      // character matrix...
0062    int TextHeight;
0063    int ClipLeft;                       // viewport clipping coords...
0064    int ClipTop;
0065    int ClipRight;
0066    int ClipBottom;
0067    char SolidFill[8];                        // 100% fill pattern.
0068    unsigned int Plane_Length;             // length of bitplane.
0069    char far * BitMap0;          // storage of hidden page in RAM...
0070    char far * BitMap1;
0071    char far * BitMap2;
0072    char far * BitMap3;
0073    union{struct {unsigned int A1; unsigned int A2;} Address;
0074        char far * FarAddress;} U1;  // union to calculate addresses.
0075    unsigned int Seg1;           // hidden bitplane segment address...
0076    unsigned int Seg2;
0077    unsigned int Seg3;
```

```
0078    unsigned int Seg4;
0079    unsigned int Off1;                   // hidden bitplane offset address...
0080    unsigned int Off2;
0081    unsigned int Off3;
0082    unsigned int Off4;
0083    int CurrentClr;                        // for Zortech's fg.lib...
0084    int WriteMode;
0085    int CurrentX;
0086    int CurrentY;
0087    int FGmaxY;
0088    int CurrentFill;
0089    int CurrentTextX;
0090    int CurrentTextY;
0091    int ArrayWidth;
0092    int ArrayDepth;
0093    char far * InitHiddenPage(void);      // initialize hidden bitmap.
0094    void FreeMemory(char far *);          // releases a block of memory.
0095    public:    // data and methods accessable by any in-scope function.
0096    PhysicalDisplay();                              // constructor.
0097    ~PhysicalDisplay();                             // destructor.
0098    friend class Viewport;      // Viewport objects have full access.
0099    friend class Layout;        // Layout objects have full access.
0100    void Init2D(int,int,int,int,int);     // sets 2D graphics state.
0101    int SetupMode(void);     // detect and set up best graphics mode.
0102    void ForceMode(int);      // forces a particular graphics mode.
0103    void ShutDownGraphics(void);            // return to text mode.
0104    void SetHue(int);          // sets the current drawing color.
0105    void SetWriteMode(int);      // sets PSET or XOR write mode.
0106    void SetRGB(int,int,int,int);     // sets RGB values for a color.
0107    void SetLine(int);          // sets the current line style.
0108    void SetFill(char *, int);      // sets the area zFill style.
0109    void BackUp(void);         // copies page 0 to hidden page.
0110    void Restore(void);        // copies hidden page to page 0.
0111    int InitUndo(void);                    // sets up undo page.
0112    void SetWritePage(int);        // sets the active page.
0113    void SetDisplayPage(int);       // sets the displayed page.
0114    void BlankPage(void);      // blanks the current active page.
0115    };
0116
0117    class Viewport                  // a viewport on the physical display.
0118    {           // has access to all members of class PhysicalDisplay.
0119        // is a virtual display using its own local coordinate system.
0120    private:   // data and methods accessable by member functions only.
0121    int ViewportReady;          // indicates if object initialized.
0122    PhysicalDisplay *GenericDisplay;                 // backward pointer.
0123    public:    // data and methods accessable by any in-scope function.
0124    Viewport(PhysicalDisplay *);                  // constructor.
0125    ~Viewport();                                  // destructor.
0126    void SetPosition(int,int);      // sets the current xy position.
0127    void DrawLine(int,int);    // draws line from current xy position.
0128    void DrawBorder(int,int,int,int);           // draws rectangle.
0129    void DrawPanel(int,int,int,int);       // draws solid rectangle.
0130    void DrawPolygon(int, int far *);          // draws solid polygon.
0131    void DrawFacet(int, int far *);      // draws transparent polygon.
0132    void DrawCircle(int,int,int);                 // draws circle.
0133    void PutText(int,int,int,char *);             // display text.
0134    void SetTextRowCol(int,int);            // set text position.
0135    void ClearTextLine(void);        // blanks the dialog text line.
0136    void Fill(int,int,int);                         // area fill.
0137    #if defined (BGI)           // if using Borland's graphics.lib...
0138    char far * MemBlock(int,int,int,int);        // allocate memory.
0139    void FreeBlock(char far *);             // deallocate memory.
```

```
0140    void GetBlock(int,int,int,int,char far *);        // save array.
0141    void PutXOR(int,int,char far *);              // show XOR array.
0142    void PutPSET(int,int,char far *);             // show PSET array.
0143    void PutAND(int,int,char far *);              // show AND array.
0144 #elif defined (FG)                  // if using Zortech's fg.lib...
0145    fg_color_t far * MemBlock(int,int,int,int);
0146    void FreeBlock(fg_color_t far *);
0147    void GetBlock(int,int,int,int,fg_color_t far *);
0148    void PutXOR(int,int,fg_color_t far *);
0149    void PutPSET(int,int,fg_color_t far *);
0150    void PutAND(int,int,fg_color_t far *);
0151 #elif defined (MS)              // if using Microsoft's graph.lib...
0152    char far * MemBlock(int,int,int,int);
0153    void FreeBlock(char far *);
0154    void GetBlock(int,int,int,int,char far *);
0155    void PutXOR(int,int,char far *);
0156    void PutPSET(int,int,char far *);
0157    void PutAND(int,int,char far *);
0158 #endif
0159    unsigned long GetBlockSize(int,int,int,int);    // size of array.
0160    void WindowOpen(int,int,int,int); // open a viewport, overloaded.
0161    void WindowOpen(int,int,int,int,int);          //...plus border.
0162    void WindowOpen(int,int,int,int,int,int);      //...plus repaint.
0163    void WindowClose(int,int);               // shuts down viewport.
0164    void WindowClear(int bgclr= 0);    // clear viewport, default 0.
0165 };
0166 /*
0167
0168 ┌─────────────────────────────────────────────────────────────┐
      │              End of LIB2DBC.HPP header file.                │
0169 └─────────────────────────────────────────────────────────────┘
0170                                                                */
```

E-16 Source code for LIB2DBC.CPP, the implementation file for class PhysicalDisplay and class Viewport, providing low-level graphics methods for Borland C++. (For Turbo C++ and Zortech C++ routines, see Fig. E-2.)

```
0001 /*
0002
0003 ┌─────────────────────────────────────────────────────────────┐
      │            Lee Adams' SUPERCHARGED C++ GRAPHICS             │
0004 │            Graphics library language bindings for C++       │
0005 ├─────────────────────────────────────────────────────────────┤
0006 │      Implementation file for low-level graphics routines    │
0007 ├─────────────────────────────────────────────────────────────┤
0008 │  Source file:  LIB2DBC.CPP        For use with Borland C++ 2.0
0009 │  Type:  implementation file for class methods.
0010 │  Include file:  LIB2DBC.HPP
0011 │  Graphics libraries:  Borland graphics library (graphics.lib)
0012 │                       Zortech graphics library (fg.lib)
0013 │                       Microsoft graphics library (graph.lib)
0014 │  Languages:  Turbo C++, Zortech C++, and all C++ compilers
0015 │              compatible with AT&T C++ specification 2.0.
0016 │  Memory model:  large.
0017 │  Graphics:  supports 640x480x16 VGA, 640x350x16 EGA, 640x200x16
0018 │    EGA, 640x480x2 MCGA, 640x200x2 CGA, and 720x348x2 Hercules.
0019 │  Output:  contains class methods that provide bindings to a
0020 │            variety of different retail C++ graphics libraries.
0021 │  Usage:  refer to the header file LIB2DBC.HPP for a guide to
0022 │          using the methods of PhysicalDisplay and Viewport.
0023 │  License:  As purchaser of the book in which this module
0024 │    appears you are granted a royalty-free license to reproduce
```

```
0025        and distribute executable files generated using this code,
0026        provided that you accept the conditions of the License
0027        Agreement and Limited Warranty described in the book.
0028     Publication: Contains material from Windcrest/McGraw-Hill
0029        book 3489, published by TAB BOOKS.
0030     U.S. Government Restricted Rights:  This software and its
0031        documentation is provided with restricted rights.  The use,
0032        duplication, or disclosure by the Government is subject to
0033        restrictions set forth in subdivision (b)(3)(ii) of The
0034        Rights in Technical Data and Computer Software clause at
0035        252.227-7013.  Contractor/manufacturer is Lee Adams and TAB
0036        BOOKS, 13311 Monterey Ave., Blue Ridge Summit PA 17214.
0037     Trademarks:  Lee Adams is a trademark of Lee Adams.
0038
0039             Copyright 1991 Lee Adams.  All rights reserved.
0040
0041
0042                     CONDITIONAL COMPILATION
0043     To compile only those blocks of code that support the C++
0044     compiler and graphics library that you are using, you should
0045     #define the appropriate tokens in the following preprocessor
0046     directives.  Use the following table as your guide:
0047            GRAPHICS LIBRARY
0048        Borland's graphics.lib            #define BGI
0049        Zortech's fg.lib or fgdebug.lib   #define FG
0050        Microsoft's graph.lib             #define MS
0051            COMPILER
0052        Borland Turbo C++ compiler        #define BORLAND
0053        Zortech C++ compiler              #define ZORTECH
0054        AT&T-compatible C++ compilers     #define MICROSOFT
0055     Be sure you define only one compiler and one graphics library.
0056
0057                                                              */
0058  #define BGI     1  // indicates the graphics library you are using.
0059  #define BORLAND 1  // indicates the C++ compiler you are using.
0060  /*
0061
0062                         CONSTANTS
0063
0064                                                              */
0065  const int zFAIL=      0;                    // boolean token.
0066  const int zVGA_12H=   1;              // VGA 640x480x16/256.
0067  const int zEGA_10H=   2;               // EGA 640x350x16/64.
0068  const int zEGA_EH=    3;                  // EGA 640x200x16.
0069  const int zMCGA_11H=  4;                  // MCGA 640x480x2.
0070  const int zCGA_6H=    5;            // CGA 640x200x2-color.
0071  const int zHERC=      6;        // Hercules 720x348x2-color.
0072  const int zYES=       1;                    // boolean token.
0073  const int zNO=        0;                    // boolean token.
0074  /*
0075
0076                        INCLUDE FILES
0077
0078                                                              */
0079  #include "LIB2DBC.HPP"     // class declarations.
0080                       // include compiler-dependent header files...
0081  #if defined (BORLAND)
0082  #include <dos.h>          // outportb().
0083  #include <alloc.h>        // farmalloc(), farfree().
0084  #include <mem.h>          // movedata().
0085  #elif defined (ZORTECH)
0086  #include <dos.h>          // outp(), farmalloc(), farfree().
```

```
0087  #include <string.h>        // movedata().
0088  #elif defined (MICROSOFT)
0089  #include <conio.h>         // outp().
0090  #include <malloc.h>        // _fmalloc(), _ffree().
0091  #include <string.h>        // movedata().
0092  #endif
0093  /*
0094
0095  ┌──────────────────────────────────────────────────────────────┐
       │           Class PhysicalDisplay:   CONSTRUCTOR                 │
0096   └──────────────────────────────────────────────────────────────┘
0097                                                                   */
0098  PhysicalDisplay::PhysicalDisplay()
0099  {
0100  ObjectReady= zYES;
0101  RAMpage= zNO;
0102  ScreenMode= 0;
0103  TextWidth= 0; TextHeight= 0;
0104  ClipLeft= 0; ClipTop= 0; ClipRight= 0; ClipBottom= 0;
0105  SolidFill[0]= 255; SolidFill[1]= 255; SolidFill[2]= 255;
0106  SolidFill[3]= 255; SolidFill[4]= 255; SolidFill[5]= 255;
0107  SolidFill[6]= 255; SolidFill[7]= 255;
0108  Plane_Length= 0; WriteMode= 0;
0109  #if defined (FG)
0110    fg_version_sync();                // ensure correct fg.lib version.
0111  #endif
0112  }
0113  /*
0114
0115  ┌──────────────────────────────────────────────────────────────┐
       │           Class PhysicalDisplay:   DESTRUCTOR                  │
0116   └──────────────────────────────────────────────────────────────┘
0117                                                                   */
0118  PhysicalDisplay::~PhysicalDisplay()
0119  {
0120  ObjectReady= zNO;
0121  }
0122  /*
0123
0124  ┌──────────────────────────────────────────────────────────────┐
       │        STARTUP AND SHUTDOWN OF THE GRAPHICS STATE              │
0125   └──────────────────────────────────────────────────────────────┘
0126                                                                   */
0127  int PhysicalDisplay::SetupMode(void)
0128  {                              // detect and set up best graphics mode.
0129  #if defined (BGI)                         // if using graphics.lib...
0130      int graphics_adapter, graphics_mode;
0131    detectgraph(&graphics_adapter,&graphics_mode);
0132      if (graphics_adapter==VGA)
0133      {
0134      graphics_adapter=VGA; graphics_mode=VGAHI;
0135      initgraph(&graphics_adapter,&graphics_mode,"");
0136      settextstyle(0,0,1);
0137      return zVGA_12H;
0138      }
0139    if (graphics_mode==EGAHI)
0140      {
0141      graphics_adapter=EGA; graphics_mode=EGAHI;
0142      initgraph(&graphics_adapter,&graphics_mode,"");
0143      settextstyle(0,0,1);
0144      return zEGA_10H;
0145      }
0146    if (graphics_mode==EGALO)
0147      {
0148      graphics_adapter=EGA; graphics_mode=EGALO;
0149      initgraph(&graphics_adapter,&graphics_mode,"");
```

```
0150       settextstyle(0,0,1);
0151       return zEGA_EH;
0152       }
0153     if (graphics_adapter==MCGA)
0154       {
0155       graphics_adapter=MCGA; graphics_mode=MCGAHI;
0156       initgraph(&graphics_adapter,&graphics_mode,"");
0157       settextstyle(0,0,1);
0158       return zMCGA_11H;
0159       }
0160     if (graphics_adapter==CGA)
0161       {
0162       graphics_adapter=CGA; graphics_mode=CGAHI;
0163       initgraph(&graphics_adapter,&graphics_mode,"");
0164       settextstyle(0,0,1);
0165       return zCGA_6H;
0166       }
0167     if (graphics_adapter==HERCMONO)
0168       {
0169       graphics_adapter=HERCMONO; graphics_mode=HERCMONOHI;
0170       initgraph(&graphics_adapter,&graphics_mode,"");
0171       return zHERC;
0172       }
0173     return zFAIL;
0174 #elif defined (FG)                         // if using fg.lib...
0175     int graphics_adapter;
0176     graphics_adapter= fg_get_type();            // detect hardware.
0177     switch(graphics_adapter)
0178       {
0179       case FG_VGA12:     fg_init_vga12(); return zVGA_12H;
0180       case FG_EGAECD:    fg_init_egaecd(); return zEGA_10H;
0181       case FG_EGACOLOR:  fg_init_egacolor(); return zEGA_EH;
0182       case FG_VGA11:     fg_init_vga11(); return zMCGA_11H;
0183       case FG_CGAHIRES:  fg_init_cga(); return zCGA_6H;
0184       case FG_HERCFULL:  fg_init_herc(); return zHERC;
0185       default: return zFAIL;
0186       }
0187 #elif defined (MS)                      // if using graph.lib...
0188     if (_setvideomoderows(_VRES16COLOR,60)!=zFAIL) return zVGA_12H;
0189     if (_setvideomoderows(_ERESCOLOR,43)!=zFAIL) return zEGA_10H;
0190     if (_setvideomoderows(_HRES16COLOR,25)!=zFAIL) return zEGA_EH;
0191     if (_setvideomoderows(_VRES2COLOR,60)!=zFAIL) return zMCGA_11H;
0192     if (_setvideomoderows(_HRESBW,25)!=zFAIL) return zCGA_6H;
0193     if (_setvideomoderows(_HERCMONO,25)!=zFAIL) return zHERC;
0194     return zFAIL;
0195 #endif
0196 }
0197
0198
0199 void PhysicalDisplay::ForceMode(int NewMode)
0200 {       // force graphics adapter into a downward-compatible mode.
0201     int graphics_adapter, graphics_mode;
0202 switch(NewMode)
0203       {
0204 #if defined (BGI)                       // if using graphics.lib...
0205     case zEGA_10H:                          // 640x350x16 mode.
0206         graphics_adapter=EGA; graphics_mode=EGAHI;
0207         initgraph(&graphics_adapter,&graphics_mode,"");
0208         settextstyle(0,0,1);
0209         break;
0210     case zEGA_EH:                           // 640x200x16 mode.
0211         graphics_adapter=EGA; graphics_mode=EGALO;
```

```
0212        initgraph(&graphics_adapter,&graphics_mode,"");
0213        settextstyle(0,0,1);
0214        break;
0215      case zMCGA_11H:                               // 640x480x2 mode.
0216        ShutDownGraphics();              // unload previous BGI driver.
0217        graphics_adapter=MCGA; graphics_mode=MCGAHI;
0218        initgraph(&graphics_adapter,&graphics_mode,"");
0219        settextstyle(0,0,1);
0220        break;
0221      case zCGA_6H:                                 // 640x200x2 mode.
0222        ShutDownGraphics();              // unload previous BGI driver.
0223        graphics_adapter=CGA; graphics_mode=CGAHI;
0224        initgraph(&graphics_adapter,&graphics_mode,"");
0225        settextstyle(0,0,1);
0226        break;
0227  #elif defined (FG)                            // if using fg.lib...
0228      case zEGA_10H:                            // 640x350x16 mode.
0229        fg_term(); fg_init_egaecd();
0230        break;
0231      case zEGA_EH:                             // 640x200x16 mode.
0232        fg_term(); fg_init_egacolor();
0233        break;
0234      case zMCGA_11H:                           // 640x480x2 mode.
0235        fg_term(); fg_init_vga11();
0236        break;
0237      case zCGA_6H:                             // 640x200x2 mode.
0238        fg_term(); fg_init_cga();
0239        break;
0240  #elif defined (MS)                            // if using graph.lib...
0241      case zEGA_10H:                            // 640x350x16 mode.
0242        _setvideomoderows(_ERESCOLOR,43);
0243        break;
0244      case zEGA_EH:                             // 640x200x16 mode.
0245        _setvideomoderows(_HRES16COLOR,25);
0246        break;
0247      case zMCGA_11H:                           // 640x480x2 mode.
0248        _setvideomoderows(_VRES2COLOR,60);
0249        break;
0250      case zCGA_6H:                             // 640x200x2 mode.
0251        _setvideomoderows(_HRESBW,25);
0252        break;
0253  #endif
0254    }
0255  return;
0256  }
0257
0258
0259  void PhysicalDisplay::Init2D(int token,int x1,int yf1,int x2,int y2)
0260  {                                // initialize various parameters.
0261  ClipLeft= x1; ClipTop= yf1; ClipRight= x2; ClipBottom= y2;
0262  FGmaxY= y2; CurrentX= 0; CurrentY= 0;        // used by fg.lib only.
0263  CurrentFill= 7; CurrentClr= 7;               // ...
0264  CurrentTextX= 0; CurrentTextY= 100;          // ...
0265  ArrayWidth= 0; ArrayDepth= 0;                // ...
0266  #if defined (FG)                      // if using Flash Graphics...
0267    fg_setlinepattern(FG_LINE_USER_DEFINED, 0xffff);
0268    WriteMode= FG_MODE_SET;
0269  #endif
0270  switch (token)
0271    {
0272    case zVGA_12H: Plane_Length=38400;ScreenMode=zVGA_12H;
0273                  #if defined (FG)
0274                      TextWidth=8;TextHeight=14;break;
```

```
0276                    TextWidth=8;TextHeight=8;break;
0277    case zEGA_10H: Plane_Length=28000;ScreenMode=zEGA_10H;
0278                    #if defined (FG)
0279                       TextWidth=8;TextHeight=14;break;
0280                    #endif
0281                    TextWidth=8;TextHeight=8;break;
0282    case zEGA_EH: Plane_Length=16000;ScreenMode=zEGA_EH;
0283                 TextWidth=8;TextHeight=8;break;
0284    case zMCGA_11H: Plane_Length=38400;ScreenMode=zMCGA_11H;
0285                      #if defined (FG)
0286                         TextWidth=8;TextHeight=14;break;
0287                      #endif
0288                      TextWidth=8;TextHeight=8;break;
0289    case zCGA_6H: Plane_Length=16384;ScreenMode=zCGA_6H;
0290                   TextWidth=8;TextHeight=8;break;
0291    case zHERC: Plane_Length=32406;ScreenMode=zHERC;
0292               TextWidth=9;TextHeight=14;break;
0293      }
0294    return;
0295    }
0296
0297
0298    void PhysicalDisplay::ShutDownGraphics(void)
0299    {                            // graceful shutdown of graphics mode.
0300    if (RAMpage==zYES)                    // if a hidden page in RAM...
0301      {                          // then release the appropriate memory...
0302      switch(ScreenMode)
0303        {
0304        case zVGA_12H:   FreeMemory(BitMap3); FreeMemory(BitMap2);
0305                         FreeMemory(BitMap1); FreeMemory(BitMap0);
0306                         break;
0307        case zMCGA_11H:  FreeMemory(BitMap0); break;
0308        case zCGA_6H:    FreeMemory(BitMap0); break;
0309        }
0310      RAMpage= zNO;
0311      }
0312    #if defined (BGI)
0313      cleardevice();                               // clear the screen.
0314      closegraph();        // shut down graphics, restore original mode.
0315    #elif defined (FG)
0316      fg_fillbox(FG_BLACK, FG_MODE_SET, ~0, fg.displaybox);
0317      fg_term();                            // restore original mode.
0318    #elif defined (MS)
0319      _clearscreen(_GCLEARSCREEN);                  // clear the screen.
0320      _setvideomode(_DEFAULTMODE);          // restore original mode.
0321    #endif
0322    return;
0323    }
0324    /*
0325
0326    ┌──────────────────────────────────────────────────────────────┐
        │          SET ATTRIBUTES FOR PENS AND BRUSHES                   │
0327    └──────────────────────────────────────────────────────────────┘
0328                                                                  */
0329    void PhysicalDisplay::SetHue(int hueclr)
0330    {                                         // set the pen color.
0331    #if defined (BGI)
0332      setcolor(hueclr);
0333    #elif defined (FG)
0334      CurrentClr= hueclr;
0335    #elif defined (MS)
0336      _setcolor(hueclr);
```

```
0337   #endif
0338   return;
0339   }
0340
0341
0342   void PhysicalDisplay::SetWriteMode(int WMode)
0343   {                                    // set PSET or XOR writing mode.
0344   #if defined (BGI)
0345     if (WMode==1) setwritemode(XOR_PUT);
0346     else setwritemode(COPY_PUT);
0347   #elif defined (FG)
0348     if (WMode==1) WriteMode= FG_MODE_XOR;
0349     else WriteMode= FG_MODE_SET;
0350   #elif defined (MS)
0351     if (WMode==1) _setwritemode(_GXOR);
0352     else _setwritemode(_GPSET);
0353   #endif
0354   return;
0355   }
0356
0357
0358   void PhysicalDisplay::SetLine(int style)
0359   {                                    // set the pen style.
0360   #if defined (BGI)
0361     setlinestyle(USERBIT_LINE,style,NORM_WIDTH);
0362   #elif defined (FG)
0363     fg_setlinepattern(FG_LINE_USER_DEFINED, style);
0364   #elif defined (MS)
0365     _setlinestyle(style);
0366   #endif
0367   return;
0368   }
0369
0370
0371   void PhysicalDisplay::SetFill(char *pattern,int hueclr)
0372   {                                    // set the brush color and pattern.
0373   #if defined (BGI)
0374     if(ScreenMode>zEGA_EH) {if(hueclr!=0) hueclr=1;}
0375     setfillpattern(pattern,hueclr);
0376     pattern++;
0377     if (*pattern==SolidFill[1]) setfillstyle(SOLID_FILL,hueclr);
0378   #elif defined (FG)
0379     CurrentFill= hueclr;
0380   #elif defined (MS)
0381     _setcolor(hueclr);
0382     _setfillmask(pattern);
0383   #endif
0384   return;
0385   }
0386
0387
0388   void PhysicalDisplay::SetRGB(int Clr,int Red,int Green,int Blue)
0389   {                          // set the hardware RGB values for a color index.
0390   #if defined (BGI)
0391     setrgbpalette(Clr,Red,Green,Blue);
0392   #elif defined (FG)
0393     fg_setpalette(Clr,Red,Green,Blue);
0394   #elif defined (MS)
0395       long int VGAcode=0;
0396       long int Rv1=0,Gv1=0,Bv1=0;
0397     Rv1=(long)RedVolts;                      // convert to long int...
0398     Gv1=(long)GrnVolts;
0399     Bv1=(long)BluVolts;
```

```
0400     VGAcode=(Bv1*65536)+(Gv1*256)+Rv1;        // calculate analog code.
0401     _remappalette(clr,VGAcode);                         // write it.
0402 #endif
0403 return;
0404 }
0405 /*
0406
0407  ┌─────────────────────────────────────────────────────────────────┐
         │                       PAGE OPERATIONS                          │
0408  └─────────────────────────────────────────────────────────────────┘
0409                                                                   */
0410 void PhysicalDisplay::SetWritePage(int Page)
0411 {                                            // set the active page.
0412 #if defined (BGI)
0413    setactivepage(Page);
0414 #elif defined (FG)
0415    fg_setactivepage(Page);
0416 #elif defined (MS)
0417    _setactivepage(Page);
0418 #endif
0419 return;
0420 }
0421
0422
0423 void PhysicalDisplay::SetDisplayPage(int Page)
0424 {                                         // set the displayed page.
0425 #if defined (BGI)
0426    setvisualpage(Page);
0427 #elif defined (FG)
0428    fg_setdisplaypage(Page);
0429 #elif defined (MS)
0430    _setvisualpage(Page);
0431 #endif
0432 return;
0433 }
0434
0435
0436 void PhysicalDisplay::BlankPage(void)
0437 {                                         // blank the active page.
0438 #if defined (BGI)
0439    cleardevice();
0440 #elif defined (FG)
0441    fg_fillbox(FG_BLACK, FG_MODE_SET, ~0, fg.displaybox);
0442 #elif defined (MS)
0443    _clearscreen(_GCLEARSCREEN);
0444 #endif
0445 return;
0446 }
0447
0448 /*
0449
0450  ┌─────────────────────────────────────────────────────────────────┐
         │                  Class Viewport:  CONSTRUCTOR                  │
0451  └─────────────────────────────────────────────────────────────────┘
0452                                                                   */
0453 Viewport::Viewport(PhysicalDisplay *Caller)
0454 {      // use physical display object referenced by pointer Caller.
0455 GenericDisplay= Caller; // GenericDisplay points to display object.
0456 ViewportReady= zYES;
0457 }
0458 /*
0459
0460  ┌─────────────────────────────────────────────────────────────────┐
         │                  Class Viewport:  DESTRUCTOR                   │
0461  └─────────────────────────────────────────────────────────────────┘
```

```
0462                                                                          */
0463    Viewport::~Viewport()
0464    {
0465    ViewportReady= zNO;
0466    }
0467    /*
0468
0469    ┌─────────────────────────────────────────────────────────────────────┐
        │                       VIEWPORT OPERATIONS                             │
0470    └─────────────────────────────────────────────────────────────────────┘
0471                                                                          */
0472    void Viewport::WindowOpen(int x1,int yf1,int x2,int y2)
0473    {           // open a viewport -- overloaded function has 3 variants.
0474    #if defined (BGI)
0475       setviewport(x1,yf1,x2,y2,1);
0476    #elif defined (FG)
0477       return;
0478    #elif defined (MS)
0479       _setviewport(x1,yf1,x2,y2);
0480    #endif
0481    GenericDisplay->ClipLeft= x1;
0482    GenericDisplay->ClipTop= yf1;
0483    GenericDisplay->ClipRight= x2;
0484    GenericDisplay->ClipBottom= y2;
0485    return;
0486    }
0487
0488
0489    void Viewport::WindowOpen(int x1,int yf1,int x2,int y2,
0490                              int borderclr)
0491    {                               // open a viewport with a border.
0492    #if defined (BGI)
0493       GenericDisplay->SetHue(borderclr);
0494       DrawBorder(x1,yf1,x2,y2);
0495       setviewport(x1+1,yf1+1,x2-1,y2-1,1);
0496    #elif defined (FG)
0497       return;
0498    #elif defined (MS)
0499       GenericDisplay->SetHue(borderclr);
0500       DrawBorder(x1,yf1,x2,y2);
0501       _setviewport(x1+1,yf1+1,x2-1,y2-1);
0502    #endif
0503    GenericDisplay->ClipLeft= x1 + 1;
0504    GenericDisplay->ClipTop= yf1 + 1;
0505    GenericDisplay->ClipRight= x2 - 1;
0506    GenericDisplay->ClipBottom= y2 - 1;
0507    return;
0508    }
0509
0510
0511    void Viewport::WindowOpen(int x1,int yf1,int x2,int y2,
0512                              int borderclr, int paintclr)
0513    {  // open a viewport with a border and clear the drawing area.
0514    #if defined (BGI)
0515       GenericDisplay->SetLine(0xffff);
0516       GenericDisplay->SetHue(paintclr);
0517       GenericDisplay->SetFill(GenericDisplay->SolidFill, paintclr);
0518       DrawPanel(x1,yf1,x2,y2);
0519       GenericDisplay->SetHue(borderclr);
0520       DrawBorder(x1,yf1,x2,y2);
0521       setviewport(x1+1,yf1+1,x2-1,y2-1,1);
0522    #elif defined (FG)
0523       return;
0524    #elif defined (MS)
```

```
0525     GenericDisplay->SetLine(0xffff);
0526     GenericDisplay->SetHue(paintclr);
0527     GenericDisplay->SetFill(GenericDisplay->SolidFill, paintclr);
0528     DrawPanel(x1,yf1,x2,y2);
0529     GenericDisplay->SetHue(borderclr);
0530     DrawBorder(x1,yf1,x2,y2);
0531     _setviewport(x1+1,yf1+1,x2-1,y2-1);
0532  #endif
0533  GenericDisplay->ClipLeft= x1 + 1;
0534  GenericDisplay->ClipTop= yf1 + 1;
0535  GenericDisplay->ClipRight= x2 - 1;
0536  GenericDisplay->ClipBottom= y2 - 1;
0537  return;
0538  }
0539
0540
0541  void Viewport::WindowClose(int xres,int yres)
0542  {                                       // close a viewport.
0543  #if defined (BGI)
0544     setviewport(0,0,xres-1,yres-1,1);
0545  #elif defined (FG)
0546     return;
0547  #elif defined (MS)
0548     _setviewport(0,0,xres-1,yres-1);
0549  #endif
0550  GenericDisplay->ClipLeft= 0;
0551  GenericDisplay->ClipTop= 0;
0552  GenericDisplay->ClipRight= xres - 1;
0553  GenericDisplay->ClipBottom= yres - 1;
0554  return;
0555  }
0556
0557
0558  void Viewport::WindowClear(int bgclr)
0559  {                                       // blank a viewport.
0560  #if defined (BGI)
0561     setfillstyle(SOLID_FILL,bgclr);
0562  #elif defined (FG)
0563     return;
0564  #elif defined (MS)
0565     zSetFill(GenericDisplay->SolidFill,bgclr);
0566  #endif
0567  DrawPanel(0,0,
0568     (GenericDisplay->ClipRight - GenericDisplay->ClipLeft),
0569     (GenericDisplay->ClipBottom - GenericDisplay->ClipTop));
0570  return;
0571  }
0572  /*
0573
0574  ┌─────────────────────────────────────────────────────────────┐
       │            LOW-LEVEL DRAWING FUNCTIONS                        │
       └─────────────────────────────────────────────────────────────┘
0575
0576                                                               */
0577  void Viewport::SetPosition(int x,int y)
0578  {                                       // set the current position.
0579  #if defined (BGI)
0580     moveto(x,y);
0581  #elif defined (FG)
0582     GenericDisplay->CurrentX= x; GenericDisplay->CurrentY= y;
0583  #elif defined (MS)
0584     _moveto(x,y);
0585  #endif
0586  return;
```

```
0587  }
0588
0589
0590  void Viewport::DrawLine(int x,int y)
0591  { // draw a line from the current position using PSET or XOR logic.
0592  #if defined (BGI)
0593    lineto(x,y);
0594  #elif defined (FG)
0595      fg_line_t Line;
0596    Line [FG_X1]= GenericDisplay->CurrentX;
0597    Line [FG_Y1]= GenericDisplay->FGmaxY - GenericDisplay->CurrentY;
0598    Line [FG_X2]= x;
0599    Line [FG_Y2]= GenericDisplay->FGmaxY - y;
0600    GenericDisplay->CurrentX= x; GenericDisplay->CurrentY= y;
0601    fg_drawline(GenericDisplay->CurrentClr,
0602                GenericDisplay->WriteMode, ~0,
0603                FG_LINE_USER_DEFINED, Line);
0604  #elif defined (MS)
0605    _lineto(x,y);
0606  #endif
0607  return;
0608  }
0609
0610
0611  void Viewport::DrawBorder(int x1,int yf1,int x2,int y2)
0612  {                      // draw a rectangle using PSET or XOR logic.
0613  #if defined (BGI)
0614    rectangle(x1,yf1,x2,y2);
0615  #elif defined (FG)
0616      fg_box_t Box;
0617    Box [FG_X1]= x1;
0618    Box [FG_Y1]= GenericDisplay->FGmaxY - y2;
0619    Box [FG_X2]= x2;
0620    Box [FG_Y2]= GenericDisplay->FGmaxY - yf1;
0621    fg_drawbox(GenericDisplay->CurrentClr,
0622                GenericDisplay->WriteMode, ~0,
0623                FG_LINE_USER_DEFINED, Box, fg.displaybox);
0624  #elif defined (MS)
0625    _rectangle(_GBORDER,x1,yf1,x2,y2);
0626  #endif
0627  return;
0628  }
0629
0630
0631  void Viewport::DrawPanel(int x1,int yf1,int x2,int y2)
0632  {                               // draw a filled rectangle.
0633  #if defined (BGI)
0634    bar(x1,yf1,x2,y2);
0635  #elif defined (FG)
0636      fg_box_t Box;
0637    Box [FG_X1]= x1;
0638    Box [FG_Y1]= GenericDisplay->FGmaxY - y2;
0639    Box [FG_X2]= x2;
0640    Box [FG_Y2]= GenericDisplay->FGmaxY - yf1;
0641    fg_fillbox(GenericDisplay->CurrentFill, FG_MODE_SET, ~0, Box);
0642  #elif defined (MS)
0643    _rectangle(_GFILLINTERIOR,x1,yf1,x2,y2);
0644  #endif
0645  return;
0646  }
0647
0648
0649  void Viewport::DrawPolygon(int NumVertices,int far *Vertices)
```

```
0650  {                                              // draw a filled polygon.
0651  #if defined (FG)
0652      int Count= 1;                              // will be used by fg.lib.
0653  #endif
0654  if (NumVertices < 4) return;          // must have at least 3 sides.
0655  #if defined (BGI)
0656      fillpoly(NumVertices, Vertices);
0657  #elif defined (FG)
0658      if (NumVertices==5)                       // if a four-sided polygon...
0659      {
0660      Vertices[1]= GenericDisplay->FGmaxY - Vertices[1];
0661      Vertices[3]= GenericDisplay->FGmaxY - Vertices[3];
0662      Vertices[5]= GenericDisplay->FGmaxY - Vertices[5];
0663      Vertices[7]= GenericDisplay->FGmaxY - Vertices[7];
0664      Vertices[9]= GenericDisplay->FGmaxY - Vertices[9];
0665      fg_fillpolygon(GenericDisplay->CurrentFill, FG_MODE_SET, ~0,
0666                      NumVertices-1, Vertices, fg.displaybox);
0667      fg_drawpolygon(GenericDisplay->CurrentClr, FG_MODE_SET, ~0,
0668                      FG_LINE_USER_DEFINED,
0669                      NumVertices-1, Vertices, fg.displaybox);
0670      }
0671      if (NumVertices!=5)               // if not a four-sided polygon...
0672      {
0673      while (Count < NumVertices*2)             // for each y coordinate...
0674          {           // ...convert to Flash Graphic's coordinate system.
0675          Vertices[Count]= GenericDisplay->FGmaxY - Vertices[Count];
0676          Count+= 2;
0677          }
0678      fg_fillpolygon(GenericDisplay->CurrentFill, FG_MODE_SET, ~0,
0679                      NumVertices-1, Vertices, fg.displaybox);
0680      fg_drawpolygon(GenericDisplay->CurrentClr, FG_MODE_SET, ~0,
0681                      FG_LINE_USER_DEFINED,
0682                      NumVertices-1, Vertices, fg.displaybox);
0683      }
0684  #elif defined (MS)
0685      _polygon(_GFILLINTERIOR, Vertices, NumVertices);
0686  #endif
0687  return;
0688  }
0689
0690
0691  void Viewport::DrawFacet(int NumVertices,int far *Vertices)
0692  {                                          // draw a transparent polygon.
0693  #if defined (FG)
0694      int Count= 1;                              // will be used by fg.lib.
0695  #endif
0696  if (NumVertices < 4) return;          // must have at least 3 sides.
0697  #if defined (BGI)
0698      drawpoly(NumVertices, Vertices);
0699  #elif defined (FG)
0700      if (NumVertices==5)                       // if a four-sided polygon.
0701      {
0702      Vertices[1]= GenericDisplay->FGmaxY - Vertices[1];
0703      Vertices[3]= GenericDisplay->FGmaxY - Vertices[3];
0704      Vertices[5]= GenericDisplay->FGmaxY - Vertices[5];
0705      Vertices[7]= GenericDisplay->FGmaxY - Vertices[7];
0706      Vertices[9]= GenericDisplay->FGmaxY - Vertices[9];
0707      fg_drawpolygon(GenericDisplay->CurrentClr, FG_MODE_SET, ~0,
0708                      FG_LINE_USER_DEFINED,
0709                      NumVertices-1, Vertices, fg.displaybox);
0710      }
0711      if (NumVertices!=5)               // if not a four-sided polygon...
```

```
0712      {
0713      while (Count < NumVertices*2)          // for each y coordinate...
0714          {              // ...convert to Flash Graphic's coordinate system.
0715          Vertices[Count]= GenericDisplay->FGmaxY - Vertices[Count];
0716          Count+= 2;
0717          }
0718      fg_drawpolygon(GenericDisplay->CurrentClr, FG_MODE_SET, ~0,
0719                       FG_LINE_USER_DEFINED,
0720                       NumVertices-1, Vertices, fg.displaybox);
0721      }
0722  #elif defined (MS)
0723      _polygon(_GBORDER, Vertices, NumVertices);
0724  #endif
0725  return;
0726  }
0727
0728
0729  void Viewport::DrawCircle(int CenterX, int CenterY, int Radius)
0730  {                                          // draw a circle.
0731  #if defined (BGI)
0732      circle(CenterX,CenterY,Radius);
0733  #elif defined (FG)
0734      fg_coord_t xradius, yradius;
0735      float Temp;
0736      xradius= Radius;
0737      CenterY= GenericDisplay->FGmaxY - CenterY;
0738      switch(GenericDisplay->ScreenMode)
0739          {              // adjust y radius to fit display aspect ratio...
0740          case zVGA_12H:  yradius= (fg_coord_t) Radius; break;
0741          case zEGA_10H:  Temp= ((float) Radius * .729);
0742                          yradius= (fg_coord_t) Temp; break;
0743          case zEGA_EH:   Temp= ((float) Radius * .417);
0744                          yradius= (fg_coord_t) Temp; break;
0745          case zMCGA_11H: yradius= (fg_coord_t) Radius; break;
0746          case zCGA_6H:   Temp= ((float) Radius * .417);
0747                          yradius= (fg_coord_t) Temp; break;
0748          case zHERC:     Temp= ((float) Radius * .64);
0749                          yradius= (fg_coord_t) Temp; break;
0750          }
0751      fg_drawellipse(GenericDisplay->CurrentClr, FG_MODE_SET, ~0,
0752                       CenterX, CenterY, xradius, yradius,
0753                       0, 3600, fg.displaybox);
0754  #elif defined (MS)
0755      int xradius;
0756      float yradius;
0757      int x1,yf1,x2,y2;
0758      xradius= Radius;
0759      switch(GenericDisplay->ScreenMode)
0760          {              // adjust y radius to fit display aspect ratio...
0761          case zVGA_12H:  yradius= (float) Radius; break;
0762          case zEGA_10H:  yradius= ((float) Radius) * .729; break;
0763          case zEGA_EH:   yradius= ((float) Radius) * .417; break;
0764          case zMCGA_11H: yradius= (float) Radius; break;
0765          case zCGA_6H:   yradius= ((float) Radius) * .417; break;
0766          case zHERC:     yradius= ((float) Radius) * .64; break;
0767          }
0768      x1= CenterX - xradius; yf1= CenterY - ((int) yradius);
0769      x2= CenterX + xradius; y2= CenterY + ((int) yradius);
0770      _ellipse(_GBORDER,x1,yf1,x2,y2);
0771  #endif
0772  return;
0773  }
0774
```

```
0775
0776   void Viewport::Fill(int x,int y,int edgeclr)
0777   {                                          // perform a flood fill.
0778   #if defined (BGI)
0779      floodfill(x,y,edgeclr);
0780   #elif defined (FG)
0781      y= GenericDisplay->FGmaxY - y;
0782      fg_fill(x,y,GenericDisplay->CurrentFill,edgeclr);
0783   #elif defined (MS)
0784      _floodfill(x,y,edgeclr);
0785   #endif
0786   return;
0787   }
0788   /*
0789
0790   ┌──────────────────────────────────────────────────────────────┐
       │                  GRAPHIC ARRAY OPERATIONS                      │
0791   └──────────────────────────────────────────────────────────────┘
0792                                                                 */
0793   #if defined (BGI)              // if using Borland's graphics.lib...
0794      char far * Viewport::MemBlock(int x1,int yf1,int x2,int y2)
0795   #elif defined (FG)                  // if using Zortech's fg.lib...
0796      fg_color_t far * Viewport::MemBlock(int x1,
0797                                       int yf1,int x2,int y2)
0798   #elif defined (MS)             // if using Microsoft's graph.lib...
0799      char far * Viewport::MemBlock(int x1,int yf1,int x2,int y2)
0800   #endif
0801   {        // allocate a block of far heap memory for a graphic array.
0802   #if defined (BGI)
0803      unsigned long blocksize;
0804      char far *blk;
0805      blocksize=(unsigned long)imagesize(x1,yf1,x2,y2);    // get size.
0806      if (blocksize==0xffff) return (char far *)zFAIL;     // if >64K.
0807      blk=(char far*)farmalloc(blocksize);          // allocate memory.
0808   #elif defined (FG)
0809      unsigned long blocksize;
0810      fg_color_t far *blk;
0811      fg_box_t Array;
0812      Array[FG_X1]= x1; Array[FG_Y1]= GenericDisplay->FGmaxY - y2;
0813      Array[FG_X2]= x2; Array[FG_Y2]= GenericDisplay->FGmaxY - yf1;
0814      blocksize=(unsigned long)(sizeof(fg_color_t)*fg_box_area(Array));
0815      blk= (fg_color_t far *) farmalloc(blocksize);
0816   #elif defined (MS)
0817      unsigned long blocksize;
0818      char far *blk;
0819      blocksize=(unsigned long)_imagesize(x1,yf1,x2,y2);   // get size.
0820      if (blocksize==0xffff) return (char far *)zFAIL;      // if >64K.
0821      blk=(char far*)_fmalloc(blocksize);           // allocate memory.
0822   #endif
0823   return blk;
0824   }
0825
0826
0827   unsigned long Viewport::GetBlockSize(int x1,int yf1,
0828                                        int x2,int y2)
0829   {              // determine storage requirements of a graphic array.
0830      unsigned long blocksize;
0831   #if defined (BGI)
0832      blocksize=(unsigned long)imagesize(x1,yf1,x2,y2);
0833   #elif defined (FG)
0834       fg_box_t Array;
0835      Array[FG_X1]= x1; Array[FG_Y1]= GenericDisplay->FGmaxY - y2;
0836      Array[FG_X2]= x2; Array[FG_Y2]= GenericDisplay->FGmaxY - yf1;
```

```
0837     blocksize=(unsigned long)(sizeof(fg_color_t*fg_box_area(Array));
0838  #elif defined (MS)
0839     blocksize=(unsigned long)_imagesize(x1,yf1,x2,y2);    // get size.
0840  #endif
0841  return blocksize;
0842  }
0843
0844
0845  #if defined (BGI)                    // if using Borland's graphics.lib...
0846     void Viewport::FreeBlock(char far *blk)
0847     {                       // deallocate a block of far heap memory.
0848     farfree(blk);
0849     return;
0850     }
0851     void Viewport::GetBlock(int x1,int yf1,int x2,
0852                              int y2,char far *blk)
0853     {                        // save graphic array in a memory block.
0854     getimage(x1,yf1,x2,y2,blk);
0855     return;
0856     }
0857     void Viewport::PutXOR(int x,int y,char far *blk)
0858     {                                      // XOR array on screen.
0859     putimage(x,y,blk,XOR_PUT);
0860     return;
0861     }
0862     void Viewport::PutPSET(int x,int y,char far *blk)
0863     {                                      // PSET array on screen.
0864     putimage(x,y,blk,COPY_PUT);
0865     return;
0866     }
0867     void Viewport::PutAND(int x,int y,char far *blk)
0868     {                                      // AND array on screen.
0869     putimage(x,y,blk,AND_PUT);
0870     return;
0871     }
0872  #elif defined (FG)                      // if using Zortech's fg.lib...
0873     void Viewport::FreeBlock(fg_color_t far *blk)
0874     {                       // deallocate a block of far heap memory.
0875     farfree(blk);
0876     return;
0877     }
0878     void Viewport::GetBlock(int x1,int yf1,int x2,
0879                              int y2,fg_color_t far *blk)
0880     {                         // save graphic array in a memory block
0881       fg_box_t Array;
0882     GenericDisplay->ArrayWidth= x2 - x1;    // save width, depth...
0883     GenericDisplay->ArrayDepth= y2 - yf1;
0884     Array[FG_X1]= x1; Array[FG_Y1]= GenericDisplay->FGmaxY - y2;
0885     Array[FG_X2]= x2; Array[FG_Y2]= GenericDisplay->FGmaxY - yf1;
0886     fg_readbox(Array, blk);
0887     return;
0888     }
0889     void Viewport::PutXOR(int x,int y,fg_color_t far *blk)
0890     {                                      // XOR array on screen.
0891     return;
0892     }
0893     void Viewport::PutPSET(int x,int y,fg_color_t far *blk)
0894     {                                      // PSET array on screen.
0895       fg_box_t Array;
0896     Array[FG_X1]= x;
0897     Array[FG_Y1]= (GenericDisplay->FGmaxY - y)
0898                  - GenericDisplay->ArrayDepth;
0899     Array[FG_X2]= x + GenericDisplay->ArrayWidth;
```

```
0900    Array[FG_Y2]= Array[FG_Y1] + GenericDisplay->ArrayDepth;
0901    fg_writebox(Array, blk);
0902    return;
0903    }
0904    void Viewport::PutAND(int x,int y,fg_color_t far *blk)
0905    {                              // AND array on screen.
0906    return;
0907    }
0908  #elif defined (MS)             // if using Microsoft's graph.lib...
0909    void Viewport::FreeBlock(char far *blk)
0910    {                    // deallocate a block of far heap memory.
0911    _ffree(blk);
0912    return;
0913    }
0914    void Viewport::GetBlock(int x1,int yf1,int x2,
0915                            int y2,char far *blk)
0916    {                        // save graphic array in a memory block.
0917    _getimage(x1,yf1,x2,y2,blk);
0918    return;
0919    }
0920    void Viewport::PutXOR(int x,int y,char far *blk)
0921    {                                   // XOR array on screen.
0922    _putimage(x,y,blk,_GXOR);
0923    return;
0924    }
0925    void Viewport::PutPSET(int x,int y,char far *blk)
0926    {                                   // PSET array on screen.
0927    _putimage(x,y,blk,_GPSET);
0928    return;
0929    }
0930    void Viewport::PutAND(int x,int y,char far *blk)
0931    {                                   // AND array on screen.
0932    _putimage(x,y,blk,_GAND);
0933    return;
0934    }
0935  #endif
0936  /*
0937
0938  ┌─────────────────────────────────────────────────────────────┐
        │            TEXT OPERATIONS USING THE DEFAULT FONT             │
0939  └─────────────────────────────────────────────────────────────┘
0940                                                              */
0941  void Viewport::PutText(int row,int col,int clr,char * tptr)
0942  {               // write a string of text at a specified position.
0943  #if defined (BGI)
0944      int TCrow,TCcol,tempclr;
0945    TCcol= (col * GenericDisplay->TextWidth)
0946          - GenericDisplay->TextWidth;          // convert col to x.
0947    TCrow= (row * GenericDisplay->TextHeight)
0948          - GenericDisplay->TextHeight;         // convert row to y.
0949    tempclr=getcolor();setcolor(clr);      // save, set active color.
0950    outtextxy(TCcol,TCrow,tptr);                // display the text.
0951    setcolor(tempclr);               // Restore previous active color.
0952  #elif defined (FG)
0953      int FGrow,FGcol;
0954    FGcol= (col * GenericDisplay->TextWidth)
0955          - GenericDisplay->TextWidth;
0956    FGrow= row * GenericDisplay->TextHeight;
0957    FGrow= GenericDisplay->FGmaxY - FGrow;
0958    fg_puts(clr, FG_MODE_SET, ~0, FG_ROT0, FGcol, FGrow,
0959          tptr, fg.displaybox);
0960  #elif defined (MS)
0961    _settextposition(row,col);_settextcolor(clr);_outtext(tptr);
```

```
0962   #endif
0963   return;
0964   }
0965
0966
0967   void Viewport::SetTextRowCol(int row,int col)
0968   {    // set current text starting position, using rows and columns.
0969   #if defined (BGI)
0970       int TCrow,TCcol;
0971     TCcol= (col * GenericDisplay->TextWidth)
0972             - GenericDisplay->TextWidth;
0973     TCrow= (row * GenericDisplay->TextHeight)
0974             - GenericDisplay->TextHeight;
0975     moveto(TCcol,TCrow);
0976   #elif defined (FG)
0977       int FGrow,FGcol;
0978     FGcol= (col * GenericDisplay->TextWidth)
0979             - GenericDisplay->TextWidth;
0980     FGrow= row * GenericDisplay->TextHeight;
0981     FGrow= GenericDisplay->FGmaxY - FGrow;
0982     GenericDisplay->CurrentTextX= FGcol;
0983     GenericDisplay->CurrentTextY= FGrow;
0984   #elif defined (MS)
0985     _settextposition(row,col);
0986   #endif
0987   return;
0988   }
0989
0990
0991   void Viewport::ClearTextLine(void)
0992   {               // blank the first text line on the graphics screen.
0993   #if defined (BGI)
0994     setfillstyle(SOLID_FILL,0);               // this is BGI-specific!
0995     if (GenericDisplay->ScreenMode==zHERC)         // if Hercules.
0996       {
0997       DrawPanel(0,0,486,13);
0998       }
0999     else DrawPanel(0,0,431,7);                 // if 8x8 characters.
1000   #elif defined (FG)
1001       fg_box_t Box;
1002     if (GenericDisplay->ScreenMode==zHERC)
1003       {
1004       Box [FG_X1]= 0;
1005       Box [FG_Y1]= GenericDisplay->FGmaxY
1006                     - GenericDisplay->TextHeight;
1007       Box [FG_X2]= 486; Box [FG_Y2]= GenericDisplay->FGmaxY;
1008       }
1009     else
1010       {
1011       Box [FG_X1]= 0;
1012       Box [FG_Y1]= GenericDisplay->FGmaxY
1013                     - GenericDisplay->TextHeight;
1014       Box [FG_X2]= 431; Box [FG_Y2]= GenericDisplay->FGmaxY;
1015       }
1016     fg_fillbox(0, FG_MODE_SET, ~0, Box);
1017   #elif defined (MS)
1018     _setcolor(0); _setfillmask(GenericDisplay->SolidFill);
1019     if (GenericDisplay->ScreenMode==zHERC)         // if Hercules.
1020       {
1021       DrawPanel(0,0,486,13);
1022       }
1023     else DrawPanel(0,0,431,7);                 // if 8x8 characters.
1024   #endif
```

```
1025   return;
1026   }
1027   /*
1028
1029   ┌─────────────────────────────────────────────────────────────┐
       │                    HIDDEN PAGE OPERATIONS                     │
1030   └─────────────────────────────────────────────────────────────┘
1031                                                                  */
1032   int PhysicalDisplay::InitUndo(void)
1033   {              // initialize a hidden page in RAM or in video memory.
1034   switch(ScreenMode)
1035     {
1036     case zVGA_12H: BitMap0=InitHiddenPage();             // 640x480x16.
1037         if(!BitMap0) return zFAIL;
1038         U1.FarAddress=BitMap0;
1039         Seg1=U1.Address.A2;Off1=U1.Address.A1;
1040         BitMap1=InitHiddenPage();
1041         if(BitMap1==0)
1042           {
1043           FreeMemory(BitMap0); return zFAIL;
1044           }
1045         U1.FarAddress=BitMap1;
1046         Seg2=U1.Address.A2;Off2=U1.Address.A1;
1047         BitMap2=InitHiddenPage();
1048         if(BitMap2==0)
1049           {
1050           FreeMemory(BitMap1); FreeMemory(BitMap0); return zFAIL;
1051           }
1052         U1.FarAddress=BitMap2;
1053         Seg3=U1.Address.A2;Off3=U1.Address.A1;
1054         BitMap3=InitHiddenPage();
1055         if(BitMap3==0)
1056           {
1057           FreeMemory(BitMap2); FreeMemory(BitMap1);
1058           FreeMemory(BitMap0); return zFAIL;
1059           }
1060         U1.FarAddress=BitMap3;
1061         Seg4=U1.Address.A2;Off4=U1.Address.A1;
1062         RAMpage= zYES; break;
1063     case zEGA_10H: break;                                // 640x350x16.
1064     case zEGA_EH: break;                                 // 640x200x16.
1065     case zMCGA_11H: BitMap0=InitHiddenPage();            // 640x480x2.
1066         if(BitMap0==0) return zFAIL;
1067         U1.FarAddress=BitMap0;
1068         Seg1=U1.Address.A2;Off1=U1.Address.A1;
1069         RAMpage= zYES; break;
1070     case zCGA_6H: BitMap0=InitHiddenPage();              // 640x200x2.
1071         if(BitMap0==0) return zFAIL;
1072         U1.FarAddress=BitMap0;
1073         Seg1=U1.Address.A2;Off1=U1.Address.A1;
1074         RAMpage= zYES; break;
1075     case zHERC: break;                                   // 720x348x2.
1076     }
1077   return zYES;
1078   }
1079
1080
1081   char far * PhysicalDisplay::InitHiddenPage(void)
1082   {                       // allocate memory for a hidden RAM bitmap.
1083     char far * vptr;      // buffer address to be returned to caller.
1084   #if defined (BORLAND)
1085     vptr=(char far *)farmalloc(Plane_Length);
1086   #elif defined (MICROSOFT)
```

```
1087    vptr=(char far *)_fmalloc(Plane_Length);
1088 #elif defined (ZORTECH)
1089    vptr=(char far *)farmalloc(Plane_Length);
1090 #endif
1091 return vptr;                      // return buffer address to caller.
1092 }
1093
1094
1095 void PhysicalDisplay::FreeMemory(char far *blk)
1096 {                                 // release a block of memory.
1097 #if defined (BGI)
1098    farfree(blk);
1099 #elif defined (FG)
1100    farfree(blk);
1101 #elif defined (MS)
1102    _ffree(blk);
1103 #endif
1104 return;
1105 }
1106
1107
1108 void PhysicalDisplay::BackUp(void)
1109 {                          // copy graphics page 0 to the hidden page.
1110 switch(ScreenMode)
1111   {
1112   case zVGA_12H:                          // VGA 640x480x16-color.
1113       #if defined (MICROSOFT)
1114          outp(0x3ce,4);outp(0x3cf,0);
1115       #elif defined (ZORTECH)
1116          outp(0x3ce,4);outp(0x3cf,0);
1117       #elif defined (BORLAND)
1118          outportb(0x03ce,(unsigned char)4);
1119          outportb(0x03cf,(unsigned char)0);
1120       #endif
1121       movedata(0xa000,0x0000,Seg1,Off1,Plane_Length);
1122       #if defined (MICROSOFT)
1123          outp(0x3ce,4);outp(0x3cf,1);
1124       #elif defined (ZORTECH)
1125          outp(0x3ce,4);outp(0x3cf,1);
1126       #elif defined (BORLAND)
1127          outportb(0x03ce,(unsigned char)4);
1128          outportb(0x03cf,(unsigned char)1);
1129       #endif
1130       movedata(0xa000,0x0000,Seg2,Off2,Plane_Length);
1131       #if defined (MICROSOFT)
1132          outp(0x3ce,4);outp(0x3cf,2);
1133       #elif defined (ZORTECH)
1134          outp(0x3ce,4);outp(0x3cf,2);
1135       #elif defined (BORLAND)
1136          outportb(0x03ce,(unsigned char)4);
1137          outportb(0x03cf,(unsigned char)2);
1138       #endif
1139       movedata(0xa000,0x0000,Seg3,Off3,Plane_Length);
1140       #if defined (MICROSOFT)
1141          outp(0x3ce,4);outp(0x3cf,3);
1142       #elif defined (ZORTECH)
1143          outp(0x3ce,4);outp(0x3cf,3);
1144       #elif defined (BORLAND)
1145          outportb(0x03ce,(unsigned char)4);
1146          outportb(0x03cf,(unsigned char)3);
1147       #endif
1148       movedata(0xa000,0x0000,Seg4,Off4,Plane_Length);
1149       #if defined (MICROSOFT)
```

```
1150          outp(0x3ce,4);outp(0x3cf,0);
1151        #elif defined (ZORTECH)
1152          outp(0x3ce,4);outp(0x3cf,0);
1153        #elif defined (BORLAND)
1154          outportb(0x03ce,(unsigned char)4);
1155          outportb(0x03cf,(unsigned char)0);
1156        #endif
1157        break;
1158      case zEGA_10H:                        // EGA 640x350x16-color.
1159        #if defined (MICROSOFT)
1160          outp(0x03ce,0x08);outp(0x03cf,0xff);outp(0x03c4,0x02);
1161          outp(0x03c5,0x0f);outp(0x03ce,0x05);outp(0x03cf,0x01);
1162          movedata(0xa000,0x0000,0xa800,0x0000,Plane_Length);
1163          outp(0x03ce,0x05);outp(0x03cf,0x00);
1164        #elif defined (ZORTECH)
1165          outp(0x03ce,0x08);outp(0x03cf,0xff);outp(0x03c4,0x02);
1166          outp(0x03c5,0x0f);outp(0x03ce,0x05);outp(0x03cf,0x01);
1167          movedata(0xa000,0x0000,0xa800,0x0000,Plane_Length);
1168          outp(0x03ce,0x05);outp(0x03cf,0x00);
1169        #elif defined (BORLAND)
1170          outportb(0x03ce,(unsigned char)4);
1171          outportb(0x03cf,(unsigned char)0);
1172          outportb(0x03c4,(unsigned char)2);
1173          outportb(0x03c5,(unsigned char)1);
1174          movedata(0xa000,0x0000,0xa800,0x0000,Plane_Length);
1175          outportb(0x03ce,(unsigned char)4);
1176          outportb(0x03cf,(unsigned char)1);
1177          outportb(0x03c4,(unsigned char)2);
1178          outportb(0x03c5,(unsigned char)2);
1179          movedata(0xa000,0x0000,0xa800,0x0000,Plane_Length);
1180          outportb(0x03ce,(unsigned char)4);
1181          outportb(0x03cf,(unsigned char)2);
1182          outportb(0x03c4,(unsigned char)2);
1183          outportb(0x03c5,(unsigned char)4);
1184          movedata(0xa000,0x0000,0xa800,0x0000,Plane_Length);
1185          outportb(0x03ce,(unsigned char)4);
1186          outportb(0x03cf,(unsigned char)3);
1187          outportb(0x03c4,(unsigned char)2);
1188          outportb(0x03c5,(unsigned char)8);
1189          movedata(0xa000,0x0000,0xa800,0x0000,Plane_Length);
1190          outportb(0x03ce,(unsigned char)4);
1191          outportb(0x03cf,(unsigned char)0);
1192          outportb(0x03c4,(unsigned char)2);
1193          outportb(0x03c5,(unsigned char)15);
1194        #endif
1195        break;
1196      case zEGA_EH:                         // EGA 640x200x16-color.
1197        #if defined (MICROSOFT)
1198          outp(0x03ce,0x08);outp(0x03cf,0xff);outp(0x03c4,0x02);
1199          outp(0x03c5,0x0f);outp(0x03ce,0x05);outp(0x03cf,0x01);
1200          movedata(0xa000,0x0000,0xa400,0x0000,Plane_Length);
1201          outp(0x03ce,0x05);outp(0x03cf,0x00);
1202        #elif defined (ZORTECH)
1203          outp(0x03ce,0x08);outp(0x03cf,0xff);outp(0x03c4,0x02);
1204          outp(0x03c5,0x0f);outp(0x03ce,0x05);outp(0x03cf,0x01);
1205          movedata(0xa000,0x0000,0xa400,0x0000,Plane_Length);
1206          outp(0x03ce,0x05);outp(0x03cf,0x00);
1207        #elif defined (BORLAND)
1208          outportb(0x03ce,(unsigned char)4);
1209          outportb(0x03cf,(unsigned char)0);
1210          outportb(0x03c4,(unsigned char)2);
1211          outportb(0x03c5,(unsigned char)1);
```

```
1212            movedata(0xa000,0x0000,0xa400,0x0000,Plane_Length);
1213            outportb(0x03ce,(unsigned char)4);
1214            outportb(0x03cf,(unsigned char)1);
1215            outportb(0x03c4,(unsigned char)2);
1216            outportb(0x03c5,(unsigned char)2);
1217            movedata(0xa000,0x0000,0xa400,0x0000,Plane_Length);
1218            outportb(0x03ce,(unsigned char)4);
1219            outportb(0x03cf,(unsigned char)2);
1220            outportb(0x03c4,(unsigned char)2);
1221            outportb(0x03c5,(unsigned char)4);
1222            movedata(0xa000,0x0000,0xa400,0x0000,Plane_Length);
1223            outportb(0x03ce,(unsigned char)4);
1224            outportb(0x03cf,(unsigned char)3);
1225            outportb(0x03c4,(unsigned char)2);
1226            outportb(0x03c5,(unsigned char)8);
1227            movedata(0xa000,0x0000,0xa400,0x0000,Plane_Length);
1228            outportb(0x03ce,(unsigned char)4);
1229            outportb(0x03cf,(unsigned char)0);
1230            outportb(0x03c4,(unsigned char)2);
1231            outportb(0x03c5,(unsigned char)15);
1232         #endif
1233         break;
1234   case zMCGA_11H: movedata(0xa000,0x0000,Seg1,Off1,Plane_Length);
1235                break;                     // MCGA 640x480x2-color.
1236   case zCGA_6H: movedata(0xb800,0x0000,Seg1,Off1,Plane_Length);
1237                break;                     // CGA 640x200x2-color.
1238   case zHERC: movedata(0xb000,0x0000,0xb800,0x0000,Plane_Length);
1239                break;                     // Herc 720x348x2-color.
1240   }
1241   return;
1242   }
1243
1244
1245   void PhysicalDisplay::Restore(void)
1246   {                        // copy the hidden page to graphics page 0.
1247   switch(ScreenMode)
1248   {
1249   case zVGA_12H:                       // VGA 640x480x16-color.
1250         #if defined (MICROSOFT)
1251            outp(0x3c4,2);outp(0x3c5,1);
1252         #elif defined (ZORTECH)
1253            outp(0x3c4,2);outp(0x3c5,1);
1254         #elif defined (BORLAND)
1255            outportb(0x03c4,(unsigned char)2);
1256            outportb(0x03c5,(unsigned char)1);
1257         #endif
1258         movedata(Seg1,Off1,0xa000,0x0000,Plane_Length);
1259         #if defined (MICROSOFT)
1260            outp(0x3c4,2);outp(0x3c5,2);
1261         #elif defined (ZORTECH)
1262            outp(0x3c4,2);outp(0x3c5,2);
1263         #elif defined (BORLAND)
1264            outportb(0x03c4,(unsigned char)2);
1265            outportb(0x03c5,(unsigned char)2);
1266         #endif
1267         movedata(Seg2,Off2,0xa000,0x0000,Plane_Length);
1268         #if defined (MICROSOFT)
1269            outp(0x3c4,2);outp(0x3c5,4);
1270         #elif defined (ZORTECH)
1271            outp(0x3c4,2);outp(0x3c5,4);
1272         #elif defined (BORLAND)
1273            outportb(0x03c4,(unsigned char)2);
1274            outportb(0x03c5,(unsigned char)4);
```

```
1275        #endif
1276        movedata(Seg3,Off3,0xa000,0x0000,Plane_Length);
1277        #if defined (MICROSOFT)
1278          outp(0x3c4,2);outp(0x3c5,8);
1279        #elif defined (ZORTECH)
1280          outp(0x3c4,2);outp(0x3c5,8);

1281        #elif defined (BORLAND)
1282          outportb(0x03c4,(unsigned char)2);
1283          outportb(0x03c5,(unsigned char)8);
1284        #endif
1285        movedata(Seg4,Off4,0xa000,0x0000,Plane_Length);
1286        #if defined (MICROSOFT)
1287          outp(0x3c4,2);outp(0x3c5,0xf);
1288        #elif defined (ZORTECH)
1289          outp(0x3c4,2);outp(0x3c5,0xf);
1290        #elif defined (BORLAND)
1291          outportb(0x03c4,(unsigned char)2);
1292          outportb(0x03c5,(unsigned char)15);
1293        #endif
1294        break;
1295    case zEGA_10H:                               // 640x350x16-color.
1296        #if defined (MICROSOFT)
1297          outp(0x03ce,0x08);outp(0x03cf,0xff);outp(0x03c4,0x02);
1298          outp(0x03c5,0x0f);outp(0x03ce,0x05);outp(0x03cf,0x01);
1299          movedata(0xa800,0x0000,0xa000,0x0000,Plane_Length);
1300          outp(0x03ce,0x05);outp(0x03cf,0x00);
1301        #elif defined (ZORTECH)
1302          outp(0x03ce,0x08);outp(0x03cf,0xff);outp(0x03c4,0x02);
1303          outp(0x03c5,0x0f);outp(0x03ce,0x05);outp(0x03cf,0x01);
1304          movedata(0xa800,0x0000,0xa000,0x0000,Plane_Length);
1305          outp(0x03ce,0x05);outp(0x03cf,0x00);
1306        #elif defined (BORLAND)
1307          outportb(0x03ce,(unsigned char)4);
1308          outportb(0x03cf,(unsigned char)0);
1309          outportb(0x03c4,(unsigned char)2);
1310          outportb(0x03c5,(unsigned char)1);
1311          movedata(0xa800,0x0000,0xa000,0x0000,Plane_Length);
1312          outportb(0x03ce,(unsigned char)4);
1313          outportb(0x03cf,(unsigned char)1);
1314          outportb(0x03c4,(unsigned char)2);
1315          outportb(0x03c5,(unsigned char)2);
1316          movedata(0xa800,0x0000,0xa000,0x0000,Plane_Length);
1317          outportb(0x03ce,(unsigned char)4);
1318          outportb(0x03cf,(unsigned char)2);
1319          outportb(0x03c4,(unsigned char)2);
1320          outportb(0x03c5,(unsigned char)4);
1321          movedata(0xa800,0x0000,0xa000,0x0000,Plane_Length);
1322          outportb(0x03ce,(unsigned char)4);
1323          outportb(0x03cf,(unsigned char)3);
1324          outportb(0x03c4,(unsigned char)2);
1325          outportb(0x03c5,(unsigned char)8);
1326          movedata(0xa800,0x0000,0xa000,0x0000,Plane_Length);
1327          outportb(0x03ce,(unsigned char)4);
1328          outportb(0x03cf,(unsigned char)0);
1329          outportb(0x03c4,(unsigned char)2);
1330          outportb(0x03c5,(unsigned char)15);
1331        #endif
1332        break;
1333    case zEGA_EH:                                // 640x200x16-color.
1334        #if defined (MICROSOFT)
1335          outp(0x03ce,0x08);outp(0x03cf,0xff);outp(0x03c4,0x02);
1336          outp(0x03c5,0x0f);outp(0x03ce,0x05);outp(0x03cf,0x01);
```

```
1337            movedata(0xa400,0x0000,0xa000,0x0000,Plane_Length);
1338            outp(0x03ce,0x05);outp(0x03cf,0x00);
1339         #elif defined (ZORTECH)
1340            outp(0x03ce,0x08);outp(0x03cf,0xff);outp(0x03c4,0x02);
1341            outp(0x03c5,0x0f);outp(0x03ce,0x05);outp(0x03cf,0x01);
1342            movedata(0xa400,0x0000,0xa000,0x0000,Plane_Length);
1343            outp(0x03ce,0x05);outp(0x03cf,0x00);
1344         #elif defined (BORLAND)
1345            outportb(0x03ce,(unsigned char)4);
1346            outportb(0x03cf,(unsigned char)0);
1347            outportb(0x03c4,(unsigned char)2);
1348            outportb(0x03c5,(unsigned char)1);
1349            movedata(0xa400,0x0000,0xa000,0x0000,Plane_Length);
1350            outportb(0x03ce,(unsigned char)4);
1351            outportb(0x03cf,(unsigned char)1);
1352            outportb(0x03c4,(unsigned char)2);
1353            outportb(0x03c5,(unsigned char)2);
1354            movedata(0xa400,0x0000,0xa000,0x0000,Plane_Length);
1355            outportb(0x03ce,(unsigned char)4);
1356            outportb(0x03cf,(unsigned char)2);
1357            outportb(0x03c4,(unsigned char)2);
1358            outportb(0x03c5,(unsigned char)4);
1359            movedata(0xa400,0x0000,0xa000,0x0000,Plane_Length);
1360            outportb(0x03ce,(unsigned char)4);
1361            outportb(0x03cf,(unsigned char)3);
1362            outportb(0x03c4,(unsigned char)2);
1363            outportb(0x03c5,(unsigned char)8);
1364            movedata(0xa400,0x0000,0xa000,0x0000,Plane_Length);
1365            outportb(0x03ce,(unsigned char)4);
1366            outportb(0x03cf,(unsigned char)0);
1367            outportb(0x03c4,(unsigned char)2);
1368            outportb(0x03c5,(unsigned char)15);
1369         #endif
1370         break;
1371     case zMCGA_11H: movedata(Seg1,Off1,0xa000,0x0000,Plane_Length);
1372                 break;                    // MCGA 640x480x2-color.
1373     case zCGA_6H: movedata(Seg1,Off1,0xb800,0x0000,Plane_Length);
1374                 break;                    // CGA 640x200x2-color.
1375     case zHERC: movedata(0xb800,0x0000,0xb000,0x0000,Plane_Length);
1376                 break;                    // Herc 720x348x2-color.
1377     }
1378     return;
1379     }
1380     /*
1381
1382     ┌─────────────────────────────────────────────────────────────┐
            │     End of LIB2DBC.CPP graphics library language bindings.    │
1383        └─────────────────────────────────────────────────────────────┘
1384                                                                   */
```

E-17 Source code for MOUSEBC.HPP, the declaration file for class PointingDevice for use with Borland C++, providing low-level input control for a mouse.

```
0001   /*
0002
0003   ┌─────────────────────────────────────────────────────────────┐
        │            Lee Adams' SUPERCHARGED C++ GRAPHICS               │
0004    │            Header file for class PointingDevice               │
0005    ├─────────────────────────────────────────────────────────────┤
0006    │  SOURCE FILE:  MOUSEBC.HPP                For Borland C++ 2.0  │
0007    │        TYPE:   include file for class PointingDevice.         │
0008    ├─────────────────────────────────────────────────────────────┤
0009    │  PointingDevice class:  PROGRAMMER'S GUIDE TO THE INTERFACE   │
```

```
0010      Detect()........ determines if a mouse is present and
0011                         initializes it if present.
0012      Data()......... returns a pointer to the struct that
0013                         holds runtime data about the mouse.
0014      Show()......... displays the mouse cursor.
0015      Hide()......... hides the mouse cursor.
0016      Pos().......... resets the xy location of the mouse.
0017      Info()......... fetches information about the status
0018                         of the mouse button and the current
0019                         xy coordinates of the mouse cursor.
0020      HLimit()....... sets the minimum and maximum horizontal
0021                         range of the mouse cursor.
0022      VLimit()....... sets the minimum and maximum vertical
0023                         range of the mouse cursor.
0024   Class declarations are located in MOUSEBC.HPP (which must be
0025      used in your program as #include "MOUSEBC.HPP").
0026   Function definitions are located in MOUSE.CPP (which uses
0027      the #include file dos.h).  Either MOUSE.CPP or MOUSE.OBJ
0028      must be named in the project list for your program.
0029
0030   LICENSE:  As purchaser of the book in which this source code
0031      appears you are granted a royalty-free license to reproduce
0032      and distribute executable files generated using this code
0033      provided that you accept the conditions of the License
0034      Agreement and Limited Warranty described in the book.
0035   PUBLICATION: Contains material from Windcrest/McGraw-Hill
0036      book 3489, published by TAB BOOKS.
0037   U.S. GOVERNMENT RESTRICTED RIGHTS:  This software and its
0038      documentation is provided with restricted rights.  The use,
0039      duplication, or disclosure by the Government is subject to
0040      restrictions set forth in subdivision (b)(3)(ii) of The
0041      Rights in Technical Data and Computer Software clause at
0042      252.227-7013.  Contractor/manufacturer is Lee Adams, c/o
0043      TAB BOOKS, 13311 Monterey Ave., Blue Ridge Summit PA 17294.
0044   TRADEMARK:  Lee Adams is a trademark of Lee Adams.
0045
0046      Copyright 1991 Lee Adams.  All rights reserved worldwide.
0047
0048                                                             */
0049   #ifndef MOUSE_HPP          // ensure this file is included only once.
0050   #define MOUSE_HPP
0051
0052   class PointingDevice                      // class declarations.
0053   {
0054   private:              // can be accessed by member functions only.
0055     struct mdata          // will contain runtime info about mouse.
0056       {
0057         int MouseFlag;        // indicates if a mouse is installed.
0058         int MouseButton;      // indicates if mouse button pressed.
0059         int MouseX;                     // current x coordinate.
0060         int MouseY;                     // current y coordinate.
0061         int MouseMinX;        // minimum allowable x coordinate.
0062         int MouseMaxX;        // maximum allowable x coordinate.
0063         int MouseMinY;        // minimum allowable y coordinate.
0064         int MouseMaxY;        // maximum allowable y coordinate.
0065       } MouseParams;          // the name of the struct variable.
0066     int MouseObjectReady;     // indicates if object initialized.
0067     void Init(void);          // low-level initialization of driver.
0068
0069   public:              // can be accessed by any in-scope function.
0070     PointingDevice();                             // constructor.
0071     ~PointingDevice();                            // destructor.
```

```
0072    int Detect(int);                              // initialize if found.
0073    mdata * Data(void);                           // returns ptr to struct.
0074    void Show(void);                              // displays cursor.
0075    void Hide(void);                              // hides cursor.
0076    void Pos(int,int);                            // sets xy coords.
0077    void Info(void);            // checks button status and xy position.
0078    void HLimit(int,int);                         // sets horiz range.
0079    void VLimit(int,int);                         // sets vert range.
0080
0081    #if defined (BORLAND)
0082      union REGS regs;                   // for register contents.
0083    #elif defined (ZORTECH)
0084      union REGS inregs,outregs;
0085    #elif defined (MICROSOFT)
0086      union REGS inregs,outregs;
0087    #endif
0088  };
0089
0090  #endif                                          // MOUSE_HPP.
0091  /*
0092
0093  ┌─────────────────────────────────────────────────────────────────┐
       │   Supercharged C++ Graphics  --  end of source file MOUSEBC.HPP   │
0094   └─────────────────────────────────────────────────────────────────┘
0095                                                                  */
```

F
Using other graphics libraries

An increasing number of professional third-party graphics libraries explicitly support C++ compilers. When this book went to press, HALO Professional 2.0 and MetaWINDOW 3.7b provided graphics support for Zortech C++ and Turbo C++. Both libraries are world-class products that deserve your attention if you are planning to migrate to a third-party graphics library.

As FIG. F-1 shows, adapting the demonstration programs in the book to call the routines of either HALO Professional or MetaWINDOW is not an unreasonably difficult task.

MetaWINDOW 3.7b

Here are some points to consider when converting the program listings in the book to run with MetaWINDOW 3.7b or MetaWINDOW/Plus 3.7b. In the interests of clarity, both products are referred to as MetaWINDOW in this appendix.

The documentation for MetaWINDOW is very well presented. If you are already familiar with the library, the only reference you will likely need while adapting the program listings is FIG. F-1. MetaWINDOW/Plus is a superset of MetaWINDOW. Be sure to check the features list for each edition carefully before you begin your programming project.

Initializing the graphics mode

MetaWINDOW offers broad support for graphics adapters, including SuperVGA modes and graphics coprocessors. The InitGrafix() function, for example, permits initialization of the standard VGA, EGA, MCGA, CGA, and Hercules modes supported by Turbo C++, Borland C++, and Zortech C++.

The InitGrafix() function returns 0 if successful and a negative value if unsuccessful. You can employ the same autodetect algorithm used in the

Class Methods Used in Demo Programs	Meta Window 3.7b	HALO Professional 1.0
Class Physical Display		
Init2D( )	[use compiler]	[use compiler]
SetupMode( )	InitGrafix( )	setdev( ) initgraphics ( )
ForceMode ( )	SetDisplay( )	setdev( ) initgraphics( )
ShutdownGraphics ( )	SetDisplay( )	closegraphics( )
SetHue( )	PenColor( )	setcolor( )
SetWriteMode ( )	PenMode( )	setxor( )
SetRGB( ) .	WritePalette( )	setcpal( ) reppal( )
SetLine( )	DefineDash( )	deflnstyle( ) setlnstyle( )
SetFill( )	DefinePattern( )	deflhatchstyle( ) sethatchstyle( )
BackUp( )	[use compiler]	imsave( )
Restore( )	[use compiler]	imrest( )
InitUndo( )	[use compiler]	[use compiler]
SetWritePage( )	SetBitmap( )	setscreen( )
SetDisplayPage( )	SetDisplay( )	display( )
BlankPage( )	EraseRect( )	clr( ) fclr( )
InitHiddenPage( )	[use compiler]	[use compiler]
FreeMemory ( )	[use compiler]	[use compiler]
Class Viewport		
SetPosition( )	MoveTo( )	movabs( )
DrawLine( )	LineTo( )	inabs( )
DrawBorder( )	FrameRect( )	box( )
DrawPanel( )	PaintRect( )	bar( )
DrawPolygon( )	FramePoly( )	polylnabs( )
DrawFacet( )	FillPoly( ) PaintPoly( )	polyfabs( )
DrawCircle( )	FrameOval( )	cir( )
PutText( )	DrawString( )	ftext( )
SetTextRowCol( )	MoveTo( )	ftlocate( )
ClearTextLine( )	PaintRect( )	bar( )
Fill( )	FillPoly( ) PaintPoly( )	flood2( ) fill( )
MemBlock( )	ImageSize( )	inqpflen( )
FreeBlock( )	[use compiler]	[use compiler]
GetBlock( )	ReadImage( )	movefrom( )
PutXOR( )	WriteImage( )	moveto( )
Put PSET( )	WriteImage( )	moveto( )
PutAND( )	WriteImage( )	moveto( )
GetBlockSize( )	ImageSize( )	inqflen( )
WindowOpen( )	MovePortTo( ) Portsize( )	setviewport( )
WindowClose( )	MovePortTo( ) Portsize( )	setviewport( )
WindowClear( )	EraseRect( )	clr( )
Notes:		
Media Cybernetics' Halo Professional 1.0 supports Zortech C++		
Metagraphics' MetaWINDOW 3.7b supports Zortech C++ and Turbo C++		

F-1 Comparison of graphics syntax for purposes of illustration only. Refer to each manufacturer's current literature for up-to-date specifications.

LIB2D.CPP class implementation listing in appendix E to support an impressive range of graphics hardware.

Line drawing

MetaWINDOW uses the MoveTo() function to reposition the current drawing position. This corresponds to the generic graphics routine SetPosition() in the program listings. Turbo C++ and Borland C++ use moveto().

MetaWINDOW's LineTo() function operates the same as the generic graphics routine zDrawLine() in this book. This maps to the lineto() of Turbo C++ and Borland C++.

The color of the line must be set in advance by a call to MetaWINDOW's PenColor() function. The line will be drawn in a style defined by the Define-Dash() function and activated by the PenDash() procedure. Refer to the user's manual for a listing of seven built-in line styles available to the PenDash() function. You use DefineDash() to redefine one of these default styles to a pattern of your own design.

Advanced line drawing

A major advantage offered by MetaWINDOW is its ability to draw lines using Boolean logic. Rather than merely drawing a line, you can change the graphics state by a call to RasterOp() and tell MetaWINDOW to exclusive-or, replace, or invert the pixels being written. This has significant performance advantages for managing your own cursors in both 2-D and 3-D applications.

Creating fill patterns

MetaWINDOW offers 32 built-in fill patterns, illustrated in the user's manual. The first eight patterns (0 through 7) are reserved for the library, but the remaining 24 styles can be redefined by the programmer by calling the procedure, DefinePattern(). Like Turbo C++ and Borland C++, patterns are defined by an 8×8 matrix, although MetaWINDOW offers a few more bells and whistles for the advanced C++ programmer.

The area fill routines provided in the MetaWINDOW toolkit are nondestructive, like those of Microsoft's graphics library, graph.lib. This means that you can layer colors and patterns on top of each other to create interesting cumulative effects.

Area fill

The two fill functions offered by MetaWINDOW are FillPoly() and PaintPoly(). They use an array of polygon vertices to control the filling operation.

Blanking the screen

Although other methods are available, the function which provides the most precise control is EraseRect(). This corresponds to the cleardevice() procedure in Turbo C++ and Borland C++.

Bitblt operations: Manipulating arrays

MetaWINDOW's array manipulators are well designed and do not pose any difficulties. ReadImage() and WriteImage() are used to save a portion of the screen to an array and to write an array to the screen, respectively. The arguments to WriteImage() control the Boolean logic during the write process. Like Turbo C++ and Borland C++, MetaWINDOW offers an ImageSize() function to calculate the size of the array required to store the rectangular image being stored, although you are still responsible for using your compiler to explicitly initialize the memory block to hold the array data.

Hidden page operations

The routines used in the program listings in the book will work with MetaWIN-DOW. The movedata() function of Turbo C++, Borland C++, and Zortech C++ is still the method to be used.

Image save/load operations

The routines provided in the program listings in the book will work with Meta-WINDOW. The movedata() function of Turbo C++, Borland C++, and Zortech C++ gets the job done.

Active page operations

To set the active, written-to graphics page, use MetaWINDOW's SetBitmap() function. To set the display page, use the SetDisplay() procedure. It is important to note that MetaWINDOW supports two graphics pages, defined by the arguments GrafPg0 and GrafPg1.

Viewports

MetaWINDOW possesses advanced viewport and windowing operations, far surpassing the routines used in the demonstration programs in this book. A familiarity with the advanced features offered by MetaWINDOW's Move-PortTo(), PortSize(), and other procedures will enhance your original programs. MetaWINDOW's MovePortTo() and PortSize() roughly correspond to the generic graphics routines WindowOpen() and WindowClose() used in the program listings in this book.

Vector fonts

MetaWINDOW offers impressive stroked font capabilities. In addition, a separately available option called MetaFONTS can be purchased for even more versatility and power. SetFont() is used to select the active text style. TextFace() chooses normal, bold, italic, underline, strikeout, proportional spacing, and other flashy parameters. TextMode() sets the Boolean operation to control the writing operation, including replace, overlay, invert, and erase. TextPath() controls the writing direction: left to right, right to left, up to down, or down to up.

Text is actually placed on the screen by the DrawString() function and the DrawChar() procedure.

The working environment

MetaWINDOW and MetaWINDOW/Plus can be used either as a TSR, as a shell to invoke your program, as linked-in functions, or as a CONFIG.SYS device driver. The MetaWINDOW driver can also be installed in high memory if RAM is critical to your application.

Metagraphics Software Corporation provides to purchasers of their libraries the royalty-free right to distribute the runtime driver with the programmer's application program. If you prefer to link the graphics library routines into your finished .exe file, then you must enter into a separate licensing agreement with Metagraphics.

Other noteworthy features

MetaWINDOW provides an impressive selection of zoombit procedures. This gives you the ability to enlarge portions of the screen. MetaWINDOW also provides object selection and object proximity capabilities. Your program can tell if a point is near an on-screen entity.

MetaWINDOW can be reconfigured to support a custom display buffer and virtual buffers in RAM. This means you can write programs which nominally support an infinite variety of graphics adapters and modes, in addition to the hardware already supported by the MetaWINDOW and MetaWINDOW/Plus libraries.

The MetaWINDOW/Plus variant of the graphics library supports DOS extenders, allowing your C++ graphics application to use memory above the 640K DOS limit.

HALO Professional 2.0

Here are some factors to consider when converting the program listings in the book to run with HALO Professional. See FIG. F-1. If you are already familiar with HALO Professional's excellent documentation, the only additional reference you will likely need while adapting the program listings is FIG. F-1.

Initializing the graphics mode

HALO Professional's initgraphics() function is used to set up the graphics mode, much like the initgraph() function of Turbo C++ and Borland C++ and the fg_init() function of Zortech C++. It is important to realize, however, that you must explicitly load the graphics driver for the particular adapter and mode you are using by calling the setdev() procedure.

Use the inqerr() function to see if the initgraphics() procedure has been successful or not. A return value of 0 indicates success.

Line drawing

HALO Professional's lnabs() function draws a line from the current position to a set of absolute xy coordinates using the current line attributes. This function is comparable to the lineto() function of Turbo C++ and Borland C++. The color of the line is set via the setcolor() function. The line style is defined by calling setlinestyle() and deflnstyle(). The zSetPosition() generic library-independent routine used in the LIB2D.CPP class implementation listing in appendix E corresponds to HALO Professional's movabs() function.

Advanced line drawing

Most graphics drawn with HALO Professional can be overwritten or XOR'd onto the screen by a preparatory call to the setxor() function. In addition, a specialized rubberbanding algorithm can be used with lines, boxes, circles, and a built-in crosshair cursor.

Creating fill patterns

HALO Professional's defhatchstyle() function is used to define a fill pattern. Five patterns can be defined. Another five default patterns are provided by the library. A call to sethatchstyle() makes a particular pattern current. HALO Professional's algorithms permit you to vary the size of the pattern matrix, unlike the fixed 8×8 matrix size of Turbo C++ and Borland C++.

Area fill

HALO Professional offers a number of functions to provide area fill capabilities. HALO Professional's flood2() function and fill() function operate similar to the floodfill functions of Turbo C++ and Borland C++. Patterns, including user-defined patterns, are supported. HALO Professional's algorithm uses a nondestructive approach similar to Microsoft's graphics library, graph.lib, meaning that different colors and patterns can be overlaid to produce an almost infinite variety of shades.

Blanking the screen

The zBlankPage() generic function used in LIB2D.CPP in appendix E can be mapped to HALO Professional's clr() and fclr() procedures. You should note that clr() will blank only the current viewport, while fclr() will always blank the entire screen.

Bitblt operations: Manipulating arrays

Versatile routines to capture and display graphic arrays are provided by HALO Professional. To store a portion of the display screen in an array, use the move-from() function. To display a previously saved graphic array, use the moveto() procedure. The moveto() function provides Boolean logic capabilities, similar to the capabilities of the putimage() function of Turbo C++ and Borland C++.

HALO Professional's inqpflen() function is useful for determining how much memory is required to store a graphic array. This corresponds to the imagesize() function of Turbo C++ and Borland C++.

Hidden page operations

The zBackUp() library-independent routine used in the class library LIB2D.CPP in this book can be replaced by HALO Professional's imsave() function, which will move a graphics page to a specified address in RAM. The zRestore() library-independent routine used in LIB2D.CPP can be replaced by HALO Professional's imrest() function. These two powerful routines can take the place of the movedata() functions necessary when Turbo C++ and Borland C++ are being used.

Image save/load operations

HALO Professional offers a good set of image save and load routines. The gwrite() function can be used to save an image to disk. The gread() procedure will load a previously saved image from disk. These two functions will always save/load the entire screen. The files written or read are binary images, which are device-dependent.

Active page operations

HALO Professional's setscreen() function is the same as the setactivepage() function in Turbo C++ and Borland C++ and the fg_setactivepage() function in Zortech C++. HALO Professional's display() procedure is similar to the setvisualpage() function of Turbo C++ and Borland C++ and the fg_setdisplay-page() function of Zortech C++.

Viewports

HALO Professional's setviewport() function is similar to the setviewport() function of Turbo C++ and Borland C++. This single function can be used to match the zWindowOpen() and zWindowClose() generic routines used in the LIB2D.CPP class implementation listing in appendix E.

Fonts

In addition to normal and fast bitmapped fonts, as well as proportionally spaced fonts, HALO Professional offers vector font capabilities. HALO Professional's vector font output includes scaling, proportional spacing, rotating, slant, and more. The .FNT font files included with the library include standard-sized bitmapped fonts called small dot text by HALO Professional, oversized bitmapped fonts called large dot text, and vector fonts called stroke text.

Vector fonts displayed by HALO Professional use the current line style and line width settings.

The HALO Professional package also provides font editors for both bitmapped and stroke text. The font editors can be used to create special symbols and icons.

The working environment

Routines from the HALO Professional graphics toolkit are linked into your applications program. HALO Professional routines expect to receive the address, not a copy of the value, of any arguments being passed by the caller. Two-byte integer values and four-byte single-precision real numbers are used.

The single-site license provided to you when you purchase the HALO Professional graphics toolkit gives you the right to use the HALO Professional routines on a single computer. Contact Media Cybernetics to arrange an additional license for distribution of the routines as part of your finished application program.

Other noteworthy features

HALO Professional's superb list of specialized features includes support for scanners, plotters, and printers, as well as a comprehensive list of supported graphics adapters, including high end graphics boards like the AT&T Image Capture Board, TARGA boards, the Number Nine Revolution boards and Pepper boards, the IBM Professional Graphics Adapter, and others. The HALO Professional library also supports all the standard VGA, EGA, MCGA, CGA, and Hercules graphics modes.

HALO Professional provides an impressive array of procedures to move graphics data, including a memcom( ) routine that compresses graphics data and a memexp( ) function to restore previously compressed data. Mouse control routines are also supplied (called locators by Media Cybernetics).

HALO Professional will also save an image to disk as a binary image, and will load a previously saved image from disk. A screen image can also be printed on a variety of printers. Any viewport can be scaled to any printed size. HALO Professional supports 256 shades on all black-and-white printers. Color printing support is also extensive.

HALO Professional provides comprehensive support for DOS extenders from Rational systems, Phar Lap, and Ergo, allowing your graphics application to take advantage of system memory past the 640K limit.

Also included with the compiler package is Dr. Proto, an interactive utility that generates source code for images you draw.

G
Trapping runtime errors:
A tutorial

The demonstration program listings and class libraries in the book lack the robust error-handling capabilities required of commercial software. A finished software product must be capable of graceful recovery from numerous runtime errors, including open drive doors, attempting to write to a nonexistent directory, math overflow, and others.

In order to compete successfully in today's competitive worldwide market, your C++ software must be intelligent enough to gently forgive users' oversights like open drive doors, disks filled to capacity, missing files, and nonexistent directories. An application program that locks up the computer when it encounters an everyday situation like this is the calling card of a rank amateur.

Exception handling

Error trapping is nothing more than exception handling. An exception is a condition that your program encounters at runtime that does not fit the norm. An exception-handling algorithm involves two steps. These steps are detection and recovery.

You can use a variety of detection procedures, including the built-in features of the C++ compiler and your own trapping routines.

The action that your application takes after detecting an error is up to you. Your alternatives range from complete system shutdown for fatal nonrecoverable errors, to simply ignoring the problem for trivial errors.

Testing

Like other algorithms in your code, you should rigorously test your error-handler routines before you distribute your program. Some of the common runtime error conditions are division by zero, math overflow, disk drive door open, insufficient space on disk, file not found, illegal drive letter or nonexistent directory, and mouse not found.

When you are building your error-handler, you should force your program to encounter each of these conditions. By simulating every anticipated runtime condition in a controlled environment, you will be reasonably confident that your error-handler is robust enough for the marketplace.

Detection of runtime errors

Before you can handle a runtime error, you must be able to detect it in the first place. And there are plenty of snares for the unwary programmer. Your code must be capable of detecting different classes of runtime errors, including user mistakes, math errors, disk and file errors, I/O hardware errors, and others.

Error detection technique 1

 Use the value returned by the runtime library function to determine if an error has occurred. The following code fragment shows how you can use Turbo C++ and Borland C++ to determine if a particular file exists.

```
if (( access("filename.ext", 0) ) = = −1 )
    {
    cout < <  "\n\rFile does not exist!";
    }
```

You can also use Zortech C++ to determine if a file exists by using the following code fragment.

```
if (( access("filename.ext", F_OK) ) = = −1 )
    {
    cout < <  "\n\rFile does not exist!";
    }
```

This method provides a reliable tool for detecting and handling runtime errors, but it has significant limitations. It cannot trap hardware I/O errors such as an open disk drive door. It will not detect an attempt to write a write-protected disk. It cannot detect a disk seek error or a bad FAT. For these types of errors you must use the harderr() function.

Error detection technique 2

 Use the harderr() function provided by Turbo C++ and Borland C++ to detect the error and to branch to an error-handler that you have written. This method will detect and trap many of the hardware errors that might slip past Error Detection Technique 1.

After your error-handler is activated, a call to hardretn() will return program control to the instruction following the statement which caused the error.

The syntax for Turbo C++ and Borland C++ is harderr() and hardretn().

You can inspect the DOS error variable named errval which is passed to your error-handler.

Although there are a number of different ways to exit your error-handling routine, the safest way is by the hardretn() function. This forces a return to the instruction immediately following the one which caused the error. Other methods of exiting your error-handler, such as hardresume() and return(), will simply branch back to the operating system and probably lock the computer.

Error detection technique 3

Use the value returned by the function to detect the occurrence of an error and then check the error code stored in the global system variables named errno and _doserrno to find out the type of error that occurred. The Turbo C++ and Borland C++ Reference Guide provides a list of errno and _doserrno values and their meanings. The Zortech C++ Function Reference provides a list of errno values and their meanings.

Suppose you want to check if a file is read-only. Assume that you have attempted to write data to the file and the write() function returned a value of −1.

```
if(errno = = EACCES)
    {
    // put desired code here.
    }
```

This global system variable method will detect conditions ranging from out-of-memory, to no-such-file-or-directory, to invalid-argument, to permission-denied, and others. It will also detect out-of-range arguments being passed to math functions.

Error detection technique 4

Use the matherr() function to catch different types of math errors at runtime. This method can be used to help your program recover gracefully from math overflow, math underflow, and other conditions.

The matherr() function is called automatically by the C++ compiler's math routines whenever an error condition is encountered. Various information concerning the error is stored in an exception type structure described in the Turbo C++ and Borland C++ manuals. The structure is defined in the header file math.h in the Turbo C++, Borland C++, and Zortech C++ runtime libraries. By inspecting this structure, you can decide upon an appropriate response.

Here is how to use Turbo C++ and Borland C++ to check if a negative value has been improperly passed to the sqrt() function, which expects only positive values as arguments.

```
int matherr(x);
struct exception *x;
```

```
if ( x->type = = DOMAIN )  // if not in legal domain.
    {
    // then do this...
    }
```

Note how the -> notation is used to inspect the type variable in the structure pointed to by x.

Error detection technique 5

You can use assert() to test for a specific logic condition and to shut down the program if the result is false. This method is handy for testing your C++ graphics programs during development. When you are ready to create your finished executable file, you can put the preprocessor directive #define NDEBUG at the beginning of your C++ source code and the compiler will automatically remove all assert() calls before it compiles your code.

Here is how to use Turbo C++, Borland C++, and Zortech C++ to ensure that a particular variable never equals zero at runtime.

```
assert (ThisVariable != 0);  // must not be zero.
```

This statement will detect if ThisVariable equals zero and will immediately shut down the program.

Error reporting

After you have detected an error, you can use the strerror() function to display an appropriate message to the user. By passing the value of the global system variables errno or _doserrno to the strerror() function, your program can print out the official system error message. You can also print your own message if you wish.

Here is how to use Turbo C++ and Borland C++ to print a system error message after you have detected an error at runtime:

```
if (( access ("thisfile.doc", 0) ) = = -1)
    {    // if file does not exist.
    cout < < "\n\r" < < strerror(errno);  // error message.
    }
```

Here is how to use Zortech C++ to print a system error message after you have detected an error at runtime:

```
if (( access ("thisfile.doc", F_OK) ) = = -1)
    {    // if file does not exist.
    cout < < "\n\r" < < strerror(errno);  // error message.
    }
```

The strerror( ) function returns a pointer to a string message, based upon the error number passed to the function. Turbo C++ and Borland C++ support an enhanced version of strerror( ) called _strerror( ), which allows you to add your own gentle message to the terse message returned by the system.

Glossary

abstract class   A C++ class intended as a base class from which other classes will be derived. No object or instance of an abstract class can ever be created.

active page   The graphics buffer to which the graphics routines are writing, also called the written-to page. Not necessarily the same as the page being displayed.

actor   A movable 3-D object in procedural animation and kinetic animation.

additive operators   The + operator and the − operator.

aggregate type   A C or C++ array, structure, or union.

algorithm   A method for solving a problem. See *heuristic*.

alias   One of several names which refer to the same memory location or variable. See *union*. Also refers to the jagged effect or jaggies produced by diagonal or curved lines on monitors with coarse resolution. See *supersampling*.

alphanumeric   A set of characters containing both letters and numbers.

ampersand   The & character.

analog   A signal that varies continuously. A digital signal is either on or off.

analog monitor   A computer monitor capable of displaying colors based upon the infinitely varying intensity of the red, green, and blue guns of the cathode ray tube. A digital monitor usually offers only three intensities: off, normal intensity, and high intensity.

animation   A rapid display of separate images that deceives the human eye into perceiving motion.

anti-aliasing   Software routines which reduce the visual impact of jagged lines on a display monitor. See *CEG*.

area fill   To fill a specified region of the display screen with a specified color or pattern. The attribute surrounding the region to be filled is generally called the boundary.

argc The first argument passed to a C or C++ program at startup by the operating system. The argument argc indicates the number of command-line arguments typed by the user.

argument A value passed to a C function or to a C++ method by the caller. The value received by a function or method is called a parameter.

argument-type list The list of arguments found in a C function prototype or C++ method definition.

arithmetic operator A mathematical operator such as addition (+), multiplication (*), and others.

array A set of data elements of similar type grouped together under a single name, usually arranged in rows and columns. An array can be scalar (consisting of numeric or string data) or graphic (consisting of pixel attributes).

assignment To assign a value to a variable. The C and C++ assignment operator is =. Avoid confusion with the C and C++ equality operator = =. In C and C++, an arithmetic operation can be performed during the assignment process using the + = addition assignment operator, the − = subtraction assignment operator, the * = multiplication assignment operator, the /= division assignment operator, and the % = remainder assignment operator. Other assignment variations include the < < = left-shift assignment operator, the > > = right-shift assignment operator, the &= bitwise-AND assignment operator, and the ^= bitwise-XOR assignment operator.

background color The underlying screen color upon which the graphics are drawn. The background is usually black or white.

backplane removal The elimination of backward-facing facets of convex polyhedra in 3-D scenes.

banner The sign-on message of an application program. The copyright notice usually appears in the banner message.

base class A C++ class from which other classes are derived.

BGI The runtime graphics drivers which are required by executable programs compiled and linked by Turbo C++ and Borland C++. An editor option allows you to build the drivers right into your finished executable file.

binary file A file stored in binary format, as opposed to ASCII character (text) format. See *image file*.

binary operator A C or C++ operator used in binary expressions. Binary operators include multiplicative operators (*,/), additive operators (+,−), shift operators (< <,> >), relational operators (<,>,< =,> =,= =,! =,), bitwise operators (&,|,^), logical operators (&&,||), and the sequential-evaluation operator (,).

BIOS Assembly language routines stored as native machine code in ROM. These routines provide basic input/output services for the operating system and for applications programs which use interrupts to call them. Also called *ROM BIOS*.

bit array A graphic array or bitblt image.

bitblt An acronym for bit boundary block transfer. Also called block graphics and graphic array.

bitblt animation   Graphic array animation.

bitblt image   A graphic array.

bit boundary block transfer   See *bitblt*.

bitmap   An arrangement of bytes in display memory whose bits correspond to the pixels on the display screen.

bitplane   One of four separate buffers which are sandwiched together by the VGA and EGA hardware in order to drive video output. Also called a color plane.

bit tiling   Mixing pixels of different colors to create patterns or shades. Also called halftone, halftoning, patterns, patterning, and dithering.

bitwise operators   &, |, and ^, which compare bits to check for true and false conditions. C's bitwise operators are AND (&), OR (|), and XOR (^). Also see C's logical operators AND (&&), OR (||), and NOT (!).

black box   Refers to a block of code which has been previously tested and debugged and is assumed to operate correctly. The programmer is no longer concerned with the algorithm or processes used by the code, only with the input and output. See *white box*.

black-box testing   Program testing which is concerned with raw input and raw output, not with the inner construction of code. See *white-box testing*.

block   A cohesive sequence of C or C++ statements, instructions, declarations, or definitions which are enclosed within braces { }.

block graphics   Same as graphic array. See *bitblt*.

bound program   A compiled program which can be run under either DOS or OS/2.

bounding box   In 3-D computer graphics, a parallelepiped that encompasses all the vertices of a 3-D model or sub-object; in 2-D computer graphics, a rectangle that surrounds the vertices of an object.

bounding box test   Using the bounding boxes of two objects to determine if a potential conflict exists.

braces   The { } tokens that enclose a block in a C or C++ program. See also parentheses and brackets.

brackets   The [ ] tokens that are used to initialize and access the elements of arrays.

B-rep   Boundary representation, a method of creating images of 3-D models by using planes, polygons, and facets. See *CSG*.

buffer   An area of memory used for temporary storage.

bump mapping   The intentional random displacement of surface normals to simulate a rough surface on a 3-D model.

camera coordinates   The xyz coordinates that describe how a 3-D model will appear to a hypothetical viewer at a given location in the 3-D scene. Also called view coordinates.

caret   The ^ character.

CEG   Continuous edge graphics. A proprietary hardware-based method for improving the resolution of VGA graphics adapters.

cel animation   Computer animation that emulates traditional methods of cel animation, where actors painted on transparent acetate are manipulated in front of static background art.

char A C or C++ variable stored in one byte of memory, capable of representing values from -128 to $+127$. An unsigned char can represent values from 0 to 255. By default, char is signed. A char type is often used to store the integer value of a member of the ASCII alphanumeric character set.

CGM The ANSI computer graphics metafile format for exchanging images between application programs or between computer systems.

CMY model The cyan-magenta-yellow color model used primarily by printers and publishers using offset lithography.

class A C++ data type consisting of data (data members) and the functions (member functions) that operate upon the data.

clipping See *line clipping*.

collision detection Detecting the moment when a vertex or facet of one solid 3-D model conflicts with the space occupied by a vertex or facet plane of another solid 3-D model. Collision response refers to the action taken by the software after collision detection.

color cycling Producing animation by swapping palette values.

color interpolation Determining the color of a pixel from its neighbors or from its distance between two known pixels.

command-line argument A keyword or other parameter passed to the program at startup by the operating system. See *argc*.

computer visualization Using graphics to interpret, manipulate, or create data. Specialized fields of computer visualization include scientific visualization, 3-D modeling and rendering, computer animation, biomedicine, fluid dynamics, tomography, computer vision, image processing, and others.

constant A value in a program which does not change during execution.

constructive solid geometry See *CSG*.

constructor A function automatically called by the compiler whenever an instance of a class is created. See destructor. A constructor can accept arguments but never returns anything.

conventional memory Up to 640K.

coordinate system The arrangement of x-axis and y-axis in a 2-D display or the arrangement of x-axis, y-axis, and z-axis in a 3-D scene.

cosine The cosine of an angle in a right-angle triangle defines the relationship between the hypotenuse and the adjacent side.

.CPP The file name extension usually appended to a C++ implementation file. See *implementation file*.

CPU An acronym for central processing unit, also called the microprocessor. IBM-compatible and DOS-compatible personal computers use Intel 8086, 8088, 80286, 80386, and 80486 microprocessors. Also see the entry for i860.

cross-compiler development software development using different compiler products, such as Borland C++, Turbo C++, and Zortech C++.

CRT A cathode ray tube, the displaying hardware of computer monitors, consisting primarily of the red, green, and blue guns.

CSG Constructive solid geometry, a method of creating images of 3-D models by using primitives such as cubes, cylinders, spheres, and cones. Contrast with B-rep.

declaration The statements that define the name and attributes of a C or C++ variable, function, structure, or class.

declaration file The .HPP file that declares the private, public, and protected members of a class.

decrement To make smaller by a specified number of units.

default A condition which is assumed to exist unless defined otherwise by the user.

default arguments In C++, arguments in a method's parameter list for which the compiler will use a default value if none is provided by the caller at runtime.

definition The actual instructions that comprise a C function or a C++ method.

depth cuing The use of colors or line styles to assist the viewer in interpreting depth in a computer-generated image.

depth sort Ordering the visible facets of a 3-D scene into a sequence which ensures that the modeler draws the facets in farthest-to-nearest order, thereby implementing the painter's algorithm.

destructor A function called by the C++ compiler whenever an object is destroyed or goes out of scope.

development platform The configuration of hardware and software used to build a software product. See *target platform*.

digital A method of representing data whereby the individual components are either fully on or fully off. See *analog*.

digital video interactive A combination of hardware and software methods for combining graphics, video, audio, titling, and other multimedia components into a computer-controlled presentation.

digitize To convert an analog image or signal to a corresponding series of bits and bytes.

display coordinates Screen coordinates. Refers primarily to the converted camera coordinates of a 3-D modeling program.

dither Used in computer rendering. To dither a line is to modify a line using line styling to match the adjacent shading pattern. Has recently come to mean the bit tiling or patterning of pixels used to implement a shading scheme. See *bit tiling*.

do-nothing routine A routine which merely returns control to the caller. Do-nothing routines are used during preliminary program development and debugging. Also called a stub.

double-buffer animation Another name for real-time animation.

DVI An acronym for digital video interactive.

ECD An acronym for enhanced color display. An ECD is a digital display capable of displaying the EGA's 640×350×16-color graphics mode.

EGA An acronym for enhanced graphics adapter.

elegant See *optimize*.

EMB Extended memory blocks.

emulation Simulation of unavailable hardware by available hardware and software.

EMS An acronym for expanded memory, which is used to provide additional physical RAM for computers which are otherwise limited to 640K RAM. Access is through a page manager. See *XMS*.

encapsulation Combining data and the functions that operate upon the data into a C++ class.

enhanced graphics adapter Same as EGA.

ensemble processing An image processing function whereby the content of two different images is compared.

entity A cohesive graphical shape such as a rectangle, circle, or subassembly (as found in a technical drawing). Sometimes called a sub-object.

ergonomics Refers to machine compatibility with human psychology and physiology.

error handler An algorithm or routine used to handle exceptions occurring at runtime.

error trapping Using a programmer-defined routine to detect and respond to errors caused by hardware or software exceptions at runtime.

Euler operators Logical or Boolean operators for the manipulation of 3-D solids. The standard operations are join, intersection, and subtraction.

expanded memory See *EMS*.

expression A combination of operators acting upon variables.

extended memory See *XMS*.

extrusion Stretching or deforming a 3-D object.

facet A polygonal planar surface used to create a solid 3-D model constructed by the B-rep method.

file pointer A variable that indicates the current position of read and write operations on a file. See *stream*.

filtering A method of color interpolation useful for anti-aliasing.

fitted curve A computer-generated curve.

font The design style of a set of alphanumeric characters, expressed either as bitmaps or vectors.

font file A file containing the bitmap data or vector formulas required to generate and display a particular style of alphanumeric characters. Usually required at runtime by C and C++ graphics programs.

force constraints The forces acting upon the actors in a kinetic animation sequence. See also *geometric constraints*.

formatting The general layout of a program listing, including tabs, spaces, indentations, and margins. See the Introduction.

forward dynamics Kinetic animation or kinematics.

Fourier analysis Using rate of change as the discriminating factor to analyze image data.

Fourier window A method of anti-aliasing.

fps An acronym for frames per second, used to measure the display rate of animation programs.

frame   A single image in an animation sequence, usually intended to mean a full-screen image.

frame animation   The rapid display of previously-created graphics images.

frame grab   The act of capturing a graphic image from an external source and storing it in a buffer or on disk.

frames per second   The rate of animation, expressed as new images per second. Also called fps.

free store   In C++, the heap (or free memory).

frequency   The rate of change found by Fourier analysis.

friend   A C++ function or class that can access the private and protected members of another class.

function declaration   Statements that define the name, return type, storage class, and parameter list of a C or C++ function. See *declaration*.

function definition   Statements that define the name, return type, storage class, parameter list, and the executable instructions which comprise a C or C++ function. See *definition*.

function overloading   See *overloaded functions*.

geometric constraints   The dimensional conditions affecting kinetic animation. See also *force constraints*.

geometric model   A mathematical definition of an object.

geometric processing   Image processing functions such as move, copy, shear, stretch.

geometry   A branch of mathematics concerned with the relationship between two triangles possessing similar angles.

global variable   A variable in a C or C++ source file that is available to all functions in that file. A variable that is declared outside of any function is global by default.

gnomon   A visual representation of the xyz axis system in a 3-D CAD program.

Gouraud shading   Smooth shading.

granular   Refers to the size of the smallest linkable element of a library, a set of routines, or collection of data. For most commercially-available libraries the granularity is at the individual function level.

granularity   See *granular*.

graphic array   A rectangular portion of the display buffer which has been saved in RAM as a bit array for later retrieval. Also called a block. See *bitblt*.

graphic array animation   Placing one or more graphic arrays into the display buffer in order to produce animation. Also called bitblt animation and block animation.

graphics driver   A module of executable code designed to interact directly with the graphics hardware.

graphics editor   The interface that allows the user to interactively create and modify computer graphics.

graphics page   An area of RAM containing the data to fill the display screen with graphics. The graphics page might or might not be the same as the display buffer, which is the page being currently displayed.

GUI   An acronym for graphical user interface.

heap   An area in RAM where data is stored. Also called the default data segment. The far heap is free memory otherwise unused by the program, but also available for data storage.

hexadecimal   The base 16 numbering system. The decimal system uses base 10. The base is also called the radix.

hex   Same as hexadecimal. A hexadecimal value is prefixed by the 0x symbol in C and C++ and is followed by the H symbol in assembly language.

HGC   An acronym for the Hercules graphics adapter, capable of displaying two pages in the $720 \times 348 \times 2$-color mode.

hidden line   In graphics programming, a line that should be hidden by another graphic.

hidden page   A graphics page that is not currently being displayed. Also called a buffer.

hidden surface   In graphics modeling, a polygonal plane surface or facet that is hidden by other surfaces.

hidden surface elimination   See *hidden surface removal*.

hidden surface removal   The process of removing from the 3-D scene all surfaces that should be hidden from view. Visible surface algorithms fall into two broad categories: image-space methods and object-space methods.

high memory   The first 64K segment of memory in RAM physically located above 1M on an 80286, 80386, or 80486 microprocessor-equipped computer. Through an addressing idiosyncracy, DOS can access this portion of memory and can use it as a page to access simulated EMS, which is actually located in XMS.

HMA   High memory area.

host graphics engine   The runtime graphics library being used.

.HPP   The file name extension usually appended to a C++ declaration file. See *declaration file*.

HSV model   The hue-saturation-value color model.

i860   An advanced microprocessor from Intel offering 3-D capabilities and z-buffer based hidden surface elimination.

illumination model   A paradigm used to explain the process whereby a 3-D scene is lighted.

image file   A binary file on diskette, hard disk, or virtual disk, that contains a graphic image or the algorithm for recreating the image.

image processing   Analyzing, interpreting, and modifying a digitized image with a computer. Typical applications include photo retouching and enhancement, blur removal, edge detection, geometric processing (stretch, invert, mirror, flop), contrast adjustment, cut and paste, computer vision, morphing and tweening, pattern recognition, target recognition, ensemble processing, and others.

image-space methods   Hidden surface algorithms which are based on the 2-D images of the display screen. See *object-space methods*.

implementation file   The file containing the definitions (source code) for the member methods of a C++ class.

include file   A text file which is logically (but not physically) merged into the user's source code at compile time.

increment   To make larger by a specified number of units.

indirection   Generally, refers to the act of addressing a variable in memory, but specifically refers to the indirection operator (*) which is used in C and C++ to declare a pointer to another variable. See *pointer*.

inheritance   Creating a C++ class (called a derived class) that possesses the characteristics of another class (called a base class).

instance   An occurrence of a graphical entity in a drawing, usually a sub-object in a 3-D scene.

instancing   Creating a complex 2-D or 3-D model by multiple occurrences of the same entity at different locations in the drawing. Also used to mean instantiation. See *instantiation*.

instantiation   Creating an instance or object of a class.

integer   A whole number with no fractional parts or decimal point.

interactive   Responsive to input from the user.

interactive graphics   Software which creates or modifies a graphical display in response to user input.

interop   Abbreviation of interoperability, which refers to the ability of software to operate on and share data across different hardware platforms.

intersection   See *Euler operators*.

join   See *Euler operators*.

keyframe   A significant frame in an animation, tweening, or morphing sequence. Typically, the programmer or the user provides a set of keyframes and the software is expected to provide the in-between images or tweens.

kinematics   The study of motion.

kinetic animation   Computer animation which is managed by algorithms conforming more or less to the laws of physics. See *procedural animation*. See *kinematics*.

kinetic-based animation   Same as kinetic animation.

knowledgebase   A specialized database used by an expert system. A knowledgebase can be created by the user of the expert system during interactive sessions or can be built in advance by the developer of the software. Useful for computer vision and image processing.

lamina   A 3-D plane which can be viewed from either side.

language binding   A module that calls compiler-dependent routines in a graphics library or runtime library.

lens distortion error field   A bitmap schematic that indicates the areas of lens distortion in a video camera attached to a computer.

library   A file that contains modules of object code comprising the functions available for use by the user's C or C++ program.

LIM   An acronym for the Lotus-Intel-Microsoft technical specification for expanded memory hardware and software components.

line clipping   Deletion of a part of a line or graphic which exceeds the physical range of the display screen or viewport.

line styling   Using a series of pixel attributes to generate dotted or dashed lines. Also refers to dithering.

linear interpolation   An algorithm for generating in-between images from keyframes whereby the movement of a vertex is assumed to follow a straight line. See *spline interpolation.*

local variable   Same as static variable. See also *global variable.*

logical operators   && and ||, which perform logical operations on bytes being compared. The && token is used to AND two bytes (the resulting bit will be on only if both the bits being evaluated were on). The || token is used to OR two bytes (the resulting bit will be on if either of the bits being evaluated were on).

mach band   An optical illusion whereby the human eye emphasizes the subtle differences between two adjacent shaded areas.

MCGA   An acronym for multicolor graphics array.

member   A data component or function component of a C++ class. A data component is called a data member. A function component is called a member function or method.

memory-mapped video   An arrangement whereby the bit contents of an area of RAM correspond directly to the pixels on the display screen.

memory model   One of the memory-management schemes used by C and C++ to set up memory space for executable code and addressable data.

merge   To combine two or more disk files, programs, or graphic images. See *overlay.*

message   In C++, calling a method of a class in the name of a particular object of that class.

metafile   In graphics programming, a file that contains the instructions and data necessary to reconstruct an image.

method   A member function of a C++ class.

modeling   Creating a geometric shape which represents a 3D object on the display screen.

module   In C and C++ usually used to mean the block of code contained in a separate source file, but can also mean a logically cohesive block of code which performs a specific function.

morphing   A gradual transformation of a graphics object to a different object. From the term metamorphosis.

motion blur   Image fuzziness caused by the subject moving faster than the refresh rate of the video camera or monitor.

mouse   A hand-held pointing device designed to be rolled across a desktop.

multi-module programming   Using separately compiled source files to build an executable file.

multiplicative operators   The * and / operators, which are multiplication and division.

native code   Executable code which is machine-specific or CPU-specific. See also *op code.*

nested loop   A program loop contained within a larger loop.

normalized coordinates   coordinates that have been expressed in the range − 1 to + 1. Normalized coordinates are device-independent.

nominal compatibility   Arbitrary compatibility, not intended to mean explicit compatibility.

NTSC   A video signal that adheres to the accepted technical standards of the broadcast industry in the United States, Canada, and Mexico: 525 lines refreshed at 30 frames per second. The European PAL standard is 625 lines at 25 fps.

null pointer   A pointer to nothing. See *pointer*.

object   In C++, an instance of a class.

object code   Machine code. A compiler or assembler takes source code (human-readable) and produces object code (machine-readable).

object file   A file containing object code.

object-space methods   Hidden surface algorithms which operate on the 3-D xyz coordinates of a 3-D scene.

objectification   Representing a phenomenon as form, color, texture, motion, and time. See *visualization*.

OEM   Original equipment manufacturer. Refers to manufacturers of computer hardware components and peripherals.

onion skin   A feature provided by animation software, whereby the previous three or four cels can be superimposed over the current cel. See *cel animation*.

online help   A context-sensitive display is available to the user while a program is running. The F1 key has become recognized as the industry standard for activating online help.

OOP   An acronym for object-oriented programming, whereby each independent module contains both executable code and the data upon which it operates.

operand   A constant or a variable that is operated upon by operators in an expression.

optimize   To improve a program's speed of execution or to lessen its memory requirements. A cleverly optimized program is said to be elegant.

overlay   A module of data or executable code that is loaded at runtime from disk into RAM over an existing section of code, thereby replacing the previous code.

overloaded functions   Methods of a C++ class that share the same name but different parameter lists.

page flipping   Using the graphics hardware to select and display a different page from display memory.

painter's algorithm   A method of hidden object removal. See *z-buffer method*.

pan   To move an image to the left or to the right. See *scroll*.

parameter   A value which a function expects to receive when it is called. Also called an argument, although Microsoft makes a distinction between the two.

pipe   The | character.

pixel   An acronym for picture element, called a pel by IBM. A pixel is the smallest addressable graphic on a display screen. In RGB systems, a pixel is comprised of a red dot, a green dot, and a blue dot.

plane equation   A vector formula that describes the qualities of a plane, including the location of a given point relative to the surface of the plane. Plane equations are useful for hidden surface removal.

plane equation test   Testing to determine if a given point is located on the inside or outside of a given facet in a 3-D scene.

platform-independent   Code that is able to execute on a wide range of different hardware configurations.

pointer   A variable that contains the address of another variable. See *null pointer*.

polygon   Usually intended to mean a plane surface used to create a 3-D solid model constructed by the B-rep method. Also used to describe a multi-sided, closed geometric shape.

preprocessor directive   An instruction that modifies the behavior of the C or C++ compiler itself. #if, #elif, #endif, #include are preprocessor directives.

private   In C++, refers to data and methods of a class accessible by member functions and by friends of the class. See *protected* and *public*.

procedural animation   Computer animation which is managed by formal or informal scripts provided by either the programmer or the user. See *kinetic animation*.

protected   In C++, refers to data and methods of a class accessible by member functions and by friends and by member functions of derived classes. See *private* and *public*.

prototype   1. The initial declaration of a function in a C or C++ program, usually containing the return type and argument list of the function. 2. A tentative mockup of a program for project planning purposes.

public   In C++, refers to data and methods of a class accessible by any in-scope function. See *private* and *protected*.

quadric primitive   A 3-D sub-object.

RAD   An acronym for rapid applications development, a method for efficient software engineering and construction whereby the use of preliminary prototypes, user feedback, and clearly defined goals is stressed.

radian   A length of arc based upon the relationship between elements of a unit circle.

radiosity   An algorithm that considers the overall energy levels from different light sources in a 3-D scene.

radix   The base of a numbering system. The radix of the hexadecimal numbering system is 16, of the decimal system is 10.

RAM   Random access memory.

RAM disk   A virtual disk which exists only in RAM memory. See *virtual disk*.

rapid applications development   See *RAD*.

ray tracing   An algorithm that calculates the illumination level of a model by tracing a ray of light back from the eye to the model and eventually to the light source.

real-time   Corresponding to the real world.

real-time animation   An animation sequence that is being created and displayed dynamically.

reflection mapping   Mathematically projecting onto the surface of a 3-D model a previously-defined bitmap containing a visual reflection of other objects in the scene. The reflection bitmap is acquired by temporarily placing the viewpoint on the surface of the mirrored object.

refresh buffer   The display buffer. The display hardware uses the display buffer to refresh the display monitor.

regen   Regeneration of a graphic entity or image. The instructions necessary to implement regen are commonly stored in a metafile. See *metafile*.

registration points   The user-specified coordinates in keyframes that will be used to create tweens. See *tweening*.

relational operators   The operators <, >, < =, > =, = =, and ! =, which in C and C++ mean less-than, greater-than, less-than-or-equal-to, greater-than-or-equal-to, equal-to, and not-equal-to. A relational operator compares the relationship between two values.

rendering   Adding illumination, shading, and color to a 3-D scene.

RGB model   The color model used by most personal computer hardware display systems.

runtime   The time during which the program is executing.

runtime library   A file containing routines which a program requires during execution.

scalar   A mathematical quantity that has quantity but not direction. A vector has quantity and direction.

SCD   An acronym for standard color display.

scientific visualization   The graphical representation of formulas or phenomena for the purpose of scientific research.

scroll   To move a graphic or alphanumeric character upwards or downwards on the display screen. See *pan*.

semantically implemented   A phrase used by compiler manufacturers to mean that their compiler recognizes a particular keyword but does not implement it. Syntactically implemented keywords are fully functional.

sequential-evaluation operator   (,) used to separate a series of sequentially evaluated expressions.

SFX   Sound effect(s).

shading   Adding the effects of illumination, shadow, and color to a 3-D model. Sometimes called rendering.

shift operators   < < and > >, which shift the bits in a byte to the left or to the right.

simulation   An imitation of a real-world event.

simulator   A program that imitates a real-world event.

sine   The sine of an angle in a right-angle triangle defines the relationship between the hypotenuse and the side opposite.

solid model   A 3-D model with hidden surfaces removed. It can be constructed by either the CSG (constructive solid geometry) method or the B-rep (boundary representation) method.

source code Program instructions written in the C or C++ programming language. Also called a program listing.

specular reflection A highlight on the surface of a 3-D model.

spline interpolation An algorithm for generating in-between images from keyframes whereby the movement of a vertex is assumed to follow a fitted curve or freeform curve. See *linear interpolation*.

statement A C or C++ instruction. Sometimes called an expression.

static variable A variable which is available to only the function in which it has been declared. Also called a local variable. See also *global variable*.

stereo vision Computer vision implemented with two video cameras.

stereolithography Using 3-D CAD software to drive one or more lasers responsible for carving prototype solids out of plastic, acrylic, wood, or light metal. Used for industrial prototypes.

stream The flow of data to or from a file or other output device.

structure A set of items grouped under a single name. The elements can be of different types. In an array, the elements must be of similar type.

stub See *do-nothing routine*.

subtraction See *Euler operators*.

supersampling Creating an image at a resolution which is greater than the actual screen resolution. When the image is scaled down to fit into the display buffer, many digital artifacts like jagged lines are suppressed as a convenient byproduct of the scaling mathematics.

super VGA Graphics adapters which extend the capabilities of the features provided by the original IBM VGA, most notably providing the $640 \times 480 \times 256$-color mode.

surface normal A line which is perpendicular to the surface of a plane in a 3-D environment. The illumination level of a surface can be derived by comparing the surface normal to the angle of incidence of incoming light rays.

syntactically implemented The full functional implementation of a particular keyword or statement by a C or C++ compiler. See the entry for semantically implemented.

syntax Grammar to be used with the C and C++ programming languages.

target platform The group of personal computer models and operating systems versions for which a software product is developed.

3-D Three-dimensional.

2-D Two-dimensional.

tilde The ~ character, which C and C++ use to mean one's complement.

toggle To change from one condition to another.

touring See *walkthrough*.

trackball A pointing device similar to a mouse, except the ball is located on the top surface of the device, meant to be activated by moving the palm of the hand over the ball.

trigonometry A branch of mathematics concerned with the relationship of two sides opposite a specific angle in a right-angle triangle. Sine and cosine are particularly useful for 3-D microcomputer graphics.

tween An in-between image which software has interpolated from keyframes provided by the programmer or the user. See *keyframe*.

tweening The act of generating tweens.

type Attribute. For example, an integer variable is of type int.

type cast The conversion of a value from one type to another type.

UMB Upper memory blocks.

unary operator An operator that manipulates a single variable. C and C++ provide the following unary operators: logical NOT (!), bitwise complement (~), arithmetic negation (–), indirection (*), address-of (&), and unary plus (or arithmetic increment) (+).

union A C or C++ structure which allocates the same memory space to different variables. The variables are often of different types.

variable A quantity whose value can change during program execution. See *constant*.

vector A mathematical value that has quantity and direction. A scalar value has only quantity.

VGA An acronym for video graphics array.

view coordinates See *camera coordinates*.

viewport A subset of the display screen.

virtual disk A simulated disk which exists only in RAM memory. Also called a RAM disk.

visibility Describes whether or not a function or a variable can be used by other parts of a C or C++ program.

visible page The graphics page currently being displayed.

visual algorithm The graphical representation of a computer function or algorithm.

visualization Using graphics to interpret, manipulate, or create data. Specialized fields of computer visualization include scientific visualization, 3-D modeling and rendering, computer animation, biomedicine, fluid dynamics, tomography, computer vision, image processing, and others. See *objectification*.

visualization graphics The graphics used for computer visualization. See *visualization*.

voice recognition software A program intended to recognize patterns of incoming voice commands and to compare those patterns with a database of previously-stored voice input.

void In C and C++ used to mean undefined.

walk-through Frame animation of a 3-D architectural model which simulates a walk-through by the viewer. Also called touring.

white box A block of code currently under development and whose algorithms and processes are being adjusted during testing. See *black box*.

white-box testing Program testing which requires access to and adjustment of the inner workings of a block of code. See *black-box testing*.

window A viewport on the display screen. Sometimes used to describe the logical relationship between the display screen and the world coordinates in 3-D graphics programming.

wire-frame   A 3-D object modeled with edges, with no hidden surfaces removed.

world coordinates   The xyz coordinates that describe the position and orientation of an object in a 3-D environment.

written-to page   The graphics page to which the graphics driver is currently writing, also called the active page.

XMS   An acronym for extended memory, which is physical memory located above 1Mb. Access requires an 80286, 80386, or 80486 microprocessor. See *EMS*.

YIQ model   The color model used by commercial television components.

z-buffer   The plane which represents near/far in the 3-D environment, often used as the criterion for the correct drawing sequence of multiple models, where nearer objects must obscure farther objects.

z-buffer method   A method of hidden surface removal. See *z-buffer*. Also called the painter's algorithm.

Index

Lee Adams' Supercharged C++ Graphics

If you are intrigued with the possibilities of the programs included in *Lee Adams' Supercharged C++ Graphics* (TAB Book No. 3489), you should definitely consider having the ready-to-run disk containing the software applications. This software is guaranteed free of manufacturer's defects. (If you have any problems, return the disk within 30 days, and we'll send you a new one.) Not only will you save the time and effort of typing the programs, but also the disk eliminates the possibility of errors that prevent the programs from functioning. Interested?

Available on either 5¼″ or 3½″ disk requiring a C compiler compatible with AT&T C++ 2.0 or equivalent at $24.95, plus $2.50 shipping and handling.